Hunting Trips of a Ranchman
&
The Wilderness Hunter

THEODORE ROOSEVELT

HUNTING TRIPS OF A RANCHMAN

SKETCHES OF SPORT ON THE NORTHERN CATTLE PLAINS

&

THE WILDERNESS HUNTER

AN ACCOUNT OF THE BIG GAME OF THE UNITED STATES AND ITS CHASE WITH HORSE, HOUND, AND RIFLE

THE MODERN LIBRARY

NEW YORK

2004 Modern Library Paperback Edition

Biographical note copyright © 1996 by Random House, Inc.
Introduction copyright © 1996 by Stephen E. Ambrose

LIBRARY OF CONGRESS CATALOGING-IN-PUBLICATION DATA
Roosevelt, Theodore.
[Hunting trips of a ranchman]
Hunting trips of a ranchman: sketches of sport on the northern
cattle plains; &, The wilderness hunter: an account of the big game
of the United States and its chase with horse, hound, and
rifle/Theodore Roosevelt.—Modern library ed.
p. cm.
First work previously published: Hunting trips of a ranchman.
Upper Saddle River, N.J.: Literature House, 1970, c. 1885. 2nd work
previously published: The wilderness hunter. Upper Saddle River,
N.J.: Literature House, 1970.
Includes indexes.
ISBN 0-375-75152-1
1. Hunting—West (U.S.)   I. Roosevelt, Theodore, 1858–1919.
Wilderness hunter.   II. Title.   III. Title: Wilderness hunter.
SK45.R6   1996
799.2'978—dc20   96-19364

Modern Library website address: www.modernlibrary.com

Printed in the United States of America

14   16   18   19   17   15

THEODORE ROOSEVELT

Theodore Roosevelt—the naturalist, writer, historian, soldier, and politician who became twenty-sixth president of the United States—was born in New York City on October 27, 1858, into a distinguished family. He was the second of four children of Theodore Roosevelt, Sr., a wealthy philanthropist of Dutch descent, and the former Martha ("Mittie") Bulloch, an aristocratic Southern belle. An endlessly inquisitive young man, he was especially interested in natural history, which became the focus of his first published works, *Summer Birds of the Adirondacks* (1877) and *Notes on Some of the Birds of Oyster Bay* (1879). Upon graduating Phi Beta Kappa from Harvard in 1880 Roosevelt briefly studied law. The next year he was elected to the New York State Assembly on the Republican ticket and soon made a name for himself as a historian with *The Naval War of 1812* (1882).

Following the death of his wife, Alice, in childbirth in 1884, Roosevelt sought change and headed west to ranch lands he had acquired in the Dakota Territory. The young outdoorsman chronicled his years in the Bad Lands in *Hunting Trips of a Ranchman* (1885), the first volume in the nature trilogy that eventually included *Ranch Life and the Hunting-Trail* (1888) and *The Wilderness Hunter* (1893). After failing to win the New York City mayoral election in 1886 as a self-styled "Cowboy Candidate," Roosevelt married childhood sweetheart Edith Kermit Carow and retired for a time to Sagamore Hill, his estate at Oyster Bay, Long Island. He wrote *Gouveneur Morris* (1888), a biography of the revolutionary-era statesman intended as a companion to the political memoir *Life of Thomas Hart Benton* (1887) and conceived the masterful four-volume history *The Winning of the West* (1889–1896).

Roosevelt returned to public life in 1889. Appointed Civil Service Commissioner he spent the next six years in Washington energetically pushing for reform of the government system, all the while propelling himself into the national spotlight. In 1895 he accepted a position as member, and later president, of the Board of Police Commissioners of New York City. Known as "a man you can't cajole, can't frighten, can't buy," Roosevelt continued to enjoy growing prestige nationwide, and within two years he was named assistant secretary of the navy under President William McKinley. Resigning this office in May 1898 at the outbreak of the Spanish-American War, Roosevelt helped organize and train the "Rough Riders," a regiment of the First U. S. Volunteer Cavalry whose legendary exploits he recorded in *The Rough Riders* (1899). A popular hero upon returning from Cuba, Roosevelt was elected governor of New York in November 1898, and two years later he became vice president of the United States in the second administration of William McKinley.

The assassination of President McKinley in September 1901 placed Roosevelt in the White House, and he was elected president in 1904. For the remainder of the decade he embodied the boundless confidence of the nation as it entered the American Century. He promised a square deal for the workingman, brought about trust-busting reforms aimed at regulating big business, and instituted modern-day environmental measures. The first American leader to play an important role in world affairs, Roosevelt guided construction of the Panama Canal, advocated a "big stick" policy to enforce the Monroe Doctrine, and sought to keep the Open Door course in China. In 1906 he was awarded the Nobel Peace Prize for resolving the Russo-Japanese War.

After leaving office in 1909 he took an almost year-long hunting trip to Africa and described his adventures in *African Game Trails* (1910). In 1912 he made a bid for reelection on the progressive Bull Moose ticket but lost to Woodrow Wilson, who became a bitter enemy. Afterward he completed *Theodore Roosevelt: An Autobiography* (1913) and *Through the Brazilian Wilderness* (1914), an account of his explorations in South America. With the outbreak of World War I, Roosevelt became an outspoken advocate of United States military preparedness in books such as *America and the World War* (1915). His last work, *The Great Adventure*, appeared in 1918. Still entertaining the idea of running again for office, Theodore Roosevelt died in his sleep at Sagamore Hill on January 6, 1919.

CONTENTS

INTRODUCTION BY
STEPHEN E. AMBROSE

Theodore Roosevelt stands in the first rank of twentieth-century American presidents by every criterion of greatness: character, intelligence, decisiveness, popularity, accomplishments, and more. His breadth and depth of knowledge was remarkable, even among presidents: he could talk about the details of their professions with a myriad of groups, including politicians, cowboys, intellectuals, historians, generals, admirals, and naturalists, among others. Imagine a conversation between Thomas Jefferson, the president who led the Republic into the nineteenth century, and Teddy Roosevelt, who led us into the twentieth. Then try to imagine a conversation between Jefferson and Richard Nixon, and you get the point.

Roosevelt stands alone, unchallenged by any other twentieth-century president, as a writer and scholar. Not even Woodrow Wilson comes close. The number of books and articles he wrote, as well as the wide variety of their subjects, is staggering. He published forty-two books and countless articles: the Harvard University *Theodore Roosevelt Collection: Dictionary Catalogue and Shelf List*, prepared in 1970, required five volumes to list all his published works. The subjects ranged from smoke-filled rooms at a political convention to the smoke of the camp-fire, from hunting elk in Montana to biographies of Oliver Cromwell and Gouverneur Morris, from the prize-winning four-volume *The Winning of the West* to impassioned pleas for conservation.

This is a productivity that only Winston Churchill could imagine; no other writer of the century has produced so much material on so many subjects, written with such originality and based on such extensive research. Yet writing was never his chief occupation. He was a lifelong politician. Still, he found time to do extensive original research in documentary collections scattered across the country for *The Winning of the West,* and was at the cutting edge of research techniques among professional historians. Indeed, he was in many ways far ahead of the professionals, obviously so in his literary skills but also as a researcher. That is why he is still read today, while the books of many professional historians are not—not even by graduate students.

His hunting books have the same winning qualities as his histories: sharp observation, revealing details, charming and illuminating anecdotes, an overview, and honesty. Henry Adams said he was "pure act," and in the hunting books—as in his political life—he certainly seems so. But rereading *Hunting Trips of a Ranchman* and *The Wilderness Hunter* has helped me see another side of TR.

He was a great listener. Many of the hunting stories he tells he heard around the campfire. He seldom identifies a specific source, probably because he often couldn't see the face of the narrator. This gives the stories a timeless quality. Storytelling began with Stone Age hunters sitting around a campfire recounting their deeds.

In *Hunting Trips of a Ranchman,* Roosevelt writes as if he had spent years on his ranches. In fact, his time there was more like months, spread over a few years. But during those months he never stopped looking around through the day, nor listening at night around the fire. And he had the most amazing memory for what he saw and heard. He absorbed impressions, details, and stories like a giant sponge. His research for these books, too, was prodigious, as is obvious from reading his bibliographic essay at the end of *The Wilderness Hunter.*

Observing, listening, and research are sedentary occupations, the opposite of action. They are receiving rather than giving, taking, or leading. They form the basis on which action can be effective, by providing knowledge, breadth of vision, and understanding. TR was a great observer, listener, and scholar, as well as a man of action.

■ ■ ■

THEODORE ROOSEVELT WAS born in New York City on October 27, 1858, into a socially prominent family of wealth and privilege. He was educated by private tutors and entered his first classroom, at Harvard University, when he was eighteen; he graduated in 1880.

As a boy, he suffered terribly from asthma; it was so bad that he often had to sleep sitting up. His eyesight was poor. The first ailment, asthma, he conquered, through prodigious effort. The second was permanent. ("I myself am not, and never will be, more than an ordinary shot," he confessed in *Hunting Trips,* "for my eyes are bad.") He was frail and his mother dressed him like a girl. His determination to overcome these handicaps was total. He led—indeed sometimes seems to have invented—"the strenuous life." That included boxing, weight-lifting, and outdoor living. From early childhood on, he spent as much time in the woods and fields as he possibly could. He was later called, with some accuracy, a perpetual Boy Scout. His enthusiasm for outdoor activities almost overwhelmed his friends.

Chief among those activities were fishing and hunting. He made his first extended hunting trip in 1880, following his graduation and just before his marriage to Alice Lee. "I think it will build me up," he told his mother. With his brother Elliott, he camped and hunted for six weeks in Illinois, Iowa, and Minnesota.

In 1883 he took the train to Dakota Territory to hunt buffalo. He got his bull and lost his heart. "I heartily enjoy this life, with its perfect freedom," he wrote his friend Henry Cabot Lodge. "I am very fond of hunting and there are few sensations I prefer to that of galloping over these rolling, limitless prairies, rifle in hand, or winding my way among the barren, fantastic and grimly picturesque deserts of the so-called Bad Lands."

He decided to go into the cattle business, partly hoping to get rich quick, mainly to provide him with a reason to continue going West. He put up $85,000 for two ranches on the Little Missouri, which was certainly putting his money where his heart was, as his inheritance from his father was $125,000 and his only paying job was as a state assemblyman in New York.

Altogether, he spent only about three years in the Bad Lands, interrupted by frequent trips back East, sometimes for lengthy stays. But when out West he lived the life to the fullest. Every cowboy who worked for him, every associate on his camping trips, every friend who came for the hunting, marveled at his energy.

He made more money writing about his experiences than he ever did as a rancher. He wrote *Hunting Trips* in 1884, following the sudden death of his wife. He was twenty-five years old and had already published *The Naval War of 1812*. *Hunting Trips* was written in New York, purely from memory, but gives evidence of an eye for detail that other writers can only envy. The first edition was limited to five hundred copies, beautifully produced, and sold for the then unheard-of price of fifteen dollars. It quickly became a collector's item. Later editions sold out on publication.

The book got rave reviews. The British *Spectator* said it "could claim an honorable place on the same shelf as Walton's *Compleat Angler.*" The reviewer added, "The charm about this ranchman as author is that he is every inch a gentleman-sportsman." Decades later, Roosevelt biographer Edmund Morris pointed to some flaws: "There are examples of Roosevelt's perennial tendency to praise himself with faint damns," anecdotes are repeated, "purplish tinges mar the otherwise crystal prose," and chapters end in anticlimax.

What sparkles is the pace and gusto of the stories, the drama of the hunts, and the warmth of the descriptive passages. And Morris gets its exactly right when he says, "The overwhelming impression left after reading *Hunting Trips of a Ranchman* is that of love for, and identity with, all living things."

I N 1893, FOLLOWING a series of political defeats, including a race for mayor of New York, Roosevelt entered a period of activity that can scarcely be believed, even of him. He was writing volumes three and four of *The Winning of the West* and simultaneously editing and contributing to an anthology, reading Kipling, addressing correspondents on subjects ranging from British court procedures to arboreal distinctions. He had become a professional lecturer—he badly needed the income—and was speaking in eastern cities regularly on history, hunting, municipal politics, and "the subject on which I feel deepest," U.S. foreign policy.

While all this was going on, he wrote what Morris calls "arguably his finest book," *The Wilderness Hunter*. It was published in late 1893, to rave reviews. *The New York Times* gave it the highest praise: "For one who intends to go a-hunting in the West this book is invaluable. One may rely upon its information. But it has better qualities. It is good reading for anybody, and people who never hunt and never will are sure to derive pleasure from its account of that part of the United States, relatively small, which is still a wilderness."

It is a richly detailed book, with all the freshness of observation of *Hunting Trips*. It has an abundance of original zoological information. The chapter on the life habits of the grizzly bear was immediately recognized as an invaluable contribution to science. Roosevelt was widely regarded as the world authority on the grizzly and other large Western species. The book contains one of his finest pieces of lyrical writing, inspired by the all-night song of a Tennessee mockingbird.

Roosevelt opens *The Wilderness Hunter* with a song to the joys of the hunting life that lay beyond the finding and killing of animals. Then he trumpets his deep belief that "the chase is among the best of all national pastimes; it cultivates that vigorous manliness for the lack of which in a nation, as in an individual, the possession of no other qualities can possibly atone." Throughout his life, TR was obsessed by manliness, which sometimes got him into trouble but far more often was beneficial to him and the nation. He was no male chauvinist, incidentally: he advocated changing the marriage ceremony to have the word "obey" eliminated; he supported equal rights for women; and nothing disgusted him more than "male sexual viciousness" or the Victorian conceit that a wife is the servant of her husband's lusts.

But he prided himself on his manliness, and he drew on it for political purposes. He once said that had he not gone to Dakota Territory, he would never have become president. He was probably right, because his association with the West gave him an identity that had a much wider appeal than that of a rich New York City intellectual. In the West he developed his lifelong passions and beliefs, and his experiences there have given us an unmatched description of a time and place that resonate with all Americans.

■ ■ ■

Roosevelt was keenly aware that he was living in a unique time. The cattle ranchers had come to the High

Plains country only five years earlier, and he predicted they would be gone in a decade, and the country would be taken over by crop farmers. "For we [ranchers] ourselves," he wrote, "[and] the life that we lead, will shortly pass away from the plains as completely as the red and white hunters who have vanished from before our herds. The free, open-air life of the ranchman, the pleasantest and healthiest life in America, is from its very nature ephemeral."

TR was a fearless predictor who was right about half the time. In 1884, in *Hunting Trips*, he had written that the cattle then prospering on the plains were vulnerable: "A winter of unusual severity will work sad havoc among the young cattle." Two years later, the worst winter ever experienced by the ranchers caused catastrophic losses; three out of four cattle died on almost all ranches (the E6 and Turkey Track ranches in Montana had 27,000 head in October 1886 and 250 head in May 1887).[1]

But he also predicted that the great ranches of the cattle country would in the end be "broken up into small patches of fenced farm land." And he thought the elk would soon follow the buffalo into near-extinction. He was wrong on both counts. He noted that with the coming of the cattle and hunters, the elk had disappeared from the plains and were now to be found only in tree-covered mountains, where they were "doomed to total destruction

---

[1] The catastrophe was immortalized by Charley Russell in his most famous drawing, "Waiting for the Chinook," depicting a three-quarters-starved heifer standing in the snow, and wolves waiting patiently.

at no distant date." But the elk adapted to the mountains, and they are thriving today. In the Bitterroot Mountains, for example, where the men of the Lewis and Clark Expedition (1804–06) almost starved because there was no game of any kind, today's hunters spend thousands of dollars to hunt elk, mule deer, bear, and other large animals that were driven into the mountains by the ranchers.

Most of the big buffalo herds of today are also no longer on the plains but in the mountains. The herd in Yellowstone National Park is so successful it has to be culled every year. That achievement, not incidentally, is thanks to TR. Together with George Bird Grinnell, he founded the Boone & Crockett Club (after Daniel Boone and Davy Crockett, two of TR's heroes). With Roosevelt as president, the club mounted a campaign to save Yellowstone. The park had been created by Congress in 1872, but there were no enforcement provisions. Hunters and promoters were killing off the big game and proposing to build a railroad through the most scenic sections of the park. In 1894 Roosevelt's wide-ranging efforts were crowned with success when Congress approved the Park Protection Act.

Casual readers of TR's hunting books may get the impression that he was engaged in a one-man slaughter of big game. Actually, he came down hard on market hunters or anyone who killed for sport. Virtually all the game he killed ended up in the pot, to be eaten around the campfire. He was one of America's first conservationists, and he is still her greatest, because of what he was able to do through the Boone & Crockett Club and as president of the United States.

Politically correct readers will find much of Roosevelt's writing on the West highly objectionable. "During the past century a good deal of sentimental nonsense has been talked about our taking the Indians' land," he complained, and pointed out that the Sioux and other tribes "had no stronger claim than that of having a few years previously butchered the original occupants." He proposed giving each Indian family a 160-acre farm, and if the man refused to work the land, "why then let him share the fate of the thousands of white hunters and trappers who have lived on the game that the settlement of the country has exterminated, and let him, like these whites, who will not work, perish from the face of the earth."

As a conservationist he also came up short by the standards of today's environmentalists. "It is always lawful to kill dangerous or noxious animals," he wrote, "like the bear, cougar, and wolf; but other game should only be shot when there is need of the meat, or for the sake of an unusually fine trophy."

He loved the cowboys. "Existence in the west seems to put the same stamp upon each and every one of them," he wrote. "Sinewy, hardy, self-reliant, their life forces them to be both daring and adventurous." Their weathered faces told of "dangers quietly fronted and hardships uncomplainingly endured." In 1898, at the time of the Spanish-American War, he recruited cowboys into his Rough Riders and led them up San Juan Hill. And he shared the cowboys' prejudice against sheep: "No man can associate with sheep and retain his self-respect. Intellectually a sheep is about on the lowest level of the brute creation."[2]

He loved the western land. "Nowhere, not even at sea, does a man feel more lonely than when riding over the far-reaching, seemingly never-ending plains," he admitted, but "after a man has lived a little while on or near them, their very vastness and loneliness and their melancholy monotony have a strong fascination for him." His opening description of the High Plains country in *Hunting Trips* is a superb piece of descriptive writing, almost a love song.

Although he was more a tourist and outside investor in the West than a permanent resident, Roosevelt and the West is one of America's great stories. His sojourns in the Dakotas, Montana, and Wyoming had a powerful influence on his outlook and politics. Most of all, his time in the West brought him great joy, a joy that is apparent in every page of *Hunting Trips of a Ranchman* and *The Wilderness Hunter*. And it is that quality more than any other—more even than what Henry Adams had in mind when he characterized TR as "pure act"—that stands out about him. So much pleasure did he take in living that he is best described as pure joy.

Nathan Miller concludes his fine biography of Roosevelt with this story: On the night of April 30, 1889, New York City celebrated the centennial of the inauguration of George Washington with a lavish dinner at the Metro-

---

[2] After the winter of 1886–87, most of the cattle ranchers on the High Plains turned to herding sheep, which were better able to survive blizzards and fetched a high return on investment.

politan Opera House. It was a long evening, with too many speeches, too many toasts, too many cigars. When it ended, most of the guests immediately headed homeward, but one of them noted a youthful figure standing on the sidewalk, talking to a circle of friends in a vigorous, eager voice that cracked with enthusiasm and excitement, and frequently raising his arm and pointing skyward.

"It was young Roosevelt," the observer reported. "He was introducing some fellows to the stars."

In these books he introduces us to a West that flourished but briefly, and to animals that are still with us, by telling us hunting stories that are timeless.

Hunting Trips
of a
Ranchman

TO THAT
KEENEST OF SPORTSMEN
AND
TRUEST OF FRIENDS
MY BROTHER
ELLIOTT ROOSEVELT

INTRODUCTORY NOTE

Most, although by no means all, of my hunting has been done on the Little Missouri River, in the neighborhood of my two ranches, the Elkhorn and Chimney Butte; the nearest town being the little hamlet of Medora—so named, I may mention for the benefit of the future local historian, in honor of the wife of the Marquis de Mores, one of the first stockmen to come to the place.

THEODORE ROOSEVELT

CHIMNEY BUTTE RANCH,
MEDORA, DAKOTA,
MAY, 1885

CONTENTS

Chapter VI: A Trip on the Prairie 178

The prong-horn antelope—Appearance, habits, and methods of hunting—Hunting on horseback—Wariness, speed, curiosity, and incapacity to make high jumps—Fawns as pets—Eagles—Horned frogs—Rattlesnakes—Trip on the prairie in June—Sights and sounds—Desolate plains—Running antelope—Night camp—Prairie dogs—Badgers—Skylarks—A long shot—Clear weather—Camping among Medicine Buttes—Sunset on plateau

Chapter VII: A Trip After Mountain Sheep 216

Spell of bitter weather—News brought of mountain sheep—Start after them—False alarm about bear—Character of Bad Lands—Description of mountain sheep or big-horn—Its wariness—Contrasted with other game—Its haunts—The hardest of all game to successfully hunt—Our trip—Cold weather and tiresome walking—Very rough ground—Slippery, ice-covered crags—Ram killed

Chapter VIII: The Lordly Buffalo 235

Extinction of the vast herds—Causes—A veritable tragedy of the animal world—Sentimental and practical sides—Traces left by buffalo—Skulls and trails—Merciless destruction by hunters and by cattle-men—Development of mountain race of the buffalo—Buffalo-hunting—Noble sport—Slight danger—A man killed—My brother charged—Adventure of my cousin with a wounded buffalo—Three of my men and wounded cow—Buffalo and cattle—Hunting them on foot—Hunting on horseback—My brother in Texas—I take a trip in buffalo country—Wounded bull escapes—Miserable night camp—Miss a cow in rain—Bad luck—Luck turns—Kill a bull—A wagon-trip

CHAPTER I

Ranching in the Bad Lands

The great middle plains of the United States, parts of which are still scantily peopled by men of Mexican parentage, while other parts have been but recently won from the warlike tribes of Horse Indians, now form a broad pastoral belt, stretching in a north and south line from British America to the Rio Grande. Throughout this great belt of grazing land almost the only industry is stock-raising, which is here engaged in on a really gigantic scale; and it is already nearly covered with the ranches of the stockmen, except on those isolated tracts (often themselves of great extent) from which the red men look hopelessly and sullenly out upon their old hunting-grounds, now roamed over by the countless herds of long-horned cattle. The northern portion of this belt is that which has been most lately thrown open to the whites; and it is with this part only that we have to do.

The northern cattle plains occupy the basin of the Upper Missouri; that is, they occupy all of the land drained by the tributaries of that river, and by the river itself, before it takes its long trend to the southeast. They stretch from the rich wheat farms of Central Dakota to the Rocky Mountains, and southward to the Black Hills and the Big Horn chain, thus including all of Montana,

Northern Wyoming, and extreme Western Dakota. The character of this rolling, broken, plains country is everywhere much the same. It is a high, nearly treeless region, of light rainfall, crossed by streams which are sometimes rapid torrents and sometimes merely strings of shallow pools. In places it stretches out into deserts of alkali and sage brush, or into nearly level prairies of short grass, extending for many miles without a break; elsewhere there are rolling hills, sometimes of considerable height; and in other places the ground is rent and broken into the most fantastic shapes, partly by volcanic action and partly by the action of water in a dry climate. These latter portions form the famous Bad Lands. Cotton-wood trees fringe the streams or stand in groves on the alluvial bottoms of the rivers; and some of the steep hills and canyon sides are clad with pines or stunted cedars. In the early spring, when the young blades first sprout, the land looks green and bright; but during the rest of the year there is no such appearance of freshness, for the short bunch grass is almost brown, and the gray-green sage bush, bitter and withered-looking, abounds everywhere, and gives a peculiarly barren aspect to the landscape.

It is but little over half a dozen years since these lands were won from the Indians. They were their only remaining great hunting-grounds, and towards the end of the last decade all of the northern plains tribes went on the warpath in a final desperate effort to preserve them. After bloody fighting and protracted campaigns they were defeated, and the country thrown open to the whites, while the building of the Northern Pacific Railroad gave immigration an immense impetus. There were great quantities of game, especially buffalo, and the hunters who thronged in to pursue the huge herds of the latter were the rough forerunners of civilization. No longer dreading the Indians, and having the railway on which to transport the robes, they followed the buffalo in season and out, until in 1883 the herds were practically destroyed. But meanwhile the cattle-men formed the vanguard of the white settlers. Already the hardy southern stockmen had pressed up with their wild-looking herds to the very border of the dangerous land, and even into it, trusting to luck and their own prowess for their safety; and the instant the danger was even partially removed, their cattle swarmed northward along the streams. Some Eastern men, seeing the extent of the grazing country, brought stock out by the railroad, and the short-horned beasts became almost as plenty as the wilder-looking southern steers. At the present time, indeed, the cattle of these northern ranges show more short-horn than long-horn blood.

Cattle-raising on the plains, as now carried on, started in Texas, where the Americans had learned it from the Mexicans whom they dispossessed. It has only become a prominent feature of Western life during the last score of years. When the Civil War was raging, there were hundreds of thousands of bony, half wild steers and cows in Texas, whose value had hitherto been very slight; but toward the middle of the struggle they became a most important source of food supply to both armies, and when the war had ended, the profits of the business were widely known and many men had gone into it. At first the stock-raising was all done in Texas, and the beef-steers, when ready for sale, were annually driven north along what became a regular cattle trail. Soon the men of Kansas and Colorado began to start ranches, and Texans who were getting crowded out moved their herds north into these lands, and afterward into Wyoming. Large herds of yearling steers also were, and still are, driven from the breeding ranches of the south to some northern range, there to be fattened for three years before selling. The cattle trail led through great wastes, and the scores of armed cowboys who, under one or two foremen, accompanied each herd, had often to do battle with bands of hostile Indians; but this danger is now a thing of the past, as, indeed, will soon be the case with the cattle trail itself, for year by year the grangers press steadily westward into it, and when they have once settled in a place, will not permit the cattle to be driven across it.

In the northern country the ranches vary greatly in size; on some there may be but a few hundred head, on others ten times as many thousand. The land is still in great part unsurveyed, and is hardly anywhere fenced in, the cattle roaming over it at will. The small ranches are often quite close to one another, say within a couple of miles; but the home ranch of a big outfit will not have another building within ten or twenty miles of it, or, indeed, if the country is dry, not within fifty. The ranch-house may be only a mud dugout, or a "shack" made of logs stuck upright into the ground; more often it is a fair-sized, well-made building of hewn logs, divided into several rooms. Around it are grouped the other buildings—log-stables, cow-sheds, and hay-ricks, an out-house in which to store things, and on large ranches another house in which the cowboys sleep. The strongly made, circular horse-corral, with a snubbing-post in the middle, stands close by; the larger cow-corral, in which the stock is branded, may be some distance off. A small patch of ground is usually enclosed as a vegetable garden, and a very large one, with water in it, as a pasture to be used only in special cases. All the work is done on horseback, and the quantity of ponies is thus of necessity very great, some of the large outfits numbering them by hundreds; on my own ranch there are eighty. Most of them are small, wiry beasts, not very speedy, but with good bottom, and able to pick up a living under the most adverse circumstances. There are usually a few large, fine horses kept for the special use of the ranchman or foremen. The best are those from Oregon; most of them come from Texas, and many are bought from the Indians. They are broken in a very rough manner, and many are in consequence vicious brutes, with the detestable habit of bucking. Of this habit I have a perfect dread, and, if I can help it, never get on a confirmed bucker. The horse puts his head down between his forefeet, arches his back, and with stiff legs gives a succession of jarring jumps, often "changing ends" as he does so. Even if a man can keep his seat, the performance gives him about as uncomfortable a shaking up as can be imagined.

The cattle rove free over the hills and prairies, picking up their own living even in winter, all the animals of each herd having certain distinctive brands on them. But little attempt is made to keep them within definite bounds, and they wander whither they wish, except that the ranchmen generally combine to keep some of their cowboys riding lines to prevent them straying away altogether. The missing ones are generally recovered in the annual round-ups, when the calves are branded. These round-ups, in which many outfits join together, and which cover hundreds of miles of territory, are the busiest period of the year for the stockmen, who then, with their cowboys, work from morning till night. In winter little is done except a certain amount of line riding.

The cowboys form a class by themselves, and are now quite as typical representatives of the wilder side of Western life, as were a few years ago the skin-clad hunters and trappers. They are mostly of native birth, and although there are among them wild spirits from every land, yet the latter soon become undistinguishable from their American companions, for these plainsmen are far from being so heterogeneous a people as is commonly supposed. On the contrary, all have a certain curious similarity to each other; existence in the west seems to put the same stamp upon each and every one of them. Sinewy, hardy, self-reliant, their life forces them to be both daring and adventurous, and the passing over their heads of a few years leaves printed on their faces certain lines which tell of dangers quietly fronted and hardships uncomplainingly endured. They are far from being as lawless as they are described; though they sometimes cut queer antics when, after many months of lonely life, they come into a frontier town in which drinking and gambling are the only recognized forms of amusement, and where pleasure and vice are considered synonymous terms. On the round-ups, or when a number get together, there is much boisterous, often foul-mouthed mirth; but they are rather silent, self-contained men when with strangers, and are frank and hospitable to a degree. The Texans are perhaps the best at the actual cowboy work. They are absolutely fearless riders and understand well the habits of the half wild cattle, being unequalled in those most trying times when, for instance, the cattle are stampeded by a thunderstorm at night, while in the use of the rope they are only excelled by the Mexicans. On the other hand, they are prone to drink, and when drunk, to shoot. Many Kansans, and others from the northern States, have also taken up the life of late years, and though these scarcely reach, in point of skill and dash, the standard of the southerners, who may be said to be born in the saddle, yet they are to the full as resolute and even more trustworthy. My own foremen were originally eastern backwoodsmen.

The cowboy's dress is both picturesque and serviceable, and, like many of the terms of his pursuit, is partly of Hispano-Mexican origin. It consists of a broad felt hat, a flannel shirt, with a bright silk handkerchief loosely knotted round the neck, trousers tucked into high-heeled boots, and a pair of leather "shaps" (chaperajos) or heavy riding overalls. Great spurs and a large-calibre revolver complete the costume. For horse gear there is a cruel curb bit, and a very strong, heavy saddle with high pommel and cantle. This saddle seems needlessly weighty, but the work is so rough as to make strength the first requisite. A small pack is usually carried behind it; also saddle pockets, or small saddle-bags; and there are leather strings wherewith to fasten the loops of the raw-hide lariat. The pommel has to be stout, as one end of the lariat is twisted round it when work is to be done, and the strain upon it is tremendous when a vigorous steer has been roped, or when, as is often the case, a wagon gets stuck and the team has to be helped out by one of the riders hauling from the saddle. A ranchman or foreman dresses precisely like the cowboys, except that the materials are finer, the saddle leather being handsomely carved, the spurs, bit, and revolver silver-mounted, the shaps of seal-skin, etc. The revolver was formerly a necessity, to protect the owner from Indians and other human foes; this is still the case in a few places, but, as a rule, it is now carried merely from habit, or to kill rattlesnakes, or on the chance of falling in with a wolf or coyote, while not unfrequently it is used to add game to the cowboy's not too varied bill of fare.

A cowboy is always a good and bold rider, but his seat in the saddle is not at all like that of one of our eastern or southern fox-hunters. The stirrups are so long that the man stands almost erect in them, from his head to his feet being a nearly straight line. It is difficult to compare the horsemanship of a western plainsman with that of an eastern or southern cross-country rider. In following hounds over fences and high walls, on a spirited horse needing very careful humoring, the latter would certainly excel; but he would find it hard work to sit a bucking horse like a cowboy, or to imitate the headlong dash with which one will cut out a cow marked with his own brand from a herd of several hundred others, or will follow at full speed the twistings and doublings of a refractory steer over ground where an eastern horse would hardly keep its feet walking.

My own ranches, the Elkhorn and the Chimney Butte, lie along the eastern border of the cattle country, where the Little Missouri flows through the heart of the Bad Lands. This, like most other plains rivers, has a broad, shallow bed, through which in times of freshets runs a muddy torrent, that neither man nor beast can pass; at other seasons of the year it is very shallow, spreading out into pools, between which the trickling water may be but a few inches deep. Even then, however, it is not always easy to cross, for the bottom is filled with quicksands and mud-holes. The river flows in long sigmoid curves through an alluvial valley of no great width. The amount of this alluvial land enclosed by a single bend is called a bottom, which may be either covered with cotton-wood trees or else be simply a great grass meadow. From the edges of the valley the land rises abruptly in steep high buttes whose crests are sharp and jagged. This broken country extends back from the river for many miles, and has been called always, by Indians, French voyageurs, and American trappers alike, the "Bad Lands," partly from its dreary and forbidding aspect and partly from the difficulty experienced in travelling through it. Every few miles it is crossed by creeks which open into the Little Missouri, of which they are simply repetitions in miniature, except that during most of the year they are almost dry, some of them having in their beds here and there a never-failing spring or muddy alkaline-water hole. From these creeks run coulies, or narrow, winding valleys, through which water flows when the snow melts; their bottoms contain patches of brush, and they lead back into the heart of the Bad Lands. Some of the buttes spread out into level plateaus, many miles in extent; others form chains, or rise as steep isolated masses. Some are of volcanic origin, being composed of masses of scoria; the others, of sandstone or clay, are worn by water into the most fantastic shapes. In coloring they are as bizarre as in form. Among the level, parallel strata which make up the land are some of coal. When a coal vein gets on fire it makes what is called a burning mine, and the clay above it is turned into brick; so that where water wears away the side of a hill sharp streaks of black and red are seen across it, mingled with the grays, purples, and browns. Some of the buttes are overgrown with gnarled, stunted cedars or small pines, and they are all cleft through and riven in every direction by deep narrow ravines, or by canyons with perpendicular sides.

In spite of their look of savage desolation, the Bad Lands make a good cattle country, for there is plenty of nourishing grass and excellent shelter from the winter storms. The cattle keep close to them in the cold months, while in the summer time they wander out on the broad prairies stretching back of them, or come down to the river bottoms.

My home ranch-house stands on the river brink. From the low, long veranda, shaded by leafy cotton-woods, one looks across sand bars and shallows to a strip of meadowland, behind which rises a line of sheer cliffs and grassy plateaus. This veranda is a pleasant place in the summer evenings when a cool breeze stirs along the river and blows in the faces of the tired men, who loll back in their rocking-chairs (what true American does not enjoy a rocking-chair?), book in hand—though they do not often read the books, but rock gently to and fro, gazing sleepily out at the weird-looking buttes opposite, until their sharp outlines grow indistinct and purple in the after-glow of the sunset. The story-high house of hewn logs is clean and neat, with many rooms, so that one can be alone if one wishes to. The nights in summer are cool and pleasant, and there are plenty of bear-skins and buffalo robes, trophies of our own skill, with which to bid defiance to the bitter cold of winter. In summer time we are not much within doors, for we rise before dawn and work hard enough to be willing to go to bed soon after nightfall. The long winter evenings are spent sitting round the hearthstone, while the pine logs roar and crackle, and the men play checkers or chess, in the fire light. The rifles stand in the corners of the room or rest across the elk antlers which jut out from over the fireplace. From the deer horns ranged along the walls and thrust into the beams and rafters hang heavy overcoats of wolf-skin or coon-skin, and otter-fur or beaver-fur caps and gauntlets. Rough board shelves hold a number of books, without which some of the evenings would be long indeed. No ranchman who loves sport can afford to be without Van Dyke's "Still Hunter," Dodge's "Plains of the Great West," or Caton's "Deer and Antelope of America"; and Coues' "Birds of the Northwest" will be valued if he cares at all for natural history. A western plainsman is reminded every day, by the names of the prominent landmarks among which he rides, that the country was known to men who spoke French long before any of his own kinsfolk came to it, and hence he reads with a double interest Parkman's histories of the early Canadians. As for Irving, Hawthorne, Cooper, Lowell, and the other standbys, I suppose no man, east or west, would willingly be long without them; while for lighter reading there are dreamy Ike Marvel, Burroughs' breezy pages, and the quaint, pathetic character-sketches of the Southern writers—Cable, Cradock, Macon, Joel Chandler Harris, and sweet Sherwood Bonner. And when one is in the Bad Lands he feels as if they somehow *look* just exactly as Poe's tales and poems *sound.*

By the way, my books have some rather unexpected foes, in the shape of the pack rats. These are larger than our house rats, with soft gray fur, big eyes, and bushy tails, like a squirrel's; they are rather pretty beasts and very tame, often coming into the shacks and log-cabins of the settlers. Woodmen and plainsmen, in their limited vocabulary, make great use of the verb "pack," which means to carry, more properly to carry on one's back; and these rats were christened pack rats, on account of their curious and inveterate habit of dragging off to their holes every object they can possibly move. From the hole of one, underneath the wall of a hut, I saw taken a small revolver, a hunting-knife, two books, a fork, a small bag, and a tin cup. The little shack mice are much more common than the rats, and among them there is a wee pocket-mouse, with pouches on the outside of its little cheeks.

In the spring, when the thickets are green, the hermit thrushes sing sweetly in them; when it is moonlight, the voluble, cheery notes of the thrashers or brown thrushes can be heard all night long. One of our sweetest, loudest songsters is the meadow-lark; this I could hardly get used to at first, for it looks exactly like the eastern meadow-lark, which utters nothing but a harsh, disagreeable chatter. But the plains air seems to give it a voice, and it will perch on the top of a bush or tree and sing for hours in rich, bubbling tones. Out on the prairie there are several kinds of plains sparrows which sing very brightly, one of them hovering in the air all the time, like a bobolink. Sometimes in the early morning, when crossing the open, grassy plateaus, I have heard the prince of them all, the Missouri skylark. The skylark sings on the wing, soaring over head and mounting in spiral curves until it can hardly be seen, while its bright, tender strains never cease for a moment. I have sat on my horse and listened to one singing for a quarter of an hour at a time without stopping. There is another bird also which sings on the wing, though I have not seen the habit put down in the books. One bleak March day, when snow covered the ground and the shaggy ponies crowded about the empty corral, a flock of snow-buntings came familiarly round the cow-shed, clambering over the ridge-pole and roof. Every few moments one of them would mount into the air, hovering about with quivering wings and warbling a loud, merry song with some very sweet notes. They were a most welcome little group of guests, and we were sorry when, after loitering around a day or two, they disappeared toward their breeding haunts.

In the still fall nights, if we lie awake we can listen to the clanging cries of the water-fowl, as their flocks speed southward; and in cold weather the coyotes occasionally come near enough for us to hear their uncanny wailing. The larger wolves, too, now and then join in, with a kind of deep, dismal howling; but this melancholy sound is more often heard when out camping than from the ranch-house.

The charm of ranch life comes in its freedom, and the vigorous, open-air existence it forces a man to lead. Except when hunting in bad ground, the whole time away from the house is spent in the saddle, and there are so many ponies that a fresh one can always be had. These ponies are of every size and disposition, and rejoice in names as different as their looks. Hackamore, Wire Fence, Steel-Trap, War Cloud, Pinto, Buckskin, Circus, and Standing Jimmie are among those that, as I write, are running frantically round the corral in the vain effort to avoid the rope, wielded by the dextrous and sinewy hand of a broad-hatted cowboy.

A ranchman is kept busy most of the time, but his hardest work comes during the spring and fall round-ups, when the calves are branded or the beeves gathered for market. Our round-up district includes the Beaver and Little Beaver creeks (both of which always contain running water, and head up toward each other), and as much of the river, nearly two hundred miles in extent, as lies between their mouths. All the ranches along the line of these two creeks and the river space between join in sending from one to three or four men to the round-up, each man taking eight ponies; and for every six or seven men there will be a four-horse wagon to carry the blankets and mess kit. The whole, including perhaps forty or fifty cowboys, is under the head of one first-class foreman, styled the captain of the round-up. Beginning at one end of the line the round-up works along clear to the other. Starting at the head of one creek, the wagons and the herd of spare ponies go down it ten or twelve miles, while the cowboys, divided into small parties, scour the neighboring country, covering a great extent of territory, and in the evening come into the appointed place with all the cattle they have seen. This big herd, together with the pony herd, is guarded and watched all night, and driven during the day.

At each home-ranch (where there is always a large corral fitted for the purpose) all the cattle of that brand are cut out from the rest of the herd, which is to continue its journey, and the cows and calves are driven into the corral, where the latter are roped, thrown, and branded. In throwing the rope from horseback, the loop, held in the right hand, is swung round and round the head by a motion of the wrist; when on foot, the hand is usually held by the side, the loop dragging on the ground. It is a pretty sight to see a man who knows how, use the rope; again and again an expert will catch fifty animals by the leg without making a mis-throw. But unless practice is begun very young it is hard to become really proficient.

Cutting out cattle, next to managing a stampeded herd at night, is that part of the cowboy's work needing the boldest and most skillful horsemanship. A young heifer or steer is very loath to leave the herd, always tries to break back into it, can run like a deer, and can dodge like a rabbit; but a thorough cattle pony enjoys the work as much as its rider, and follows a beast like a four-footed fate through every double and turn. The ponies for the cutting-out or afternoon work are small and quick; those used for the circle-riding in the morning have need rather to be strong and rangey.

The work on a round-up is very hard, but although the busiest it is also the pleasantest part of a cowboy's existence. His food is good, though coarse, and his sleep is sound indeed; while the work is very exciting, and is done in company, under the stress of an intense rivalry between all the men, both as to their own skill, and as to the speed and training of their horses. Clumsiness, and still more the slightest approach to timidity, expose a man to the roughest and most merciless raillery; and the unfit are weeded out by a very rapid process of natural selection. When the work is over for the day the men gather round the fire for an hour or two to sing songs, talk, smoke, and tell stories; and he who has a good voice, or, better still, can play a fiddle or banjo, is sure to receive his meed of most sincere homage.

Though the ranchman is busiest during the round-up, yet he is far from idle at other times. He rides round among the cattle to see if any are sick, visits any outlying camp of his men, hunts up any band of ponies which may stray—and they are always straying,—superintends the haying, and, in fact, does not often find that he has too much leisure time on his hands. Even in winter he has work which must be done. His ranch supplies milk, butter, eggs, and potatoes, and his rifle keeps him, at least intermittently, in fresh meat; but coffee, sugar, flour, and whatever else he may want, has to be hauled in, and this is generally done when the ice will bear. Then firewood must be chopped; or, if there is a good coal vein, as on my ranch, the coal must be dug out and hauled in. Altogether, though the ranchman will have time enough to take shooting trips, he will be very far from having time to make shooting a business, as a stranger who comes for nothing else can afford to do.

There are now no Indians left in my immediate neighborhood, though a small party of harmless Grosventres occasionally passes through; yet it is but six years since the Sioux surprised and killed five men in a log station just south of me, where the Fort Keogh trail crosses the river;

and, two years ago, when I went down on the prairies toward the Black Hills, there was still danger from Indians. That summer the buffalo hunters had killed a couple of Crows, and while we were on the prairie a long-range skirmish occurred near us between some Cheyennes and a number of cowboys. In fact, we ourselves were one day scared by what we thought to be a party of Sioux; but on riding toward them they proved to be half-breed Crees, who were more afraid of us than we were of them.

During the past century a good deal of sentimental nonsense has been talked about our taking the Indians' land. Now, I do not mean to say for a moment that gross wrong has not been done the Indians, both by government and individuals, again and again. The government makes promises impossible to perform, and then fails to do even what it might toward their fulfilment; and where brutal and reckless frontiersmen are brought into contact with a set of treacherous, revengeful, and fiendishly cruel savages a long series of outrages by both sides is sure to follow. But as regards taking the land, at least from the western Indians, the simple truth is that the latter never had any real ownership in it at all. Where the game was plenty, there they hunted; they followed it when it moved away to new hunting-grounds, unless they were prevented by stronger rivals; and to most of the land on which we found them they had no stronger claim than that of having a few years previously butchered the original occupants. When my cattle came to the Little Missouri the region was only inhabited by a score or so of white hunters; their title to it was quite as good as that of most Indian tribes to the lands they claim; yet nobody dreamed of saying that these hunters owned the country. Each could eventually have kept his own claim of 160 acres, and no more. The Indians should be treated in just the same way that we treat the white settlers. Give each his little claim; if, as would generally happen, he declined this, why then let him share the fate of the thousands of white hunters and trappers who have lived on the game that the settlement of the country has exterminated, and let him, like these whites, who will not work, perish from the face of the earth which he cumbers.

The doctrine seems merciless, and so it is; but it is just and rational for all that. It does not do to be merciful to a few, at the cost of justice to the many. The cattle-men at least keep herds and build houses on the land; yet I would not for a moment debar settlers from the right of entry to the cattle country, though their coming in means in the end the destruction of us and our industry.

For we ourselves, and the life that we lead, will shortly pass away from the plains as completely as the red and white hunters who have vanished from before our herds. The free, open-air life of the ranchman, the pleasantest and healthiest life in America, is from its very nature ephemeral. The broad and boundless prairies have already been bounded and will soon be made narrow. It is scarcely a figure of speech to say that the tide of white settlement during the last few years has risen over the west like a flood; and the cattle-men are but the spray from the crest of the wave, thrown far in advance, but soon to be overtaken. As the settlers throng into the lands and seize the good ground, especially that near the streams, the great fenceless ranches, where the cattle and their mounted herdsmen wandered unchecked over hundreds of thousands of acres, will be broken up and divided into corn land, or else into small grazing farms where a few hundred head of stock are closely watched and taken care of. Of course the most powerful ranches, owned by wealthy corporations or individuals, and already firmly rooted in the soil, will long resist this crowding; in places, where the ground is not suited to agriculture, or where, through the old Spanish land-grants, title has been acquired to a great tract of territory, cattle ranching will continue for a long time, though in a greatly modified form; elsewhere I doubt if it outlasts the present century. Immense sums of money have been made at it in the past, and it is still fairly profitable; but the good grounds (aside from those reserved for the Indians) are now almost all taken up, and it is too late for new men to start at it on their own account, unless in exceptional cases, or where an Indian reservation is thrown open. Those that are now in will continue to make money; but most of those who hereafter take it up will lose.

The profits of the business are great; but the chances for loss are great also. A winter of unusual severity will work sad havoc among the young cattle, especially the heifers; sometimes a disease like the Texas cattle fever will take off a whole herd; and many animals stray and are not recovered. In fall, when the grass is like a mass of dry and brittle tinder, the fires do much damage, reducing the prairies to blackened deserts as far as the eye can see, and destroying feed which would keep many thousand head of stock during winter. Then we hold in about equal abhorrence the granger who may come in to till the land, and the sheep-owner who drives his flocks over it. The former will gradually fill up the country to our own exclusion, while the latter's sheep nibble the grass off so close to the ground as to starve out all other animals.

Then we suffer some loss—in certain regions very severe loss—from wild beasts, such as cougars, wolves, and lynxes. The latter, generally called "bob-cats," merely make inroads on the hen-roosts (one of them destroyed half my poultry, coming night after night with most praiseworthy regularity), but the cougars and wolves destroy many cattle.

The wolf is not very common with us; nothing like as plentiful as the little coyote. A few years ago both wolves and coyotes were very numerous on the plains, and as Indians and hunters rarely molested them, they were then very unsuspicious. But all this is changed now. When the cattle-men came in they soon perceived in the wolves their natural foes, and followed them unrelentingly. They shot at and chased them on all occasions, and killed great numbers by poisoning; and as a consequence the comparatively few that are left are as wary and cunning beasts as exist anywhere. They hardly ever stir abroad by day, and hence are rarely shot or indeed seen. During the last three years these brutes have killed nearly a score of my cattle, and in return we have poisoned six or eight wolves and a couple of dozen coyotes; yet in all our riding we have not seen so much as a single wolf, and only rarely a coyote. The coyotes kill sheep and occasionally very young calves, but never meddle with any thing larger. The stockman fears only the large wolves.

According to my experience, the wolf is rather solitary. A single one or a pair will be found by themselves, or possibly with one or more well-grown young ones, and will then hunt over a large tract where no other wolves will be found; and as they wander very far, and as their melancholy howlings have a most ventriloquial effect, they are often thought to be much more plentiful than they are. During the daytime they lie hid in caves or in some patch of bush, and will let a man pass right by them without betraying their presence. Occasionally somebody runs across them by accident. A neighboring ranchman to me once stumbled, while riding an unshod pony, right into the midst of four wolves who were lying in some tall, rank grass, and shot one with his revolver and crippled another before they could get away. But such an accident as this is very rare; and when, by any chance, the wolf is himself abroad in the daytime he keeps such a sharp look-out, and is so wary, that it is almost impossible to get near him, and he gives every human being a wide berth. At night it is different. The wolves then wander far and wide, often coming up round the outbuildings of the ranches; I have seen in light snow the tracks of two that had walked round the house within fifty feet of it. I have never heard of an instance where a man was attacked or threatened by them, but they will at times kill every kind of domestic animal. They are fond of trying to catch young foals, but do not often succeed, for the mares and foals keep together in a kind of straggling band, and the foal is early able to run at good speed for a short distance. When attacked, the mare and foal dash off towards the rest of the band, which gathers together at once, the foals pressing into the middle and the mares remaining on the outside, not in a ring with their heels out, but moving in and out, and forming a solid mass into which the wolves do not venture. Full-grown horses are rarely molested, while a stallion becomes himself the assailant.

In early spring when the cows begin to calve the wolves sometimes wait upon the herds as they did of old on the buffalo, and snap up any calf that strays away from its mother. When hard pressed by hunger they will kill a steer or a heifer, choosing the bitterest and coldest night to make the attack. The prey is invariably seized by the haunch or flank, and its entrails afterwards torn out; while a cougar, on the contrary, grasps the neck or throat. Wolves have very strong teeth and jaws and inflict a most severe bite. They will in winter come up to the yards and carry away a sheep, pig, or dog without much difficulty; I have known one which had tried to seize a sheep and been prevented by the sheep dogs to canter off with one of the latter instead. But a spirited dog will always attack a wolf. On the ranch next below mine there was a plucky bull terrier, weighing about twenty-five pounds, who lost his life owing to his bravery. On one moonlight night three wolves came round the stable, and the terrier sallied out promptly. He made such a quick rush as to take his opponents by surprise, and seized one by the throat; nor did he let go till the other two tore him almost asunder across the loins. Better luck attended a large mongrel called a sheep dog by his master, but whose blood was apparently about equally derived from collie, Newfoundland, and bulldog. He was a sullen, but very intelligent and determined brute, powerfully built and with strong jaws, and though neither as tall nor as heavy as a wolf he had yet killed two of these animals single-handed. One of them had come into the farm-yard at night, and had taken a young pig, whose squeals roused everybody. The wolf loped off with his booty, the dog running after and overtaking him in the darkness. The struggle was short, for the dog had seized the wolf by the throat and the latter could not shake him off, though he made the most desperate efforts, rising on his hind legs and pressing the dog down with his fore paws. This time the victor escaped scatheless, but in his second fight, when he strangled a still larger wolf, he was severely punished. The wolf had seized a sheep, when the dog, rushing on him, caused him to leave his quarry. Instead of running he turned to bay at once, taking off one of the assailant's ears with a rapid snap. The dog did not get a good hold, and the wolf scored him across the shoulders and flung him off. They then faced each other for a minute and at the next dash the dog made good his throat hold, and throttled the wolf, though the latter contrived to get his foe's foreleg into his jaws and broke it clear through. When I saw the dog he had completely recovered, although pretty well scarred.

On another neighboring ranch there is a most ill-favored hybrid, whose mother was a Newfoundland and whose father was a large wolf. It is stoutly built, with erect ears, pointed muzzle, rather short head, short bushy tail, and of a brindled color; funnily enough it looks more like a hyena than like either of its parents. It is familiar with people and a good cattle dog, but rather treacherous; it both barks and howls. The parent wolf carried on a long courtship with the Newfoundland. He came round the ranch, regularly and boldly, every night, and she would at once go out to him. In the daylight he would lie hid in the bushes at some little distance. Once or twice his hiding-place was discovered and then the men would amuse themselves by setting the Newfoundland on him. She would make at him with great apparent ferocity; but when they were a good way from the men he would turn round and wait for her and they would go romping off together, not to be seen again for several hours.

The cougar is hardly ever seen round my ranch; but toward the mountains it is very destructive both to horses and horned cattle. The ranchmen know it by the name of mountain lion; and it is the same beast that in the east is called panther or "painter." The cougar is the same size and build as the Old World leopard, and with very much the same habits. One will generally lie in wait for the heifers or young steers as they come down to water, and singling out an animal, reach it in a couple of bounds and fasten its fangs in the throat or neck. I have seen quite a large cow that had been killed by a cougar; and on another occasion, while out hunting over light snow, I came across a place where two bucks, while fighting, had been stalked up to by a cougar which pulled down one and tore him in pieces. The cougar's gait is silent and stealthy to an extra-ordinary degree; the look of the animal when creeping up to his prey has been wonderfully caught by the sculptor, Kemeys, in his bronzes: "The Still Hunt" and "The Silent Footfall."

I have never myself killed a cougar, though my brother shot one in Texas, while still-hunting some deer, which the cougar itself was after. It never attacks man, and even when hard pressed and wounded turns to bay with extreme reluctance, and at the first chance again seeks safety in flight. This was certainly not the case in old times, but the nature of the animal has been so changed by constant contact with rifle-bearing hunters, that timidity toward them has become a hereditary trait deeply engrained in its nature. When the continent was first settled, and for long afterward, the cougar was quite as dangerous an antagonist as the African or Indian leopard, and would even attack men unprovoked. An instance of this occurred in the annals of my mother's family. Early in the present century one of my ancestral relatives, a Georgian, moved down to the wild and almost unknown country bordering on Florida. His plantation was surrounded by jungles in which all kinds of wild beasts swarmed. One of his negroes had a sweetheart on another plantation, and in visiting her, instead of going by the road he took a short cut through the swamps, heedless of the wild beasts, and armed only with a long knife—for he was a man of colossal strength, and of fierce and determined temper. One night he started to return late, expecting to reach the plantation in time for his daily task on the morrow. But he never reached home, and it was thought he had run away. However, when search was made for him his body was found in the path through the swamp, all gashed and torn, and but a few steps from him the body of a cougar, stabbed and cut in many places. Certainly that must have been a grim fight, in the gloomy, lonely recesses of the swamp, with no one to watch the midnight death struggle between the powerful, naked man and the ferocious brute that was his almost unseen assailant.

When hungry, a cougar will attack any thing it can

master. I have known of their killing wolves and large dogs. A friend of mine, a ranchman in Wyoming, had two grizzly bear cubs in his possession at one time, and they were kept in a pen outside the ranch. One night two cougars came down, and after vain efforts to catch a dog which was on the place, leaped into the pen and carried off the two young bears!

Two or three powerful dogs, however, will give a cougar all he wants to do to defend himself. A relative of mine in one of the Southern States had a small pack of five blood-hounds, with which he used to hunt the canebrakes for bear, wildcats, etc. On one occasion they ran across a cougar, and after a sharp chase treed him. As the hunters drew near he leaped from the tree and made off, but was overtaken by the hounds and torn to pieces after a sharp struggle in which one or two of the pack were badly scratched.

Cougars are occasionally killed by poisoning, and they may be trapped much more easily than a wolf. I have never known them to be systematically hunted in the West, though now and then one is accidentally run across and killed with the rifle while the hunter is after some other game.

As already said, ranchmen do not have much idle time on their hands, for their duties are manifold, and they need to be ever on the watch against their foes, both animate and inanimate. Where a man has so much to do he cannot spare a great deal of his time for any amusement; but a good part of that which the ranchman can spare he is very apt to spend in hunting. His quarry will be one of the seven kinds of plains game—bear, buffalo, elk, bighorn, antelope, blacktail or whitetail deer. Moose, caribou, and white goat never come down into the cattle country; and it is only on the southern ranches near the Rio Grande and the Rio Colorado that the truculent peccary and the great spotted jaguar are found.

Until recently all sporting on the plains was confined to army officers, or to men of leisure who made extensive trips for no other purpose; leaving out of consideration the professional hunters, who trapped and shot for their livelihood. But with the incoming of the cattle-men, there grew up a class of residents, men with a stake in the welfare of the country, and with a regular business carried on in it, many of whom were keenly devoted to sport,—a class whose members were in many respects closely akin to the old Southern planters. In this book I propose to give some description of the kind of sport that can be had by the average ranchman who is fond of the rifle. Of course no man with a regular business can have such opportunities as fall to the lot of some who pass their lives in hunting only; and we cannot pretend to equal the achievements of such men, for with us it is merely a pleasure, to be eagerly sought after when we have the chance, but not to be allowed to interfere with our business. No ranchmen have time to make such extended trips as are made by some devotees of sport who are so fortunate as to have no every-day work to which to attend. Still, ranch life undoubtedly offers more chance to a man to get sport than is now the case with any other occupation in America, and those who follow it are apt to be men of game spirit, fond of excitement and adventure, who perforce lead an open-air life, who must needs ride well, for they are often in the saddle from sunrise to sunset, and who naturally take kindly to that noblest of weapons, the rifle. With such men hunting is one of the chief of pleasures; and they follow it eagerly when their work will allow them. And with some of them it is at times more than a pleasure. On many of the ranches—on my own, for instance—the supply of fresh meat depends mainly on the skill of the riflemen, and so, both for pleasure and profit, most ranchmen do a certain amount of hunting each season. The buffalo are now gone forever, and the elk are rapidly sharing their fate; but antelope and deer are still quite plenty, and will remain so for some years; and these are the common game of the plainsman. Nor is it likely that the game will disappear much before ranch life itself is a thing of the past. It is a phase of American life as fascinating as it is evanescent, and one well deserving an historian. But in these pages I propose to dwell on only one of its many pleasant sides, and to give some idea of the game shooting which forms perhaps the chief of the cattle-man's pleasures, aside from those more strictly connected with his actual work. I have to tell of no unusual adventures, but merely of just such hunting as lies within reach of most of the sport-loving ranchmen whose cattle range along the waters of the Powder and the Bighorn, the Little Missouri and the Yellowstone.

Of course I have never myself gone out hunting under the direction of a professional guide or professional hunter, unless it was to see one of the latter who was reputed a crack shot; all of my trips have been made either by myself or else with one of my cowboys as a companion. Most of the so-called hunters are not worth much. There are plenty of men hanging round the frontier settlements who claim to be hunters, and who bedizen themselves in all the traditional finery of the craft, in the hope of getting a job at guiding some "tender-foot"; and there are plenty of skin-hunters, or meat-hunters, who, after the Indians have been driven away and when means of communication have been established, mercilessly slaughter the game in season and out, being too lazy to work at any regular trade, and keeping on hunting until the animals become too scarce and shy to be taken without more skill than they possess; but these are all mere temporary excrescences, and the true old Rocky Mountain hunter and trapper, the plainsman, or mountain-man, who, with all his faults, was a man of iron nerve and will, is now almost a thing of the past. In the place of these heroes of a bygone age, the men who were clad in buckskin and who carried long rifles, stands, or rather rides, the bronzed and sinewy cowboy, as picturesque and self-reliant, as dashing and resolute as the saturnine Indian fighters whose place he has taken; and, alas that it should be written! he in his turn must at no distant time share the fate of the men he has displaced. The ground over which he so gallantly rides his small, wiry horse will soon know him no more, and in his stead there will be the plodding grangers and husbandmen. I suppose it is right and for the best that the great cattle country, with its broad extent of fenceless land, over which the ranchman rides as free as the game that he follows or the horned herds that he guards, should be in the end broken up into small patches of fenced farm land and grazing land; but I hope against hope that I myself shall not live to see this take place, for when it does one of the pleasantest

and freest phases of western American life will have come
to an end.

The old hunters were a class by themselves. They penetrated, alone or in small parties, to the farthest and
wildest haunts of the animals they followed, leading a solitary, lonely life, often never seeing a white face for months
and even years together. They were skilful shots, and were
cool, daring, and resolute to the verge of recklessness. On
any thing like even terms they very greatly overmatched
the Indians by whom they were surrounded, and with
whom they waged constant and ferocious war. In the government expeditions against the plains tribes they were of
absolutely invaluable assistance as scouts. They rarely had
regular wives or white children, and there are none to take
their places, now that the greater part of them have gone.
For the men who carry on hunting as a business where it
is perfectly safe have all the vices of their prototypes, but,
not having to face the dangers that beset the latter, so neither need nor possess the stern, rough virtues that were required in order to meet and overcome them. The ranks of
the skin-hunters and meat-hunters contain some good
men; but as a rule they are a most unlovely race of beings,
not excelling even in the pursuit which they follow because they are too shiftless to do any thing else; and the
sooner they vanish the better.

A word as to weapons and hunting dress. When I
first came to the plains I had a heavy Sharps rifle, 45–120,
shooting an ounce and a quarter of lead, and a 50-calibre,
double-barrelled English express. Both of these, especially the latter, had a vicious recoil; the former was very
clumsy; and above all they were neither of them repeaters;

for a repeater or magazine gun is as much superior to a single- or double-barrelled breech-loader as the latter is to a muzzle-loader. I threw them both aside: and have instead a 40–90 Sharps for very long range work; a 50–115 6-shot Bullard express, which has the velocity, shock, and low trajectory of the English gun; and, better than either, a 45–75 half-magazine Winchester. The Winchester, which is stocked and sighted to suit myself, is by all odds the best weapon I ever had, and I now use it almost exclusively, having killed every kind of game with it, from a grizzly bear to a big-horn. It is as handy to carry, whether on foot or on horseback, and comes up to the shoulder as readily as a shot-gun; it is absolutely sure, and there is no recoil to jar and disturb the aim, while it carries accurately quite as far as a man can aim with any degree of certainty; and the bullet, weighing three quarters of an ounce, is plenty large enough for any thing on this continent. For shooting the very large game (buffalo, elephants, etc.) of India and South Africa, much heavier rifles are undoubtedly necessary; but the Winchester is the best gun for any game to be found in the United States, for it is as deadly, accurate, and handy as any, stands very rough usage, and is unapproachable for the rapidity of its fire and the facility with which it is loaded.

Of course every ranchman carries a revolver, a long 45 Colt or Smith & Wesson, by preference the former. When after game a hunting-knife is stuck in the girdle. This should be stout and sharp, but not too long, with a round handle. I have two double-barrelled shot-guns: a No. 10 choke-bore for ducks and geese, made by Thomas of Chicago; and a No. 16 hammerless, built for me by

Kennedy of St. Paul, for grouse and plover. On regular hunting trips I always carry the Winchester rifle; but in riding round near home, where a man may see a deer and is sure to come across ducks and grouse, it is best to take the little ranch gun, a double-barrel No. 16, with a 40–70 rifle underneath the shot-gun barrels.

As for clothing, when only off on a day's trip, the ordinary ranchman's dress is good enough: flannel shirt, and overalls tucked into alligator boots, the latter being of service against the brambles, cacti, and rattlesnakes. Such a costume is good in warm weather. When making a long hunting trip, where there will be much rough work, especially in the dry cold of fall and winter, there is nothing better than a fringed buckskin tunic or hunting-shirt, (held in at the waist by the cartridge belt,) buckskin trowsers, and a fur cap, with heavy moccasins for use in the woods, and light alligator-hide shoes if it is intended to cross rocks and open ground. Buckskin is most durable, keeps out wind and cold, and is the best possible color for the hunter—no small point in approaching game. For wet it is not as good as flannel, and it is hot in warm weather. On very cold days, fur gloves and either a coon-skin overcoat or a short riding jacket of fisher's fur may be worn. In cold weather, if travelling light with only what can be packed behind the horse, I sleep in a big buffalo-robe, sewed up at the sides and one end into the form of a bag, and very warm. When, as is sometimes the case, the spirit in the thermometer sinks to 60°–65° Fahrenheit, it is necessary to have more wraps and bedding, and we use beaver-robes and bear-skins. An oilskin "slicker" or water-proof overcoat and a pair of shaps keep out the rain almost completely.

Where most of the hunting is done on horseback the hunting-pony is a very important animal. Many people seem to think that any broken-down pony will do to hunt, but this seems to me a very great mistake. My own hunting-horse, Manitou, is the best and most valuable animal on the ranch. He is stoutly built and strong, able to carry a good-sized buck behind his rider for miles at a lope without minding it in the least; he is very enduring and very hardy, not only picking up a living but even growing fat when left to shift for himself under very hard conditions; and he is perfectly surefooted and as fast as any horse on the river. Though both willing and spirited, he is very gentle, with an easy mouth, and will stay grazing in one spot when left, and will permit himself to be caught without difficulty. Add to these virtues the fact that he will let any dead beast or thing be packed on him, and will allow a man to shoot off his back or right by him without moving, and it is evident that he is as nearly perfect as can be the case with hunting-horseflesh. There is a little sorrel mare on the ranch, a perfect little pet, that is almost as good, but too small. We have some other horses we frequently use, but all have faults. Some of the quiet ones are slow, lazy, or tire easily; others are gun shy; while others plunge and buck if we try to pack any game on their backs. Others cannot be left standing untied, as they run away; and I can imagine few forms of exercise so soul-harrowing as that of spending an hour or two in running, in shaps, top boots, and spurs over a broken prairie, with the ther-

mometer at 90°, after an escaped horse. Most of the
hunting-horses used by my friends have one or more of
these tricks, and it is rare to find one, like Manitou, who
has none of them. Manitou is a treasure and I value him
accordingly. Besides, he is a sociable old fellow, and a great
companion when off alone, coming up to have his head
rubbed or to get a crust of bread, of which he is very fond.

To be remarkably successful in killing game a man
must be a good shot; but a good target shot may be a very
poor hunter, and a fairly successful hunter may be only a
moderate shot. Shooting well with the rifle is the highest
kind of skill, for the rifle is the queen of weapons; and it is
a difficult art to learn. But many other qualities go to make
up the first-class hunter. He must be persevering, watchful, hardy, and with good judgment; and a little dash and
energy at the proper time often help him immensely. I
myself am not, and never will be, more than an ordinary
shot; for my eyes are bad and my hand not over-steady; yet
I have killed every kind of game to be found on the plains,
partly because I have hunted very perseveringly, and partly
because by practice I have learned to shoot about as well
at a wild animal as at a target. I have killed rather more
game than most of the ranchmen who are my neighbors,
though at least half of them are better shots than I am.

Time and again I have seen a man who had, as he
deemed, practised sufficiently at a target, come out "to kill
a deer," hot with enthusiasm; and nine out of ten times he
has gone back unsuccessful, even when deer were quite
plenty. Usually he has been told by the friend who advised
him to take the trip, or by the guide who inveigled him
into it, that "the deer were so plenty you saw them all

round you," and, this not proving quite true, he lacks perseverance to keep on; or else he fails to see the deer at the right time; or else if he does see it he misses it, making the discovery that to shoot at a gray object, not overdistinctly seen, at a distance merely guessed at, and with a background of other gray objects, is very different from firing into a target, brightly painted and a fixed number of yards off. A man must be able to hit a bull's-eye eight inches across every time to do good work with deer or other game; for the spot around the shoulders that is fatal is not much bigger than this; and a shot a little back of that merely makes a wound which may in the end prove mortal, but which will in all probability allow the animal to escape for the time being. It takes a good shot to hit a bull's-eye off-hand several times in succession at a hundred yards, and if the bull's-eye was painted the same color as the rest of the landscape, and was at an uncertain distance, and, moreover, was alive, and likely to take to its heels at any moment, the difficulty of making a good shot would be greatly enhanced. The man who can kill his buck right along at a hundred yards has a right to claim that he is a good shot. If he can shoot off-hand standing up, that is much the best way, but I myself always drop on one knee, if I have time, unless the animal is very close. It is curious to hear the nonsense that is talked and to see the nonsense that is written about the distances at which game is killed. Rifles now carry with deadly effect the distance of a mile, and most middle-range hunting-rifles would at least kill at half a mile; and in war firing is often begun at these ranges. But in war there is very little accurate aiming, and the fact that there is a variation of thirty or forty feet in the flight of the ball makes no difference; and, finally, a thousand bullets are fired for every man that is killed—and usually many more than a thousand. How would that serve for a record on game? The truth is that three hundred yards is a very long shot, and that even two hundred yards is a long shot. On looking over my game-book I find that the average distance at which I have killed game on the plains is less than a hundred and fifty yards. A few years ago, when the buffalo would stand still in great herds, half a mile from the hunter, the latter, using a long-range Sharp's rifle, would often, by firing a number of shots into the herd at that distance, knock over two or three buffalo; but I have hardly ever known single animals to be killed six hundred yards off, even in antelope hunting, the kind in which most long-range shooting is done; and at half that distance a very good shot, with all the surroundings in his favor, is more apt to miss than to hit. Of course old hunters—the most inveterate liars on the face of the earth—are all the time telling of their wonderful shots at even longer distances, and they do occasionally, when shooting very often, make them, but their performances, when actually tested, dwindle amazingly. Others, amateurs, will brag of their rifles. I lately read in a magazine about killing antelopes at eight hundred yards with a Winchester express, a weapon which cannot be depended upon at over two hundred, and is wholly inaccurate at over three hundred, yards.

The truth is that, in almost all cases the hunter merely guesses at the distance, and, often perfectly honestly, just about doubles it in his own mind. Once a man told me of an extraordinary shot by which he killed a deer at four hundred yards. A couple of days afterward we happened to pass the place, and I had the curiosity to step off the distance, finding it a trifle over a hundred and ninety. I always make it a rule to pace off the distance after a successful shot, whenever practicable—that is, when the animal has not run too far before dropping,—and I was at first both amused and somewhat chagrined to see how rapidly what I had supposed to be remarkably long shots shrank under actual pacing. It is a good rule always to try to get as near the game as possible, and in most cases it is best to risk startling it in the effort to get closer rather than to risk missing it by a shot at long range. At the same time, I am a great believer in powder-burning, and if I cannot get near, will generally try a shot anyhow, if there is a chance of the rifle's carrying to it. In this way a man will now and then, in the midst of many misses, make a very good long shot, but he should not try to deceive himself into the belief that these occasional long shots are to be taken as samples of his ordinary skill. Yet it is curious to see how a really truthful man will forget his misses, and his hits at close quarters, and, by dint of constant repetition, will finally persuade himself that he is in the habit of killing his game at three or four hundred yards. Of course in different kinds of ground the average range for shooting varies. In the Bad Lands most shots will be obtained much closer than on the prairie, and in the timber they will be nearer still.

Old hunters who are hardy, persevering, and well acquainted with the nature of the animals they pursue, will often kill a great deal of game without being particularly good marksmen; besides, they are careful to get up close, and are not flurried at all, shooting as well at a deer as they do at a target. They are, as a rule, fair shots—that is, they shoot a great deal better than Indians or soldiers, or than the general run of Eastern amateur sportsmen; but I have never been out with one who has not missed a great deal, and the "Leather-stocking" class of shooting stories are generally untrue, at least to the extent of suppressing part of the truth—that is, the number of misses. Beyond question our Western hunters are, as a body, to the full as good marksmen as, and probably much better than, any other body of men in the world, not even excepting the Dutch Boers or Tyrolese Jägers, and a certain number of them who shoot a great deal at game, and are able to squander cartridges very freely, undoubtedly become crack shots, and perform really wonderful feats. As an instance there is old "Vic," a former scout and Indian fighter, and concededly the best hunter on the Little Missouri; probably there are not a dozen men in the West who are better shots or hunters than he is, and I have seen him do most skilful work. He can run the muzzle of his rifle through a board so as to hide the sights, and yet do quite good shooting at some little distance; he will cut the head off a chicken at eighty or ninety yards, shoot a deer running through brush at that distance, kill grouse on the wing early in the season, and knock over antelopes when they are so far off that I should not dream of shooting. He firmly believes, and so do most men that speak of him, that he never misses. Yet I have known him make miss after miss at game, and some that were not such especially difficult shots either. One secret of his success is his constant practice. He is firing all the time, at marks, small birds, etc., etc., and will average from fifty to a hundred cartridges a day; he certainly uses nearly twenty thousand a year, while a man who only shoots for sport, and that occasionally, will, in practising at marks and every thing else, hardly get through with five hundred. Besides, he was cradled in the midst of wild life, and has handled a rifle and used it against both brute and human foes almost since his infancy; his nerves and sinews are like iron, and his eye is naturally both quick and true.

Vic is an exception. With practice an amateur will become nearly as good a shot as the average hunter; and, as I said before, I do not myself believe in taking out a professional hunter as a shooting companion. If I do not go alone I generally go with one of my foremen, Merrifield, who himself came from the East but five years ago. He is a good-looking fellow, daring and self-reliant, a good rider and first-class shot, and a very keen sportsman. Of late years he has been my *fidus Achates* of the hunting field. I can kill more game with him than I can alone; and in hunting on the plains there are many occasions on which it is almost a necessity to have a companion along.

It frequently happens that a solitary hunter finds himself in an awkward predicament, from which he could be extricated easily enough if there were another man with him. His horse may fall into a wash-out, or may get stuck in a mud-hole or quicksand in such a manner that a man working by himself will have great difficulty in getting it out; and two heads often prove better than one in an emergency, especially if a man gets hurt in any way. The first thing that a western plainsman has to learn is the capacity for self-help, but at the same time he must not forget that occasions may arise when the help of others will be most grateful.

CHAPTER II

Waterfowl

O ne cool afternoon in the early fall, while sitting on the veranda of the ranch-house, we heard a long way off the ha-ha-honk, ha-honk, of a gang of wild geese; and shortly afterward they came in sight, in a V-shaped line, flying low and heavily toward the south, along the course of the stream. They went by within a hundred yards of the house, and we watched them for some minutes as they flew up the valley, for they were so low in the air that it seemed certain that they would soon alight; and light they did when they were less than a mile past us. As the ground was flat and without much cover where they had settled, I took the rifle instead of a shot-gun and hurried after them on foot. Wild geese are very watchful and wary, and as I came toward the place where I thought they were I crept along with as much caution as if the game had been a deer. At last, peering through a thick clump of bullberry bushes I saw them. They were clustered on a high sandbar in the middle of the river, which here ran in a very wide bed between low banks. The only way to get at them was to crawl along the river-bed, which was partly dry, using the patches of rushes and the sand hillocks and drift-wood to shield myself from their view. As it was already late and the sun was just sinking, I hastily retreated a few paces, dropped over the bank, and began to creep along on my hands and knees through the sand and gravel. Such work is always tiresome, and it is especially so when done against time. I kept in line with a great log washed up on the shore, which was some seventy-five yards from the geese. On reaching it and looking over I was annoyed to find that in the fading light I could not distinguish the birds clearly enough to shoot, as the dark river bank was behind them. I crawled quickly back a few yards, and went off a good bit to the left into a hollow. Peeping over the edge I could now see the geese, gathered into a clump with their necks held straight out, sharply outlined against the horizon; the sand flats stretching out on either side, while the sky above was barred with gray and faint crimson. I fired into the thickest of the bunch, and as the rest flew off, with discordant clamor, ran forward and picked up my victim, a fat young wild goose (or Canada goose), the body badly torn by the bullet.

On two other occasions I have killed geese with the rifle. Once while out riding along the river bottoms, just at dawn, my attention was drawn to a splashing and low cackling in the stream, where the water deepened in a wide bend, which swept round a low bluff. Leaving my horse where he was, I walked off towards the edge of the stream, and lying on the brink of the bank looked over into the water of the bend. Only a faint streak of light was visible in the east, so that objects on the water could hardly be made out; and the little wreaths of mist that rose from the river made the difficulty even greater. The birds were some distance above me, where the water made a long straight stretch through a sandy level. I could not see them, but could plainly hear their low murmuring and splashing, and once one of them, as I judged by the sound, stood up on end and flapped its wings vigorously. Pretty soon a light puff of wind blew the thin mist aside, and I caught a glimpse of them; as I had supposed, they were wild geese, five of them, swimming slowly, or rather resting on the water, and being drifted down with the current. The fog closed over them again, but it was growing light very rapidly, and in a short time I knew they would be in the still water of the bend just below me, so I rose on my elbows and held my rifle ready at the poise. In a few minutes, before the sun was above the horizon, but when there was plenty of light by which to shoot, another eddy in the wind blew away the vapor and showed the five geese in a cluster, some thirty yards off. I fired at once, and one of the geese, kicking and flapping frantically, fell over, its neck half cut from the body, while the others, with laborious effort, got under way. Before they could get their heavy bodies fairly off the water and out of range, I had taken three more shots, but missed. Waiting till the dead goose drifted into shore, I picked it up and tied it on the saddle of my horse to carry home to the ranch. Being young and fat it was excellent eating.

The third goose I killed with the rifle was of a different kind. I had been out after antelopes, starting before there was any light in the heavens, and pushing straight out towards the rolling prairie. After two or three hours, when the sun was well up, I neared where a creek ran in a broad, shallow valley. I had seen no game, and before coming up to the crest of the divide beyond which lay the creek bottom, I dismounted and crawled up to it, so as to see if any animal had come down to drink. Field glasses are almost always carried while hunting on the plains, as the distances at which one can see game are so enormous. On looking over the crest with the glasses the valley of the creek for about a mile was stretched before me. At my feet the low hills came closer together than in other places, and shelved abruptly down to the bed of the valley, where there was a small grove of box-alders and cotton-woods. The beavers had, in times gone by, built a large dam at this place across the creek, which must have produced a great back-flow and made a regular little lake in the times of freshets. But the dam was now broken, and the beavers, or most of them, gone, and in the place of the lake was a long green meadow. Glancing towards this my eye was at once caught by a row of white objects stretched straight across it, and another look showed me that they were snow-geese. They were feeding, and were moving abreast of one another slowly down the length of the meadow towards the end nearest me, where the patch of small trees and brushwood lay. A goose is not as big game as an antelope; still I had never shot a snow-goose, and we needed fresh meat, so I slipped back over the crest and ran down to the bed of the creek, round a turn of the hill, where the geese were out of sight. The creek was not an entirely dry one, but there was no depth of water in it except in certain deep holes; elsewhere it was a muddy ditch with steep sides, difficult to cross on horseback because of the quicksands. I walked up to the trees without any special care, as they screened me from view, and looked cautiously out from behind them. The geese were acting just as our tame geese act in feeding on a common, moving along with their necks stretched out before them, nibbling and jerking at the grass as they tore it up by mouthfuls. They were very watchful, and one or the other of them had its head straight in the air looking sharply round all the time. Geese will not come near any cover in which foes may be lurking if they can help it, and so I feared that they would turn before coming near enough to the brush to give me a good shot. I therefore dropped into the bed of the creek, which wound tortuously along the side of the meadow, and crept on all fours along one of its banks until I came to where it made a loop out towards the middle of the bottom. Here there was a tuft of tall grass, which served as a good cover, and I stood upright, dropping my hat, and looking through between the blades. The geese, still in a row, with several yards' interval between each one and his neighbor, were only sixty or seventy yards off, still feeding towards me. They came along quite slowly, and the ones nearest, with habitual suspicion, edged away from the scattered tufts of grass and weeds which marked the brink of the creek. I tried to get two in line, but could not. There was one gander much larger than any other bird in the lot, though not the closest to me; as he went by just opposite my hiding-place, he stopped still, broadside to me, and I aimed just at the root of the neck—for he was near enough for any one firing a rifle from a rest to hit him about where he pleased. Away flew the others, and in a few minutes I was riding along with the white gander dangling behind my saddle.

The beaver meadows spoken of above are not common, but, until within the last two or three years, beavers themselves were very plentiful, and there are still a good many left. Although only settled for so short a period, the land has been known to hunters for half a century, and throughout that time it has at intervals been trapped over by whites or half-breeds. If fur was high and the Indians peaceful quite a number of trappers would come in, for the Little Missouri Bad Lands were always famous both for fur and game; then if fur went down, or an Indian war broke out, or if the beaver got pretty well thinned out, the place would be forsaken and the animals would go unmolested for perhaps a dozen years, when the process would be repeated. But the incoming of the settlers and the driving out of the Indians have left the ground clear for the trappers to work over unintermittently, and the extinction of the beaver throughout the plains country is a question of but a short time. Excepting an occasional otter or mink, or a few musk-rats, it is the only fur-bearing animal followed by the western plains trapper; and its large size and the marked peculiarities of its habits, together with the accessibility of its haunts on the plains, as compared with its haunts in the deep woods and mountains, render its pursuit and capture comparatively easy. We have trapped (or occasionally shot) on the ranch during the past three years several score beaver; the fur is paler and less valuable than in the forest animal. Those that live in the river do not build dams all across it, but merely extending up some distance against the current, so as to make a deep pool or eddy, beside which are the burrows and houses. It would seem to be a simple feat to break into a beaver house, but in reality it needs no little toil with both spade and axe, for the house has very thick roof and walls, made of clay and tough branches, twisted together into a perfect mat, which, when frozen, can withstand any thing but the sharpest and best of tools. At evening beaver often come out to swim, and by waiting on the bank perfectly quietly for an hour or so a close shot can frequently be obtained.

Beaver are often found in the creeks, not only in those which always contain running water, but also in the dry ones. Here they build dams clean across, making ponds which always contain water, even if the rest of the bed is almost dry; and I have often been surprised to find fresh traces of beaver in a pond but a few feet across, a mile away from any other body of water. On one occasion I was deer-hunting in a rough, broken country, which was little more than a tangle of ravines and clefts, with very steep sides rising into sharp hills. The sides of the ravines were quite densely overgrown with underbrush and young trees, and through one or two of them ran, or rather trickled, small streams, but an inch or two in depth, and often less. Directly across one of these ravines, at its narrowest and steepest part, the beaver had built an immense, massive dam, completely stopping the course of a little brooklet. The dam was certainly eight feet high, and strong enough and broad enough to cross on horseback; and it had turned back the stream until a large pond, almost a little lake, had been formed by it. This was miles from any other body of water, but, judging from the traces of their work, it had once held a large colony of beavers; when I saw it they had all been trapped out, and the pond had been deserted for a year and over. Though clumsy on dry ground, and fearing much to be caught upon it, yet beaver can make, if necessary, quite long overland journeys, and that at a speed with which it will give a man trouble to keep up.

As there are few fish in the plains streams, otters are naturally not at all common, though occasionally we get one. Musk-rats are quite plenty in all the pools of water. Sometimes a little pool out on the prairie will show along its edges numerous traces of animal life; for, though of small extent, and a long distance from other water, it may be the home of beavers and musk-rats, the breeding-place of different kinds of ducks, and the drinking-place for the denizens of the dry country roundabouts, such as wolves, antelopes, and badgers.

Although the plains country is in most places very dry, yet there are here and there patches of prairie land where the reverse is true. One such is some thirty miles distant from my ranch. The ground is gently rolling, in some places almost level, and is crossed by two or three sluggish, winding creeks, with many branches, always holding water, and swelling out into small pools and lakelets wherever there is a hollow. The prairie round about is wet, at times almost marshy, especially at the borders of the great reedy slews. These pools and slews are favorite breeding-places for water-fowl, especially for mallard, and a good bag can be made at them in the fall, both among the young flappers (as tender and delicious birds for the table as any I know), and among the flights of wild duck that make the region a stopping-place on their southern migration. In these small pools, with little cover round the edges, the poor flappers are at a great disadvantage; we never shoot them unless we really need them for the table. But quite often, in August or September, if near the place, I have gone down to visit one or two of the pools, and have brought home half a dozen flappers, killed with the rifle if I had been out after large game, or with the revolver if I had merely been among the cattle,—each duck, in the latter case, representing the expenditure of a vast number of cartridges.

Later in the fall, when the young ducks are grown and the flocks are coming in from the north, fair shooting may be had by lying in the rushes on the edge of some large pond, and waiting for the evening flight of the birds; or else by taking a station on some spot of low ground across which the ducks fly in passing from one sheet of water to another. Frequently quite a bag of mallard, widgeon, and pintail can be made in this manner, although nowhere in the Bad Lands is there any such duck-shooting as is found farther east. Ducks are not very easy to kill, or even to hit, when they fly past. My duck-gun, the No. 10 choke-bore, is a very strong and close shooting piece, and such a one is needed when the strong-flying birds are at any distance; but the very fact of its shooting so close makes it necessary that the aim should be very true; and as a consequence my shooting at ducks has varied from bad to indifferent, and my bags have been always small.

Once I made an unusually successful right and left, however. In late summer and early fall large flocks of both green-winged and blue-winged teal are often seen both on the ponds and on the river, flying up and down the latter. On one occasion while out with the wagon we halted for the mid-day meal on the bank of the river. Travelling across the plains in company with a wagon, especially if

making a long trip, as we were then doing, is both tiresome and monotonous. The scenery through the places
where the wagon must go is everywhere much the same,
and the pace is very slow. At lunch-time I was glad to get
off the horse, which had been plodding along at a walk for
hours, and stretch my muscles; and, noticing a bunch of
teal fly past and round a bend in the river, I seized the
chance for a little diversion, and taking my double-barrel,
followed them on foot. The banks were five or six feet
high, edged with a thick growth of cotton-wood saplings;
so the chance to creep up was very good. On getting round
the bend I poked my head through the bushes, and saw
that the little bunch I was after had joined a great flock of
teal, which was on a sand bar in the middle of the stream.
They were all huddled together, some standing on the bar,
and others in the water right by it, and I aimed for the
thickest part of the flock. At the report they sprang into
the air, and I leaped to my feet to give them the second
barrel, when, from under the bank right beneath me, two
shoveller or spoon-bill ducks rose, with great quacking,
and, as they were right in line, I took them instead, knocking both over. When I had fished out the two shovellers, I
waded over to the sand bar and picked up eleven teal,
making thirteen ducks with the two barrels.

On one occasion my brother and myself made a short
wagon trip in the level, fertile, farming country, whose
western edge lies many miles to the east of the Bad Lands
around my ranch. There the land was already partially settled by farmers, and we had one or two days' quite fair
duck-shooting. It was a rolling country of mixed prairie
land and rounded hills, with small groves of trees and nu-

merous little lakes in the hollows. The surface of the natural prairie was broken in places by great wheat fields, and when we were there the grain was gathered in sheaves and stacks among the stubble. At night-time we either put up at the house of some settler, or, if there were none round, camped out.

One night we had gone into camp among the dense timber fringing a small river, which wound through the prairie in a deep narrow bed with steep banks. Until people have actually camped out themselves it is difficult for them to realize how much work there is in making or breaking camp. But it is very quickly done if every man has his duties assigned to him and starts about doing them at once. In choosing camp there are three essentials to be looked to—wood, water, and grass. The last is found everywhere in the eastern prairie land, where we were on our duck-shooting trip, but in many places on the great dry plains farther west, it is either very scanty or altogether lacking; and I have at times been forced to travel half a score miles farther than I wished to get feed for the horses. Water, again, is a commodity not by any means to be found everywhere on the plains. If the country is known and the journeys timed aright, water can easily be had, at least at the night camps, for on a pinch a wagon can be pushed along thirty miles or so at a stretch, giving the tough ponies merely a couple of hours' rest and feed at mid-day; but in going through an unknown country it has been my misfortune on more than one occasion to make a dry camp—that is, one without any water either for men or horses, and such camps are most uncomfortable. The thirst seems to be most annoying just after sundown; after one has gotten to sleep and the air has become cool, he is not troubled much by it again until within two or three hours of noon next day, when the chances are that he will have reached water, for of course by that time he will have made a desperate push to get to it. When found, it is more than likely to be bad, being either from a bitter alkaline pool, or from a hole in a creek, so muddy that it can only be called liquid by courtesy. On the great plains wood is even scarcer, and at least half the time the only material from which to make a fire will be buffalo chips and sage brush; the long roots of the latter if dug up make a very hot blaze. Of course when wood is so scarce the fire is a small one, used merely to cook by, and is not kept up after the cooking is over.

When a place with grass, wood, and water is found, the wagon is driven up to the windward side of where the beds are to be laid, and the horses are unhitched, watered, and turned out to graze freely until bedtime, when a certain number of them are picketed or hobbled. If danger from white or red horse-thieves is feared, a guard is kept over them all night. The ground is cleared of stones and cacti where the beds are to be placed, and the blankets and robes spread. Generally we have no tent, and the wagon-cover is spread over all to keep out rain. Meanwhile some one gathers the wood and starts a fire. The coffee-pot is set among the coals, and the frying-pan with bacon and whatever game has been shot is placed on top. Like Eastern backwoodsmen, all plainsmen fry about every thing they can get hold of to cook; for my own use I always have a broiler carried along in the wagon. One evening in every three or four is employed in baking bread in the Dutch oven; if there is no time for this, biscuits are made in the frying-pan. The food carried along is very simple, consisting of bacon, flour, coffee, sugar, baking-powder, and salt; for all else we depend on our guns. On a long trip every old hand carries a water-proof canvas bag, containing his few spare clothes and necessaries; on a short trip a little oilskin one, for the toothbrush, soap, towel, etc., will do.

On the evening in question our camping-ground was an excellent one; we had no trouble about any thing, except that we had to bring water to the horses in pails, for the banks were too steep and rotten to get them down to the river. The beds were made under a great elm, and in a short time the fire was roaring in front of them, while the tender grouse were being roasted on pointed sticks. One of the pleasantest times of camping out is the period immediately after supper, when the hunters lie in the blaze of the firelight, talking over what they have done during the day and making their plans for the morrow. And how soundly a man who has worked hard sleeps in the open, none but he who has tried it knows.

Before we had risen in the morning, when the blackness of the night had barely changed to gray, we were roused by the whistle of wings, as a flock of ducks flew by along the course of the stream, and lit in the water just above the camp. Some kinds of ducks in lighting strike the water with their tails first, and skitter along the surface for a few feet before settling down. Lying in our blankets we could plainly hear all the motions: first of all, the whistle—whistle of their wings; then a long-drawn splash-h-h—plump; and then a low, conversational quacking. It was too dark to shoot, but we got up and ready, and strolled down along the brink of the river opposite where we could hear them; and as soon as we could see we gave them four barrels and picked up half a dozen scaup-ducks. Breakfast was not yet ready, and we took a turn out on the prairie before coming back to the wagon. In a small pool, down in a hollow, were a couple of little dipper ducks or buffleheads; they rose slowly against the wind, and offered such fair marks that it was out of the question to miss them.

The evening before we had lain among the reeds near a marshy lake and had killed quite a number of ducks, mostly widgeon and teal; and this morning we intended to try shooting among the cornfields. By sunrise we were a good distance off, on a high ridge, across which we had noticed that the ducks flew in crossing from one set of lakes to another. The flight had already begun, and our arrival scared off the birds for the time being; but in a little while, after we had hidden among the sheaves, stacking the straw up around us, the ducks began to come back, either flying over in their passage from the water, or else intending to light and feed. They were for the most part mallards, which are the commonest of the Western ducks, and the only species customarily killed in this kind of shooting. They are especially fond of the corn, of which there was a small patch in the grain field. To this flocks came again and again, and fast though they flew we got many before they left the place, scared by the shooting. Those that were merely passing from one point to another flew low, and among them we shot a couple of gadwall, and also knocked over a red-head from a little bunch that went by, their squat, chunky forms giving them a very different look from the longer, lighter-built mallard. The mallards that came to feed flew high in the air, wheeling round in gradually lowering circles when they had reached the spot where they intended to light. In shooting in the grain fields there is usually plenty of time to aim, a snap shot being from the nature of the sport exceptional. Care must be taken to lie quiet until the ducks are near enough; shots are most often lost through shooting too soon. Heavy guns with heavy loads are necessary, for the ducks are generally killed at long range; and both from this circumstance as well as from the rapidity of their flight, it is imperative to hold well ahead of the bird fired at. It has one advantage over shooting in a marsh, and that is that a wounded bird which drops is of course hardly ever lost. Corn-fed mallards are most delicious eating; they rank on a par with teal and red-head, and second only to the canvas-back—a bird, by the way, of which I have never killed but one or two individuals in the West.

In going out of this field we got a shot at a gang of wild geese. We saw them a long way off, coming straight toward us in a head and tail line. Down we dropped, flat on our faces, remaining perfectly still without even looking up (for wild geese are quick to catch the slightest motion) until the sound of the heavy wing strokes and the honking seemed directly overhead. Then we rose on our knees and fired all four barrels, into which we had slipped buckshot cartridges. They were away up in the air, much beyond an ordinary gunshot; and we looked regretfully after them as they flew off. Pretty soon one lagged a little behind; his wings beat slower; suddenly his long neck dropped, and he came down like a stone, one of the buckshot having gone clean through his breast.

We had a long distance to make that day, and after leaving the grain fields travelled pretty steadily, only getting out of the wagon once or twice after prairie chickens. At lunch time we halted near a group of small ponds and reedy sloughs. In these were quite a number of teal and wood-duck, which were lying singly, in pairs, or small bunches, on the edges of the reeds, or where there were thick clusters of lily pads; and we had half an hour's good sport in "jumping" these little ducks, moving cautiously along the margin of the reeds, keeping as much as possible concealed from view, and shooting four teal and a wood-duck, as, frightened at our near approach, they sprang into the air and made off. Late in the evening, while we were passing over a narrow neck of land that divided two small lakes, with reedy shores, from each other, a large flock of the usually shy pintail duck passed over us at close range, and we killed two from the wagon, making in all a bag of twenty-one and a half couple of water-fowl during the day, two thirds falling to my brother's gun. Of course this is a very small bag indeed compared to those made in the Chesapeake, or in Wisconsin and the Mississippi valley; but the day was so perfect, and there were so many varieties of shooting, that I question if any bag, no matter how large, ever gave much more pleasure to the successful sportsman than did our forty-three ducks to us.

Though ducks fly so fast, and need such good shooting to kill them, yet their rate of speed, as compared to that of other birds, is not so great as is commonly supposed. Hawks, for instance, are faster. Once, on the prairie, I saw a mallard singled out of a flock, fairly overtaken, and struck down, by a large, light-colored hawk, which I supposed to be a lanner, or at any rate one of the long-winged falcons; and I saw a duck hawk, on the coast of Long Island, perform a similar feat with the swift-flying long-tailed duck—the old squaw, or sou'-sou'-southerly, of the baymen. A more curious instance was related to me by a friend. He was out along a river, shooting ducks as they flew by him, and had noticed a bald eagle perched on the top of a dead tree some distance from him. While looking at it a little bunch of teal flew swiftly by, and to his astonishment the eagle made after them. The little ducks went along like bullets, their wings working so fast that they whistled; flop, flop came the great eagle after them, with labored-looking flight; and yet he actually gained so rapidly on his seemingly fleeter quarry that he was almost up to them when opposite my friend. Then the five teal went down headlong into the water, diving like so many shot. The eagle kept hovering over the spot, thrusting with its claws at each little duck as it came up; but he was unsuccessful, all of the teal eventually getting into the reeds, where they were safe. In the East, by the way, I have seen the same trick of hovering over the water where a flock of ducks had disappeared, performed by a Cooper's hawk. He had stooped at some nearly grown flappers of the black duck; they all went under water, and he remained just above, grasping at any one that appeared, and forcing them to go under without getting a chance to breathe. Soon he had singled out one, which kept down a shorter and shorter time at each dive; it soon grew exhausted, was a little too slow in taking a dive, and was grasped in the claws of its foe.

In duck-shooting where there are reeds, grass and

water-lilies the cripples should be killed at once, even at the cost of burning some additional powder, many kinds of waterfowl being very expert at diving. Others, as widgeon, shoveller, and teal, do not dive, merely trying to hide in some hole in the bank; and these are generally birds that fall to the touch of shot much more easily than is the case with their tougher relatives.

There are two or three species of birds tolerably common over the plains which we do not often regularly hunt, but which are occasionally shot for the table. These are the curlew, the upland or grass plover, and the golden plover. All three kinds belong to the family of what are called wading birds; but with us it is rare to see any one of them near water.

The curlew is the most conspicuous; indeed its loud, incessant clamor, its erect carriage, and the intense curiosity which possesses it, and which makes it come up to circle around any strange object, all combine to make it in springtime one of the most conspicuous features of plains life. At that time curlews are seen in pairs or small parties, keeping to the prairies and grassy uplands. They are never silent, and their discordant noise can be heard half a mile off. Whenever they discover a wagon or a man on horseback, they fly toward him, though usually taking good care to keep out of gunshot. They then fly over and round the object, calling all the time, and sometimes going off to one side, where they will light and run rapidly through the grass; and in this manner they will sometimes accompany a hunter or traveller for miles, scaring off all game. By the end of July or August they have reared their young; they then go in small flocks, are comparatively silent, and are very good eating. I have never made a practice of shooting them, though I have fired at them sometimes with the rifle, and in this way have now and then killed one; twice I have hit them on the wing with this weapon, while they were soaring slowly about above me, occasionally passing pretty near.

The grass plover is found in the same places as the curlew, and like it breeds with us. Its flesh is just as good, and it has somewhat the same habits; but is less wary, noisy, and inquisitive. The golden plover is only found during the migrations, when large flocks may sometimes be seen. They are delicious eating; the only ones I have ever shot have been killed with the little ranch gun, when riding round the ranch, or travelling from one point to another.

Like the grouse, and other ground-nesting birds, the curlews and plovers during breeding-time have for their chief foes the coyotes, badgers, skunks, and other flesh-eating prowlers; and as all these are greatly thinned off by the cattle-men, with their fire-arms and their infinitely more deadly poison, the partial and light settlement of the country that accompanies the cattle industry has had the effect of making all these birds more plentiful than before; and most unlike the large game, game birds bid fair to increase in numbers during the next few years.

The skunks are a nuisance in more ways than one. They are stupid, familiar beasts, with a great predilection for visiting camps, and the shacks or huts of the settlers, to pick up any scraps of meat that may be lying round. I have time and again known a skunk to actually spend several hours of the night in perseveringly digging a hole underneath the logs of a hut, so as to get inside among the inmates. The animal then hunts about among them, and of course no one will willingly molest it; and it has often been known to deliberately settle down upon and begin to eat one of the sleepers. The strange and terrible thing about these attacks is that in certain districts and at certain times the bite of the skunk is surely fatal, producing hydrophobia; and many cowmen, soldiers, and hunters have annually died from this cause. There is no wild beast in the West, no matter what its size and ferocity, so dreaded by old plainsmen as this seemingly harmless little beast.

I remember one rather ludicrous incident connected with a skunk. A number of us, among whom was a huge, happy-go-lucky Scotchman, who went by the name of Sandy, were sleeping in a hut, when a skunk burrowed under the logs and got in. Hearing it moving about among the tin pans Sandy struck a light, was much taken by the familiarity of the pretty black and white little animal, and, as it seemed in his eyes a curiosity, took a shot at it with his revolver. He missed; the skunk, for a wonder, retired promptly without taking any notice of the attack; and the rest of the alarmed sleepers, when informed of the cause of the shot, cursed the Scotchman up hill and down dale for having so nearly brought dire confusion on them all. The latter took the abuse very philosophically, merely remarking: "I'm glad a did na kill him mysel'; he seemed such a dacent wee beastie." The sequel proved that neither the skunk nor Sandy had learned any wisdom by the encounter, for half an hour later the "dacent wee beastie" came back, and this time Sandy fired at him with fatal effect. Of course the result was a frantic rush of all hands from the hut, Sandy exclaiming with late but sincere repentance: "A did na ken't wad cause such a tragadee."

Besides curlew and plover there are at times, especially during the migrations, a number of species of other waders to be found along the streams and pools in the cattle region. Yellowlegs, yelper, willet, marlin, dough bird, stilt, and avocet are often common, but they do not begin to be as plentiful as they are in the more fertile lands to the eastward, and the ranchmen never shoot at them or follow them as game birds.

A more curious bird than any of these is the plains plover, which avoids the water and seems to prefer the barren plateaus and almost desert-like reaches of sagebrush and alkali. Plains plovers are pretty birds, and not at all shy. In fall they are fat and good eating, but they are not plentiful enough to be worth going after. Sometimes they are to be seen in the most seemingly unlikely places for a wader to be. Last spring one pair nested in a broken piece of Bad Lands near my ranch, where the ground is riven and twisted into abrupt, steep crests and deep canyons. The soil is seemingly wholly unfitted to support bird life, as it is almost bare of vegetation, being covered with fossil plants, shells, fishes, etc.—all of which objects, by the way, the frontiersman, who is much given to broad generalization, groups together under the startling title of "stone clams."

CHAPTER III

The Grouse of the Northern Cattle Plains

To my mind there is no comparison between sport with the rifle and sport with the shot-gun. The rifle is the freeman's weapon. The man who uses it well in the chase shows that he can at need use it also in war with human foes. I would no more compare the feat of one who bags his score of ducks or quail with that of him who fairly hunts down and slays a buck or bear, than I would compare the skill necessary to drive a buggy with that required to ride a horse across country; or the dexterity acquired in handling a billiard cue with that shown by a skilful boxer or oarsman. The difference is not one of degree; it is one of kind.

I am far from decrying the shot-gun. It is always pleasant as a change from the rifle, and in the Eastern States it is almost the only fire-arm which we now have a chance to use. But out in the cattle country it is the rifle that is always carried by the ranchman who cares for sport. Large game is still that which is sought after, and most of the birds killed are either simply slaughtered for the pot, or else shot for the sake of variety, while really after deer or antelope; though every now and then I have taken a day with the shot-gun after nothing else but prairie fowl.

The sharp-tailed prairie fowl is much the most plentiful of the feathered game to be found on the northern cattle plains, where it replaces the common prairie chicken so abundant on the prairies to the east and south-east of the range of our birds. In habits it is much like the latter, being one of the grouse which keep to the open, treeless tracts, though it is far less averse to timber than is its nearest relative, and often is found among the cotton-wood trees and thick brush which fringe the streams. I have never noticed that its habits when pursued differ much from those of the common prairie chicken, though it is perhaps a little more shy, and is certainly much more apt to light on a tree like the ruffed grouse. It is, however, essentially a bird of the wilds, and it is a curious fact that it seems to retreat before civilization, continually moving westward as the wheat fields advance, while its place is taken by the common form, which seems to keep pace with the settlement of the country. Like the latter bird, and unlike the ruffed grouse and blue grouse, which have white meat, its flesh is dark, and it is very good eating from about the middle of August to the middle of November, after which it is a little tough.

As already said, the ranchmen do not often make a regular hunt after these grouse. This is partly because most of them look with something akin to contempt upon any fire-arm but the rifle or revolver, and partly because it is next to impossible to keep hunting-dogs very long on the plains. The only way to check in any degree the ravages of the wolves is by the most liberal use of strychnine, and the offal of any game killed by a cattle-man is pretty sure to be poisoned before being left, while the "wolfer," or profes-sional wolf-killer strews his bait everywhere. It thus comes about that any dog who is in the habit of going any distance from the house is almost sure to run across and eat some of the poisoned meat, the effect of which is certain death. The only time I have ever shot sharp-tailed prairie fowl over dogs was during a trip to the eastward with my brother, which will be described further on. Out on the plains I have occasionally taken a morning with the shotgun after them, but more often have either simply butchered them for the pot, when out of meat, or else have killed a few with the rifle when I happened to come across them while after deer or antelope.

Occasions frequently arise, in living a more or less wild life, when a man has to show his skill in shifting for himself; when, for instance, he has to go out and make a foray upon the grouse, neither for sport, nor yet for a change of diet, but actually for food. Under such circumstances he of course pays no regard to the rules of sport which would govern his conduct on other occasions. If a man's dinner for several consecutive days depends upon a single shot, he is a fool if he does not take every advantage he can. I remember, for instance, one time when we were travelling along the valley of the Powder River, and got entirely out of fresh meat, owing to my making a succession of ludicrously bad misses at deer. Having had my faith in my capacity to kill any thing whatever with the rifle a good deal shaken, I started off one morning on horseback with the shot-gun. Until nearly noon I saw nothing; then, while riding through a barren-looking bottom, I happened to spy some prairie fowl squatting close to the ground underneath a sage-brush. It was some minutes before I could make out what they were, they kept so low and so quiet, and their color harmonized so well with their surroundings. Finally I was convinced that they were grouse, and rode my horse slowly by them. When opposite, I reined him in and fired, killing the whole bunch of five birds. Another time at the ranch our supply of fresh meat gave out entirely, and I sallied forth with the ranch gun, intent, not on sport, but on slaughter. It was late fall, and as I rode along in the dawn (for the sun was not up) a small pack of prairie fowl passed over my head and lit on a dead tree that stood out some little distance from a grove of cotton-woods. They paid little attention to me, but they are so shy at that season that I did not dare to try to approach them on foot, but let the horse jog on at the regular cow-pony gait—a kind of single-foot pace, between a walk and a trot,—and as I passed by fired into the tree and killed four birds. Now, of course I would not have dreamed of taking either of these shots had I been out purely for sport, and neither needed any more skill than would be shown in killing hens in a barn-yard; but, after all, when one is hunting for one's dinner he takes an interest in his success which he would otherwise lack, and on both occasions I felt a most unsportsman-like glee when I found how many I had potted.

The habits of this prairie fowl vary greatly at different seasons of the year. It is found pretty much everywhere within moderate distance of water, for it does not frequent the perfectly dry wastes where we find the great sage cock. But it is equally at home on the level prairie and among the steep hills of the Bad Lands. When on the ground it has rather a comical look, for it stands very high on its legs, carries its sharp little tail cocked up like a wren's, and when startled stretches its neck out straight; altogether it gives one the impression of being a very angular bird. Of course it crouches, and moves about when feeding, like any other grouse.

One of the strangest, and to me one of the most attractive, sounds of the prairie is the hollow booming made by the cocks in spring. Before the snow has left the ground they begin, and at the break of morning their deep resonant calls sound from far and near, for in still weather they can be heard at an immense distance. I hardly know how to describe the call; indeed it cannot be described in words. It has a hollow, vibrant sound like that of some wind instrument, and would hardly be recognized as a bird note at all. I have heard it at evening, but more often shortly after dawn; and I have often stopped and listened to it for many minutes, for it is as strange and weird a form of natural music as any I know. At the time of the year when they utter these notes the cocks gather together in certain places and hold dancing rings, posturing and strutting about as they face and pass each other.

The nest is generally placed in a tuft of grass or under a sage-brush in the open, but occasionally in the brush wood near a stream. The chicks are pretty little balls of mottled brown and yellow down. The mother takes great care of them, leading them generally into some patch of brushwood, but often keeping them out in the deep grass. Frequently when out among the cattle I have ridden my horse almost over a hen with a brood of chicks. The little chicks first attempt to run off in single file; if discovered they scatter and squat down under clods of earth or tufts of grass. Holding one in my hand near my pocket it scuttled into it like a flash. The mother, when she sees her brood discovered, tumbles about through the grass as if wounded, in the effort to decoy the foe after her. If she is successful in this, she takes a series of short flights, keeping just out of reach of her pursuer, and when the latter has been lured far enough from the chicks the hen rises and flies off at a humming speed.

By the middle of August the young are well enough grown to shoot, and are then most delicious eating. Different coveys at this time vary greatly in their behavior if surprised feeding in the open. Sometimes they will not permit of a very close approach, and will fly off after one or two have been shot; while again they will show perfect indifference to the approach of man, and will allow the latter to knock off the heads of five or six with his rifle before the rest take the alarm and fly off. They now go more or less all over the open ground, but are especially fond of frequenting the long grass in the bottoms of the coulies and ravines and the dense brush along the edges of the creeks and in the valleys; there they will invariably be found at mid-day, and will lie till they are almost trodden on before rising.

Late in the month of August one year we had been close-herding a small bunch of young cattle on a bottom about a mile square, walled in by bluffs, and with, as an inlet, a long, dry creek running back many miles into the Bad Lands, where it branched out into innumerable smaller creeks and coulies. We wished to get the cattle accustomed to the locality, for animals are more apt to stray when first brought on new ground than at any later period; so each night we "bedded" them on the level bottom—that is, gathering them together on the plain, one of us would ride slowly and quietly round and round the herd, heading off and turning back into it all beasts that tried to stray off, but carefully avoiding disturbing them or making any unusual noise; and by degrees they would all lie down, close together. This "bedding down" is always done when travelling with a large herd, when, of course, it needs several cowboys to do it; and in such cases some of the cowboys keep guard all the time, walking their horses round the herd, and singing and calling to the cattle all night long. The cattle seem to like to hear the human voice, and it tends to keep them quiet and free from panic. Often when camping near some great cattle outfit I have lain awake at night for an hour or over listening to the wild, not unmusical, calls of the cowboys as they rode round the half-slumbering steers. In the clear, still night air the calls can be heard for a mile and more, and I like to listen to them as they come through the darkness, half mellowed by the distance, for they are one of the characteristic sounds of plains life. Texan steers often give considerable trouble before they can be bedded, and are prone to stampede, especially in a thunder-storm. But with the little herd we were at this time guarding there was no difficulty whatever, the animals being grade short-horns of Eastern origin. After seeing them quiet we would leave them for the night, again riding out early in the morning.

On every occasion when we thus rode out in the morning we saw great numbers of prairie fowl feeding in the open plain in small flocks, each evidently composed of a hen and her grown brood. They would often be right round the cattle, and went indifferently among the sage-brush or out on the short prairie grass. They flew into the bottom from some distance off about daybreak, fed for a couple of hours, and soon after sunrise again took wing and flew up along the course of the dry creek mentioned above. While on the bottom they were generally quite shy, not permitting any thing like a close approach before taking wing. Their habit of crowing or clucking while flying off is very noticeable; it is, by the way, a most strongly characteristic trait of this species. I have been especially struck by it when shooting in Minnesota, where both the sharp-tail and the common prairie fowl are found; the contrast between the noisiness of one bird and the quiet of the other was very marked. If one of us approached a covey on horseback the birds would, if they thought they were unobserved, squat down close to the ground; more often they would stand very erect, and walk off. If we came too close to one it would utter a loud kuk-kuk-kuk, and be off, at every few strokes of its wings repeating the sound—a kind of crowing cluck. This is the note they utter when alarmed, or when calling to one another. When a flock are together and undisturbed they keep up a sociable garrulous cackling.

Every morning by the time the sun had been up a little while the grouse had all gone from the bottom, but later in the day while riding along the creek among the cattle we often stumbled upon little flocks. We fired at them with our revolvers whenever we were close enough, but the amount we got in this way was very limited, and as we were rather stinted for fresh meat, the cattle taking up so much of our time as to prevent our going after deer, I made up my mind to devote a morning to hunting up the creeks and coulies for grouse, with the shot-gun.

Accordingly the next morning I started, just about the time the last of the flocks were flying away from their feeding-ground on the bottom. I trudged along on foot, not wanting to be bothered by a horse. The air was fresh and cool, though the cloudless sky boded a hot noon. As I walked by the cattle they stopped grazing and looked curiously at me, for they were unused to seeing any man not on horseback. But they did not offer to molest me; Texan or even northern steers bred on the more remote ranges will often follow and threaten a foot-man for miles. While passing among the cattle it was amusing to see the actions of the little cow buntings. They were very familiar little birds, lighting on the backs of the beasts, and keeping fluttering round their heads as they walked through the grass, hopping up into the air all the time. At first I could not make out what they were doing; but on watching them closely saw that they were catching the grasshoppers and moths which flew into the air to avoid the cattle's hoofs. They are as tame with horsemen; while riding through a patch of tall grass a flock of buntings will often keep circling within a couple of yards of the horse's head, seizing the insects as they fly up before him.

The valley through which the creek ran was quite wide, bordered by low buttes. After a heavy rainfall the water rushes through the at other times dry bed in a foaming torrent, and it thus cuts it down into a canyon-like shape, making it a deep, winding, narrow ditch, with steep sides. Along the edges of this ditch were dense patches, often quite large, of rose-bushes, bullberry bushes, ash, and wild cherry, making almost impenetrable thickets, generally not over breast high. In the bottom of the valley, along the edges of the stream bed, the grass was long and coarse, entirely different from the short fine bunch grass a little farther back, the favorite food of the cattle.

Almost as soon as I had entered the creek, in walking through a small patch of brush I put up an old cock, as strong a flyer as the general run of October birds. Off he went, with a whirr, clucking and crowing; I held the little 16-bore fully two feet ahead of him, pulled the trigger, and down he came into the bushes. The sharp-tails fly strongly and steadily, springing into the air when they rise, and then going off in a straight line, alternately sailing and giving a succession of rapid wing-beats. Sometimes they will sail a long distance with set wings before alighting, and when they are passing overhead with their wings outstretched each of the separate wing feathers can be seen, rigid and distinct.

Picking up and pocketing my bird I walked on, and on turning round a shoulder of the bluffs saw a pair of sharptails sitting sunning themselves on the top of a bullberry bush. As soon as they saw me they flew off a short distance and lit in the bed of the creek. Rightly judging that there were more birds than those I had seen I began to beat with great care the patches of brush and long grass on both sides of the creek, and soon was rewarded by some very pretty shooting. The covey was a large one, composed of two or three broods of young prairie fowl, and I struck on the exact place, a slight hollow filled with low brush and tall grass, where they were lying. They lay very close, and my first notice of their presence was given by one that I almost trod on, which rose from fairly between my feet. A young grouse at this season offers an easy shot, and he was dropped without difficulty. At the report two others rose and I got one. When I had barely reloaded the rest began to get up, singly or two or three at a time, rising straight up to clear the edge of the hollow, and making beautiful marks; when the last one had been put up I had down seven birds, of which I picked up six, not being able to find the other. A little farther on I put up and shot a single grouse, which fell into a patch of briars I could not penetrate. Then for some time I saw nothing, although beating carefully through every likely-looking place. One patch of grass, but a few feet across, I walked directly through without rousing any thing; happening to look back when I had gone some fifty yards, I was surprised to see a dozen heads and necks stretched up, and eying me most inquisitively; their owners were sharp-tails, a covey of which I had almost walked over without their making a sign. I strode back; but at my first step they all stood up straight, with their absurd little tails held up in the air, and at the next step away they went, flying off a quarter of a mile and then scattering in the brushy hollows where a coulie headed up into the buttes. (Grouse at this season hardly ever light in a tree.) I marked them down carefully and tramped all through the place, yet I only succeeded in putting up two, of which I got one and missed the other with both barrels. After that I walked across the heads of the coulies, but saw nothing except in a small swale of high grass, where there was a little covey of five, of which I got two with a right and left. It was now very hot, and I made for a spring which I knew ran out of a cliff a mile or two off. There I stayed till long after the shadows began to lengthen, when I started homeward. For some miles I saw nothing, but as the evening came on the grouse began to stir. A small party flew over my head, and though I missed them with both barrels, either because I miscalculated the distance or for some other reason, yet I marked them down very well, and when I put them up again got two. Three times afterward I came across coveys, either flying or walking out from the edges of the brushes, and I got one bird out of each, reaching home just after sunset with fifteen sharptails strung over my back. Of course working after grouse on an August day in this manner, without a dog, is very tiring, and no great bag can be made without a pointer or setter.

In September the sharp-tails begin to come out from the brushy coulies and creek bottoms, and to wander out among the short grass of the ravines and over the open prairie. They are at first not very shy, and in the early part of the month I have once or twice had good sport with them. Once I took a companion in the buck-board, and drove during the course of the day twenty or twenty-five miles along the edge of the rolling prairie, crossing the creeks, and skirting the wooded basins where the Bad Lands began. We came across quite a number of coveys, which in almost all cases waited for us to come up, and as the birds did not rise all together, I got three or four shots at each covey, and came home with ten and a half couple.

A little later the birds become shy and acquire their full strength of wing. They now wander far out on the prairie, and hardly ever make any effort to squat down and conceal themselves in the marvellous way which they have earlier in the season, but, on the contrary, trust to their vigilance and their powers of flight for their safety. On bare ground it is now impossible to get anywhere near them, but if they are among sage-brush or in other low cover they afford fine sport to a good shot, with a close-shooting, strong-hitting gun. I remember one evening, while coming over with a wagon team from the head waters of O'Fallon Creek, across the Big Sandy, when it became a matter of a good deal of interest for us to kill something, as otherwise we would have had very little to eat. We had camped near a succession of small pools, containing one or two teal, which I shot; but a teal is a small bird when placed before three hungry men. Sharp-tails, however, were quite numerous, having come in from round about, as evening came on, to drink. They were in superb condition, stout and heavy, with clean, bright plumage, but very shy; and they rose so far off and flew so strongly and swiftly that a good many cartridges were spent before four of the plump, white-bellied birds were brought back to the wagon in my pockets.

Later than this they sometimes unite into great packs, containing hundreds of individuals, and then show a strong preference for the timbered ravines and the dense woods and underbrush of the river bottoms, the upper branches of the trees being their favorite resting-places. On very cold mornings, when they are feeling numb and chilled, a man can sometimes get very close up to them, but as a rule they are very wild, and the few I have killed at this season of the year have been shot with the rifle, either from a tree or when standing out on the bare hillsides, at a considerable distance. They offer very pretty marks for target practice with the rifle, and it needs a good shot to hit one at eighty or a hundred yards.

But though the shot-gun is generally of no use late in the season, yet last December I had a good afternoon's sport with it. There was a light snow falling, and having been in the house all the morning, I determined to take a stroll out in the afternoon with the shot-gun. A couple of miles from the house was a cedar canyon; that is, a canyon one of whose sides was densely wooded with gnarled, stunted evergreens. This had been a favorite resort for the sharp-tails for some time, and it was especially likely that they would go to it during a storm, as it afforded fine shelter, and also food. The buttes bounding it on the side where the trees were, rose to a sharp crest, which extended along with occasional interruptions for over a mile, and by walking along near this and occasionally looking out over it, I judged I would get up close to the grouse, while the falling snow and the wind would deaden the report of the gun, and not let it scare all the prairie fowl out of the canyon at the first fire. It came out as I had planned and expected. I clambered up to the crest near the mouth of the gorge, braced myself firmly, and looked over the top. At once a dozen sharp-tails, who had perched in the cedar tops almost at my feet, took wing, crossed over the canyon, and as they rose all in a bunch to clear the opposite wall I fired both barrels into the brown, and two of the birds dropped down to the bottom of the ravine. They fell on the snow-covered open ground where I could easily find them again, and as it would have been a great and useless labor to have gone down for them, I left them where they were and walked on along the crest. Before I had gone a hundred yards I had put up another sharp-tail from a cedar and killed him in fine style as he sailed off below me. The snow and bad weather seemed to make the prairie fowl disinclined to move. There must have been a good many score of them scattered in bunches among the cedars, and as I walked along I put up a covey or a single bird every two or three hundred yards. They were always started when I was close up to them, and the nature of the place made them offer excellent shots as they went off, while when killed they dropped down on the snow-covered canyon bottom where they could be easily recovered on my walk home. When the sharp-tails had once left the canyon they scattered among the broken buttes. I tried to creep up to one or two, but they were fully as wild and watchful as deer, and would not let me come within a hundred yards of them; so I turned back, climbed down into the canyon, and walked homeward through it, picking up nine birds on the way, the result of a little over an hour's shooting. Most of them were dead outright; and the two or three who had been only wounded were easily followed by the tracks they made in the tell-tale snow.

Most of the prairie fowl I have killed, however, have not been obtained in the course of a day or an afternoon regularly spent after them for the sake of the sport, but have simply been shot with whatever weapon came handy, because we actually needed them for immediate use. On more than one occasion I would have gone supperless or dinnerless had it not been for some of these grouse; and one such instance I will give.

One November, about the middle of the month, we

had driven in a beef herd (which we wished to ship to the cattle yards), round the old cantonment building, in which a few years ago troops had been stationed to guard against Indian outbreaks. Having taken care of the beef herd, I

tle bunch of cattle which was some
the river, under the care of one of
fellow, born in Maine, whose ca-
an extent only possible in Amer-
vely followed the occupations of
buffalo hunter, and cowboy.

bout noon, but there was so much
was an hour and a half afterwards
smart little cow-pony and loped
It was a sharp day, the mercury
; and the pony, fresh and untired,
ing in the cold, went along at a
sets in so early at this season that
iles before I began to fear that I
ack by nightfall. The well-beaten
e bottoms for some distance and
the Bad Lands, leading up and
ines and over the ridge crests of
oken country, and crossing a great
the wind blew savagely, sweeping
off of the bent blades of short,
king a wide circle of some twelve
e back to the Little Missouri, and

led along the bottoms between the rows of high bluffs, continually crossing and recrossing the river. These crossings were difficult and disagreeable for the horse, as they always are when the ice is not quite heavy enough to bear.

The water had not frozen until two or three days before, and the cold snap had not yet lasted long enough to make the ice solid, besides which it was covered with about half an inch of light snow that had fallen, concealing all bad-looking places. The ice after bearing the cautiously stepping pony for a few yards would suddenly break and let him down to the bottom, and he would then have to plunge and paw his way through to the opposite shore. Often it is almost impossible to make a pony attempt the crossing under such circumstances; and I have seen ponies which had to be knocked down and pulled across glare ice on their sides. If the horse slips and falls it is a serious matter to the rider; for a wetting in such cold weather, with a long horseback journey to make, is no joke.

I was still several miles from the hut I was striving to reach when the sun set; and for some time previous the valley had been in partial darkness, though the tops of the sombre bluffs around were still lit up. The pony loped steadily on along the trail, which could be dimly made out by the starlight. I hurried the willing little fellow all I could without distressing him, for though I knew the road pretty well, yet I doubted if I could find it easily in perfect darkness; and the clouds were gathering overhead with a rapidity which showed that the starlight would last but a short while. The light snow rendered the hoof beats of my horse muffled and indistinct; and almost the only sound that broke the silence was the long-drawn, melancholy howling of a wolf, a quarter of a mile off. When we came to the last crossing the pony was stopped and watered; and we splashed through over a rapid where the ice had formed only a thin crust. On the opposite side was a large patch of cotton-woods thickly grown up with underbrush, the whole about half a mile square. In this was the cow-boy's shack, but as it was now pitch dark I was unable to find it until I rode clean through to the cow-corral, which was out in the open on the other side. Here I dismounted, groped around till I found the path, and then easily fol-lowed it to the shack.

Rather to my annoyance the cowboy was away, having run out of provisions, as I afterwards learned; and of course he had left nothing to eat behind him. The tough little pony was, according to custom, turned loose to shift for himself; and I went into the low, windowless hut, which was less than twelve feet square. In one end was a great chimney-place, and it took but a short time to start a roaring fire, which speedily made the hut warm and comfortable. Then I went down to the river with an axe and a pail, and got some water; I had carried a paper of tea in my pocket, and the tea-kettle was soon simmering away. I should have liked something to eat, but as I did not have it, the hot tea did not prove such a bad substitute for a cold and tired man.

Next morning I sallied out at break of day with the rifle, for I was pretty hungry. As soon as I stepped from the hut I could hear the prairie fowl crowing and calling to one another from the tall trees. There were many score— many hundreds would perhaps be more accurate—scat-tered through the wood. Evidently they had been attracted by the good cover and by the thick growth of choke-cherries and wild plums. As the dawn brightened the sharp-tails kept up incessantly their hoarse clucking, and small parties began to fly down from their roosts to the berry bushes. While perched up among the bare limbs of the trees, sharply outlined against the sky, they were very conspicuous. Generally they crouched close down, with the head drawn in to the body and the feathers ruffled, but when alarmed or restless they stood up straight with their necks stretched out, looking very awkward. Later in the day they would have been wild and hard to approach, but I kept out of their sight, and sometimes got two or three shots at the same bird before it flew off. They offered beautiful marks, and I could generally get a rest for my rifle, while in the gray morning, before sunrise, I was not very conspicuous myself, and could get up close beneath where they were; so I did not have much trouble in killing five, almost all of them shot very nearly where the neck joins the body, one having the head fairly cut off. Salt, like tea, I had carried with me, and it was not long before two of the birds, plucked and cleaned, were split open and roasting before the fire. And to me they seemed most delicious food, although even in November the sharp-tails, while keeping their game flavor, have begun to be dry and tough, most unlike the tender and juicy young of August and September.

The best day's work I ever did after sharp-tails was in the course of the wagon trip, already mentioned, which my brother and I made through the fertile farming country to the eastward. We had stopped over night with a Norwegian settler who had taken and adapted to a farmhouse an old log trading-post of one of the fur companies, lying in the timber which fringed a river, and so stoutly built as to have successfully withstood the assaults of time. We were travelling in a light covered wagon, in which we could drive anywhere over the prairie. Our dogs would have made an Eastern sportsman blush, for when roughing it in the West we have to put up with any kind of mongrel makeshift, and the best dog gets pretty well battered after a season or two. I never had a better duck retriever than a little yellow cur, with hardly a trace of hunting blood in his veins. On this occasion we had a stiff-jointed old pointer with a stub tail, and a wild young setter pup, tireless and ranging very free (a Western dog on the prairies should cover five times the ground necessary for an Eastern one to get over), but very imperfectly trained.

Half of the secret of success on a shooting trip lies in getting up early and working all day; and this at least we had learned, for we we were off as soon as there was light enough by which to drive. The ground, of course, was absolutely fenceless, houses being many miles apart. Through the prairie, with its tall grass, in which the sharp-tails lay at night and during the day, were scattered great grain fields, their feeding-grounds in the morning and evening. Our plan was to drive from one field to another, getting out at each and letting the dogs hunt it over. The birds were in small coveys and lay fairly well to the dogs, though they rose much farther off from us in the grain fields than they did later in the day when we flushed them from the tall grass of the prairie (I call it tall grass in contradistinction to the short bunch grass of the cattle plains to the westward). Old stub-tail, though slow, was very staunch and careful, never flushing a bird, while the puppy, from pure heedlessness, and with the best intentions, would sometimes bounce into the midst of a covey before he knew of their presence. On the other hand, he covered twice the ground that the pointer did. The actual killing the birds was a good deal like quail shooting in the East, except that it was easier, the marks being so much larger. When we came to a field we would beat through it a hundred yards apart, the dogs ranging in long diagonals. When either the setter or the pointer came to a stand, the other generally backed him. If the covey was near enough, both of us, otherwise, whichever was closest, walked cautiously up. The grouse generally flushed before we came up to the dog, rising all together, so as to give only a right and left.

When the morning was well advanced the grouse left the stubble fields and flew into the adjoining prairie. We marked down several coveys into one spot, where the ground was rolling and there were here and there a few bushes in the hollows. Carefully hunting over this, we found two or three coveys and had excellent sport out of each. The sharp-tails in these places lay very close, and we had to walk them up, when they rose one at a time, and thus allowed us shot after shot; whereas, as already said, earlier in the day we merely got a quick right and left at each covey. At least half the time we were shooting in our rubber overcoats, as the weather was cloudy and there were frequent flurries of rain.

We rested a couple of hours at noon for lunch, and the afternoon's sport was simply a repetition of the morning's, except that we had but one dog to work with; for shortly after mid-day the stub-tail pointer, for his sins, encountered a skunk, with which he waged prompt and valiant battle—thereby rendering himself, for the balance of the time, wholly useless as a servant and highly offensive as a companion.

The setter pup did well, ranging very freely, but naturally got tired and careless, flushing his birds half the time; and we had to stop when we still had a good hour of daylight left. Nevertheless we had in our wagon, when we came in at night, a hundred and five grouse, of which sixty-two had fallen to my brother's gun, and forty-three to mine. We would have done much better with more serviceable dogs; besides, I was suffering all day long from a most acute colic, which was anything but a help to good shooting.

Besides the sharp-tail there is but one kind of grouse found in the northern cattle plains. This is the sage cock, a bird the size of a young turkey, and, next to the Old World capercailzie or cock of the woods, the largest of the grouse family. It is a handsome bird with a long pointed tail and black belly, and is a very characteristic form of the regions which it inhabits.

It is peculiarly a desert grouse, for though sometimes found in the grassy prairies and on the open river bottoms, it seems really to prefer the dry arid wastes where the withered-looking sage-brush and the spiney cactus are almost the only plants to be found, and where the few pools of water are so bitterly alkaline as to be nearly undrinkable. It is pre-eminently the grouse of the plains, and, unlike all of its relatives, is never found near trees; indeed no trees grow in its haunts.

As is the case with the two species of prairie fowl the cocks of this great bird become very noisy in the early spring. If a man happens at that season to be out in the dry plains which are frequented by the sage fowl he will hear in the morning, before sunrise, the deep, sonorous booming of the cocks, as they challenge one another or call to their mates. This call is uttered in a hollow, bass tone, and can be heard a long distance in still weather; it is difficult to follow up, for it has a very ventriloquial effect.

Unlike the sharp-tail the habits and haunts of the sage fowl are throughout the year the same, except that it grows shyer as the season advances, and occasionally wanders a little farther than formerly from its birthplace. It is only found where the tough, scraggly wild sage abounds, and it feeds for most of the year solely on sage leaves, varying this diet in August and September by quantities of grasshoppers. Curiously enough it does not possess any gizzard, such as most gallinaceous birds have, but has in its place a membranous stomach, suited to the digestion of its peculiar food.

The little chicks follow their mother as soon as hatched, and she generally keeps them in the midst of some patch of sage-brush so dense as to be almost impenetrable to man or beast. The little fellows skulk and dodge through the crooked stems so cleverly that it is almost impossible to catch them. Early in August, when the brood is well grown, the mother leads them out, and during the next two months they are more often found out on the grassy prairies than is the case at any other season. They do not form into packs like the prairie fowl as winter comes on, two broods at the outside occasionally coming together; and they then again retire to the more waste parts of the plains, living purely on sage leaves, and keeping closely to the best-sheltered hollows until the spring-time.

In the early part of the season the young, and indeed their parents also, are tame and unsuspicious to the very verge of stupidity, and at this time are often known by the name of "fool-hens" among the frontiers-men. They grow shyer as the season advances, and after the first of October are difficult to approach, but even then are rarely as wild as the sharp-tails.

It is commonly believed that the flesh of the sage fowl is uneatable, but this is very far from being the truth, and, on the contrary, it is excellent eating in August and September, when grasshoppers constitute their chief food, and, if the birds are drawn as soon as shot, is generally perfectly palatable at other seasons of the year. The first time I happened to find this out was on the course of a trip taken with one of my foremen as a companion through the arid plains to the westward of the Little Missouri. We had been gone for two or three days and camped by a mud hole, which was almost dry, what water it still held being almost as thick as treacle. Our luxuries being limited, I bethought me of a sage cock which I had shot during the day and had hung to the saddle. I had drawn it as soon as it was picked up, and I made up my mind to try how it tasted. A good deal to our surprise, the meat, though dark and coarse-grained, proved perfectly well flavored, and was quite as good as wild-goose, which it much resembled. Some young sage fowl, shot shortly afterward, proved tender and juicy, and tasted quite as well as sharp-tails. All of these birds had their crops crammed with grasshoppers, and doubtless the nature of their food had much to do with their proving so good for the table. An old bird, which had fed on nothing but sage, and was not drawn when shot, would, beyond question, be very poor eating. Like the spruce grouse and the two kinds of prairie fowl, but unlike the ruffed grouse and blue grouse, the sage fowl has dark meat.

In walking and running on the ground, sage fowl act much like common hens, and can skulk through the sage-brush so fast that it is often difficult to make them take wing. When surprised they will sometimes squat flat down with their heads on the ground, when it is very difficult to make them out, as their upper parts harmonize curiously in color with the surroundings. I have never known of their being shot over a dog, and, indeed, the country where they are found is so dry and difficult that no dog would be able to do any work in it.

When flushed, they rise with a loud whirring, laboring heavily, often clucking hoarsely; when they get fairly under way they move along in a strong, steady flight, sailing most of the time, but giving, every now and then, a succession of powerful wing-beats, and their course is usually sustained for a mile or over before they light. They are very easy marks, but require hard hitting to bring them down, for they are very tenacious of life. On one occasion I came upon a flock and shot an old cock through the body with the rifle. He fell over, fluttering and kicking, and I shot a young one before the rest of the flock rose. To my astonishment the old cock recovered himself and made off after them, actually flying for half a mile before he dropped. When I found him he was quite dead, the ball having gone clean through him. It was a good deal as if a man had run a mile with a large grapeshot through his body.

Most of the sage fowl I have killed have been shot with the rifle when I happened to run across a covey while out riding, and wished to take two or three of them back for dinner. Only once did I ever make a trip with the shotgun for the sole purpose of a day's sport with these birds.

This was after having observed that there were several small flocks of sage fowl at home on a great plateau or high plain, crossed by several dry creeks, which was about eight miles from the cow-camp where I was staying; and I concluded that I would devote a day to their pursuit. Accordingly, one morning I started out on horseback with my double-barrel 10-bore and a supply of cartridges loaded with No. 4 shot; one of my cowboys went with me carrying a rifle so as to be ready if we ran across any antelope. Our horses were fresh, and the only way to find the birds was to cover as much ground as possible; so as soon as we reached the plateau we loped across it in parallel lines till we struck one of the creeks, when we went up it, one on each side, at a good gait, and then crossed over to another, where we repeated the operation. It was nearly noon when, while going up the third creek, we ran into a covey of about fifteen sage fowl—a much larger covey than ordinary. They were down in the bottom of the creek, which here exhibited a formation very common on the plains. Although now perfectly dry, every series of heavy rainfalls changed it into a foaming torrent, which flowed down the valley in sharp curves, eating away the land into perpendicular banks on the outside of each curve. Thus a series of small bottoms was formed, each fronted by a semicircular bluff, highest in the middle, and rising perfectly sheer and straight. At the foot of these bluffs, which varied from six to thirty feet in height, was the bed of the stream. In many of these creeks there will be a growth of small trees by the stream bed, where it runs under the bluffs, and perhaps pools of water will be found in such places even in times of drought. But on the creek where we found the sage fowl there were neither trees nor water, and the little bottoms were only covered with stunted sage-brush. Dismounting and leaving my horse with the cowboy I walked down to the edge of the bottom, which was not more than thirty or forty yards across. The covey retreated into the brush, some of the birds crouching flat down, while the others walked or ran off among the bushes. They were pretty tame, and rose one at a time as I walked on. They had to rise over the low, semicircular bluff in front of them, and, it being still early in the season, they labored heavily as they left the ground. I fired just as they topped the bluff, and as they were so close and large, and were going so slowly, I was able to knock over eight birds, hardly moving from my place during the entire time. On our way back we ran into another covey, a much smaller one, on the side of another creek; of these I got a couple; and I got another out of still a third covey, which we found out in the open, but of which the birds all rose and made off together. We carried eleven birds back, most of them young and tender, and all of them good eating.

In shooting grouse we sometimes run across rabbits. There are two kinds of these. One is the little cotton-tail, almost precisely similar in appearance to the common gray rabbit of the Eastern woods. It abounds in all the patches of dense cover along the river bottoms and in the larger creeks, and can be quite easily shot at all times, but especially when there is any snow on the ground. It is eatable but hardly ever killed except to poison and throw out as bait for the wolves.

The other kind is the great jack-rabbit. This is a characteristic animal of the plains; quite as much so as the antelope or prairie dog. It is not very abundant, but is found everywhere over the open ground, both on the prairie or those river bottoms which are not wooded, and in the more open valleys and along the gentle slopes of the Bad Lands. Sometimes it keeps to the patches of sage-brush, and in such cases will lie close to the ground when approached; but more often it is found in the short grass where there is no cover at all to speak of, and relies upon its speed for its safety. It is a comical-looking beast with its huge ears and long legs, and runs very fast, with a curious lop-sided gait, as if it was off its balance. After running a couple of hundred yards it will generally stop and sit up erect on its haunches to look round and see if it is pursued. In winter it turns snow-white except that the tips of the ears remain black. The flesh is dry, and I have never eaten it unless I could get nothing else.

Jack-rabbits are not plentiful enough nor valuable enough to warrant a man's making a hunting trip solely for their sakes; and the few that I have shot have been killed with the rifle while out after other game. They offer beautiful marks for target practice when they sit upon their haunches. But though hardly worth powder they afford excellent sport when coursed with greyhounds, being very fleet, and when closely pressed able to double so quickly that the dogs shoot by them. For reasons already given, however, it is difficult to keep sporting dogs on the plains, though doubtless in the future coursing with greyhounds will become a recognized Western sport.

This finishes the account of the small game of the northern cattle country. The wild turkey is not found with us; but it is an abundant bird farther south, and eagerly followed by the ranchmen in whose neighborhood it exists. And as it is easily the king of all game birds, and as its pursuit is a peculiarly American form of sport, some account of how it is hunted in the southern plains country may be worth reading. The following is an extract from a letter written to me by my brother, in December, 1875, while he was in Texas, containing an account of some of his turkey-hunting experience in that State. The portion relating how the birds are coursed with greyhounds is especially markworthy; it reminds one of the method of killing the great bustard with gaze-hounds, as described in English sporting books of two centuries back.

"Here, some hundred miles south and west of Fort McKavett, are the largest turkey roosts in the world. This beautiful fertile valley, through which the deep, silent stream of the Llano flows, is densely wooded with grand old pecan trees along its banks; as are those of its minor tributaries which come boiling down from off the immense upland water-shed of the staked plains, cutting the sides of the 'divide' into narrow canyons. The journey to this sportsman's paradise was over the long-rolling plains of Western Texas. Hour after hour through the day's travel we would drop into the trough of some great plains-wave only to toil on up to the crest of the next, and be met by an endless vista of boundless, billowy-looking prairie. We were following the old Fort Terret trail, its ruts cut so deep in the prairie soil by the heavy supply wagons that these ten years have not healed the scars in the earth's face. At last, after journeying for leagues through the stunted live oaks, we saw from the top of one of the larger divides a dark bluish line against the horizon,—the color of distant leafless trees,—and knew that it meant we should soon open out the valley. Another hour brought us over the last divide, and then our hunting grounds lay before and below us. All along through the unbroken natural fields the black-tail and prong-horn abound, and feast to their hearts' content all the winter through on the white, luscious, and nutritious mesquite grass. Through the valley with its flashing silver stream ran the dark line of the famous pecan-tree forests—the nightly resting-place of that king of game birds, the wild turkey. It would sound like romancing to tell of the endless number and variety of the waterfowl upon the river; while the multitude of game fish inhabiting the waters make the days spent on the river with the rod rival in excitement and good sport the nights passed gun in hand among the trees in the roosts. Of course, as we are purely out on a turkey shoot, during the day no louder sport is permitted than whipping the stream, or taking the greyhounds well back on the plains away from the river to course antelope, jack-rabbit, or maybe even some fine old gobbler himself.

"When, after our journey, we reached the brink of the canyon, to drop down into the valley, pass over the lowlands, and settle ourselves comfortably in camp under the shadow of the old stockade fort by the river, was a matter of but a few hours. There we waited for the afternoon shadows to lengthen and the evening to come, when off we went up the stream for five or six miles to a spot where some mighty forest monarchs with huge, bare, spreading limbs had caught the eye of one of our sporting scouts in the afternoon. Leaving our horses half a mile from the place, we walked silently along the river bank through the jungle to the roosting trees, where we scattered, and each man secreted himself as best he could in the underbrush, or in a hollow stump, or in the reeds of the river itself. The sun was setting, and over the hills and from the lowlands came the echoes of the familiar gobble, gobble, gobble, as each strutting, foolishly proud cock headed his admiring family for the roost, after their day's feeding on the uplands. Soon, as I lay close and hushed in my hiding-place, sounds like the clinking of silver, followed by what seemed like a breath of the wind rushing through the trees, struck my ears. I hardly dared breathe, for the sounds were made by the snapping of a gobbler's quills and his rustling feathers; and immediately a magnificent old bird, swelling and clucking, bullying his wives and abusing his weaker children to the last, trod majestically down to the water's edge, and, after taking his evening drink, winged his way to his favorite bough above, where he was joined, one by one, by his family and relations and friends, who came by tens and dozens from the surrounding country. Soon in the rapidly darkening twilight the superb old pecan trees looked as if they were bending under a heavy crop of the most odd-shaped and lively kind of fruit. The air was filled with the peevish pi-ou! pi-ou! of the sleepy birds. Gradually the noisy fluttering subsided, and the last faint unsettled peep even was hushed. Dead silence reigned, and we waited and watched. The moon climbed up, and in an another hour, as we looked through the tree-tops, we could make out against the light background of the sky, almost as clearly as by day, the sleeping victims of our guns and rifles. A low soft whistle was passed along from man to man; and the signal given, how different the scene became! A deafening report suddenly rang out into the silent night, a flash of light belched from the gun muzzle, and a heavy thud followed as twenty pounds of turkey struck the ground. In our silent moccasins we flitted about under the roost, and report after report on all sides told how good the sport was and how excellent the chance that the boys at McKavett would have plenty of turkeys at their Christmas dinner. The turkeys were so surprised by the sudden noise, so entirely unprepared for the visit of the sportsman to their secluded retreat, that they did not know what to make of it, often remaining stupidly on their branch after a companion five feet off had been shot down. With the last bird shot or flown away ended our evening's sport. All the dead birds were gathered together and strapped in bunches by our saddles and on the pack-mules. It does not take many pecan- and grass-fed turkeys to make a load, and back we trotted to camp, the steel hoofs striking into the prairie soil with a merry ring of triumph over the night's work. The hour was nearly midnight when we sat down to the delicately browned turkey steaks in the mess tent, and realized that we had enjoyed the delights of one of the best sports in Texas—turkey-shooting in the roosts.

"Early in the afternoon following the night's sport we

left the fort mounted on fine three-quarter Kentucky thorough-breds, and taking the eleven greyhounds, struck off six or eight miles into the plains. Then spreading into line we alternated dogs and horses, and keeping a general direction, beat up the small oak clumps, grass clusters, or mesquite jungles as we went along. Soon, with a loud whirr of wings, three or four turkeys rose out of the grass ahead, started up by one of the greyhounds; the rest of the party closed in from all sides; dogs and men choosing each the bird they marked as theirs. The turkey, after towering a bit, with wings set struck off at a pace like a bullet, and with eyes fixed upwards the hounds coursed after him. It was whip and spur for a mile as hard as horse, man, and hound could make the pace. The turkey at last came down nearer and nearer the ground, its small wings refusing to bear the weight of the heavy body. Finally, down he came and began running; then the hounds closed in on him and forced him up again as is always the case. The second flight was not a strong one, and soon he was skimming ten or even a less number of feet from the ground. Now came the sport of it all; the hounds were bunched and running like a pack behind him. Suddenly old 'Grimbeard,' in the heart of the pack, thought it was time for the supreme effort; with a rush he went to the front, and as a mighty spring carried him up in the air, he snapped his clean, cruel fangs under the brave old gobbler, who by a great effort rose just out of reach. One after another in the next twenty-five yards each hound made his trial and failed. At last the old hound again made his rush, sprang up a wonderful height into the air, and cut the bird down as with a knife.

"The first flight of a turkey when being coursed is rarely more than a mile, and the second about half as long. After that, if it gets up at all again, it is for very short flights so near the ground that it is soon cut down by any hound. The astonishing springs a greyhound who is an old hand at turkey coursing will make are a constant source of surprise and wonder to those fond of the sport. A turkey, after coming down from his first flight, will really perform the feat which fable attributes to the ostrich; that is, will run its head into a clump of bushes and stand motionless as if, since it cannot see its foes, it were itself equally invisible. During the day turkeys are scattered all over the plains, and it is no unusual thing to get in one afternoon's ride eight or ten of them."

CHAPTER IV

The Deer of the River Bottoms

Of all the large game of the United States, the white-tail deer is the best known and the most widely distributed. Taking the Union as a whole, fully ten men will be found who have killed white-tail for one who has killed any other kind of large game. And it is the only ruminant animal which is able to live on in the land even when it has been pretty thickly settled. There is hardly a State wherein it does not still exist, at least in some out-of-the-way corner; and long after the elk and the buffalo have passed away, and when the big-horn and prong-horn have become rare indeed, the white-tail deer will still be common in certain parts of the country.

When, less than five years ago, cattle were first driven on to the northern plains, the white-tail were the least plentiful and the least sought after of all the large game; but they have held their own as none of the others have begun to do, and are already in certain localities more common than any other kind, and indeed in many places are more common than all other kinds put together. The ranchmen along the Powder River, for instance, now have to content themselves with white-tail venison unless they make long trips back among the hills. The same is rapidly getting to be true of the Little Missouri. This is partly because the skin and meat hunters find the chase of this deer to be the most tedious and least remunerative species of hunting, and therefore only turn their attention to it when there is nothing else left to hunt, and partly because the sheep and cattle and the herdsmen who follow them are less likely to trespass on their grounds than on the grounds of other game. The white-tail is the deer of the river bottoms and the large creeks, whose beds contain plenty of brush and timber running down into them. It prefers the densest cover, in which it lies hid all day, and it is especially fond of wet, swampy places, where a horse runs the risk of being engulfed. Thus it is very rarely jumped by accident, and when the cattle stray into its haunts, which is but seldom, the cowboys are not apt to follow them. Besides, unlike most other game, it has no aversion to the presence of cattle, and in the morning and evening will come out and feed freely among them.

This last habit was the cause of our getting a fine buck a few days before last Christmas. The weather was bitterly cold, the spirit in the thermometer sometimes going down at night to 50° below zero and never for over a fortnight getting above −10° (Fahrenheit). Snow covered the ground, to the depth, however, of but a few inches, for in the cattle country the snowfall is always light. When the cold is so great it is far from pleasant to be out-of-doors. Still a certain amount of riding about among the cattle and ponies had to be done, and almost every day was spent by at least one of us in the saddle. We wore the heaviest kind of all-wool under-clothing, with flannels, lined boots, and great fur coats, caps, and gauntlets or mittens, but yet after each ride one or the other of us would be almost sure to come in with a touch of the frost somewhere about him. On one ride I froze my nose and one cheek, and each of the men froze his ears, fingers, or toes at least once during the fortnight. This generally happened while riding over a plain or plateau with a strong wind blowing in our faces. When the wind was on our backs it was not bad fun to gallop along through the white weather, but when we had to face it, it cut through us like a keen knife. The ponies did not seem to mind the cold much, but the cattle were very uncomfortable, standing humped up in the bushes except for an hour or two at mid-day when they ventured out to feed; some of the young stock which were wintering on the range for the first time died from the exposure. A very weak animal we would bring into the cow-shed and feed with hay; but this was only done in cases of the direst necessity, as such an animal has then to be fed for the rest of the winter, and the quantity of hay is limited. In the Bad Lands proper, cattle do not wander far, the deep ravines affording them a refuge from the bitter icy blasts of the winter gales; but if by any accident caught out on the open prairie in a blizzard, a herd will drift before it for maybe more than a hundred miles, until it finds a shelter capable of holding it. For this reason it is best to keep more or less of a look-out over all the bunches of beasts, riding about among them every few days, and turning back any herd that begins to straggle toward the open plains; though in winter, when weak and emaciated, the cattle must be disturbed and driven as little as possible, or the loss among them will be fearful.

One afternoon, while most of us were away from the ranch-house, one of the cowboys, riding in from his day's outing over the range, brought word that he had seen two white-tail deer, a buck and a doe, feeding with some cattle on the side of a hill across the river, and not much more than half a mile from the house. There was about an hour of daylight left, and one of the foremen, a tall, fine-looking fellow named Ferris, the best rider on the ranch but not an unusually good shot, started out at once after the deer; for in the late fall and early winter we generally kill a good deal of game, as it then keeps well and serves as a food supply throughout the cold months; after January we hunt as little as possible. Ferris found the deer easily enough, but they started before he could get a standing shot at them, and when he fired as they ran, he only broke one of the buck's hind legs, just above the ankle. He followed it in the snow for several miles, across the river, and down near the house to the end of the bottom, and then back toward the house. The buck was a cunning old beast, keeping in the densest cover, and often doubling back on his trail and sneaking off to one side as his pursuer passed by. Finally it grew too dark to see the tracks any longer, and Ferris came home.

Next morning early we went out to where he had left the trail, feeling very sure from his description of the place (which was less than a mile from the house) that we would get the buck; for when he had abandoned the pursuit the deer was in a copse of bushes and young trees some hundreds of yards across, and in this it had doubtless spent the night, for it was extremely unlikely that, wounded and tired as it was, it would go any distance after finding that it was no longer pursued.

When we got to the thicket we first made a circuit

round it to see if the wounded animal had broken cover, but though there were fresh deer tracks leading both in and out of it, none of them were made by a cripple; so we knew he was still within. It would seem to be a very easy task to track up and kill a broken-legged buck in light snow; but we had to go very cautiously, for though with only three legs he could still run a good deal faster than either of us on two, and we were anxious not to alarm him and give him a good start. Then there were several well-beaten cattle trails through the thicket, and in addition to that one or two other deer had been walking to and fro within it; so that it was hard work to follow the tracks. After working some little time we hit on the right trail, finding where the buck had turned into the thickest growth. While Ferris followed carefully in on the tracks, I stationed myself farther on toward the outside, knowing that the buck would in all likelihood start up wind. In a minute or two Ferris came on the bed where he had passed the night, and which he had evidently just left; a shout informed me that the game was on foot, and immediately afterward the crackling and snapping of the branches were heard as the deer rushed through them. I ran as rapidly and quietly as possible toward the place where the sounds seemed to indicate that he would break cover, stopping under a small tree. A minute afterward he appeared, some thirty yards off on the edge of the thicket, and halted for a second to look round before going into the open. Only his head and antlers were visible above the bushes which hid from view the rest of his body. He turned his head sharply toward me as I raised the rifle, and the bullet went fairly into his throat, just under the jaw, breaking his neck, and bringing him down in his tracks with hardly a kick. He was a fine buck of eight points, unusually fat, considering that the rutting season was just over. We dressed it at once, and, as the house was so near, determined we would drag it there over the snow ourselves, without going back for a horse. Each took an antler, and the body slipped along very easily; but so intense was the cold that we had to keep shifting sides all the time, the hand which grasped the horn becoming numb almost immediately.

White-tail are very canny, and know perfectly well what threatens danger and what does not. Their larger, and to my mind nobler, relation, the black-tail, is if any thing easier to approach and kill, and yet is by no means so apt to stay in the immediate neighborhood of a ranch, where there is always more or less noise and confusion. The bottom on which my ranch-house stands is a couple of miles in length, and well wooded; all through last summer it was the home of a number of white-tails, and most of them are on it to this moment. Two fawns in especial were really amusingly tame, at one time spending their days hid in an almost impenetrable tangle of bullberry bushes, whose hither edge was barely a hundred yards from the ranch-house; and in the evening they could frequently be seen from the door, as they came out to feed. In walking out after sunset, or in riding home when night had fallen, we would often run across them when it was too dark to make out any thing but their flaunting white tails as they cantered out of the way. Yet for all their seeming familiarity they took good care not to expose themselves to danger. We were reluctant to molest them, but one day, having performed our usual weekly or fortnightly feat of eating up about every thing there was in the house, it was determined that the two deer (for it was late in autumn and they were then well grown) should be sacrificed. Accordingly one of us sallied out, but found that the sacrifice was not to be consummated so easily, for the should-be victims appeared to distinguish perfectly well between a mere passer-by, whom they regarded with absolute indifference, and any one who harbored sinister designs. They kept such a sharp look-out, and made off so rapidly if any one tried to approach them, that on two evenings the appointed hunter returned empty-handed, and by the third some one else had brought in a couple of black-tail. After that no necessity arose for molesting the two "tame deer," for whose sound common-sense we had all acquired a greatly increased respect.

When not much molested white-tail feed in the evening or late afternoon; but if often shot at and chased they only come out at night. They are very partial to the water, and in the warm summer nights will come down into the prairie ponds and stand knee-deep in them, eating the succulent marsh plants. Most of the plains rivers flow through sandy or muddy beds with no vegetable growth, and to these, of course, the deer merely come down to drink or refresh themselves by bathing, as they contain nothing to eat.

Throughout the day the white-tails keep in the densest thickets, choosing if possible those of considerable extent. For this reason they are confined to the bottoms of the rivers and the mouths of the largest creeks, the cover elsewhere being too scanty to suit them. It is very difficult to make them leave one of their haunts during the day-time. They lie very close, permitting a man to pass right by them; and the twigs and branches surrounding them are so thick and interlaced that they can hear the approach of any one from a long distance off, and hence are rarely sur-prised. If they think there is danger that the intruder will discover them, they arise and skulk silently off through the thickest part of the brush. If followed, they keep well ahead, moving perfectly noiselessly through the thicket, often going round in a circle and not breaking cover until hard pressed; yet all the time stepping with such sharp-eyed caution that the pursuing hunter will never get a glimpse of the quarry, though the patch of brush may not be fifty rods across.

At times the white-tail will lie so close that it may al-most be trodden on. One June morning I was riding down along the river, and came to a long bottom, crowded with rose-bushes, all in bloom. It was crossed in every direction by cattle paths, and a drove of long-horned Texans were scattered over it. A cow-pony gets accustomed to travel-ling at speed along the cattle trails, and the one I bestrode threaded its way among the twisted narrow paths with perfect ease, loping rapidly onward through a sea of low rose-bushes, covered with the sweet, pink flowers. They gave a bright color to the whole plain, while the air was filled with the rich, full songs of the yellow-breasted meadow larks, as they perched on the topmost sprays of the little trees. Suddenly a white-tail doe sprang up almost from under the horse's feet, and scudded off with her white flag flaunting. There was no reason for harming her, and she made a pretty picture as she bounded lightly off among the rose-red flowers, passing without heed through the ranks of the long-horned and savage-looking steers.

Doubtless she had a little spotted fawn not far away. These wee fellows soon after birth grow very cunning and able to take care of themselves, keeping in the densest part of the brush, through which they run and dodge like a rabbit. If taken young they grow very tame and are most dainty pets. One which we had round the house answered well to its name. It was at first fed with milk, which it lapped eagerly from a saucer, sharing the meal with the two cats, who rather resented its presence and cuffed it heartily when they thought it was greedy and was taking more than its share. As it grew older it would eat bread or potatoes from our hands, and was perfectly fearless. At night it was let go or put in the cow-shed, whichever was handiest, but it was generally round in time for breakfast next morning. A blue ribbon with a bell attached was hung around its neck, so as to prevent its being shot; but in the end it shared the fate of all pets, for one night it went off and never came back again. Perhaps it strayed away of its own accord, but more probably some raw hand at hunting saw it, and slaughtered it without noticing the bell hanging from its neck.

The best way to kill white-tail is to still-hunt carefully through their haunts at dusk, when the deer leave the deep recesses in which their day-beds lie, and come out to feed in the more open parts. For this kind of hunting, no dress is so good as a buckskin suit and moccasins. The moccasins enable one to tread softly and noiselessly, while the buckskin suit is of a most inconspicuous color, and makes less rustling than any other material when passing among projecting twigs. Care must be taken to always hunt up wind, and to advance without any sudden motions, walking close in to the edge of the thickets, and keeping a sharp look-out, as it is of the first importance to see the game before the game sees you. The feeding-grounds of the deer may vary. If they are on a bottom studded with dense copses, they move out on the open between them; if they are in a dense wood, they feed along its edges; but, by preference, they keep in the little glades and among the bushes underneath the trees. Wherever they may be found, they are rarely far from thick cover, and are always on the alert, lifting up their heads every few bites they take to see if any danger threatens them. But, unlike the antelope, they seem to rely for safety even more upon escaping observation than upon discovering danger while it is still far off, and so are usually in sheltered places where they cannot be seen at any distance. Hence, shots at them are generally obtained, if obtained at all, at very much closer range than at any other kind of game; the average distance would be nearer fifty than a hundred yards. On the other hand, more of the shots obtained are running ones than is the case with the same number taken at antelope or black-tail.

If the deer is standing just out of a fair-sized wood, it can often be obtained by creeping up along the edge; if seen among the large trees, it is even more easily still-hunted, as a tree trunk can be readily kept in line with the quarry, and thus prevent its suspecting any approach. But only a few white-tail are killed by regular and careful stalking; in much the greater number of instances the hunter simply beats patiently and noiselessly from the leeward, carefully through the clumps of trees and bushes, always prepared to see his game, and with his rifle at the ready. Sooner or later, as he steals round a corner, he either sees the motionless form of a deer, not a great distance off, regarding him intently for a moment before taking flight; or else he hears a sudden crash, and catches a glimpse of the animal as it lopes into the bushes. In either case, he must shoot quick; but the shot is a close one.

If he is heard or seen a long way off, the deer is very apt, instead of running away at full speed, to skulk off quietly through the bushes. But when suddenly startled, the white-tail makes off at a great rate, at a rolling gallop, the long, broad tail, pure white, held up in the air. In the dark or in thick woods, often all that can be seen is the flash of white from the tail. The head is carried low and well forward in running; a buck, when passing swiftly through thick underbrush, usually throws his horns back almost on his shoulders, with his nose held straight in front. White-tail venison is, in season, most delicious eating, only inferior to the mutton of the mountain sheep.

Among the places which are most certain to contain white-tails may be mentioned the tracts of swampy ground covered with willows and the like, which are to be found in a few (and but a few) localities through the plains country; there are, for example, several such along the Powder River, just below where the Little Powder empties into it. Here there is a dense growth of slim-stemmed young trees, sometimes almost impenetrable, and in other places opening out into what seem like arched passageways, through which a man must at times go almost on all fours. The ground may be covered with rank shrubbery, or it may be bare mud with patches of tall reeds. Here and there, scattered through these swamps, are pools of water, and sluggish ditches occasionally cut their way deep below the surface of the muddy soil. Game trails are abundant all through them, and now and then there is a large path beaten out by the cattle; while at intervals there are glades and openings. A horse must be very careful in going through such a swamp or he will certainly get mired, and even a man must be cautious about his footing. In the morning or late afternoon a man stands a good chance of killing deer in such a place, if he hunts carefully through it. It is comparatively easy to make but little noise in the mud and among the wet, yielding swamp plants; and by moving cautiously along the trails and through the openings, one can see some little distance ahead; and toward evening the pools should be visited, and the borders as far back as possible carefully examined, for any deer that come to drink, and the glades should be searched through for any that may be feeding. In the soft mud, too, a fresh track can be followed as readily as if in snow, and without exposing the hunter to such probability of detection. If a shot is obtained at all, it is at such close quarters as to more than counterbalance the dimness of the light, and to render the chance of a miss very unlikely. Such hunting is for a change very pleasant, the perfect stillness of the place, the quiet with which one has to move, and the constant expectation of seeing game keeping one's nerves always on the stretch; but after a while it grows tedious, and it makes a man feel cramped to be always ducking and crawling through such places. It is not to be compared, in cool weather, with still-hunting on the open hills; nevertheless, in the furious heat of the summer sun it has its advantages, for it is not often so oppressingly hot in the swamp as it is on the open prairie or in the dry thickets.

The white-tail is the only kind of large game for which the shot-gun can occasionally be used. At times in the dense brush it is seen, if seen at all, at such short distances, and the shots have to be taken so hurriedly, that the shot-gun is really the best weapon wherewith to attempt its death. One method of taking it is to have trained dogs hunt through a valley and drive the deer to guns stationed at the opposite end. With a single slow hound, given to baying, a hunter can often follow the deer on foot in the method adapted in most of the Eastern States for the capture of both the gray and the red fox. If the dog is slow and noisy the deer will play round in circles and can be cut off and shot from a stand. Any dog will soon put a deer out of a thicket, or drive it down a valley; but without a dog it is often difficult to drive deer toward the runaway or place at which the guns are stationed, for the white-tail will often skulk round and round a thicket instead of putting out of it when a man enters; and even when started it may break back past the driver instead of going toward the guns.

In all these habits white-tail are the very reverse of such game as antelope. Antelope care nothing at all about being seen, and indeed rather court observation, while the chief anxiety of a white-tail is to go unobserved. In passing through a country where there are antelope, it is almost impossible not to see them; while where there are an equal number of white-tail, the odds are manifold against travellers catching a glimpse of a single individual. The prong-horn is perfectly indifferent as to whether the pursuer sees him, so long as in his turn he is able to see the pursuer; and he relies entirely upon his speed and wariness for his safety; he never trusts for a moment to eluding observation. White-tail on the contrary rely almost exclusively either upon lying perfectly still and letting the danger pass by, or else upon skulking off so slyly as to be unobserved; it is only when hard pressed or suddenly startled that they bound boldly and freely away.

In many of the dense jungles without any opening the brush is higher than a man's head, and one has then practically no chance at all of getting a shot on foot when crossing through such places. But I have known instances where a man had himself driven in a tall light wagon through a place like this, and got several snap shots at the deer, as he caught momentary glimpses of them stealing off through the underbrush; and another method of pursuit in these jungles is occasionally followed by one of my foremen, who, mounted on a quiet horse, which will stand fire, pushes through the bushes and now and then gets a quick shot at a deer from horseback. I have tried this method myself, but without success, for though my hunting-horse, old Manitou, stands as steady as a rock, yet I find it impossible to shoot the rifle with any degree of accuracy from the saddle.

Except on such occasions as those just mentioned, the white-tail is rarely killed while hunting on horseback. This last term, by-the-way, must not be understood in the sense in which it would be taken by the fox-hunter of the South, or by the Californian and Texan horsemen who course hare, antelope, and wild turkey with their fleet greyhounds. With us hunting on horseback simply means that the horse is ridden not only to the hunting grounds, but also through them, until the game is discovered; then the hunter immediately dismounts, shooting at once if the animal is near enough and has seen him, or stalking up to it on foot if it is a good distance off and he is still unobserved. Where great stretches of country have to be covered, as in antelope shooting, hunting on horseback is almost the only way followed; but the haunts and habits of the white-tail deer render it nearly useless to try to kill them in this way, as the horse would be sure to alarm them by making a noise, and even if he did not there would hardly be time to dismount and take a snap shot. Only once have I ever killed a white-tail buck while hunting on horseback; and at that time I had been expecting to fall in with black-tail.

This was while we had been making a wagon trip to the westward, following the old Keogh trail, which was made by the heavy army wagons that journeyed to Fort Keogh in the old days when the soldiers were, except a few daring trappers, the only white men to be seen on the last great hunting-ground of the Indians. It was abandoned as a military route several years ago, and is now only rarely travelled over, either by the canvas-topped ranch-wagon of some wandering cattle-men—like ourselves,—or else by a small party of emigrants, in two or three prairie schooners, which contain all their household goods. Nevertheless, it is still as plain and distinct as ever. The two deep parallel ruts, cut into the sod by the wheels of the heavy wagon, stretch for scores of miles in a straight line across the level prairie, and take great turns and doublings to avoid the impassable portions of the Bad Lands. The track is always perfectly plain, for in the dry climate of the western plains the action of the weather tends to preserve rather than to obliterate it; where it leads downhill, the snow water has cut and widened the ruts into deep gullies, so that a wagon has at those places to travel alongside the road. From any little rising in the prairie the road can be seen, a long way off, as a dark line, which, when near, resolves itself into two sharply defined parallel cuts. Such a road is a great convenience as a landmark. When travelling along it, or one like it, the hunters can separate in all directions, and no matter how long or how far they hunt, there is never the least difficulty about finding camp. For the general direction in which the road lies, is, of course, kept in mind, and it can be reached whether the sun is down or not; then a glance tells if the wagon has passed, and all that remains to be done is to gallop along the trail until camp is found.

On the trip in question we had at first very bad weather. Leaving the ranch in the morning, two of us, who were mounted, pushed on ahead to hunt, the wagon following slowly, with a couple of spare saddle ponies leading behind it. Early in the afternoon, while riding over the crest of a great divide, which separates the drainage basins of two important creeks, we saw that a tremendous storm was brewing with that marvellous rapidity which is so marked a characteristic of weather changes on the plains. A towering mass of clouds gathered in the northwest, turning that whole quarter of the sky to an inky blackness. From there the storm rolled down toward us at a furious speed, obscuring by degrees the light of the sun, and extending its wings toward each side, as if to overlap any that tried to avoid its path. Against the dark background of the mass could be seen pillars and clouds of gray mist, whirled hither and thither by the wind, and sheets of level rain driven before it. The edges of the wings tossed to and fro, and the wind shrieked and moaned as it swept over the prairie. It was a storm of unusual intensity; the prairie fowl rose in flocks from before it, scudding with spread wings toward the thickest cover, and the herds of antelope ran across the plain like race-horses to gather in the hollows and behind the low ridges.

We spurred hard to get out of the open, riding with loose reins for the creek. The centre of the storm swept by behind us, fairly across our track, and we only got a wipe from the tail of it. Yet this itself we could not have faced in the open. The first gust caught us a few hundred yards from the creek, almost taking us from the saddle, and driving the rain and hail in stinging level sheets against us. We galloped to the edge of a deep wash-out, scrambled into it at the risk of our necks, and huddled up with our horses underneath the windward bank. Here we remained pretty well sheltered until the storm was over. Although it was August, the air became very cold. The wagon was fairly caught, and would have been blown over if the top had been on; the driver and horses escaped without injury, pressing under the leeward side, the storm coming so level that they did not need a roof to protect them from the hail. Where the centre of the whirlwind struck it did great damage, sheets of hailstones as large as pigeons' eggs striking the earth with the velocity of bullets; next day the hailstones could have been gathered up by the bushel from the heaps that lay in the bottom of the gullies and ravines. One of my cowboys was out in the storm, during whose continuance he crouched under his horse's belly; coming home he came across some antelope so numb and stiffened that they could barely limp out of the way.

Near my ranch the hail killed quite a number of lambs. These were the miserable remnants of a flock of twelve thousand sheep driven into the Bad Lands a year before, four fifths of whom had died during the first winter, to the delight of all the neighboring cattle-men. Cattle-men hate sheep, because they eat the grass so close that cattle cannot live on the same ground. The sheepherders are a morose, melancholy set of men, generally afoot, and with no companionship except that of the bleating idiots they are hired to guard. No man can associate with sheep and retain his self-respect. Intellectually a sheep is about on the lowest level of the brute creation; why the early Christians admired it, whether young or old, is to a good cattle-man always a profound mystery.

The wagon came on to the creek, along whose banks we had taken shelter, and we then went into camp. It rained all night, and there was a thick mist, with continual sharp showers, all the next day and night. The wheeling was, in consequence, very heavy, and after striking the Keogh trail we were able to go along it but a few miles before the fagged-out look of the team and the approach of evening warned us that we should have to go into camp while still a dozen miles from any pool or spring. Accordingly we made what would have been a dry camp had it not been for the incessant downpour of rain, which we gathered in the canvas wagon-sheet and in our oilskin overcoats in sufficient quantity to make coffee, having with infinite difficulty started a smouldering fire just to leeward of the wagon. The horses, feeding on the soaked grass, did not need water. An antelope, with the bold and heedless curiosity sometimes shown by its tribe, came up within two hundred yards of us as we were building the fire; but though one of us took a shot at him, it missed. Our shaps and oilskins had kept us perfectly dry, and as soon as our frugal supper was over, we coiled up among the boxes and bundles inside the wagon and slept soundly till daybreak.

When the sun rose next day, the third we were out, the sky was clear, and we two horsemen at once prepared to make a hunt. Some three miles off to the south of where we were camped, the plateau on which we were sloped off into a great expanse of broken ground, with chains upon chains of steep hills, separated by deep valleys, winding and branching in every direction, their bottoms filled with trees and brushwood. Toward this place we rode, intending to go into it some little distance, and then to hunt along through it near the edge. As soon as we got down near the brushy ravine we rode along without talking, guiding the horses as far as possible on earthy places, where they would neither stumble nor strike their feet against stones, and not letting our rifle-barrels or spurs clink against any thing. Keeping outside of the brush, a little up the side of the hill, one of us would ride along each side of the ravine, examining intently with our eyes every clump of trees or brushwood. For some time we saw nothing, but, finally, as we were riding both together round the jutting spur of a steep hill, my companion suddenly brought his horse to a halt, and pointing across the shelving bend to a patch of trees well up on the opposite side of a broad ravine, asked me if I did not see a deer in it. I was off the horse in a second, throwing the reins over his head. We were in the shadow of the cliff-shoulder, and with the wind in our favor; so we were unlikely to be observed by the game. I looked long and eagerly toward the spot indicated, which was about a hundred and twenty-five yards from us, but at first could see nothing. By this time, however, the experienced plainsman who was with me was satisfied that he was right in his supposition, and he told me to try again and look for a patch of red. I saw the patch at once, just glimmering through the bushes, but should certainly never have dreamed it was a deer if left to myself. Watching it attentively I soon saw it move enough to satisfy me where the head lay; kneeling on one knee and (as it was a little beyond point-blank range) holding at the top of the portion visible, I pulled trigger, and the bright-colored patch disappeared from among the bushes. The aim was a good one, for, on riding up to the brink of the ravine, we saw a fine white-tail buck lying below us, shot through just behind the shoulder; he was still in the red coat, with his antlers in the velvet.

A deer is far from being such an easy animal to see as the novice is apt to suppose. Until the middle of September he is in the red coat; after that time he is in the gray; but it is curious how each one harmonizes in tint with certain of the surroundings. A red doe lying down is, at a little distance, undistinguishable from the soil on which she is; while a buck in the gray can hardly be made out in dead timber. While feeding quietly or standing still, they rarely show the proud, free port we are accustomed to associate with the idea of a buck, and look rather ordinary, humble-seeming animals, not at all conspicuous or likely to attract the hunter's attention; but once let them be frightened, and as they stand facing the danger, or bound away from it, their graceful movements and lordly bearing leave nothing to be desired. The black-tail is a still nobler-looking animal; while an antelope, on the contrary, though as light and quick on its feet as is possible for any animal not possessing wings to be, yet has an angular, goat-like look, and by no means conveys to the beholder the same idea of grace that a deer does.

In coming home, on this wagon trip, we made a long moonlight ride, passing over between sunset and sunrise what had taken us three days' journey on the outward march. Of our riding horses, two were still in good condition and well able to stand a twenty-four hours' jaunt, in spite of hard work and rough usage; the spare ones, as well as the team, were pretty well done up and could get along but slowly. All day long we had been riding beside the wagon over barren sage-brush plains, following the dusty trails made by the beef-herds that had been driven toward one of the Montana shipping towns.

When we halted for the evening meal we came near learning by practical experience how easy it is to start a prairie fire. We were camped by a dry creek on a broad bottom covered with thick, short grass, as dry as so much tinder. We wished to burn a good circle clear for the campfire; lighting it, we stood round with branches to keep it under. While thus standing a puff of wind struck us; the fire roared like a wild beast as it darted up; and our hair and eyelashes were well singed before we had beaten it out. At one time it seemed as if, though but a very few feet in extent, it would actually get away from us; in which case the whole bottom would have been a blazing furnace within five minutes.

After supper, looking at the worn-out condition of the team, we realized that it would take three more days travelling at the rate we had been going to bring us in, and as the country was monotonous, without much game, we concluded we would leave the wagon with the driver, and taking advantage of the full moon, push through the whole distance before breakfast next morning. Accordingly, we at nine o'clock again saddled the tough little ponies we had ridden all day and loped off out of the circle of firelight. For nine hours we rode steadily, generally at a quick lope, across the moon-lit prairie. The hoof-beats of our horses rang out in steady rhythm through the silence of the night, otherwise unbroken save now and then by the wailing cry of a coyote. The rolling plains stretched out on all sides of us, shimmering in the clear moonlight; and occasionally a band of spectral-looking antelope swept silently away from before our path. Once we went by a drove of Texan cattle, who stared wildly at the intruders; as we passed they charged down by us, the ground rumbling beneath their tread, while their long horns knocked against each other with a sound like the clattering of a multitude of castanets. We could see clearly enough to keep our general course over the trackless plain, steering by the stars where the prairie was perfectly level and without landmarks; and our ride was timed well, for as we galloped down into the valley of the Little Missouri the sky above the line of level bluffs in our front was crimson with the glow of the unrisen sun.

CHAPTER V

The Black-Tail Deer

Far different from the low-scudding, brush-loving white-tail, is the black-tail deer, the deer of the ravines and the rocky uplands. In general shape and form, both are much alike; but the black-tail is the larger of the two, with heavier antlers, of which the prongs start from one another, as if each of the tines of a two-pronged pitchfork had bifurcated; and in some cases it looks as if the process had been again repeated. The tail, instead of being broad and bushy as a squirrel's, spreading from the base, and pure white to the tip, is round and close haired, with the end black, though the rest is white. If an ordinary deer is running, its flaunting flag is almost its most conspicuous part; but no one would notice the tail of a black-tail deer.

All deer vary greatly in size; and a small black-tail buck will be surpassed in bulk by many white-tails; but the latter never reaches the weight and height sometimes attained by the former. The same holds true of the antlers borne by the two animals; on the average those of the black-tail are the heavier, and exceptionally large antlers of this species are larger than any of the white-tail. Bucks of both kinds very often have, when full-grown, more than the normal number of ten points; sometimes these many-pronged antlers will be merely deformities, while in other instances the points are more symmetrical, and add greatly to the beauty and grandeur of the head. The venison of the black-tail is said to be inferior in quality to that of the white-tail; but I have never been able to detect much difference, though, perhaps, on the whole, the latter is slightly better.

The gaits of the two animals are widely different. The white-tail runs at a rolling gallop, striking the ground with the forward feet first, the head held forward. The black-tail, on the contrary, holds its head higher up, and progresses by a series of prodigious bounds, striking the earth with all four feet at once, the legs held nearly stiff. It seems like an extraordinary method of running; and the violent exertion tires the deer sooner than does the more easy and natural gait of the white-tail; but for a mile or so these rapidly succeeding bounds enable the black-tail to get over the ground at remarkable speed. Over rough ground, along precipitous slopes, and among the boulders of rocky cliffs, it will go with surprising rapidity and surefootedness, only surpassed by the feats of the big-horn in similar localities, and not equalled by those of any other plains game.

One of the noticeable things in western plains hunting is the different zones or bands of territory inhabited by different kinds of game. Along the alluvial land of the rivers and large creeks is found the white-tail. Back of these alluvial lands generally comes a broad tract of broken, hilly country, scantily clad with brush in some places; this is the abode of the black-tail deer. And where these hills rise highest, and where the ground is most rugged and barren, there the big-horn is found. After this hilly country is passed, in travelling away from the river, we come to the broad, level plains, the domain of the antelope. Of course the habitats of the different species overlap at the edges; and this overlapping is most extended in the cases of the big-horn and the black-tail.

The Bad Lands are the favorite haunts of the black-tail. Here the hills are steep and rugged, cut up and crossed in every direction by canyon-like ravines and valleys, which branch out and subdivide in the most intricate and perplexing manner. Here and there are small springs, or pools, marked by the greener vegetation growing round them. Along the bottoms and sides of the ravines there are patches of scrubby undergrowth, and in many of the pockets or glens in the sides of the hills the trees grow to some little height. High buttes rise here and there, naked to the top, or else covered with stunted pines and cedars, which also grow in the deep ravines and on the edges of the sheer canyons. Such lands, where the ground is roughest, and where there is some cover, even though scattered and scanty, are the best places to find the black-tail. Naturally their pursuit needs very different qualities in the hunter from those required in the chase of the white-tail. In the latter case stealth and caution are the prime requisites; while the man who would hunt and kill the deer of the uplands has more especial need of energy, activity, and endurance, of good judgment and of skill with the rifle. Hunting the black-tail is beyond all comparison the nobler sport. Indeed, there is no kind of plains hunting, except only the chase of the big-horn, more fitted to bring out the best and hardiest of the many qualities which go to make up a good hunter.

It is still a moot question whether it is better to hunt on horseback or on foot; but the course of events is rapidly deciding it in favor of the latter method. Undoubtedly it is easier and pleasanter to hunt on horseback; and it has the advantage of covering a great deal of ground. But it is impossible to advance with such caution, and it is difficult to shoot as quickly, as when on foot; and where the deer are shy and not very plenty, the most enthusiastic must, slowly and reluctantly but surely, come to the conclusion that a large bag can only be made by the still-hunter who goes on foot. Of course, in the plains country it is not as in mountainous or thickly wooded regions, and the horse should almost always be taken as a means of conveyance to the hunting-grounds and from one point to another; but the places where game is expected should, as a rule, be hunted over on foot. This rule is by no means a general one, however. There are still many localities where the advantage of covering a great deal of ground more than counterbalances the disadvantage of being on horseback. About one third of my hunts are still made on horseback; and in almost all the others I take old Manitou to carry me to and from the grounds and to pack out any game that may be killed. A hunting-horse is of no use whatever unless he will permit a man to jump from his back and fire with the greatest rapidity; and nowhere does practice have more to do with success than in the case of jumping off a horse to shoot at game which has just been seen. The various movements take a novice a good deal of time; while an old hand will be off and firing with the most instantaneous quickness. Manitou can be left anywhere at a moment's warning, while his rider leaps off, shoots at a deer from almost under his head, and perhaps chases the wounded animal a mile or over; and on his return the good old fellow will be grazing away, perfectly happy and contented, and not making a movement to run off or evade being caught.

One method of killing deer on horseback is very exciting. Many of the valleys or ravines extend with continual abrupt turns and windings for several miles, the brush and young trees stretching with constant breaks down the middle of the bottom, and leaving a space on each side along which a surefooted horse can gallop at speed. Two men, on swift, hardy horses, can hunt down such a ravine very successfully at evening, by each taking a side and galloping at a good speed the whole length against the wind. The patter of the unshod hoofs over the turf makes but little noise; and the turns are so numerous and abrupt, and the horses go so swiftly, that the hunters come on the deer almost before the latter are aware of their presence. If it is so late in the day that the deer have begun to move they will find the horses close up before they have a suspicion of danger, while if they are still lying in the cover the suddenness of the appearance of their foe is apt to so startle them as to make them break out and show themselves instead of keeping hid, as they would probably do if they perceived the approach from afar. One thus gets a close running shot, or if he waits a minute he will generally get a standing shot at some little distance, owing to a very characteristic habit of the black-tail. This is its custom of turning round, apparently actuated simply by curiosity, to look at the object which startled it, after it has run off a hundred and fifty yards or so. It then stands motionless for a few seconds, and offers a chance for a steady shot. If the chance is not improved, no other will offer, for as soon as the deer has ended its scrutiny it is off again, and this time will not halt till well out of danger. Owing to its singular gait, a succession of buck jumps, the black-tail is a peculiarly difficult animal to hit while on the run; and it is best to wait until it stops and turns before taking the shot, as if fired at, the report will generally so alarm it as to make it continue its course without halting to look back. Some of the finest antlers in my possession come from bucks killed by this method of hunting; and it is a most exhilarating form of sport, the horse galloping rapidly over what is often very broken ground, and the senses being continually on the alert for any sign of game. The rush and motion of the horse, and the care necessary to guide it and at the same time be in constant readiness for a shot, prevent the chase having any of the monotony that is at times inseparable from still-hunting proper.

Nevertheless, it is by still-hunting that most deer are killed, and the highest form of hunting craft is shown in the science of the skilful still-hunter. With sufficient practice any man who possesses common-sense and is both hardy and persevering can become, to a certain extent, a still-hunter. But the really *good* still-hunter is born rather than made; though of course in addition to possessing the gifts naturally he must also have developed them, by constant practice, to the highest point possible. One of the foremen on my ranch is a really remarkably good hunter and game shot, and another does almost as well; but the rest of us are not, and never will be, any thing very much out of the common. By dint of practice we have learned to shoot as well at game as at a target; and those of us who are fond of the sport hunt continually and so get a good deal of game at one time or another. Hunting through good localities, up wind, quietly and perseveringly, we come upon quite a number of animals; and we can kill a standing shot at a fair distance and a running shot close up, and by good luck every now and then kill far off; but to much more than is implied in the description of such modest feats we cannot pretend.

After the disappearance of the buffalo and the thinning out of the elk, the black-tail was, and in most places it still is, the game most sought after by the hunters; I have myself shot as many of them as of all other kinds of plains game put together. But for this very reason it is fast disappearing; and bids fair to be the next animal, after the buffalo and elk, to vanish from the places that formerly knew it. The big-horn and the prong-horn are more difficult to stalk and kill, partly from their greater natural wariness, and partly from the kind of ground on which they are found. But it seems at first sight strange that the black-tail should be exterminated or driven away so much more quickly than the white-tail, when it has sharper ears and nose, is more tenacious of life, and is more wary. The main reason is to be found in the difference in the character of the haunts of the two creatures. The black-tail is found on much more open ground, where the animals can be seen farther off, where it is much easier to take advantage of the direction of the wind and to get along without noise, and where far more country can be traversed in a given time; and though the average length of the shots taken is in one case two or three times as great as in the other, yet this is more than counterbalanced by the fact that they are more often standing ones, and that there is usually much more time for aiming. Moreover, one kind of sport can be followed on horseback, while the other must be followed on foot; and then the chase of the white-tail, in addition, is by far the more tedious and patience-trying. And the black-tail are much the more easily scared or driven out of a locality by persecution or by the encroaching settlements. All these qualities combine to make it less able to hold its own against mankind than its smaller rival. It is the favorite game of the skin hunters and meat hunters, and has, in consequence, already disappeared from many places, while in others its extermination is going on at a frightfully rapid rate, owing to its being followed in season and out of season without mercy. Besides, the cattle are very fond of just the places to which it most often resorts; and wherever cattle go the cowboys ride about after them, with their ready six-shooters at their hips. They blaze away at any deer they see, of course, and in addition to now and then killing or wounding one, continually harry and disturb the poor animals. In the more remote and inaccessible districts the black-tail will long hold its own, to be one of the animals whose successful pursuit will redound most to the glory of the still-hunter; but in a very few years it will have ceased entirely to be one of the common game animals of the plains.

Its great curiosity is one of the disadvantages under which it labors in the fierce struggle for existence, compared to the white-tail. The latter, when startled, does not often stop to look round; but, as already said, the former will generally do so after having gone a few hundred feet. The first black-tail I ever killed—unfortunately killed, for the body was not found until spoiled—was obtained owing solely to this peculiarity. I had been riding up along the side of a brushy coulie, when a fine buck started out some thirty yards ahead. Although so close, my first shot, a running one, was a miss; when a couple of hundred yards off, on the very crest of the spur up which he had run, he stopped and turned partially round. Firing again from a rest, the bullet broke his hind leg far up and went into his body. Off he went on three legs, and I after him as fast as the horse could gallop. He went over the spur and down into the valley of the creek from which the coulie branched up, in very bad ground. My pony was neither fast nor surefooted, but of course in half a mile overhauled the three-legged deer, which turned short off and over the side of the hill flanking the valley. Instead of running right up on it I foolishly dismounted and began firing; after the first shot—a miss—it got behind a boulder hitherto un-seen, and thence over the crest. The pony meanwhile had slipped its hind leg into the rein; when, after some time, I got it out and galloped up to the ridge, the most careful scrutiny of which my unpractised eyes were capable failed to discover a track on the dry ground, hard as granite. A day or two afterwards the place where the carcass lay was made known by the vultures, gathered together from all parts to feed upon it.

When fired at from a place of hiding, deer which have not been accustomed to the report of a gun will often appear confused and uncertain what to do. On one occasion, while hunting in the mountains, I saw an old buck with remarkably large horns, of curious and beautiful shape, more symmetrical than in most instances where the normal form is departed from. The deer was feeding in a wide, gently sloping valley, containing no cover from behind which to approach him. We were in no need of meat, but the antlers were so fine that I felt they justified the death of their bearer. After a little patient waiting, the buck walked out of the valley, and over the ridge on the other side, moving up wind; I raced after him, and crept up behind a thick growth of stunted cedars, which had started up from among some boulders. The deer was about a hundred yards off, down in the valley. Out of breath, and over-confident, I fired hastily, overshooting him. The wind blew the smoke back away from the ridge, so that he saw nothing, while the echo prevented his placing the sound. He took a couple of jumps nearer, when he stood still and was again overshot. Again he took a few jumps, and the third shot went below him; and the fourth just behind him. This was too much, and away he went. In despair I knelt down (I had been firing off-hand), took a steady aim well-forward on his body, and fired, bringing him down, but with small credit to the shot, for the bullet had gone into his hip, paralyzing his hind-quarters. The antlers are the finest pair I ever got, and form a magnificent ornament for the hall; but the shooting is hardly to be recalled with pleasure. Still, though certainly very bad, it was not quite as discreditable as the mere target shot would think. I have seen many a crack marksman at the target do quite as bad missing when out in the field, and that not once, but again and again.

Of course, in those parts of the wilderness where the black-tail are entirely unused to man, they are as easy to approach (from the leeward side) as is any and every other kind of game under like conditions. In lonely spots, to which hunters rarely or never penetrate, deer of this species will stand and look at a hunter without offering to run away till he is within fifty yards of them, if he will advance quietly. In a far-off mountain forest I have more than once shot a young buck at less than that distance as he stood motionless, gazing at me, although but little caution had been used in approaching him.

But a short experience of danger on the part of the black-tail changes all this; and where hunters are often afoot, he becomes as wild and wary as may be. Then the successful still-hunter shows that he is indeed well up in the higher forms of hunting craft. For the man who can, not once by accident, but again and again, as a regular thing, single-handed, find and kill his black-tail, has shown that he is no mere novice in his art; still-hunting the black-tail is a sport that only the skilful can follow with good results, and one which implies in the successful sportsman the presence of most of the still-hunter's rarest attributes. All of the qualities which a still-hunter should possess are of service in the pursuit of any kind of game; but different ones will be called into especial play in hunting different kinds of animals. Thus, to be a successful hunter after any thing, a man should be patient, resolute, hardy, and with good judgment; he should have good lungs and stout muscles; he should be able to move with noiseless stealth; and he should be keen-eyed, and a first-rate marksman with the rifle. But in different kinds of shooting, the relative importance of these qualities varies greatly. In hunting white-tail deer, the two prime requisites are stealth and patience. If the quarry is a big-horn, a man needs especially to be sound in wind and limbs, and to be both hardy and resolute. Skill in the use of the long-range rifle counts for more in antelope hunting than in any other form of sport; and it is in this kind of hunting alone that good marksmanship is more important than any thing else. With dangerous game, cool and steady nerves are of the first consequence; all else comes after. Then, again, in the use of the rifle, the *kind* of skill—not merely the *degree* of skill—required to hunt different animals may vary greatly. In shooting white-tail, it is especially necessary to be a good snap shot at running game; when the distance is close, quickness is an essential. But at antelope there is plenty of time, and what is necessary is ability to judge distance, and capacity to hit a small stationary object at long range.

The different degrees of estimation in which the chase of the various kinds of plains game is held depend less upon the difficulty of capture than upon the nature of the qualities in the hunter which each particular form of hunting calls into play. A man who is hardy, resolute, and a good shot, has come nearer to realizing the ideal of a bold and free hunter than is the case with one who is merely stealthy and patient; and so, though to kill a white-tail is rather more difficult than to kill a black-tail, yet the chase of the latter is certainly the nobler form of sport, for it calls into play, and either develops or implies the presence of, much more manly qualities than does the other. Most hunters would find it nearly as difficult to watch in silence by a salt-lick throughout the night, and then to butcher with a shot-gun a white-tail, as it would be to walk on foot through rough ground from morning till evening, and to fairly approach and kill a black-tail; yet there is no comparison between the degree of credit to be attached to one feat and that to be attached to the other. Indeed, if difficulty in killing is to be taken as a criterion, a mink or even a weasel would have to stand as high up in the scale as a deer, were the animals equally plenty.

Ranged in the order of the difficulty with which they are approached and slain, plains game stand as follows: big-horn, antelope, white-tail, black-tail, elk, and buffalo. But, as regards the amount of manly sport furnished by the chase of each, the white-tail should stand at the bottom of the list, and the elk and black-tail abreast of the antelope.

Other things being equal, the length of an animal's stay in the land, when the arch foe of all lower forms of animal life has made his appearance therein, depends upon the difficulty with which he is hunted and slain. But other influences have to be taken into account. The big-horn is shy and retiring; very few, compared to the whole number, will be killed; and yet the others vanish completely. Apparently they will not remain where they are hunted and disturbed. With antelope and white-tail this does not hold; they will cling to a place far more tenaciously, even if often harassed. The former being the more conspicuous, and living in such open ground, is apt to be more persecuted; while the white-tail, longer than any other animal, keeps its place in the land in spite of the swinish game butchers, who hunt for hides and not for sport or actual food, and who murder the gravid doe and the spotted fawn with as little hesitation as they would kill a buck of ten points. No one who is not himself a sportsman and lover of nature can realize the intense indignation with which a true hunter sees these butchers at their brutal work of slaughtering the game, in season and out, for the sake of the few dollars they are too lazy to earn in any other and more honest way.

All game animals rely upon both eyes, ears, and nose to warn them of the approach of danger; but the amount of reliance placed on each sense varies greatly in different species. Those found out on the plains pay very little attention to what they hear; indeed, in the open they can hardly be approached near enough to make of much account any ordinary amount of noise caused by the stalker, especially as the latter is walking over little but grass and soft earth. The buffalo, whose shaggy frontlet of hair falls over his eyes and prevents his seeing at any great distance, depends mainly upon his exquisite sense of smell. The antelope, on the other hand, depends almost entirely on his great, bulging eyes, and very little on his nose. His sight is many times as good as that of deer, both species of which, as well as elk, rely both upon sight and hearing, but most of all upon their sense of smell, for their safety. The bighorn has almost as keen eyesight as an antelope, while his ears and nose are as sensitive to sound and scent as are those of an elk.

Black-tail, like other members of the deer family, do

not pay much attention to an object which is not moving. A hunter who is standing motionless or squatting down is not likely to receive attention, while a big-horn or prong-horn would probably see him and take the alarm at once; and if the black-tail is frightened and running he will run almost over a man standing in plain sight, without paying any heed to him, if the latter does not move. But the very slightest movement at once attracts a deer's attention, and deer are not subject to the panics that at times overtake other kinds of game. The black-tail has much curiosity, which often proves fatal to it; but which with it is after all by no means the ungovernable passion that it is with antelope. The white-tail and the big-horn are neither over-afflicted with morbid curiosity, nor subject to panics or fits of stupidity; and both these animals, as well as the black-tail, seem to care very little for the death of the leader of the band, going their own ways with small regard for the fate of the chief, while elk will huddle together in a confused group, and remain almost motionless when their leader is struck down. Antelope and more especially elk are subject to perfect panics of unreasoning terror, during which they will often put themselves completely in the power of the hunter; while buffalo will frequently show a downright stupidity almost unequalled.

The black-tail suffers from no such peculiarities. His eyes are good; his nose and ears excellent. He is ever alert and wary; his only failing is his occasional over-curiosity; and his pursuit taxes to the utmost the skill and resources of the still-hunter.

By all means the best coverings for the feet when still-hunting are moccasins, as with them a man can go noiselessly through ground where hobnailed boots would clatter like the hoofs of a horse; but in hunting in winter over the icy buttes and cliffs it is best to have stout shoes, with nails in the soles, and if the main work is done on horseback it is best to wear high boots, as they keep the trousers down. Indeed in the Bad Lands boots have other advantages, for rattlesnakes abound, and against these they afford perfect protection—unless a man should happen to stumble on a snake while crawling along on all fours. But moccasins are beyond all comparison the best footgear for hunting. In very cold weather a fur cap which can be pulled down over the ears is a necessity; but at other times a brimmed felt hat offers better protection against both sun and rain. The clothes should be of some neutral tint—buckskin is on this account excellent—and very strong.

The still-hunter should be well acquainted with, at any rate, certain of the habits of his quarry. There are seasons when the black-tail is found in bands; such is apt to be the case when the rutting time is over. At this period, too, the deer wander far and wide, making what may almost be called a migration; and in rutting time the bucks follow the does at speed for miles at a stretch. But except at these seasons each individual black-tail has a certain limited tract of country to which he confines himself unless disturbed or driven away, not, of course, keeping in the same spot all the time, but working round among a particular set of ravines and coulies, where the feed is good, and where water can be obtained without going too far out of the immediate neighborhood.

Throughout the plains country the black-tail lives in the broken ground, seldom coming down to the alluvial bottoms or out on the open prairies and plateaus. But he is found all through this broken ground. Sometimes it is rolling in character with rounded hills and gentle valleys, dotted here and there with groves of trees; or the hills may rise into high chains, covered with an open pine forest, sending off long spurs and divided by deep valleys and basins. Such places are favorite resorts of this deer; but it is as plentiful in the Bad Lands proper. There are tracts of these which are in part or wholly of volcanic origin; then the hills are called scoria buttes. They are high and very steep, but with rounded tops and edges, and are covered, as is the ground round about, with scoriac boulders. Bushes, and sometimes a few cedar, grow among them, and though they would seem to be most unlikely places for deer, yet black-tail are very fond of them, and are very apt to be found among them. Often in the cold fall mornings they will lie out among the boulders, on the steep side of such a scoria butte, sunning themselves, far from any cover except a growth of brushwood in the bottom of the dry creeks or coulies. The grass on top of and between these scoria buttes is often very nutritious, and cattle are also fond of it. The higher buttes are choice haunts of the mountain sheep.

Nineteen twentieths of the Bad Lands, however, owe their origin not to volcanic action but to erosion and to the peculiar weathering forces always at work in the dry climate of the plains. Geologically the land is for the most part composed of a set of parallel, perfectly horizontal strata, of clay, marl, or sandstone, which, being of different degrees of hardness, offer some more and some less resistance to the action of the weather. The table-lands, peaks, cliffs, and jagged ridges are caused solely by the rains and torrents cutting away the land into channels, which at first are merely wash-outs, and at last grow into deep canyons, winding valleys, and narrow ravines or basins. The sides of these cuts are at first perpendicular, exposing to view the various bands of soil, perhaps of a dozen different colors; the hardest bands resist the action of the weather best and form narrow ledges stretching along the face of the cliff. Peaks of the most fantastic shape are formed in this manner; and where a ridge is worn away on each side its crest may be as sharp as a knife blade, but all notched and jagged. The peaks and ridges vary in height from a few feet to several hundred; the sides of the buttes are generally worn down in places so as to be steeply sloping instead of perpendicular. The long wash-outs and the canyons and canyon-like valleys stretch and branch out in every direction; the dryness of the atmosphere, the extremes of intense heat and bitter cold, and the occasional furious rain-storms keep the edges and angles sharp and jagged, and pile up boulders and masses of loose detritus at the foot of the cliffs and great lonely crags. Sometimes the valleys are quite broad, with steep sides and with numerous pockets, separated by spurs jutting out into the bottom from the lateral ridges. Other ravines or clefts taper down to a ditch, a foot or so wide, from which the banks rise at an angle of sixty degrees to the tops of the enclosing ridges.

The faces of the terraced cliffs and sheer crags are bare of all but the scantiest vegetation, and where the Bad Lands are most rugged and broken the big-horn is the only game found. But in most places the tops of the buttes, the sides of the slopes, and the bottoms of the valleys are more or less thickly covered with the nutritious grass which is the favorite food of the black-tail.

Of course, the Bad Lands grade all the way from those that are almost rolling in character to those that are so fantastically broken in form and so bizarre in color as to seem hardly properly to belong to this earth. If the weathering forces have not been very active, the ground will look, from a little distance, almost like a level plain, but on approaching nearer, it will be seen to be crossed by straight-sided gullies and canyons, miles in length, cutting across the land in every direction and rendering it almost impassable for horsemen or wagon-teams. If the forces at work have been more intense, the walls between the different gullies have been cut down to thin edges, or broken through, leaving isolated peaks of strange shape, while the hollows have been channelled out deeper and deeper; such places show the extreme and most characteristic Bad Lands formation. When the weathering has gone on further, the angles are rounded off, grass begins to grow, bushes and patches of small trees sprout up, water is found in places, and the still very rugged country becomes the favorite abode of the black-tail.

During the daytime, these deer lie quietly in their beds, which are sometimes in the brush and among the matted bushes in the bottoms of the small branching coulies, or heads of the crooked ravines. More often they will be found in the thickets of stunted cedars clothing the brinks of the canyons or the precipitous slopes of the great chasms into which the ground is cleft and rent; or else among the groves of gnarled pines on the sides of the buttes, and in the basins and pockets between the spurs. If the country is not much hunted over, a buck or old doe will often take its mid-day rest out in the open, lying down among the long grass or shrubbery on one of the bare benches at the head of a ravine, at the edge of the dense brush with which its bottom and sides are covered. In such a case, a position is always chosen from which a look-out can be kept all around; and the moment any suspicious object is seen, the deer slips off into the thicket below him. Perhaps the favorite resting-places are the rounded edges of gorges, just before the sides of the latter break sheer off. Here the deer lies, usually among a few straggling pines or cedars, on the very edge of the straight side-wall of the canyon, with a steep-shelving slope above him, so that he cannot be seen from the summit; and in such places it is next to impossible to get at him. If lying on a cedar-grown spur or ridge-point, the still-hunter has a better chance, for the evergreen needles with which the ground is covered enable a man to walk noiselessly, and, by stooping or going on all fours, he can keep under the branches. But it is at all times hard and unsatisfactory work to find and successfully still-hunt a deer that is enjoying its day rest. Generally, the only result is to find the warm, fresh bed from which the deer has just sneaked off, the blades of grass still slowly rising, after the hasty departure of the weight that has flattened them down; or else, if in dense cover, the hunter suddenly hears a scramble, a couple of crashing bounds through the twigs and dead limbs, and gets a momentary glimpse of a dark outline vanishing into the thicket as the sole reward of his labor. Almost the only way to successfully still-hunt a deer in the middle of the day, is to find its trail and follow it up to the resting-places, and such a feat needs an expert tracker and a noiseless and most skilful stalker.

The black-tail prefers to live in the neighborhood of water, where he can get it every twenty-four hours; but he is perfectly willing to drink only every other day, if, as is often the case, he happens to be in a very dry locality. Nor does he stay long in the water or near it, like the white-tail, but moves off as soon as he is no longer thirsty. On moonlight nights he feeds a good deal of the time, and before dawn he is always on foot for his breakfast; the hours around daybreak are those in which most of his grazing is done. By the time the sun has been up an hour he is on his way homeward, grazing as he goes; and he will often stay for some little time longer, if there has been no distrubance from man or other foes, feeding among the scattered scrub cedars skirting the thicket in which he intends to make his bed for the day. Having once made his bed he crouches very close in it, and is difficult to put up during the heat of the day; but as the afternoon wears on he becomes more restless, and will break from his bed and bound off at much smaller provocation, while if the place is lonely he will wander out into the open hours before sunset. If, however, he is in much danger of being molested, he will keep close to his hiding-place until nearly nightfall, when he ventures out to feed. Owing to the lateness of his evening appearance in localities where there is much hunting, it is a safer plan to follow him in the early morning, being on the ground and ready to start out by the time the first streak of dawn appears. Often I have lost deer when riding home in the evening, because the dusk had deepened so that it was impossible to distinguish clearly enough to shoot.

One day one of my cowboys and myself were returning from an unsuccessful hunt, about nightfall, and were still several miles from the river, when a couple of yearling black-tails jumped up in the bed of the dry creek down which we were riding. Our horses though stout and swift were not well trained; and the instant we were off their backs they trotted off. No sooner were we on the ground and trying to sight the deer, one of which was cantering slowly off among the bushes, than we found we could not catch the bead sights of our rifles, the outlines of the animals seeming vague, and shadowy, and confounding themselves with the banks and dull green sage bushes behind them. Certainly six or eight shots were fired, we doing our best to aim, but without any effect; and when we gave it up and turned to look for our horses we were annoyed to see the latter trotting off down the valley half a mile away. We went after at a round pace; but darkness closed in before we had gained at all on them. There was nothing left to do but to walk on down the valley to the bottoms, and then to wade the river; as the latter was quite high, we had to take off our clothes, and it is very uncomfortable to feel one's way across a river at night, in bare feet, with the gun and the bundle of clothes held high over head. However, when across the river and half a mile from home, we ran into our horses—a piece of good luck, as otherwise we should have had to spend the next day in looking for them.

Almost the only way in which it is possible to aim after dark is to get the object against the horizon, toward the light. One of the finest bucks I ever killed was shot in this way. It was some little time after the sun had set, and I was hurrying home, riding down along a winding creek at a gallop. The middle of the bottom was covered with brush, while the steep, grassy, rounded hills on each side sent off spurs into the valley, the part between every two spurs making a deep pocket. The horse's feet were unshod and he made very little noise, coming down against the wind. While passing a deep pocket I heard from within it a snort and stamping of feet, the well-known sounds made by a startled deer. Pulling up short I jumped off the horse—it was Manitou,—who instantly began feeding with perfect indifference to what he probably regarded as an irrational freak of his master; and, aiming as well as I could in the gathering dusk, held the rifle well ahead of a shadowy gray object which was scudding along the base of the hill towards the mouth of the pocket. The ball struck in front of and turned the deer, which then started obliquely up the hill. A second shot missed it; and I then (here comes in the good of having a repeater) knelt down and pointed the rifle against the sky line, at the place where the deer seemed likely to top the bluff. Immediately afterwards the buck appeared, making the last jump with a great effort which landed him square on the edge, as sharply outlined as a silhouette against the fading western light. My rifle bead was just above him; pulling it down I fired, as the buck paused for a second to recover himself from his last great bound, and with a crash the mighty antlered beast came rolling down the hill, the bullet having broken his back behind the shoulders, afterwards going out through his chest.

At times a little caution must be used in approaching a wounded buck, for if it is not disabled it may be a rather formidable antagonist. In my own experience I have never known a wounded buck to do more than make a pass with his horns, or, in plunging when the knife enters his throat, to strike with his forefeet. But one of my men was regularly charged by a great buck, which he had wounded, and which was brought to bay on the ice by a dog. It seemed to realize that the dog was not the main antagonist, and knocking him over charged straight past him at the man, and as the latter had in his haste not reloaded his rifle, he might have been seriously injured had it not been for the dog, a very strong and plucky one, which caught the buck by the hock and threw him. The buck got up and again came straight at his foe, uttering a kind of grunting bleat, and it was not till after quite a scuffle that the man, by the help of the dog, got him down and thrust the knife in his throat. Twice I have known hounds to be killed by bucks which they had brought to bay in the rutting season. One of these bucks was a savage old fellow with great thick neck and sharp-pointed antlers. He came to bay in a stream, under a bank thickly matted with willows which grew down into the water, guarding his rear and flanks, while there was a small pool in his front across which the hounds had to swim. Backing in among the willows he rushed out at every dog that came near, striking it under water with his forefeet, and then again retreating to his fortress. In this way he kept the whole pack off, and so injured one hound that he had to be killed. Indeed, a full-grown buck with antlers would be a match for a wolf, unless surprised, and could not improbably beat off a cougar if he received the latter's spring fairly on his prong points.

Bucks fight fiercely among themselves during the rutting season. At that time the black-tail, unlike the white-tail, is found in bands, somewhat like those of the elk, but much smaller, and the bucks of each band keep up an incessant warfare. A weak buck promptly gets out of the way if charged by a large one; but when two of equal strength come together the battle is well fought. Instances occasionally occur, of a pair of these duellists getting their horns firmly interlocked and thus perishing; but these instances are much rarer, owing to the shape of the antlers, than with the white-tail, of which species I have in my own experience come across two or three sets of skulls held together by their interlacing antlers, the bearers of which had doubtless died owing to their inability to break away from each other.

A black-tail buck is one of the most noble-looking of all deer. His branching and symmetrically curved antlers are set on a small head, carried with beautiful poise by the proud, massive neck. The body seems almost too heavy for the slender legs, and yet the latter bear it as if they were rods of springing steel. Every movement is full of alert, fiery life and grace, and he steps as lightly as though he hardly trod the earth. The large, sensitive ears are thrown forward to catch the slightest sound; and in the buck they are not too conspicuous, though they are the only parts of his frame which to any eye can be said to take away from his beauty. They give the doe a somewhat mulish look; at a distance, the head of a doe peering out from among twigs looks like a great black V. To me, however, even in the case of the doe, they seem to set off and strengthen by contrast the delicate, finely-moulded look of the head. Owing to these ears the species is called in the books the Mule Deer, and every now and then a plainsman will speak of it by this title. But all plainsmen know it generally, and ninety-nine out of a hundred know it only, as the Black-tail Deer; and as this is the title by which it is known among all who hunt it or live near it, it should certainly be called by the same name in the books.

But though so grand and striking an object when startled, or when excited, whether by curiousity or fear, love or hate, a black-tail is nevertheless often very hard to make out when standing motionless among the trees and brushwood, or when lying down among the boulders. A raw hand at hunting has no idea how hard it is to see a deer when at rest. The color of the hair is gray, almost the same tint as that of the leafless branches and tree trunks; for of course the hunting season is at its height only when the leaves have fallen. A deer standing motionless looks black or gray, according as the sunlight strikes it; but always looks exactly the same color as the trees around it. It generally stands or lies near some tree trunks; and the eye may pass over it once or twice without recognizing its real nature. In the brush it is still more difficult, and there a deer's form is often absolutely indistinguishable from the surroundings, as one peers through the mass of interlacing limbs and twigs. Once an old hunter and myself in walking along the ridge of a scoria butte passed by without seeing them, three black-tail lying among the scattered boulders of volcanic rock on the hillside, not fifty yards from us. After a little practical experience a would-be hunter learns not to expect deer always, or even generally, to appear as they do when near by or suddenly startled; but on the contrary to keep a sharp look-out on every dull-looking red or yellow patch he sees in a thicket, and to closely examine any grayish-looking object observed on the hillsides, for it is just such small patches or obscure-looking objects which are apt, if incautiously approached, to suddenly take to themselves legs, and go bounding off at a rate which takes them out of danger before the astonished tyro has really waked up to the fact that they are deer. The first lesson to be learned in still-hunting is the knowledge of how to tell what objects are and what are not deer; and to learn it is by no means as easy a task as those who have never tried it would think.

When he has learned to see a deer, the novice then has to learn to hit it, and this again is not the easy feat it seems. That he can do well with a shot-gun proves very little as to a man's skill with the rifle, for the latter carries but one bullet, and can therefore hit in but one place, while with a shot-gun, if you hold a foot off your mark you will be nearly as apt to hit as if you held plumb centre. Nor does *mere* practice at a mark avail, though excellent in its way; for a deer is never seen at a fixed and ascertained distance, nor is its outline often clearly and sharply defined as with a target. Even if a man keeps cool—and for the first shot or two he will probably be flurried—he may miss an absurdly easy shot by not taking pains. I remember on one occasion missing two shots in succession where it seemed really impossible for a man to help hitting. I was out hunting on horseback with one of my men, and on loping round the corner of a brushy valley came suddenly in sight of a buck with certainly more than a dozen points on his great spreading antlers. I jumped off my horse instantly, and fired as he stood facing me not over forty yards off; fired, as I supposed, perfectly coolly, though without dropping on my knee as I should have done. The shot must have gone high, for the buck bounded away unharmed, heedless of a second ball; and immediately his place was taken by another, somewhat smaller, who sprang out of a thicket into almost the identical place where the big buck had stood. Again I fired and missed; again the buck ran off, and was shot at and missed while running—all four shots being taken within fifty yards. I clambered on to the horse without looking at my companion, but too conscious of his smothered disfavor; after riding a few hundred yards, he said with forced politeness and a vague desire to offer some cheap consolation, that he supposed I had done my best; to which I responded with asperity that I'd be damned if I had; and we finished our journey homeward in silence. A man is likely to overshoot at any distance; but at from twenty-five to seventy-five yards he is certain to do so if he is at all careless.

Moreover, besides not missing, a man must learn to hit his deer in the right place; the first two or three times he shoots he will probably see the whole deer in the rifle sights, instead of just the particular spot he wishes to strike; that is, he will aim in a general way at the deer's whole body—which will probably result in a wound not disabling the animal in the least for the time, although ensuring its finally dying a lingering and painful death. The most instantaneously fatal places are the brain and any part of the spinal column; but these offer such small marks that it is usually only by accident they are hit. The mark at any part of which one can fire with safety is a patch about eight inches or a foot square, including the shoulder-blades, lungs, and heart. A kidney-shot is very fatal; but a black-tail will go all day with a bullet through its entrails, and in cold weather I have known one to run several miles with a portion of its entrails sticking out of a wound and frozen solid. To break both shoulders by a shot as the deer stands sideways to the hunter, brings the buck down in its tracks; but perhaps the best place at which to aim is the point in the body right behind the shoulder-blade. On receiving a bullet in this spot the deer will plunge forward for a jump or two, and then go some fifty yards in a labored gallop; will then stop, sway unsteadily on its legs for a second, and pitch forward on its side. When the hunter comes up he will find his quarry stone dead. If the deer stands facing the hunter it offers only a narrow mark, but either a throat or chest shot will be fatal.

Good shooting is especially necessary after black-tail, because it is so very tenacious of life; much more so than the white-tail, or, in proportion to its bulk, than the elk. For this reason it is of the utmost importance to give an immediately fatal or disabling wound, or the game will almost certainly be lost. It is wonderful to see how far and how fast a seemingly crippled deer will go. Of course, a properly trained dog would be of the greatest use in tracking and bringing to bay wounded black-tail; but, unless properly trained to come in to heel, a dog is worse than useless; and, anyhow, it will be hard to keep one, as long as the wolf-hunters strew the ground so plentifully with poisoned bait. We have had several hunting dogs on our ranch at different times; generally wirehaired deer-hounds, fox-hounds, or greyhounds, by no means absolutely pure in blood; but they all, sooner or later, succumbed to the effects of eating poisoned meat. Some of them were quite good hunting dogs, the rough deer-hounds being perhaps the best at following and tackling a wounded buck. They were all very eager for the sport, and when in the morning we started out on a hunt the dogs were apparently more interested than the men; but their judgement did not equal their zeal, and lack of training made them on the whole more bother than advantage.

But much more than good shooting is necessary before a man can be called a good hunter. Indians, for example, get a great deal of game, but they are in most cases very bad shots. Once, while going up the Clear Fork of the Powder, in Northern Wyoming, one of my men, an excellent hunter, and myself rode into a large camp of Cheyennes; and after a while started a shooting-match with some of them. We had several trials of skill with the rifle, and, a good deal to my astonishment, I found that most of the Indians (quite successful hunters, to judge by the quantity of smoked venison lying round) were very bad shots indeed. None of them came anywhere near the hunter who was with me; nor, indeed, to myself. An Indian gets his game by his patience, his stealth, and his tireless perseverance; and a white to be really successful in still-hunting must learn to copy some of the Indian's traits.

While the game butchers, the skin hunters, and their like, work such brutal slaughter among the plains animals that these will soon be either totally extinct or so thinned out as to cease being prominent features of plains life yet, on the other hand, the nature of the country debars them from following certain murderous and unsportsman-like forms of hunting much in vogue in other quarters of our land. There is no deep water into which a deer can be driven by hounds, and then shot at arm's-length from a boat, as is the fashion with some of the city sportsmen who infest the Adirondack forests during the hunting season; nor is the winter snow ever deep enough to form a crust over which a man can go on snow-shoes, and after running down a deer, which plunges as if in a quagmire, knock the poor, worn-out brute on the head with an axe. Fire-hunting is never tried in the cattle country; it would be far more likely to result in the death of a steer or pony than in the death of a deer, if attempted on foot with a torch, as is done in some of the Southern States; while the streams are not suited to the floating or jacking with a lantern in the bow of the canoe, as practised in the Adirondacks. Floating and fire-hunting, though by no means to be classed among the nobler kinds of sport, yet have a certain fascination of their own, not so much for the sake of the actual hunting, as for the novelty of being out in the wilderness at night; and the noiselessness absolutely necessary to insure success often enables the sportsman to catch curious glimpses of the night life of the different kinds of wild animals.

If it were not for the wolf poison, the plains country would be peculiarly fitted for hunting with hounds; and, if properly carried on, there is no manlier form of sport. It does not imply in the man who follows it the skill that distinguishes the successful still-hunter, but it has a dash and excitement all its own, if the hunter follows the hounds on horseback. But, as carried on in the Adirondacks and in the Eastern and Southern mountains generally, hounding deer is not worthy of much regard. There the hunter is stationed at a runaway over which deer will probably pass, and has nothing to do but sit still for a number of weary hours and perhaps put a charge of buckshot into a deer running by but a few yards off. If a rifle instead of a shotgun is used, a certain amount of skill is necessary, for then it is hard to hit a deer running, no matter how close up; but even with this weapon all the sportsman has to do is to shoot well; he need not show knowledge of a single detail of hunting craft, nor need he have any trait of mind or body such as he must possess to follow most other kinds of the chase.

Deer-hunting on horseback is something widely different. Even if the hunters carry rifles and themselves kill the deer, using the dogs merely to drive it out of the brush, they must be bold and skilful horsemen, and must show good judgment in riding to cut off the quarry, so as to be able to get a shot at it. This is the common American method of hunting the deer in those places where it is followed with horse and hound; but it is also coursed with greyhounds in certain spots where the lay of the land permits this form of sport, and in many districts, even where ordinary hounds are used, the riders go unarmed and merely follow the pack till the deer is bayed and pulled down. All kinds of hunting on horseback—and most hunting on horseback is done with hounds—tend to bring out the best and manliest qualities in the men who follow them, and they should be encouraged in every way. Long after the rifleman, as well as the game he hunts, shall have vanished from the plains, the cattle country will afford fine sport in coursing hares; and both wolves and deer could be followed and killed with packs of properly-trained hounds, and such sport would be even more exciting than still-hunting with the rifle. It is on the great plains lying west of the Missouri that riding to hounds will in the end receive its fullest development as a national pastime.

But at present, for the reasons already stated, it is almost unknown in the cattle country; and the ranchman who loves sport must try still-hunting—and by still-hunting is meant pretty much every kind of chase where a single man, unaided by a dog, and almost always on foot, outgenerals a deer and kills it with the rifle. To do this successfully, unless deer are very plenty and tame, implies a certain knowledge of the country, and a good knowledge of the habits of the game. The hunter must keep a sharp look-out for deer sign; for, though a man soon gets to have a general knowledge of the kind of places in which deer are likely to be, yet he will also find that they are either very capricious, or else than no man has more than a partial understanding of their tastes and likings; for many spots apparently just suited to them will be almost uninhabited, while in others they will be found where it would hardly occur to any one to suspect their presence. Any cause may temporarily drive deer out of a given locality. Still-hunting, especially, is sure to send many away, while rendering the others extremely wild and shy, and where deer have become used to being pursued in only one way, it is often an excellent plan to try some entirely different method.

A certain knowledge of how to track deer is very useful. To become a really skilful tracker is most difficult; and there are some kinds of ground, where, for instance, it is very hard and dry, or frozen solid, on which almost any man will be at fault. But any one with a little practice can learn to do a certain amount of tracking. On snow, of course, it is very easy; but on the other hand it is also peculiarly difficult to avoid being seen by the deer when the ground is white. After deer have been frightened once or twice, or have even merely been disturbed by man, they get the habit of keeping a watch back on their trail; and when snow has fallen, a man is such a conspicuous object deer see him a long way off, and even the tamest become wild. A deer will often, before lying down, take a half circle back to one side and make its bed a few yards from its trail, where it can, itself unseen, watch any person tracing it up. A man tracking in snow needs to pay very little heed to the footprints, which can be followed without effort, but requires to keep up the closest scrutiny over the ground ahead of him, and on either side of the trail.

In the early morning when there is a heavy dew the footprints will be as plain as possible in the grass, and can then be followed readily; and in any place where the ground is at all damp they will usually be plain enough to be made out without difficulty. When the ground is hard or dry the work is very much less easy, and soon becomes so difficult as not to be worth while following up. Indeed, at all times, even in the snow, tracks are chiefly of use to show the probable locality in which a deer may be found; and the still-hunter instead of laboriously walking along a trail will do far better to merely follow it until, from its freshness and direction, he feels confident that the deer is in some particular space of ground, and then hunt through it, guiding himself by his knowledge of the deer's habits and by the character of the land. Tracks are of most use in showing whether deer are plenty or scarce, whether they have been in the place recently or not. Generally, signs of deer are infinitely more plentiful than the animals themselves—although in regions where tracking is especially difficult deer are often jumped without any sign having been seen at all. Usually, however, the rule is the reverse, and as deer are likely to make any quantity of tracks the beginner is apt, judging purely from the sign, greatly to over-estimate their number. Another mistake of the beginner is to look for the deer during the daytime in the places where their tracks were made in the morning, when their day beds will probably be a long distance off. In the night-time deer will lie down almost anywhere, but during the day they go some distance from their feeding- or watering-places, as already explained.

If deer are at all plenty—and if scarce only a master in the art can succeed at still-hunting—it is best not to try to follow the tracks at all, but merely to hunt carefully through any ground which from its looks seems likely to contain the animals. Of course the hunting must be done either against or across the wind, and the greatest care must be taken to avoid making a noise. Moccasins should be worn, and not a twig should be trodden on, nor should the dress be allowed to catch in a brush. Especial caution should be used in going over a ridge or crest; no man should ever let his whole body appear at once, but should first carefully peep over, not letting his rifle barrel come into view, and closely inspect every place in sight in which a deer could possibly stand or lie, always remembering that a deer is when still a most difficult animal to see, and that it will be completely hidden in cover which would apparently hardly hold a rabbit. The rifle should be carried habitually so that the sun will not glance upon it. Advantage must be taken, in walking, of all cover, so that the hunter will not be a conspicuous object at any distance. The heads of a series of brushy ravines should always be crossed; and a narrow, winding valley, with patches of bushes and young trees down through the middle, is always a likely place. Caution should never for a moment be forgotten, especially in the morning or evening, the times when a hunter will get nine tenths of his shots; for it is just then, when moving and feeding, that deer are most watchful. One will never browse for more than a minute or two without raising its head and peering about for any possible foe, the great, sensitive ears thrown forward to catch the slightest sound. But while using such caution it is also well to remember that as much ground should be crossed as possible; other things being equal, the number of shots obtained will correspond to the amount of country covered. And of course a man should be on the hunting ground—not starting for the hunting ground—by the time there is enough light by which to shoot.

Deer are in season for hunting from August first to January first. August is really too early to get full enjoyment out of the sport. The bucks, though fat and good eating, are still in the velvet; and neither does nor fawns should be killed, as many of the latter are in the spotted coat. Besides it is very hot in the middle of the day, though pleasant walking in the early morning and late evening, and with cool nights. December is apt to be too cold, although with many fine days. The true time for the chase of the black-tail is in the three fall months. Then the air is fresh and bracing, and a man feels as if he could walk or ride all day long without tiring. In the bright fall weather the country no longer keeps its ordinary look of parched desolation, and the landscape loses its sameness at the touch of the frost. Where every thing before had been gray or dull green there are now patches of russet red and bright yellow. The clumps of ash, wild plum-trees, and rose-bushes in the heads and bottoms of the sloping valleys become spots of color that glow among the stretches of brown and withered grass; the young cotton-woods, growing on the points of land round which flow the rivers and streams, change to a delicate green or yellow, on which the eye rests with pleasure after having so long seen only the dull drab of the prairies. Often there will be days of bitter cold, when a man who sleeps out in the open feels the need of warm furs; but still more often there will be days and days of sunny weather, not cold enough to bring discomfort, but yet so cool that the blood leaps briskly through a man's veins and makes him feel that to be out and walking over the hills is a pleasure in itself, even were he not in hopes of any moment seeing the sun glint on the horns and hide of some mighty buck, as it rises to face the intruder. On days such as these, mere life is enjoyment; and on days such as these, the life of a hunter is at its pleasantest and best.

Many black-tail are sometimes killed in a day. I have never made big bags myself, for I rarely hunt except for a fine head or when we need meat, and if it can be avoided do not shoot at fawns or does; so the greatest number I have ever killed in a day was three. This was late one November, on an occasion when our larder was running low. My foreman and I, upon discovering this fact, determined to make a trip next day back in the broken country, away from the river, where black-tail were almost sure to be found.

We breakfasted hours before sunrise, and then mounted our horses and rode up the river bottom. The bright prairie moon was at the full, and was sunk in the west till it hung like a globe of white fire over the long row of jagged bluffs that rose from across the river, while its beams brought into fantastic relief the peaks and crests of the buttes upon our left. The valley of the river itself was in partial darkness, and the stiff, twisted branches of the sage-brush seemed to take on uncanny shapes as they stood in the hollows. The cold was stinging, and we let our willing horses gallop with loose reins, their hoofs ringing on the frozen ground. After going up a mile or two along the course of the river we turned off to follow the bed of a large dry creek. At its mouth was a great space of ground much cut up by the hoofs of the cattle, which was in summer overflowed and almost a morass; but now the frostbound earth was like wrinkled iron beneath the horses' feet. Behind us the westering moon sank down out of sight; and with no light but that of the stars, we let our horses thread their own way up the creek bottom. When we had gone a couple of miles from the river the sky in front of our faces took on a faint grayish tinge, the forerunner of dawn. Every now and then we passed by bunches of cattle, lying down or standing huddled together in the patches of brush or under the lee of some shelving bank or other wind-break; and as the eastern heavens grew brighter, a dark form suddenly appeared against the sky-line, on the crest of a bluff directly ahead of us. Another and another came up beside it. A glance told us that it was a troop of ponies, which stood motionless, like so many silhouettes, their outstretched necks and long tails vividly outlined against the light behind them. All in the valley was yet dark when we reached the place where the creek began to split up and branch out into the various arms and ravines from which it headed. We galloped smartly over the divide into a set of coulies and valleys which ran into a different creek, and selected a grassy place where there was good feed to leave the horses. My companion picketed his; Manitou needed no picketing.

The tops of the hills were growing rosy, but the sun was not yet above the horizon when we started off, with our rifles on our shoulders, walking in cautious silence, for we were in good ground and might at any moment see a deer. Above us was a plateau of some size, breaking off sharply at the rim into a surrounding stretch of very rough and rugged country. It sent off low spurs with notched crests into the valleys round about, and its edges were indented with steep ravines and half-circular basins, their sides covered with clusters of gnarled and wind-beaten cedars, often gathered into groves of some size. The ground was so broken as to give excellent cover under which a man could approach game unseen; there were plenty of fresh signs of deer; and we were confident we should soon get a shot. Keeping at the bottom of the gullies, so as to be ourselves inconspicuous, we walked noise-lessly on, cautiously examining every pocket or turn before we rounded the corner, and looking with special care along the edges of the patches of brush.

At last, just as the sun had risen, we came out by the mouth of a deep ravine or hollow, cut in the flank of the plateau, with steep, cedar-clad sides; and on the crest of a jutting spur, not more than thirty yards from where I stood, was a black-tail doe, half facing me. I was in the shadow, and for a moment she could not make me out, and stood motionless with her head turned toward me and her great ears thrown forward. Dropping on my knee, I held the rifle a little back of her shoulder—too far back, as it proved, as she stood quartering and not broadside to me. No fairer chance could ever fall to the lot of a hunter; but, to my intense chagrin, she bounded off at the report as if unhurt, disappearing instantly. My companion had now come up, and we ran up a rise of ground, and crouched down beside a great block of sandstone, in a position from which we overlooked the whole ravine or hollow. After some minutes of quiet watchfulness, we heard a twig snap—the air was so still we could hear any thing—some rods up the ravine, but below us; and immediately after-ward a buck stole out of the cedars. Both of us fired at once, and with a convulsive spring he rolled over back-ward, one bullet having gone through his neck, and the other—probably mine—having broken a hind leg. Imme-diately afterward, another buck broke from the upper edge of the cover, near the top of the plateau, and, though I took a hurried shot at him, bounded over the crest, and was lost to sight.

We now determined to go down into the ravine and look for the doe, and as there was a good deal of snow in the bottom and under the trees, we knew we could soon tell if she were wounded. After a little search we found her track, and walking along it a few yards, came upon some drops and then a splash of blood. There being no need to hurry, we first dressed the dead buck—a fine, fat fellow, but with small, misshapen horns,—and then took up the trail of the wounded doe. Here, however, I again committed an error, and paid too much heed to the trail and too little to the country round about; and while following it with my eyes down on the ground in a place where it was faint, the doe got up some distance ahead and to one side of me, and bounded off round a corner of the ravine. The bed where she had lain was not very bloody, but from the fact of her having stopped so soon, I was sure she was badly wounded. However, after she got out of the snow the ground was as hard as flint, and it was impossible to track her; the valley soon took a turn, and branched into a tangle of coulies and ravines. I deemed it probable that she would not go up hill, but would run down the course of the main valley; but as it was so uncertain, we thought it would pay us best to look for a new deer.

Our luck, however, seemed—very deservedly—to have ended. We tramped on, as swiftly as was compatible with quiet, for hour after hour; beating through the valleys against the wind, and crossing the brushy heads of the ravines, sometimes close together, and sometimes keeping about a hundred yards apart, according to the nature of the ground. When we had searched all through the country round the head of the creek, into which we had come down, we walked over to the next, and went over it with equal care and patience. The morning was now well advanced, and we had to change our method of hunting. It was no longer likely that we should find the deer feeding or in the open, and instead we looked for places where they might be expected to bed, following any trails that led into thick patches of brush or young trees, one of us then hunting through the patch while the other kept watch without. Doubtless we must have passed close to more than one deer, and doubtless others heard us and skulked off through the thick cover; but, although we saw plenty of signs, we saw neither hoof nor hair of living thing. It is under such circumstances that a still-hunter needs to show resolution, and to persevere until his luck turns— this being a euphemistic way of saying, until he ceases to commit the various blunders which alarm the deer and make them get out of the way. Plenty of good shots become disgusted if they do not see a deer early in the morning, and go home; still more, if they do not see one in two or three days. Others will go on hunting, but become careless, stumble and step on dried sticks, and let their eyes fall to the ground. It is a good test of a man's resolution to see if, at the end of a long and unsuccessful tramp after deer, he moves just as carefully, and keeps just as sharp a lookout as he did at the beginning. If he does this, and exercises a little common-sense—in still-hunting, as in every thing else, common-sense is the most necessary of qualities,—he may be sure that his reward will come some day; and when it does come, he feels a gratification that only his fellow-sportsmen can understand.

We lunched at the foot of a great clay butte, where

there was a bed of snow. Fall or winter hunting in the Bad
Lands has one great advantage: the hunter is not annoyed
by thirst as he is almost sure to be if walking for long hours
under the blazing summer sun. If he gets very thirsty, a
mouthful or two of snow from some hollow will moisten
his lips and throat; and anyhow thirstiness is largely a
mere matter of habit. For lunch, the best thing a hunter
can carry is dried or smoked venison, with not too much
salt in it. It is much better than bread, and not nearly so
dry; and it is easier to carry, as a couple of pieces can be
thrust into the bosom of the hunting-shirt or the pocket,
or in fact anywhere; and for keeping up a man's strength
there is nothing that comes up to it.

After lunch we hunted until the shadows began to
lengthen out, when we went back to our horses. The buck
was packed behind good old Manitou, who can carry any
amount of weight at a smart pace, and does not care at all
if a strap breaks and he finds his load dangling about his
feet, an event that reduces most horses to a state of frantic
terror. As soon as loaded we rode down the valley into
which the doe had disappeared in the morning, one taking each side and looking into every possible lurking
place. The odds were all against our finding any trace of
her; but a hunter soon learns that he must take advantage
of every chance, however slight. This time we were rewarded for our care; for after riding about a mile our attention was attracted by a white patch in a clump of low
briars. On getting off and looking in it proved to be the
white rump of the doe, which lay stretched out inside,
stark and stiff. The ball had gone in too far aft and had
come out on the opposite side near her hip, making a mor-

tal wound, but one which allowed her to run over a mile before dying. It was little more than an accident that we in the end got her; and my so nearly missing at such short range was due purely to carelessness and bad judgment. I had killed too many deer to be at all nervous over them, and was as cool with a buck as with a rabbit; but as she was so close I made the common mistake of being too much in a hurry, and did not wait to see that she was standing quartering to me and that consequently I should aim at the point of the shoulder. As a result the deer was nearly lost.

Neither of my shots had so far done me much credit; but at any rate I had learned where the error lay, and this is going a long way toward correcting it. I kept wishing that I could get another chance to see if I had not profited by my lessons; and before we reached home my wish was gratified. We were loping down a grassy valley, dotted with clumps of brush, the wind blowing strong in our faces, and deadening the noise made by the hoofs on the grass. As we passed by a piece of broken ground a yearling black-tail buck jumped into view and cantered away. I was off Manitou's back in an instant. The buck was moving slowly, and was evidently soon going to stop and look round, so I dropped on one knee, with my rifle half raised, and waited. When about sixty yards off he halted and turned sideways to me, offering a beautiful broadside shot. I aimed at the spot just behind the shoulder and felt I had him. At the report he went off, but with short, weak bounds, and I knew he would not go far; nor did he, but stopped short, swayed unsteadily about, and went over on his side, dead, the bullet clean through his body.

Each of us already had a deer behind his saddle, so we could not take the last buck along with us. Accordingly we dressed him, and hung him up by the heels to a branch of a tree, piling the brush around as if building a slight pen or trap, to keep off the coyotes; who, anyhow, are not apt to harm game that is hanging up, their caution seeming to make them fear that it will not be safe to do so. In such cold weather a deer hung up in this way will keep an indefinite length of time; and the carcass was all right when a week or two afterwards we sent out the buck-board to bring it back.

A stout buck-board is very useful on a ranch, where men are continually taking short trips on which they do not wish to be encumbered by the heavy ranch wagon. Pack ponies are always a nuisance, though of course an inevitable one in making journeys through mountains or forests. But on the plains a buck-board is far more handy. The blankets and provisions can be loaded upon it, and it can then be given a definite course to travel or point to reach; and meanwhile the hunters, without having their horses tired by carrying heavy packs, can strike off and hunt wherever they wish. There is little or no difficulty in going over the prairie; but it needs a skilful plainsman, as well as a good teamster, to take a wagon through the Bad Lands. There are but two courses to follow. One is to go along the bottoms of the valleys; the other is to go along the tops of the divides. The latter is generally the best; for each valley usually has at its bottom a deep winding ditch with perpendicular banks, which wanders first to one side and then to the other, and has to be crossed again and again, while a little way from it begin the gullies and gulches which come down from the side hills. It is no easy matter to tell which is the main divide, as it curves and twists about, and is all the time splitting up into lesser ones, which merely separate two branches of the same creek. If the teamster does not know the lay of the land he will be likely to find himself in a *cul-de-sac*, from which he can only escape by going back a mile or two and striking out afresh. In very difficult country the horsemen must be on hand to help the team pull up the steep places. Many horses that will not pull a pound in harness will haul for all there is in them from the saddle; Manitou is a case in point. Often obstacles will be encountered across which it is simply impossible for any team to drag a loaded or even an empty wagon. Such are steep canyons, or muddy-bottomed streams with sheer banks, especially if the latter have rotten edges. The horses must then be crossed first and the wagon dragged over afterward by the aid of long ropes. Often it may be needful to build a kind of rude bridge or causeway on which to get the animals over; and if the canyon is very deep the wagon may have to be taken in pieces, let down one side, and hauled up the other. An immense amount of labor may be required to get over a very trifling distance. Pack animals, however, can go almost anywhere that a man can.

Although still-hunting on foot, as described above, is on the whole the best way to get deer, yet there are many places where from the nature of the land the sport can be followed quite as well on horseback, than which there is no more pleasant kind of hunting. The best shot I ever made in my life—a shot into which, however, I am afraid the element of chance entered much more largely than the element of skill—was made while hunting black-tail on horseback.

We were at that time making quite a long trip with the wagon, and were going up the fork of a plains river in Western Montana. As we were out of food, those two of our number who usually undertook to keep the camp supplied with game determined to make a hunt off back of the river after black-tail; for though there were some white-tail in the more densely timbered river bottoms, we had been unable to get any. It was arranged that the wagon should go on a few miles, and then halt for the night, as it was already the middle of the afternoon when we started out. The country resembled in character other parts of the cattle plains, but it was absolutely bare of trees except along the bed of the river. The rolling hills sloped steeply off into long valleys and deep ravines. They were sparsely covered with coarse grass, and also with an irregular growth of tall sage-brush, which in some places gathered into dense thickets. A beginner would have thought the country entirely too barren of cover to hold deer, but a very little experience teaches one that deer will be found in thickets of such short and sparse growth that it seems as if they could hide nothing; and, what is more, that they will often skulk round in such thickets without being discovered. And a black-tail is a bold, free animal, liking to go out in comparatively open country, where he must trust to his own powers, and not to any concealment, to protect him from danger.

Where the hilly country joined the alluvial river bottom, it broke short off into steep bluffs, up which none but a Western pony could have climbed. It is really wonderful to see what places a pony can get over, and the indifference with which it regards tumbles. In getting up from the bottom we went into a wash-out, and then led our ponies along a clay ledge, from which we turned off and went straight up a very steep sandy bluff. My companion was ahead; just as he turned off the ledge, and as I was right underneath him, his horse, in plunging to try to get up the sand bluff, overbalanced itself, and, after standing erect on its hind legs for a second, came over backward. The second's pause while it stood bolt upright, gave me time to make a frantic leap out of the way with my pony, which scrambled after me, and we both clung with hands and hoofs to the side of the bank, while the other horse took two as complete somersaults as I ever saw, and landed with a crash at the bottom of the wash-out, feet uppermost. I thought it was done for, but not a bit. After a moment or two it struggled to its legs, shook itself, and looked round in rather a shamefaced way, apparently not in the least the worse for the fall. We now got my pony up to the top by vigorous pulling, and then went down for the other, which at first strongly objected to making another trial, but, after much coaxing and a good deal of abuse, took a start and went up without trouble.

For some time after reaching the top of the bluffs we rode along without seeing any thing. When it was possible, we kept one on each side of a creek, avoiding the tops of the ridges, because while on them a horseman can be seen at a very long distance, and going with particular caution whenever we went round a spur or came up over a crest. The country stretched away like an endless, billowy sea of dull-brown soil and barren sage-brush, the valleys making long parallel furrows, and every thing having a look of dreary sameness. At length, as we came out on a rounded ridge, three black-tail bucks started up from a lot of sage-brush some two hundred yards away and below us, and made off down hill. It was a very long shot, especially to try running, but, as game seemed scarce and cartridges were plenty, I leaped off the horse, and, kneeling, fired. The bullet went low, striking in line at the feet of the hindmost. I held very high next time, making a wild shot above and ahead of them, which had the effect of turning them, and they went off round a shoulder of a bluff, being by this time down in the valley. Having plenty of time I elevated the sights (a thing I hardly ever do) to four hundred yards and waited for their reappearance. Meanwhile they had evidently gotten over their fright, for pretty soon one walked out from the other side of the bluff, and came to a standstill, broadside toward me. He was too far off for me to see his horns. As I was raising the rifle another stepped out and began to walk towards the first. I thought I might as well have as much of a target as possible to shoot at, and waited for the second buck to come out farther, which he did immediately and stood still just alongside of the first. I aimed above his shoulders and pulled the trigger. Over went the two bucks! And when I rushed down to where they lay I found I had pulled a little to one side, and the bullet had broken the backs of both. While my companion was dressing them I went back and paced off the distance. It was just four hundred and thirty-one long paces; over four hundred yards. Both were large bucks and very fat, with the velvet hanging in shreds from their antlers, for it was late in August. The day was waning and we had a long ride back to the wagon, each with a buck behind his saddle. When we came back to the river valley it was pitch dark, and it was rather ticklish work for our heavily laden horses to pick their way down the steep bluffs and over the rapid stream; nor were we sorry when we saw ahead under a bluff the gleam of the camp fire, as it was reflected back from the canvas-topped prairie schooner, that for the time being represented home to us.

This was much the best shot I ever made; and it is just such a shot as any one will occasionally make if he takes a good many chances and fires often at ranges where the odds are greatly against his hitting. I suppose I had fired a dozen times at animals four or five hundred yards off, and now, by the doctrine of chances, I happened to hit; but I would have been very foolish if I had thought for a moment that I had learned how to hit at over four hundred yards. I have yet to see the hunter who can hit with any regularity at that distance, when he has to judge it for himself; though I have seen plenty who could make such a long range hit now and then. And I have noticed that such a hunter, in talking over his experience, was certain soon to forget the numerous misses he made, and to say, and even to actually think, that his occasional hits represented his average shooting.

One of the finest black-tail bucks I ever shot was killed while lying out in a rather unusual place. I was hunting mountain-sheep, in a stretch of very high and broken country, and about mid-day, crept cautiously up to the edge of a great gorge, whose sheer walls went straight down several hundred feet. Peeping over the brink of the chasm I saw a buck, lying out on a ledge so narrow as to barely hold him, right on the face of the cliff wall opposite, some distance below, and about seventy yards diagonally across from me. He lay with his legs half stretched out, and his head turned so as to give me an exact centre-shot at his forehead; the bullet going in between his eyes, so that his legs hardly so much as twitched when he received it. It was toilsome and almost dangerous work climbing out to where he lay; I have never known any other individual, even of this bold and adventurous species of deer, to take its noonday siesta in a place so barren of all cover and so difficult of access even to the most sure-footed climber. This buck was as fat as a prize sheep, and heavier than any other I have ever killed; while his antlers also were, with two exceptions, the best I ever got.

CHAPTER VI

A Trip on the Prairie

No antelope are found, except rarely, immediately round my ranch-house, where the ground is much too broken to suit them; but on the great prairies, ten or fifteen miles off, they are plentiful, though far from as abundant as they were a few years ago when the cattle were first driven into the land. By plainsmen they are called either prong-horn or antelope, but are most often known by the latter and much less descriptive title. Where they are found they are always very conspicuous figures in the landscape; for, far from attempting to conceal itself, an antelope really seems anxious to take up a prominent position, caring only to be able to itself see its foes. It is the smallest in size of the plains game, even smaller than a white-tail deer; and its hide is valueless, being thin and porous, and making very poor buckskin. In its whole appearance and structure it is a most singular creature. Unlike all other hollow-horned animals, it sheds its horns annually, exactly as the deer shed their solid antlers; but the shedding process in the prong-horn occupies but a very few days, so short a time, indeed, that many hunters stoutly deny that it takes place at all. The hair is of remarkable texture, very long, coarse, and brittle; in the spring it comes off in handfuls. In strong contrast to the reddish yellow of the other parts of the body, the rump is pure white, and when alarmed or irritated every hair in the white patch bristles up on end, greatly increasing the apparent area of the color. The flesh, unlike that of any other plains animal, is equally good all through the year, In the fall it is hardly so juicy as deer venison, but in the spring, when no other kind of game is worth eating, it is perfectly good; and at that time of the year, if we have to get fresh meat, we would rather kill antelope than any thing else; and as the bucks are always to be instantly distinguished from the does by their large horns, we confine ourselves to them, and so work no harm to the species.

The antelope is a queer-looking rather than a beautiful animal. The curious pronged horns, great bulging eyes, and strange bridle-like marks and bands on the face and throat are more striking, but less handsome, than the delicate head and branching antlers of a deer; and it entirely lacks the latter animal's grace of movement. In its form and look, when standing still, it is rather angular and goat-like, and its movements merely have the charm that comes from lightness, speed, and agility. Its gait is singularly regular and even, without any of the bounding, rolling movement of a deer; and it is, consequently, very easy to hit running, compared with other kinds of game.

Antelope possess a most morbid curiosity. The appearance of any thing out of the way, or to which they are not accustomed, often seems to drive them nearly beside themselves with mingled fright and desire to know what it is, a combination of feelings that throws them into a perfect panic, during whose continuance they will at times seem utterly unable to take care of themselves. In very remote, wild places, to which no white man often penetrates, the appearance of a white-topped wagon will be enough to excite this feeling in the prong-horn, and in such cases it is not unusual for a herd to come up and circle round the strange object heedless of rifle-shots. This curiosity is particularly strong in the bucks during rutting-time, and one method of hunting them is to take advantage of it, and "flag" them up to the hunters by waving a red handkerchief or some other object to and fro in the air. In very wild places they can sometimes be flagged up, even after they have seen the man; but, elsewhere, the latter must keep himself carefully concealed behind a ridge or hillock, or in tall grass, and keep cautiously waving the handkerchief overhead. The antelope will look fixedly at it, stamp, snort, start away, come nearer by fits and starts, and run from one side to the other, the better to see it. Sometimes a wary old buck will keep this up for half an hour, and at the end make off; but, again, the attraction may prove too strong, and the antelope comes slowly on until within rifle-shot. This method of hunting, however, is not so much practised now as formerly, as the antelope are getting continually shyer and more difficult to flag. I have never myself shot one in this manner, though I have often seen the feat performed, and have several times tried it myself, but always with the result that after I had made my arm really weak with waving the handkerchief to and fro, the antelope, which had been shifting about just out of range, suddenly took to its heels and made off.

No other kind of plains game, except the big-horn, is

as shy and sharp-sighted as the antelope; and both its own habits and the open nature of the ground on which it is found render it peculiarly difficult to stalk. There is no cover, and if a man is once seen by the game the latter will not let him get out of sight again, unless it decides to go off at a gait that soon puts half a dozen miles between them. It shifts its position, so as to keep the hunter continually in sight, Thus, if it is standing on a ridge, and the hunter disappear into a ravine up which he intends to crawl, the antelope promptly gallops off to some other place of observation from which its foe is again visible; and this is repeated until the animal at last makes up its mind to start for good. It keeps up an incessant watch, being ever on the look-out for danger, far or near; and as it can see an immense distance, and has its home on ground so level that a horseman can be made out a mile off, its attention is apt to be attracted when still four or five rifle-shots beyond range, and after it has once caught a glimpse of the foe, the latter might as well give up all hopes of getting the game.

But while so much more wary than deer, it is also at times much more foolish, and has certain habits—some of which, such as its inordinate curiosity and liability to panic, have already been alluded to—that tend to its destruction. Ordinarily, it is a far more difficult feat to kill an antelope than it is to kill a deer, but there are times when the former can be slaughtered in such numbers that it becomes mere butchery.

The prong-horn is pre-eminently a gregarious animal. It is found in bands almost all the year through. During the two or three days after he has shed his horns and while the new ones are growing the buck retires to some out-of-the-way spot, and while bringing forth her fawns the doe stays by herself. But as soon as possible each again rejoins the band; and the fawns become members of it at a remarkably early age. In the late fall, when the bitter cold has begun, a large number of these bands collect together, and immense herds are formed which last throughout the winter. Thus at this season a man may travel for days through regions where antelope are most plentiful during the hot months and never see one; but if he does come across any they will be apt to be in great numbers, most probably along the edge of the Bad Lands, where the ground is rolling rather than broken, but where there is some shelter from the furious winter gales. Often they will even come down to the river bottom or find their way up to some plateau. They now always hang closely about the places they have chosen for their winter haunts, and seem very reluctant to leave them. They go in dense herds, and when starved and weak with cold are less shy; and can often be killed in great numbers by any one who has found out where they are—though a true sportsman will not molest them at this season.

Sometimes a small number of individuals will at this time get separated from the main herd and take up their abode in some place by themselves; and when they have once done so it is almost impossible to drive them away. Last winter a solitary prong-horn strayed into the river bottom at the mouth of a wide creek-valley, half a mile from my ranch, and stayed there for three months, keeping with the cattle, and always being found within a mile of the same spot. A little band at the same time established itself on a large plateau, about five miles long by two miles wide, some distance up the river above me, and afforded fine sport to a couple of ranchmen who lived not far from its base. The antelope, twenty or thirty in number, would not leave the plateau, which lies in the midst of broken ground; for it is a peculiarity of these animals, which will be spoken of further on, that they will try to keep in the open ground at any cost or hazard. The two ranchmen agreed never to shoot at the antelope on foot, but only to try to kill them from horseback, either with their revolvers or their Winchesters. They thus hunted them for the sake of the sport purely; and certainly they got plenty of fun out of them. Very few horses indeed are as fast as a prong-horn; and these few did not include any owned by either of my two friends. But the antelope were always being obliged to break back from the edge of the plateau, and so were forced constantly to offer opportunities for cutting them off; and these opportunities were still further increased by the two hunters separating. One of them would go to the upper end of the plateau and start the band, riding after them at full speed. They would distance him, but would be checked in their career by coming to the brink of the cliff; then they would turn at an angle and give their pursuer a chance to cut them off; and if they kept straight up the middle the other hunter would head them. When a favorable moment came the hunters would dash in as close as possible and empty their revolvers or repeaters into the herd; but it is astonishing how hard it is, when riding a horse at full speed, to hit any object, unless it is directly under the muzzle of the weapon. The number of cartridges spent compared to the number of prong-horn killed was enormous; but the fun and excitement of the chase were the main objects with my friends, to whom the actual killing of the game was of entirely secondary importance. They went out after them about a dozen times during the winter, and killed in all ten or fifteen prong-horns.

A prong-horn is by far the fleetest animal on the plains; one can outrun and outlast a deer with the greatest ease. Very swift greyhounds can overtake them, if hunted in leashes or couples; but only a remarkably good dog can run one down single-handed. Besides prong-horn are most plucky little creatures, and will make a most resolute fight against a dog or wolf, striking with their forefeet and punching with their not very formidable horns, and are so quick and wiry as to be really rather hard to master.

Antelope have the greatest objection to going on any thing but open ground, and seem to be absolutely unable to make a high jump. If a band is caught feeding in the bottom of a valley leading into a plain they invariably make a rush straight to the mouth, even if the foe is stationed there, and will run heedlessly by him, no matter how narrow the mouth is, rather than not try to reach the open country. It is almost impossible to force them into even a small patch of brush, and they will face almost certain death rather than try to leap a really very trifling obstacle. If caught in a glade surrounded by a slight growth of brushwood, they make no effort whatever to get through or over this growth, but dash frantically out through the way by which they got in. Often the deer, especially the black-tail, will wander out on the edge of the plain frequented by antelope; and it is curious to see the two animals separate the second there is an alarm, the deer making for the broken country, while the antelope scud for the level plains. Once two of my men nearly caught a couple of antelope in their hands. They were out driving in the buck-board, and saw two antelope, a long distance ahead, enter the mouth of a wash-out (a canyon *in petto*); they had strayed away from the prairie to the river bottom, and were evidently feeling lost. My two men did not think much of the matter but when opposite the mouth of the wash-out, which was only thirty feet or so wide, they saw the two antelope starting to come out, having found that it was a blind passage, with no outlet at the other end. Both men jumped out of the buck-board and ran to the entrance; the two antelope dashed frantically to and fro inside the wash-out. The sides were steep, but a deer would have scaled them at once; yet the antelope seemed utterly unable to do this, and finally broke out past the two men and got away. They came so close that the men were able to touch each of them, but their movements were too quick to permit of their being caught.

However, though unable to leap any height, an antelope can skim across a level jump like a bird, and will go over water-courses and wash-outs that very few horses indeed will face. A mountain-sheep, on the other hand, is a marvellous vertical leaper; the black-tail deer comes next; the white-tail is pretty good, and the elk is at any rate better than the antelope; but when it comes to horizontal jumping the latter can beat them all.

In May or early June the doe brings forth her fawns, usually two in number, for she is very prolific. She makes her bed in some valley or hollow, and keeps with the rest of the band, only returning to the fawns to feed them. They lie out in the grass or under some slight bush, but are marvellously hard to find. By instinct they at once know how to crouch down so as to be as inconspicuous as possible. Once we scared away a female prong-horn from an apparently perfectly level hill-side; and in riding along passed over the spot she had left and came upon two little fawns that could have been but a few hours old. They lay flat in the grass, with their legs doubled under them and their necks and heads stretched out on the ground. When we took them up and handled them, they soon got used to us and moved awkwardly round, but at any sudden noise or motion they would immediately squat flat down again. But at a very early age the fawns learn how to shift for themselves, and can then run almost as fast as their parents, even when no larger than a jack-rabbit. Once, while we were haying, a couple of my cowboys spent half an hour in trying to run down and capture a little fawn, but they were unable to catch it, it ran so fast and ducked about so quickly. Antelope fawns are very easily tamed and make most amusing pets. We have had two or three, but have never succeeded in rearing any of them; but some of the adjoining ranchmen have been more fortunate. They are not nearly so pretty as deer fawns, having long, gangling legs and angular bodies, but they are much more familiar and interesting. One of my neighbors has three live prong-horns, as well as two little spotted white-tail deer. The deer fawns are always skulking about, and are by no means such bold inquisitive little creatures as the small antelope are. The latter have a nurse in the shape of a fat old ewe; and it is funny to see her, when alarmed, running off at a waddling gait, while her ungainly little foster-children skip round and round her, cutting the most extraordinary antics. There are a couple of very large dogs, mastiffs, on the place, whose natural solemnity is completely disconcerted by the importunities and fearlessness of the little antelope fawns. Where one goes the other two always follow; and so one of the mastiffs, while solemnly blinking in the sun, will suddenly find himself charged at full speed by the three queer little creatures, who will often fairly butt up against him. The uneasy look of the dog, and his efforts to get out of the way without compromising his dignity, are really very comical.

Young fawns seem to give out no scent, and thus many of them escape from the numerous carnivorous beasts that are ever prowling about at night over the prairie, and which, during the spring months, are always fat from feeding on the bodies of the innocents they have murdered. If discovered by a fox or coyote during its first few days of existence a little fawn has no chance of life, although the mother, if present, will fight desperately for it; but after it has acquired the use of its legs it has no more to fear than have any of the older ones.

Sometimes the fawns fall victims to the great Golden Eagle. This grand bird, the War Eagle of the Sioux, is not very common in the Bad Lands, but is sometimes still seen with us; and, as everywhere else, its mere presence adds a certain grandeur to its lonely haunts. Two or three years ago a nest was found by one of my men on the face of an almost inaccessible cliff, and a young bird was taken out from it and reared in a roughly extemporized cage. Wherever the eagle exists it holds undisputed sway over every thing whose size does not protect it from the great bird's beak and talons; not only does it feed on hares, grouse, and ducks, but it will also attack the young fawns of the deer and antelope. Still, the eagle is but an occasional foe, and aside from man, the only formidable enemies the antelope has to fear are the wolves and coyotes. These are very destructive to the young, and are always lounging about the band to pick up any wounded straggler; in winter, when the ground is slippery and the antelope numbed and weak, they will often commit great havoc even among those that are grown up.

The voice of the antelope is not at all like that of the deer. Instead of bleating it utters a quick, harsh noise, a kind of bark; a little like the sound "kau," sharply and clearly repeated. It can be heard a long distance off; and is usually uttered when the animal is a little startled or surprised by the presence of something it does not understand.

The prong-horn cannot go without water any longer than a deer can, and will go great distances to get it; for space is nothing to a traveller with such speed and such last. No matter how dry and barren may be the desert in which antelope are found, it may be taken for granted that they are always within reaching distance of some spring or pool of water, and that they visit it once a day. Once or twice I have camped out by some pool, which was the only one for miles around, and in every such case have been surprised at night by the visits of the antelope, who, on finding that their drinking-place was tenanted, would hover round at a short distance, returning again and again and continually uttering the barking "kau, kau," until they became convinced that there was no hope of their getting in, when they would set off at a run for some other place.

Prong-horn perhaps prefer the rolling prairies of short grass as their home, but seem to do almost equally well on the desolate and monotonous wastes where the sage-brush and prickly pear and a few blades of coarse grass are the only signs of plant life to be seen. In such places, the prong-horn, the sage cock, the rattlesnake, and the horned frog alone are able to make out a livelihood.

The horned frog is not a frog at all, but a lizard,—a queer, stumpy little fellow with spikes all over the top of its head and back, and given to moving in the most leisurely manner imaginable. Nothing will make it hurry. If taken home it becomes a very tame and quaint but also very uninteresting little pet.

Rattlesnakes are only too plentiful everywhere; along the river bottoms, in the broken, hilly ground, and on the prairies and the great desert wastes alike. Every cowboy kills dozens each season. To a man wearing top-boots there is little or no danger while he is merely walking about, for the fangs cannot get through the leather, and the snake does not strike as high as the knee. Indeed the rattlesnake is not nearly as dangerous as are most poisonous serpents, for it always gives fair warning before striking, and is both sluggish and timid. If it can it will get out of the way, and only coils up in its attitude of defence when it believes that it is actually menaced. It is, of course, however, both a dangerous and a disagreeable neighbor, and one of its annoying traits is the fondness it displays for crawling into a hut or taking refuge among the blankets left out on the ground. Except in such cases men are rarely in danger from it, unless they happen to be stooping over, as was the case with one of my cowboys who had leaned over to pick up a log, and was almost bitten by a snake which was underneath it; or unless the snake is encountered while stalking an animal. Once I was creeping up to an antelope under cover of some very low sage-brush—so low that I had to lie flat on my face and push myself along with my hands and feet. While cautiously moving on in this way I was electrified by hearing almost by my ears the well-known, ominous "whir-r-r" of a rattlesnake, and on hastily glancing up there was the reptile, not ten feet away from me, all coiled up and waiting. I backed off and crawled to one side, the rattler turning its head round to keep watch over my movements; when the stalk was over (the antelope took alarm and ran off before I was within rifle-shot) I came back, hunted up the snake, and killed it. Although I have known of several men being bitten, I know of but one case where the bite caused the death of a human being. This was a girl who had been out milking, and was returning, in bare feet; the snake struck her just above the ankle, and in her fright she fell and was struck again in the neck. The double wound was too much for her, and the poison killed her in the course of a couple of hours.

Occasionally one meets a rattlesnake whose rattle has been lost or injured; and such a one is always dangerous, because it strikes without warning. I once nearly lost a horse by the bite of one of these snakes without rattles. I was riding along a path when my horse gave a tremendous start and jump; looking back I saw that it had been struck at by a rattlesnake with an injured tail, which had been lying hid in a bunch of grass, directly beside the path. Luckily it had merely hit the hard hoof, breaking one of its fangs.

Horses differ very much in their conduct toward snakes. Some show great fright at sight of them or on hearing their rattles, plunging and rearing and refusing to go anywhere near the spot; while others have no fear of them at all, being really perfectly stupid about them. Manitou does not lose his wits at all over them, but at the same time takes very good care not to come within striking distance.

Ranchmen often suffer some loss among their stock owing to snake-bites; both horned cattle and horses, in grazing, frequently coming on snakes and having their noses or cheeks bitten. Generally, these wounds are not fatal, though very uncomfortable; it is not uncommon to see a woe-begone looking mule with its head double the natural size, in consequence of having incautiously browsed over a snake. A neighbor lost a weak pony in this way; and one of our best steers also perished from the same cause. But in the latter case, the animal, like the poor girl spoken of above, had received two wounds with the poison fangs; apparently it had, while grazing with its head down, been first struck in the nose, and been again struck in the foreleg as it started away.

Of all kinds of hunting, the chase of the antelope is pre-eminently that requiring skill in the use of the rifle at long range. The distance at which shots have to be taken in antelope hunting is at least double the ordinary distance at which deer are fired at. In pursuing most other kinds of game, a hunter who is not a good shot may still do excellent work; but in prong-horn hunting, no man can make even a fairly good record unless he is a skilful marksman. I have myself done but little hunting after antelopes, and have not, as a rule, been very successful in the pursuit.

Ordinary hounds are rarely, or never, used to chase this game; but coursing it with greyhounds is as manly and exhilarating a form of sport as can be imagined,—a much better way of hunting it than is shooting it with the rifle, which latter, though needing more skill in the actual use of the weapon, is in every other respect greatly inferior as a sport to still-hunting the black-tail or big-horn.

I never but once took a trip of any length with antelope hunting for its chief object. This was one June, when all the men were away on the round-up. As is usual during the busy half of the ranchman's year, the spring and summer, when men have no time to hunt and game is out of condition, we had been living on salt pork, beans, potatoes, and bread; and I had hardly had a rifle in my hand for months; so, finding I had a few days to spare, I thought I should take a short trip on the prairie, in the beautiful June weather, and get a little sport and a little fresh meat out of the bands of prong-horn bucks, which I was sure to encounter. Intending to be gone but a couple of days, it was not necessary to take many articles. Behind my saddle I carried a blanket for bedding, and an oil-skin coat to ward off the wet; a large metal cup with the handle riveted, not soldered, on, so that water could be boiled in it; a little tea and salt, and some biscuits; and a small water-proof bag containing my half dozen personal necessaries—not forgetting a book. The whole formed a small, light pack, very little encumbrance to stout old Manitou. In June, fair weather can generally be counted on in the dry plains country.

I started in the very earliest morning, when the intense brilliancy of the stars had just begun to pale before the first streak of dawn. By the time I left the river bottom and struck off up the valley of a winding creek, which led through the Bad Lands, the eastern sky was growing rosy; and soon the buttes and cliffs were lit up by the level rays of the cloudless summer sun. The air was fresh and sweet, and odorous with the sweet scents of the spring-time that was but barely passed; the dew lay heavy, in glittering drops, on the leaves and the blades of grass, whose vivid green, at this season, for a short time brightens the desolate and sterile-looking wastes of the lonely western plains. The rose-bushes were all in bloom, and their pink blossoms clustered in every point and bend of the stream; and the sweet, sad songs of the hermit thrushes rose from the thickets, while the meadow larks perched boldly in sight as they uttered their louder and more cheerful music. The round-up had passed by our ranch, and all the cattle with our brands, the maltese cross and cut dewlap, or the elk-horn and triangle, had been turned loose; they had not yet worked away from the river, and I rode by long strings of them, walking in single file off to the hills, or standing in groups to look at me as I passed.

Leaving the creek I struck off among a region of scoria buttes, the ground rising into rounded hills through whose grassy covering the red volcanic rock showed in places, while boulder-like fragments of it were scattered all through the valleys between. There were a few clumps of bushes here and there, and near one of them were two magpies, who lit on an old buffalo skull, bleached white by sun and snow. Magpies are birds that catch the eye at once from their bold black and white plumage and long tails; and they are very saucy and at the same time very cunning and shy. In spring we do not often see them; but in the late fall and winter they will come close round the huts and out-buildings on the look-out for any thing to eat. If a deer is hung up and they can get at it they will pick it to pieces with their sharp bills; and their carnivorous tastes and their habit of coming round hunters' camps after the game that is left out, call to mind their kinsman, the whiskey-jack or moose-bird of the northern forests.

After passing the last line of low, rounded scoria buttes, the horse stepped out on the border of the great, seemingly endless stretches of rolling or nearly level prairie, over which I had planned to travel and hunt for the next two or three days. At intervals of ten or a dozen miles this prairie was crossed by dry creeks, with, in places in their beds, pools or springs of water, and alongside a spindling growth of trees and bushes; and my intention was to hunt across these creeks, and camp by some water-hole in one of them at night.

I rode over the land in a general southerly course, bending to the right or left according to the nature of the ground and the likelihood of finding game. Most of the time the horse kept on a steady single-foot, but this was varied by a sharp lope every now and then, to ease the muscles of both steed and rider. The sun was well up, and its beams beat fiercely down on our heads from out of the cloudless sky; for at this season, though the nights and the early morning and late evening are cool and pleasant, the hours around noon are very hot. My glass was slung alongside the saddle, and from every one of the scattered hillocks the country was scanned carefully far and near; and the greatest caution was used in riding up over any divide, to be sure that no game on the opposite side was scared by the sudden appearance of my horse or myself.

Nowhere, not even at sea, does a man feel more lonely than when riding over the far-reaching, seemingly never-ending plains; and, after a man has lived a little while on or near them, their very vastness and loneliness and their melancholy monotony have a strong fascination for him. The landscape seems always the same, and after the traveller has plodded on for miles and miles he gets to feel as if the distance was indeed boundless. As far as the eye can see there is no break; either the prairie stretches out into perfectly level flats, or else there are gentle, rolling slopes, whose crests mark the divides between the drainage systems of the different creeks; and when one of these is ascended, immediately another precisely like it takes its place in the distance, and so roll succeeds roll in a succession as interminable as that of the waves of the ocean. Nowhere else does one seem so far off from all mankind; the plains stretch out in death-like and measure-less expanse, and as he journeys over them they will for many miles be lacking in all signs of life. Although he can see so far, yet all objects on the outermost verge of the horizon, even though within the ken of his vision, look unreal and strange; for there is no shade to take away from the bright glare, and at a little distance things seem to shimmer and dance in the hot rays of the sun. The ground is scorched to a dull brown, and against its monotonous expanse any objects stand out with a prominence that makes it difficult to judge of the distance at which they are. A mile off one can see, through the strange shimmering haze, the shadowy white outlines of something which looms vaguely up till it looks as large as the canvas-top of a prairie wagon; but as the horseman comes nearer it shrinks and dwindles and takes clearer form, until at last it changes into the ghastly staring skull of some mighty buffalo, long dead and gone to join the rest of his vanished race.

When the grassy prairies are left and the traveller enters a region of alkali desert and sage-brush, the look of the country becomes even more grim and forbidding. In places the alkali forms a white frost on the ground that glances in the sunlight like the surface of a frozen lake; the dusty little sage-brush, stunted and dried up, sprawls over the parched ground, from which it can hardly extract the small amount of nourishment necessary for even its weazened life; the spiny cactus alone seems to be really in its true home. Yet even in such places antelope will be found, as alert and as abounding with vivacious life as elsewhere. Owing to the magnifying and distorting power of the clear, dry plains air, every object, no matter what its shape or color or apparent distance, needs the closest examination. A magpie sitting on a white skull, or a couple of ravens, will look, a quarter of a mile off, like some curious beast; and time and again a raw hunter will try to stalk a lump of clay or a burnt stick; and after being once or twice disappointed he is apt to rush to the other extreme, and conclude too hastily that a given object is not an antelope, when it very possibly is.

During the morning I came in sight of several small

bands or pairs of antelope. Most of them saw me as soon as or before I saw them, and after watching me with intense curiosity as long as I was in sight and at a distance, made off at once as soon as I went into a hollow or appeared to be approaching too near. Twice, in scanning the country narrowly with the glasses, from behind a sheltering divide, bands of prong-horn were seen that had not discovered me. In each case the horse was at once left to graze, while I started off after the game, nearly a mile distant. For the first half mile I could walk upright or go along half stooping; then, as the distance grew closer, I had to crawl on all fours and keep behind any little broken bank, or take advantage of a small, dry watercourse; and toward the end work my way flat on my face, wriggling like a serpent, using every stunted sage-brush or patch of cactus as a cover, bare-headed under the blazing sun. In each case, after nearly an hour's irksome, thirsty work, the stalk failed. One band simply ran off without a second's warning, alarmed at some awkward movement on my part, and without giving a chance for a shot. In the other instance, while still at very long and uncertain range, I heard the sharp barking alarm-note of one of the prong-horn; the whole band instantly raising their heads and gazing intently at their would-be destroyer. They were a very long way off; but, seeing it was hopeless to try to get nearer I rested my rifle over a little mound of earth and fired. The dust came up in a puff to one side of the nearest antelope; the whole band took a few jumps and turned again; the second shot struck at their feet, and they went off like so many race-horses, being missed again as they ran. I sat up by a sage-brush thinking they would of course not come back, when to my surprise I saw them wheel round with the precision of a cavalry squadron, all in line and fronting me, the white and brown markings on their heads and throats showing like the facings on soldiers' uniforms; and then back they came charging up till again within long range, when they wheeled their line as if on a pivot and once more made off, this time for good, not heeding an ineffectual fusillade from the Winchester. Antelope often go through a series of regular evolutions, like so many trained horsemen, wheeling, turning, halting, and running as if under command; and their coming back to again run the (as it proved very harmless) gauntlet of my fire was due either to curiosity or to one of those panicky freaks which occasionally seize those ordinarily wary animals, and cause them to run into danger easily avoided by creatures commonly much more readily approached than they are. I had fired half a dozen shots without effect; but while no one ever gets over his feeling of self-indignation at missing an easy shot at close quarters, any one who hunts antelope and is not of a disposition so timid as never to take chances, soon learns that he has to expect to expend a good deal of powder and lead before bagging his game.

By mid-day we reached a dry creek and followed up its course for a mile or so, till a small spot of green in the side of a bank showed the presence of water, a little pool of which lay underneath. The ground was so rotten that it was with difficulty I could get Manitou down where he could drink; but at last both of us satisfied our thirst, and he was turned loose to graze, with his saddle off, so as to cool his back, and I, after eating a biscuit, lay on my face on the ground—there was no shade of any sort near—and dozed until a couple of hours' rest and feed had put the horse in good trim for the afternoon ride. When it came to crossing over the dry creek on whose bank we had rested, we almost went down in a quicksand, and it was only by frantic struggles and flounderings that we managed to get over.

On account of these quicksands and mud-holes, crossing the creeks on the prairie is often very disagreeable work. Even when apparently perfectly dry the bottom may have merely a thin crust of hard mud and underneath a fathomless bed of slime. If the grass appears wet and with here and there a few tussocks of taller blades in it, it is well to avoid it. Often a man may have to go along a creek nearly a mile before he can find a safe crossing, or else run the risk of seeing his horse mired hard and fast. When a horse is once in a mud-hole it will perhaps so exhaust itself by its first desperate and fruitless struggle that it is almost impossible to get it out. Its bridle and saddle have to be taken off; if another horse is along the lariat is drawn from the pommel of the latter's saddle to the neck of the one that is in, and it is hauled out by main force. Otherwise a man may have to work half a day, fixing the horse's legs in the right position and then taking it by the forelock and endeavoring to get it to make a plunge; each plunge bringing it perhaps a few inches nearer the firm ground. Quicksands are even more dangerous than these mud-holes, as, if at all deep, a creature that cannot get out immediately is sure to be speedily engulfed. Many parts of the Little Missouri are impassable on account of these quicksands. Always in crossing unknown ground that looks dangerous it is best to feel your way very cautiously along, and, if possible, to find out some cattle trail or even game trail which can be followed.

For some time after leaving the creek nothing was seen; until, on coming over the crest of the next great divide, I came in sight of a band of six or eight prong-horn about a quarter of a mile off to my right hand. There was a slight breeze from the southeast, which blew diagonally across my path towards the antelopes. The latter, after staring at me a minute, as I rode slowly on, suddenly started at full speed to run directly up wind, and therefore in a direction that would cut the line of my course less than half a mile ahead of where I was. Knowing that when antelope begin running in a straight line they are very hard to turn, and seeing that they would have to run a longer distance than my horse would to intercept them, I clapped spurs into Manitou, and the game old fellow, a very fleet runner, stretched himself down to the ground and seemed to go almost as fast as the quarry. As I had expected, the latter, when they saw me running, merely straightened themselves out and went on, possibly even faster than before, without changing the line of their flight, keeping right up wind. Both horse and antelope fairly flew over the ground, their courses being at an angle that would certainly bring them together. Two of the antelope led, by some fifty yards or so, the others, who were all bunched together. Nearer and nearer we came, Manitou, in spite of carrying myself and the pack behind the saddle, gamely holding his own, while the antelope, with outstretched necks, went at an even, regular gait that offered a strong contrast to the springing bounds with which a deer runs. At last the two leading animals crossed the line of my flight ahead of me; when I pulled short up, leaped from Manitou's back, and blazed into the band as they went by not forty yards off, aiming well ahead of a fine buck who was on the side nearest me. An antelope's gait is so even that it offers a good running mark; and as the smoke blew off I saw the buck roll over like a rabbit, with both shoulders broken. I then emptied the Winchester at the rest of the band, breaking one hind leg of a young buck. Hastily cutting the throat of, and opening, the dead buck, I again mounted and started off after the wounded one. But, though only on three legs, it went astonishingly fast, having had a good start; and after following it over a mile I gave up the pursuit, though I had gained a good deal; for the heat was very great, and I did not deem it well to tire the horse at the beginning of the trip. Returning to the carcass, I cut off the hams and strung them beside the saddle; an antelope is so spare that there is very little more meat on the body.

This trick of running in a straight line is another of the antelope's peculiar characteristics which frequently lead it into danger. Although with so much sharper eyes than a deer, antelope are in many ways far stupider animals, more like sheep, and they especially resemble the latter in their habit of following a leader, and in their foolish obstinacy in keeping to a course they have once adopted. If a horseman starts to head off a deer the latter will always turn long before he has come within range, but quite often an antelope will merely increase his speed and try to pass ahead of his foe. Almost always, however, one if alone will keep out of gunshot, owing to the speed at which he goes, but if there are several in a band which is well strung out, the leader only cares for his own safety and passes well ahead himself. The others follow like sheep, without turning in the least from the line the first followed, and thus may pass within close range. If the leader bounds into the air, those following will often go through exactly the same motions; and if he turns, the others are very apt to each in succession run up and turn in the same place, unless the whole band are manœuvring together, like a squadron of cavalry under orders, as has already been spoken of.

After securing the buck's hams and head (the latter for the sake of the horns, which were unusually long and fine), I pushed rapidly on without stopping to hunt, to reach some large creek which should contain both wood and water, for even in summer a fire adds greatly to the comfort and cosiness of a night camp. When the sun had nearly set we went over a divide and came in sight of a creek fulfilling the required conditions. It wound its way through a valley of rich bottom land, cotton-wood trees of no great height or size growing in thick groves along its banks, while its bed contained many deep pools of water, some of it fresh and good. I rode into a great bend, with a grove of trees on its right and containing excellent feed. Manitou was loosed, with the lariat round his neck, to feed where he wished until I went to bed, when he was to be taken to a place where the grass was thick and succulent, and tethered out for the night. There was any amount of wood with which a fire was started for cheerfulness, and some of the coals were soon raked off apart to cook over. The horse blanket was spread on the ground, with the oil-skin over it as a bed, underneath a spreading cotton-wood tree, while the regular blanket served as covering. The metal cup was soon filled with water and simmering over the coals to make tea, while an antelope steak was roasting on a forked stick. It is wonderful how cosy a camp, in clear weather, becomes if there is a good fire and enough to eat, and how sound the sleep is afterwards in the cool air, with the brilliant stars glimmering through the branches overhead. In the country where I was there was absolutely no danger from Indian horse-thieves, and practically none from white ones, for I felt pretty sure no one was anywhere within a good many miles of me, and none could have seen me come into the valley. Besides, in the cattle country stealing horses is a hazardous profession, as any man who is found engaged in it is at once, and very properly, strung up to the nearest tree, or shot if no trees are handy; so very few people follow it, at least for any length of time, and a man's horses are generally safe.

Near where we had halted for the night camp was a large prairie-dog town. Prairie-dogs are abundant all over the cattle country; they are in shape like little woodchucks, and are the most noisy and inquisitive animals imaginable. They are never found singly, but always in towns of several hundred inhabitants; and these towns are found in all kinds of places where the country is flat and treeless. Sometimes they will be placed on the bottoms of the creeks or rivers, and again far out on the prairie or among the Bad Lands, a long distance from any water. Indeed, so dry are some of the localities in which they exist, that it is a marvel how they can live at all; yet they seem invariably plump and in good condition. They are exceedingly destructive to grass, eating away every thing round their burrows, and thus each town is always extending at the borders, while the holes in the middle are deserted; in many districts they have become a perfect bane to the cattle-men, for the incoming of man has been the means of causing a great falling off in the ranks of their four-footed foes, and this main check to their increase being gone, they multiply at a rate that threatens to make them a serious pest in the future. They are among the few plains animals who are benefited instead of being injured by the presence of man; and it is most difficult to exterminate them or to keep their number in any way under, as they are prolific to a most extraordinary degree; and the quantity of good feed they destroy is very great, and as they eat up the roots of the grass it is a long time before it grows again. Already in many districts the stockmen are seriously considering the best way in which to take steps against them. Prairie-dogs wherever they exist are sure to attract attention, all the more so because, unlike most other rodents, they are diurnal and not nocturnal, offering therein a curious case of parallelism to their fellow denizen of the dry plains, the antelope, which is also a creature loving to be up and stirring in the bright daylight, unlike its relatives, the dusk-loving deer. They are very noisy, their shrill yelping resounding on all sides whenever a man rides through a town. None go far from their homes, always keeping close enough to be able to skulk into them at once; and as soon as a foe appears they take refuge on the hillocks beside their burrows, yelping continuously, and accompanying each yelp by a spasmodic jerking of the tail and body. When the man comes a little nearer they disappear inside and then thrust their heads out, for they are most inquisitive. Their burrows form one of the chief dangers to riding at full speed over the plains country; hardly any man can do much riding on the prairie for more than a year or two without coming to grief on more than one occasion by his horse putting its foot in a prairie-dog hole. A badger hole is even worse. When a horse gets his foot in such a hole, while going at full speed, he turns a complete somersault, and is lucky if he escape without a broken leg, while I have time and again known the rider to be severely injured. There are other smaller animals whose burrows sometimes cause a horseman to receive a sharp tumble. These are the pocket-gophers, queer creatures, shaped like moles and having the same subterranean habits, but with teeth like a rat's, and great pouches on the outside of their jaws, whose long, rambling tunnels cover the ground in certain places, though the animals themselves are very rarely seen; and the little striped gophers and gray gophers, entirely different animals, more like ground squirrels. But the prairie-dog is always the main source of danger to the horseman, as well as of mischief to the cattle-herder.

Around the prairie-dog towns it is always well to keep a look-out for the smaller carnivora, especially coyotes and badgers, as they are very fond of such neighborhoods, and almost always it is also a favorite resort for the larger kinds of hawks, which are so numerous throughout the cattle country. Rattlesnakes are quite plenty, living in the deserted holes, and the latter are also the homes of the little burrowing owls, which will often be seen standing at the opening, ready to run in as quick as any of the prairie-dogs if danger threatens. They have a funny habit of gravely bowing or posturing at the passer-by, and stand up very erect on their legs. With the exception of this species, owls are rare in the cattle country.

A prairie-dog is rather a difficult animal to get, as it stands so close to its burrow that a spasmodic kick, even if at the last gasp, sends the body inside, where it cannot be recovered. The cowboys are always practising at them with their revolvers, and as they are pretty good shots, mortally wound a good many, but unless the force of the blow fairly knocks the prairie-dog away from the mouth of the burrow, it almost always manages to escape inside. But a good shot with the rifle can kill any number by lying down quietly and waiting a few minutes until the dogs get a little distance from the mouths of their homes.

Badgers are more commonly found round prairie-dog towns than anywhere else; and they get their chief food by digging up the prairie-dogs and gophers with their strong forearms and long, stout claws. They are not often found wandering away from their homes in the daytime, but if so caught are easily run down and killed. A badger is a most desperate fighter, and an overmatch for a coyote, his hide being very thick and his form so squat and strong that it is hard to break his back or legs, while his sharp teeth grip like a steel trap. A very few seconds allow him to dig a hole in the ground, into which he can back all except his head; and when placed thus, with his rear and flanks protected, he can beat off a dog many times his own size. A young badger one night came up round the ranch-house, and began gnawing at some bones that had been left near the door. Hearing the noise one of my men took a lantern and went outside. The glare of the light seemed to make the badger stupid, for after looking at the lantern a few moments, it coolly turned and went on eating the scraps of flesh on the bones, and was knocked on the head without attempting to escape.

To come back to my trip. Early in the morning I was awakened by the shrill yelping of the prairie-dogs whose town was near me. The sun had not yet risen, and the air had the peculiar chill it always takes on toward morning, while little wreaths of light mist rose from the pools. Getting up and loosing Manitou to let him feed round where he wished and slake his thirst, I took the rifle, strolled up the creek valley a short distance, and turned off out on the prairie. Nothing was in sight in the way of game; but overhead a skylark was singing, soaring up above me so high that I could not make out his form in the gray morning light. I listened for some time, and the music never ceased for a moment, coming down clear, sweet, and tender from the air above. Soon the strains of another answered from a little distance off, and the two kept soaring and singing as long as I stayed to listen; and when I walked away I could still hear their notes behind me. In some ways the skylark is the sweetest singer we have; only certain of the thrushes rival it, but though the songs of the latter have perhaps even more melody, they are far from being as uninterrupted and well sustained, being rather a succession of broken bursts of music.

The sun was just appearing when I walked back to the creek bottom. Coming slowly out of a patch of brushwood, was a doe, going down to drink; her great, sensitive ears thrown forward as she peered anxiously and timidly round. She was very watchful, lifting her head and gazing about between every few mouthfuls. When she had drunk her fill she snatched a hasty mouthful or two of the wet grass, and then cantered back to the edge of the brush, when a little spotted fawn came out and joined her. The two stood together for a few moments, and then walked off into the cover. The little pond at which they had drunk was within fifty yards of my night bed; and it had other tenants in the shape of a mallard duck, with a brood of little ducklings, balls of fuzzy yellow down, that bobbed off into the reeds like little corks as I walked by.

Breaking camp is a simple operation for one man; and but a few minutes after breakfast Manitou and I were off; the embers of the fire having been extinguished with the care that comes to be almost second nature with the cattleman, one of whose chief dreads is the prairie fire, that sometimes robs his stock of such an immense amount of feed. Very little game was seen during the morning, as I rode in an almost straight line over the hot, parched plains, the ground cracked and seamed by the heat, and the dull brown blades bending over as if the sun was too much even for them. The sweat drenched the horse even when we were walking; and long before noon we halted for rest by a bitter alkaline pool with border so steep and rotten that I had to bring water up to the horse in my hat; having taken some along in a canteen for my own use. But there was a steep bank near, overgrown with young trees, and thus giving good shade; and it was this that induced me to stop. When leaving this halting-place, I spied three figures in the distance, loping towards me; they turned out to be cowboys, who had been out a couple of days looking up a band of strayed ponies, and as they had exhausted their supply of food, I gave them the antelope hams, trusting to shoot another for my own use.

Nor was I disappointed. After leaving the cowboys I headed the horse towards the more rolling country where the prairies begin to break off into the edges of the Bad Lands. Several bands of antelope were seen, and I tried one unsuccessful stalk, not being able to come within rifle range; but towards evening, when only about a mile from a wooded creek on whose banks I intended to sleep, I came across a solitary buck, just as I was topping the ridge of the last divide. As I was keeping a sharp lookout at the time, I reined in the horse the instant the head of the antelope came in sight, and jumping off crept up till I could see his whole body, when I dropped on my knee and took steady aim. He was a long way off (three hundred yards by actual pacing), and not having made out exactly what we were he stood still, looking intently in our direction and broadside to us. I held well over his shoulder, and at the report he dropped like a shot, the ball having broken his neck. It was a very good shot; the best I ever made at antelope, of which game, as already said, I have killed but very few individuals. Taking the hams and saddle I rode on down to the creek and again went into camp among timber. Thus on this trip I was never successful in outwitting antelope on the several occasions when I pitted my craft and skill against their wariness and keen senses, always either failing to get within range or else missing them; but nevertheless I got two by taking advantage of the stupidity and curiosity which they occasionally show.

The middle part of the days having proved so very

hot, and as my store of biscuits was nearly gone, and as I knew, moreover, that the antelope meat would not keep over twenty-four hours, I decided to push back home next day; and accordingly I broke camp at the first streak of dawn, and took Manitou back to the ranch at a smart lope.

A solitary trip such as this was, through a comparatively wild region in which game is still plentiful, always has great attraction for any man who cares for sport and for nature, and who is able to be his own companion, but the pleasure after all depends a good deal on the weather. To be sure, after a little experience in roughing it, the hardships seem a good deal less formidable than they formerly did, and a man becomes able to roll up in a wet blanket and sleep all night in a pelting rain without hurting himself—though he will shiver a good deal, and feel pretty numb and stiff in those chill and dreary hours just before dawn. But when a man's clothes and bedding and rifle are all wet, no matter how philosophically he may bear it, it may be taken for granted that he does not enjoy it. So fair weather is a very vital and important element among those that go to make up the pleasure and success of such a trip. Luckily fair weather can be counted on with a good deal of certainty in late spring and throughout most of the summer and fall on the northern cattle plains. The storms that do take place, though very violent, do not last long.

Every now and then, however, there will be in the fall a three-days' storm in which it is almost impossible to travel, and then the best thing to be done is to lie up under any shelter that is at hand until it blows over. I remember one such camp which was made in the midst of the most singular and picturesque surroundings. It was toward the end of a long wagon trip that we had been taking, and all of the horses were tired by incessant work. We had come through country which was entirely new to us, passing nearly all day in a long flat prairie through which flowed a stream that we supposed to be either the Box Alder or the Little Beaver. In leaving this we had struck some heavy sand-hills, and while pulling the loaded wagon up them one of the team played out completely, and we had to take her out and put in one of the spare saddle-ponies, a tough little fellow. Night came on fast, and the sun was just setting when we crossed the final ridge and came in sight of as singular a bit of country as I have ever seen. The cowboys, as we afterward found, had christened the place "Medicine Buttes." In plains dialect, I may explain, "Medicine" has been adopted from the Indians, among whom it means any thing supernatural or very unusual. It is used in the sense of "magic," or "out of the common."

Over an irregular tract of gently rolling sandy hills, perhaps about three quarters of a mile square, were scattered several hundred detached and isolated buttes or cliffs of sandstone, each butte from fifteen to fifty feet high, and from thirty to a couple of hundred feet across. Some of them rose as sharp peaks or ridges, or as connected chains, but much the greater number had flat tops like little table-lands. The sides were perfectly perpendicular, and were cut and channelled by the weather into the most extraordinary forms; caves, columns, battlements, spires, and flying buttresses were mingled in the strangest confusion. Many of the caves were worn clear through the buttes, and they were at every height in the sides, while ledges ran across the faces, and shoulders and columns jutted out from the corners. On the tops and at the bases of most of the cliffs grew pine trees, some of considerable height, and the sand gave every thing a clean, white look.

Altogether it was as fantastically beautiful a place as I have ever seen: it seemed impossible that the hand of man should not have had something to do with its formation. There was a spring of clear cold water a few hundred yards off, with good feed for the horses round it; and we made our camp at the foot of one of the largest buttes, building a roaring pine-log fire in an angle in the face of the cliff, while our beds were under the pine trees. It was the time of the full moon, and the early part of the night was clear. The flame of the fire leaped up the side of the cliff, the red light bringing out into lurid and ghastly relief the bold corners and strange-looking escarpments of the rock, while against it the stiff limbs of the pines stood out like rigid bars of iron. Walking off out of sight of the circle of firelight, among the tall crags, the place seemed almost as unreal as if we had been in fairy-land. The flood of clear moonlight turned the white faces of the cliffs and the grounds between them into shining silver, against which the pines showed dark and sombre, while the intensely black shadows of the buttes took on forms that were grimly fantastic. Every cave or cranny in the crags looked so black that it seemed almost to be thrown out from the surface, and when the branches of the trees moved, the bright moonlight danced on the ground as if it were a sheet of molten metal. Neither in shape nor in color did our surroundings seem to belong to the dull gray world through which we had been travelling all day.

But by next morning every thing had changed. A furious gale of wind was blowing, and we were shrouded in a dense, drizzling mist, through which at times the rain drove in level sheets. Now and then the fog would blow away, and then would come on thicker than ever; and when it began to clear off a steady rain took its place, and the wind increased to a regular hurricane. With its canvas top on, the wagon would certainly have been blown over if on open ground, and it was impossible to start or keep a fire except under the sheltered lee of the cliff. Moreover, the wind kept shifting, and we had to shift too, as fast as ever it started to blow from a new quarter; and thus in the course of the twenty-four hours we made a complete circle of the cliff at whose base we were. Our blankets got wet during the night; and they got no drier during the day; and the second night, as we slept on them they got steadily damper. Our provisions were pretty nearly out, and so, with little to eat and less to do, wet and uncomfortable, we cowered over the sputtering fire, and whiled the long day away as best we might with our own thoughts; fortunately we had all learned that no matter how bad things are, grumbling and bad temper can always be depended upon to make them worse, and so bore our ill-fortune, if not with stoical indifference, at least in perfect quiet. Next day the storm still continued, but the fog was gone and the wind somewhat easier; and we spent the whole day looking up the horses, which had drifted a long distance before the storm; nor was it till the morning of the third day that we left our beautiful but, as events had made it, uncomfortable camping-ground.

In midsummer the storms are rarely of long duration,

but are very severe while they last. I remember well one day when I was caught in such a storm. I had gone some twenty-five miles from the ranch to see the round-up, which had reached what is known as the Oxbow of the Little Missouri, where the river makes a great loop round a flat grassy bottom, on which the cattle herd was gathered. I stayed, seeing the cattle cut out and the calves branded, until after dinner; for it was at the time of the year when the days were longest.

At last the work was ended, and I started home in the twilight. The horse splashed across the shallow ford, and then spent half an hour in climbing up through the rugged side hills, till we reached the top of the first great plateau that had to be crossed. As soon as I got on it I put in the spurs and started off at a gallop. In the dusk the brown level land stretched out in formless expanse ahead of me, unrelieved, except by the bleached white of a buffalo's skull, whose outlines glimmered indistinctly to one side of the course I was riding. On my left the sun had set behind a row of jagged buttes, that loomed up in sharp relief against the western sky; above them it had left a bar of yellow light, which only made more intense the darkness of the surrounding heavens. In the quarter towards which I was heading there had gathered a lowering mass of black storm-clouds, lit up by the incessant play of the lightning. The wind had totally died away, and the death-like stillness was only broken by the continuous, measured beat of the horse's hoofs as he galloped over the plain, and at times by the muttered roll of the distant thunder.

Without slacking pace I crossed the plateau, and as I came to the other edge the storm burst in sheets and torrents of water. In five minutes I was drenched through, and to guide myself had to take advantage of the continual flashes of lightning; and I was right glad, half an hour afterward, to stop and take shelter in the log hut of a couple of cowboys, where I could get dry and warm.

CHAPTER VII

A Trip After Mountain Sheep

Late one fall a spell of bitter weather set in, and lasted on through the early part of the winter. For many days together the cold was fierce in its intensity; and the wheels of the ranch-wagon, when we drove out for a load of fire-wood, creaked and sang as they ground through the powdery snow that lay light on the ground. At night in the clear sky the stars seemed to snap and glitter; and for weeks of cloudless white weather the sun shone down on a land from which his beams glanced and glistened as if it had been the surface of a mirror, till the glare hurt the eyes that looked upon it. In the still nights we could hear the trees crack and jar from the strain of the biting frost; and in its winding bed the river lay fixed like a huge bent bar of blue steel.

We had been told that a small band of big-horn was hanging around some very steep and broken country about twenty-five miles from the ranch-house. I had been out after them once alone, but had failed to find even their tracks, and had made up my mind that in order to hunt them it would be necessary to make a three- or four-days' trip, taking along the buck-board with our bedding and eatables. The trip had been delayed owing to two of my men, who had been sent out to buy ponies, coming in with a bunch of fifty, for the most part hardly broken. Some of them were meant for the use of the lower ranch, and the men from the latter had come up to get them. At night the ponies were let loose, and each day were gathered into the horse corral and broken as well as we could break them in such weather. It was my intention not to start on the hunt until the ponies were separated into the two bands, and the men from the lower ranch (the Elkhorn) had gone off with theirs. Then one of the cowboys was to take the buck-board up to a deserted hunter's hut, which lay on a great bend of the river near by the ground over which the big-horn were said to wander, while my foreman, Merrifield, and myself would take saddle-horses, and each day ride to the country through which we intended to hunt, returning at night to the buck-board and hut. But we started a little sooner than we had intended, owing to a funny mistake made by one of the cowboys.

The sun did not rise until nearly eight, but each morning we breakfasted at five, and the men were then sent out on the horses which had been kept in overnight, to find and drive home the pony band; of course they started in perfect darkness, except for the starlight. On the last day of our proposed stay the men had come in with the ponies before sunrise; and, leaving the latter in the corral, they entered the house and crowded round the fire, stamping and beating their numbed hands together. In the midst of the confusion word was brought by one of the cowboys, that while hunting for the horses he had seen two bears go down into a wash-out; and he told us that he could bring us right to the place where he had seen them, for as soon as he left it he had come in at speed on his swift, iron-gray horse—a vicious, clean-limbed devil, with muscles like bundles of tense wire; the cold had made the brute savage, and it had been punished with the cruel curb bit until long, bloody icicles hung from its lips.

At once Merrifield and I mounted in hot haste, and rode off with the bringer of good tidings, leaving hasty instructions where we were to be joined by the buck-board. The sun was still just below the horizon as we started, wrapped warmly in our fur coats and with our caps drawn down over our ears to keep out the cold. The cattle were standing in the thickets and sheltered ravines, huddled together with their heads down, the frost lying on their backs and the icicles hanging from their muzzles; they stared at us as we rode along, but were too cold to move a hand's breadth out of our way; indeed it is a marvel how they survive the winter at all. Our course at first lay up a long valley, cut up by cattle trails; then we came out, just as the sun had risen, upon the rounded, gently-sloping highlands, thickly clad with the short, nutritious grass, which curls on the stalk into good hay, and on which the cattle feed during winter. We galloped rapidly over the hills, our blood gradually warming up from the motion; and soon came to the long wash-out, cutting down like a miniature canyon for a space of two or three miles through the bottom of a valley, into which the cowboy said he had seen the bears go. One of us took one side and one the other, and we rode along up wind, but neither the bears nor any traces of them could we see; at last, half a mile ahead of us, two dark objects suddenly emerged from the wash-out, and came out on the plain. For a second we thought they

were the quarry; then we saw that they were merely a couple of dark-colored ponies. The cowboy's chapfallen face
was a study; he had seen, in the dim light, the two ponies
going down with their heads held near the ground, and
had mistaken them for bears (by no means the unnatural
mistake that it seems; I have known an experienced hunter
fire twice at a black calf in the late evening, thinking it was
a bear). He knew only too well the merciless chaff to
which he would be henceforth exposed; and a foretaste of
which he at once received from my companion. The
ponies had strayed from the main herd, and the cowboy
was sent back to drive them to the home corral, while
Merrifield and myself continued our hunt.

We had all day before us, and but twenty miles or so
to cover before reaching the hut where the buck-board
was to meet us; but the course we intended to take was
through country so rough that no Eastern horse could
cross it, and even the hardy Western hunting-ponies, who
climb like goats, would have difficulty in keeping their
feet. Our route lay through the heart of the Bad Lands,
but of course the country was not equally rough in all
parts. There were tracts of varying size, each covered with
a tangled mass of chains and peaks, the buttes in places
reaching a height that would in the East entitle them to
be called mountains. Every such tract was riven in all directions by deep chasms and narrow ravines, whose sides
sometimes rolled off in gentle slopes, but far more often
rose as sheer cliffs, with narrow ledges along their fronts.
A sparse growth of grass covered certain portions of these
lands, and on some of the steep hillsides, or in the
canyons, were scanty groves of coniferous evergreens, so

stunted by the thin soil and bleak weather that many of them were bushes rather than trees. Most of the peaks and ridges, and many of the valleys, were entirely bare of vegetation, and these had been cut by wind and water into the strangest and most fantastic shapes. Indeed it is difficult, in looking at such formations, to get rid of the feeling that their curiously twisted and contorted forms are due to some vast volcanic upheavals or other subterranean forces; yet they are merely caused by the action of the various weathering forces of the dry climate on the different strata of sandstones, clays, and marls. Isolated columns shoot up into the air, bearing on their summits flat rocks like tables; square buttes tower high above surrounding depressions, which are so cut up by twisting gullies and low ridges as to be almost impassable; shelving masses of sandstone jut out over the sides of the cliffs; some of the ridges, with perfectly perpendicular sides, are so worn away that they stand up like gigantic knife blades; and gulches, washouts, and canyons dig out the sides of each butte, while between them are thrust out long spurs, with sharp ragged tops. All such patches of barren, broken ground, where the feed seems too scant to support any large animal, are the favorite haunts of the big-horn, though it also wanders far into the somewhat gentler and more fertile, but still very rugged, domain of the black-tail deer.

Between all such masses of rough country lay wide, grassy plateaus or long stretches of bare plain, covered with pebbly shingle. We loped across all these open places; and when we came to a reach of broken country would leave our horses and hunt through it on foot. Except where the wind had blown it off, there was a thin coat of snow over every thing, and the icy edges and sides of the cliffs gave only slippery and uncertain foothold, so as to render the climbing doubly toilsome. Hunting the big-horn is at all times the hardest and most difficult kind of sport, and is equally trying to both wind and muscle; and for that very reason the big-horn ranks highest among all the species of game that are killed by still-hunting, and its chase constitutes the noblest form of sport with the rifle, always excepting, of course, those kinds of hunting where the quarry is itself dangerous to attack. Climbing kept us warm in spite of the bitter weather; we only wore our fur coats and shaps while on horseback, leaving them where we left the horses, and doing our still-hunting in buckskin shirts, fur caps, and stout shoes.

Big-horn, more commonly known as mountain sheep, are extremely wary and cautious animals, and are plentiful in but few places. This is rather surprising, for they seem to be fairly prolific (although not as much so as deer and antelope), and comparatively few are killed by the hunters; indeed, much fewer are shot than of any other kind of western game in proportion to their numbers. They hold out in a place long after the elk and buffalo have been exterminated, and for many years after both of these have become things of the past the big-horn will still exist to afford sport to the man who is a hardy moun-taineer and skilful with the rifle. For it is the only kind of game on whose haunts cattle do not trespass. Good buf-falo or elk pasture is sure to be also good pasture for steers and cows; and in summer the herds of the ranchman wan-der far into the prairies of the antelope, while in winter their chosen and favorite resorts are those of which the black-tail is equally fond. Thus, the cattle-men are almost as much foes of these kinds of game as are the hunters, but neither cattle nor cowboys penetrate into the sterile and rocky wastes where the big-horn is found. And it is too wary game, and the labor of following it is too great, for it ever to be much persecuted by the skin or market hunters.

In size the big-horn comes next to buffalo and elk, averaging larger than the black-tail deer, while an old ram will sometimes be almost as heavy as a small cow elk. In his movements he is not light and graceful like the prong-horn and other antelopes, his marvellous agility seeming rather to proceed from sturdy strength and wonderful command over iron sinews and muscles. The huge horns are carried proudly erect by the massive neck; every motion of the body is made with perfect poise; and there seems to be no ground so difficult that the big-horn cannot cross it. There is probably no animal in the world his superior in climbing; and his only equals are the other species of mountain sheep and the ibexes. No matter how sheer the cliff, if there are ever so tiny cracks or breaks in the surface, the big-horn will bound up or down it with wonderful ease and seeming absence of effort. The perpendicular bounds it can make are truly startling—in strong contrast with its distant relative the prong-horn which can leap almost any level jump but seems unable to clear the smallest height. In descending a sheer wall of rock the big-horn holds all four feet together and goes down in long jumps, bounding off the surface almost like a rubber ball every time he strikes it. The way that one will vanish over the roughest and most broken ground is a perpetual surprise to any one that has hunted them; and the ewes are quite as skilful as the rams, while even the very young lambs seem almost as well able to climb, and certainly follow wherever their elders lead. Time and again one will rush over a cliff to what appears certain death, and will gallop away from the bottom unharmed. Their perfect self-confidence seems to be justified, however, for they never slip or make a misstep, even on the narrowest ledges when covered with ice and snow. And all their marvelous jumping and climbing is done with an apparent ease that renders it the more wonderful. Rapid though the movements of one are they are made without any of the nervous hurry so characteristic of the antelopes and smaller deer; the on-looker is really as much impressed with the animal's sinewy power and self-command as with his agility. His strength and his self-reliance seem to fit him above all other kinds of game to battle with the elements and with his brute foes; he does not care to have the rough ways of his life made smooth; were his choice free his abode would still be the vast and lonely wilderness in which he is found. To him the barren wastes of the Bad Lands offer a most attractive home; yet to other living creatures they are at all times as grimly desolate and forbidding as any spot on earth can be; at all seasons they seem hostile to every form of life. In the raging heat of summer the dry earth cracks and crumbles, and the sultry, lifeless air sways and trembles as if above a furnace. Through the high, clear atmosphere, the intense sunlight casts unnaturally deep shadows; and where there are no shadows, brings out in glaring relief the weird, fantastic shapes and bizarre coloring of the buttes. In winter snow and ice coat the thin crests and sharp sides of the cliffs, and increase their look of savage wildness; the cold turns the ground into ringing iron; and the icy blasts sweep through the clefts and over the ridges with an angry fury even more terrible than is the intense, death-like, silent heat of midsummer. But the mountain ram is alike proudly indifferent to the hottest summer sun and to the wildest winter storm.

The lambs are brought forth late in May or early in June. Like the antelope, the dam soon leads her kids to join the herd, which may range in size from a dozen to four or five times as many individuals, generally approaching nearer the former number. The ewes, lambs, and yearling or two-year-old rams go together. The young but full-grown rams keep in small parties of three or four, while the old fellows, with monstrous heads, keep by themselves, except when they join the ewes in the rutting season. At this time they wage savage war with each other. The horns of the old rams are always battered and scarred from these butting contests—which appearance, by the way, has given rise to the ridiculous idea that they were in the habit of jumping over precipices and landing on their heads.

Occasionally the big-horn come down into the valleys or along the grassy slopes to feed, but this is not often, and in such cases every member of the band is always keeping the sharpest look-out, and at the slightest alarm they beat a retreat to their broken fastnesses. At night-time or in the early morning they come down to drink at the small pools or springs, but move off the instant they have satisfied their thirst. As a rule, they spend their time among the rocks and rough ground, and it is in these places that they must be hunted. They cover a good deal of ground when feeding, for the feed is scanty in their haunts, and they walk quite rapidly along the ledges or peaks, by preference high up, as they graze or browse. When through feeding they always choose as a resting-place some point from which they can command a view over all the surrounding territory. An old ram is peculiarly wary. The crest of a ridge or the top of a peak is a favorite resting-bed; but even more often they choose some ledge, high up, but just below the crest, or lie on a shelf of rock that juts out from where a ridge ends, and thus enables them to view the country on three sides of them. In color they harmonize curiously with the grayish or yellowish brown of the ground on which they are found, and it is often very difficult to make them out when lying motionless on a ledge of rock. Time and again they will be mistaken for boulders, and, on the other hand, I have more than once stalked up to masses of sandstone that I have mistaken for sheep.

When lying down the big-horn can thus scan every thing below it; and both while feeding and resting it invariably keeps the sharpest possible look-out for all danger from beneath, and this trait makes it needful for the hunter to always keep on the highest ground and try to come on it from above. For protection against danger it relies on ears, eyes, and nose alike. The slightest sound startles it and puts it on its guard, while if it sees or smells any thing which it deems may bode danger it is off like a flash. It is as wary and quick-sighted as the antelope, and its senses are as keen as are those of the elk, while it is not afflicted by the occasional stupidity nor heedless recklessness of these two animals, nor by the intense curiosity of the black-tail, and it has all the white-tail's sound common-sense, coupled with a much shyer nature and much sharper faculties, so that it is more difficult to kill than are any of these creatures. And the climbing is rendered all the more tiresome by the traits above spoken of, which make it necessary for the hunter to keep above it. The first thing to do is to clamber up to the top of a ridge, and after that to keep on the highest crests.

At all times, and with all game, the still-hunter should be quiet, and should observe caution, but when after mountain sheep he must be absolutely noiseless and must not neglect a single chance. He must be careful not to step on a loose stone or to start any crumbling earth; he must always hunt up or across wind, and he must take advantage of every crag or boulder to shelter himself from the gaze of his watchful quarry. While keeping up as high as possible, he should not go on the very summit, as that brings him out in too sharp relief against the sky. And all the while he will be crossing land where he will need to pay good heed to his own footing or else run the risk of breaking his neck.

As far as lay in us, on our first day's hunt we paid proper heed to all the rules of hunting-craft; but without success. Up the slippery, ice-covered buttes we clambered, clinging to the rocks, and slowly working our way across the faces of the cliffs, or cautiously creeping along the narrow ledges, peering over every crest long and carefully, and from the peaks scanning the ground all about with the field-glasses. But we saw no sheep, and but little sign of them. Still we did see some sign, and lost a shot, either through bad luck or bad management. This was while going through a cluster of broken buttes, whose peaks rose up like sharp cones. On reaching the top of one at the leeward end, we worked cautiously up the side, seeing nothing, to the other end, and then down along the middle. When about half-way back we came across the fresh footprints of a ewe or yearling ram in a little patch of snow. On tracing them back we found that it had been lying down on the other side of a small bluff, within a hundred yards of where we had passed, and must have either got our wind, or else have heard us make some noise. At any rate it had gone off, and though we followed its tracks a little in the snow, they soon got on the bare, frozen ground and we lost them.

After that we saw nothing. The cold, as the day wore on, seemed gradually to chill us through and through; our hands and feet became numb, and our ears tingled under our fur caps. We hunted carefully through two or three masses of jagged buttes which seemed most likely places for the game we were after, taking a couple of hours to each place; and then, as the afternoon was beginning to wane, mounted our shivering horses for good, and pushed toward the bend of the river where we were to meet the buck-board. Our course lay across a succession of bleak, wind-swept plateaus, broken by deep and narrow pine-clad gorges. We galloped swiftly over the plateaus, where the footing was good and the going easy, for the gales had driven the feathery snow off the withered brown grass; but getting on and off these table-lands was often a real labor, their sides were so sheer. The horses plunged and scrambled after us as we led them up; while in descending they would sit back on their haunches and half-walk, half-slide, down the steep inclines. Indeed, one or two of the latter were so very straight that the horses would not face them, and we had to turn them round and back them over the edge, and then all go down with a rush. At any rate it warmed our blood to keep out of the way of the hoofs. On one of the plateaus I got a very long shot at a black-tail, which I missed.

Finally we struck the head of a long, winding valley with a smooth bottom, and after cantering down it four or five miles, came to the river, just after the cold, pale-red sun had sunk behind the line of hills ahead of us. Our horses were sharp shod, and crossed the ice without difficulty; and in a grove of leafless cotton-woods, on the opposite side, we found the hut for which we had been making, the cowboy already inside with the fire started. Throughout the night the temperature sank lower and lower, and it was impossible to keep the crazy old hut anywhere near freezing-point; the wind whistled through the chinks and crannies of the logs, and, after a short and by no means elaborate supper, we were glad to cower down with our great fur coats still on, under the pile of buffalo robes and bear-skins. My sleeping-bag came in very handily, and kept me as warm as possible, in spite of the bitter frost.

We were up and had taken breakfast next morning by the time the first streak of dawn had dimmed the brilliancy of the stars, and immediately afterwards strode off on foot, as we had been hampered by the horses on the day before. We walked briskly across the plain until, by the time it was light enough to see to shoot, we came to the

foot of a great hill, known as Middle Butte, a huge, isolated mass of rock, several miles in length, and with high
sides, very steep towards the nearly level summit; it would
be deemed a mountain of no inconsiderable size in the
East. We hunted carefully through the outlying foothills
and projecting spurs around its base, without result, finding but a few tracks, and those very old ones, and then
toiled up to the top, which, though narrow in parts, in
others widened out into plateaus half a mile square. Having made a complete circuit of the top, peering over the
edge and closely examining the flanks of the butte with
the field-glass, without having seen any thing, we slid
down the other side and took off through a streak of very
rugged but low country. This day, though the weather had
grown even colder, we did not feel it, for we walked all the
while with a quick pace, and the climbing was very hard
work. The shoulders and ledges of the cliffs had become
round and slippery with the ice, and it was no easy task to
move up and along them, clutching the gun in one hand,
and grasping each little projection with the other. Climbing through the Bad Lands is just like any other kind of
mountaineering, except that the precipices and chasms are
much lower; but this really makes very little difference
when the ground is frozen as solid as iron, for it would be
almost as unpleasant to fall fifty feet as to fall two hundred, and the result to the person who tried it would be
very much the same in each case.

Hunting for a day or two without finding game where
the work is severe and toilsome, is a good test of the
sportsman's staying qualities; the man who at the end of
the time is proceeding with as much caution and determi-

nation as at the beginning, has got the right stuff in him. On this day I got rather tired, and committed one of the blunders of which no hunter ought ever to be guilty; that is, I fired at small game while on ground where I might expect large. We had seen two or three jack-rabbits scudding off like noiseless white shadows, and finally came upon some sharp-tail prairie fowl in a hollow. One was quite near me, perched on a bush, and with its neck stretched up offered a beautiful mark; I could not resist it, so knelt and fired. At the report of the rifle (it was a miss, by the by) a head suddenly appeared over a ridge some six hundred yards in front—too far off for us to make out what kind of animal it belonged to,—looked fixedly at us, and then disappeared. We feared it might be a mountain sheep, and that my unlucky shot had deprived us of the chance of a try at it; but on hurrying up to the place where it had been we were relieved to find that the tracks were only those of a black-tail. After this lesson we proceeded in silence, making a long circle through the roughest kind of country. When on the way back to camp, where the buttes rose highest and steepest, we came upon fresh tracks, but as it was then late in the afternoon, did not try to follow them that day. When near the hut I killed a sharp-tail for supper, making rather a neat shot, the bird being eighty yards off. The night was even colder than the preceding one, and all signs told us that we would soon have a change for the worse in the weather, which made me doubly anxious to get a sheep before the storm struck us. We determined that next morning we would take the horses and make a quick push for the chain of high buttes where we had seen the fresh tracks, and hunt them through with thorough care.

We started in the cold gray of the next morning and pricked rapidly off over the frozen plain, columns of white steam rising from the nostrils of the galloping horses. When we reached the foot of the hills where we intended to hunt, and had tethered the horses, the sun had already risen, but it was evident that the clear weather of a fortnight past was over. The air was thick and hazy, and away off in the northwest a towering mass of grayish white clouds looked like a weather-breeder; every thing boded a storm at no distant date. The country over which we now hunted was wilder and more mountainous than any we had yet struck. High, sharp peaks and ridges broke off abruptly into narrow gorges and deep ravines; they were bare of all but the scantiest vegetation, save on some of the sheltered sides where grew groves of dark pines, now laden down with feathery snow. The climbing was as hard as ever. At first we went straight up the side of the tallest peak, and then along the knife-like ridge which joined it with the next. The ice made the footing very slippery as we stepped along the ledges or crawled round the jutting shoulders, and we had to look carefully for our footholds; while in the cold, thin air every quick burst we made up a steep hill caused us to pant for breath. We had gone but a little way before we saw fresh signs of the animals we were after, but it was some time before we came upon the quarry itself.

We left the high ground and descending into a narrow chasm walked along its bottom, which was but a couple of feet wide, while the sides rose up from it at an acute angle. After following this for a few hundred yards, we turned a sharp corner, and shortly afterward our eyes were caught by some grains of fresh earth lying on the snow in front of our feet. On the sides, some feet above our heads, were marks in the snow which a moment's glance showed us had been made by a couple of mountain sheep that had come down one side of the gorge and had leaped across to the other, their sharp toes going through the thin snow and displacing the earth that had fallen to the bottom. The tracks had evidently been made just before we rounded the corner, and as we had been advancing noiselessly on the snow with the wind in our favor, we knew that the animals could have no suspicion of our presence. They had gone up the cliff on our right, but as that on our left was much lower, and running for some distance parallel to the other, we concluded that by running along its top we would be most certain to get a good shot. Clambering instantly up the steep side, digging my hands and feet into the loose snow, and grasping at every little rock or frozen projection, I reached the top; and then ran forward along the ridge a few paces, crouching behind the masses of queerly-shaped sandstone; and saw, about ninety yards off across the ravine, a couple of mountain rams. The one with the largest horns was broadside toward me, his sturdy, massive form outlined clearly against the sky, as he stood on the crest of the ridge. I dropped on my knee, raising the rifle as I did so; for a second he did not quite make me out, turning his head half round to look. I held the sight fairly on the point just behind his shoulder and pulled the trigger. At the report he staggered and pitched forward, but recovered himself and crossed over the ridge out of sight. We jumped and slid down into the ravine again, and clambered up the opposite side as fast as our lungs and the slippery ice would let us; then taking the trail of the wounded ram we trotted along it. We had not far to go; for, as I expected, we found him lying on his side a couple of hundred yards beyond the ridge, his eyes already glazed in death. The bullet had gone in behind the shoulder and ranged clean through his body crosswise, going a little forward; no animal less tough than a mountain ram could have gone any distance at all with such a wound. He had most obligingly run round to a part of the hill where we could bring up one of the horses without very much difficulty. Accordingly I brought up old Manitou, who can carry any thing and has no fear, and the bighorn was soon strapped across his back. It was a fine ram, with perfectly-shaped but not very large horns.

The other ram, two years old, with small horns, had bounded over the ridge before I could get a shot at him; we followed his trail for half a mile, but as he showed no signs of halting, and we were anxious to get home, we then gave up the pursuit.

It was still early in the day, and we made up our minds to push back for the home ranch, as we did not wish to be caught out in a long storm. The lowering sky was already overcast by a mass of leaden-gray clouds; and it was evident that we had no time to lose. In a little over an hour we were back at the log camp, where the ram was shifted from Manitou's back to the buck-board. A very few minutes sufficed to pack up our bedding and provisions, and we started home. Merrifield and I rode on ahead, not sparing the horses; but before we got home the storm had burst, and a furious blizzard blew in our teeth as we galloped along the last mile of the river bottom, before coming to the home ranch house; and as we warmed our stiffened limbs before the log fire, I congratulated myself upon the successful outcome of what I knew would be the last hunting trip I should take during that season.

The death of this ram was accomplished without calling for any very good shooting on our part. He was standing still, less than a hundred yards off, when the shot was fired; and we came across him so close merely by accident. Still, we fairly deserved our luck, for we had hunted with the most patient and painstaking care from dawn till nightfall for the better part of three days, spending most of the time in climbing at a smart rate of speed up sheer cliffs and over rough and slippery ground. Still-hunting the big-horn is always a toilsome and laborious task, and the very bitter weather during which we had been out had not lessened the difficulty of the work, though in the cold it was much less exhausting than it would have been to have hunted across the same ground in summer. No other kind of hunting does as much to bring out the good qualities, both moral and physical, of the sportsmen who follow it. If a man keeps at it, it is bound to make him both hardy and resolute; to strengthen his muscles and fill out his lungs.

Mountain mutton is in the fall the most delicious eating furnished by any game animal. Nothing else compares with it for juiciness, tenderness, and flavor; but at all other times of the year it is tough, stringy, and worthless.

CHAPTER VIII

The Lordly Buffalo

Gone forever are the mighty herds of the lordly buffalo. A few solitary individuals and small bands are still to be found scattered here and there in the wilder parts of the plains; and though most of these will be very soon destroyed, others will for some years fight off their doom and lead a precarious existence either in remote and almost desert portions of the country near the Mexican frontier, or else in the wildest and most inaccessible fastnesses of the Rocky Mountains; but the great herds, that for the first three quarters of this century formed the distinguishing and characteristic feature of the Western plains, have vanished forever.

It is only about a hundred years ago that the white man, in his march westward, first encroached upon the lands of the buffalo, for these animals had never penetrated in any number to the Appalachian chain of mountains. Indeed, it was after the beginning of the century before the inroads of the whites upon them grew at all serious. Then, though constantly driven westward, the diminution in their territory, if sure, was at least slow, although growing progressively more rapid. Less than a score of years ago the great herds, containing many millions of individuals, ranged over a vast expanse of country that stretched in an unbroken line from near Mexico to far into British America; in fact, over almost all the plains that are now known as the cattle region. But since that time their destruction has gone on with appalling rapidity and thoroughness; and the main factors in bringing it about have been the railroads, which carried hordes of hunters into the land and gave them means to transport their spoils to market. Not quite twenty years since, the range was broken in two, and the buffalo herds in the middle slaughtered or thrust aside; and thus there resulted two ranges, the northern and the southern. The latter was the larger, but being more open to the hunters, was the sooner to be depopulated; and the last of the great southern herds was destroyed in 1878, though scattered bands escaped and wandered into the desolate wastes to the southwest. Meanwhile equally savage war was waged on the northern herds, and five years later the last of these was also destroyed or broken up. The bulk of this slaughter was done in the dozen years from 1872 to 1883; never before in all history were so many large wild animals of one species slain in so short a space of time.

The extermination of the buffalo has been a veritable tragedy of the animal world. Other races of animals have been destroyed within historic times, but these have been species of small size, local distribution, and limited numbers, usually found in some particular island or group of islands; while the huge buffalo, in countless myriads, ranged over the greater part of a continent. Its nearest relative, the Old World aurochs, formerly found all through the forests of Europe, is almost as near the verge of extinction, but with the latter the process has been slow, and has extended over a period of a thousand years, instead of being compressed into a dozen. The destruction of the various larger species of South African game is much more local, and is proceeding at a much slower rate. It may truthfully be said that the sudden and complete extermination of the vast herds of the buffalo is without a parallel in historic times.

No sight is more common on the plains than that of a bleached buffalo skull; and their countless numbers attest the abundance of the animal at a time not so very long past. On those portions where the herds made their last stand, the carcasses, dried in the clear, high air, or the mouldering skeletons, abound. Last year, in crossing the country around the heads of the Big Sandy, O'Fallon Creek, Little Beaver, and Box Alder, these skeletons or dried carcasses were in sight from every hillock, often lying over the ground so thickly that several score could be seen at once. A ranchman who at the same time had made a journey of a thousand miles across Northern Montana, along the Milk River, told me that, to use his own expression, during the whole distance he was never out of sight of a dead buffalo, and never in sight of a live one.

Thus, though gone, the traces of the buffalo are still thick over the land. Their dried dung is found everywhere, and is in many places the only fuel afforded by the plains; their skulls, which last longer than any other part of the animal, are among the most familiar of objects to the plainsman; their bones are in many districts so plentiful that it has become a regular industry, followed by hundreds of men (christened "bone hunters" by the frontiersmen), to go out with wagons and collect them in great numbers for the sake of the phosphates they yield; and Bad Lands, plateaus, and prairies alike, are cut up in all directions by the deep ruts which were formerly buffalo trails.

These buffalo trails were made by the herds travelling strung out in single file, and invariably taking the same route each time they passed over the same piece of ground. As a consequence, many of the ruts are worn so deeply into the ground that a horseman riding along one strikes his stirrups on the earth. In moving through very broken country they are often good guides; for though buffalo can go easily over the roughest places, they prefer to travel where it is smooth, and have a remarkable knack at finding out the best passage down a steep ravine, over a broken cliff, or along a divide. In a pass, or, as it is called in the West, "draw," between two feeding grounds, through which the buffalo were fond of going, fifteen or twenty deep trails may be seen; and often, where the great beasts have travelled in parallel files, two ruts will run side by side over the prairie for a mile's length. These old trails are frequently used by the cattle herds at the present time, or are even turned into pony paths by the ranchmen. For many long years after the buffalo die out from a place, their white skulls and well-worn roads remain as melancholy monuments of their former existence.

The rapid and complete extermination of the buffalo affords an excellent instance of how a race, that has thriven and multiplied for ages under conditions of life to which it has slowly fitted itself by a process of natural selection continued for countless generations, may succumb at once when these surrounding conditions are varied by the introduction of one or more new elements, immediately becoming the chief forces with which it has to contend in the struggle for life. The most striking characteristics of the buffalo, and those which had been found most useful in maintaining the species until the white man entered upon the scene, were its phenomenal gregariousness—surpassed by no other four-footed beast, and only equalled, if equalled at all, by one or two kinds of South African antelope,—its massive bulk, and unwieldy strength. The fact that it was a plains and not a forest or mountain animal was at that time also greatly in its favor. Its toughness and hardy endurance fitted it to contend with purely natural forces: to resist cold and the winter blasts, or the heat of a thirsty summer, to wander away to new pastures when the feed on the old was exhausted, to plunge over broken ground, and to plough its way through snow-drifts or quagmires. But one beast of prey existed sufficiently powerful to conquer it when full grown and in health; and this, the grizzly bear, could only be considered an occasional foe. The Indians were its most dangerous enemies, but they were without horses, and their weapons, bows and arrows, were only available at close range; so that a slight degree of speed enabled buffalo to get out of the way of their human foes when discovered, and on the open plains a moderate development of the senses was sufficient to warn them of the approach of the latter before they had come up to the very close distance required for their primitive weapons to take effect. Thus the strength, size, and gregarious habits of the brute were sufficient for a protection against most foes; and a slight degree of speed and moderate development of the senses served as adequate guards against the grizzlies and bow-bearing foot Indians. Concealment and the habit of seeking lonely and remote places for a dwelling would have been of no service.

But the introduction of the horse, and shortly afterwards the incoming of white hunters carrying long-range rifles, changed all this. The buffaloes' gregarious habits simply rendered them certain to be seen, and made it a matter of perfect ease to follow them up; their keeping to the open plains heightened their conspicuousness, while their senses were too dull to discover their foes at such a distance as to nullify the effects of the long rifles; their speed was not such as to enable them to flee from a horseman; and their size and strength merely made them too clumsy either to escape from or to contend with their foes. Add to this the fact that their hides and flesh were valuable, and it is small wonder that under the new order of things they should have vanished with such rapidity.

The incoming of the cattle-men was another cause of the completeness of their destruction. Wherever there is good feed for a buffalo, there is good feed for a steer or cow; and so the latter have penetrated into all the pastures of the former; and of course the cowboys follow. A cowboy is not able to kill a deer or antelope unless in exceptional cases, for they are too fleet, too shy, or keep themselves too well hidden. But a buffalo neither tries nor is able to do much in the way of hiding itself; its senses are too dull to give it warning in time; and it is not so swift as a horse, so that a cowboy, riding round in the places where cattle, and therefore buffalo, are likely to be, is pretty sure to see any of the latter that may be about, and then can easily approach near enough to be able to overtake them when they begin running. The size and value of the animal makes the chase after it very keen. Hunters will follow the trail of a band for days, when they would not follow that of deer or antelope for a half hour.

Events have developed a race of this species, known either as the wood or mountain buffalo, which is acquiring, and has already largely acquired, habits widely different from those of the others of its kind. It is found in the wooded and most precipitous portions of the mountains, instead of on the level and open plains; it goes singly or in small parties, instead of in huge herds; and it is more agile and infinitely more wary than is its prairie cousin. The formation of this race is due solely to the extremely severe process of natural selection that has been going on among the buffalo herds for the last sixty or seventy years; the vast majority of the individuals were utterly unable to accommodate themselves to the sudden and complete change in the surrounding forces with which they had to cope, and therefore died out; while a very few of the more active and wary, and of those most given to wandering off into mountainous and out-of-the-way places, in each generation survived, and among these the wariness continually increased, partly by personal experience, and still more by inheriting an increasingly suspicious nature from their ancestors. The sense of smell always was excellent in the buffalo; the sense of hearing becomes much quicker in any woods animal than it is in one found on the plains; while in beasts of the forest the eyesight does not have to be as keen as is necessary for their protection in open country. On the mountains the hair grows longer and denser, and the form rather more thickset. As a result, a new race has been built up; and we have an animal far better fitted to "harmonize with the environment," to use the scientific cant of the day. Unfortunately this race has developed too late. With the settlement of the country it will also disappear, unless very stringent laws are made for its protection; but at least its existence will for some years prevent the total extermination of the species as a whole. It must be kept in mind that even this shyer kind of buffalo has not got the keen senses of other large game, such as moose; and it is more easily followed and much more keenly and eagerly sought after than would be any other animal smaller and less valuable to the hunter than itself.

While the slaughter of the buffalo has been in places needless and brutal, and while it is to be greatly regretted that the species is likely to become extinct, and while, moreover, from a purely selfish standpoint many, including myself, would rather see it continue to exist as the chief feature in the unchanged life of the Western wilderness; yet, on the other hand, it must be remembered that its continued existence in any numbers was absolutely incompatible with any thing but a very sparse settlement of the country; and that its destruction was the condition precedent upon the advance of white civilization in the West, and was a positive boon to the more thrifty and industrious frontiersmen. Where the buffalo were plenty, they ate up all the grass that could have supported cattle. The country over which the huge herds grazed during the last year or two of their existence was cropped bare, and the grass did not grow to its normal height and become able to support cattle for, in some cases two, in others three, seasons. Every buffalo needed as much food as an ox or cow; and if the former abounded, the latter perforce would have to be scarce. Above all, the extermination of the buffalo was the only way of solving the Indian question. As long as this large animal of the chase existed, the Indians simply could not be kept on reservations, and always had an ample supply of meat on hand to support them in the event of a war; and its disappearance was the only method of forcing them to at least partially abandon their savage mode of life. From the standpoint of humanity at large, the extermination of the buffalo has been a blessing. The many have been benefited by it; and I suppose the comparatively few of us who would have preferred the continuance of the old order of things, merely for the sake of our own selfish enjoyment, have no right to complain.

The buffalo is easier killed than is any other kind of plains game; but its chase is very far from being the tame amusement it has been lately represented. It is genuine sport; it needs skill, marksmanship, and hardihood in the man who follows it, and if he hunts on horseback, it needs also pluck and good riding. It is in no way akin to various forms of so-called sport in vogue in parts of the East, such as killing deer in a lake or by fire hunting, or even by watching at a runaway. No man who is not of an adventurous temper, and able to stand rough food and living, will penetrate to the haunts of the buffalo. The animal is so tough and tenacious of life that it must be hit in the right spot; and care must be used in approaching it, for its nose is very keen, and though its sight is dull, yet, on the other hand, the plains it frequents are singularly bare of cover; while, finally, there is just a faint spice of danger in the pursuit, for the bison, though the least dangerous of all bovine animals, will, on occasions, turn upon the hunter, and though its attack is, as a rule, easily avoided, yet in rare cases it manages to charge home. A ranchman of my acquaintance once, many years ago, went out buffalo hunting on horseback, together with a friend who was unused to the sport, and who was mounted on a large, untrained, nervous horse. While chasing a bull, the friend's horse became unmanageable, and when the bull turned, proved too clumsy to get out of the way, and was caught on the horns, one of which entered its flank, while the other inflicted a huge, bruised gash across the man's thigh, tearing the muscles all out. Both horse and rider were flung to the ground with tremendous violence. The horse had to be killed, and the man died in a few hours from the shock, loss of blood, and internal injuries. Such an accident, however, is very exceptional.

My brother was in at the death of the great southern herds in 1877, and had a good deal of experience in buffalo hunting; and once or twice was charged by old bulls, but never had any difficulty in either evading the charge or else killing the brute as it came on. My cousin, John Roosevelt, also had one adventure with a buffalo, in which he received rather a fright. He had been out on foot with a dog and had severely wounded a buffalo bull, which nevertheless, with the wonderful tenacity of life and ability to go over apparently inaccessible places that this species shows, managed to clamber up a steep, almost perpendicular, cliff. My cousin climbed up after it, with some difficulty; on reaching the top he got his elbows over and drew himself up on them only to find the buffalo fronting him with lowered head not a dozen feet off. Immediately upon seeing him it cocked up its tail and came forward. He was clinging with both hands to the edge and could not use his rifle; so, not relishing what was literally a tête-à-tête, he promptly let go and slid or rather rolled head over heels to the foot of the cliff, not hurting himself much in the sand, though of course a good deal jarred by the fall. The buffalo came on till its hoofs crumbled the earth at the brink, when the dog luckily got up and distracted its attention; meanwhile, my cousin, having bounced down to the bottom, picked himself up, shook himself, and finding that nothing was broken, promptly scrambled up the bluff at another place a few yards off and shot his antagonist.

When my cattle first came on the Little Missouri three of my men took a small bunch of them some fifty miles to the south and there wintered with them, on what were then the outskirts of the buffalo range, the herds having been pressed up northwards. In the intervals of tending the cattle—work which was then entirely new to them—they occupied themselves in hunting buffalo, killing during the winter sixty or seventy, some of them on horseback, but mostly by still-hunting them on foot. Once or twice the bulls when wounded turned to bay; and a couple of them on one occasion charged one of the men and forced him to take refuge upon a steep isolated butte. At another time the three of them wounded a cow so badly that she broke down and would run no farther, turning to bay in a small clump of thick trees. As this would have been a very bad place in which to skin the body, they wished to get her out and tried to tease her into charging;

but she seemed too weak to make the effort. Emboldened by her apathy one of the men came up close to her behind, while another was standing facing her; and the former finally entered the grove of trees and poked her with a long stick. This waked her up most effectually, and instead of turning on her assailant she went headlong at the man in front. He leaped to one side just in time, one of her horns grazing him, ripping away his clothes and knocking him over; as he lay she tried to jump on him with her forefeet, but he rolled to one side, and as she went past she kicked at him like a vicious mule. The effort exhausted her, however, and she fell before going a dozen yards farther. The man who was charged had rather a close shave; thanks to the rashness and contempt of the game's prowess which they all felt—for all three are very quiet men and not afraid of any thing. It is always a good rule to be cautious in dealing with an apparently dead or dying buffalo. About the time the above incident occurred a party of hunters near my ranch killed a buffalo, as they thought, and tied a pony to its foreleg, to turn it over, as its position was a very bad one for skinning. Barely had the pony been tied when the buffalo came to with a jump, killed the unfortunate pony, and needed a dozen more balls before he fell for good.

At that time the buffalo would occasionally be scattered among the cattle, but, as a rule, avoided the latter and seemed to be afraid of them; while the cattle, on the contrary, had no apparent dread of the buffalo, unless it happened that on some occasion they got caught by a herd of the latter that had stampeded. A settler or small ranchman, not far from my place, was driving in a team of oxen in a wagon one day three years since, when, in crossing a valley, he encountered a little herd of stampeded buffalo, who, in their blind and heedless terror, ran into him and knocked over the wagon and oxen. The oxen never got over the fright the rough handling caused them, and ever afterward became unmanageable and tore off at sight or smell of a buffalo. It is said that the few buffalo left in the country through which the head waters of the Belle Fourche flow, have practically joined themselves to the great herds of cattle now found all over that region.

Buffalo are very easily tamed. On a neighboring ranch there are four which were taken when very young calves. They wander about with the cattle, and are quite as familiar as any of them, and do not stray any farther away. One of them was captured when a yearling, by the help of a large yellow hound. The cowboy had been chasing it some time and, finally, fearing it might escape, hied on the hound, which dashed in, caught the buffalo by the ear, and finally brought it down to its knees, when the cowboy, by means of his lariat secured it, and, with the help of a companion, managed to get it back to the ranch. Buffalo can be trained to draw a wagon, and are valuable for their great strength; but they are very headstrong and stupid. If thirsty, for instance, and they smell or see water, it is absolutely impossible to prevent their going to it, no matter if it is in such a place that they have to upset the wagon to get down to it, nor how deep the mud is. When tamed they do not seem to be as ferocious as ordinary cattle that are allowed to go free; but they are such strong, blundering brutes that very few fences will hold them.

My men, in hunting buffalo, which was with them an

occasional occupation and not a regular pursuit, used light Winchesters; but the professional buffalo hunters carried either 40–90 or 45–120 Sharps, than which there are in the world no rifles more accurate or powerful; with the larger calibred ones (45 or 50) a man could easily kill an elephant. These weapons are excellent for very long range work, being good for half a mile and over; and sometimes the hunters were able to kill very many buffalo at a time, owing to their curious liability to fits of stupid, panic terror. Sometimes when these panics seize them they stampede and run off in headlong, heedless flight, going over any thing in their way. Once, in mid-winter, one of my men was lying out in the open, under a heavy roll of furs, the wagon sheet over all. During the night a small herd of stampeded buffalo passed by, and one of them jumped on the bed, almost trampling on the sleeper, and then bounded off, as the latter rose with a yell. The others of the herd passed almost within arm's length on each side.

Occasionally these panic fits have the opposite effect and make them run together and stand still in a stupid, frightened manner. This is now and then the result when a hunter fires at a herd while keeping himself concealed; and on rare occasions (for buffalo act very differently at different times, according to their moods) it occurs even when he is in full sight. When they are made to act thus it is called in hunters' parlance getting a "stand" on them; and often thirty or forty have been killed in one such stand, the hunter hardly shifting his position the whole time. Often, with their long-range heavy rifles, the hunters would fire a number of shots into a herd half a mile off, and on approaching would find that they had bagged several—for the Sharps rifle has a very long range, and the narrow, heavy conical bullets will penetrate almost any thing. Once while coming in over the plains with an ox wagon two of my cowboys surprised a band of buffaloes, which on being fired at ran clear round them and then made a stand in nearly their former position; and there they stood until the men had fired away most of their ammunition, but only half a dozen or so were killed, the Winchesters being too light for such a distance. Hunting on foot is much the most destructive way of pursuing buffaloes; but it lacks the excitement of chasing them with horses.

When in Texas my brother had several chances to hunt them on horseback, while making a trip as guest of a captain of United States cavalry. The country through which they hunted was rolling and well watered, the buffalo being scattered over it in bands of no great size. While riding out to look for the game they were mounted on large horses; when a band was spied they would dismount and get on the smaller buffalo ponies which the orderlies had been leading behind them. Then they would carefully approach from the leeward side, if possible keeping behind some hill or divide. When this was no longer possible they trotted gently towards the game, which usually gathered together and stood for a moment looking at them. The instant the buffalo turned, the spurs were put in and the ponies raced forward for all there was in them, it being an important point to close as soon as possible, as buffalo, though not swift, are very enduring. Usually a half a mile took the hunters up to the game, when each singled out his animal, rode alongside on its left flank, so close as almost to be able to touch it with the hand, and fired the heavy revolver into the loins or small of the back, the bullet ranging forward. At the instant of firing, the trained pony swerved off to the left, almost at right angles to its former course, so as to avoid the lunging charge sometimes made by the wounded brute. If the animal kept on, the hunter, having made a half circle, again closed up and repeated the shot; very soon the buffalo came to a halt, then its head dropped, it straddled widely with its forelegs, swayed to and fro, and pitched heavily forward on its side. The secret of success in this sort of hunting is to go right up by the side of the buffalo; if a man stays off at a distance of fifteen or twenty feet he may fire a score of shots and not kill or cripple his game.

While hunting this, the largest of American animals, on horseback is doubtless the most exciting way in which its chase can be carried on, we must beware of crying down its pursuit on foot. To be sure, in the latter case, the actual stalking and shooting the buffalo does not need on the part of the hunter as much skill and as good marksmanship as is the case in hunting most other kinds of large game, and is but a trifle more risky; yet, on the other hand, the fatigue of following the game is much greater, and the country is usually so wild as to call for some hardihood and ability to stand rough work on the part of the man who penetrates it.

One September I determined to take a short trip after bison. At that time I was staying in a cow-camp a good many miles up the river from my ranch; there were then no cattle south of me, where there are now very many thousand head, and the buffalo had been plentiful in the country for a couple of winters past, but the last of the herds had been destroyed or driven out six months before, and there were only a few stragglers left. It was one of my first hunting trips; previously I had shot with the rifle very little, and that only at deer or antelope. I took as a companion one of my best men, named Ferris (a brother of the Ferris already mentioned); we rode a couple of ponies, not very good ones, and each carried his roll of blankets and a very small store of food in a pack behind the saddle.

Leaving the cow-camp early in the morning, we crossed the Little Missouri and for the first ten miles threaded our way through the narrow defiles and along the tortuous divides of a great tract of Bad Lands. Although it was fall and the nights were cool the sun was very hot in the middle of the day, and we jogged along at a slow pace, so as not to tire our ponies. Two or three black-tail deer were seen, some distance off, and when we were a couple of hours on our journey, we came across the fresh track of a bull buffalo. Buffalo wander a great distance, for, though they do not go fast, yet they may keep travelling, as they graze, all day long; and though this one had evidently passed but a few hours before, we were not sure we would see him. His tracks were easily followed as long as he had kept to the soft creek bottom, crossing and recrossing the narrow wet ditch which wound its way through it; but when he left this and turned up a winding coulie that branched out in every direction, his hoofs scarcely made any marks in the hard ground. We rode up the ravine, carefully examining the soil for nearly half an hour, however; finally, as we passed the mouth of a little side coulie, there was a plunge and crackle through the bushes at its head, and a shabby-looking old bull bison galloped out of it and, without an instant's hesitation, plunged over a steep bank into a patch of rotten, broken ground which led around the base of a high butte. So quickly did he disappear that we had not time to dismount and fire. Spurring our horses we galloped up to the brink of the cliff down which he had plunged; it was remarkable that he should have gone down it unhurt. From where we stood we could see nothing; so, getting our horses over the broken ground as fast as possible, we ran to the butte and rode round it, only to see the buffalo come out of the broken land and climb up the side of another butte over a quarter of a mile off. In spite of his great weight and cumbersome, heavy-looking gait, he climbed up the steep bluff with ease and even agility, and when he had reached the ridge stood and looked back at us for a moment; while so doing he held his head high up, and at that distance his great shaggy mane and huge fore-quarter made him look like a lion. In another second he again turned away and made off; and, being evidently very shy and accustomed to being harassed by hunters, must have travelled a long distance before stopping, for we followed his trail for some miles until it got on such hard, dry ground that his hoofs did not leave a scrape in the soil, and yet did not again catch so much as a glimpse of him.

Soon after leaving his trail we came out on the great, broken prairies that lie far back from the river. These are by no means everywhere level. A flat space of a mile or two will be bounded by a low cliff or a row of small round-topped buttes; or will be interrupted by a long, gently sloping ridge, the divide between two creeks; or by a nar-

row canyon, perhaps thirty feet deep and not a dozen
wide, stretching for miles before there is a crossing place.
The smaller creeks were dried up, and were merely sinu-
ous hollows in the prairie; but one or two of the larger
ones held water here and there, and cut down through the
land in bold, semicircular sweeps, the outside of each
curve being often bounded by a steep bluff with trees at its
bottom, and occasionally holding a miry pool. At one of
these pools we halted, about ten o'clock in the morning,
and lunched; the banks were so steep and rotten that we
had to bring water to the more clumsy of the two ponies
in a hat.

Then we remounted and fared on our way, scanning
the country far and near from every divide, but seeing no
trace of game. The air was hot and still, and the brown,
barren land stretched out on every side for leagues of
dreary sameness. Once we came to a canyon which ran
across our path, and followed along its brink for a mile to
find a place where we could get into it; when we finally
found such a place, we had to back the horses down to the
bottom and then lead them along it for some hundred
yards before finding a break through which we could
climb out.

It was late in the afternoon before we saw any game;
then we made out in the middle of a large plain three
black specks, which proved to be buffalo—old bulls. Our
horses had come a good distance, under a hot sun, and as
they had had no water except from the mud-hole in the
morning they were in no condition for running. They
were not very fast anyhow; so, though the ground was unfavorable, we made up our minds to try to creep up to the

buffalo. We left the ponies in a hollow half a mile from the game, and started off on our hands and knees, taking advantage of every sage-brush as cover. After a while we had to lie flat on our bodies and wriggle like snakes; and while doing this I blundered into a bed of cactus, and filled my hands with the spines. After taking advantage of every hollow, hillock, or sage-brush, we got within about a hundred and twenty-five or fifty yards of where the three bulls were unconsciously feeding, and as all between was bare ground I drew up and fired. It was the first time I ever shot at buffalo, and confused by the bulk and shaggy hair of the beast, I aimed too far back at one that was standing nearly broadside on towards me. The bullet told on his body with a loud crack, the dust flying up from his hide; but it did not work him any immediate harm, or in the least hinder him from making off; and away went all three, with their tails up, disappearing over a slight rise in the ground.

Much disgusted, we trotted back to where the horses were picketed, jumped on them, a good deal out of breath, and rode after the flying game. We thought that the wounded one might turn out and leave the others; and so followed them, though they had over a mile's start. For seven or eight miles we loped our jaded horses along at a brisk pace, occasionally seeing the buffalo far ahead; and finally, when the sun had just set, we saw that all three had come to a stand in a gentle hollow. There was no cover anywhere near them; and, as a last desperate resort, we concluded to try to run them on our worn-out ponies.

As we cantered toward them they faced us for a second and then turned round and made off, while with spurs and quirts we made the ponies put on a burst that enabled us to close in with the wounded one just about the time that the lessening twilight had almost vanished; while the rim of the full moon rose above the horizon. The pony I was on could barely hold its own, after getting up within sixty or seventy yards of the wounded bull; my companion, better mounted, forged ahead, a little to one side. The bull saw him coming and swerved from his course, and by cutting across I was able to get nearly up to him. The ground over which we were running was fearful, being broken into holes and ditches, separated by hillocks; in the dull light, and at the speed we were going, no attempt could be made to guide the horses, and the latter, fagged out by their exertions, floundered and pitched forward at every stride, hardly keeping their legs. When up within twenty feet I fired my rifle, but the darkness, and especially the violent, labored motion of my pony, made me miss; I tried to get in closer, when suddenly up went the bull's tail, and wheeling, he charged me with lowered horns. My pony, frightened into momentary activity, spun round and tossed up his head; I was holding the rifle in both hands, and the pony's head, striking it, knocked it violently against my forehead, cutting quite a gash, from which, heated as I was, the blood poured into my eyes. Meanwhile the buffalo, passing me, charged my companion, and followed him as he made off, and, as the ground was very bad, for some little distance his lowered head was unpleasantly near the tired pony's tail. I tried to run in on him again, but my pony stopped short, dead beat; and by no spurring could I force him out of a slow trot. My companion jumped off and took a couple of shots at the buffalo, which missed in the dim moonlight; and to our unutterable chagrin the wounded bull labored off and vanished in the darkness. I made after him on foot, in hopeless and helpless wrath, until he got out of sight.

Our horses were completely done out; we did not mount them again, but led them slowly along, trembling, foaming, and sweating. The ground was moist in places, and after an hour's search we found in a reedy hollow a little mud-pool, with water so slimy that it was almost gelatinous. Thirsty though we were, for we had not drunk for twelve hours, neither man nor horse could swallow more than a mouthful or two of this water. We unsaddled the horses, and made our beds by the hollow, each eating a biscuit; there was not a twig from which to make a fire, nor any thing to which we might fasten the horses. Spreading the saddle-blankets under us, and our own over us, we lay down, with the saddles as pillows, to which we had been obliged to lariat our steeds.

The ponies stood about almost too tired to eat; but in spite of their fatigue they were very watchful and restless, continually snorting or standing with their ears forward, peering out into the night; wild beasts, or some such things, were about. The day before we had had a false alarm from supposed hostile Indians, who turned out to be merely half-breed Crees; and, as we were in a perfectly lonely part of the wilderness, we knew we were in the domain of both white and red horse-thieves, and that the latter might in addition to our horses try to take our scalps. It was some time before we dozed off; waking up with a start whenever we heard the horses stop grazing and stand motionless with heads raised, looking out into the darkness. But at last, tired out, we fell sound asleep.

About midnight we were rudely awakened by having our pillows whipped out from under our heads; and as we started from the bed we saw, in the bright moonlight, the horses galloping madly off with the saddles, tied to the lariats whose other ends were round their necks, bounding and trailing after them. Our first thought was that they had been stampeded by horse-thieves, and we rolled over and crouched down in the grass with our rifles; but nothing could be seen, except a shadowy four-footed form in the hollow, and in the end we found that the horses must have taken alarm at a wolf or wolves that had come up to the edge of the bank and looked over at us, not being able at first to make out what we were.

We did not expect to find the horses again that night, but nevertheless took up the broad trail made by the saddles as they dragged through the dewy grass, and followed it well in the moonlight. Our task proved easier than we had feared; for they had not run much over half a mile, and we found them standing close together and looking intently round when we came up. Leading them back we again went to sleep; but the weather was rapidly changing, and by three o'clock a fine rain began to come steadily down, and we cowered and shivered under our wet blankets till morning. At the first streak of dawn, having again eaten a couple of biscuits, we were off, glad to bid goodbye to the inhospitable pool, in whose neighborhood we had spent such a comfortless night. A fine, drizzling mist shrouded us and hid from sight all distant objects; and at times there were heavy downpours of rain. Before we had gone any distance we became what is termed by backwoodsmen or plainsmen, "turned round," and the creeks suddenly seemed to be running the wrong way; after which we travelled purely by the compass.

For some hours we kept a nearly straight course over the formless, shapeless plain, drenched through, and thoroughly uncomfortable; then as we rose over a low divide the fog lifted for a few minutes, and we saw several black objects slowly crossing some rolling country ahead of us, and a glance satisfied us they were buffalo. The horses were picketed at once, and we ran up as near the game as we dared, and then began to stalk them, creeping forward on our hands and knees through the soft, muddy prairie soil, while a smart shower of rain blew in our faces, as we advanced up wind. The country was favorable, and we got within less than a hundred yards of the nearest, a large cow, though we had to creep along so slowly that we were chilled through, and our teeth chattered behind our blue lips. To crown my misfortunes, I now made one of those misses which a man to his dying day always looks back upon with wonder and regret. The rain was beating in my eyes, and the drops stood out in the sights of the rifle so that I could hardly draw a bead; and I either overshot or else at the last moment must have given a nervous jerk and pulled the rifle clear off the mark. At any rate I missed clean, and the whole band plunged down into a hollow and were off before, with my stiffened and numbed fingers, I could get another shot; and in wet, sullen misery we plodded back to the ponies.

All that day the rain continued, and we passed another wretched night. Next morning, however, it had cleared off, and as the sun rose brightly we forgot our hunger and sleepiness, and rode cheerily off up a large dry creek, in whose bottom pools of rain-water still stood. During the morning, however, our ill-luck continued. My companion's horse almost trod on a rattlesnake, and narrowly escaped being bitten. While riding along the face of a steeply-inclined bluff the sandy soil broke away under the ponies' hoofs, and we slid and rolled down to the bottom, where we came to in a heap, horses and men. Then while galloping through a brush-covered bottom my pony put both forefeet in a hole made by the falling and uprooting of a tree, and turned a complete somersault, pitching me a good ten feet beyond his head. And finally, while crossing what looked like the hard bed of a dry creek, the earth gave way under my horse as if he had stepped on a trap-door, and let him down to his withers in soft, sticky mud. I was off at once and floundered to the bank, loosening the lariat from the saddle-bow; and both of us turning to with a will, and bringing the other pony in to our aid, hauled him out by the rope, pretty nearly strangling him in so doing; and he looked rather a melancholy object as he stood up, trembling and shaking, and plastered with mire from head to tail.

So far the trip had certainly not been a success, although sufficiently varied as regards its incidents; we had been confined to moist biscuits for three days as our food; had been wet and cold at night, and sunburned till our faces peeled in the day; were hungry and tired, and had met with bad weather, and all kinds of accidents; in addition to which I had shot badly. But a man who is fond of sport, and yet is not naturally a good hunter, soon learns that if he wishes any success at all he must both keep in memory and put in practice Anthony Trollope's famous precept: "It's dogged as does it." And if he keeps doggedly on in his course the odds are heavy that in the end the longest lane will prove to have a turning. Such was the case on this occasion.

Shortly after mid-day we left the creek bottom, and skirted a ridge of broken buttes, cut up by gullies and winding ravines, in whose bottoms grew bunch grass. While passing near the mouth, and to leeward of one of these ravines, both ponies threw up their heads, and snuffed the air, turning their muzzles towards the head of the gully. Feeling sure that they had smelt some wild beast, either a bear or a buffalo, I slipped off my pony, and ran quickly but cautiously up along the valley. Before I had gone a hundred yards, I noticed in the soft soil at the bottom the round prints of a bison's hoofs; and immediately afterwards got a glimpse of the animal himself, as he fed slowly up the course of the ravine, some distance ahead of me. The wind was just right, and no ground could have been better for stalking. Hardly needing to bend down, I walked up behind a small sharp-crested hillock, and peeping over, there below me, not fifty yards off, was a great bison bull. He was walking along, grazing as he walked. His glossy fall coat was in fine trim, and shone in the rays of the sun; while his pride of bearing showed him to be in the lusty vigor of his prime. As I rose above the crest of the hill, he held up his head and cocked his tail in the air. Before he could go off, I put the bullet in behind his shoulder. The wound was an almost immediately fatal one, yet with surprising agility for so large and heavy an animal, he bounded up the opposite side of the ravine, heedless of two more balls, both of which went into his flank and ranged forwards, and disappeared over the ridge at a lumbering gallop, the blood pouring from his mouth and nostrils. We knew he could not go far, and trotted leisurely along on his bloody trail; and in the next gully we found him stark dead, lying almost on his back, having pitched over the side when he tried to go down it. His head was a remarkably fine one, even for a fall buffalo. He was lying in a very bad position, and it was most tedious and tiresome work to cut it off and pack it out. The flesh of a cow or calf is better eating than is that of a bull; but the so-called hump meat—that is, the strip of steak on each side of the backbone—is excellent, and tender and juicy. Buffalo meat is with difficulty to be distinguished from ordinary beef. At any rate, the flesh of this bull tasted uncommonly good to us, for we had been without fresh meat for a week; and until a healthy, active man has been without it for some little time, he does not know how positively and almost painfully hungry for flesh he becomes, no matter how much farinaceous food he may have. And the very toil I had been obliged to go through, in order to procure the head, made me feel all the prouder of it when it was at last in my possession.

A year later I made another trip, this time with a wagon, through what had once been a famous buffalo range, the divide between the Little Missouri and the Powder, at its northern end, where some of the creeks flowing into the Yellowstone also head up; but though in most places throughout the range the grass had not yet grown from the time a few months before when it had been cropped off down close to the roots by the grazing herds, and though the ground was cut up in all directions by buffalo trails, and covered by their innumerable skulls and skeletons, not a living one did we see, and only one moderately fresh track, which we followed until we lost it. Some of the sharper ridges were of soft, crumbling sandstone, and when a buffalo trail crossed such a one, it generally made a curious, heart-shaped cut, the feet of the animals sinking the narrow path continually deeper and deeper, while their bodies brushed out the sides. The profile of a ridge across which several trails led had rather a curious look when seen against the sky.

Game was scarce on this broken plains country, where the water supply was very scanty, and where the dull brown grass that grew on the parched, sun-cracked ground had been already cropped close; still we found enough to keep us in fresh meat; and though no buffalo were seen, the trip was a pleasant one. There was a certain charm in the very vastness and the lonely, melancholy desolation of the land over which every day we galloped far and wide from dawn till nightfall; while the heavy canvas-covered wagon lumbered slowly along to the appointed halting-place. On such a trip one soon gets to feel that the wagon is home; and after a tiresome day it is pleasant just to lie still in the twilight by the side of the smouldering fire and watch the men as they busy themselves cooking or arranging the beds, while the solemn old ponies graze around or stand quietly by the great white-topped prairie schooner.

The blankets and rubbers being arranged in a carefully chosen spot to leeward of the wagon, we were not often bothered at night, even by quite heavy rainfalls; but once or twice, when in peculiarly exposed places, we were struck by such furious gusts of wind and rain that we were forced to gather up our bedding and hastily scramble into the wagon, where we would at least be dry, even though in pretty cramped quarters.

CHAPTER IX

Still-Hunting Elk on the Mountains

After the buffalo the elk are the first animals to disappear from a country when it is settled. This arises from their size and consequent conspicuousness, and the eagerness with which they are followed by hunters; and also because of their gregariousness and their occasional fits of stupid panic during whose continuance hunters can now and then work great slaughter in a herd. Five years ago elk were abundant in the valley of the Little Missouri, and in fall were found wandering in great bands of over a hundred individuals each. But they have now vanished completely, except that one or two may still lurk in some of the most remote and broken places, where there are deep, wooded ravines.

Formerly the elk were plentiful all over the plains, coming down into them in great bands during the fall months and traversing their entire extent. But the incoming of hunters and cattle-men has driven them off the ground as completely as the buffalo; unlike the latter, however, they are still very common in the dense woods that cover the Rocky Mountains and the other great western chains. In the old days running elk on horseback was a highly esteemed form of plains sport; but now that it has become a beast of the timber and the craggy ground, instead of a beast of the open, level prairie, it is followed almost solely on foot and with the rifle. Its sense of smell is very acute, and it has good eyes and quick ears; and its wariness makes it under ordinary circumstances very difficult to approach. But it is subject to fits of panic folly, and during their continuance great numbers can be destroyed. A band places almost as much reliance upon the leaders as does a flock of sheep; and if the leaders are shot down, the others will huddle together in a terrified mass, seemingly unable to make up their minds in which direction to flee. When one, more bold than the rest, does at last step out, the hidden hunter's at once shooting it down will produce a fresh panic; I have known of twenty elk (or wapiti, as they are occasionally called) being thus procured out of one band. And at times they show a curious indifference to danger, running up on a hunter who is in plain sight, or standing still for a few fatal seconds to gaze at one that unexpectedly appears.

In spite of its size and strength and great branching antlers, the elk is but little more dangerous to the hunter than is an ordinary buck. Once, in coming up to a wounded one, I had it strike at me with its forefeet, bristling up the hair on the neck, and making a harsh, grating noise with its teeth; as its back was broken it could not get at me, but the savage glare in its eyes left me no doubt as to its intentions. Only in a single instance have I ever known of a hunter being regularly charged by one of these great deer. He had struck a band of elk and wounded an old bull, which, after going a couple of miles, received another ball and then separated from the rest of the herd and took refuge in a dense patch of small timber. The hunter went in on its trail and came upon it lying down; it jumped to its feet and, with hair all bristling, made a regular charge upon its pursuer, who leaped out of the way behind a tree just in time to avoid it. It crashed past through the undergrowth without turning, and he killed it with a third and last shot. But this was a very exceptional case, and in most instances the elk submits to death with hardly an effort at resistance; it is by no means as dangerous an antagonist as is a bull moose.

The elk is unfortunately one of those animals seemingly doomed to total destruction at no distant date. Already its range has shrunk to far less than one half its former size. Originally it was found as far as the Atlantic sea-board; I have myself known of several sets of antlers preserved in the house of a Long Island gentleman, whose ancestors had killed the bearers shortly after the first settlement of New York. Even so late as the first years of this century elk were found in many mountainous and densely wooded places east of the Mississippi, in New York, Pennsylvania, Virginia, Kentucky, Tennessee, and all of what were then the Northwestern States and Territories. The last individual of the race was killed in the Adirondacks in 1834; in Pennsylvania not till nearly thirty years later; while a very few are still to be found in Northern Michigan. Elsewhere they must now be sought far to the west of the Mississippi; and even there they are almost gone from the great plains, and are only numerous in the deep mountain forests. Wherever it exists the skin hunters and meat butchers wage the most relentless and unceasing war upon it for the sake of its hide and flesh, and their unremitting persecution is thinning out the herds with terrible rapidity.

The gradual extermination of this, the most stately and beautiful animal of the chase to be found in America, can be looked upon only with unmixed regret by every sportsman and lover of nature. Excepting the moose, it is the largest and, without exception, it is the noblest of the deer tribe. No other species of true deer, in either the Old or the New World, comes up to it in size and in the shape, length, and weight of its mighty antlers; while the grand, proud carriage and lordly bearing of an old bull make it perhaps the most majestic-looking of all the animal creation. The open plains have already lost one of their great attractions, now that we no more see the long lines of elk trotting across them; and it will be a sad day when the lordly, antlered beasts are no longer found in the wild rocky glens and among the lonely woods of towering pines that cover the great western mountain chains.

The elk has other foes besides man. The grizzly will always make a meal of one if he gets a chance; and against his ponderous weight and savage prowess hoofs and antlers avail but little. Still he is too clumsy and easily avoided ever to do very much damage in the herds. Cougars, where they exist, work more havoc. A bull elk in rutting season, if on his guard, would with ease beat off a cougar; but the sly, cunning cat takes its quarry unawares, and once the cruel fangs are fastened in the game's throat or neck, no plunging or struggling can shake it off. The gray timber wolves also join in twos and threes to hunt down and hamstring the elk, if other game is scarce. But these great deer can hold their own and make head against all their brute foes; it is only when pitted against Man the Destroyer, that they succumb in the struggle for life.

I have never shot any elk in the immediate neighborhood of where my cattle range; but I have had very good sport with them in a still wilder and more western region; and this I will now describe.

During last summer we found it necessary to leave my ranch on the Little Missouri and take quite a long trip through the cattle country of Southeastern Montana and Northern Wyoming; and, having come to the foot of the Bighorn Mountains, we took a fortnight's hunt through them after elk and bear.

We went into the mountains with a pack train, leaving the ranch wagon at the place where we began to go up the first steep rise. There were two others, besides myself, in the party; one of them, the teamster, a weather-beaten old plainsman, who possessed a most extraordinary stock of miscellaneous misinformation upon every conceivable subject, and the other my ranch foreman, Merrifield. None of us had ever been within two hundred miles of the Bighorn range before; so that our hunting trip had the added zest of being also an exploring expedition.

Each of us rode one pony, and the packs were carried on four others. We were not burdened by much baggage. Having no tent we took the canvas wagon sheet instead; our bedding, plenty of spare cartridges, some flour, bacon, coffee, sugar and salt, and a few very primitive cooking utensils, completed the outfit.

The Bighorn range is a chain of bare, rocky peaks stretching lengthwise along the middle of a table-land which is about thirty miles wide. At its edges this table-land falls sheer off into the rolling plains country. From the rocky peaks flow rapid brooks of clear, icy water, which take their way through deep gorges that they have channelled out in the surface of the plateau; a few miles from the heads of the streams these gorges become regular canyons, with sides so steep as to be almost perpendicular; in travelling, therefore, the trail has to keep well up toward timber line, as lower down horses find it difficult or impossible to get across the valleys. In strong contrast to the treeless cattle plains extending to its foot, the sides of the table-land are densely wooded with tall pines. Its top forms what is called a park country; that is, it is covered with alternating groves of trees and open glades, each grove or glade varying in size from half a dozen to many hundred acres.

We went in with the pack train two days' journey before pitching camp in what we intended to be our hunting grounds, following an old Indian trail. No one who has not tried it can understand the work and worry that it is to drive a pack train over rough ground and through timber. We were none of us very skilful at packing, and the loads were all the time slipping; sometimes the ponies would stampede with the pack half tied, or they would get caught among the fallen logs, or in a ticklish place would suddenly decline to follow the trail, or would commit some one of the thousand other tricks which seem to be all a pack-pony knows. Then at night they were a bother; if picketed out they fed badly and got thin, and if they were not picketed they sometimes strayed away. The most valuable one of the lot was also the hardest to catch. Accordingly we used to let him loose with a long lariat tied round his neck, and one night this lariat twisted up in a sage-brush, and in struggling to free himself the pony got a half hitch round his hind leg, threw himself, and fell over a bank into a creek on a large stone. We found him in the morning very much the worse for wear, and his hind legs swelled up so that his chief method of progression was by a series of awkward hops. Of course no load could be put upon him, but he managed to limp along behind the other horses, and actually in the end reached the ranch on the Little Missouri three hundred miles off. No sooner had he got there and been turned loose to rest than he fell down a big wash-out and broke his neck. Another time one of the mares—a homely beast with a head like a camel's—managed to flounder into the very centre of a mud-hole, and we spent the better part of a morning in fishing her out.

It was on the second day of our journey into the mountains, while leading the pack-ponies down the pre-cipitous side of a steep valley, that I obtained my first sight of elk. The trail wound through a forest of tall, slender pines, standing very close together, and with dead trees lying in every direction. The narrow trunks or overhang-ing limbs threatened to scrape off the packs at every mo-ment, as the ponies hopped and scrambled over the fallen trunks; and it was difficult work, and most trying to the temper, to keep them going along straight and prevent them from wandering off to one side or the other. At last we got out into a succession of small, open glades, with boggy spots in them; the lowest glade was of some size, and as we reached it we saw a small band of cow elk disappearing into the woods on its other edge. I was riding a restive horse, and when I tried to jump off to shoot, it reared and turned round, before I could get my left foot out of the stirrup; when I at last got free I could get a glimpse of but one elk, vanishing behind a dead trunk, and my hasty shot missed. I was a good deal annoyed at this, my opening experience with mountain game, feeling that it was an omen of misfortune; but it did not prove so, for during the rest of my two weeks' stay, I with one exception got every animal I fired at.

A beautiful, clear mountain brook ran through the bottom of the valley, and in an open space by its side we pitched camp. We were entirely out of fresh meat, and after lunch all three of us separated to hunt, each for his own hand. The teamster went up stream, Merrifield went down, while I followed the tracks of the band of cows and calves that we had started in the morning; their trail led along the wooded hill-crests parallel to the stream, and therefore to Merrifield's course. The crests of the hills formed a wavy-topped but continuous ridge between two canyon-like valleys, and the sides fell off steeper and steeper the farther down stream I went, until at last they were broken in places by sheer precipices and cliffs; the groves of trees too, though with here and there open glades, formed a continuous forest of tall pines. There was a small growth of young spruce and other evergreen, thick enough to give cover, but not to interfere with seeing and shooting to some distance. The pine trunks rose like straight columns, standing quite close together; and at their bases the ground was carpeted with the sweet-scented needles, over which, in my moccasined feet, I trod without any noise. It was but a little past noon, and the sun in the open was very hot; yet underneath the great archways of the pine woods the air though still was cool, and the sunbeams that struggled down here and there through the interlacing branches, and glinted on the rough trunks, only made bright spots in what was elsewhere the uniform, grayish half-light of the mountain forest. Game trails threaded the woods in all directions, made for the most part by the elk. These animals, when not disturbed, travel strung out in single file, each one stepping very nearly in the tracks of the one before it; they are great wanderers, going over an immense amount of country during the course of a day, and so they soon wear regular, well-beaten paths in any place where they are at all plentiful.

The band I was following had, as is their custom, all run together into a wedge-shaped mass when I fired, and crashed off through the woods in a bunch during the first moments of alarm. The footprints in the soil showed that they had in the beginning taken a plunging gallop, but after a few strides had settled into the swinging, ground-covering trot that is the elk's most natural and characteristic gait. A band of elk when alarmed is likely to go twenty miles without halting; but these had probably been very little molested, and there was a chance that they would not go far without stopping. After getting through the first grove, the huddled herd had straightened itself out into single file, and trotted off in a nearly straight line. A mile or two of ground having been passed over in this way, the animals had slackened their pace into a walk, evidently making up their minds that they were out of danger. Soon afterwards they had begun to go slower, and to scatter out on each side, browsing or grazing.

It was not difficult work to follow up the band at first. While trotting, their sharp hoofs came down with sufficient force to leave very distinct footprints, and, moreover, the trail was the more readily made out as all the animals trod nearly in each other's steps. But when the band spread out the tracking was much harder, as each single one, walking slowly along, merely made here and there a slight scrape in the soil or a faint indentation in the bed of pine needles. Besides, I had to advance with the greatest caution, keeping the sharpest look-out in front and on all sides of me. Even as it was, though I got very close up to my game, they were on foot before I saw them, and I did not get a standing shot. While carefully looking to my footsteps I paid too little heed to the rifle which I held in my right hand, and let the barrel tap smartly on a tree trunk. Instantly there was a stamp and movement among the bushes ahead and to one side of me; the elk had heard but had neither seen nor smelt me; and a second afterward I saw the indistinct, shadowy outlines of the band as they trotted down hill, from where their beds had been made on the very summit of the crest, taking a course diagonal to mine. I raced forward and also down hill, behind some large mossy boulders, and cut them fairly off, the band passing directly ahead of me and not twenty yards away, at a slashing trot, which a few of them changed for a wild gallop, as I opened fire. I was so hemmed in by the thick tree trunks, and it was so difficult to catch more than a fleeting glimpse of each animal, that though I fired four shots I only brought down one elk, a full-grown cow, with a broken neck, dead in its tracks; but I also broke the hind leg of a bull calf. Elk offer easy marks when in motion, much easier than deer, because of their trotting gait, and their regular, deliberate movements. They look very handsome as they trot through a wood, stepping lightly and easily over the dead trunks and crashing through the underbrush, with the head held up and nose pointing forward. In galloping, however, the neck is thrust straight out in front, and the animal moves with labored bounds, which carry it along rapidly but soon tire it out.

After thrusting the hunting-knife into the throat of the cow, I followed the trail of the band; and in an open glade, filled with tall sage-brush, came across and finished the wounded calf. Meanwhile the others ran directly across Merrifield's path, and he shot two. This gave us much more meat than we wished; nor would we have shot as many, but neither of us could reckon upon the other's getting as much game, and flesh was a necessity. Leaving Merrifield to skin and cut up the dead animals, I walked back to camp where I found the teamster, who had brought in the hams and tongues of two deer he had shot, and sent him back with a pack-pony for the hides and meat of the elk. Elk tongues are most delicious eating, being juicy, tender, and well flavored; they are excellent to take out as a lunch on a long hunting trip.

We now had more than enough meat in camp, and did not shoot at another cow or calf elk while on the mountains, though we saw quite a number; the last day of my stay I was within fifty yards of two that were walking quietly through a very dense, swampy wood. But it took me some time longer before I got any fine heads.

The day after killing the cow and calf I went out in the morning by myself and hunted through the woods up toward the rocky peaks, going above timber line, and not reaching camp until after nightfall. In hunting through a wild and unknown country a man must always take great care not to get lost. In the first place he should never, under any conceivable circumstances, stir fifty yards from camp without a compass, plenty of matches, and his rifle; then he need never feel nervous, even if he is lost, for he can keep himself from cold and hunger, and can steer a straight course until he reaches some settlement. But he should not get lost at all. Old plainsmen or backwoodsmen get to have almost an instinct for finding their way, and are able to tell where they are and the way home in almost any place; probably they keep in their heads an accurate idea of their course and of the general lay of the land. But most men cannot do this. In hunting through a new country a man should, if possible, choose some prominent landmarks, and then should learn how they look from different sides—for they will with difficulty be recognized as the same objects, if seen from different points of view. If he gets out of sight of these, he should choose another to work back to, as a kind of half-way point; and so on. He should keep looking back; it is wonderful how different a country looks when following back on one's trail. If possible, he should locate his camp, in his mind, with reference to a line, and not a point; he should take a river or a long ridge, for example. Then at any time he can strike back to this line and follow it up or down till he gets home.

If possible, I always spend the first day, when on new ground, in hunting up-stream. Then, so long as I am sure

I do not wander off into the valleys or creeks of another water-course, I am safe, for, no matter on what remote branch, all I have to do is to follow down-stream until I reach camp; while if I was below camp, it would be difficult to tell which fork to follow up every time the stream branched. A man should always notice the position of the sun, the direction from which the wind blows, the slope of the water-courses, prominent features in the landscape, and so forth, and should keep in mind his own general course; and he had better err on the side of caution rather than on that of boldness. Getting lost is very uncomfortable, both for the man himself and for those who have to break up their work and hunt for him. Deep woods or perfectly flat, open country are almost equally easy places in which to get lost; while if the country is moderately open and level, with only here and there a prominent and easily recognized hill or butte, a man can safely go where he wishes, hardly paying any heed to his course. But even here he should know his general direction from camp, so as to be able to steer for it with a compass if a fog comes up. And if he leaves his horse hidden in a gully or pocket while he goes off to hunt on foot, he must recollect to keep the place well in his mind; on one occasion, when I feared that somebody might meddle with my horse, I hid him so successfully that I spent the better part of a day in finding him.

Keeping in mind the above given rules, when I left camp the morning after the breaking up of the band of cows and calves, I hunted up-stream, and across and through the wooded spurs dividing the little brooks that formed its head waters. No game was encountered, except some blue grouse, which I saw when near camp on my return, and shot for the pot. These blue grouse are the largest species found in America, except the sage fowl. They are exclusively birds of the deep mountain forests, and in their manners remind one of the spruce grouse of the Northeastern woods, being almost equally tame. When alarmed, they fly at once into a tree, and several can often be shot before the remainder take fright and are off. On this trip we killed a good many, shooting off their heads with our rifles. They formed a most welcome addition to our bill of fare, the meat being white and excellent. A curious peculiarity in their flesh is that the breast meat has in it a layer of much darker color. They are very handsome birds, and furnish dainty food to men wearied of venison; but, unless their heads are knocked off with a rifle, they do not furnish much sport, as they will not fly off when flushed, but simply rise into a fairly tall tree, and there sit, motionless, except that the head is twisted and bobbed round to observe the acts of the foe.

All of the sights and sounds in these pine woods that clothed the Bighorn Mountains reminded me of the similar ones seen and heard in the great, sombre forests of Maine and the Adirondacks. The animals and birds were much the same. As in the East, there were red squirrels, chipmunks, red hares, and woodchucks, all of them differing but slightly from our common kinds; woodpeckers, chickadees, nuthatches, and whisky jacks came about camp; ravens and eagles flew over the rocky cliffs. There were some new forms, however. The nutcracker, a large, noisy, crow-like bird, with many of the habits of a woodpecker, was common, and in the rocks above timber line, we came upon the Little Chief hare, a wee animal, with a shrill, timorous squeak.

During our stay upon the mountains the weather was generally clear, but always cold, thin ice covering the dark waters of the small mountain tarns, and there were slight snow-falls every two or three days; but we were only kept in camp one day, when it sleeted, snowed, and rained from dawn till nightfall. We passed this day very comfortably, however. I had far too much forethought to go into the woods without a small supply of books for just such occasions. We had rigged the canvas wagon sheet into a tent, at the bottom of the ravine, near the willow-covered brink of the brook that ran through it. The steep hill-sides bounding the valley, which a little below us became sheer cliffs, were partly covered with great pines and spruces, and partly open ground grown up with tall grass and safe-brush. We were thus well sheltered from the wind; and when one morning we looked out and saw the wet snow lying on the ground, and with its weight bending down the willow bushes and loading the tall evergreens, while the freezing sleet rattled against the canvas, we simply started a roaring fire of pine logs in front of the tent, and passed a cosy day inside, cleaning guns, reading, and playing cards. Blue grouse, elk hams, and deer saddles hung from the trees around, so we had no fear of starvation. Still, towards evening we got a little tired, and I could not resist taking a couple of hours' brisk ride in the mist, through a chain of open glades that sloped off from our camp.

Later on we made a camp at the head of a great natural meadow, where two streams joined together, and in times long gone by had been dammed by the beaver. This had at first choked up the passage and made a small lake; then dams were built higher and higher up, making chains of little ponds. By degrees these filled up, and the whole valley became a broad marshy meadow, through which the brook wound between rows of willows and alders. These beaver meadows are very common; but are not usually of such large size. Around this camp there was very little game; but we got a fine mess of spotted trout by taking a long and most toilsome walk up to a little lake lying very near timber line. Our rods and lines were most primitive, consisting of two clumsy dead cedars (the only trees within reach), about six feet of string tied to one and a piece of catgut to the other, with preposterous hooks; yet the trout were so ravenous that we caught them at the rate of about one a minute; and they formed another welcome change in our camp fare. This lake lay in a valley whose sides were so steep and boulder-covered as to need hard climbing to get into and out of it. Every day in the cold, clear weather we tramped miles and miles through the woods and mountains, which, after a snow-storm took on a really wintry look; while in the moonlight the snow-laden forests shone and sparkled like crystal. The dweller in cities has but a faint idea of the way we ate and slept.

One day Merrifield and I went out together and had a rather exciting chase after some bull elk. The previous evening, toward sunset, I had seen three bulls trotting off across an open glade toward a great stretch of forest and broken ground, up near the foot of the rocky peaks. Next morning early we started off to hunt through this country. The walking was hard work, especially up and down the steep cliffs, covered with slippery pine needles; or among the windfalls, where the rows of dead trees lay piled up across one another in the wildest confusion. We saw nothing until we came to a large patch of burnt ground, where we at once found the soft, black soil marked up by elk hoofs; nor had we penetrated into it more than a few hundred yards before we came to tracks made but a few minutes before, and almost instantly afterward saw three bull elk, probably those I had seen on the preceding day. We had been running briskly up-hill through the soft, heavy loam, in which our feet made no noise but slipped and sank deeply; as a consequence, I was all out of breath and my hand so unsteady that I missed my first shot. Elk, however, do not vanish with the instantaneous rapidity of frightened deer, and these three trotted off in a direction quartering to us. I doubt if I ever went through more violent exertion than in the next ten minutes. We raced after them at full speed, opening fire; I wounded all three, but none of the wounds were immediately disabling. They trotted on and we panted afterwards, slipping on the wet earth, pitching headlong over charred stumps, leaping on dead logs that broke beneath our weight, more than once measuring our full-length on the ground, halting and firing whenever we got a chance. At last one bull fell; we passed him by after the others which were still running up-hill. The sweat streamed into my eyes and made furrows in the sooty mud that covered my face, from having fallen full length down on the burnt earth; I sobbed for breath as I toiled at a shambling trot after them, as nearly done out as could well be. At this moment they turned down-hill. It was a great relief; a man who is too done up to go a step up-hill can still run fast enough down; with a last spurt I closed in near enough to fire again; one elk fell; the other went off at a walk. We passed the second elk and I kept on alone after the third, not able to go at more than a slow trot myself, and too much winded to dare risk a shot at any distance. He got out of the burnt patch, going into some thick timber in a deep ravine; I closed pretty well, and rushed after him into a thicket of young evergreens. Hardly was I in when there was a scramble and bounce among them and I caught a glimpse of a yellow body moving out to one side; I ran out toward the edge and fired through the twigs at the moving beast. Down it went, but when I ran up, to my disgust I found that I had jumped and killed, in my haste, a black-tail deer, which must have been already roused by the passage of the wounded elk. I at once took up the trail of the latter again, but after a little while the blood grew less, and ceased, and I lost the track; nor could I find it, hunt as hard as I might. The poor beast could not have gone five hundred yards; yet we never found the carcass.

Then I walked slowly back past the deer I had slain by so curious a mischance, to the elk. The first one shot down was already dead. The second was only wounded, though it could not rise. When it saw us coming it sought to hide from us by laying its neck flat on the ground, but when we came up close it raised its head and looked proudly at us, the heavy mane bristling up on the neck, while its eyes glared and its teeth grated together. I felt really sorry to kill it. Though these were both well-grown elks, their antlers, of ten points, were small, twisted, and ill-shaped; in fact hardly worth preserving, except to call to mind a chase in which during a few minutes I did as much down-right hard work as it has often fallen to my lot to do. The burnt earth had blackened our faces and hands till we looked like negroes.

The bull elk had at this time begun calling, and several times they were heard right round camp at night, challenging one another or calling to the cows. Their calling is known to hunters as "whistling"; but this is a most inappropriate name for it. It is a most singular and beautiful sound, and is very much the most musical cry uttered by any four-footed beast. When heard for the first time it is almost impossible to believe that it is the call of an animal; it sounds far more as if made by an Æolian harp or some strange wind instrument. It consists of quite a series of notes uttered continuously, in a most soft, musical, vibrant tone, so clearly that they can be heard half a mile off. Heard in the clear, frosty moonlight from the depths of the rugged and forest-clad mountains the effect is most beautiful; for its charm is heightened by the wild and desolate surroundings. It has the sustained, varied melody of some bird songs, with, of course, a hundred-fold greater power. Now and then, however, the performance is marred by the elk's apparently getting out of breath towards the close, and winding up with two or three gasping notes which have an unpleasantly mule-like sound.

The great pine-clad mountains, their forests studded with open glades, were the best of places for the still-hunter's craft. Going noiselessly through them in our dull-colored buckskin and noiseless moccasins, we kept getting glimpses, as it were, of the inner life of the mountains. Each animal that we saw had its own individuality.

Aside from the thrill and tingle that a hunter experiences at the sight of his game, I by degrees grew to feel as if I had a personal interest in the different traits and habits of the wild creatures. The characters of the animals differed widely, and the differences were typified by their actions; and it was pleasant to watch them in their own homes, myself unseen, when after stealthy, silent progress through the sombre and soundless depths of the woods I came upon them going about the ordinary business of their lives. The lumbering, self-confident gait of the bears, their burly strength, and their half-humorous, half-ferocious look, gave me a real insight into their character; and I never was more impressed by the exhibition of vast, physical power, than when watching from an ambush a grizzly burying or covering up an elk carcass. His motions looked awkward, but it was marvellous to see the ease and absence of effort with which he would scoop out great holes in the earth, or twitch the heavy carcass from side to side. And the proud, graceful, half-timid, half-defiant bearing of the elk was in its own way quite as noteworthy; they seemed to glory in their own power and beauty, and yet to be ever on the watch for foes against whom they knew they might not dare to contend. The true still-hunter should be a lover of nature as well as of sport, or he will miss half the pleasure of being in the woods.

The finest bull, with the best head that I got, was killed in the midst of very beautiful and grand surroundings. We had been hunting through a great pine wood which ran up to the edge of a broad canyon-like valley, bounded by sheer walls of rock. There were fresh tracks of elk about, and we had been advancing up-wind with even more than our usual caution when, on stepping out into a patch of open ground, near the edge of the cliff, we came upon a great bull, beating and thrashing his antlers against a young tree, about eighty yards off. He stopped and faced us for a second, his mighty antlers thrown in the air, as he held his head aloft. Behind him towered the tall and sombre pines, while at his feet the jutting crags overhung the deep chasm below, that stretched off between high walls of barren and snow-streaked rocks, the evergreens clinging to their sides, while along the bottom the rapid torrent gathered in places into black and sullen mountain lakes. As the bull turned to run I struck him just behind the shoulder; he reeled to the death-blow, but staggered gamely on a few rods into the forest before sinking to the ground, with my second bullet through his lungs.

Two or three days later than this I killed another bull, nearly as large, in the same patch of woods in which I had slain the first. A bear had been feeding on the carcass of the latter, and, after a vain effort to find his den, we determined to beat through the woods and try to start him up. Accordingly Merrifield, the teamster, and myself took parallel courses some three hundred yards apart, and started at one end to walk through to the other. I doubt if the teamster much wished to meet a bear alone (while nothing would have given Merrifield more hearty and unaffected enjoyment than to have encountered an entire family), and he gradually edged in pretty close to me. Where the woods became pretty open I saw him suddenly lift his rifle and fire, and immediately afterwards a splendid bull elk trotted past in front of me, evidently untouched, the teamster having missed. The elk ran to the other side of two trees that stood close together some seventy yards off, and stopped for a moment to look round. Kneeling down I fired at the only part of his body I could see between the two trees, and sent a bullet into his flank. Away he went, and I after, running in my moccasins over the moss and pine needles for all there was in me. If a wounded elk gets fairly started he will go at a measured trot for many hours, and even if mortally hurt may run twenty miles before falling; while at the same time he does not start off at full speed, and will often give an active hunter a chance for another shot as he turns and changes his course preparatory to taking a straight line. So I raced along after the elk at my very best speed for a few hundred feet, and then got another shot as he went across a little glade, injuring his hip somewhat. This made it all right for me, and another hundred yards' burst took me up to where I was able to put a ball in a fatal spot, and the grand old fellow sank down and fell over on his side.

No sportsman can ever feel much keener pleasure and self-satisfaction than when, after a successful stalk and good shot, he walks up to a grand elk lying dead in the cool shade of the great evergreens, and looks at the massive and yet finely moulded form, and at the mighty antlers which are to serve in the future as the trophy and proof of his successful skill. Still-hunting the elk on the mountains is as noble a kind of sport as can well be imagined; there is nothing more pleasant and enjoyable, and at the same time it demands that the hunter shall bring into play many manly qualities. There have been few days of my hunting life that were so full of unalloyed happiness as were those spent on the Bighorn range. From morning till night I was on foot, in cool, bracing air, now moving silently through the vast, melancholy pine forests, now treading the brink of high, rocky precipices, always amid the most grand and beautiful scenery; and always after as noble and lordly game as is to be found in the Western world.

Since writing the above I killed an elk near my ranch; probably the last of his race that will ever be found in our neighborhood. It was just before the fall round-up. An old hunter, who was under some obligation to me, told me that he had shot a cow elk and had seen the tracks of one or two others not more than twenty-five miles off, in a place where the cattle rarely wandered. Such a chance was not to be neglected; and, on the first free day, one of my Elk-horn foremen, Will Dow by name, and myself, took our hunting horses and started off, accompanied by the ranch wagon, in the direction of the probable haunts of the doomed deer. Towards nightfall we struck a deep spring pool, near by the remains of an old Indian encampment. It was at the head of a great basin, several miles across, in which we believed the game to lie. The wagon was halted and we pitched camp; there was plenty of dead wood, and soon the venison steaks were broiling over the coals raked from beneath the crackling cottonwood logs, while in the narrow valley the ponies grazed almost within the circle of the flickering fire-light. It was in the cool and pleasant month of September; and long after going to bed we lay awake under the blankets watching the stars that on clear nights always shine with such intense brightness over the lonely Western plains.

We were up and off by the gray of the morning. It was

a beautiful hunting day; the sundogs hung in the red dawn; the wind hardly stirred over the crisp grass; and though the sky was cloudless yet the weather had that queer, smoky, hazy look that it is most apt to take on during the time of the Indian summer. From a high spur of the table-land we looked out far and wide over a great stretch of broken country, the brown of whose hills and valleys was varied everywhere by patches of dull red and vivid yellow, tokens that the trees were already putting on the dress with which they greet the mortal ripening of the year. The deep and narrow but smooth ravines running up towards the edges of the plateaus were heavily wooded, the bright green tree-tops rising to a height they rarely reach in the barren plains-country; and the rocky sides of the sheer gorges were clad with a thick growth of dwarfed cedars, while here and there the trailing Virginia creepers burned crimson among their sombre masses.

We hunted stealthily up-wind, across the line of the heavily timbered coulies. We soon saw traces of our quarry; old tracks at first, and then the fresh footprints of a single elk—a bull, judging by the size—which had come down to drink at a mirey alkali pool, its feet slipping so as to leave the marks of the false hoofs in the soft soil. We hunted with painstaking and noiseless care for many hours; at last as I led old Manitou up to look over the edge of a narrow ravine, there was a crash and movement in the timber below me, and immediately afterwards I caught a glimps of a great bull elk trotting up through the young trees as he gallantly breasted the steep hill-side opposite. When clear of the woods, and directly across the valley from me, he stopped and turned half round, throwing his head in the air to gaze for a moment at the intruder. My bullet struck too far back, but, nevertheless, made a deadly wound, and the elk went over the crest of the hill at a wild, plunging gallop. We followed the bloody trail for a quarter of a mile, and found him dead in a thicket. Though of large size, he yet had but small antlers, with few points.

CHAPTER X

Old Ephraim

B ut few bears are found in the immediate neighborhood of my ranch; and though I have once or twice
seen their tracks in the Bad Lands, I have never had any
experience with the animals themselves except during the
elk-hunting trip on the Bighorn Mountains, described in
the preceding chapter.

The grizzly bear undoubtedly comes in the category
of dangerous game, and is, perhaps, the only animal in the
United States that can be fairly so placed, unless we count
the few jaguars found north of the Rio Grande. But the
danger of hunting the grizzly has been greatly exaggerated, and the sport is certainly very much safer than it was
at the beginning of this century. The first hunters who
came into contact with this great bear were men belonging to that hardy and adventurous class of backwoodsmen
which had filled the wild country between the Appalachian Mountains and the Mississippi. These men carried but one weapon: the long-barrelled, small-bored
pea-rifle, whose bullets ran seventy to the pound, the
amount of powder and lead being a little less than that
contained in the cartridge of a thirty-two calibre Winchester. In the Eastern States almost all the hunting was
done in the woodland; the shots were mostly obtained at
short distance, and deer and black bear were the largest

game; moreover, the pea-rifles were marvellously accurate for close range, and their owners were famed the world over for their skill as marksmen. Thus these rifles had so far proved plenty good enough for the work they had to do, and indeed had done excellent service as military weapons in the ferocious wars that the men of the border carried on with their Indian neighbors, and even in conflict with more civilized foes, as at the battles of King's Mountain and New Orleans. But when the restless frontiersmen pressed out over the Western plains, they encountered in the grizzly a beast of far greater bulk and more savage temper than any of those found in the Eastern woods, and their small-bore rifles were utterly inadequate weapons with which to cope with him. It is small wonder that he was considered by them to be almost invulnerable, and extraordinarily tenacious of life. He would be a most unpleasant antagonist now to a man armed only with a thirty-two calibre rifle, that carried but a single shot and was loaded at the muzzle. A rifle, to be of use in this sport, should carry a ball weighing from half an ounce to an ounce. With the old pea-rifles the shot had to be in the eye or heart; and accidents to the hunter were very common. But the introduction of heavy breech-loading repeaters has greatly lessened the danger, even in the very few and far-off places where the grizzlies are as ferocious as formerly. For nowadays these great bears are undoubtedly much better aware of the death-dealing power of men, and, as a consequence, much less fierce, than was the case with their forefathers, who so unhesitatingly attacked the early Western travellers and explorers. Constant contact with rifle-carrying hunters, for a period extending over many generations of bear-life, has taught the grizzly by bitter experience that man is his undoubted overlord, as far as fighting goes; and this knowledge has become an hereditary characteristic. No grizzly will assail a man now unprovoked, and one will almost always rather run than fight; though if he is wounded or thinks himself cornered he will attack his foes with a headlong, reckless fury that renders him one of the most dangerous of wild beasts. The ferocity of all wild animals depends largely upon the amount of resistance they are accustomed to meet with, and the quantity of molestation to which they are subjected.

The change in the grizzly's character during the last half century has been precisely paralleled by the change in the characters of his northern cousin, the polar bear, and of the South African lion. When the Dutch and Scandinavian sailors first penetrated the Arctic seas, they were kept in constant dread of the white bear, who regarded a man as simply an erect variety of seal, quite as good eating as the common kind. The records of these early explorers are filled with examples of the ferocious and man-eating propensities of the polar bears; but in the accounts of most of the later Arctic expeditions they are portrayed as having learned wisdom, and being now most anxious to keep out of the way of the hunters. A number of my sporting friends have killed white bears, and none of them were ever even charged. And in South Africa the English sportsmen and Dutch boers have taught the lion to be a very different creature from what it was when the first white man reached that continent. If the Indian tiger had been a native of the United States, it would now be one of the most shy of beasts. Of late years our estimate of the grizzly's ferocity has been lowered; and we no longer accept the tales of uneducated hunters as being proper authority by which to judge it. But we should make a parallel reduction in the cases of many foreign animals and their describers. Take, for example, that purely melodramatic beast, the North African lion, as portrayed by Jules Gérard, who bombastically describes himself as "le tueur des lions." Gérard's accounts are self-evidently in large part fictitious, while if true they would prove less for the bravery of the lion than for the phenomenal cowardice, incapacity, and bad marksmanship of the Algerian Arabs. Doubtless Gérard was a great hunter; but so is many a Western plainsman, whose account of the grizzlies he has killed would be wholly untrustworthy. Take for instance the following from page 223 of "La Chasse au Lion": "The inhabitants had assembled one day to the number of two or three hundred with the object of killing (the lion) or driving it out of the country. The attack took place at sunrise; at mid-day five hundred cartridges had been expended; the Arabs carried off one of their number dead and six wounded, and the lion remained master of the field of battle." Now if three hundred men could fire five hundred shots at a lion without hurting him, it merely shows that they were wholly incapable of hurting any thing, or else that M. Gérard was more expert with the long-bow than with the rifle. Gérard's whole book is filled with equally preposterous nonsense; yet a great many people seriously accept this same book as trustworthy authority for the manners and ferocity of the North African lion. It would be quite as sensible to accept M. Jules Verne's stories as being valuable contributions to science. A good deal of the lion's reputation is built upon just such stuff.

How the prowess of the grizzly compares with that of the lion or tiger would be hard to say; I have never shot either of the latter myself, and my brother, who has killed tigers in India, has never had a chance at a grizzly. Any one of the big bears we killed on the mountains would, I should think, have been able to make short work of either a lion or a tiger; for the grizzly is greatly superior in bulk and muscular power to either of the great cats, and its teeth are as large as theirs, while its claws, though blunter, are much longer; nevertheless, I believe that a lion or a tiger would be fully as dangerous to a hunter or other human being, on account of the superior speed of its charge, the lightning-like rapidity of its movements, and its apparently sharper senses. Still, after all is said, the man should have a thoroughly trustworthy weapon and a fairly cool head, who would follow into his own haunts and slay grim Old Ephraim.

A grizzly will only fight if wounded or cornered, or, at least, if he thinks himself cornered. If a man by accident stumbles on to one close up, he is almost certain to be attacked really more from fear than from any other motive; exactly the same reason that makes a rattlesnake strike at a passer-by. I have personally known of but one instance of a grizzly turning on a hunter before being wounded. This happened to a friend of mine, a Californian ranchman, who, with two or three of his men, was following a bear that had carried off one of his sheep. They got the bear into a cleft in the mountain from which there was no escape, and he suddenly charged back through the line of his pursuers, struck down one of the horsemen, seized the arm of the man in his jaws and broke it as if it had been a pipestem, and was only killed after a most lively fight, in which, by repeated charges, he at one time drove every one of his assailants off the field.

But two instances have come to my personal knowledge where a man has been killed by a grizzly. One was that of a hunter at the foot of the Bighorn Mountains who had chased a large bear and finally wounded him. The animal turned at once and came straight at the man, whose second shot missed. The bear then closed and passed on, after striking only a single blow; yet that one blow, given with all the power of its thick, immensely muscular forearm, armed with nails as strong as so many hooked steel spikes, tore out the man's collar-bone and snapped through three or four ribs. He never recovered from the shock, and died that night.

The other instance occurred to a neighbor of mine—who has a small ranch on the Little Missouri—two or three years ago. He was out on a mining trip, and was prospecting with two other men near the head-water of the Little Missouri, in the Black Hills country. They were walking down along the river, and came to a point of land, thrust out into it, which was densely covered with brush and fallen timber. Two of the party walked round by the edge of the stream, but the third, a German, and a very powerful fellow, followed a well-beaten game trail, leading through the bushy point. When they were some forty yards apart the two men heard an agonized shout from the German, and at the same time the loud coughing growl, or roar, of a bear. They turned just in time to see their companion struck a terrible blow on the head by a grizzly, which must have been roused from its lair by his almost stepping on it; so close was it that he had no time to fire his rifle, but merely held it up over his head as a guard. Of course it was struck down, the claws of the great brute at the same time shattering his skull like an egg-shell. Yet the man staggered on some ten feet before he fell; but when he did he never spoke or moved again. The two others killed the bear after a short, brisk struggle, as he was in the midst of a most determined charge.

In 1872, near Fort Wingate, New Mexico, two soldiers of a cavalry regiment came to their death at the claws of a grizzly bear. The army surgeon who attended them told me the particulars, as far as they were known. The men were mail carriers, and one day did not come in at the appointed time. Next day, a relief party was sent out to look for them, and after some search found the bodies of both, as well as that of one of the horses. One of the men still showed signs of life; he came to his senses before dying, and told the story. They had seen a grizzly and pursued it on horseback, with their Spencer rifles. On coming close, one had fired into its side, when it turned with marvellous quickness for so large and unwieldy an animal, and struck down the horse, at the same time inflicting a ghastly wound on the rider. The other man dismounted and came up to the rescue of his companion. The bear then left the latter and attacked the other. Although hit by the bullet, it charged home and threw the man down, and then lay on him and deliberately bit him to death, while his groans and cries were frightful to hear. Afterward it walked off into the bushes without again offering to molest the already mortally wounded victim of its first assault.

At certain times the grizzly works a good deal of havoc among the herds of the stockmen. A friend of mine, a ranchman in Montana, told me that one fall bears became very plenty around his ranches, and caused him severe loss, killing with ease even full-grown beef-steers. But one of them once found his intended quarry too much for him. My friend had a stocky, rather vicious range stallion, which had been grazing one day near a small thicket of bushes, and, towards evening, came galloping in with three or four gashes in his haunch, that looked as if they had been cut with a dull axe. The cowboys knew at once that he had been assailed by a bear, and rode off to the thicket near which he had been feeding. Sure enough a bear, evidently in a very bad temper, sallied out as soon as the thicket was surrounded, and, after a spirited fight and a succession of charges, was killed. On examination, it was found that his under jaw was broken, and part of his face smashed in, evidently by the stallion's hoofs. The horse had been feeding when the bear leaped out at him but failed to kill at the first stroke; then the horse lashed out behind, and not only freed himself, but also severely damaged his opponent.

Doubtless, the grizzly could be hunted to advantage with dogs, which would not, of course, be expected to seize him, but simply to find and bay him, and distract his attention by barking and nipping. Occasionally a bear can be caught in the open and killed with the aid of horses. But nine times out of ten the only way to get one is to put on moccasins and still-hunt it in its own haunts, shooting it at close quarters. Either its tracks should be followed until the bed wherein it lies during the day is found, or a given locality in which it is known to exist should be carefully beaten through, or else a bait should be left out and a watch kept on it to catch the bear when he has come to visit it.

■ ■ ■

FOR SOME DAYS after our arrival on the Bighorn range we did not come across any grizzly.

Although it was still early in September, the weather was cool and pleasant, the nights being frosty; and every two or three days there was a flurry of light snow, which rendered the labor of tracking much more easy. Indeed, throughout our stay on the mountains, the peaks were snow-capped almost all the time. Our fare was excellent, consisting of elk venison, mountain grouse, and small trout; the last caught in one of the beautiful little lakes that lay almost up by timber line. To us, who had for weeks been accustomed to make small fires from dried brush, or from sage-brush roots, which we dug out of the ground, it was a treat to sit at night before the roaring and crackling pine logs; as the old teamster quaintly put it, we had at last come to a land "where the wood grew on trees." There were plenty of black-tail deer in the woods, and we came across a number of bands of cow and calf elk, or of young bulls; but after several days' hunting, we were still without any head worth taking home, and had seen no sign of grizzly, which was the game we were especially anxious to kill; for neither Merrifield nor I had ever seen a wild bear alive.

Sometimes we hunted in company; sometimes each of us went out alone; the teamster, of course, remaining in to guard camp and cook. One day we had separated; I reached camp early in the afternoon, and waited a couple of hours before Merrifield put in an appearance.

At last I heard a shout—the familiar long-drawn *Ei-koh-h-h* of the cattle-men,—and he came in sight galloping at speed down an open glade, and waving his hat, evidently having had good luck; and when he reined in his small, wiry, cow-pony, we saw that he had packed behind his saddle the fine, glossy pelt of a black bear. Better still, he announced that he had been off about ten miles to a perfect tangle of ravines and valleys where bear sign was very thick; and not of black bear either but of grizzly. The black bear (the only one we got on the mountains) he had run across by accident, while riding up a valley in which there was a patch of dead timber grown up with berry bushes. He noticed a black object which he first took to be a stump; for during the past few days we had each of us made one or two clever stalks up to charred logs which our imagination converted into bears. On coming near, however, the object suddenly took to its heels; he followed over frightful ground at the pony's best pace, until it stumbled and fell down. By this time he was close on the bear, which had just reached the edge of the wood. Picking himself up, he rushed after it, hearing it growling ahead of him; after running some fifty yards the sounds stopped, and he stood still listening. He saw and heard nothing, until he hap-

pened to cast his eyes upwards, and there was the bear, almost overhead, and about twenty-five feet up a tree; and
in as many seconds afterwards it came down to the ground
with a bounce, stone dead. It was a young bear, in its second year, and had probably never before seen a man,
which accounted for the ease with which it was treed and
taken. One minor result of the encounter was to convince
Merrifield—the list of whose faults did not include lack of
self-confidence—that he could run down any bear; in
consequence of which idea we on more than one subsequent occasion went through a good deal of violent exertion.

Merrifield's tale made me decide to shift camp at
once, and go over to the spot where the bear-tracks were
so plenty. Next morning we were off, and by noon pitched
camp by a clear brook, in a valley with steep, wooded sides,
but with good feed for the horses in the open bottom. We
rigged the canvas wagon sheet into a small tent, sheltered
by the trees from the wind, and piled great pine logs near
by where we wished to place the fire; for a night camp in
the sharp fall weather is cold and dreary unless there is a
roaring blaze of flame in front of the tent.

That afternoon we again went out, and I shot a fine
bull elk. I came home alone toward nightfall, walking
through a reach of burnt forest, where there was nothing
but charred tree-trunks and black mould. When nearly
through it I came across the huge, half-human footprints
of a great grizzly, which must have passed by within a few
minutes. It gave me rather an eerie feeling in the silent,
lonely woods, to see for the first time the unmistakable
proofs that I was in the home of the mighty lord of the

wilderness. I followed the tracks in the fading twilight until it became too dark to see them any longer, and then shouldered my rifle and walked back to camp.

That evening we almost had a visit from one of the animals we were after. Several times we had heard at night the musical calling of the bull elk—a sound to which no writer has as yet done justice. This particular night, when we were in bed and the fire was smouldering, we were roused by a ruder noise—a kind of grunting or roaring whine, answered by the frightened snorts of the ponies. It was a bear which had evidently not seen the fire, as it came from behind the bank, and had probably been attracted by the smell of the horses. After it made out what we were it stayed round a short while, again uttered its peculiar roaring grunt, and went off; we had seized our rifles and had run out into the woods, but in the darkness could see nothing; indeed it was rather lucky we did not stumble across the bear, as he could have made short work of us when we were at such a disadvantage.

Next day we went off on a long tramp through the woods and along the sides of the canyons. There were plenty of berry bushes growing in clusters; and all around these there were fresh tracks of bear. But the grizzly is also a flesh-eater, and has a great liking for carrion. On visiting the place where Merrifield had killed the black bear, we found that the grizzlies had been there before us, and had utterly devoured the carcass, with cannibal relish. Hardly a scrap was left, and we turned our steps toward where lay the bull elk I had killed. It was quite late in the afternoon when we reached the place. A grizzly had evidently been at the carcass during the preceding night, for his great footprints were in the ground all around it, and the carcass itself was gnawed and torn, and partially covered with earth and leaves—for the grizzly has a curious habit of burying all of his prey that he does not at the moment need. A great many ravens had been feeding on the body, and they wheeled about over the tree tops above us, uttering their barking croaks.

The forest was composed mainly of what are called ridge-pole pines, which grow close together, and do not branch out until the stems are thirty or forty feet from the ground. Beneath these trees we walked over a carpet of pine needles, upon which our moccasined feet made no sound. The woods seemed vast and lonely, and their silence was broken now and then by the strange noises always to be heard in the great forests, and which seem to mark the sad and everlasting unrest of the wilderness. We climbed up along the trunk of a dead tree which had toppled over until its upper branches struck in the limb crotch of another, that thus supported it at an angle half-way in its fall. When above the ground far enough to prevent the bear's smelling us, we sat still to wait for his approach; until, in the gathering gloom, we could no longer see the sights of our rifles, and could but dimly make out the carcass of the great elk. It was useless to wait longer; and we clambered down and stole out to the edge of the woods. The forest here covered one side of a steep, almost canyon-like ravine, whose other side was bare except of rock and sage-brush. Once out from under the trees there was still plenty of light, although the sun had set, and we crossed over some fifty yards to the opposite hill-side, and crouched down under a bush to see if perchance some animal might not also leave the cover. To our right the ravine sloped downward toward the valley of the Bighorn River, and far on its other side we could catch a glimpse of the great main chain of the Rockies, their snow peaks glinting crimson in the light of the set sun. Again we waited quietly in the growing dusk until the pine trees in our front blended into one dark, frowning mass. We saw nothing; but the wild creatures of the forest had begun to stir abroad. The owls hooted dismally from the tops of the tall trees, and two or three times a harsh wailing cry, probably the voice of some lynx or wolverine, arose from the depths of the woods. At last, as we were rising to leave, we heard the sound of the breaking of a dead stick, from the spot where we knew the carcass lay. It was a sharp, sudden noise, perfectly distinct from the natural creaking and snapping of the branches; just such a sound as would be made by the tread of some heavy creature. "Old Ephraim" had come back to the carcass. A minute afterward, listening with strained ears, we heard him brush by some dry twigs. It was entirely too dark to go in after him; but we made up our minds that on the morrow he should be ours.

Early next morning we were over at the elk carcass, and, as we expected, found that the bear had eaten his fill at it during the night. His tracks showed him to be an immense fellow, and were so fresh that we doubted if he had left long before we arrived; and we made up our minds to follow him up and try to find his lair. The bears that lived on these mountains had evidently been little disturbed; indeed, the Indians and most of the white hunters are rather chary of meddling with "Old Ephraim," as the mountain men style the grizzly, unless they get him at a disadvantage; for the sport is fraught with some danger and but small profit. The bears thus seemed to have very little fear of harm, and we thought it likely that the bed of the one who had fed on the elk would not be far away.

My companion was a skilful tracker, and we took up the trail at once. For some distance it led over the soft, yielding carpet of moss and pine needles, and the footprints were quite easily made out, although we could follow them but slowly; for we had, of course, to keep a sharp look-out ahead and around us as we walked noiselessly on in the sombre half-light always prevailing under the great pine trees, through whose thickly interlacing branches stray but few beams of light, no matter how bright the sun may be outside. We made no sound ourselves, and every little sudden noise sent a thrill through me as I peered about with each sense on the alert. Two or three of the ravens that we had scared from the carcass flew overhead, croaking hoarsely; and the pine tops moaned and sighed in the slight breeze—for pine trees seem to be ever in motion, no matter how light the wind.

After going a few hundred yards the tracks turned off on a well-beaten path made by the elk; the woods were in many places cut up by these game trails, which had often become as distinct as ordinary foot-paths. The beast's footprints were perfectly plain in the dust, and he had lumbered along up the path until near the middle of the hill-side, where the ground broke away and there were hollows and boulders. Here there had been a windfall, and the dead trees lay among the living, piled across one another in all directions; while between and around them sprouted up a thick growth of young spruces and other evergreens. The trail turned off into the tangled thicket, within which it was almost certain we would find our quarry. We could still follow the tracks, by the slight scrapes of the claws on the bark, or by the bent and broken twigs; and we advanced with noiseless caution, slowly climbing over the dead tree trunks and upturned stumps, and not letting a branch rustle or catch on our clothes. When in the middle of the thicket we crossed what was almost a breastwork of fallen logs, and Merrifield, who was leading, passed by the upright stem of a great pine. As soon as he was by it he sank suddenly on one knee, turning half round, his face fairly aflame with excitement; and as I strode past him, with my rifle at the ready, there, not ten steps off, was the great bear, slowly rising from his bed among the young spruces. He had heard us, but apparently hardly knew exactly where or what we were, for he reared up on his haunches sideways to us. Then he saw us and dropped down again on all fours, the shaggy hair on his neck and shoulders seeming to bristle as he turned toward us. As he sank down on his forefeet I had raised the rifle; his head was bent slightly down, and when I saw the top of the white bead fairly between his small, glittering, evil eyes, I pulled trigger. Half-rising up, the huge beast fell over on his side in the death throes, the ball having gone into his brain, striking as fairly between the eyes as if the distance had been measured by a carpenter's rule.

The whole thing was over in twenty seconds from the time I caught sight of the game; indeed, it was over so quickly that the grizzly did not have time to show fight at all or come a step toward us. It was the first I had ever seen, and I felt not a little proud, as I stood over the great brindled bulk, which lay stretched out at length in the cool shade of the evergreens. He was a monstrous fellow, much larger than any I have seen since, whether alive or brought in dead by the hunters. As near as we could estimate (for of course we had nothing with which to weigh more than very small portions) he must have weighed about twelve hundred pounds, and though this is not as large as some of his kind are said to grow in California, it is yet a very unusual size for a bear. He was a good deal heavier than any of our horses; and it was with the greatest difficulty that we were able to skin him. He must have been very old, his teeth and claws being all worn down and blunted; but nevertheless he had been living in plenty, for he was as fat as a prize hog, the layers on his back being a finger's length in thickness. He was still in the summer coat, his hair being short, and in color a curious brindled brown, somewhat like that of certain bull-dogs; while all the bears we shot afterward had the long thick winter fur, cinnamon or yellowish brown. By the way, the name of this bear has reference to its character and not to its color, and should, I suppose, be properly spelt grisly—in the sense of horrible, exactly as we speak of a "grisly spectre"—and not grizzly; but perhaps the latter way of spelling it is too well established to be now changed.

In killing dangerous game steadiness is more needed than good shooting. No game is dangerous unless a man is close up, for nowadays hardly any wild beast will charge from a distance of a hundred yards, but will rather try to run off; and if a man is close it is easy enough for him to shoot straight if he does not lose his head. A bear's brain is about the size of a pint bottle; and any one can hit a pint bottle off-hand at thirty or forty feet. I have had two shots at bears at close quarters, and each time I fired into the brain, the bullet in one case striking fairly between the eyes, as told above, and in the other going in between the eye and ear. A novice at this kind of sport will find it best and safest to keep in mind the old Norse viking's advice in reference to a long sword: "If you go in close enough your sword will be long enough." If a poor shot goes in close enough he will find that he shoots straight enough.

I was very proud over my first bear; but Merrifield's chief feeling seemed to be disappointment that the animal had not had time to show fight. He was rather a reckless fellow, and very confident in his own skill with the rifle; and he really did not seem to have any more fear of the grizzlies than if they had been so many jack-rabbits. I did not at all share his feelings, having a hearty respect for my foes' prowess, and in following and attacking them always took all possible care to get the chances on my side. Merrifield was sincerely sorry that we never had to stand a regular charge; while on this trip we killed five grizzlies with seven bullets, and except in the case of the she and cub, spoken of further on, each was shot about as quickly as it got sight of us. The last one we got was an old male, which was feeding on an elk carcass. We crept up to within about sixty feet, and as Merrifield had not yet killed a grizzly purely to his own gun, and I had killed three, I told him to take the shot. He at once whispered gleefully: "I'll break his leg, and we'll see what he'll do!" Having no ambition to be a participator in the antics of a three-legged bear, I hastily interposed a most emphatic veto; and with a rather injured air he fired, the bullet going through the neck just back of the head. The bear fell to the shot, and could not get up from the ground, dying in a few minutes; but first he seized his left wrist in his teeth and bit clean through it, completely separating the bones of the paw and arm. Although a smaller bear than the big one I first shot, he would probably have proved a much more ugly foe, for he was less unwieldy, and had much longer and sharper teeth and claws. I think that if my companion had merely broken the beast's leg he would have had his curiosity as to its probable conduct more than gratified.

We tried eating the grizzly's flesh but it was not good, being coarse and not well flavored; and besides, we could not get over the feeling that it had belonged to a carrion feeder. The flesh of the little black bear, on the other hand, was excellent; it tasted like that of a young pig. Doubtless, if a young grizzly, which had fed merely upon fruits, berries, and acorns, was killed, its flesh would prove good eating; but even then, it would probably not be equal to a black bear.

A day or two after the death of the big bear, we went out one afternoon on horseback, intending merely to ride down to see a great canyon lying some six miles west of our camp; indeed, we went more to look at the scenery than for any other reason, though, of course, neither of us ever stirred out of camp without his rifle. We rode down the valley in which we had camped, through alternate pine groves and open glades, until we reached the canyon, and then skirted its brink for a mile or so. It was a great chasm, many miles in length, as if the table-land had been rent asunder by some terrible and unknown force; its sides were sheer walls of rock, rising three or four hundred feet straight up in the air, and worn by the weather till they looked like the towers and battlements of some vast fortress. Between them at the bottom was a space, in some places nearly a quarter of a mile wide, in others very narrow, through whose middle foamed a deep, rapid torrent of which the sources lay far back among the snow-topped mountains around Cloud Peak. In this valley, dark-green, sombre pines stood in groups, stiff and erect; and here and there among them were groves of poplar and cottonwood, with slender branches and trembling leaves, their bright green already changing to yellow in the sharp fall weather. We went down to where the mouth of the canyon opened out, and rode our horses to the end of a great jutting promontory of rock, thrust out into the plain; and in the cold, clear air we looked far over the broad valley of the Bighorn as it lay at our very feet, walled in on the other side by the distant chain of the Rocky Mountains.

Turning our horses, we rode back along the edge of another canyon-like valley, with a brook flowing down its centre, and its rocky sides covered with an uninterrupted pine forest—the place of all others in whose inaccessible wildness and ruggedness a bear would find a safe retreat. After some time we came to where other valleys, with steep, grass-grown sides, covered with sage-brush, branched out from it, and we followed one of these out. There was plenty of elk sign about, and we saw several black-tail deer. These last were very common on the mountains, but we had not hunted them at all, as we were in no need of meat. But this afternoon we came across a buck with remarkably fine antlers, and accordingly I shot it, and we stopped to cut off and skin out the horns, throwing the reins over the heads of the horses and leaving them to graze by themselves. The body lay near the crest of one side of a deep valley, or ravine, which headed up on the plateau a mile to our left. Except for scattered trees and bushes the valley was bare; but there was heavy timber along the crests of the hills on its opposite side. It took some time to fix the head properly, and we were just ending when Merrifield sprang to his feet and exclaimed: "Look at the bears!" pointing down into the valley below us. Sure enough there were two bears (which afterwards proved to be an old she and a nearly full-grown cub) travelling up the bottom of the valley, much too far off for us to shoot. Grasping our rifles and throwing off our hats we started off as hard as we could run, diagonally down the hill-side, so as to cut them off. It was some little time before they saw us, when they made off at a lumbering gallop up the valley. It would seem impossible to run into two grizzlies in the open, but they were going up-hill and we down, and moreover the old one kept stopping. The cub would forge ahead and could probably have escaped us, but the mother now and then stopped to sit up on her haunches and look round at us, when the cub would run back to her. The upshot was that we got ahead of them, when they turned and went straight up one hill-side as we ran straight down the other behind them. By this time I was pretty nearly done out, for running along the steep ground through the sage-brush was most exhausting work; and Merrifield kept gaining on me and was well in front. Just as he disappeared over a bank, almost at the bottom of the valley, I tripped over a bush and fell full-length. When I got up I knew I could never make up the ground I had lost, and besides, could hardly run any longer; Merrifield was out of sight below, and the bears were laboring up the steep hill-side directly opposite and about three hundred yards off, so I sat down and began to shoot over Merrifield's head, aiming at the big bear. She was going very steadily and in a straight line, and each bullet sent up a puff of dust where it struck the dry soil, so that I could keep correcting my aim; and the fourth ball crashed into the old bear's flank. She lurched heavily forward, but recovered herself and reached the timber, while Merrifield, who had put on a spurt, was not far behind.

I toiled up the hill at a sort of trot, fairly gasping and sobbing for breath; but before I got to the top I heard a couple of shots and a shout. The old bear had turned as soon as she was in the timber, and came towards Merrifield, but he gave her the death wound by firing into her chest, and then shot at the young one, knocking it over. When I came up he was just walking towards the latter to finish it with the revolver, but it suddenly jumped up as lively as ever and made off at a great pace—for it was nearly full-grown. It was impossible to fire where the tree trunks were so thick, but there was a small opening across which it would have to pass, and collecting all my energies I made a last run, got into position, and covered the opening with my rifle. The instant the bear appeared I fired, and it turned a dozen somersaults downhill, rolling over and over; the ball had struck it near the tail and had ranged forward through the hollow of the body. Each of us had thus given the fatal wound to the bear into which the other had fired the first bullet. The run, though short, had been very sharp, and over such awful country that we were completely fagged out, and could hardly speak for lack of breath. The sun had already set, and it was too late to skin the animals; so we merely dressed them, caught the ponies—with some trouble, for they were frightened at the smell of the bear's blood on our hands,—and rode home through the darkening woods. Next day we brought the teamster and two of the steadiest pack-horses to the carcasses, and took the skins into camp.

The feed for the horses was excellent in the valley in which we were camped, and the rest after their long journey across the plains did them good. They had picked up wonderfully in condition during our stay on the mountains; but they were apt to wander very far during the night, for there were so many bears and other wild beasts around that they kept getting frightened and running off. We were very loath to leave our hunting grounds, but time was pressing, and we had already many more trophies than we could carry; so one cool morning, when the branches of the evergreens were laden with the feathery snow that had fallen overnight, we struck camp and started out of the mountains, each of us taking his own bedding behind his saddle, while the pack-ponies were loaded down with bearskins, elk and deer antlers, and the hides and furs of other game. In single file we moved through the woods, and across the canyons to the edge of the great table-land, and then slowly down the steep slope to its foot, where we found our canvas-topped wagon; and next day saw us setting out on our long journey homewards, across the three hundred weary miles of treeless and barren-looking plains country.

Last spring, since the above was written, a bear killed

a man not very far from my ranch. It was at the time of the floods. Two hunters came down the river, by our ranch, on a raft, stopping to take dinner. A score or so of miles below, as we afterwards heard from the survivor, they landed, and found a bear in a small patch of brushwood. After waiting in vain for it to come out, one of the men rashly attempted to enter the thicket, and was instantly struck down by the beast, before he could so much as fire his rifle. It broke in his skull with a blow of its great paw, and then seized his arm in its jaws, biting it through and through in three places, but leaving the body and retreating into the bushes as soon as the unfortunate man's companion approached. We did not hear of the accident until too late to go after the bear, as we were just about starting to join the spring round-up.

ADDENDUM

In speaking of the trust antelope place in their eyesight as a guard against danger, I do not mean to imply that their noses are not also very acute; it is as important with them as with all other game to prevent their getting the hunter's wind. So with deer; while their eyes are not as sharp as those of big-horn and prong-horn, they are yet quite keen enough to make it necessary for the still-hunter to take every precaution to avoid being seen.

Although with us antelope display the most rooted objection to entering broken or wooded ground, yet a friend of mine, whose experience in the hunting-field is many times as great as my own, tells me that in certain parts of the country they seem by preference to go among the steepest and roughest placcs (of course, in so doing, being obliged to make vertical as well as horizontal leaps), and even penetrate into thick woods. Indeed, no other species seems to show such peculiar "freakiness" of character, both individually and locally.

The Wilderness Hunter

TO
E.K.R.

"They saw the silences
Move by and beckon; saw the forms,
The very beards, of burly storms,
And heard them talk like sounding seas . . .
They saw the snowy mountains rolled
And heaved along the nameless lands
Like mighty billows; saw the gold
Of awful sunsets; saw the blush
Of sudden dawn, and felt the hush
Of heaven when the day sat down
And hid his face in dusky hands."

Joaquin Miller

"In vain the speeding or shyness;
In vain the elk takes to the inner passes of the woods. . .
    . . . where geese nip their food with short jerks,
Where sundown shadows lengthen over the limitless
    prairie,
Where herds of buffalo make a crawling spread of the
    square miles, far and near,
Where winter wolves bark amid wastes of snow and ice-
    clad trees . . .
The moose, large as an ox, cornered by hunters plunging
    with his forefeet, the hoofs as sharp as knives . . .
The blazing fire at night, the sweet taste of supper, the
    talk, the bed of hemlock boughs, and the bear-skin."

Walt Whitman

CONTENTS

trip—A shot from the ranch-house verandah—The Columbian blacktail

dawn—Young ram shot—A hunt in the Rocky Mountains—
An old bighorn stalked and shot—Habits of the game

chipmunks—Clarke's crow—Lewis' woodpecker—Whisky-jack—Trout—The Yellowstone canyon

In the Shoshones—Travelling with a pack-train—Scenery—Flowers—A squaw-man—Bull elk shot in rain while challenging—Storm—Breaking camp in rain—Two-Ocean Pass—Our camp—A young ten-pointer shot—The mountains in moonlight—Blue grouse—Snow-shoe rabbits—Death of a master bull—The Tetons—Following a bull by scent—Ill luck—Luck changes—Death of spike bull—Three bulls killed—Travelling home—Heavy snowstorm—Bucking horse—Various hunts compared—Number cartridges used—Still-hunting the elk

The moose of the Rocky Mountains—Its habits—Difficult nature of its haunts—Repeated failures while hunting it—Watching a marsh at dawn—A moose in the reeds—Stalking and shooting him—Travelling light with a pack-train—A beaver meadow—Shooting a big bull at dawn—The moose in summer; in winter—Young moose—Pugnacity of moose—Still-hunting moose—Rather more easy to kill than whitetail deer—At times a dangerous antagonist—The winter yards—Hunting on snow-shoes—A narrow escape—A fatal encounter

Extermination of the bison—My brother and cousin take a hunting trip in Texas—Hardships—Hunting on the Brazos—Many buffalo slain—Following four bulls—A stampede—

Splitting the herd—Occasional charges—A Comanche war party—Great herds on the Arkansas—Adventure of Clarence King—The bison of the mountains—At the vanishing point—A hunt for mountain bison—A trail discovered—Skilful tracking—A band of six—Death of the bull—A camp in the canyon on second day—Shot at a grisly—His resolute charge and death—Danger in hunting the grisly—Exaggerated, but real—Rogers charged—Difference in ferocity in different bears—Dr. Merrill's queer experience—Tazewell Woody's adventures—Various ways in which bears attack—Examples—Men maimed and slain—Instances—Mr. Whitney's experience—A bear killed on the round-up—Ferocity of old-time bears—Occasional unprovoked attacks—A French trapper attacked—Cowboys and bears—Killing them with a revolver—Feat of General Jackson

Difficulty of killing the cougar—My own failures—Kill one in the mountains—Hunting the cougar with hounds—Experience of General Wade Hampton and Col. Cecil Clay—"Hold on, Penny"—What the cougar preys on—Its haunts—Its calls—Rarely turns on man—Occasionally dangerous—Instances

A trip in southern Texas—A ranch on the Frio—Roping cattle—Extermination of the peccary—Odd habits—Occasionally attacks unprovoked—We drive south to the Nueces—Flower prairies—Semi-tropical landscape—Hunting on horseback—Half-blood hounds—Find a small band of peccaries—Kill two—How they act when at bay—Their occasional freaks

Old-time hunters rarely used dogs—The packs of the southern planters—Coursing in the West—Hunting with greyhounds near my ranch—Jack-rabbits, foxes, coyotes, antelope, and

PREFACE

For a number of years much of my life was spent either in the wilderness or on the borders of the settled country—if, indeed, "settled" is a term that can rightly be applied to the vast, scantily peopled regions where cattle-ranching is the only regular industry. During this time I hunted much, among the mountains and on the plains, both as a pastime and to procure hides, meat, and robes for use on the ranch; and it was my good luck to kill all the various kinds of large game that can properly be considered to belong to temperate North America.

In hunting, the finding and killing of the game is after all but a part of the whole. The free, self-reliant, adventurous life, with its rugged and stalwart democracy; the wild surroundings, the grand beauty of the scenery, the chance to study the ways and habits of the woodland creatures—all these unite to give to the career of the wilderness hunter its peculiar charm. The chase is among the best of all national pastimes; it cultivates that vigorous manliness for the lack of which in a nation, as in an individual, the possession of no other qualities can possibly atone.

No one, but he who has partaken thereof, can understand the keen delight of hunting in lonely lands. For him is the joy of the horse well ridden and the rifle well held; for him the long days of toil and hardship, resolutely endured, and crowned at the end with triumph. In after years there shall come forever to his mind the memory of endless prairies shimmering in the bright sun; of vast snowclad wastes lying desolate under gray skies; of the melancholy marshes; of the rush of mighty rivers; of the breath of the evergreen forest in summer; of the crooning of ice-armored pines at the touch of the winds of winter; of cataracts roaring between hoary mountain masses; of all the innumerable sights and sounds of the wilderness; of its immensity and mystery; and of the silences that brood in its still depths.

THEODORE ROOSEVELT

SAGAMORE HILL,
JUNE, 1893

The American Wilderness; Wilderness Hunters and Wilderness Game

Manifold are the shapes taken by the American wilderness. In the east, from the Atlantic coast to the Mississippi valley, lies a land of magnificent hardwood forest. In endless variety and beauty, the trees cover the ground, save only where they have been cleared away by man, or where towards the west the expanse of the forest is broken by fertile prairies. Towards the north, this region of hardwood trees merges insensibly into the southern extension of the great subarctic forest; here the silver stems of birches gleam against the sombre background of coniferous evergreens. In the southeast again, by the hot, oozy coasts of the South Atlantic and the Gulf, the forest becomes semi-tropical; palms wave their feathery fronds, and the tepid swamps teem with reptile life.

Some distance beyond the Mississippi, stretching from Texas to North Dakota, and westward to the Rocky Mountains, lies the plains country. This is a region of light rainfall, where the ground is clad with short grass, while cottonwood trees fringe the courses of the winding plains streams; streams that are alternately turbid torrents and mere dwindling threads of water. The great stretches of natural pasture are broken by gray sage-brush plains, and tracts of strangely shaped and colored Bad Lands; sun-scorched wastes in summer, and in winter arctic in their iron desolation. Beyond the plains rise the Rocky Mountains, their flanks covered with coniferous woods; but the trees are small, and do not ordinarily grow very closely together. Towards the north the forest becomes denser, and the peaks higher; and glaciers creep down towards the valleys from the fields of everlasting snow. The brooks are brawling, trout-filled torrents; the swift rivers foam over rapid and cataract, on their way to one or the other of the two great oceans.

Southwest of the Rockies evil and terrible deserts stretch for leagues and leagues, mere waterless wastes of sandy plain and barren mountain, broken here and there by narrow strips of fertile ground. Rain rarely falls, and there are no clouds to dim the brazen sun. The rivers run in deep canyons, or are swallowed by the burning sand; the smaller watercourses are dry throughout the greater part of the year.

Beyond this desert region rise the sunny Sierras of California, with their flower-clad slopes and groves of giant trees; and north of them, along the coast, the rain-shrouded mountain chains of Oregon and Washington, matted with the towering growth of the mighty evergreen forest.

The white hunters, who from time to time first penetrated the different parts of this wilderness, found themselves in such hunting grounds as those wherein, long ages before, their Old-World forefathers had dwelt; and the game they chased was much the same as that their lusty barbarian ancestors followed, with weapons of bronze and of iron, in the dim years before history dawned. As late as the end of the seventeenth century the turbulent village nobles of Lithuania and Livonia hunted the bear, the bison, the elk, the wolf, and the stag, and hung the spoils in their smoky wooden palaces; and so, two hundred years later, the free hunters of Montana, in the interludes between hazardous mining quests and bloody Indian campaigns, hunted game almost or quite the same in kind, through the cold mountain forests surrounding the Yellowstone and Flathead lakes, and decked their log cabins and ranch houses with the hides and horns of the slaughtered beasts.

Zoölogically speaking, the north temperate zones of the Old and New Worlds are very similar, differing from one another much less than they do from the various regions south of them, or than these regions differ among themselves. The untrodden American wilderness resembles both in game and physical character the forests, the mountains, and the steppes of the Old World as it was at the beginning of our era. Great woods of pine and fir, birch and beech, oak and chestnut; streams where the chief game fish are spotted trout and silvery salmon; grouse of various kinds as the most common game birds; all these the hunter finds as characteristic of the New World as of the Old. So it is with most of the beasts of the chase, and so also with the fur-bearing animals that furnish to the trapper alike his life work and his means of livelihood. The bear, wolf, bison, moose, caribou, wapiti, deer, and bighorn, the lynx, fox, wolverine, sable, mink, ermine, beaver, badger, and otter of both worlds are either identical or more or less closely kin to one another. Sometimes of the two forms, that found in the Old World is the largest. Perhaps more often the reverse is true, the American beast being superior in size. This is markedly the case with the wapiti, which is merely a giant brother of the European stag, exactly as the fisher is merely a very large cousin of the European sable or marten. The extraordinary prong-buck, the only hollow-horned ruminant which sheds its horns annually, is a distant representative of the Old-World antelopes of the steppes; the queer white antelope-goat has for its nearest kinsfolk certain Himalayan species. Of the animals commonly known to our hunters and trappers, only a few, such as the cougar, peccary, raccoon, possum (and among birds the wild turkey), find their nearest representatives and type forms in tropical America.

Of course this general resemblance does not mean identity. The differences in plant life and animal life, no less than in the physical features of the land, are sufficiently marked to give the American wilderness a character distinctly its own. Some of the most characteristic of the woodland animals, some of those which have most vividly impressed themselves on the imagination of the hunters and pioneer settlers, are the very ones which have no Old-World representatives. The wild turkey is in every way the king of American game birds. Among the small beasts the coon and the possum are those which have left the deepest traces in the humbler lore of the frontier; exactly as the cougar—usually under the name of panther or mountain lion—is a favorite figure in the wilder hunting tales. Nowhere else is there anything to match the wealth of the eastern hardwood forests, in number, variety, and beauty of trees; nowhere else is it possible to find conifers approaching in size the giant redwoods and sequoias of the Pacific slope. Nature here is generally on a larger scale than in the Old-World home of our race. The lakes are like inland seas, the rivers like arms of the sea. Among stupendous mountain chains there are valleys and canyons of fathomless depth and incredible beauty and majesty. There are tropical swamps, and sad, frozen marshes; deserts and Death Valleys, weird and evil, and the strange wonderland of the Wyoming geyser region. The waterfalls are rivers rushing over precipices; the prairies seem without limit, and the forest never ending.

At the time when we first became a nation, nine tenths of the territory now included within the limits of the United States was wilderness. It was during the stirring and troubled years immediately preceding the outbreak of the Revolution that the most adventurous hunters, the vanguard of the hardy army of pioneer settlers, first crossed the Alleghanies, and roamed far and wide through the lonely, danger-haunted forests which filled the No-man's-land lying between the Tennessee and the Ohio. They waged ferocious warfare with Shawnee and Wyandott and wrought huge havoc among the herds of game with which the forests teemed. While the first Continental Congress was still sitting, Daniel Boone, the archetype of the American hunter, was leading his bands of tall backwoods riflemen to settle in the beautiful country of Kentucky, where the red and the white warriors strove with such obstinate rage that both races alike grew to know it as "the dark and bloody ground."

Boone and his fellow-hunters were the heralds of the oncoming civilization, the pioneers in that conquest of the wilderness which has at last been practically achieved in our own day. Where they pitched their camps and built their log huts or stockaded hamlets, towns grew up, and men who were tillers of the soil, not mere wilderness wanderers, thronged in to take and hold the land. Then, ill-at-ease among the settlements for which they had themselves made ready the way, and fretted even by the slight restraints of the rude and uncouth semi-civilization of the border, the restless hunters moved onward into the yet unbroken wilds where the game dwelt and the red tribes marched forever to war and hunting. Their untamable souls ever found something congenial and beyond measure attractive in the lawless freedom of the lives of the very savages against whom they warred so bitterly.

Step by step, often leap by leap, the frontier of settlement was pushed westward; and ever from before its advance fled the warrior tribes of the red men and the scarcely less intractable array of white Indian fighters and game hunters. When the Revolutionary war was at its height, George Rogers Clarke, himself a mighty hunter of the old backwoods type, led his handful of hunter-soldiers to the conquest of the French towns of the Illinois. This was but one of the many notable feats of arms performed by the wild soldiery of the backwoods. Clad in their fringed and tasselled hunting shirts of buckskin or homespun, with coonskin caps and deer-hide leggings and moccasins, with tomahawk and scalping knife thrust into their bead-worked belts, and long rifles in hand, they fought battle after battle of the most bloody character, both against the Indians, as at the Great Kanawha, at the Fallen Timbers, and at Tippecanoe, and against more civilized foes, as at King's Mountain, New Orleans, and the River Thames.

Soon after the beginning of the present century Louisiana fell into our hands, and the most daring hunters and explorers pushed through the forests of the Mississippi valley to the great plains, steered across these vast seas of grass to the Rocky Mountains, and then through their rugged defiles onwards to the Pacific Ocean. In every work of exploration, and in all the earlier battles with the original lords of the western and southwestern lands, whether Indian or Mexican, the adventurous hunters played the leading part; while close behind came the swarm of hard, dogged, border-farmers,—a masterful race, good fighters and good breeders, as all masterful races must be.

Very characteristic in its way was the career of quaint, honest, fearless Davy Crockett, the Tennessee rifleman and Whig Congressman, perhaps the best shot in all our country, whose skill in the use of his favorite weapon passed into a proverb, and who ended his days by a hero's death in the ruins of the Alamo. An even more notable man was another mighty hunter, Houston, who when a boy ran away to the Indians; who while still a lad returned to his own people to serve under Andrew Jackson in the campaigns which that greatest of all the backwoods leaders waged against the Creeks, the Spaniards, and the British. He was wounded at the storming of one of the strongholds of Red Eagle's doomed warriors, and returned to his Tennessee home to rise to high civil honor, and become the foremost man of his State. Then, while Governor of Tennessee, in a sudden fit of moody anger, and of mad longing for the unfettered life of the wilderness, he abandoned his office, his people, and his race, and fled to the Cherokees beyond the Mississippi. For years he lived as one of their chiefs; until one day, as he lay in ignoble ease and sloth, a rider from the south, from the rolling plains of the San Antonio and Brazos, brought word that the Texans were up, and in doubtful struggle striving to wrest their freedom from the lancers and carbineers of Santa Anna. Then his dark soul flamed again into burning life; riding by night and day he joined the risen Texans, was hailed by them as a heaven-sent leader, and at the San Jacinto led them on to the overthrow of the Mexican host. Thus the stark hunter, who had been alternately Indian fighter and Indian chief, became the President of the new Republic, and, after its admission into the United States, a Senator at Washington; and, to his high honor, he remained to the end of his days staunchly loyal to the flag of the Union.

By the time that Crockett fell, and Houston became the darling leader of the Texans, the typical hunter and Indian fighter had ceased to be a backwoodsman; he had become a plains-man, or mountain-man; for the frontier, east of which he never willingly went, had been pushed beyond the Mississippi. Restless, reckless, and hardy, he spent years of his life in lonely wanderings through the Rockies as a trapper; he guarded the slow-moving caravans, which for purposes of trade journeyed over the dangerous Santa Fé trail; he guided the large parties of frontier settlers who, driving before them their cattle, with all their household goods in their white-topped wagons, spent perilous months and seasons on their weary way to

Oregon or California. Joining in bands, the stalwart, skin-clad riflemen waged ferocious war on the Indians scarcely more savage than themselves, or made long raids for plunder and horses against the outlying Mexican settlements. The best, the bravest, the most modest of them all was the renowned Kit Carson. He was not only a mighty hunter, a daring fighter, a finder of trails, and maker of roads through the unknown, untrodden wilderness, but also a real leader of men. Again and again he crossed and re-crossed the continent, from the Mississippi to the Pacific; he guided many of the earliest military and exploring expeditions of the United States Government; he himself led the troops in victorious campaigns against Apache and Navahoe; and in the Civil War he was made a colonel of the Federal army.

After him came many other hunters. Most were pure-blooded Americans, but many were Creole Frenchmen, Mexicans, or even members of the so-called civilized Indian tribes, notably the Delawares. Wide were their wanderings, many their strange adventures in the chase, bitter their unending warfare with the red lords of the land. Hither and thither they roamed, from the desolate, burning deserts of the Colorado to the grassy plains of the Upper Missouri; from the rolling Texas prairies, bright beneath their sunny skies, to the high snow peaks of the northern Rockies, or the giant pine forests, and soft rainy weather, of the coasts of Puget Sound. Their main business was trapping, furs being the only articles yielded by the wilderness, as they knew it, which were both valuable and portable. These early hunters were all trappers likewise, and, indeed, used their rifles only to procure meat or repel attacks. The chief of the fur-bearing animals they followed was the beaver, which abounded in the streams of the plains and mountains; in the far north they also trapped otter, mink, sable, and fisher. They married squaws from among the Indian tribes with which they happened for the moment to be at peace; they acted as scouts for the United States troops in their campaigns against the tribes with which they happened to be at war.

Soon after the Civil War the life of these hunters, taken as a class, entered on its final stage. The Pacific coast was already fairly well settled, and there were a few mining camps in the Rockies; but most of this Rocky Mountains region, and the entire stretch of plains country proper, the vast belt of level or rolling grass land lying between the Rio Grande and the Saskatchewan, still remained primeval wilderness, inhabited only by roving hunters and formidable tribes of Indian nomads, and by the huge herds of game on which they preyed. Beaver swarmed in the streams and yielded a rich harvest to the trapper; but trapping was no longer the mainstay of the adventurous plainsmen. Foremost among the beasts of the chase, on account of its numbers, its size, and its economic importance, was the bison or American buffalo: its innumerable multitudes darkened the limitless prairies. As the transcontinental railroads were pushed towards completion, and the tide of settlement rolled onwards with ever increasing rapidity, buffalo robes became of great value. The hunters forthwith turned their attention mainly to the chase of the great clumsy beasts, slaughtering them by hundreds of thousands for their hides; sometimes killing them on horseback, but more often on foot, by still-hunting, with the heavy long-range Sharp's rifle. Throughout the fifteen years during which this slaughter lasted, a succession of desperate wars was waged with the banded tribes of the Horse Indians. All the time, in unending succession, long trains of big white-topped wagons crept slowly westward across the prairies, marking the steady oncoming of the frontier settlers.

By the close of 1883 the last buffalo herd was destroyed. The beaver were trapped out of all the streams, or their numbers so thinned that it no longer paid to follow them. The last formidable Indian war had been brought to a successful close. The flood of the incoming whites had risen over the land; tongues of settlement reached from the Mississippi to the Rocky Mountains, and from the Rocky Mountains to the Pacific. The frontier had come to an end; it had vanished. With it vanished also the old race of wilderness hunters, the men who spent all their days in the lonely wilds, and who killed game as their sole means of livelihood. Great stretches of wilderness still remain in the Rocky Mountains, and here and there in the plains country, exactly as much smaller tracts of wild land are to be found in the Alleghanies and northern New York and New England; and on these tracts occasional hunters and trappers still linger; but as a distinctive class, with a peculiar and important position in American life, they no longer exist.

There were other men beside the professional hunters, who lived on the borders of the wilderness, and followed hunting, not only as a pastime, but also as yielding an important portion of their subsistence. The frontier farmers were all hunters. In the eastern backwoods, and in certain places in the west, as in Oregon, these adventurous tillers of the soil were the pioneers among the actual settlers; in the Rockies their places were taken by the miners, and on the great plains by the ranchmen and cowboys, the men who lived in the saddle, guarding their branded herds of horses and horned stock. Almost all of the miners and cowboys were obliged on occasions to turn hunters.

Moreover, the regular army which played so important a part in all the later stages of the winning of the west produced its full share of mighty hunters. The later Indian wars were fought principally by the regulars. The West Point officer and his little company of trained soldiers appeared abreast of the first hardy cattlemen and miners. The ordinary settlers rarely made their appearance until in campaign after campaign, always inconceivably wearing and harassing, and often very bloody in character, the scarred and tattered troops had broken and overthrown the most formidable among the Indian tribes. Faithful, uncomplaining, unflinching, the soldiers wearing the national uniform lived for many weary years at their lonely little posts, facing unending toil and danger with quiet endurance, surrounded by the desolation of vast solitudes, and menaced by the most merciless of foes. Hunting was followed not only as a sport, but also as the only means of keeping the posts and the expeditionary trains in meat. Many of the officers became equally proficient as marksmen and hunters. The three most famous Indian fighters since the Civil War, Generals Custer, Miles, and Crook, were all keen and successful followers of the chase.

Of American big game the bison, almost always

known as the buffalo, was the largest and most important to man. When the first white settlers landed in Virginia the bison ranged east of the Alleghanies almost to the sea-coast, westward to the dry deserts lying beyond the Rocky Mountains, northward to the Great Slave Lake and southward to Chihuahua. It was a beast of the forests and mountains, in the Alleghanies no less than in the Rockies; but its true home was on the prairies, and the high plains. Across these it roamed, hither and thither, in herds of enormous, of incredible magnitude; herds so large that they covered the waving grass land for hundreds of square leagues, and when on the march occupied days and days in passing a given point. But the seething myriads of shaggy-maned wild cattle vanished with remarkable and melancholy rapidity before the inroads of the white hunters, and the steady march of the oncoming settlers. Now they are on the point of extinction. Two or three hundred are left in that great national game preserve, the Yellowstone Park; and it is said that others still remain in the wintry desolation of Athabasca. Elsewhere only a few individuals exist—probably considerably less than half a hundred all told—scattered in small parties in the wildest and most remote and inaccessible portions of the Rocky Mountains. A bison bull is the largest American animal. His huge bulk, his short, curved black horns, the shaggy mane clothing his great neck and shoulders, give him a look of ferocity which his conduct belies. Yet he is truly a grand and noble beast, and his loss from our prairies and forest is as keenly regretted by the lover of nature and of wild life as by the hunter.

Next to the bison in size, and much superior in height

to it and to all other American game—for it is taller than the tallest horse—comes the moose, or broad-horned elk. It is a strange, uncouth-looking beast, with very long legs, short thick neck, a big, ungainly head, a swollen nose, and huge shovel horns. Its home is in the cold, wet pine and spruce forests, which stretch from the sub-arctic region of Canada southward in certain places across our frontier. Two centuries ago it was found as far south as Massachusetts. It has now been exterminated from its former haunts in northern New York and Vermont, and is on the point of vanishing from northern Michigan. It is still found in northern Maine and northeastern Minnesota and in portions of northern Idaho and Washington; while along the Rockies it extends its range southward through western Montana to northwestern Wyoming, south of the Tetons. In 1884 I saw the fresh hide of one that was killed in the Bighorn Mountains.

The wapiti, or round-horned elk, like the bison, and unlike the moose, had its centre of abundance in the United States, though extending northward into Canada. Originally its range reached from ocean to ocean and it went in herds of thousands of individuals; but it has suffered more from the persecution of hunters than any other game except the bison. By the beginning of this century it had been exterminated in most localities east of the Mississippi; but a few lingered on for many years in the Alleghanies. Col. Cecil Clay informs me that an Indian whom he knew killed one in Pennsylvania in 1869. A very few still exist here and there in northern Michigan and Minnesota, and in one or two spots on the western boundary of Nebraska and the Dakotas; but it is now properly a beast of the wooded western mountains. It is still plentiful in western Colorado, Wyoming, and Montana, and in parts of Idaho, Washington, and Oregon. Though not as large as the moose it is the most beautiful and stately of all animals of the deer kind, and its antlers are marvels of symmetrical grandeur.

The woodland caribou is inferior to the wapiti both in size and symmetry. The tips of the many branches of its long, irregular antlers are slightly palmated. Its range is the same as that of the moose, save that it does not go so far southward. Its hoofs are long and round; even larger than the long, oval hoofs of the moose, and much larger than those of the wapiti. The tracks of all three can be told apart at a glance, and cannot be mistaken for the footprints of other game. Wapiti tracks, however, look much like those of yearling and two-year-old cattle, unless the ground is steep or muddy, in which case the marks of the false hoofs appear, the joints of wapiti being more flexible than those of domestic stock.

The whitetail deer is now, as it always has been, the best known and most abundant of American big game, and though its numbers have been greatly thinned it is still found in almost every State of the Union. The common blacktail or mule deer, which has likewise been sadly thinned in numbers, though once extraordinarily abundant, extends from the great plains to the Pacific; but is supplanted on the Puget Sound coast by the Columbian blacktail. The delicate, heart-shaped footprints of all three are nearly indistinguishable; when the animal is running the hoof prints are of course separated. The track of the antelope is more oval, growing squarer with age. Mountain sheep leave footmarks of a squarer shape, the points of the hoof making little indentations in the soil, well apart, even when the animal is only walking; and a yearling's track is not unlike that made by a big prong-buck when striding rapidly with the toes well apart. White-goat tracks are also square, and as large as those of the sheep; but there is less indentation of the hoof points, which come nearer together.

The antelope, or prong-buck, was once found in abundance from the eastern edge of the great plains to the Pacific, but it has everywhere diminished in numbers, and has been exterminated along the eastern and western borders of its former range. The bighorn, or mountain sheep, is found in the Rocky Mountains from northern Mexico to Alaska; and in the United States from the Coast and Cascade ranges to the Bad Lands of the western edges of the Dakotas, wherever there are mountain chains or tracts of rugged hills. It was never very abundant, and, though it has become less so, it has held its own better than most game. The white goat, however, alone among our game animals, has positively increased in numbers since the advent of settlers; because white hunters rarely follow it, and the Indians who once sought its skin for robes now use blankets instead. Its true home is in Alaska and Canada, but it crosses our borders along the lines of the Rockies and Cascades, and a few small isolated colonies are found here and there southward to California and New Mexico.

The cougar and wolf, once common throughout the United States, have now completely disappeared from all save the wildest regions. The black bear holds its own better; it was never found on the great plains. The huge grisly ranges from the great plains to the Pacific. The little peccary or Mexican wild hog merely crosses our southern border.

The finest hunting ground in America was, and indeed is, the mountainous region of western Montana and northwestern Wyoming. In this high, cold land, of lofty mountains, deep forests, and open prairies, with its beautiful lakes and rapid rivers, all the species of big game mentioned above, except the peccary and Columbian blacktail, are to be found. Until 1880 they were very abundant, and they are still, with the exception of the bison, fairly plentiful. On most of the long hunting expeditions which I made away from my ranch, I went into this region.

The bulk of my hunting has been done in the cattle country, near my ranch on the Little Missouri, and in the adjoining lands round the lower Powder and Yellowstone. Until 1881 the valley of the Little Missouri was fairly thronged with game, and was absolutely unchanged in any respect from its original condition of primeval wildness. With the incoming of the stockmen all this changed, and the game was wofully slaughtered; but plenty of deer and antelope, a few sheep and bear, and an occasional elk are still left.

Since the professional hunters have vanished, with the vast herds of game on which they preyed, the life of the ranchman is that which yields most chance of hunting. Life on a cattle ranch, on the great plains or among the foothills of the high mountains, has a peculiar attraction for those hardy, adventurous spirits who take most kindly to a vigorous out-of-doors existence, and who are therefore most apt to care passionately for the chase of big game. The free ranchman lives in a wild, lonely country, and exactly as he breaks and tames his own horses, and guards and tends his own branded herds, so he takes the keenest enjoyment in the chase, which is to him not merely the pleasantest of sports but also a means of adding materially to his comforts, and often his only method of providing himself with fresh meat.

Hunting in the wilderness is of all pastimes the most attractive, and it is doubly so when not carried on merely as a pastime. Shooting over a private game preserve is of course in no way to be compared to it. The wilderness hunter must not only show skill in the use of the rifle and address in finding and approaching game, but he must also show the qualities of hardihood, self-reliance, and resolution needed for effectively grappling with his wild surroundings. The fact that the hunter needs the game, both for its meat and for its hide, undoubtedly adds a zest to the pursuit. Among the hunts which I have most enjoyed were those made when I was engaged in getting in the winter's stock of meat for the ranch, or was keeping some party of cowboys supplied with game from day to day.

CHAPTER II

Hunting from the Ranch; The Blacktail Deer

No life can be pleasanter than life during the months of fall on a ranch in the northern cattle country. The weather is cool; in the evenings and on the rare rainy days we are glad to sit by the great fireplace, with its roaring cottonwood logs. But on most days not a cloud dims the serene splendor of the sky; and the fresh pure air is clear with the wonderful clearness of the high plains. We are in the saddle from morning to night.

The long, low, roomy ranch house, of clean hewed logs, is as comfortable as it is bare and plain. We fare simply but well; for the wife of my foreman makes excellent bread and cake, and there are plenty of potatoes, grown in the forlorn little garden-patch on the bottom. We also have jellies and jams, made from wild plums and buffalo berries; and all the milk we can drink. For meat we depend on our rifles; and, with an occasional interlude of ducks or prairie chickens, the mainstay of each meal is venison, roasted, broiled, or fried.

Sometimes we shoot the deer when we happen on them while about our ordinary business,—indeed throughout the time that I have lived on the ranch, very many of the deer and antelope I killed were thus obtained. Of course while doing the actual round-up work it is impossible to attend to anything else; but we generally carry rifles while riding after the saddle band in the early morning, while visiting the line camps, or while in the saddle among the cattle on the range; and get many a shot in this fashion.

In the fall of 1890 some friends came to my ranch; and one day we took them to see a round-up. The OX, a Texan steer-outfit, had sent a couple of wagons to work down the river, after beef cattle, and one of my men had gone along to gather any of my own scattered steers that were ready for shipping, and to brand the late calves. There were perhaps a dozen riders with the wagons; and they were camped for the day on a big bottom where Blacktail and Whitetail creeks open into the river, several miles below my ranch.

At dawn one of the men rode off to bring in the saddle band. The rest of us were up by sunrise; and as we stood on the verandah under the shimmering cottonwood trees, revelling in the blue of the cloudless sky, and drinking in the cool air before going to breakfast, we saw the motley-colored string of ponies file down from the opposite bank of the river, and splash across the broad, shallow ford in front of the ranch house. Cantering and trotting the band swept towards the high, round horse-corral, in the open glade to the rear of the house. Guided by the jutting wing which stuck out at right angles, they entered the open gate, which was promptly closed by the cowboy who had driven them in.

After breakfast we strolled over to the corral, with our lariats, and, standing by the snubbing-post in the middle, roped the horses we wished for the party—some that were gentle, and others that were not. Then every man saddled his horse; and at the moment of mounting for the start there was, as always, a thrill of mild excitement, each rider hoping that his own horse would not buck, and that his neighbor's would. I had no young horses on the ranch at the time; but a number of the older ones still possessed some of the least amiable traits of their youth.

Once in the saddle we rode off down river, along the bottoms, crossing the stream again and again. We went in Indian file, as is necessary among the trees and in broken ground, following the cattle-trails—which themselves had replaced or broadened the game paths that alone crossed the plateaus and bottoms when my ranch house was first built. Now we crossed open reaches of coarse grass, thinly sprinkled with large, brittle cottonwood trees, their branches torn and splintered; now we wound our way through a dense jungle where the gray, thorny buffalo bushes, spangled with brilliant red berry clusters, choked the spaces between the thick-growing box-alders; and again the sure-footed ponies scrambled down one cut bank and up another, through seemingly impossible rifts, or with gingerly footsteps trod a path which cut the side of a butte or overhung a bluff. Sometimes we racked, or shacked along at the fox trot which is the cow-pony's ordinary gait; and sometimes we loped or galloped and ran.

At last we came to the ford beyond which the riders of the round-up had made their camp. In the bygone days of the elk and buffalo, when our branded cattle were first driven thus far north, this ford had been dangerous from quicksand; but the cattle, ever crossing and re-crossing, had trodden down and settled the sand, and had found out the firm places; so that it was now easy to get over.

Close beyond the trees on the farther bank stood the two round-up wagons; near by was the cook's fire, in a trench, so that it might not spread; the bedding of the riders and horse-wranglers lay scattered about, each roll of blankets wrapped and corded in a stout canvas sheet. The cook was busy about the fire; the night-wrangler was snatching an hour or two's sleep under one of the wagons. Half a mile away, on the plain of sage-brush and long grass, the day-wrangler was guarding the grazing or resting horse herd, of over a hundred head. Still farther distant, at the mouth of a ravine, was the day-herd of cattle, two or three cowboys watching it as they lolled drowsily in their saddles. The other riders were off on circles to bring in cattle to the round-up; they were expected every moment.

With the ready hospitality always shown in a cow-camp we were pressed to alight and take dinner, or at least a lunch; and accordingly we jumped off our horses and sat down. Our tin plates were soon heaped with fresh beef, bread, tomatoes, rice, and potatoes, all very good; for the tall, bearded, scrawny cook knew his work, and the OX outfit always fed its men well,—and saw that they worked well too.

Before noon the circle riders began to appear on the plain, coming out of the ravines, and scrambling down the steep hills, singly or in twos and threes. They herded before them bunches of cattle, of varying size; these were driven together and left in charge of a couple of cowpunchers. The other men rode to the wagon to get a hasty dinner—lithe, sinewy fellows, with weather-roughened faces and fearless eyes; their broad felt hats flapped as they galloped, and their spurs and bridle chains jingled. They rode well, with long stirrups, sitting straight in the deep stock saddles, and their wiry ponies showed no signs of fatigue from the long morning's ride.

The horse-wrangler soon drove the saddle band to the wagons, where it was caught in a quickly improvised rope-corral. The men roped fresh horses, fitted for the cutting-work round the herd, with its attendant furious galloping and flash-like turning and twisting. In a few minutes all were in the saddle again and riding towards the cattle.

Then began that scene of excitement and turmoil, and seeming confusion, but real method and orderliness, so familiar to all who have engaged in stock-growing on the great plains. The riders gathered in a wide ring round the herd of uneasy cattle, and a couple of men rode into their midst to cut out the beef steers and the cows that were followed by unbranded calves. As soon as the animal was picked out the cowboy began to drive it slowly towards the outside of the herd, and when it was near the edge he suddenly raced it into the open. The beast would then start at full speed and try to double back among its fellows; while the trained cow-pony followed like a shadow, heading it off at every turn. The riders round that part of the herd opened out and the chosen animal was speedily hurried off to some spot a few hundred yards distant, where it was left under charge of another cowboy. The latter at first had his hands full in preventing his charge from rejoining the herd; for cattle dread nothing so much as being separated from their comrades. However, as soon as two or three others were driven out, enough to form a little bunch, it became a much easier matter to hold the "cut" as it is called. The cows and calves were put in one place, the beeves in another; the latter were afterwards run into the day-herd.

Meanwhile from time to time some clean-limbed young steer or heifer, able to run like an antelope and double like a jack-rabbit, tried to break out of the herd that was being worked, when the nearest cowboy hurried in pursuit at top speed and brought it back, after a headlong, break-neck race, in which no heed was paid to brush, fallen timber, prairie-dog holes, or cut banks. The dust rose in little whirling clouds, and through it dashed bolting cattle and galloping cowboys, hither and thither, while the air was filled with the shouts and laughter of the men, and the bellowing of the herd.

As soon as the herd was worked it was turned loose, while the cows and calves were driven over to a large corral, where the branding was done. A fire was speedily kindled, and in it were laid the branding irons of the different outfits represented on the round-up. Then two of the best ropers rode into the corral and began to rope the calves, round the hind legs by preference, but sometimes round the head. The other men dismounted to "wrestle" and brand them. Once roped, the calf, bawling and struggling, was swiftly dragged near the fire, where one or two of the calf-wrestlers grappled with and threw the kicking, plunging little beast, and held it while it was branded. If the calf was large the wrestlers had hard work; and one or two young maverick bulls—that is, unbranded yearling bulls, which had been passed by in the round-ups of the preceding year—fought viciously, bellowing and charging, and driving some of the men up the sides of the corral, to the boisterous delight of the others.

After watching the work for a little while we left and rode homewards. Instead of going along the river bottoms we struck back over the buttes. From time to time we came out on some sharp bluff overlooking the river. From these points of vantage we could see for several miles up and down the valley of the Little Missouri. The level bottoms were walled in by rows of sheer cliffs, and steep, grassy slopes. These bluff lines were from a quarter of a mile to a mile apart; they did not run straight, but in a succession of curves, so as to look like the halves of many amphitheatres. Between them the river swept in great bends from side to side; the wide bed, brimful during the time of freshets, now held but a thin stream of water. Some of the bottoms were covered only with grass and sage-brush; others with a dense jungle of trees; while yet others looked like parks, the cottonwoods growing in curved lines or in clumps scattered here and there.

On our way we came across a bunch of cattle, among which the sharp eyes of my foreman detected a maverick two-year-old heifer. He and one of the cowboys at once got down their ropes and rode after her; the rest of us first rounding up the bunch so as to give a fair start. After a sharp run one of the men, swinging his lariat round his head, got close up; in a second or two the noose settled round the heifer's neck, and as it became taut she was brought to with a jerk; immediately afterwards the other man made his throw and cleverly heeled her. In a trice the red heifer was stretched helpless on the ground, the two fierce little ponies, a pinto and a buckskin, keeping her down on their own account, tossing their heads and backing so that the ropes which led from the saddle-horns to her head and hind feet never slackened. Then we kindled a fire; one of the cinch rings was taken off to serve as a branding iron, and the heifer speedily became our property—for she was on our range.

When we reached the ranch it was still early, and after finishing dinner it lacked over an hour of sundown. Accordingly we went for another ride; and I carried my rifle. We started up a winding coulie which opened back of the ranch house; and after half an hour's canter clambered up the steep head-ravines, and emerged on a high ridge which went westward, straight as an arrow, to the main divide between the Little Missouri and the Big Beaver. Along this narrow, grassy crest we loped and galloped; we were so high that we could look far and wide over all the country round about. To the southward, across a dozen leagues of rolling and broken prairie, loomed Sentinel Butte, the chief landmark of all that region. Behind us, beyond the river, rose the weird chaos of Bad Lands which at this point lie for many miles east of the Little Missouri. Their fantastic outlines were marked against the sky as sharply as if cut with a knife; their grim and forbidding desolation warmed into wonderful beauty by the light of the dying sun. On our right, as we loped onwards, the land sunk away in smooth green-clad slopes and valleys; on our left it fell in sheer walls. Ahead of us the sun was sinking behind a mass of blood-red clouds; and on either hand the flushed skies were changing their tint to a hundred hues of opal and amethyst. Our tireless little horses sprang under us, thrilling with life; we were riding through a fairy world of beauty and color and limitless space and freedom.

Suddenly a short hundred yards in front three black-tail leaped out of a little glen and crossed our path, with the peculiar bounding gait of their kind. At once I sprang from my horse and, kneeling, fired at the last and largest of the three. My bullet sped too far back, but struck near the hip, and the crippled deer went slowly down a ravine. Running over a hillock to cut it off, I found it in some brush a few hundred yards beyond and finished it with a second ball. Quickly dressing it, I packed it on my horse, and trotted back leading him; an hour afterwards we saw through the waning light the quaint, home-like outlines of the ranch house.

After all, however, blacktail can only at times be picked up by chance in this way. More often it is needful to kill them by fair still-hunting, among the hills or wooded mountains where they delight to dwell. If hunted they speedily become wary. By choice they live in such broken country that it is difficult to pursue them with hounds; and they are by no means such water-loving animals as whitetail. On the other hand, the land in which they dwell is very favorable to the still-hunter who does not rely merely on stealth, but who can walk and shoot well. They do not go on the open prairie, and, if possible, they avoid deep forests, while, being good climbers, they like hills. In the mountains, therefore, they keep to what is called park country, where glades alternate with open groves. On the great plains they avoid both the heavily timbered river bottoms and the vast treeless stretches of level or rolling grass land; their chosen abode being the broken and hilly region, scantily wooded, which skirts almost every plains river and forms a belt, sometimes very narrow, sometimes many miles in breadth, between the alluvial bottom land and the prairies beyond. In these Bad Lands dwarfed pines and cedars grow in the canyon-like ravines and among the high steep hills; there are also basins and winding coulies, filled with brush and shrubbery and small elm or ash. In all such places the blacktail loves to make its home.

I have not often hunted blacktail in the mountains, because while there I was generally after larger game; but round my ranch I have killed more of them than of any other game, and for me their chase has always possessed a peculiar charm. We hunt them in the loveliest season of the year, the fall and early winter, when it is keen pleasure merely to live out-of-doors. Sometimes we make a regular trip, of several days' duration, taking the ranch wagon, with or without a tent, to some rugged and little disturbed spot where the deer are plenty; perhaps returning with eight or ten carcasses, or even more—enough to last a long while in cold weather. We often make such trips while laying in our winter supply of meat.

At other times we hunt directly from the ranch house. We catch our horses overnight, and are in the saddle for an all-day's hunt long before the first streak of dawn, possibly not returning until some hours after nightfall. The early morning and late evening are the best time for hunting game, except in regions where it is hardly ever molested, and where in consequence it moves about more or less throughout the day.

During the rut, which begins in September, the deer are in constant motion, and are often found in bands. The necks of the bucks swell and their sides grow gaunt; they chase the does all night, and their flesh becomes strong and stringy—far inferior to that of the barren does and yearlings. The old bucks then wage desperate conflicts with one another, and bully their smaller brethren unmercifully. Unlike the elk, the blacktail, like the whitetail, are generally silent in the rutting season. They occasionally grunt when fighting; and once, on a fall evening, I heard two young bucks barking in a ravine back of my ranch house, and crept up and shot them; but this was a wholly exceptional instance.

At this time I hunt on foot, only using the horse to carry me to and from the hunting ground; for while rutting, the deer, being restless, do not try to escape observation by lying still, and on the other hand are apt to wander about and so are easily seen from a distance. When I have reached a favorable place I picket my horse and go from vantage point to vantage point, carefully scanning the hillsides, ravines, and brush coulies from every spot that affords a wide outlook. The quarry once seen it may be a matter of hours, or only of minutes, to approach it, accordingly as the wind and cover are or are not favorable. The walks for many miles over the hills, the exercise of constant watchfulness, the excitement of the actual stalk, and the still greater excitement of the shot, combine to make still-hunting the blacktail, in the sharp fall weather, one of the most attractive of hardy outdoor sports. Then after the long, stumbling walk homewards, through the cool gloom of the late evening, comes the meal of smoking venison and milk and bread, and the sleepy rest, lying on the bear-skins, or sitting in the rocking chair before the roaring fire, while the icy wind moans outside.

Earlier in the season, while the does are still nursing the fawns, and until the bucks have cleaned the last vestiges of velvet from their antlers, the deer lie very close, and wander round as little as may be. In the spring and early summer, in the ranch country, we hunt big game very little, and then only antelope; because in hunting antelope there is no danger of killing aught but bucks. About the first of August we begin to hunt blacktail, but do not kill does until a month later—and then only when short of meat. In the early weeks of the deer season we frequently do even the actual hunting on horseback instead of on foot; because the deer at this time rarely appear in view, so as to afford chance for a stalk, and yet are reluctant to break cover until very closely approached. In consequence we keep on our horses', and so get over much more ground than on foot, beating through or beside all likely-looking cover, with the object of jumping the deer close by. Under such circumstances bucks sometimes lie until almost trodden on.

One afternoon in mid-August, when the ranch was entirely out of meat, I started with one of my cow-hands, Merrifield, to kill a deer. We were on a couple of stout, quiet ponies, accustomed to firing and to packing game. After riding a mile or two down the bottoms we left the river and struck off up a winding valley, which led back among the hills. In a short while we were in a blacktail country, and began to keep a sharp lookout for game, riding parallel to, but some little distance from, one another.

The sun, beating down through the clear air, was very hot; the brown slopes of short grass, and still more the white clay walls of the Bad Lands, threw the heat rays in our faces. We skirted closely all likely-looking spots, such as the heavy brush-patches in the bottoms of the winding valleys, and the groves of ash and elm in the basins and pockets flanking the high plateaus; sometimes we followed a cattle trail which ran down the middle of a big washout, and again we rode along the brink of a deep cedar canyon. After a while we came to a coulie with a small muddy pool at its mouth; and round this pool there was much fresh deer sign. The coulie was but half a mile long, heading into and flanked by the spurs of some steep, bare hills. Its bottom, which was fifty yards or so across, was choked by a dense growth of brush, chiefly thorny bullberries, while the sides were formed by cut banks twelve or fifteen feet high. My companion rode up the middle, while I scrambled up one of the banks, and, dismounting, led my horse along its edge, that I might have a clear shot at whatever we roused. We went nearly to the head, and then the cowboy reined up and shouted to me that he "guessed there were no deer in the coulie." Instantly there was a smashing in the young trees midway between us, and I caught a glimpse of a blacktail buck speeding round a shoulder of the cut bank; and though I took a hurried shot I missed. However, another buck promptly jumped up from the same place; evidently the two had lain secure in their day-beds, shielded by the dense cover, while the cowboy rode by them, and had only risen when he halted and began to call to me across them. This second buck, a fine fellow with big antlers not yet clear of velvet, luckily ran up the opposite bank and I got a fair shot at him as he galloped broadside to me along the open hillside. When I fired he rolled over with a broken back. As we came up he bleated loudly, an unusual thing for a buck to do.

Now these two bucks must have heard us coming, but reckoned on our passing them by without seeing them; which we would have done had they not been startled when the cowboy halted and spoke. Later in the season they would probably not have let us approach them, but would have run as soon as they knew of our presence. Of course, however, even later in the season, a man may by chance stumble across a deer close by. I remember one occasion when my ranch partner, Robert Munro Ferguson, and I almost corralled an unlucky deer in a small washout.

It was October, and our meat supply unexpectedly gave out; on our ranch, as on most ranches, an occasional meat famine of three or four days intervenes between the periods of plenty. So Ferguson and I started together, to get venison; and at the end of two days' hard work, leaving the ranch by sunrise, riding to the hunting grounds and tramping steadily until dark, we succeeded. The weather was stormy and there were continual gusts of wind and of cold rain, sleet, or snow. We hunted through a large tract of rough and broken country, six or eight miles from the ranch. As often happens in such wild weather the deer were wild too; they were watchful and were on the move all the time. We saw a number, but either they ran off before we could get a shot, or if we did fire it was at such a distance or under such unfavorable circumstances that we missed. At last, as we were plodding drearily up a bare valley, the sodden mud caking round our shoes, we roused three deer from the mouth of a short washout but a few paces from us. Two bounded off; the third by mistake rushed into the washout, where he found himself in a regular trap and was promptly shot by my companion. We slung the carcass on a pole and carried it down to where we had left the horses; and then we loped homewards, bending to the cold slanting rain.

Although in places where it is much persecuted the blacktail is a shy and wary beast, the successful pursuit of which taxes to the uttermost the skill and energy of the hunter, yet, like the elk, if little molested it often shows astonishing tameness and even stupidity. In the Rockies I have sometimes come on blacktail within a very short distance, which would merely stare at me, then trot off a few yards, turn and stare again, and wait for several minutes before really taking alarm. What is much more extraordinary I have had the same thing happen to me in certain little hunted localities in the neighborhood of my ranch, even of recent years. In the fall of 1890 I was riding down a canyon-coulie with my foreman, Sylvane Ferris, and a young friend from Boston, when we almost rode over a barren blacktail doe. She only ran some fifty yards, round a corner of the coulie, and then turned and stood until we ran forward and killed her—for we were in need of fresh meat. One October, a couple of years before this, my cousin, West Roosevelt, and I took a trip with the wagon to a very wild and rugged country, some twenty miles from the ranch. We found that the deer had evidently been but little disturbed. One day while scrambling down a steep, brushy hill, leading my horse, I came close on a doe and fawn; they merely looked at me with curiosity for some time, and then sauntered slowly off, remaining within shot for at least five minutes. Fortunately we had plenty of meat at the time, and there was no necessity to harm the graceful creatures. A few days later we came on two bucks sunning themselves in the bottom of a valley. My companion killed one. The other was lying but a dozen rods off; yet it never moved, until several shots had been fired at the first. It was directly under me and in my anxiety to avoid overshooting, to my horror I committed the opposite fault, and away went the buck.

Every now and then any one will make most unaccountable misses. A few days after thus losing the buck I spent nearly twenty cartridges in butchering an unfortunate yearling, and only killed it at all because it became so bewildered by the firing that it hardly tried to escape. I never could tell why I used so many cartridges to such little purpose. During the next fortnight I killed seven deer without making a single miss, though some of the shots were rather difficult.

CHAPTER III

The Whitetail Deer; And the Blacktail of the Columbia

The whitetail deer is much the commonest game animal of the United States, being still found, though generally in greatly diminished numbers throughout most of the Union. It is a shrewd, wary, knowing beast; but it owes its prolonged stay in the land chiefly to the fact that it is an inveterate skulker, and fond of the thickest cover. Accordingly it usually has to be killed by stealth and stratagem, and not by fair, manly hunting; being quite easily slain in any one of half a dozen unsportsmanlike ways. In consequence I care less for its chase than for the chase of any other kind of American big game. Yet in the few places where it dwells in open, hilly forests and can be killed by still-hunting as if it were a blacktail; or better still, where the nature of the ground is such that it can be run down in fair chase on horseback, either with greyhounds, or with a pack of trackhounds, it yields splendid sport.

Killing a deer from a boat while the poor animal is swimming in the water, or on snow-shoes as it flounders helplessly in the deep drifts, can only be justified on the plea of hunger. This is also true of lying in wait at a lick. Whoever indulges in any of these methods save from necessity, is a butcher, pure and simple, and has no business in the company of true sportsmen.

Fire hunting may be placed in the same category; yet it is possibly allowable under exceptional circumstances to indulge in a fire hunt, if only for the sake of seeing the wilderness by torch-light. My first attempt at big-game shooting, when a boy, was "jacking" for deer in the Adirondacks, on a pond or small lake surrounded by the grand northern forests of birch and beech, pine, spruce, and fir. I killed a spike buck; and while I have never been willing to kill another in this manner, I cannot say that I regret having once had the experience. The ride over the glassy, black water, the witchcraft of such silent progress through the mystery of the night, cannot but impress one. There is pleasure in the mere buoyant gliding of the birch-bark canoe, with its curved bow and stern; nothing else that floats possesses such grace, such frail and delicate beauty, as this true craft of the wilderness, which is as much a creature of the wild woods as the deer and bear themselves. The light streaming from the bark lantern in the bow cuts a glaring lane through the gloom; in it all objects stand out like magic, shining for a moment white and ghastly and then vanishing into the impenetrable darkness; while all the time the paddler in the stern makes not so much as a ripple, and there is never a sound but the occasional splash of a muskrat, or the moaning *uloo-oo—uloo-uloo* of an owl from the deep forests; and at last perchance the excitement of a shot at a buck, standing at gaze, with luminous eye-balls.

The most common method of killing the whitetail is by hounding; that is, by driving it with hounds past runways where hunters are stationed—for all wild animals when on the move prefer to follow certain definite routes. This is a legitimate, but inferior, kind of sport.

However, even killing driven deer may be good fun at certain times. Most of the whitetail we kill round the ranch are obtained in this fashion. On the Little Missouri—as throughout the plains country generally—these deer cling to the big wooded river bottoms, while the blacktail are found in the broken country back from the river. The tangled mass of cottonwoods, box-alders, and thorny bullberry bushes which cover the bottoms afford the deer a nearly secure shelter from the still-hunter; and it is only by the aid of hounds that they can be driven from their wooded fastnesses. They hold their own better than any other game. The great herds of buffalo, and the bands of elk, have vanished completely; the swarms of antelope and blacktail have been wofully thinned; but the whitetail, which were never found in such throngs as either buffalo or elk, blacktail or antelope, have suffered far less from the advent of the white hunters, ranchmen, and settlers. They are of course not as plentiful as formerly; but some are still to be found in almost all their old haunts. Where the river, winding between rows of high buttes, passes my ranch house, there is a long succession of heavily wooded bottoms; and on all of these, even on the one whereon the house itself stands, there are a good many whitetail yet left.

When we take a day's regular hunt we usually wander afar, either to the hills after blacktail or to the open prairie after antelope. But if we are short of meat, and yet have no time for a regular hunt, being perhaps able to spare only a couple of hours after the day's work is over, then all hands turn out to drive a bottom for whitetail. We usually have one or two trackhounds at the ranch; true southern deerhounds, black and tan, with lop ears and hanging lips, their wrinkled faces stamped with an expression of almost ludicrous melancholy. They are not fast, and have none of the alert look of the pied and spotted modern foxhound; but their noses are very keen, their voices deep and mellow, and they are wonderfully staunch on a trail.

All is bustle and laughter as we start on such a hunt. The baying hounds bound about, as the rifles are taken down; the wiry ponies are roped out of the corral, and each broad-hatted hunter swings joyfully into the saddle. If the pony bucks or "acts mean" the rider finds that his rifle adds a new element of interest to the performance, which is of course hailed with loud delight by all the men on quiet horses. Then we splash off over the river, scramble across the faces of the bluffs, or canter along the winding cattle paths, through the woods, until we come to the bottom we intend to hunt. Here a hunter is stationed at each runway along which it is deemed likely that the deer will pass; and one man, who has remained on horseback, starts into the cover with the hounds; occasionally this horseman himself, skilled, as most cowboys are, in the use of the revolver, gets a chance to kill a deer. The deep baying of the hounds speedily gives warning that the game is afoot; and the watching hunters, who have already hid their horses carefully, look to their rifles. Sometimes the deer comes far ahead of the dogs, running very swiftly with neck stretched straight out; and if the cover is thick such an animal is hard to hit. At other times, especially if the quarry is a young buck, it plays along not very far ahead of its baying pursuers, bounding and strutting with head up and white flag flaunting. If struck hard, down goes the flag at once, and the deer plunges into a staggering run, while the hounds yell with eager ferocity as they follow the bloody trail. Usually we do not have to drive more than one or two bottoms before getting a deer, which is forthwith packed behind one of the riders, as the distance is not great, and home we come in triumph. Sometimes, however, we fail to find game, or the deer take unguarded passes, or the shot is missed. Occasionally I have killed deer on these hunts; generally I have merely sat still a long while, listened to the hounds, and at last heard somebody else shoot. In fact such hunting, though good enough fun if only tried rarely, would speedily pall if followed at all regularly.

Personally the chief excitement I have had in connection therewith has arisen from some antic of my horse; a half-broken bronco is apt to become unnerved when a man with a gun tries to climb on him in a hurry. On one hunt in 1890 I rode a wild animal named Whitefoot. He had been a confirmed and very bad bucker three years before, when I had him in my string on the round-up; but had grown quieter with years. Nevertheless I found he had some fire left; for a hasty vault into the saddle on my part, was followed on his by some very resolute pitching. I lost my rifle and hat, and my revolver and knife were bucked out of my belt; but I kept my seat all right, and finally got his head up and mastered him without letting him throw himself over backwards, a trick he sometimes practised.

Nevertheless, in the first jump when I was taken unawares, I strained myself across the loins, and did not get
entirely over it for six months.

To shoot running game with the rifle it is always necessary to be a good and quick marksman; for it is never
easy to kill an animal, when in rapid motion, with a single
bullet. If on a runway a man who is a fairly skilful rifleman, has plenty of time for a clear shot, on open ground,
at comparatively short distance, say under eighty yards,
and if the deer is cantering, he ought to hit: at least I generally do under such circumstances, by remembering to
hold well forward, in fact just in front of the deer's chest.
But I do not always kill by any means; quite often when I
thought I held far enough ahead, my bullet has gone into
the buck's hips or loins. However, one great feature in the
use of dogs is that they enable one almost always to recover wounded game.

If the animal is running at full speed a long distance
off, the difficulty of hitting is of course very much increased; and if the country is open the value of a repeating
rifle is then felt. If the game is bounding over logs or
dodging through underbrush, the difficulty is again increased. Moreover, the natural gait of the different kinds
of game must be taken into account. Of course the larger
kinds, such as elk and moose, are the easiest to hit; then
comes the antelope, in spite of its swiftness, and the sheep,
because of the evenness of their running; then the white-
tail, with its rolling gallop; and last and hardest of all, the
blacktail, because of its extraordinary stiff-legged bounds.

Sometimes on a runway the difficulty is not that the
game is too far, but that it is too close; for a deer may ac-

tually almost jump on the hunter, surprising him out of all accuracy of aim. Once something of the sort happened to me.

Winter was just beginning. I had been off with the ranch wagon on a last round-up of the beef steers; and had suffered a good deal, as one always does on these cold weather round-ups, sleeping out in the snow, wrapped up in blankets and tarpaulin, with no tent and generally no fire. Moreover, I became so weary of the interminable length of the nights, that I almost ceased to mind the freezing misery of standing night guard round the restless cattle; while roping, saddling, and mastering the rough horses each morning, with numbed and stiffened limbs, though warming to the blood was harrowing to the temper.

On my return to the ranch I found a strange hunter staying there; a clean, square-built, honest-looking little fellow, but evidently not a native American. As a rule, nobody displays much curiosity about any one else's antecedents in the Far West; but I happened to ask my foreman who the new-comer was,—chiefly because the said new-comer, evidently appreciating the warmth and comfort of the clean, roomy, ranch house, with its roaring fires, books, and good fare, seemed inclined to make a permanent stay, according to the custom of the country. My foreman, who had a large way of looking at questions of foreign ethnology and geography, responded with indifference: "Oh, he's a kind of a Dutchman; but he hates the other Dutch, mortal. He's from an island Germany took from France in the last war!" This seemed puzzling; but it turned out that the "island" in question was Alsace. Native

Americans predominate among the dwellers in and on the borders of the wilderness, and in the wild country over which the great herds of the cattle-men roam; and they take the lead in every way. The sons of the Germans, Irish, and other European new-comers are usually quick to claim to be "straight United States," and to disavow all kinship with the fellow-countrymen of their fathers. Once, while with a hunter bearing a German name, we came by chance on a German hunting party from one of the eastern cities. One of them remarked to my companion that he must be part German himself, to which he cheerfully answered: "Well, my father was a Dutchman, but my mother was a white woman! I'm pretty white myself!" whereat the Germans glowered at him gloomily.

As we were out of meat the Alsatian and one of the cowboys and I started down the river with a wagon. The first day in camp it rained hard, so that we could not hunt. Towards evening we grew tired of doing nothing, and as the rain had become a mere fine drizzle, we sallied out to drive one of the bottoms for whitetail. The cowboy and our one trackhound plunged into the young cottonwood, which grew thickly over the sandy bottom; while the little hunter and I took our stands on a cut bank, twenty feet high and half a mile long, which hedged in the trees from behind. Three or four game trails led up through steep, narrow clefts in this bank; and we tried to watch these. Soon I saw a deer in an opening below, headed towards one end of the bank, round which another game trail led; and I ran hard towards this end, where it turned into a knife-like ridge of clay. About fifty yards from the point there must have been some slight irregularities in the face of the bank, enough to give the deer a foothold; for as I ran along the animal suddenly bounced over the crest, so close that I could have hit it with my right hand. As I tried to pull up short and swing round, my feet slipped from under me in the wet clay, and down I went; while the deer literally turned a terrified somersault backwards. I flung myself to the edge and missed a hurried shot as it raced back on its tracks. Then, wheeling, I saw the little hunter running towards me along the top of the cut bank, his face on a broad grin. He leaped over one of the narrow clefts, up which a game trail led; and hardly was he across before the frightened deer bolted up it, not three yards from his back. He did not turn, in spite of my shouting and handwaving, and the frightened deer, in the last stage of panic at finding itself again almost touching one of its foes, sped off across the grassy slopes like a quarter horse. When at last the hunter did turn, it was too late; and our long-range fusillade proved harmless. During the next two days I redeemed myself, killing four deer.

Coming back our wagon broke down, no unusual incident in ranch-land, where there is often no road, while the strain is great in hauling through quicksands, and up or across steep broken hills; it rarely makes much difference beyond the temporary delay, for plains-men and mountain-men are very handy and self-helpful. Besides, a mere break-down sinks into nothing compared to having the team play out; which is, of course, most apt to happen at the times when it insures hardship and suffering, as in the middle of a snowstorm, or when crossing a region with no water. However, the reinsmen of the plains must needs face many such accidents, not to speak of runaways, or

having the wagon pitchpole over on to the team in dropping down too steep a hillside. Once after a three days'
rainstorm some of us tried to get the ranch wagon along a
trail which led over the ridge of a gumbo or clay butte. The
sticky stuff clogged our shoes, the horses' hoofs, and the
wheels; and it was even more slippery than it was sticky.
Finally we struck a sloping shoulder; with great struggling, pulling, pushing, and shouting, we reached the middle of it, and then, as one of my men remarked, "the whole
darned outfit slid into the coulie."

These hunting trips after deer or antelope with the
wagon usually take four or five days. I always ride some
tried hunting horse; and the wagon itself when on such a
hunt is apt to lead a chequered career, as half the time
there is not the vestige of a trail to follow. Moreover we
often make a hunt when the good horses are on the
round-up, or otherwise employed, and we have to get together a scrub team of cripples or else of outlaws—vicious
devils, only used from dire need. The best teamster for
such a hunt that we ever had on the ranch was a weather-
beaten old fellow known as "Old Man Tompkins." In the
course of a long career as lumberman, plains teamster, buffalo hunter, and Indian fighter, he had passed several years
as a Rocky Mountain stage driver; and a stage driver of the
Rockies is of necessity a man of such skill and nerve that
he fears no team and no country. No matter how wild the
unbroken horses, Old Tompkins never asked help; and he
hated to drive less than a four-in-hand. When he once
had a grip on the reins, he let no one hold the horses'
heads. All he wished was an open plain for the rush at the
beginning. The first plunge might take the wheelers' fore-

feet over the cross-bars of the leaders, but he never stopped for that; on went the team, running, bounding, rearing, tumbling, while the wagon leaped behind, until gradually things straightened out of their own accord. I soon found, however, that I could not allow him to carry a rifle; for he was an inveterate game butcher. In the presence of game the old fellow became fairly wild with excitement, and forgot the years and rheumatism which had crippled him. Once, after a long and tiresome day's hunt, we were walking home together; he was carrying his boots in his hands, bemoaning the fact that his feet hurt him. Suddenly a whitetail jumped up; down dropped Old Tompkins' boots, and away he went like a college sprinter, entirely heedless of stones and cactus. By some indiscriminate firing at long range we dropped the deer; and as Old Tompkins cooled down he realized that his bare feet had paid full penalty for his dash.

One of these wagon trips I remember because I missed a fair running shot which I much desired to hit; and afterwards hit a very much more difficult shot about which I cared very little. Ferguson and I, with Sylvane and one or two others, had gone a day's journey down the river for a hunt. We went along the bottoms, crossing the stream every mile or so, with an occasional struggle through mud or quicksand, or up the steep, rotten banks. An old buffalo hunter drove the wagon, with a couple of shaggy, bandy-legged ponies; the rest of us jogged along in front on horseback, picking out a trail through the bottoms and choosing the best crossing places. Some of the bottoms were grassy pastures; on others great, gnarled cotton-woods, with shivered branches, stood in clumps; yet others were choked with a true forest growth. Late in the afternoon we went into camp, choosing a spot where the cottonwoods were young; their glossy leaves trembled and rustled unceasingly. We speedily picketed the horses—changing them about as they ate off the grass,—drew water, and hauled great logs in front of where we had pitched the tent, while the wagon stood nearby. Each man laid out his bed; the food and kitchen kit were taken from the wagon; supper was cooked and eaten; and we then lay round the camp-fire, gazing into it, or up at the brilliant stars, and listening to the wild, mournful wailing of the coyotes. They were very plentiful round this camp; before sunrise and after sundown they called unceasingly.

Next day I took a long tramp and climb after mountain sheep and missed a running shot at a fine ram, about a hundred yards off; or rather I hit him and followed his bloody trail a couple of miles, but failed to find him; whereat I returned to camp much cast down.

Early the following morning Sylvane and I started for another hunt, this time on horseback. The air was crisp and pleasant; the beams of the just-risen sun struck sharply on the umber-colored hills and white cliff walls guarding the river, bringing into high relief their strangely carved and channelled fronts. Below camp the river was little but a succession of shallow pools strung along the broad sandy bed which in spring-time was filled from bank to bank with foaming muddy water. Two mallards sat in one of these pools; and I hit one with the rifle, so nearly missing that the ball scarcely ruffled a feather; yet in some way the shock told, for the bird after flying thirty yards dropped on the sand.

Then we left the river and our active ponies scrambled up a small canyon-like break in the bluffs. All day we rode among the hills; sometimes across rounded slopes, matted with short buffalo grass; sometimes over barren buttes of red or white clay, where only sage brush and cactus grew; or beside deep ravines, black with stunted cedar; or along beautiful winding coulies, where the grass grew rankly, and the thickets of ash and wild plum made brilliant splashes of red and yellow and tender green. Yet we saw nothing.

As evening drew on we rode riverwards; we slid down the steep bluff walls, and loped across a great bottom of sage brush and tall grass, our horses now and then leaping like cats over the trunks of dead cottonwoods. As we came to the brink of the cut bank which forms the hither boundary of the river in freshet time, we suddenly saw two deer, a doe and a well grown fawn—of course long out of the spotted coat. They were walking with heads down along the edge of a sand-bar, near a pool, on the farther side of the stream bed, over two hundred yards distant. They saw us at once, and turning, galloped away, with flags aloft, the pictures of springing, vigorous beauty. I jumped off my horse in an instant, knelt, and covered the fawn. It was going straight away from me, running very evenly, and I drew a coarse sight at the tip of the white flag. As I pulled trigger down went the deer, the ball having gone into the back of its head. The distance was a good three hundred yards; and while of course there was much more chance than skill in the shot I felt well pleased with it—though I could not help a regret that while making such a difficult shot at a mere whitetail I should have missed a much easier shot at a noble bighorn. Not only I, but all the camp, had a practical interest in my success; for we had no fresh meat, and a fat whitetail fawn, killed in October, yields the best of venison. So after dressing the deer I slung the carcass behind my saddle, and we rode swiftly back to camp through the dark; and that evening we feasted on the juicy roasted ribs.

The degree of tameness and unsuspiciousness shown by whitetail deer depends, of course, upon the amount of molestation to which they are exposed. Their times for sleeping, feeding, and coming to water vary from the same cause. Where they are little persecuted they feed long after sunrise and before sunset, and drink when the sun is high in the heavens, sometimes even at midday; they then show but little fear of man, and speedily become indifferent to the presence of deserted dwellings.

In the cattle country the ranch houses are often shut during the months of warm weather, when the round-ups succeed one another without intermission, as the calves must be branded, the beeves gathered and shipped, long trips made to collect strayed animals, and the trail stock driven from the breeding to the fattening grounds. At that time all the men-folk may have to be away in the white-topped wagons, working among the horned herds, whether plodding along the trail, or wandering to and fro on the range. Late one summer, when my own house had been thus closed for many months, I rode thither with a friend to pass a week. The place already wore the look of having slipped away from the domain of man. The wild forces, barely thrust back beyond the threshold of our habitation, were prompt to spring across it to renewed possession the moment we withdrew. The rank grass grew tall in the yard, and on the sodded roofs of the stable and sheds; the weather-beaten long walls of the house itself were one in tint with the trunks of the gnarled cotton-woods by which it was shaded. Evidently the woodland creatures had come to regard the silent, deserted buildings as mere outgrowths of the wilderness, no more to be feared than the trees around them or the gray, strangely shaped buttes behind.

Lines of delicate, heart-shaped footprints in the muddy reaches of the half-dry river-bed showed where the deer came to water; and in the dusty cattle-trails among the ravines many round tracks betrayed the passing and repassing of timber wolves,—once or twice in the late evening we listened to their savage and melancholy howling. Cotton-tail rabbits burrowed under the verandah. Within doors the bushy-tailed pack-rats had possession, and at night they held a perfect witches' sabbath in the garret and kitchen; while a little white-footed mouse, having dragged half the stuffing out of a mattress, had made thereof a big fluffy nest, entirely filling the oven.

Yet, in spite of the abundant sign of game, we at first suffered under one of those spells of ill-luck which at times befall all hunters, and for several days we could kill nothing, though we tried hard, being in need of fresh meat. The moon was full—each evening, sitting on the ranch verandah, or walking homeward, we watched it rise over the line of bluffs beyond the river—and the deer were feeding at night; moreover in such hot weather they lie very close, move as little as possible, and are most difficult to find. Twice we lay out from dusk until dawn, in spite of the mosquitoes, but saw nothing; and the chances we did get we failed to profit by.

One morning, instead of trudging out to hunt I stayed at home, and sat in a rocking-chair on the verandah reading, rocking, or just sitting still listening to the low rustling of the cottonwood branches overhead, and gazing across the river. Through the still, clear, hot air, the faces of the bluffs shone dazzling white; no shadow fell from the cloudless sky on the grassy slopes, or on the groves of timber; only the faraway cooing of a mourning dove broke the silence. Suddenly my attention was arrested by a slight splashing in the water; glancing up from my book I saw three deer, which had come out of the thick fringe of bushes and young trees across the river, and were strolling along the sand-bars directly opposite me. Slipping stealthily into the house I picked up my rifle, and slipped back again. One of the deer was standing motionless, broadside to me; it was a long shot, two hundred and fifty yards, but I had a rest against a pillar of the verandah. I held true, and as the smoke cleared away the deer lay struggling on the sands.

■ ■ ■

As the whitetail is the most common and widely distributed of American game, so the Columbian blacktail has the most sharply limited geographical range; for it is confined to the northwest coast, where it is by far the most abundant deer. In antlers it is indistinguishable from the common blacktail of the Rockies and the great plains, and it has the regular blacktail gait, a succession of stiff-legged bounds on all four feet at once; but its tail is more like a whitetail's in shape, though black above. As regards methods of hunting, and the amount of sport yielded, it stands midway between its two brethren. It lives in a land of magnificent timber, where the trees tower far into the sky, the giants of their kind; and there are few more attractive sports than still-hunting on the mountains, among these forests of marvellous beauty and grandeur. There are many lakes among the mountains where it dwells, and as it cares more for water than the ordinary blacktail, it is comparatively easy for hounds to drive it into some pond where it can be killed at leisure. It is thus often killed by hounding.

The only one I ever killed was a fine young buck. We had camped near a little pond, and as evening fell I strolled off towards it and sat down. Just after sunset the buck came out of the woods. For some moments he hesitated and then walked forward and stood by the edge of the water, about sixty yards from me. We were out of meat, so I held right behind his shoulder, and though he went off, his bounds were short and weak, and he fell before he reached the wood.

CHAPTER IV

On the Cattle Ranges; The Prong-horn Antelope

Early one June just after the close of the regular spring round-up, a couple of wagons, with a score of riders between them, were sent to work some hitherto untouched country, between the little Missouri and the Yellowstone. I was to go as the representative of our own and of one or two neighboring brands; but as the round-up had halted near my ranch I determined to spend a day there, and then to join the wagons;—the appointed meeting-place being a cluster of red scoria buttes, some forty miles distant, where there was a spring of good water.

Most of my day at the ranch was spent in slumber; for I had been several weeks on the round-up, where nobody ever gets quite enough sleep. This is the only drawback to the work; otherwise it is pleasant and exciting, with just that slight touch of danger necessary to give it zest, and without the wearing fatigue of such labor as lumbering or mining. But there is never enough sleep, at least on the spring and mid-summer round-ups. The men are in the saddle from dawn until dusk, at the time when the days are longest on these great northern plains; and in addition there is the regular night guarding and now and then a furious storm or a stampede, when for twenty-four hours at a stretch the riders only dismount to change horses or snatch a mouthful of food.

I started in the bright sunrise, riding one horse and driving loose before me eight others, one carrying my bedding. They travelled strung out in single file. I kept them trotting and loping, for loose horses are easiest to handle when driven at some speed, and moreover the way was long. My rifle was slung under my thigh; the lariat was looped on the saddle-horn.

At first our trail led through winding coulies, and sharp grassy defiles; the air was wonderfully clear, the flowers were in bloom, the breath of the wind in my face was odorous and sweet. The patter and beat of the unshod hoofs, rising in half-rhythmic measure, frightened the scudding deer; but the yellow-breasted meadow larks, perched on the budding tops of the bushes, sang their rich full songs without heeding us as we went by.

When the sun was well on high and the heat of the day had begun we came to a dreary and barren plain, broken by rows of low clay buttes. The ground in places was whitened by alkali; elsewhere it was dull gray. Here there grew nothing save sparse tufts of coarse grass, and cactus, and sprawling sage brush. In the hot air all things seen afar danced and wavered. As I rode and gazed at the shimmering haze the vast desolation of the landscape bore on me; it seemed as if the unseen and unknown powers of the wastes were moving by and marshalling their silent forces. No man save the wilderness dweller knows the strong melancholy fascination of these long rides through lonely lands.

At noon, that the horses might graze and drink, I halted where some box-alders grew by a pool in the bed of a half-dry creek; and shifted my saddle to a fresh beast. When we started again we came out on the rolling prairie, where the green sea of wind-rippled grass stretched limitless as far as the eye could reach. Little striped gophers scuttled away, or stood perfectly straight at the mouths of their burrows, looking like picket pins. Curlews clamored mournfully as they circled overhead. Prairie fowl swept off, clucking and calling, or strutted about with their sharp tails erect. Antelope were very plentiful, running like racehorses across the level, or uttering their queer, barking grunt as they stood at gaze, the white hairs on their rumps all on end, their neck bands of broken brown and white vivid in the sunlight. They were found singly or in small straggling parties; the master bucks had not yet begun to drive out the younger and weaker ones as later in the season, when each would gather into a herd as many does as his jealous strength could guard from rivals. The nursing does whose kids had come early were often found with the bands; the others kept apart. The kids were very conspicuous figures on the prairies, across which they scudded like jack-rabbits, showing nearly as much speed and alertness as their parents; only the very young sought safety by lying flat to escape notice.

The horses cantered and trotted steadily over the mat of buffalo grass, steering for the group of low scoria mounds which was my goal. In mid-afternoon I reached it. The two wagons were drawn up near the spring; under them lay the night-wranglers, asleep; nearby the teamster-cooks were busy about the evening meal. A little way off the two day-wranglers were watching the horse-herd; into which I speedily turned my own animals. The riders had already driven in the bunches of cattle; and were engaged in branding the calves, and turning loose the animals that were not needed, while the remainder were kept, forming the nucleus of the herd which was to accompany the wagon.

As soon as the work was over the men rode to the wagons; sinewy fellows, with tattered broad-brimmed hats and clanking spurs, some wearing leather shaps or leggings, others having their trousers tucked into their high-heeled top-boots, all with their flannel shirts and loose neckerchiefs dusty and sweaty. A few were indulging in rough, good-natured horse play, to an accompaniment of yelling mirth; most were grave and taciturn, greeting me with a silent nod or a "How! friend." A very talkative man, unless the acknowledged wit of the party, according to the somewhat florid frontier notion of wit, is always looked on with disfavor in a cow-camp. After supper, eaten in silent haste, we gathered round the embers of the small fires, and the conversation glanced fitfully over the threadbare subjects common to all such camps; the antics of some particularly vicious bucking bronco, how the different brands of cattle were showing up, the smallness of the calf drop, the respective merits of rawhide lariats and grass ropes, and bits of rather startling and violent news concerning the fates of certain neighbors. Then one by one we began to turn in under our blankets.

Our wagon was to furnish the night guards for the cattle; and each of us had his gentlest horse tied ready to hand. The night guards went on duty two at a time for two-hour watches. By good luck my watch came last. My comrade was a happy-go-lucky young Texan who for some inscrutable reason was known as "Latigo Strap"; he had just come from the south with a big drove of trail cattle.

A few minutes before two one of the guards who had gone on duty at midnight rode into camp and wakened us by shaking our shoulders. Fumbling in the dark I speedily saddled my horse; Latigo had left his saddled, and he started ahead of me. One of the annoyances of night guarding, at least in thick weather, is the occasional difficulty of finding the herd after leaving camp, or in returning to camp after the watch is over; there are few things more exasperating than to be helplessly wandering about in the dark under such circumstances. However, on this occasion there was no such trouble; for it was a brilliant starlight night and the herd had been bedded down by a sugar-loaf butte which made a good landmark. As we reached the spot we could make out the loom of the cattle lying close together on the level plain; and then the dim figure of a horseman rose vaguely from the darkness and moved by in silence; it was the other of the two midnight guards, on his way back to his broken slumber.

At once we began to ride slowly round the cattle in opposite directions. We were silent, for the night was clear, and the herd quiet; in wild weather, when the cattle are restless, the cowboys never cease calling and singing as they circle them, for the sounds seem to quiet the beasts.

For over an hour we steadily paced the endless round, saying nothing, with our great-coats buttoned, for the air is chill towards morning on the northern plains, even in summer. Then faint streaks of gray appeared in the east. Latigo Strap began to call merrily to the cattle. A coyote came sneaking over the butte nearby, and halted to yell and wail; afterwards he crossed the coulie and from the hillside opposite again shrieked in dismal crescendo. The dawn brightened rapidly; the little skylarks of the plains began to sing, soaring far overhead, while it was still much too dark to see them. Their song is not powerful, but it is so clear and fresh and long-continued that it always appeals to one very strongly; especially because it is most often heard in the rose-tinted air of the glorious mornings, while the listener sits in the saddle, looking across the endless sweep of the prairies.

As it grew lighter the cattle became restless, rising and stretching themselves, while we continued to ride round them.

> "Then the bronc' began to pitch
> And I began to ride;
> He bucked me off a cut bank,
> Hell! I nearly died!"

sang Latigo from the other side of the herd. A yell from the wagons told that the cook was summoning the sleeping cow-punchers to breakfast; we were soon able to distinguish their figures as they rolled out of their bedding, wrapped and corded it into bundles, and huddled sullenly round the little fires. The horse wranglers were driving in the saddle bands. All the cattle got on their feet and started feeding. In a few minutes the hasty breakfast at the wagons had evidently been despatched for we could see the men forming rope corrals into which the ponies were driven; then each man saddled, bridled, and mounted his horse, two or three of the half-broken beasts bucking, rearing, and plunging frantically in the vain effort to unseat their riders.

The two men who were first in the saddle relieved Latigo and myself and we immediately galloped to camp, shifted our saddles to fresh animals, gulped down a cup or two of hot coffee, and some pork, beans, and bread, and rode to the spot where the others were gathered, lolling loosely in their saddles, and waiting for the round-up boss to assign them their tasks. We were the last, and as soon as we arrived the boss divided all into two parties for the morning work, or "circle riding," whereby the cattle were to be gathered for the round-up proper. Then, as the others started, he turned to me and remarked: "We've got enough hands to drive this open country without you; but we're out of meat, and I don't want to kill a beef for such a small outfit; can't you shoot some antelope this morning? We'll pitch camp by the big blasted cottonwood at the foot of the ash coulies, over yonder, below the breaks of Dry Creek."

Of course I gladly assented, and was speedily riding alone across the grassy slopes. There was no lack of the game I was after, for from every rise of ground I could see antelope scattered across the prairie, singly, in couples, or in bands. But their very numbers, joined to the lack of cover on such an open, flattish country, proved a bar to success; while I was stalking one band another was sure to see me and begin running, whereat the first would likewise start; I missed one or two very long shots, and noon found me still without game.

However, I was then lucky enough to see a band of a dozen feeding to windward of a small butte, and by galloping in a long circle I got within a quarter of a mile of them before having to dismount. The stalk itself was almost too easy; for I simply walked to the butte, climbed carefully up a slope where the soil was firm and peered over the top to see the herd, a little one, a hundred yards off. They saw me at once and ran, but I held well ahead of a fine young prong-buck, and rolled him over like a rabbit, with both shoulders broken. In a few minutes I was riding onwards once more with the buck lashed behind my saddle.

The next one I got, a couple of hours later, offered a much more puzzling stalk. He was a big fellow in company with four does or small bucks. All five were lying in the middle of a slight basin, at the head of a gentle valley. At first sight it seemed impossible to get near them, for there was not so much cover as a sage brush, and the smooth, shallow basin in which they lay was over a thousand yards across, while they were looking directly down the valley. However, it is curious how hard it is to tell, even from nearby, whether a stalk can or cannot be made; the difficulty being to estimate the exact amount of shelter yielded by little inequalities of ground. In this instance a small shallow watercourse, entirely dry, ran along the valley, and after much study I decided to try to crawl up it, although the big bulging telescopic eyes of the prong-buck—which have much keener sight than deer or any other game—would in such case be pointed directly my way.

Having made up my mind I backed cautiously down from the coign of vantage whence I had first seen the game, and ran about a mile to the mouth of a washout which formed the continuation of the watercourse in question. Protected by the high clay banks of this washout I was able to walk upright until within half a mile of the prong-bucks; then my progress became very tedious and toilsome, as I had to work my way up the watercourse flat on my stomach, dragging the rifle beside me. At last I reached a spot beyond which not even a snake could crawl unnoticed. In front was a low bank, a couple of feet high, crested with tufts of coarse grass. Raising my head very cautiously I peered through these and saw the prong-horn about a hundred and fifty yards distant. At the same time I found that I had crawled to the edge of a village of prairie dogs, which had already made me aware of their presence by their shrill yelping. They saw me at once; and all those away from their homes scuttled towards them, and dived down the burrows, or sat on the mounds at the entrances, scolding convulsively and jerking their fat little bodies and short tails. This commotion at once attracted the attention of the antelope. They rose forthwith, and immediately caught a glimpse of the black muzzle of the rifle which I was gently pushing through the grass tufts. The fatal curiosity which so often in this species offsets wariness and sharp sight, proved my friend; evidently the antelope could not quite make me out and wished to know what I was. They moved nervously to and fro, striking the earth with their fore hoofs, and now and then uttering a sudden bleat. At last the big buck stood still broadside to me, and I fired. He went off with the others, but lagged behind as they passed over the hill crest, and when I reached it I saw him standing, not very far off, with his head down. Then he walked backwards a few steps, fell over on his side, and died.

As he was a big buck I slung him across the saddle, and started for camp afoot, leading the horse. However my hunt was not over, for while still a mile from the wagons, going down a coulie of Dry Creek, a yearling prong-buck walked over the divide to my right and stood still until I sent a bullet into its chest; so that I made my appearance in camp with three antelope.

I spoke above of the sweet singing of the western meadow lark and plains skylark; neither of them kin to the true skylark, by the way, one being a cousin of the grakles and hang-birds, and the other a kind of pipit. To me both of these birds are among the most attractive singers to which I have ever listened; but with all bird-music much must be allowed for the surroundings, and much for the mood, and the keenness of sense, of the listener. The lilt of the little plains skylark is neither very powerful nor very melodious; but it is sweet, pure, long-sustained, with a ring of courage befitting a song uttered in highest air.

The meadow lark is a singer of a higher order, deserving to rank with the best. Its song has length, variety, power and rich melody; and there is in it sometimes a cadence of wild sadness, inexpressibly touching. Yet I cannot say that either song would appeal to others as it appeals to me; for to me it comes forever laden with a hundred memories and associations; with the sight of dim hills redden-

ing in the dawn, with the breath of cool morning winds
blowing across lonely plains, with the scent of flowers on
the sunlit prairie, with the motion of fiery horses, with all
the strong thrill of eager and buoyant life. I doubt if any
man can judge dispassionately the bird songs of his own
country; he cannot disassociate them from the sights and
sounds of the land that is so dear to him.

This is not a feeling to regret, but it must be taken into
account in accepting any estimate of bird music—even in
considering the reputation of the European skylark and
nightingale. To both of these birds I have often listened in
their own homes; always with pleasure and admiration,
but always with a growing belief that relatively to some
other birds they were ranked too high. They are pre-
eminently birds with literary associations; most people
take their opinions of them at second-hand, from the
poets.

No one can help liking the lark; it is such a brave, honest, cheery bird, and moreover its song is uttered in the air,
and is very long-sustained. But it is by no means a musi-
cian of the first rank. The nightingale is a performer of a
very different and far higher order; yet though it is indeed
a notable and admirable singer, it is an exaggeration to call
it unequalled. In melody, and above all in that finer, higher
melody where the chords vibrate with the touch of eternal
sorrow, it cannot rank with such singers as the wood
thrush and hermit thrush. The serene, ethereal beauty of
the hermit's song, rising and falling through the still
evening, under the archways of hoary mountain forests
that have endured from time everlasting; the golden,
leisurely chiming of the wood thrush, sounding on June

afternoons, stanza by stanza, through sun-flecked groves of tall hickories, oaks, and chestnuts; with these there is nothing in the nightingale's song to compare. But in volume and continuity, in tuneful, voluble, rapid outpouring and ardor, above all in skilful and intricate variation of theme, its song far surpasses that of either of the thrushes. In all these respects it is more just to compare it with the mocking-bird's, which, as a rule, likewise falls short precisely on those points where the songs of the two thrushes excel.

The mocking-bird is a singer that has suffered much in reputation from its powers of mimicry. On ordinary occasions, and especially in the daytime, it insists on playing the harlequin. But when free in its own favorite haunts at night in the love season it has a song, or rather songs, which are not only purely original, but are also more beautiful than any other bird music whatsoever. Once I listened to a mocking-bird singing the livelong spring night, under the full moon, in a magnolia tree; and I do not think I shall ever forget its song.

It was on the plantation of Major Campbell Brown, near Nashville, in the beautiful, fertile mid-Tennessee country. The mocking-birds were prime favorites on the place; and were given full scope for the development, not only of their bold friendliness towards mankind, but also of that marked individuality and originality of character in which they so far surpass every other bird as to become the most interesting of all feathered folk. One of the mockers, which lived in the hedge bordering the garden, was constantly engaged in an amusing feud with an honest old setter dog, the point of attack being the tip of the dog's tail. For some reason the bird seemed to regard any hoisting of the setter's tail as a challenge and insult. It would flutter near the dog as he walked; the old setter would become interested in something and raise his tail. The bird would promptly fly at it and peck the tip; whereupon down went the tail until in a couple of minutes the old fellow would forget himself, and the scene would be repeated. The dog usually bore the assaults with comic resignation; and the mocker easily avoided any momentary outburst of clumsy resentment.

On the evening in question the moon was full. My host kindly assigned me a room of which the windows opened on a great magnolia tree, where, I was told, a mocking-bird sang every night and all night long. I went to my room about ten. The moonlight was shining in through the open window, and the mocking-bird was already in the magnolia. The great tree was bathed in a flood of shining silver; I could see each twig, and mark every action of the singer, who was pouring forth such a rapture of ringing melody as I have never listened to before or since. Sometimes he would perch motionless for many minutes, his body quivering and thrilling with the outpour of music. Then he would drop softly from twig to twig, until the lowest limb was reached, when he would rise, fluttering and leaping through the branches, his song never ceasing for an instant, until he reached the summit of the tree and launched into the warm, scent-laden air, floating in spirals, with outspread wings, until, as if spent, he sank gently back into the tree and down through the branches, while his song rose into an ecstasy of ardor and passion. His voice rang like a clarionet, in rich, full tones, and his execution covered the widest possible compass; theme followed theme, a torrent of music, a swelling tide of harmony, in which scarcely any two bars were alike. I stayed till midnight listening to him; he was singing when I went to sleep; he was still singing when I woke a couple of hours later; he sang through the livelong night.

There are many singers beside the meadow lark and little skylark in the plains country; that brown and desolate land, once the home of the thronging buffalo, still haunted by the bands of the prong-buck, and roamed over in ever increasing numbers by the branded herds of the ranchman. In the brush of the river bottoms there are the thrasher and song sparrow; on the grassy uplands the lark finch, vesper sparrow, and lark bunting; and in the rough canyons the rock wren, with its ringing melody.

Yet in certain moods a man cares less for even the loveliest bird songs than for the wilder, harsher, stronger sounds of the wilderness; the guttural booming and clucking of the prairie fowl and the great sage fowl in spring; the honking of gangs of wild geese, as they fly in rapid wedges; the bark of an eagle, wheeling in the shadow of storm-scarred cliffs; or the far-off clanging of many sand-hill cranes, soaring high overhead in circles which cross and recross at an incredible altitude. Wilder yet, and stranger, are the cries of the great four-footed beasts; the rhythmic pealing of a bull-elk's challenge; and that most sinister and mournful sound, ever fraught with foreboding of murder and rapine, the long-drawn baying of the gray wolf.

Indeed, save to the trained ear most mere bird songs are not very noticeable. The ordinary wilderness dweller, whether hunter or cowboy, scarcely heeds them; and in fact knows but little of the smaller birds. If a bird has some conspicuous peculiarity of look or habit he will notice its existence; but not otherwise. He knows a good deal about magpies, whiskey jacks, or water ousels; but nothing whatever concerning the thrushes, finches, and warblers.

It is the same with mammals. The prairie-dogs he cannot help noticing. With the big pack-rats also he is well acquainted; for they are handsome, with soft gray fur, large eyes, and bushy tails; and, moreover, no one can avoid remarking their extraordinary habit of carrying to their burrows everything bright, useless, and portable, from an empty cartridge case to a skinning knife. But he knows nothing of mice, shrews, pocket gophers, or weasels; and but little even of some larger mammals with very marked characteristics. Thus I have met but one or two plainsmen who knew anything of the curious plains ferret, that rather rare weasel-like animal, which plays the same part on the plains that the mink does by the edges of all our streams and brooks, and the tree-loving sable in the cold northern forests. The ferret makes its home in burrows, and by preference goes abroad at dawn and dusk, but sometimes even at mid-day. It is as blood-thirsty as the mink itself, and its life is one long ramble for prey, gophers, prairie-dogs, sage rabbits, jack-rabbits, snakes, and every kind of ground bird furnishing its food. I have known one to fairly depopulate a prairie-dog town, it being the arch foe of these little rodents, because of its insatiable blood lust and its capacity to follow them into their burrows. Once I found the bloody body and broken eggs of a poor prairie-hen which a ferret had evidently surprised on her nest. Another time one of my men was eye-witness to a more remarkable instance of the little animal's blood-thirsty ferocity. He was riding the range, and being attracted by a slight commotion in a clump of grass, he turned his horse thither to look, and to his astonishment found an antelope fawn at the last gasp, but still feebly struggling, in the grasp of a ferret, which had throttled it and was sucking its blood with hideous greediness. He avenged the murdered innocent by a dexterous blow with the knotted end of his lariat.

That mighty bird of rapine, the war eagle, which on the great plains and among the Rockies supplants the bald-headed eagle of better-watered regions, is another dangerous foe of the young antelope. It is even said that under exceptional circumstances eagles will assail a full grown prong-horn; and a neighboring ranchman informs me that he was once an eye-witness to such an attack. It was a bleak day in the late winter, and he was riding home across a wide dreary plateau, when he saw two eagles worrying and pouncing on a prong-buck—seemingly a yearling. It made a gallant fight. The eagles hovered over it with spread wings, now and then swooping down, their talons out-thrust, to strike at the head, or to try to settle on the loins. The antelope reared and struck with hoofs and horns like a goat; but its strength was failing rapidly, and doubtless it would have succumbed in the end had not the approach of the ranchman driven off the marauders.

I have likewise heard stories of eagles attacking badgers, foxes, bob-cats, and coyotes; but I am inclined to think all such cases exceptional. I have never myself seen an eagle assail anything bigger than a fawn, lamb, kid, or jack-rabbit. It also swoops at geese, sage fowl, and prairie fowl. On one occasion while riding over the range I witnessed an attack on a jack-rabbit. The eagle was soaring overhead, and espied the jack while the latter was crouched motionless. Instantly the great bird rushed down through the humming air, with closed wings; checked itself when some forty yards above the jack, hovered for a moment, and again fell like a bolt. Away went long-ears, running as only a frightened jack can; and after him the eagle, not with the arrowy rush of its descent from high air, but with eager, hurried flapping. In a short time it had nearly overtaken the fugitive, when the latter dodged sharply to one side, and the eagle over-shot it precisely as a greyhound would have done, stopping itself by a powerful, setting motion of the great pinions. Twice this manœuvre was repeated; then the eagle made a quick rush, caught and overthrew the quarry before it could turn, and in another moment was sitting triumphant on the quivering body, the crooked talons driven deep into the soft, furry sides.

Once while hunting mountain sheep in the Bad Lands I killed an eagle on the wing with the rifle. I was walking beneath a cliff of gray clay, when the eagle sailed into view over the crest. As soon as he saw me he threw his wings aback, and for a moment before wheeling poised motionless, offering a nearly stationary target; so that my bullet grazed his shoulder, and down he came through the air, tumbling over and over. As he struck the ground he threw himself on his back, and fought against his death with the undaunted courage proper to his brave and cruel nature.

Indians greatly prize the feathers of this eagle. With them they make their striking and beautiful war bonnets, and bedeck the manes and tails of their spirited war ponies. Every year the Grosventres and Mandans from the Big Missouri come to the neighborhood of my ranch to hunt. Though not good marksmen they kill many whitetail deer, driving the bottoms for them in bands, on horseback; and they catch many eagles. Sometimes they take these alive by exposing a bait near which a hole is dug, where one of them lies hidden for days, with Indian patience, until an eagle lights on the bait and is noosed.

Even eagles are far less dangerous enemies to antelope than are wolves and coyotes. These beasts are always prowling round the bands, to snap up the sick or unwary; and in spring they revel in carnage of the kids and fawns. They are not swift enough to overtake the grown animals by sheer speed; but they are superior in endurance, and especially in winter, often run them down in fair chase. A prong-buck is a plucky little beast, and when cornered it often makes a gallant, though not a very effectual, fight.

CHAPTER V

Hunting the Prong-Buck; Frost, Fire, and Thirst

As with all other American game man is a worse foe to the prong-horns than all their brute enemies combined. They hold their own much better than the bigger game; on the whole even better than the blacktail; but their numbers have been wofully thinned, and in many places they have been completely exterminated. The most exciting method of chasing them is on horseback with greyhounds; but they are usually killed with the rifle. Owing to the open nature of the ground they frequent the shots must generally be taken at long range; hence this kind of hunting is pre-eminently that needing judgment of distance and skill in the use of the long-range rifle at stationary objects. On the other hand the antelope are easily seen, making no effort to escape observation, as deer do, and are so curious that in very wild districts to this day they can sometimes be tolled within rifle shot by the judicious waving of a red flag. In consequence, a good many very long, but tempting, shots can be obtained. More cartridges are used, relatively to the amount of game killed, on antelope, than in any other hunting.

Often I have killed prong-bucks while riding between the outlying line camps, which are usually stationed a dozen miles or so back from the river, where the Bad

Lands melt into the prairie. In continually trying long shots, of course one occasionally makes a remarkable hit. Once I remember while riding down a broad, shallow coulie with two of my cow-hands—Seawell and Dow, both keen hunters and among the staunchest friends I have ever had,—rousing a band of antelope which stood irresolute at about a hundred yards until I killed one. Then they dashed off, and I missed one shot, but with my next, to my own utter astonishment, killed the last of the band, a big buck, just as he topped a rise four hundred yards away. To offset such shots I have occasionally made an unaccountable miss. Once I was hunting with the same two men, on a rainy day, when we came on a bunch of antelope some seventy yards off, lying down on the side of a coulie, to escape the storm. They huddled together a moment to gaze, and, with stiffened fingers I took a shot, my yellow oilskin slicker flapping around me in the wind and rain. Down went one buck, and away went the others. One of my men walked up to the fallen beast, bent over it, and then asked, "Where did you aim?" Not reassured by the question, I answered doubtfully, "Behind the shoulder"; whereat he remarked drily, "Well, you hit it in the eye!" I never did know whether I killed the antelope I aimed at or another. Yet that same day I killed three more bucks at decidedly long shots; at the time we lacked meat at the ranch, and were out to make a good killing.

Besides their brute and human foes, the prong-horn must also fear the elements, and especially the snows of winter. On the northern plains the cold weather is of polar severity, and turns the green, grassy prairies of mid-

summer into ironbound wastes. The blizzards whirl and
sweep across them with a shrieking fury which few living
things may face. The snow is like fine ice dust, and the
white waves glide across the grass with a stealthy, crawling
motion which has in it something sinister and cruel. Accordingly, as the bright fall weather passes, and the dreary
winter draws nigh, when the days shorten, and the nights
seem interminable, and gray storms lower above the gray
horizon, the antelope gather in bands and seek sheltered
places, where they may abide through the winter-time of
famine and cold and deep snow. Some of these bands
travel for many hundred miles, going and returning over
the same routes, swimming rivers, crossing prairies, and
threading their way through steep defiles. Such bands
make their winter home in places like the Black Hills, or
similar mountainous regions, where the shelter and feed
are good, and where in consequence antelope have wintered in countless thousands for untold generations.
Other bands do not travel for any very great distance, but
seek some sheltered grassy table-land in the Bad Lands, or
some well-shielded valley, where their instinct and experience teach them that the snow does not lie deep in winter.
Once having chosen such a place they stand much persecution before leaving it.

One December, an old hunter whom I knew told me
that such a band was wintering a few miles from a camp
where two line-riders of the W Bar brand were stationed;
and I made up my mind to ride thither and kill a couple.
The line camp was twenty miles from my ranch; the shack
in which the old hunter lived was midway between, and I
had to stop there to find out the exact lay of the land.

At dawn, before our early breakfast, I saddled a tough, shaggy sorrel horse; hastening in-doors as soon as the job was over, to warm my numbed fingers. After breakfast I started, muffled in my wolf-skin coat, with beaver-fur cap, gloves, and shaps, and great felt over-shoes. The windless air was bitter cold, the thermometer showing well below zero. Snow lay on the ground, leaving bare patches here and there, but drifted deep in the hollows. Under the steel-blue heavens the atmosphere had a peculiar glint as if filled with myriads of tiny crystals. As I crossed the frozen river, immediately in front of the ranch house, the strangely carved tops of the bluffs were reddening palely in the winter sunrise. Prairie fowl were perched in the bare cottonwoods along the river brink, showing large in the leafless branches; they called and clucked to one another.

Where the ground was level and the snow not too deep I loped, and before noon I reached the sheltered coulie where, with long poles and bark, the hunter had built his tepee—wigwam, as eastern woodsmen would have called it. It stood in a loose grove of elms and box-alders; from the branches of the nearest trees hung saddles of frozen venison. The smoke rising from the funnel-shaped top of the tepee showed that there was more fire than usual within; it is easy to keep a good tepee warm, though it is so smoky that no one therein can stand up-right. As I drew rein the skin door was pushed aside, and the hard old face and dried, battered body of the hunter appeared. He greeted me with a surly nod, and a brief re-quest to "light and hev somethin' to eat"—the invariable proffer of hospitality on the plains. He wore a greasy buckskin shirt or tunic, and an odd cap of badger skin,

from beneath which strayed his tangled hair; age, rheumatism, and the many accidents and incredible fatigue, hardship, and exposure of his past life had crippled him, yet he
still possessed great power of endurance, and in his
seamed weather-scarred face his eyes burned fierce and
piercing as a hawk's. Ever since early manhood he had
wandered over the plains, hunting and trapping; he had
waged savage private war against half the Indian tribes of
the north; and he had wedded wives in each of the tribes
of the other half. A few years before this time the great
buffalo herds had vanished, and the once swarming beaver
had shared the same fate; the innumerable horses and
horned stock of the cattlemen, and the daring rough riders of the ranches, had supplanted alike the game and the
red and white wanderers who had followed it with such
fierce rivalry. When the change took place the old fellow,
with failing bodily powers, found his life-work over. He
had little taste for the career of the desperado, horse-thief,
highwayman, and man-killer, which not a few of the old
buffalo hunters adopted when their legitimate occupation
was gone; he scorned still more the life of vicious and idle
semi-criminality led by others of his former companions
who were of weaker mould. Yet he could not do regular
work. His existence had been one of excitement, adventure, and restless roaming, when it was not passed in lazy
ease; his times of toil and peril varied by fits of brutal rev-
elry. He had no kin, no ties of any kind. He would accept
no help, for his wants were very few, and he was utterly
self-reliant. He got meat, clothing, and bedding from the
antelope and deer he killed; the spare hides and venison he
bartered for what little else he needed. So he built him his

tepee in one of the most secluded parts of the Bad Lands, where he led the life of a solitary hunter, awaiting in grim loneliness the death which he knew to be near at hand.

I unsaddled and picketed my horse, and followed the old hunter into his smoky tepee; sat down on the pile of worn buffalo robes which formed his bedding, and waited in silence while he fried some deer meat, and boiled some coffee—he was out of flour. As I ate, he gradually unbent and talked quite freely, and before I left he told me exactly where to find the band, which he assured me was located for the winter, and would not leave unless much harried.

After a couple of hours' rest I again started, and pushed out to the end of the Bad Lands. Here, as there had been no wind, I knew I should find in the snow the tracks of one of the riders from the line camp, whose beat lay along the edge of the prairie for some eight miles, until it met the beat of a rider from the line camp next above. As nightfall came on it grew even colder; long icicles hung from the lips of my horse; and I shivered slightly in my fur coat. I had reckoned the distance ill, and it was dusk when I struck the trail; but my horse at once turned along it of his own accord and began to lope. Half an hour later I saw through the dark what looked like a spark on the side of a hill. Toward this my horse turned; and in another moment a whinneying from in front showed I was near the camp. The light was shining through a small window, the camp itself being a dugout with a log roof and front—a kind of frontier building always warm in winter. After turning my horse into the rough log stable with the horses of the two cowboys, I joined the latter at supper inside the dugout; being received of course with hearty cordiality. After the

intense cold outside the warmth within was almost oppressive, for the fire was roaring in the big stone fireplace.
The bunks were broad; my two friends turned into one,
and I was given the other, with plenty of bedding; so that
my sleep was sound.

We had breakfasted and saddled our horses and were
off by dawn next morning. My companions, muffled in
furs, started in opposite directions to ride their lonely
beats, while I steered for my hunting-ground. It was a
lowering and gloomy day; at sunrise pale, lurid sundogs
hung in the glimmering mist; gusts of wind moaned
through the ravines.

At last I reached a row of bleak hills, and from a ridge
looked cautiously down on the chain of plateaus, where I
had been told I should see the antelope. Sure enough,
there they were, to the number of several hundred, scattered over the level snow-streaked surface of the nearest
and largest plateau, greedily cropping the thick, short
grass. Leaving my horse tied in a hollow I speedily stalked
up a coulie to within a hundred yards of the nearest band
and killed a good buck. Instantly all the antelope in sight
ran together into a thick mass and raced away from me,
until they went over the opposite edge of the plateau; but
almost as soon as they did so they were stopped by deep
drifts of powdered snow, and came back to the summit of
the table-land. They then circled round the edge at a gallop, and finally broke madly by me, jostling one another in
their frantic haste and crossed by a small ridge into the
next plateau beyond; as they went by I shot a yearling.

I now had all the venison I wished, and would shoot
no more, but I was curious to see how the antelope would

act, and so walked after them. They ran about half a mile, and then the whole herd, of several hundred individuals, wheeled into line fronting me, like so many cavalry, and stood motionless, the white and brown bands on their necks looking like the facings on a uniform. As I walked near they again broke and rushed to the end of the valley. Evidently they feared to leave the flats for the broken country beyond, where the rugged hills were riven by gorges, in some of which snow lay deep even thus early in the season. Accordingly, after galloping a couple of times round the valley, they once more broke by me, at short range, and tore back along the plateaus to that on which I had first found them. Their evident and extreme reluctance to venture into the broken country round about made me readily understand the tales I had heard of game butchers killing over a hundred individuals at a time out of a herd so situated.

I walked back to my game, dressed it, and lashed the saddles and hams behind me on my horse; I had chosen old Sorrel Joe for the trip because he was strong, tough, and quiet. Then I started for the ranch, keeping to the prairie as long as I could, because there the going was easier; sometimes I rode, sometimes I ran on foot leading Sorrel Joe.

Late in the afternoon, as I rode over a roll in the prairie I saw ahead of me a sight very unusual at that season; a small emigrant train going westward. There were three white-topped prairie schooners, containing the household goods, the tow-headed children, and the hard-faced, bony women; the tired horses were straining wearily in the traces; the bearded, moody men walked alongside.

They had been belated by sickness, and the others of their company had gone ahead to take up claims along the Yellowstone; now they themselves were pushing forward in order to reach the holdings of their friends before the first deep snows stopped all travel. They had no time to halt; for there were still two or three miles to go that evening before they could find a sheltered resting-place with fuel, grass, and water. A little while after passing them I turned in the saddle and looked back. The lonely little train stood out sharply on the sky-line, the wagons looming black against the cold red west as they toiled steadily onward across the snowy plain.

Night soon fell; but I cared little, for I was on ground I knew. The old horse threaded his way at a lope along the familiar game trails and cattle paths; in a couple of hours I caught the gleam from the firelit windows of the ranch house. No man who, for his good-fortune, has at times in his life endured toil and hardship, ever fails to appreciate the strong elemental pleasures of rest after labor, food after hunger, warmth and shelter after bitter cold.

So much for the winter hunting. But in the fall, when the grass is dry as tinder, the antelope hunter, like other plainsmen, must sometimes face fire instead of frost. Fire is one of the most dreaded enemies of the ranchmen on the cattle ranges; and fighting a big prairie fire is a work of extraordinary labor, and sometimes of danger. The line of flame, especially when seen at night, undulating like a serpent, is very beautiful; though it lacks the terror and grandeur of the great forest fires.

One October, Ferguson and I, with one of the cowhands, and a friend from the East, took the wagon for an antelope hunt in the broken country between the Little Missouri and the Beaver. The cowboy drove the wagon to a small spring, near some buttes which are well distinguished by a number of fossil tree-stumps; while the rest of us, who were mounted on good horses, made a circle after antelope. We found none, and rode on to camp, reaching it about the middle of the afternoon. We had noticed several columns of smoke in the southeast, showing that prairie fires were under way; but we thought that they were too far off to endanger our camp, and accordingly unsaddled our horses and sat down to a dinner of bread, beans, and coffee. Before we were through the smoke began to pour over a ridge a mile distant in such quantities that we ran thither with our slickers, hoping to find some stretch of broken ground where the grass was sparse, and where we could fight the fire with effect. Our hopes were vain. Before we reached the ridge the fire came over its crest, and ran down in a long tongue between two scoria buttes. Here the grass was quite short and thin, and we did our best to beat out the flames; but they gradually gained on us, and as they reached the thicker grass lower down the slope, they began to roar and dart forward in a way that bade us pay heed to our own safety. Finally they reached a winding line of brushwood in the bottom of the coulie; and as this burst into a leaping blaze we saw it was high time to look to the safety of our camp, and ran back to it at top speed. Ferguson, who had been foremost in fighting the fire, was already scorched and blackened.

We were camped on the wagon trail which leads along the divide almost due south to Sentinel Butte. The line of fire was fanned by a southeasterly breeze, and was therefore advancing diagonally to the divide. If we could drive the wagon southward on the trail in time to get it past the fire before the latter reached the divide, we would be to windward of the flames, and therefore in safety. Accordingly, while the others were hastily harnessing the team, and tossing the bedding and provisions into the wagon, I threw the saddle on my horse, and galloped down the trail, to see if there was yet time to adopt this expedient. I soon found that there was not. Half a mile from camp the trail dipped into a deep coulie, where fair-sized trees and dense undergrowth made a long winding row of brush and timber. The trail led right under the trees at the upper end of this coulie. As I galloped by I saw that the fire had struck the trees a quarter of a mile below me; in the dried timber it instantly sprang aloft like a giant, and roared in a thunderous monotone as it swept up the coulie. I galloped to the hill ridge ahead, saw that the fire line had already reached the divide, and turned my horse sharp on his haunches. As I again passed under the trees, the fire, running like a racehorse in the brush, had reached the road; its breath was hot in my face; tongues of quivering flame leaped over my head and kindled the grass on the hillside fifty yards away.

When I got back to camp Ferguson had taken measures for the safety of the wagon. He had moved it across the coulie, which at this point had a wet bottom, making a bar to the progress of the flames until they had time to work across lower down. Meanwhile we fought to keep the fire from entering a well-grassed space on the hither side of the coulie, between it and a row of scoria buttes. Favored by a streak of clay ground, where the grass was sparse, we succeeded in beating out the flame as it reached this clay streak, and again beating it out when it ran round the buttes and began to back up towards us against the wind. Then we recrossed the coulie with the wagon, before the fire swept up the farther side; and so, when the flames passed by, they left us camped on a green oasis in the midst of a charred, smoking desert. We thus saved some good grazing for our horses.

But our fight with the fire had only begun. No stockman will see a fire waste the range and destroy the winter feed of the stock without spending every ounce of his strength in the effort to put a stop to its ravages—even when, as in our case, the force of men and horses at hand is so small as to offer only the very slenderest hope of success.

We set about the task in the way customary in the cattle country. It is impossible for any but a very large force to make head against a prairie fire while there is any wind; but the wind usually fails after nightfall, and accordingly the main fight is generally waged during the hours of darkness.

Before dark we drove to camp and shot a stray steer, and then split its carcass in two lengthwise with an axe. After sundown the wind lulled; and we started towards the line of fire, which was working across a row of broken grassy hills, three quarters of a mile distant. Two of us were on horseback, dragging a half carcass, bloody side down, by means of ropes leading from our saddle-horns to the fore and hind legs; the other two followed on foot with slickers and wet saddle blankets. There was a reddish glow in the night air, and the waving, bending lines of flame

showed in great bright curves against the hillsides ahead
of us.

When we reached them, we found the fire burning
in a long, continuous line. It was not making rapid headway, for the air was still, and the flames stood upright,
two or three feet high. Lengthening the ropes, one of us
spurred his horse across the fire line and then, wheeling,
we dragged the carcass along it; one horseman being on
the burnt ground, and one on the unburnt grass, while the
body of the steer lay lengthwise across the line. The
weight and the blood smothered the fire as we twitched
the carcass over the burning grass; and the two men following behind with their blankets and slickers readily
beating out any isolated tufts of flame.

The fire made the horses wild, and it was not always
easy to manage both them and the ropes, so as to keep the
carcass true on the line. Sometimes there would be a slight
puff of wind, and then the man on the grass side of the line
ran the risk of a scorching. We were blackened with
smoke, and the taut ropes hurt our thighs; while at times
the plunging horses tried to buck or bolt. It was worse
when we came to some deep gully or ravine, breaking the
line of fire. Into this we of course had to plunge, so as to
get across to the fire on the other side. After the glare of
the flame the blackness of the ravine was Stygian; we
could see nothing, and simply spurred our horses into it
anywhere, taking our chances. Down we would go, stumbling, sliding, and pitching, over cut banks and into holes
and bushes, while the carcass bounded behind, now catching on a stump, and now fetching loose with a "pluck" that
brought it full on the horses' haunches, driving them

nearly crazy with fright. The pull up the opposite bank was, if anything, worse.

By midnight the half carcass was worn through; but we had stifled the fire in the comparatively level country to the eastwards. Back we went to camp, drank huge draughts of muddy water, devoured roast ox-ribs, and dragged out the other half carcass to fight the fire on the west. But after hours of wearing labor we found ourselves altogether baffled by the exceeding roughness of the ground. There was some little risk to us who were on horseback, dragging the carcass; we had to feel our way along knife-like ridges in the dark, one ahead and the other behind, while the steer dangled over the precipice on one side; and in going down the buttes and into the canyons only by extreme care could we avoid getting tangled in the ropes and rolling down in a heap. Moreover the fire was in such rough places that the carcass could not be twitched fairly over it, and so we could not put it out. Before dawn we were obliged to abandon our fruitless efforts and seek camp, stiffened and weary. From a hill we looked back through the pitchy night at the fire we had failed to conquer. It had been broken into many lines by the roughness of the chasm-strewn and hilly country. Of these lines of flame some were in advance, some behind, some rushing forward in full blast and fury, some standing still; here and there one wheeling towards a flank, or burning in a semicircle, round an isolated hill. Some of the lines were flickering out; gaps were showing in others. In the darkness it looked like the rush of a mighty army, bearing triumphantly onwards, in spite of a resistance so stubborn as to break its formation into many fragments and cause each one of them to wage its own battle for victory or defeat.

On the wide plains where the prong-buck dwells the hunter must sometimes face thirst, as well as fire and frost. The only time I ever really suffered from thirst was while hunting prong-buck.

It was late in the summer. I was with the ranch wagon on the way to join a round-up, and as we were out of meat I started for a day's hunt. Before leaving in the morning I helped to haul the wagon across the river. It was fortunate I stayed, as it turned out. There was no regular ford where we made the crossing; we anticipated no trouble, as the water was very low, the season being dry. However, we struck a quicksand, in which the wagon settled, while the frightened horses floundered helplessly. All the riders at once got their ropes on the wagon, and hauling from the saddle, finally pulled it through. This took time; and it was ten o'clock when I rode away from the river, at which my horse and I had just drunk—our last drink for over twenty-four hours as it turned out.

After two or three hours' ride, up winding coulies, and through the scorched desolation of patches of Bad Lands, I reached the rolling prairie. The heat and drought had long burned the short grass dull brown; the bottoms of what had been pools were covered with hard, dry, cracked earth. The day was cloudless, and the heat oppressive. There were many antelope, but I got only one shot, breaking a buck's leg; and though I followed it for a couple of hours I could not overtake it. By this time it was late in the afternoon, and I was far away from the river; so I pushed for a creek, in the bed of which I had always found pools of water, especially towards the head, as is usual with plains watercourses. To my chagrin, however, they all proved to be dry; and though I rode up the creek bed toward the head, carefully searching for any sign of water, night closed on me before I found any. For two or three hours I stumbled on, leading my horse, in my fruitless search; then a tumble over a cut bank in the dark warned me that I might as well stay where I was for the rest of the warm night. Accordingly I unsaddled the horse, and tied him to a sage brush; after awhile he began to feed on the dewy grass. At first I was too thirsty to sleep. Finally I fell into slumber, and when I awoke at dawn I felt no thirst. For an hour or two more I continued my search for water in the creek bed; then abandoned it and rode straight for the river. By the time we reached it my thirst had come back with redoubled force, my mouth was parched, and the horse was in quite as bad a plight; we rushed down to the brink, and it seemed as if we could neither of us ever drink our fill of the tepid, rather muddy water. Of course this experience was merely unpleasant; thirst is not a source of real danger in the plains country proper, whereas in the hideous deserts that extend from southern Idaho through Utah and Nevada to Arizona, it ever menaces with death the hunter and explorer.

In the plains the weather is apt to be in extremes; the heat is tropical, the cold arctic, and the droughts are relieved by furious floods. These are generally most severe and lasting in the spring, after the melting of the snow; and fierce local freshets follow the occasional cloudbursts. The large rivers then become wholly impassable, and even the smaller are formidable obstacles. It is not easy to get cattle across a swollen stream, where the current runs like a turbid mill-race over the bed of shifting quicksand. Once five of us took a thousand head of trail steers across the Little Missouri when the river was up, and it was no light task. The muddy current was boiling past the banks, covered with driftwood and foul yellow froth, and the frightened cattle shrank from entering it. At last, by hard riding, with much loud shouting and swinging of ropes, we got the leaders in, and the whole herd followed. After them we went in our turn, the horses swimming at one moment, and the next staggering and floundering through the quicksand. I was riding my pet cutting horse, Muley, which has the provoking habit of making great bounds where the water is just not deep enough for swimming; once he almost unseated me. Some of the cattle were caught by the currents and rolled over and over; most of these we were able, with the help of our ropes, to put on their feet again; only one was drowned, or rather choked in a quicksand. Many swam down stream, and in consequence struck a difficult landing, where the river ran under a cut bank; these we had to haul out with our ropes. Both men and horses were well tired by the time the whole herd was across.

Although I have often had a horse down in quicksand, or in crossing a swollen river, and have had to work hard to save him, I have never myself lost one under such circumstances. Yet once I saw the horse of one of my men drown under him directly in front of the ranch house, while he was trying to cross the river. This was in early spring, soon after the ice had broken.

When making long wagon trips over the great plains, antelope often offer the only source of meat supply, save for occasional water fowl, sage fowl, and prairie fowl—the sharp-tailed prairie fowl, be it understood. This is the characteristic grouse of the cattle country; the true prairie fowl is a bird of the farming land farther east.

Towards the end of the summer of '92 I found it necessary to travel from my ranch to the Black Hills, some two hundred miles south. The ranch wagon went with me, driven by an all-round plainsman, a man of iron nerves and varied past, the sheriff of our county. He was an old friend of mine; at one time I had served as deputy-sheriff for the northern end of the county. In the wagon we carried our food and camp kit, and our three rolls of bedding, each wrapped in a thick, nearly waterproof canvas sheet; we had a tent, but we never needed it. The load being light, the wagon was drawn by but a span of horses, a pair of wild runaways, tough, and good travellers. My foreman and I rode beside the wagon on our wiry, unkempt, unshod cattle-ponies. They carried us all day at a rack, pace, single-foot or slow lope, varied by rapid galloping when we made long circles after game; the trot, the favorite gait with eastern park-riders, is disliked by all peoples who have to do much of their life-work in the saddle.

The first day's ride was not attractive. The heat was intense and the dust stifling, as we had to drive some loose horses for the first few miles, and afterwards to ride up and down the sandy river bed, where the cattle had gathered, to look over some young steers we had put on the range the preceding spring. When we did camp it was by a pool of stagnant water, in a creek bottom, and the mosquitoes were a torment. Nevertheless, as evening fell, it was pleasant to climb a little knoll nearby and gaze at the rows of strangely colored buttes, grass-clad, or of bare earth and scoria, their soft reds and purples showing as through a haze, and their irregular outlines gradually losing their sharpness in the fading twilight.

Next morning the weather changed, growing cooler, and we left the tangle of ravines and Bad Lands, striking out across the vast sea-like prairies. Hour after hour, under the bright sun, the wagon drew slowly ahead, over the immense rolling stretches of short grass, dipping down each long slope until it reached the dry, imperfectly outlined creek bed at the bottom,—wholly devoid of water and without so much as a shrub of wood,—and then ascending the gentle rise on the other side until at last it topped the broad divide, or watershed, beyond which lay the shallow winding coulies of another creek system. From each rise of ground we looked far and wide over the sunlit prairie, with its interminable undulations. The sicklebill curlews which in spring, while breeding, hover above the travelling horseman with ceaseless clamor, had for the most part gone southward. We saw only one small party of half a dozen birds; they paid little heed to us, but piped to one another, making short flights, and on alighting stood erect, first spreading and then folding and setting their wings with a slow, graceful motion. Little horned larks continually ran along the ruts of the faint wagon track, just ahead of the team, and twittered plaintively as they rose, while flocks of long-spurs swept hither and thither, in fitful, irregular flight.

My foreman and I usually rode far off to one side of the wagon, looking out for antelope. Of these we at first saw few, but they grew more plentiful as we journeyed on-

ward, approaching a big scantily wooded creek, where I
had found the prong-horn abundant in previous seasons.
They were very wary and watchful whether going singly
or in small parties, and the lay of the land made it exceedingly difficult to get within range. The last time I had
hunted in this neighborhood was in the fall, at the height
of the rutting season. Prong-bucks, even more than other
game, seem fairly maddened by erotic excitement. At the
time of my former hunt they were in ceaseless motion;
each master buck being incessantly occupied in herding
his harem, and fighting would-be rivals, while single
bucks chased single does as greyhounds chase hares, or
else, if no does were in sight, from sheer excitement ran to
and fro as if crazy, racing at full speed in one direction,
then halting, wheeling, and tearing back again just as hard
as they could go.

At this time, however, the rut was still some weeks off,
and all the bucks had to do was to feed and keep a look-
out for enemies. Try my best, I could not get within less
than four or five hundred yards, and though I took a number of shots at these, or at even longer, distances, I missed.
If a man is out merely for a day's hunt, and has all the time
he wishes, he will not scare the game and waste cartridges
by shooting at such long ranges, preferring to spend half a
day or more in patient waiting and careful stalking; but if
he is travelling, and is therefore cramped for time, he must
take his chances, even at the cost of burning a good deal
of powder.

I was finally helped to success by a characteristic freak
of the game I was following. No other animals are as keen-
sighted, or are normally as wary as prong-horns; but no

others are so whimsical and odd in their behavior at times, or so subject to fits of the most stupid curiosity and panic. Late in the afternoon, on topping a rise I saw two good bucks racing off about three hundred yards to one side; I sprang to the ground, and fired three shots at them in vain, as they ran like quarter-horses until they disappeared over a slight swell. In a minute, however, back they came, suddenly appearing over the crest of the same swell, immediately in front of me, and, as I afterwards found by pacing, some three hundred and thirty yards away. They stood side by side facing me, and remained motionless, unheeding the crack of the Winchester; I aimed at the right-hand one, but a front shot of the kind, at such a distance, is rather difficult, and it was not until I fired for the fourth time that he sank back out of sight. I could not tell whether I had killed him, and took two shots at his mate, as the latter went off, but without effect. Running forward, I found the first one dead, the bullet having gone through him lenghtwise; the other did not seem satisfied even yet, and kept hanging round in the distance for some minutes, looking at us.

I had thus bagged one prong-buck, as the net outcome of the expenditure of fourteen cartridges. This was certainly not good shooting; but neither was it as bad as it would seem to the man inexperienced in antelope hunting. When fresh meat is urgently needed, and when time is too short, the hunter who is after antelope in an open flattish country must risk many long shots. In no other kind of hunting is there so much long-distance shooting, or so many shots fired for every head of game bagged.

Throwing the buck into the wagon we continued our

journey across the prairie, no longer following any road, and before sunset jolted down towards the big creek for which we had been heading. There were many waterholes therein, and timber of considerable size; box alder and ash grew here and there in clumps and fringes, beside the serpentine curves of the nearly dry torrent bed, the growth being thickest under the shelter of the occasional low bluffs. We drove down to a heavily grassed bottom, near a deep, narrow pool, with, at one end, that rarest of luxuries in the plains country, a bubbling spring of pure, cold water. With plenty of wood, delicious water, ample feed for the horses, and fresh meat we had every comfort and luxury incident to camp life in good weather. The bedding was tossed out on a smooth spot beside the wagon; the horses were watered and tethered to picket pins where the feed was best; water was fetched from the spring; a deep hole was dug for the fire, and the grass roundabout carefully burned off; and in a few moments the bread was baking in the Dutch oven, the potatoes were boiling, antelope steaks were sizzling in the frying-pan, and the kettle was ready for the tea. After supper, eaten with the relish known well to every hard-working and successful hunter, we sat for half an hour or so round the fire, and then turned in under the blankets, pulled the tarpaulins over us, and listened drowsily to the wailing of the coyotes until we fell sound asleep.

We determined to stay in this camp all day, so as to try and kill another prong-buck, as we would soon be past the good hunting grounds. I did not have to go far for my game next morning, for soon after breakfast, while sitting on my canvas bag cleaning my rifle, the sheriff suddenly called to me that a bunch of antelope were coming towards us. Sure enough there they were, four in number, rather over half a mile off, on the first bench of the prairie, two or three hundred yards back from the creek, leisurely feeding in our direction. In a minute or two they were out of sight, and I instantly ran along the creek towards them for a quarter of a mile, and then crawled up a short shallow coulie, close to the head of which they seemed likely to pass. When nearly at the end I cautiously raised my hatless head, peered through some straggling weeds, and at once saw the horns of the buck. He was a big fellow, about a hundred and twenty yards off; the others, a doe and two kids, were in front. As I lifted myself on my elbows he halted and turned his raised head towards me; the sunlight shone bright on his supple, vigorous body with its markings of sharply contrasted brown and white. I pulled trigger, and away he went; but I could see that his race was nearly run, and he fell after going a few hundred yards.

Soon after this a wind storm blew up so violent that we could hardly face it. In the late afternoon it died away, and I again walked out to hunt, but saw only does and kids, at which I would not shoot. As the sun set, leaving bars of amber and pale red in the western sky, the air became absolutely calm. In the waning evening the low, far-off ridges were touched with a violet light; then the hues grew sombre, and still darkness fell on the lonely prairie.

Next morning we drove to the river, and kept near it for several days, most of the time following the tracks made by the heavy wagons accompanying the trail herds—this being one of the regular routes followed by the great throng of slow-moving cattle yearly driven from the south. At other times we made our own road. Twice or thrice we passed ranch houses; the men being absent on the round-up they were shut, save one which was inhabited by two or three lean Texan cow-punchers, with sunburned faces and reckless eyes, who had come up with a trail herd from the Cherokee strip. Once, near the old Sioux crossing, where the Dakota war bands used to ford the river on their forays against the Crows and the settlers along the Yellowstone, we met a large horse herd. The tough, shabby, tired-looking animals, one or two of which were loaded with bedding and a scanty supply of food, were driven by three travel-worn, hard-faced men, with broad hats, shaps, and long pistols in their belts. They had brought the herd over plain and mountain pass all the way from far distant Oregon.

It was a wild, rough country, bare of trees save for a fringe of cottonwoods along the river, and occasional clumps of cedar on the jagged, brown buttes; as we went farther the hills turned the color of chalk, and were covered with a growth of pine. We came upon acres of sunflowers as we journeyed southward; they are not as tall as they are in the rich bottom lands of Kansas, where the splendid blossoms, on their strong stalks, stand as high as the head of a man on horseback.

Though there were many cattle here, big game was scarce. However, I killed plenty of prairie chickens and sage hens for the pot; and as the sage hens were still feeding largely on crickets and grasshoppers, and not exclusively on sage, they were just as good eating as the prairie chickens. I used the rifle, cutting off their heads or necks, and, as they had to be shot on the ground, and often while in motion, or else while some distance away, it was more difficult than shooting off the heads of grouse in the mountains, where the birds sit motionless in trees. The head is a small mark, while to hit the body is usually to spoil the bird; so I found that I averaged three or four cartridges for every head neatly taken off, the remaining shots representing spoiled birds and misses.

For the last sixty or seventy miles of our trip we left the river and struck off across a great, desolate gumbo prairie. There was no game, no wood for fuel, and the rare water-holes were far apart, so that we were glad when, as we toiled across the monotonous succession of long, swelling ridges, the dim, cloud-like mass, looming vague and purple on the rim of the horizon ahead of us, gradually darkened and hardened into the bold outline of the Black Hills.

CHAPTER VI

Among the High Hills; The Bighorn or Mountain Sheep

During the summer of 1886 I hunted chiefly to keep the ranch in meat. It was a very pleasant summer; although it was followed by the worst winter we ever witnessed on the plains. I was much at the ranch, where I had a good deal of writing to do; but every week or two I left, to ride among the line camps, or spend a few days on any round-up which happened to be in the neighborhood.

These days of vigorous work among the cattle were themselves full of pleasure. At dawn we were in the saddle, the morning air cool in our faces; the red sunrise saw us loping across the grassy reaches of prairie land, or climbing in single file among the rugged buttes. All the forenoon we spent riding the long circle with the cowpunchers of the round-up; in the afternoon we worked the herd, cutting the cattle, with much breakneck galloping and dextrous halting and wheeling. Then came the excitement and hard labor of roping, throwing, and branding the wild and vigorous range calves; in a corral, if one was handy, otherwise in a ring of horsemen. Soon after nightfall we lay down, in a log hut or tent, if at a line camp; under the open sky, if with the round-up wagon.

After ten days or so of such work, in which every man had to do his full share—for laggards and idlers, no matter who, get no mercy in the real and healthy democracy of the round-up—I would go back to the ranch to turn to my books with added zest for a fortnight. Yet even during these weeks at the ranch there was some out-door work; for I was breaking two or three colts. I took my time, breaking them gradually and gently, not, after the usual cowboy fashion, in a hurry, by sheer main strength and rough riding, with the attendant danger to the limbs of the man and very probable ruin to the manners of the horse. We rose early; each morning I stood on the low-roofed verandah, looking out under the line of murmuring, glossy-leaved cottonwoods, across the shallow river, to see the sun flame above the line of bluffs opposite. In the evening I strolled off for an hour or two's walk, rifle in hand. The roomy, homelike ranch house, with its log walls, shingled roof, and big chimneys and fireplaces, stands in a glade, in the midst of the thick forest, which covers half the bottom; behind rises, bare and steep, the wall of peaks, ridges, and table-lands.

During the summer in question, I once or twice shot a whitetail buck right on this large bottom; once or twice I killed a blacktail in the hills behind, not a mile from the ranch house. Several times I killed and brought in prong-bucks, rising before dawn, and riding off on a good horse for an all day's hunt in the rolling prairie country twelve or fifteen miles away. Occasionally I took the wagon and one of the men, driving to some good hunting ground and spending a night or two; usually returning with two or three prong-bucks, and once with an elk—but this was later in the fall. Not infrequently I went away by myself on horseback for a couple of days, when all the men were on the round-up, and when I wished to hunt thoroughly some country quite a distance from the ranch. I made one such hunt in late August, because I happened to hear that a small bunch of mountain sheep were haunting a tract of very broken ground, with high hills, about fifteen miles away.

I left the ranch early in the morning, riding my favorite hunting horse, old Manitou. The blanket and oil-skin slicker were rolled and strapped behind the saddle; for provisions I carried salt, a small bag of hard tack, and a little tea and sugar, with a metal cup in which to boil my water. The rifle and a score of cartridges in my woven belt completed my outfit. On my journey I shot two prairie chickens from a covey in the bottom of a brush coulie.

I rode more than six hours before reaching a good spot to camp. At first my route lay across grassy plateaus, and along smooth, wooded coulies; but after a few miles the ground became very rugged and difficult. At last I got into the heart of the Bad Lands proper, where the hard, wrinkled earth was torn into shapes as sullen and grotesque as those of dreamland. The hills rose high, their barren flanks carved and channelled, their tops mere needles and knife crests. Bands of black, red, and purple varied the gray and yellow-brown of their sides; the tufts of scanty vegetation were dull green. Sometimes I rode my horse at the bottom of narrow washouts, between straight walls of clay, but a few feet apart; sometimes I had to lead him as he scrambled up, down, and across the sheer faces of the buttes. The glare from the bare clay walls dazzled the eye; the air was burning under the hot August sun. I saw nothing living except the rattlesnakes, of which there were very many.

At last, in the midst of this devil's wilderness, I came on a lovely valley. A spring trickled out of a cedar canyon, and below this spring the narrow, deep ravine was green with luscious grass and was smooth for some hundred of yards. Here I unsaddled, and turned old Manitou loose to drink and feed at his leisure. At the edge of the dark cedar wood I cleared a spot for my bed, and drew a few dead sticks for the fire. Then I lay down and watched drowsily until the afternoon shadows filled the wild and beautiful gorge in which I was camped. This happened early, for the valley was very narrow and the hills on either hand were steep and high.

Springing to my feet, I climbed the nearest ridge, and then made my way, by hard clambering, from peak to peak and from crest to crest, sometimes crossing and sometimes skirting the deep washouts and canyons. When possible I avoided appearing on the sky-line, and I moved with the utmost caution, walking in a wide sweep so as to hunt across and up wind. There was much sheep sign, some of it fresh, though I saw none of the animals themselves; the square slots, with the indented marks of the toe points wide apart, contrasting strongly with the heart-shaped and delicate footprints of deer. The animals had, according to their habit, beaten trails along the summits of the higher crests; little side trails leading to any spur, peak, or other vantage-point from which there was a wide outlook over the country round-about.

The bighorns of the Bad Lands, unlike those of the mountains, shift their range but little, winter or summer. Save in the breeding season, when each master ram gets together his own herd, the ewes, lambs, and yearlings are apt to go in bands by themselves, while the males wander in small parties; now and then a very morose old fellow lives by himself, in some precipitous, out-of-the-way retreat. The rut begins with them much later than with deer; the exact time varies with the locality, but it is always after the bitter winter weather has set in. Then the old rams fight fiercely together, and on rare occasions utter a long grunting bleat or call. They are marvellous climbers, and dwell by choice always among cliffs and jagged, broken ground, whether wooded or not. An old bighorn ram is heavier than the largest buck; his huge, curved horns, massive yet supple build, and proud bearing mark him as one of the noblest beasts of the chase. He is wary; great skill and caution must be shown in approaching him; and no one but a good climber, with a steady head, sound lungs, and trained muscles, can successfully hunt him in his own rugged fastnesses. The chase of no other kind of American big game ranks higher, or more thoroughly tests the manliest qualities of the hunter.

I walked back to camp in the gloaming, taking care to reach it before it grew really dark; for in the Bad Lands it is entirely impossible to travel, or to find any given locality, after nightfall. Old Manitou had eaten his fill, and looked up at me with pricked ears, and wise, friendly face as I climbed down the side of the cedar canyon; then he came slowly towards me to see if I had not something for him. I rubbed his soft nose and gave him a cracker; then I picketed him to a solitary cedar, where the feed was good. Afterwards I kindled a small fire, roasted both prairie fowl, ate one, and put the other by for breakfast; and soon rolled myself in my blanket, with the saddle for a pillow, and the oilskin beneath. Manitou was munching the grass nearby. I lay just outside the line of stiff black cedars; the night air was soft in my face; I gazed at the shining and brilliant multitude of stars until my eyelids closed.

The chill breath which comes before dawn awakened me. It was still and dark. Through the gloom I could indistinctly make out the loom of the old horse, lying down. I was speedily ready, and groped and stumbled slowly up the hill, and then along its crest to a peak. Here I sat down and waited a quarter of an hour or so, until gray appeared in the east, and the dim light-streaks enabled me to walk farther. Before sunrise I was two miles from camp; then I crawled cautiously to a high ridge and crouching behind it scanned all the landscape eagerly. In a few minutes a movement about a third of a mile to the right, midway down a hill, caught my eye. Another glance showed me three white specks moving along the hillside. They were the white rumps of three fine mountain sheep, on their way to drink at a little alkaline pool in the bottom of a deep, narrow valley. In a moment they went out of sight round a bend of the valley; and I rose and trotted briskly towards them, along the ridge. There were two or three deep gullies to cross, and a high shoulder over which to clamber; so I was out of breath when I reached the bend beyond which they had disappeared. Taking advantage of a scrawny sage brush as cover I peeped over the edge, and at once saw the sheep, three big young rams. They had finished drinking and were standing beside the little mirey pool, about three hundred yards distant. Slipping back I dropped down into the bottom of the valley, where a narrow washout zigzagged from side to side, between straight walls of clay. The pool was in the upper end of this washout, under a cut bank.

An indistinct game trail, evidently sometimes used by both bighorn and blacktail, ran up this washout; the bottom was of clay so that I walked noiselessly; and the crookedness of the washout's course afforded ample security against discovery by the sharp eyes of the quarry. In a couple of minutes I stalked stealthily round the last bend, my rifle cocked and at the ready, expecting to see the rams by the pool. However, they had gone, and the muddy water was settling in their deep hoof marks. Running on I looked over the edge of the cut bank and saw them slowly quartering up the hillside, cropping the sparse tufts of coarse grass. I whistled, and as they stood at gaze I put a bullet into the biggest, a little too far aft of the shoulder, but ranging forward. He raced after the others, but soon fell behind, and turned off on his own line, at a walk, with drooping head. As he bled freely I followed his tracks, found him, very sick, in a washout a quarter of a mile beyond, and finished him with another shot. After dressing him, and cutting off the saddle and hams, as well as the head, I walked back to camp, breakfasted, and rode Manitou to where the sheep lay. Packing it securely behind the saddle, and shifting the blanket roll to in front of the saddle-horn, I led the horse until we were clear of the Bad Lands; then mounted him, and was back at the ranch soon after midday. The mutton of a fat young mountain ram, at this season of the year, is delicious.

Such quick success is rare in hunting sheep. Generally each head has cost me several days of hard, faithful work; and more than once I have hunted over a week without any reward whatsoever. But the quarry is so noble that the ultimate triumph—sure to come, if the hunter will but persevere long enough—atones for all previous toil and failure.

Once a lucky stalk and shot at a bighorn was almost all that redeemed a hunt in the Rockies from failure. I was high among the mountains at the time, but was dogged by ill luck; I had seen but little, and I had not shot very well. One morning I rose early, and hunted steadily until mid-day without seeing anything. A mountain hunter was with me. At noon we sat down to rest, and look over the country, from behind a shield of dwarf evergreens, on the brink of a mighty chasm. The rocks fell downwards in huge cliffs, stern and barren; from far below rose the strangled roaring of the torrent, as the foaming masses of green and white water churned round the boulders in the stream bed. Except this humming of the wild water, and the soughing of the pines, there was no sound. We were sitting on a kind of jutting promontory of rock so that we could scan the cliffs far and near. First I took the glasses and scrutinized the ground almost rod by rod, for nearly half an hour; then my companion took them in turn. It is very hard to make out game, especially when lying down, and still; and it is curious to notice how, after fruitlessly scanning a country through the glasses for a considerable period, a herd of animals will suddenly appear in the field of vision as if by magic. In this case, while my companion held the glasses for the second time, a slight motion caught his eye; and looking attentively he made out, five or six hundred yards distant, a mountain ram lying among some loose rocks and small bushes at the head of a little grassy cove or nook, in a shallow break between two walls of the cliff. So well did the bluish gray of its body harmonize in tint with the rocks and shrubbery that it was some time before I could see it, even when pointed out to me.

The wind was favorable, and we at once drew back and began a cautious stalk. It was impossible, owing to the nature of the cliffs above and below the bighorn's resting-place, to get a shot save by creeping along nearly on a level with him. Accordingly we worked our way down through a big cleft in the rocks, being forced to go very slowly and carefully lest we should start a loose stone; and at last reached a narrow terrace of rock and grass along which we walked comparatively at our ease. Soon it dwindled away, and we then had to do our only difficult piece of climbing—a clamber for fifty or sixty feet across a steep cliff shoulder. Some little niches and cracks in the rock and a few projections and diminutive ledges on its surface, barely enabled us to swarm across, with painstaking care—not merely to avoid alarming the game this time, but also to avoid a slip which would have proved fatal. Once across we came on a long, grassy shelf, leading round a shoulder into the cleft where the ram lay. As I neared the end I crept forward on hands and knees, and then crawled flat, shoving the rifle ahead of me, until I rounded the shoulder and peered into the rift. As my eyes fell on the ram he sprang to his feet, with a clatter of loose stones, and stood facing me, some sixty yards off, his dark face and white muzzle brought out finely by the battered, curved horns. I shot into his chest, hitting him in the sticking place; and after a few mad bounds he tumbled headlong, and fell a very great distance, unfortunately injuring one horn.

When much hunted, bighorn become the wariest of all American game, and their chase is then peculiarly laborious and exciting. But where they have known nothing of men, not having been molested by hunters, they are exceedingly tame. Professor John Bache McMaster informs me that in 1877 he penetrated to the Uintah Mountains of Wyoming, which were then almost unknown to hunters; he found all the game very bold, and the wild sheep in particular so unsuspicious that he could walk up to within short rifle range of them in the open.

On the high mountains bighorn occasionally get killed by a snow-slide. My old friend, the hunter Woody, once saw a band which started such an avalanche by running along a steep sloping snow field, it being in the spring; for several hundred yards it thundered at their heels, but by desperate racing they just managed to get clear. Woody was also once an eye-witness to the ravages the cougar commits among these wild sheep. He was stalking a band in the snow when he saw them suddenly scatter at a run in every direction. Coming up he found the traces of a struggle, and the track of a body being dragged through the snow, together with the round footmarks of the cougar; a little farther on lay a dead ewe, the blood flowing from the fang wounds in her throat.

Mountain Game;
The White Goat

Late one August I started on a trip to the Big Hole Basin, in Western Montana, to hunt white goats. With me went a friend of many hunts, John Willis, a tried mountain man.

We left the railroad at the squalid little hamlet of Divide, where we hired a team and wagon from a "busted" granger, suspected of being a Mormon, who had failed, even with the help of irrigation, in raising a crop. The wagon was in fairly good order; the harness was rotten, and needed patching with ropes; while the team consisted of two spoiled horses, overworked and thin, but full of the devil the minute they began to pick up condition. However, on the frontier one soon grows to accept little facts of this kind with bland indifference; and Willis was not only an expert teamster, but possessed that inexhaustible fertility of resource and unfailing readiness in an emergency so characteristic of the veteran of the border. Through hard experience he had become master of plainscraft and woodcraft, skilled in all frontier lore.

For a couple of days we jogged up the valley of the Big Hole River, along the mail road. At night we camped under our wagon. At the mouth of the stream the valley was a mere gorge, but it broadened steadily the farther up we went, till the rapid river wound through a wide expanse of hilly, treeless prairie. On each side the mountains rose, their lower flanks and the foot-hills covered with the ever-green forest. We got milk and bread at the scattered log-houses of the few settlers; and for meat we shot sage fowl, which abounded. They were feeding on grasshoppers at this time, and the flesh, especially of the young birds, was as tender and well tasting as possible; whereas, when we again passed through the valley in September, we found the birds almost uneatable, being fairly bitter with sage. Like all grouse they are far tamer earlier in the season than later, being very wild in winter; and, of course, they are boldest where they are least hunted; but for some unex-plained reason they are always tamer than the sharp-tail prairie fowl which are to be found in the same locality.

Finally we reached the neighborhood of the Battle Ground, where a rude stone monument commemorates the bloody drawn fight between General Gibbons' sol-diers and the Nez Percés warriors of Chief Joseph. Here, on the third day of our journey, we left the beaten road and turned towards the mountains, following an indistinct trail made by wood-choppers. We met with our full share of the usual mishaps incident to prairie travel; and towards evening our team got mired in crossing a slough. We at-tempted the crossing with some misgivings, which were warranted by the result; for the second plunge of the horses brought them up to their bellies in the morass, where they stuck. It was freezing cold, with a bitter wind blowing, and the bog holes were skimmed with ice; so that we passed a thoroughly wretched two hours while freeing the horses and unloading the wagon. However, we even-tually got across; my companion preserving an absolutely unruffled temper throughout, perseveringly whistling the "Arkansas Traveller." At one period, when we were up to our waists in the icy mud, it began to sleet and hail, and I muttered that I would "rather it didn't storm"; whereat he stopped whistling for a moment to make the laconic rejoinder, "We're not having our rathers this trip."

At nightfall we camped among the willow bushes by a little brook. For firewood we had only dead willow sticks; they made a hot blaze which soon died out; and as the cold grew intense, we rolled up in our blankets as soon as we had eaten our supper. The climate of the Big Hole Basin is alpine; that night, though it was the 20th of August, the thermometer sank to 10° F.

Early next morning we struck camp, shivering with cold as we threw the stiff, frozen harness on the horses. We soon got among the foot-hills, where the forest was open and broken by large glades, forming what is called a park country. The higher we went the smaller grew the glades and the denser the woodland; and it began to be very difficult to get the wagon forward. In many places one man had to go ahead to pick out the way, and if necessary do a little chopping and lopping with the axe, while the other followed driving the team. At last we were brought to a standstill, and pitched camp beside a rapid, alder-choked brook in the uppermost of a series of rolling glades, hemmed in by mountains and the dense coniferous forest. Our tent stood under a grove of pines, close to the brook; at night we built in front of it a big fire of crackling, resinous logs. Our goods were sheltered by the wagon, or covered with a tarpaulin; we threw down sprays of odorous evergreens to make a resting-place for our bedding; we built small scaffolds on which to dry the flesh of elk and deer. In an hour or two we had round us all the many real comforts of such a little wilderness home.

Whoever has long roamed and hunted in the wilderness always cherishes with wistful pleasure the memory of some among the countless camps he has made. The camp by the margin of the clear, mountain-hemmed lake; the camp in the dark and melancholy forest, where the gusty wind booms through the tall pine tops; the camp under gnarled cottonwoods, on the bank of a shrunken river, in the midst of endless grassy prairies,—of these, and many like them, each has had its own charm. Of course in hunting one must expect much hardship and repeated disappointment; and in many a camp, bad weather, lack of shelter, hunger, thirst, or ill success with game, renders the days and nights irksome and trying. Yet the hunter worthy of the name always willingly takes the bitter if by so doing he can get the sweet, and gladly balances failure and success, spurning the poorer souls who know neither.

We turned our horses loose, hobbling one; and as we did not look after them for several days, nothing but my companion's skill as a tracker enabled us to find them again. There was a spell of warm weather which brought out a few of the big bull-dog flies, which drive a horse— or indeed a man—nearly frantic; we were in the haunts of these dreaded and terrible scourges, which up to the beginning of August render it impossible to keep stock of any description unprotected where they abound, but which are never formidable after the first frost. In many parts of the wilderness these pests, or else the incredible swarms of mosquitoes, blackflies, and buffalo gnats, render life not worth living during the last weeks of spring and the early months of summer.

There were elk and deer in the neighborhood; also ruffed, blue, and spruce grouse; so that our camp was soon stocked with meat. Early one morning while Willis was washing in the brook, a little black bear thrust its sharp nose through the alders a few feet from him, and then hastily withdrew and was seen no more. The smaller wild-folk were more familiar. As usual in the northern mountains, the gray moose-birds and voluble, nervous little chipmunks made themselves at home in the camp. Parties of chickadees visited us occasionally. A family of flying squirrels lived overhead in the grove; and at nightfall they swept noiselessly from tree to tree, in long graceful curves. There were sparrows of several kinds moping about in the alders; and now and then one of them would sing a few sweet, rather mournful bars.

After several days' preliminary exploration we started on foot for white goat. We took no packs with us, each carrying merely his jacket, with a loaf of bread and a paper of salt thrust into the pockets. Our aim was to get well to one side of a cluster of high, bare peaks, and then to cross them and come back to camp; we reckoned that the trip would take three days.

All the first day we tramped through dense woods and across and around steep mountain spurs. We caught glimpses of two or three deer and a couple of elk, all does or fawns, however, which we made no effort to molest. Late in the afternoon we stumbled across a family of spruce grouse, which furnished us material for both supper and breakfast. The mountain men call this bird the fool-hen; and most certainly it deserves the name. The members of this particular flock, consisting of a hen and her three-parts grown chickens, acted with a stupidity unwonted even for their kind. They were feeding on the ground among some young spruce, and on our approach flew up and perched in the branches four or five feet above our heads. There they stayed, uttering a low, complaining whistle, and showed not the slightest suspicion when we came underneath them with long sticks and knocked four off their perches—for we did not wish to alarm any large game that might be in the neighborhood by firing. One particular bird was partially saved from my first blow by the intervening twigs; however, it merely flew a few yards, and then sat with its bill open,—having evidently been a little hurt,—until I came up and knocked it over with a better directed stroke.

Spruce grouse are plentiful in the mountain forests of the northern Rockies, and, owing to the ease with which they are killed, they have furnished me my usual provender when off on trips of this kind, where I carried no pack. They are marvellously tame and stupid. The young birds are the only ones I have ever killed in this manner with a stick; but even a full plumaged old cock in September is easily slain with a stone by any one who is at all a good thrower. A man who has played much base-ball need never use a gun when after spruce grouse. They are the smallest of the grouse kind; the cock is very handsome, with red eyebrows and dark, glossy plumage. Moreover, he is as brave as he is stupid and good-looking, and in the love season becomes fairly crazy: at such time he will occasionally make a feint of attacking a man, strutting, fluttering, and ruffling his feathers. The flesh of the spruce grouse is not so good as that of his ruffed and blue kinsfolk; and in winter, when he feeds on spruce buds, it is ill tasting. I have never been able to understand why closely allied species, under apparently the same surroundings, should differ so radically in such important traits as wariness and capacity to escape from foes. Yet the spruce grouse in this respect shows the most marked contrast to the blue grouse and the ruffed grouse. Of course all three kinds vary greatly in their behavior accordingly as they do or do not live in localities where they have been free from man's persecutions. The ruffed grouse, a very wary game bird in all old-settled regions, is often absurdly tame in the wilderness; and under persecution, even the spruce grouse gains some little wisdom; but the latter never becomes as wary as the former, and under no circumstances is it possible to outwit the ruffed grouse by such clumsy means as serve for his simple-minded brother. There is a similar difference between the sage fowl and prairie fowl, in favor of the latter. It is odd that the largest and the smallest kinds of grouse found in the United States should be the tamest; and also the least savory.

After tramping all day through the forest, at nightfall we camped in its upper edge, just at the foot of the steep rock walls of the mountain. We chose a sheltered spot, where the small spruce grew thick, and there was much dead timber; and as the logs, though long, were of little girth, we speedily dragged together a number sufficient to keep the fire blazing all night. Having drunk our full at a brook we cut two forked willow sticks, and then each plucked a grouse, split it, thrust the willow-fork into it, and roasted it before the fire. Besides this we had salt, and bread; moreover we were hungry and healthily tired; so the supper seemed, and was, delicious. Then we turned up the collars of our jackets, and lay down, to pass the night in broken slumber; each time the fire died down the chill waked us, and we rose to feed it with fresh logs.

At dawn we rose, and cooked and ate the two remaining grouse. Then we turned our faces upwards, and passed a day of severe toil in climbing over the crags. Mountaineering is very hard work; and when we got high among the peaks, where snow filled the rifts, the thinness of the air forced me to stop for breath every few hundred yards of the ascent. We found much sign of white goats, but in spite of steady work and incessant careful scanning of the rocks, we did not see our quarry until early in the afternoon.

We had clambered up one side of a steep saddle of naked rock, some of the scarped ledges being difficult, and indeed dangerous, of ascent. From the top of the saddle a careful scrutiny of the neighboring peaks failed to reveal any game, and we began to go down the other side. The mountain fell away in a succession of low cliffs, and we had to move with the utmost caution. In letting ourselves down from ledge to ledge one would hold the guns until the other got safe footing, and then pass them down to him. In many places we had to work our way along the cracks in the faces of the frost-riven rocks. At last, just as we reached a little smooth shoulder, my companion said, pointing down beneath us, "Look at the white goat!"

A moment or two passed before I got my eyes on it. We were looking down into a basin-like valley, surrounded by high mountain chains. At one end of the basin was a low pass, where the ridge was cut up with the zigzag trails made by the countless herds of game which had travelled it for many generations. At the other end was a dark gorge, through which a stream foamed. The floor of the basin was bright emerald green, dotted with darker bands where belts of fir trees grew; and in its middle lay a little lake.

At last I caught sight of the goat, feeding on a terrace rather over a hundred and twenty-five yards below me. I promptly fired, but overshot. The goat merely gave a few jumps and stopped. My second bullet went through its lungs; but fearful lest it might escape to some inaccessible cleft or ledge I fired again, missing; and yet again, breaking its back. Down it went, and the next moment began to roll over and over, from ledge to ledge. I greatly feared it would break its horns; an annoying and oft-recurring incident of white-goat shooting, where the nature of the ground is such that the dead quarry often falls hundreds of feet, its body being torn to ribbons by the sharp crags. However in this case the goat speedily lodged unharmed in a little dwarf evergreen.

Hardly had I fired my fourth shot when my companion again exclaimed, "Look at the white goats! look at the white goats!" Glancing in the direction in which he pointed I speedily made out four more goats standing in a bunch rather less than a hundred yards off, to one side of my former line of fire. They were all looking up at me. They stood on a slab of white rock, with which the color of their fleece harmonized well; and their black horns, muzzles, eyes, and hoofs looked like dark dots on a light-colored surface, so that it took me more than one glance to determine what they were. White goat invariably run up-hill when alarmed, their one idea seeming to be to escape danger by getting above it; for their brute foes are able to overmatch them on anything like level ground, but are helpless against them among the crags. Almost as soon as I saw them these four started up the mountain, nearly in my direction, while I clambered down and across to meet them. They halted at the foot of a cliff, and I at the top, being unable to see them; but in another moment they came bounding and cantering up the sheer rocks, not moving quickly, but traversing the most seemingly impossible places by main strength and sure-footedness. As they broke by me, some thirty yards off, I fired two shots at the rearmost, an old buck, somewhat smaller than the one I had just killed; and he rolled down the mountain dead. Two of the others, a yearling and a kid, showed more alarm than their elders, and ran off at a brisk pace. The remaining one, an old she, went off a hundred yards, and then deliberately stopped and turned round to gaze at us for a couple of minutes! Verily the white goat is the fool-hen among beasts of the chase.

Having skinned and cut off the heads we walked rapidly onwards, slanting down the mountain side, and then over and down the pass of the game trails; for it was growing late and we wished to get well down among the timber before nightfall. On the way an eagle came soaring over head, and I shot at it twice without success. Having once killed an eagle on the wing with a rifle, I always have a lurking hope that sometime I may be able to repeat the feat. I revenged myself for the miss by knocking a large blue goshawk out of the top of a blasted spruce, where it was sitting in lazy confidence, its crop stuffed with rabbit and grouse.

A couple of hours' hard walking brought us down to timber; just before dusk we reached a favorable camping spot in the forest, beside a brook, with plenty of dead trees for the night-fire. Moreover, the spot fortunately yielded us our supper too, in the shape of a flock of young spruce grouse, of which we shot off the heads of a couple. Immediately afterwards I ought to have procured our breakfast, for a cock of the same kind suddenly flew down nearby; but it was getting dark, I missed with the first shot, and with the second must have merely creased the neck, for though the tough old bird dropped, it fluttered and ran off among the underbrush and escaped.

We broiled our two grouse before our fire, dragged plenty of logs into a heap beside it, and then lay down to sleep fitfully, an hour or so at a time, throughout the night. We were continually wakened by the cold, when we had to rise and feed the flames. In the early morning we again started, walking for some time along the fresh trail made by a large band of elk, cows and calves. We thought we knew exactly the trend and outlet of the valley in which we were, and that therefore we could tell where the camp was; but, as so often happens in the wilderness, we had not reckoned aright, having passed over one mountain spur too many, and entered the ravines of an entirely different watercourse-system. In consequence we became entangled in a network of hills and valleys, making circle after circle to find our bearings; and we only reached camp after twelve hours' tiresome tramp without food.

On another occasion I shot a white goat while it was in a very curious and characteristic attitude. I was hunting, again with an old mountain man as my sole companion, among the high mountains of the Kootenai country, near the border of Montana and British Columbia. We had left our main camp, pitched by the brink of the river, and were struggling wearily on foot through the tangled forest and over the precipitous mountains, carrying on our backs light packs, consisting of a little food and two or three indispensable utensils, wrapped in our blankets. One day we came to the foot of a great chain of bare rocks, and climbed laboriously to its crest, up cliff after cliff, some of which were almost perpendicular. Swarming round certain of the rock shoulders, crossing an occasional sheer chasm, and in many places clinging to steep, smooth walls by but slight holds, we reached the top. The climbing at such a height was excessively fatiguing; moreover, it was in places difficult and even dangerous. Of course it was not to be compared to the ascent of towering, glacier-bearing peaks, such as those of the Selkirks and Alaska, where climbers must be roped to one another and carry ice axes.

Once at the top we walked very cautiously, being careful not to show ourselves against the sky-line, and scanning the mountain sides through our glasses. At last we made out three goats, grazing unconcernedly on a narrow grassy terrace, which sloped abruptly to the brink of a high precipice. They were not very far off, and there was a little rock spur above them which offered good cover for a stalk; but we had to crawl so slowly, partly to avoid falling, and partly to avoid detaching loose rocks, that it was nearly an hour before we got in a favorable position above them, and some seventy yards off. The frost-disintegrated mountains in which they live are always sending down showers of detached stones, so that the goats are not very sensitive to this noise; still, they sometimes pay instantaneous heed to it, especially if the sound is repeated.

When I peeped over the little ridge of rock, shoving my rifle carefully ahead of me, I found that the goats had finished feeding and were preparing to leave the slope. The old billy saw me at once, but evidently could not quite make me out. Thereupon, gazing intently at me, he rose gravely on his haunches, sitting up almost in the attitude of a dog when begging. I know no other horned animal that ever takes this position.

As I fired he rolled backwards, slipped down the grassy slope, and tumbled over the brink of the cliff, while the other two, a she and a kid, after a moment's panic-struck pause, and a bewildered rush in the wrong direction, made off up a little rocky gully, and were out of sight in a moment. To my chagrin when I finally reached the carcass, after a tedious and circuitous climb to the foot of the cliff, I found both horns broken off.

It was late in the afternoon, and we clambered down to the border of a little marshy alpine lake, which we reached in an hour or so. Here we made our camp about sunset, in a grove of stunted spruces, which furnished plenty of dead timber for the fire. There were many white-goat trails leading to this lake, and from the slide rock roundabout we heard the shrill whistling of hoary rock-woodchucks, and the querulous notes of the little conies—two of the sounds most familiar to the white-goat hunter. These conies had gathered heaps of dried plants, and had stowed them carefully away for winter use in the cracks between the rocks.

While descending the mountain we came on a little pack of snow grouse or mountain ptarmigan, birds which, save in winter, are always found above timber line. They were tame and fearless, though hard to make out as they ran among the rocks, cackling noisily, with their tails cocked aloft; and we had no difficulty in killing four, which gave us a good breakfast and supper. Old white goats are intolerably musky in flavor, there being a very large musk-pod between the horn and ear. The kids are eatable, but of course are rarely killed; the shot being usually taken at the animal with best horns—and the shes and young of any game should only be killed when there is a real necessity.

These two hunts may be taken as samples of most expeditions after white goat. There are places where the goats live in mountains close to bodies of water, either ocean fiords or large lakes; and in such places canoes can be used, to the greatly increased comfort and lessened labor of the hunters. In other places, where the mountains are low and the goats spend all the year in the timber, a pack-train can be taken right up to the hunting grounds. But generally one must go on foot, carrying everything on one's back, and at night lying out in the open or under a brush lean-to; meanwhile living on spruce grouse and ptarmigan, with an occasional meal of trout, and in times of scarcity squirrels, or anything else. Such a trip entails severe fatigue and not a little hardship. The actual hunting, also, implies difficult and laborious climbing, for the goats live by choice among the highest and most inaccessible mountains; though where they are found, as they sometimes are, in comparatively low forest-clad ranges, I have occasionally killed them with little trouble by lying in wait beside the well-trodden game trails they make in the timber.

In any event the hard work is to get up to the grounds where the game is found. Once the animals are spied there is but little call for the craft of the still-hunter in approaching them. Of all American game the white goat is the least wary and most stupid. In places where it is much hunted it of course gradually grows wilder and becomes difficult to approach and kill; and much of its silly tameness is doubtless due to the inaccessible nature of its haunts, which renders it ordinarily free from molestation; but aside from this it certainly seems as if it was naturally less wary than either deer or mountain sheep. The great point is to get above it. All its foes live in the valleys, and while it is in the mountains, if they strive to approach it at all, they must do so from below. It is in consequence always on the watch for danger from beneath; but it is easily approached from above, and then, as it generally tries to escape by running up hill, the hunter is very apt to get a shot.

Its chase is thus laborious rather than exciting; and to my mind it is less attractive than is the pursuit of most of our other game. Yet it has an attraction of its own after all; while the grandeur of the scenery amid which it must be carried on, the freedom and hardihood of the life and the pleasure of watching the queer habits of the game, all combine to add to the hunter's enjoyment.

White goats are self-confident, pugnacious beings.

An old billy, if he discovers the presence of a foe without being quite sure what it is, often refuses to take flight, but walks around, stamping, and shaking his head. The needle-pointed black horns are alike in both sexes, save that the males' are a trifle thicker; and they are most effective weapons when wielded by the muscular neck of a resolute and wicked old goat. They wound like stilettos and their bearer is in consequence a much more formidable foe in a hand-to-hand struggle than either a branching-antlered deer or a mountain ram, with his great battering head. The goat does not butt; he thrusts. If he can cover his back by a tree trunk or boulder he can stand off most carnivorous animals, no larger than he is.

Though awkward in movement, and lacking all semblance of lightness or agility, goats are excellent climbers. One of their queer traits is their way of getting their fore-hoofs on a slight ledge, and then drawing or lifting their bodies up by simple muscular exertion, stretching out their elbows, much as a man would. They do a good deal of their climbing by strength and command over their muscles; although they are also capable of making astonishing bounds. If a cliff surface has the least slope, and shows any inequalities or roughness whatever, goats can go up and down it with ease. With their short, stout legs, and large, sharp-edged hoofs they clamber well over ice, passing and repassing the mountains at a time when no man would so much as crawl over them. They bear extreme cold with indifference, but are intolerant of much heat; even when the weather is cool they are apt to take their noontide rest in caves; I have seen them solemnly retiring, for this purpose, to great rents in the rocks, at a time when my own teeth chattered because of the icy wind.

They go in small flocks; sometimes in pairs or little family parties. After the rut the bucks often herd by themselves, or go off alone, while the young and the shes keep together throughout the winter and the spring. The young are generally brought forth above timber line, or at its uppermost edge, save of course in those places where the goats live among mountains wooded to the top. Throughout the summer they graze on the short mountain plants which in many places form regular mats above timber line; the deep winter snows drive them low down in the wooded valleys, and force them to subsist by browsing. They are so strong that they plough their way readily through deep drifts; and a flock of goats at this season, when their white coat is very long and thick, if seen waddling off through the snow, have a comical likeness to so many diminutive polar bears. Of course they could easily be run down in the snow by a man on snowshoes, in the plain; but on a mountain side there are always bare rocks and cliff shoulders, glassy with winter ice, which give either goats or sheep an advantage over their snowshoe-bearing foes that deer and elk lack. Whenever the goats pass the winter in woodland they leave plenty of sign in the shape of patches of wool clinging to all the sharp twigs and branches against which they have brushed. In the spring they often form the habit of drinking at certain low pools, to which they beat deep paths; and at this season, and to a less extent in the summer and fall, they are very fond of frequenting mineral licks. At any such lick the ground is tramped bare of vegetation, and is filled with pits and hollows, actually dug by the tongues of innumerable generations of animals; while the game paths lead from them in a dozen directions.

In spite of the white goat's pugnacity, its clumsiness renders it no very difficult prey when taken unawares by either wolf or cougar, its two chief enemies. They cannot often catch it when it is above timber line; but it is always in sore peril from them when it ventures into the forest. Bears, also, prey upon it in the early spring; and one midwinter my friend Willis found a wolverine eating a goat which it had killed in a snowdrift at the foot of a cliff. The savage little beast growled and showed fight when he came near the body. Eagles are great enemies of the young kids, as they are of the young lambs of the bighorn.

The white goat is the only game beast of America which has not decreased in numbers since the arrival of the white man. Although in certain localities it is now decreasing, yet, taken as a whole, it is probably quite as plentiful now as it was fifty years back; for in the early part of the present century there were Indian tribes who hunted it perseveringly to make the skins into robes, whereas now they get blankets from the traders and no longer persecute the goats. The early trappers and mountain-men knew but little of the animal. Whether they were after beaver, or were hunting big game, or were merely exploring, they kept to the valleys; there was no inducement for them to climb to the tops of the mountains; so it resulted that there was no animal with which the old hunters were so unfamiliar as with the white goat. The professional hunters of to-day likewise bother it but little; they do not care to undergo severe toil for an animal with worthless flesh and a hide of little value—for it is only in the late fall and winter that the long hair and fine wool give the robe any beauty.

So the quaint, sturdy, musky beasts, with their queer and awkward ways, their boldness and their stupidity, with their white coats and big black hoofs, black muzzles, and sharp, gently-curved span-long black horns, have held their own well among the high mountains that they love. In the Rockies and the Coast ranges they abound from Alaska south to Montana, Idaho, and Washington; and here and there isolated colonies are found among the high mountains to the southward, in Wyoming, Colorado, even in New Mexico, and, strangest of all, in one or two spots among the barren coast mountains of southern California. Long after the elk has followed the buffalo to the happy hunting grounds the white goat will flourish among the towering and glacier-riven peaks, and, grown wary with succeeding generations, will furnish splendid sport to those hunters who are both good riflemen and hardy cragsmen.

Hunting in the Selkirks; The Caribou

In September, 1888, I was camped on the shores of Kootenai Lake, having with me as companions, John Willis and an impassive-looking Indian named Ammál. Coming across through the dense coniferous forests of northern Idaho we had struck the Kootenai River. Then we went down with the current as it wound in half circles through a long alluvial valley of mixed marsh and woodland, hemmed in by lofty mountains. The lake itself, when we reached it, stretched straight away like a great fiord, a hundred miles long and about three in breadth. The frowning and rugged Selkirks came down sheer to the water's edge. So straight were the rock walls that it was difficult for us to land with our batteau, save at the places where the rapid mountain torrents entered the lake. As these streams of swift water broke from their narrow gorges they made little deltas of level ground, with beaches of fine white sand; and the stream-banks were edged with cottonwood and poplar, their shimmering foliage relieving the sombre coloring of the evergreen forest.

Close to such a brook, from which we drew strings of large silver trout, our tent was pitched, just within the forest. From between the trunks of two gnarled, wind-beaten trees, a pine and a cottonwood, we looked out across the lake. The little bay in our front, in which we bathed and swam, was sometimes glassily calm; and again heavy wind squalls arose, and the surf beat strongly on the beach where our boat was drawn up. Now and then great checker-back loons drifted buoyantly by, stopping with bold curiosity to peer at the white tent gleaming between the tree-trunks, and at the smoke curling above their tops; and they called to one another, both at dawn and in the daytime, with shrieks of unearthly laughter. Troops of noisy, parti-colored Clark's crows circled over the tree-tops or hung from among the pine cones; jays and chick-adees came round camp, and woodpeckers hammered lustily in the dead timber. Two or three times parties of In-dians passed down the lake, in strangely shaped bark ca-noes, with peaked, projecting prows and sterns; craft utterly unlike the graceful, feather-floating birches so beloved by both the red and the white woodsmen of the northeast. Once a couple of white men, in a dugout or pirogue made out of a cottonwood log, stopped to get lunch. They were mining prospectors, French Canadians by birth, but beaten into the usual frontier-mining stamp; doomed to wander their lives long, ever hoping, in the quest for metal wealth.

With these exceptions there was nothing to break the silent loneliness of the great lake. Shrouded as we were in the dense forest, and at the foot of the first steep hills, we could see nothing of the country on the side where we were camped; but across the water the immense mountain masses stretched away from our vision, range upon range, until they turned to a glittering throng of ice peaks and snow fields, the feeding beds of glaciers. Between the lake and the snow range were chains of gray rock peaks, and the mountain sides and valleys were covered by the primeval forest. The woods were on fire across the lake from our camp, burning steadily. At night the scene was very grand, as the fire worked slowly across the mountain sides in immense zigzags of quivering red; while at times isolated pines of unusual size kindled, and flamed for hours, like the torches of a giant. Finally the smoke grew so thick as to screen from our views the grand landscape opposite.

We had come down from a week's fruitless hunting in the mountains; a week of excessive toil, in a country where we saw no game—for in our ignorance we had wasted time, not going straight back to the high ranges, from which the game had not yet descended. After three or four days of rest, and of feasting on trout—a welcome relief to the monotony of frying-pan bread and coarse salt pork— we were ready for another trial; and early one morning we made the start. Having to pack everything for a fortnight's use on our backs, through an excessively rough country, we of course travelled as light as possible, leaving almost all we had with the tent and boat. Each took his own blanket; and among us we carried a frying-pan, a teapot, flour, pork, salt, tea, and matches. I also took a jacket, a spare pair of socks, some handkerchiefs, and my washing kit. Fifty cartridges in my belt completed my outfit.

We walked in single file, as is necessary in thick woods. The white hunter led and I followed, each with rifle on shoulder and pack on back. Ammál, the Indian, pigeon-toed along behind, carrying his pack, not as we did ours, but by help of a forehead-band, which he sometimes shifted across his breast. The travelling through the tangled, brush-choked forest, and along the boulder-strewn and precipitous mountain sides, was inconceivably rough and difficult. In places we followed the valley, and when this became impossible we struck across the spurs. Every step was severe toil. Now we walked through deep moss and rotting mould, every few feet clambering over huge trunks; again we pushed through a stiff jungle of bushes and tall, prickly plants—called "devil's clubs,"—which stung our hands and faces. Up the almost perpendicular hill-sides we in many places went practically on all fours, forcing our way over the rocks and through the dense thickets of laurels or young spruce. Where there were windfalls or great stretches of burnt forest, black and barren wastes, we balanced and leaped from log to log, sometimes twenty or thirty feet above the ground; and when such a stretch was on a steep hill-side, and especially if the logs were enveloped in a thick second growth of small evergreens, the footing was very insecure, and the danger from a fall considerable. Our packs added greatly to our labor, catching on the snags and stubs; and where a grove of thick-growing young spruces or balsams had been burned, the stiff and brittle twigs pricked like so much coral. Most difficult of all were the dry water-courses, choked with alders, where the intertwined tangle of tough stems formed an almost literally impenetrable barrier to our progress. Nearly every movement—leaping, climbing, swinging one's self up with one's hands, bursting through stiff bushes, plunging into and out of bogs—was one of strain and exertion; the fatigue was tremendous, and steadily continued, so that in an hour every particle of clothing I had on was wringing wet with sweat.

At noon we halted beside a little brook for a bite of lunch—a chunk of cold frying-pan bread, which was all we had.

While at lunch I made a capture. I was sitting on a great stone by the edge of the brook, idly gazing at a water-wren which had come up from a short flight—I can call it nothing else—underneath the water, and was singing sweetly from a spray-splashed log. Suddenly a small animal swam across the little pool at my feet. It was less in size than a mouse, and as it paddled rapidly underneath the water its body seemed flattened like a disc and was spangled with tiny bubbles, like specks of silver. It was a water-shrew, a rare little beast. I sat motionless and watched both the shrew and the water-wren—waterousel, as it should rightly be named. The latter, emboldened by my quiet, presently flew by me to a little rapids close at hand, lighting on a round stone, and then slipping unconcernedly into the swift water. Anon he emerged, stood on another stone, and trilled a few bars, though it was late in the season for singing; and then dove again into the stream. I gazed at him eagerly; for this strange, pretty water-thrush is to me one of the most attractive and interesting birds to be found in the gorges of the great Rockies. Its haunts are romantically beautiful, for it always dwells beside and in the swift-flowing mountain brooks; it has a singularly sweet song; and its ways render it a marked bird at once, for though looking much like a sober-colored, ordinary woodland thrush, it spends half its time under the water, walking along the bottom, swimming and diving, and flitting through as well as over the cataracts.

In a minute or two the shrew caught my eye again. It got into a little shallow eddy and caught a minute fish, which it carried to a half-sunken stone and greedily devoured, tugging voraciously at it as it held it down with its paws. Then its evil genius drove it into a small puddle alongside the brook, where I instantly pounced on and slew it; for I knew a friend in the Smithsonian at Washington who would have coveted it greatly. It was a soft, pretty creature, dark above, snow-white below, with a very long tail. I turned the skin inside out and put a bent twig in, that it might dry; while Ammál, who had been intensely interested in the chase and capture, meditatively shook his head and said "wagh," unable to fathom the white man's medicine. However, my labor came to nought, for that evening I laid the skin out on a log, Ammál threw the log into the fire, and that was the end of the shrew.

When this interlude was over we resumed our march, toiling silently onwards through the wild and rugged country. Towards evening the valley widened a little, and we were able to walk in the bottoms, which much lightened our labor. The hunter, for greater ease, had tied the thongs of his heavy pack across his breast, so that he could not use his rifle; but my pack was lighter, and I carried it in a manner that would not interfere with my shooting, lest we should come unawares on game.

It was well that I did so. An hour or two before sunset we were travelling, as usual, in Indian file, beside the stream, through an open wood of great hemlock trees.

There was no breeze, and we made no sound as we marched, for our feet sunk noiselessly into the deep sponge of moss, while the incessant dashing of the torrent, churning among the stones, would have drowned a far louder advance.

Suddenly the hunter, who was leading, dropped down in his tracks, pointing forward; and some fifty feet beyond I saw the head and shoulders of a bear as he rose to make a sweep at some berries. He was in a hollow where a tall, rank, prickly plant, with broad leaves, grew luxuriantly; and he was gathering its red berries, rising on his hind legs and sweeping them down into his mouth with his paw, and was much too intent on his work to notice us, for his head was pointed the other way. The moment he rose again I fired, meaning to shoot through the shoulders, but instead, in the hurry, taking him in the neck. Down he went, but whether hurt or not we could not see, for the second he was on all fours he was no longer visible. Rather to my surprise he uttered no sound—for bear when hit or when charging often make a great noise—so I raced forward to the edge of the hollow, the hunter close behind me, while Ammál danced about in the rear, very much excited, as Indians always are in the presence of big game. The instant we reached the hollow and looked down into it from the low bank on which we stood we saw by the swaying of the tall plants that the bear was coming our way. The hunter was standing some ten feet distant, a hemlock trunk being between us; and the next moment the bear sprang clean up the bank the other side of the hemlock, and almost within arm's length of my companion. I do not think he had intended to charge; he was probably confused by the bullet through his neck, and had by chance blundered out of the hollow in our direction; but when he saw the hunter so close he turned for him, his hair bristling and his teeth showing. The man had no cartridge in his weapon, and with his pack on could not have used it anyhow; and for a moment it looked as if he stood a fair chance of being hurt, though it is not likely that the bear would have done more than knock him down with his powerful forepaw, or perchance give him a single bite in passing. However, as the beast sprang out of the hollow he poised for a second on the edge of the bank to recover his balance, giving me a beautiful shot, as he stood sideways to me; the bullet struck between the eye and ear, and he fell as if hit with a pole axe.

Immediately the Indian began jumping about the body, uttering wild yells, his usually impassive face lit up with excitement, while the hunter and I stood at rest, leaning on our rifles and laughing. It was a strange scene, the dead bear lying in the shade of the giant hemlocks, while the fantastic-looking savage danced round him with shrill whoops, and the tall frontiersman looked quietly on.

Our prize was a large black bear, with two curious brown streaks down his back, one on each side of the spine. We skinned him and camped by the carcass, as it was growing late. To take the chill off the evening air we built a huge fire, the logs roaring and crackling. To one side of it we made our beds—of balsam and hemlock boughs; we did not build a brush lean-to, because the night seemed likely to be clear. Then we supped on sugarless tea, frying-pan bread, and quantities of bear meat, fried or roasted—and how very good it tasted only those know who have gone through much hardship and some little hunger, and have worked violently for several days without flesh food. After eating our fill we stretched ourselves around the fire; the leaping sheets of flame lit the tree-trunks round about, causing them to start out against the cavernous blackness beyond, and reddened the interlacing branches that formed a canopy overhead. The Indian sat on his haunches, gazing steadily and silently into the pile of blazing logs, while the white hunter and I talked together.

The morning after killing Bruin, we again took up our march, heading up stream, that we might go to its sources amidst the mountains, where the snow fields fed its springs. It was two full days' journey thither, but we took much longer to make it, as we kept halting to hunt the adjoining mountains. On such occasions Ammál was left as camp guard, while the white hunter and I would start by daybreak and return at dark utterly worn out by the excessive fatigue. We knew nothing of caribou, nor where to hunt for them; and we had been told that thus early in the season they were above tree limit on the mountain sides. Accordingly we would climb up to the limits of the forests, but never found a caribou trail; and once or twice we went on to the summits of the crag-peaks, and across the deep snow fields in the passes. There were plenty of white goats, however, their trails being broad paths, especially at one spot where they led down to a lick in the valley; round the lick, for a space of many yards, the ground was trampled as if in a sheepfold.

The mountains were very steep, and the climbing was in places dangerous, when we were above the timber and had to make our way along the jagged knife-crests and

across the faces of the cliffs; while our hearts beat as if
about to burst in the high, thin air. In walking over rough
but not dangerous ground—across slides or in thick timber—my companion was far more skilful than I was; but
rather to my surprise I proved to be nearly as good as he
when we came to the really dangerous places, where we
had to go slowly, and let one another down from ledge to
ledge, or crawl by narrow cracks across the rock walls.

The view from the summits was magnificent, and I
never tired of gazing at it. Sometimes the sky was a dome
of blue crystal, and mountain, lake, and valley lay spread in
startling clearness at our very feet; and again snow-peak
and rock-peak were thrust up like islands through a sea of
billowy clouds. At the feet of the topmost peaks, just
above the edge of the forest, were marshy alpine valleys,
the boggy ground soaked with water, and small bushes or
stunted trees fringing the icy lakes. In the stony mountain
sides surrounding these lakes there were hoary woodchucks, and conies. The former resembled in their habits
the alpine marmot, rather than our own common eastern
woodchuck. They lived alone or in couples among the
rocks, their gray color often making them difficult to see
as they crouched at the mouths of their burrows, or sat
bolt upright; and as an alarm note they uttered a loud
piercing whistle, a strong contrast to the querulous, plaintive "p-a-a-y" of the timid conies. These likewise loved to
dwell where the stones and slabs of rock were heaped on
one another; though so timid, they were not nearly as wary
as the woodchucks. If we stood quite still the little brown
creatures would venture away from their holes and hop
softly over the rocks as if we were not present.

The white goats were too musky to eat, and we saw nothing else to shoot; so we speedily became reduced to tea, and to bread baked in the frying-pan, save every now and then for a feast on the luscious mountain blueberries. This rather meagre diet, coupled with incessant fatigue and exertion, made us fairly long for meat food; and we fell off in flesh, though of course in so short a time we did not suffer in either health or strength. Fortunately the nights were too cool for mosquitoes; but once or twice in the afternoons, while descending the lower slopes of the mountains, we were much bothered by swarms of gnats; they worried us greatly, usually attacking us at a time when we had to go fast in order to reach camp before dark, while the roughness of the ground forced us to use both hands in climbing, and thus forbade us to shield our faces from our tiny tormentors. Our chief luxury was, at the end of the day, when footsore and weary, to cast aside our sweat-drenched clothes and plunge into the icy mountain torrent for a moment's bath that freshened us as if by magic. The nights were generally pleasant, and we slept soundly on our beds of balsam boughs, but once or twice there were sharp frosts, and it was so cold that the hunter and I huddled together for warmth and kept the fires going till morning. One day, when we were on the march, it rained heavily, and we were soaked through, and stiff and chilly when we pitched camp; but we speedily built a great brush lean-to, made a roaring fire in front, and grew once more to warmth and comfort as we sat under our steaming shelter. The only discomfort we really minded was an occasional night in wet blankets.

In the evening the Indian and the white hunter played

interminable games of seven-up with a greasy pack of cards. In the course of his varied life the hunter had been a professional gambler; and he could have easily won all the Indian's money, the more speedily inasmuch as the untutored red man was always attempting to cheat, and was thus giving his far more skilful opponent a certain right to try some similar deviltry in return. However, it was distinctly understood that there should be no gambling, for I did not wish Ammál to lose all his wages while in my employ; and the white man stood loyally by his agreement. Ammál's people, just before I engaged him, had been visited by their brethren, the Upper Kootenais, and in a series of gambling matches had lost about all their belongings.

Ammál himself was one of the Lower Kootenais; I had hired him for the trip, as the Indians west of the Rockies, unlike their kinsman of the plains, often prove hard and willing workers. His knowledge of English was almost nil; and our very scanty conversation was carried on in the Chinook jargon, universally employed between the mountains and the Pacific. Apparently he had three names: for he assured us that his "Boston" (*i.e.,* American) name was Ammál; his "Siwash" (*i.e.,* Indian) name was Appák; and that the priest called him Abél—for the Lower Kootenais are nominally Catholics. Whatever his name he was a good Indian, as Indians go. I often tried to talk with him about game and hunting, but we understood each other too little to exchange more than the most rudimentary ideas. His face brightened one night when I happened to tell him of my baby boys at home; he must have been an affectionate father in his way, this dark Ammál, for he at once proceeded to tell me about his own papoose, who had also seen one snow, and to describe how the little fellow was old enough to take one step and then fall down. But he never displayed so much vivacity as on one occasion when the white hunter happened to relate to him a rather gruesome feat of one of their mutual acquaintances, an Upper Kootenai Indian named Three Coyotes. The latter was a quarrelsome, adventurous Indian, with whom the hunter had once had a difficulty—"I had to beat the cuss over the head with my gun a little," he remarked parenthetically. His last feat had been done in connection with a number of Chinamen who had been working among some placer mines, where the Indians came to visit them. Now the astute Chinese are as fond of gambling as any of the borderers, white or red, and are very successful, generally fleecing the Indians unmercifully. Three Coyotes lost all he possessed to one of the pigtailed gentry; but he apparently took his losses philosophically, and pleasantly followed the victor round, until the latter had won all the cash and goods of several other Indians. Then he suddenly fell on the exile from the Celestial Empire, slew him and took all his plunder, retiring unmolested, as it did not seem any one's business to avenge a mere Chinaman. Ammál was immensely interested in the tale, and kept recurring to it again and again, taking two little sticks and making the hunter act out the whole story. The Kootenais were then only just beginning to consider the Chinese as human. They knew they must not kill white people, and they had their own code of morality among themselves; but when the Chinese first appeared they evidently thought that there could not be any especial objection to killing them, if any reason arose for doing so. I think the hunter himself sympathized somewhat with this view.

Ammál objected strongly to leaving the neighborhood of the lake. He went the first day's journey willingly enough, but after that it was increasingly difficult to get him along, and he gradually grew sulky. For some time we could not find out the reason; but finally he gave us to understand that he was afraid because up in the high mountains there were "little bad Indians" who would kill him if they caught him alone, especially at night. At first we thought he was speaking of stray warriors of the Blackfeet tribe; but it turned out that he was not thinking of human beings at all, but of hobgoblins.

Indeed the night sounds of these great stretches of mountain woodland were very weird and strange. Though I have often and for long periods dwelt and hunted in the wilderness, yet I never before so well understood why the people who live in lonely forest regions are prone to believe in elves, wood spirits, and other beings of an unseen world. Our last camp, whereat we spent several days, was pitched in a deep valley nearly at the head of the stream. Our brush shelter stood among the tall coniferous trees that covered the valley bottom; but the altitude was so great that the forest extended only a very short distance up the steep mountain slopes. Beyond, on either hand, rose walls of gray rock, with snow beds in their rifts, and, high above, toward the snow peaks, the great white fields dazzled the eyes. The torrent foamed swiftly by but a short distance below the mossy level space on which we had built our slight weather-shield of pine boughs; other streams poured into it, from ravines through which they leaped down the mountain sides.

After nightfall, round the camp fire, or if I awakened after sleeping a little while, I would often lie silently for many minutes together, listening to the noises of the wilderness. At times the wind moaned harshly through the tops of the tall pines and hemlocks; at times the branches were still; but the splashing murmur of the torrent never ceased, and through it came other sounds—the clatter of huge rocks falling down the cliffs, the dashing of cataracts in far-off ravines, the hooting of owls. Again, the breeze would shift, and bring to my ears the ringing of other brooks and cataracts and wind-stirred forests, and perhaps at long intervals the cry of some wild beast, the crash of a falling tree, or the faint rumble of a snow avalanche. If I listened long enough, it would almost seem that I heard thunderous voices laughing and calling to one another, and as if at any moment some shape might stalk out of the darkness into the dim light of the embers.

Until within a couple of days of turning our faces back towards the lake we did not come across any caribou, and saw but a few old signs; and we began to be fearful lest we should have to return without getting any, for our shoes had been cut to ribbons by the sharp rocks, we were almost out of flour, and therefore had but little to eat. However, our perseverance was destined to be rewarded.

The first day after reaching our final camp, we hunted across a set of spurs and hollows but saw nothing living; yet we came across several bear tracks, and in a deep, mossy quagmire, by a spring, found where a huge silver-tip had wallowed only the night before.

Next day we started early, determined to take a long walk and follow the main stream up to its head, or at least above timber line. The hunter struck so brisk a pace, plunging through thickets and leaping from log to log in the slashes of fallen timber, and from boulder to boulder in crossing the rock-slides, that I could hardly keep up to him, struggle as I would, and we each of us got several ugly tumbles, saving our rifles at the expense of scraped hands and bruised bodies. We went up one side of the stream, intending to come down the other; for the forest belt was narrow enough to hunt thoroughly. For two or three hours we toiled through dense growth, varied by rock-slides, and once or twice by marshy tracts, where water oozed and soaked through the mossy hillsides, studded rather sparsely with evergreens. In one of these places we caught a glimpse of an animal which the track showed to be a wolverine.

Then we came to a spur of open hemlock forest; and no sooner had we entered it than the hunter stopped and pointed exultingly to a well-marked game trail, in which it was easy at a glance to discern the great round footprints of our quarry. We hunted carefully over the spur and found several trails, generally leading down along the ridge; we also found a number of beds, some old and some recent, usually placed where the animal could keep a lookout for any foe coming up from the valley. They were merely slight hollows or indentations in the pine-needles; and, like the game trails, were placed in localities similar to those that would be chosen by blacktail deer. The caribou droppings were also very plentiful; and there were signs of where they had browsed on the blueberry bushes, cropping off the berries, and also apparently of where they had here and there plucked a mouthful of a peculiar kind of moss, or cropped off some little mushrooms. But the beasts themselves had evidently left the hemlock ridge, and we went on.

We were much pleased at finding the sign in open timber, where the ground was excellent for still-hunting; for in such thick forest as we had passed through, it would have been by mere luck only that we could have approached game.

After a little while the valley became so high that the large timber ceased, and there were only occasional groves of spindling evergreens. Beyond the edge of the big timber was a large boggy tract, studded with little pools; and here again we found plenty of caribou tracks. A caribou has an enormous foot, bigger than a cow's, and admirably adapted for travelling over snow or bogs; hence they can pass through places where the long slender hoofs of moose or deer, or the rounded hoofs of elk, would let their owners sink at once; and they are very difficult to kill by following on snow-shoes—a method much in vogue among the brutal game butchers for slaughtering the more helpless animals. Spreading out his great hoofs, and bending his legs till he walks almost on the joints, a caribou will travel swiftly over a crust through which a moose breaks at every stride, or through deep snow in which a deer cannot flounder fifty yards. Usually he trots; but when pressed he will spring awkwardly along, leaving tracks in the snow almost exactly like magnified imprints of those of a great rabbit, the long marks of the two hind legs forming an angle with each other, while the forefeet make a large point almost between.

The caribou had wandered all over the bogs and through the shallow pools, but evidently only at night or in the dusk, when feeding or in coming to drink; and we again went on. Soon the timber disappeared almost entirely, and thick brushwood took its place; we were in a high, bare alpine valley, the snow lying in drifts along the sides. In places there had been enormous rock-slides, entirely filling up the bottom, so that for a quarter of a mile at a stretch the stream ran underground. In the rock masses of this alpine valley we, as usual, saw many conies and hoary woodchucks.

The caribou trails had ceased, and it was evident that the beasts were not ahead of us in the barren, treeless recesses between the mountains of rock and snow; and we turned back down the valley, crossing over to the opposite or south side of the stream. We had already eaten our scanty lunch, for it was afternoon. For several miles of hard walking, through thicket, marsh, and rock-slide, we saw no traces of the game. Then we reached the forest, which soon widened out, and crept up the mountain sides; and we came to where another stream entered the one we were following. A high, steep shoulder between the two valleys was covered with an open growth of great hemlock timber, and in this we again found the trails and beds plentiful. There was no breeze, and after beating through the forest nearly to its upper edge, we began to go down the ridge, or point of the shoulder. The comparative freedom from brushwood made it easy to walk without noise, and we descended the steep incline with the utmost care, scanning every object, and using every caution not to slip on the hemlock needles, nor to strike a stone or break a stick with our feet. The sign was very fresh, and when still half a mile or so from the bottom we at last came on three bull caribou.

Instantly the hunter crouched down, while I ran noiselessly forward behind the shelter of a big hemlock trunk until within fifty yards of the grazing and unconscious quarry. They were feeding with their heads up-hill, but so greedily that they had not seen us; and they were rather difficult to see themselves, for their bodies harmonized well in color with the brown tree-trunks and lichen-covered boulders. The largest, a big bull with a good but by no means extraordinary head, was nearest. As he stood fronting me with his head down I fired into his neck, breaking the bone, and he turned a tremendous back somersault. The other two halted a second in stunned terror; then one, a yearling, rushed past us up the valley down which we had come, while the other, a large bull with small antlers, crossed right in front of me, at a canter, his neck thrust out, and his head—so coarse-looking compared to the delicate outlines of an elk's—turned towards me. His movements seemed clumsy and awkward, utterly unlike those of a deer; but he handled his great hoofs cleverly enough, and broke into a headlong, rattling gallop as he went down the hillside, crashing through the saplings and leaping over the fallen logs. There was a spur a little beyond, and up this he went at a swinging trot, halting when he reached the top, and turning to look at me once more. He was only a hundred yards away; and though I had not intended to shoot him (for his head was not good), the temptation was sore; and I was glad when, in another second, the stupid beast turned again and went off up the valley at a slashing run.

Then we hurried down to examine with pride and pleasure the dead bull—his massive form, sleek coat, and fine antlers. It was one of those moments that repay the hunter for days of toil and hardship; that is if he needs repayment, and does not find life in the wilderness pleasure enough in itself.

It was getting late, and if we expected to reach camp that night it behooved us not to delay; so we merely halted long enough to dress the caribou, and take a steak with us—which we did not need, by the way, for almost immediately we came on a band of spruce grouse and knocked off the heads of five with our rifles. The caribou's stomach was filled with blueberries, and with their leaves, and with a few small mushrooms also, and some mouthfuls of moss. We went home very fast, too much elated to heed scratches and tumbles; and just as it was growing so dark that further travelling was impossible we came opposite our camp, crossed the river on a fallen hemlock, and walked up to the moody Indian, as he sat crouched by the fire.

He lost his sullenness when he heard what we had done; and next day we all went up and skinned and butchered the caribou, returning to camp and making ready to start back to the lake the following morning; and that night we feasted royally.

We were off by dawn, the Indian joyfully leading. Coming up into the mountains he had always been the rear man of the file; but now he went first and struck a pace that, continued all day long, gave me a little trouble to follow. Each of us carried his pack; to the Indians' share fell the caribou skull and antlers, which he bore on his head. At the end of the day he confessed to me that it had made his head "heap sick"—as well it might. We had made four short days', or parts of days', march coming up; for we had stopped to hunt, and moreover we knew nothing of the country, being probably the first white men in it, while none of the Indians had ever ventured a long distance from the lake. Returning we knew how to take the shortest route, we were going down hill, and we walked or trotted very fast; and so we made the whole distance in twelve hours' travel. At sunset we came out on the last range of steep foot-hills, overlooking the cove where we had pitched our permanent camp; and from a bare cliff shoulder we saw our boat on the beach, and our white tent among the trees, just as we had left them, while the glassy mirror of the lake reflected the outlines of the mountains opposite.

Though this was the first caribou I had ever killed, it was by no means the first I had ever hunted. Among my earliest hunting experiences, when a lad, were two fruitless and toilsome expeditions after caribou in the Maine woods. One I made in the fall, going to the head of the Munsungin River in a pirogue, with one companion. The water was low, and all the way up we had to drag the pirogue, wet to our middles, our ankles sore from slipping on the round stones under the rushing water, and our muscles aching with fatigue. When we reached the head-waters we found no caribou sign, and came back without slaying anything larger than an infrequent duck or grouse.

The following February I made a trip on snow-shoes after the same game, and with the same result. However, I enjoyed the trip, for the northland woods are very beautiful and strange in winter, as indeed they are at all other times—and it was my first experience on snow-shoes. I used the ordinary webbed racquets, and as the snow, though very deep, was only imperfectly crusted, I found that for a beginner the exercise was laborious in the extreme, speedily discovering that, no matter how cold it was, while walking through the windless woods I stood in no need of warm clothing. But at night, especially when lying out, the cold was bitter. Our plan was to drive in a sleigh to some logging camp, where we were always received with hearty hospitality, and thence make hunting trips, in very light marching order, through the heart of the surrounding forest. The woods, wrapped in their heavy white mantle, were still and lifeless. There were a few chickadees and woodpeckers; now and then we saw flocks of red-polls, pine linnets, and large, rosy grossbeaks; and once or twice I came across a grouse or white rabbit, and killed it for supper; but this was nearly all. Yet, though bird life was scarce, and though we saw few beasts beyond an occasional porcupine or squirrel, every morning the snow was dotted with a network of trails made during the hours of darkness; the fine tracery of the footprints of the little red wood-mouse, the marks which showed the loping progress of the sable, the V and dot of the rabbit, the round pads of the lucivee, and many others. The snow reveals, as nothing else does, the presence in the forest of the many shy woodland creatures which lead their lives abroad only after nightfall. Once we saw a coon, out early after its winter nap, and following I shot it in a hollow tree. Another time we came on a deer and the frightened beast left its "yard," a tangle of beaten paths, or deep furrows. The poor animal made but slow headway through the powdery snow; after going thirty or forty rods it sank exhausted in a deep drift, and lay there in helpless panic as we walked close by. Very different were the actions of the only caribou we saw—a fine beast which had shed its antlers. I merely caught a glimpse of it as it leaped over a breastwork of down timbers; and we never saw it again. Alternately trotting and making a succession of long jumps, it speedily left us far behind; with its great splay-hoofs it could snow-shoe better than we could. It is among deer the true denizen of the regions of heavy snowfall; far more so than the moose. Only under exceptional conditions of crust-formation is it in any danger from a man on snow-shoes.

In other ways it is no better able to take care of itself than moose and deer; in fact I doubt whether its senses are quite as acute, or at least whether it is as wary and knowing, for under like conditions it is rather easier to still-hunt. In the fall caribou wander long distances, and are fond of frequenting the wet barrens which break the expanse of the northern forest in tracts of ever increasing size as the subarctic regions are neared. At this time they go in bands, each under the control of a master bull, which wages repeated and furious battles for his harem; and in their ways of life they resemble the wapiti more than they do the moose or deer. They sometimes display a curious boldness, the bulls especially showing both stupidity and pugnacity when in districts to which men rarely penetrate.

On our way out of the woods, after this hunt, there was a slight warm spell, followed by rain and then by freezing weather, so as to bring about what is known as a silver thaw. Every twig was sheathed in glittering ice, and in the moonlight the forest gleamed as if carved out of frosted silver.

CHAPTER IX

The Wapiti or Round-Horned Elk

Once, while on another hunt with John Willis, I spent a week in a vain effort to kill moose among the outlying mountains at the southern end of the Bitter Root range. Then, as we had no meat, we determined to try for elk, of which we had seen much sign.

We were camped with a wagon, as high among the foot-hills as wheels could go, but several hours' walk from the range of the game; for it was still early in the season, and they had not yet come down from the upper slopes. Accordingly we made a practice of leaving the wagon for two or three days at a time to hunt; returning to get a night's rest in the tent, preparatory to a fresh start. On these trips we carried neither blankets nor packs, as the walking was difficult and we had much ground to cover. Each merely put on his jacket with a loaf of frying-pan bread and a paper of salt stuffed into the pockets. We were cumbered with nothing save our rifles and cartridges.

On the morning in question we left camp at sunrise. For two or three hours we walked up-hill through a rather open growth of small pines and spruces, the travelling being easy. Then we came to the edge of a deep valley, a couple of miles across. Into this we scrambled, down a steep slide, where the forest had grown up among the im-

mense boulder masses. The going here was difficult to a
degree; the great rocks, dead timber, slippery pine needles,
and loose gravel entailing caution at every step, while we
had to guard our rifles carefully from the consequences of
a slip. It was not much better at the bottom, which was
covered by a tangled mass of swampy forest. Through this
we hunted carefully, but with no success, in spite of our
toil; for the only tracks we saw that were at all fresh were
those of a cow and calf moose. Finally, in the afternoon,
we left the valley and began to climb a steep gorge, down
which a mountain torrent roared and foamed in a succession of cataracts.

Three hours' hard climbing brought us to another valley, but of an entirely different character. It was several
miles long, but less than a mile broad. Save at the mouth,
it was walled in completely by chains of high rock-peaks,
their summits snow-capped; the forest extended a short
distance up their sides. The bottom of the valley was in
places covered by open woodland, elsewhere by marshy
meadows, dotted with dense groves of spruce.

Hardly had we entered this valley before we caught a
glimpse of a yearling elk walking rapidly along a game
path some distance ahead. We followed as quickly as we
could without making a noise, but after the first glimpse
never saw it again; for it is astonishing how fast an elk
travels, with its ground-covering walk. We went up the
valley until we were well past its middle, and saw abundance of fresh elk sign. Evidently two or three bands had
made the neighborhood their headquarters. Among them
were some large bulls, which had been trying their horns
not only on the quaking-asp and willow saplings, but also

on one another, though the rut had barely begun. By one pool they had scooped out a kind of wallow or bare spot in the grass, and had torn and tramped the ground with their hoofs. The place smelt strongly of their urine.

By the time the sun set we were sure the elk were towards the head of the valley. We utilized the short twilight in arranging our sleeping place for the night, choosing a thick grove of spruce beside a small mountain tarn, at the foot of a great cliff. We were chiefly influenced in our choice by the abundance of dead timber of a size easy to handle; the fuel question being all-important on such a trip, where one has to lie out without bedding, and to keep up a fire, with no axe to cut wood.

Having selected a smooth spot, where some low-growing firs made a wind break, we dragged up enough logs to feed the fire throughout the night. Then we drank our fill at the icy pool, and ate a few mouthfuls of bread. While it was still light we heard the querulous bleat of the conies, from among the slide rocks at the foot of the mountain; and the chipmunks and chickarees scolded at us. As dark came on, and we sat silently gazing into the flickering blaze, the owls began muttering and hooting.

Clearing the ground of stones and sticks, we lay down beside the fire, pulled our soft felt hats over our ears, buttoned our jackets, and went to sleep. Of course our slumbers were fitful and broken, for every hour or two the fire got low and had to be replenished. We wakened shivering out of each spell of restless sleep to find the logs smouldering; we were alternately scorched and frozen.

As the first faint streak of dawn appeared in the dark sky my companion touched me lightly on the arm. The fire was nearly out; we felt numbed by the chill air. At once we sprang up, stretched our arms, shook ourselves, examined our rifles, swallowed a mouthful or two of bread, and walked off through the gloomy forest.

At first we could scarcely see our way, but it grew rapidly lighter. The gray mist rose and wavered over the pools and wet places; the morning voices of the wilderness began to break the death-like stillness. After we had walked a couple of miles the mountain tops on our right hand reddened in the sun-rays.

Then, as we trod noiselessly over the dense moss, and on the pine needles under the scattered trees, we heard a sharp clang and clatter up the valley ahead of us. We knew this meant game of some sort; and stealing lightly and cautiously forward we soon saw before us the cause of the noise.

In a little glade, a hundred and twenty-five yards from us, two bull elk were engaged in deadly combat, while two others were looking on. It was a splendid sight. The great beasts faced each other with lowered horns, the manes that covered their thick necks, and the hair on their shoulders, bristling and erect. Then they charged furiously, the crash of the meeting antlers resounding through the valley. The shock threw them both on their haunches; with locked horns and glaring eyes they strove against each other, getting their hind legs well under them, straining every muscle in their huge bodies, and squealing savagely. They were evenly matched in weight, strength, and courage; and push as they might, neither got the upper hand, first one yielding a few inches, then the other, while they swayed to and fro in their struggles, smashing the bushes and ploughing up the soil.

Finally they separated and stood some little distance apart, under the great pines; their sides heaving, and columns of steam rising from their nostrils through the frosty air of the brightening morning. Again they rushed together with a crash, and each strove mightily to over-throw the other, or get past his guard; but the branching antlers caught every vicious lunge and thrust. This set-to was stopped rather curiously. One of the onlooking elk was a yearling; the other, though scarcely as heavy-bodied as either of the fighters, had a finer head. He was evidently much excited by the battle, and he now began to walk to-wards the two combatants, nodding his head and uttering a queer, whistling noise. They dared not leave their flanks uncovered to his assault; and as he approached they promptly separated, and walked off side by side a few yards apart. In a moment, however, one spun round and jumped at his old adversary, seeking to stab him in his un-protected flank; but the latter was just as quick, and as be-fore caught the rush on his horns. They closed as furiously as ever; but the utmost either could do was to inflict one or two punches on the neck and shoulders of his foe, where the thick hide served as a shield. Again the peace-maker approached, nodding his head, whistling, and threatening; and again they separated.

This was repeated once or twice; and I began to be afraid lest the breeze which was very light and puffy should shift and give them my wind. So, resting my rifle on my knee I fired twice, putting one bullet behind the shoulder of the peace-maker, and the other behind the shoulder of one of the combatants. Both were deadly shots, but, as so often with wapiti, neither of the wounded animals at the moment showed any signs of being hit. The yearling ran off unscathed. The other three crowded together and trotted behind some spruce on the left, while we ran forward for another shot. In a moment one fell; whereupon the remaining two turned and came back across the glade, trotting to the right. As we opened fire they broke into a lumbering gallop, but were both downed before they got out of sight in the timber.

As soon as the three bulls were down we busied ourselves taking off their heads and hides, and cutting off the best portions of the meat—from the saddles and hams—to take back to camp, where we smoked it. But first we had breakfast. We kindled a fire beside a little spring of clear water and raked out the coals. Then we cut two willow twigs as spits, ran on each a number of small pieces of elk loin, and roasted them over the fire. We had salt; we were very hungry; and I never ate anything that tasted better.

The wapiti is, next to the moose, the most quarrelsome and pugnacious of American deer. It cannot be said that it is ordinarily a dangerous beast to hunt; yet there are instances in which wounded wapiti, incautiously approached to within striking distance, have severely misused their assailants, both with their antlers and their forefeet. I myself knew one man who had been badly mauled in this fashion. When tamed the bulls are dangerous to human life in the rutting season. In a grapple they are of course infinitely more to be dreaded than ordinary deer, because of their great strength.

However, the fiercest wapiti bull, when in a wild state,

flees the neighborhood of man with the same panic terror shown by the cows; and he makes no stand against a grisly, though when his horns are grown he has little fear of either wolf or cougar if on his guard and attacked fairly. The chief battles of the bulls are of course waged with one another. Before the beginning of the rut they keep by themselves: singly, while the sprouting horns are still very young, at which time they lie in secluded spots and move about as little as possible; in large bands, later in the season. At the beginning of the fall these bands join with one another and with the bands of cows and calves, which have likewise been keeping to themselves during the late winter, the spring, and the summer. Vast herds are thus sometimes formed, containing, in the old days when wapiti were plenty, thousands of head. The bulls now begin to fight furiously with one another, and the great herd becomes split into smaller ones. Each of these has one master bull, who has won his position by savage battle, and keeps it by overcoming every rival, whether a solitary bull, or the lord of another harem, who challenges him. When not fighting or love-making he is kept on the run, chasing away the young bulls who venture to pay court to the cows. He has hardly time to eat or sleep, and soon becomes gaunt and worn to a degree. At the close of the rut many of the bulls become so emaciated that they retire to some secluded spot to recuperate. They are so weak that they readily succumb to the elements, or to their brute foes; many die from sheer exhaustion.

The battles between the bulls rarely result fatally. After a longer or shorter period of charging, pushing, and struggling the heavier or more enduring of the two begins to shove his weaker antagonist back and round; and the latter then watches his chance and bolts, hotly, but as a rule harmlessly, pursued for a few hundred yards. The massive branching antlers serve as effective guards against the most wicked thrusts. While the antagonists are head on, the worst that can happen is a punch on the shoulder which will not break the thick hide, though it may bruise the flesh underneath. It is only when a beast is caught while turning that there is a chance to deliver a possibly deadly stab in the flank, with the brow prongs, the "dog-killers" as they are called in bucks. Sometimes, but rarely, fighting wapiti get their antlers interlocked and perish miserably; my own ranch, the Elkhorn, was named from finding on the spot where the ranch house now stands two splendid pairs of elk antlers thus interlocked.

Wapiti keep their antlers until the spring, whereas deer and moose lose theirs by midwinter. The bull's behavior in relation to the cow is merely that of a vicious and brutal coward. He bullies her continually, and in times of danger his one thought is for sneaking off to secure his own safety. For all his noble looks he is a very unamiable beast, who behaves with brutal ferocity to the weak, and shows abject terror of the strong. According to his powers, he is guilty of rape, robbery, and even murder. I never felt the least compunction at shooting a bull, but I hate to shoot a cow, even when forced by necessity. Maternity must always appeal to any one. A cow has more courage than a bull. She will fight valiantly for her young calf, striking such blows with her forefeet that most beasts of prey at once slink away from the combat. Cougars and wolves commit great ravages among the bands; but they often secure their quarry only at the cost of sharp preliminary tussles—and in tussles of this kind they do not always prove victors or escape scathless.

During the rut the bulls are very noisy; and their notes of amorous challenge are called "whistling" by the frontiersmen,—very inappropriately. They begin to whistle about ten days before they begin to run; and they have in addition an odd kind of bark, which is only heard occasionally. The whistling is a most curious, and to me a most attractive sound, when heard in the great lonely mountains. As with so many other things, much depends upon the surroundings. When listened to nearby and under unfavorable circumstances, the sound resembles a succession of hoarse whistling roars, ending with two or three gasping grunts.

But heard at a little distance, and in its proper place, the call of the wapiti is one of the grandest and most beautiful sounds in nature. Especially is this the case when several rivals are answering one another, on some frosty moonlight night in the mountains. The wild melody rings from chasm to chasm under the giant pines, sustained and modulated, through bar after bar, filled with challenge and proud anger. It thrills the soul of the listening hunter.

Once, while in the mountains, I listened to a peculiarly grand chorus of this kind. We were travelling with pack ponies at the time, and our tent was pitched in a grove of yellow pine, by a brook in the bottom of a valley. On either hand rose the mountains, covered with spruce forest. It was in September, and the first snow had just fallen.

The day before we had walked long and hard; and

during the night I slept the heavy sleep of the weary. Early in the morning, just as the east began to grow gray, I waked; and as I did so, the sounds that smote on my ear, caused me to sit up and throw off the warm blankets. Bull elk were challenging among the mountains on both sides of the valley, a little way from us, their notes echoing like the calling of silver bugles. Groping about in the dark, I drew on my trousers, an extra pair of thick socks, and my moccasins, donned a warm jacket, found my fur cap and gloves, and stole out of the tent with my rifle.

The air was very cold; the stars were beginning to pale in the dawn; on the ground the snow glimmered white, and lay in feathery masses on the branches of the balsams and young pines. The air rang with the challenges of many wapiti; their incessant calling came pealing down through the still, snow-laden woods. First one bull challenged; then another answered; then another and another. Two herds were approaching one another from opposite sides of the valley, a short distance above our camp; and the master bulls were roaring defiance as they mustered their harems.

I walked stealthily up the valley, until I felt that I was nearly between the two herds; and then stood motionless under a tall pine. The ground was quite open at this point, the pines, though large, being scattered; the little brook ran with a strangled murmur between its rows of willows and alders, for the ice along its edges nearly skimmed its breadth. The stars paled rapidly, the gray dawn brightened, and in the sky overhead faint rose-colored streaks were turning blood-red. What little wind there was breathed in my face and kept me from discovery.

I made up my mind, from the sound of the challenging, now very near me, that one bull on my right was advancing towards a rival on my left, who was answering
every call. Soon the former approached so near that I
could hear him crack the branches, and beat the bushes
with his horns; and I slipped quietly from tree to tree, so
as to meet him when he came out into the more open
woodland. Day broke, and crimson gleams played across
the snow-clad mountains beyond.

At last, just as the sun flamed red above the hill-tops,
I heard the roar of the wapiti's challenge not fifty yards
away; and I cocked and half raised my rifle, and stood motionless. In a moment more, the belt of spruces in front of
me swayed and opened, and the lordly bull stepped out.
He bore his massive antlers aloft; the snow lay thick on his
mane; he snuffed the air and stamped on the ground as he
walked. As I drew a bead, the motion caught his eye; and
instantly his bearing of haughty and warlike self-
confidence changed to one of alarm. My bullet smote
through his shoulder-blades, and he plunged wildly forward, and fell full length on the blood-stained snow.

Nothing can be finer than a wapiti bull's carriage
when excited or alarmed; he then seems the embodiment
of strength and stately grace. But at ordinary times his
looks are less attractive, as he walks with his neck level
with his body and his head outstretched, his horns lying
almost on his shoulders. The favorite gait of the wapiti is
the trot, which is very fast, and which they can keep up for
countless miles; when suddenly and greatly alarmed, they
break into an awkward gallop, which is faster, but which
speedily tires them.

I have occasionally killed elk in the neighborhood of my ranch on the Little Missouri. They were very plentiful along this river until 1881, but the last of the big bands were slaughtered or scattered about that time. Smaller bunches were found for two or three years longer; and to this day, scattered individuals, singly or in parties of two or three, linger here and there in the most remote and inaccessible parts of the broken country. In the old times they were often found on the open prairie, and were fond of sunning themselves on the sand bars by the river, even at midday, while they often fed by daylight (as they do still in remote mountain fastnesses). Nowadays the few survivors dwell in the timber of the roughest ravines, and only venture abroad at dusk or even after nightfall. Thanks to their wariness and seclusiveness, their presence is often not even suspected by the cowboys or others who occasionally ride through their haunts; and so the hunters only know vaguely of their existence. It thus happens that the last individuals of a species may linger in a locality for many years after the rest of their kind have vanished; on the Little Missouri to-day every elk (as in the Rockies every buffalo) killed is at once set down as "the last of its race." For several years in succession I myself kept killing one or two such "last survivors."

A yearling bull which I thus obtained was killed while in company with my staunch friend Will Dow, on one of the first trips which I took with that prince of drivers, old man Tompkins. We were laying in our stock of winter meat; and had taken the wagon to go to a knot of high and very rugged hills where we knew there were deer, and thought there might be elk. Old Tompkins drove the wagon with unmoved composure up, down, and across frightful-looking hills, and when they became wholly impassable, steered the team over a cut bank and up a kind of winding ravine or wooded washout, until it became too rough and narrow for farther progress. There was good grass for the horses on a hill off to one side of us; and stunted cottonwood trees grew between the straight white walls of clay and sandstone which hemmed in the washout. We pitched our tent by a little trickling spring and kindled a great fire, the fitful glare lighting the bare cliffs and the queer, sprawling tops of the cottonwoods; and after a dinner of fried prairie-chicken went to bed. At dawn we were off, and hunted till nearly noon; when Dow, who had been walking to one side, beckoned to me and remarked, "There's something mighty big in the timber down under the cliff; I guess it's an elk" (he had never seen one before); and the next moment, as old Tompkins expressed it, "the elk came bilin' out of the coulie." Old Tompkins had a rifle on this occasion and the sight of game always drove him crazy; as I aimed I heard Dow telling him "to let the boss do the shooting"; and I killed the elk to a savage interjectional accompaniment of threats delivered at old man Tompkins between the shots.

Elk are sooner killed off than any other game save buffalo, but this is due to their size and the nature of the ground they frequent rather than to their lack of shyness. They like open woodland, or mountainous park country, or hills riven by timber coulies; and such ground is the most favorable to the hunter, and the most attractive in which to hunt. On the other hand moose, for instance, live in such dense cover that it is very difficult to get at them;

when elk are driven by incessant persecution to take refuge in similar fastnesses they become almost as hard to kill. In fact, in this respect the elk stands to the moose much as the blacktail stands to the whitetail. The moose and whitetail are somewhat warier than the elk and blacktail; but it is the nature of the ground which they inhabit that tells most in their favor. On the other hand, as compared to the blacktail, it is only the elk's size which puts it at a disadvantage in the struggle for life when the rifle-bearing hunter appears on the scene. It is quite as shy and difficult to approach as the deer; but its bulk renders it much more eagerly hunted, more readily seen, and more easily hit. Occasionally elk suffer from fits of stupid tameness or equally stupid panic; but the same is true of blacktail. In two or three instances, I have seen elk show silly ignorance of danger; but half a dozen times I have known blacktail behave with an even greater degree of stupid familiarity.

There is another point in which the wapiti and blacktail agree in contrast to the moose and whitetail. Both the latter delight in water-lilies, entering the ponds to find them, and feeding on them greedily. The wapiti is very fond of wallowing in the mud, and of bathing in pools and lakes; but as a rule it shows as little fondness as the blacktail for feeding on water-lilies or other aquatic plants.

In reading of the European red deer, which is nothing but a diminutive wapiti, we often see a "stag of ten" alluded to as if a full-grown monarch. A full-grown wapiti bull, however, always has twelve, and may have fourteen, regular normal points on his antlers, besides irregular additional prongs; and he occasionally has ten points when a two-year-old, as I have myself seen with calves captured young and tamed. The calf has no horns. The yearling carries two foot-long spikes, sometimes bifurcated, so as to make four points. The two-year-old often has six or eight points on his antlers; but sometimes ten, although they are always small. The three-year-old has eight or ten points, while his body may be nearly as large as that of a full-grown animal. The four-year-old is normally a ten or twelve pointer, but as yet with much smaller antlers than those so proudly borne by the old bulls.

Frontiersmen only occasionally distinguish the prongs by name. The brow and bay points are called dog-killers or war-tines; the tray is known simply as the third point; and the most characteristic prong, the long and massive fourth, is now and then called the dagger-point; the others being known as the fifth and sixth.

In the high mountain forest into which the wapiti has been driven, the large, heavily furred northern lynx, the lucivee, takes the place of the smaller, thinner-haired lynx of the plains and of the more southern districts, the bobcat or wildcat. On the Little Missouri the latter is the common form; yet I have seen a lucivee which was killed there. On Clarke's Fork of the Columbia both occur, the lucivee being the most common. They feed chiefly on hares, squirrels, grouse, fawns, etc.; and the lucivee, at least, also occasionally kills foxes and coons, and has in its turn to dread the pounce of the big timber wolf. Both kinds of lynx can most easily be killed with dogs, as they tree quite readily when thus pursued. The wildcat is often followed on horseback, with a pack of hounds, when the country is favorable; and when chased in this fashion yields excellent sport. The skin of both these lynxes is tender. They often maul an inexperienced pack quite badly, inflicting severe scratches and bites on any hound which has just resolution enough to come to close quarters, but not to rush in furiously; but a big fighting dog will readily kill either. At Thompson's Falls two of Willis' hounds killed a lucivee unaided, though one got torn. Archibald Rogers' dog Sly, a cross between a greyhound and a bull mastiff, killed a bobcat single-handed. He bayed the cat and then began to threaten it, leaping from side to side; suddenly he broke the motion, and rushing in got his foe by the small of the back and killed it without receiving a scratch.

The porcupine is sure to attract the notice of any one going through the mountains. It is also found in the timber belts fringing the streams of the great plains, where it lives for a week at a time in a single tree or clump of trees, peeling the bark from the limbs. But it is the easiest of all animals to exterminate, and is now abundant only in deep mountain forests. It is very tame and stupid; it goes on the ground, but its fastest pace is a clumsy waddle, and on trees, but is the poorest of tree-climbers,—grasping the trunk like a small, slow bear. It can neither escape nor hide. It trusts to its quills for protection, as the skunk does to its odor; but it is far less astute and more helpless than the skunk. It is readily made into a very unsuspicious and familiar, but uninteresting, pet. I have known it come into camp in the daytime, and forage round the fire by which I was sitting. Its coat protects it against most foes. Bears sometimes eat it when very hungry, as they will eat anything; and I think that elk occasionally destroy it in sheer wantonness. One of its most resolute foes is the fisher, that big sable—almost a wolverine—which preys on everything, from a coon to a fawn, or even a small fox.

The noisy, active little chickarees and chipmunks, however, are by far the most numerous and lively denizens of these deep forests. They are very abundant and very noisy; scolding the travellers exactly as they do the bears when the latter dig up the caches of ants. The chipmunks soon grow tame and visit camp to pick up the crusts. The chickarees often ascend to the highest pine tops, where they cut off the cones, dropping them to the ground with a noise which often for a moment puzzles the still-hunter.

Two of the most striking and characteristic birds to be seen by him who hunts and camps among the pine-clad and spruce-clad slopes of the northern Rockies are a small crow and a rather large woodpecker. The former is called Clark's crow, and the latter Lewis' woodpecker. Their names commemorate their discoverers, the explorers Lewis and Clark, the first white men who crossed the United States to the Pacific, the pioneers of that great army of adventurers who since then have roamed and hunted over the Great Plains and among the Rocky Mountains.

These birds are nearly of a size, being about as large as a flicker. The Clark's crow, an ash-colored bird with black wings and white tail and forehead, is as common as it is characteristic, and is sure to attract attention. It is as knowing as the rest of its race, and very noisy and active. It flies sometimes in a straight line, with regular wing-beats, sometimes in a succession of loops like a wood-pecker, and often lights on rough bark or a dead stump in an attitude like the latter; and it is very fond of scrambling and clinging, often head downwards, among the outermost cones on the top of a pine, chattering loudly all the while. One of the noticeable features of its flight is the hollow, beating sound of the wings. It is restless and fond of company, going by preference in small parties. These little parties often indulge in regular plays, assembling in some tall tree-top and sailing round and round it, in noisy pursuit of one another, lighting continually among the branches.

The Lewis' woodpecker, a handsome, dark-green bird, with white breast and red belly, is much rarer, quite as shy, and generally less noisy and conspicuous. Its flight is usually strong and steady, like a jay's, and it perches upright among the twigs, or takes short flights after passing insects, as often as it scrambles over the twigs in the ordinary woodpecker fashion. Like its companion, the Clark's crow, it is ordinarily a bird of the high tree-tops, and around these it indulges in curious aërial games, again like those of the little crow. It is fond of going in troops, and such a troop frequently choose some tall pine and soar round and above it in irregular spirals.

The remarkable and almost amphibious little water wren, with its sweet song, its familiarity, and its very curious habit of running on the bottom of the stream, several feet beneath the surface of the race of rapid water, is the most noticeable of the small birds of the Rocky Mountains. It sometimes sings loudly while floating with half-spread wings on the surface of a little pool. Taken as a whole, small birds are far less numerous and noticeable in the wilderness, especially in the deep forests, than in the groves and farmland of the settled country. The hunter and trapper are less familiar with small-bird music than with the screaming of the eagle and the large hawks, the croaking bark of the raven, the loon's cry, the crane's guttural clangor, and the unearthly yelling and hooting of the big owls.

No bird is so common around camp, so familiar, so amusing on some occasions, and so annoying on others, as that drab-colored imp of iniquity, the whisky-jack—also known as the moose bird and camp robber. The familiarity of these birds is astonishing, and the variety of their cries,—generally harsh, but rarely musical—extraordinary. They snatch scraps of food from the entrances of the tents, and from beside the camp fire; and they shred the venison hung in the trees unless closely watched. I have seen an irate cook of accurate aim knock one off an elk-haunch, with a club seized at random; and I have known another to be killed with a switch, and yet another to be caught alive in the hand. When game is killed they are the first birds to come to the carcass. Following them come the big jays, of a uniform dark-blue color, who bully them, and are bullied in turn by the next arrivals, the magpies; while when the big ravens come, they keep all the others in the background, with the exception of an occasional wide-awake magpie.

For a steady diet no meat tastes better or is more nourishing than elk venison; moreover the different kinds of grouse give variety to the fare, and delicious trout swarm throughout the haunts of the elk in the Rockies. I have never seen them more numerous than in the wonderful and beautiful Yellowstone Canyon, a couple of miles below where the river pitches over the Great Falls, in wind-swayed cataracts of snowy foam. At this point it runs like a mill-race, in its narrow winding bed, between immense walls of queerly carved and colored rock which tower aloft in almost perpendicular cliffs. Late one afternoon in the fall of '90 Ferguson and I clambered down into the canyon, with a couple of rods, and in an hour caught all the fish we could carry. It then lacked much less than an hour of nightfall, and we had a hard climb to get out of the canyon before darkness overtook us; as there was not a vestige of a path, and as the climbing was exceedingly laborious and at one or two points not entirely without danger, the rocks being practicable in very few places, we could hardly have made much progress after it became too dark to see. Each of us carried the bag of trout in turn, and I personally was nearly done out when we reached the top; and then had to trot three miles to the horses.

CHAPTER X

An Elk-Hunt at
Two-Ocean Pass

In September, 1891, with my ranch-partner, Ferguson, I
made an elk-hunt in northwestern Wyoming among
the Shoshone Mountains, where they join the Hoodoo
and Absoraka ranges. There is no more beautiful game-
country in the United States. It is a park land, where
glades, meadows, and high mountain pastures break the
evergreen forest; a forest which is open compared to the
tangled density of the woodland farther north. It is a high,
cold region of many lakes and clear rushing streams. The
steep mountains are generally of the rounded form so
often seen in the ranges of the Cordilleras of the United
States; but the Hoodoos, or Goblins, are carved in fantastic and extraordinary shapes; while the Tetons, a group of
isolated rock-peaks, show a striking boldness in their lofty
outlines.

This was one of the pleasantest hunts I ever made. As
always in the mountains, save where the country is so
rough and so densely wooded that one must go a-foot, we
had a pack-train; and we took a more complete outfit than
we had ever before taken on such a hunt, and so travelled
in much comfort. Usually when in the mountains I have
merely had one companion, or at most a couple, and two
or three pack-ponies; each of us doing his share of the
packing, cooking, fetching water, and pitching the small

square of canvas which served as tent. In itself packing is both an art and a mystery, and a skilful professional packer, versed in the intricaies of the "diamond hitch," packs with a speed which no non-professional can hope to rival, and fixes the side packs and top packs with such scientific nicety, and adjusts the doubles and turns of the lash-rope so accurately, that everything stays in place under any but the most adverse conditions. Of course, like most hunters, I can myself in case of need throw the diamond hitch after a fashion, and pack on either the off or near side. Indeed, unless a man can pack it is not possible to make a really hard hunt in the mountains, if alone, or with only a single companion. The mere fair-weather hunter, who trusts entirely to the exertions of others, and does nothing more than ride or walk about under favorable circumstances, and shoot at what somebody else shows him, is a hunter in name only. Whoever would really deserve the title must be able at a pinch to shift for himself, to grapple with the difficulties and hardships of wilderness life unaided, and not only to hunt, but at times to travel for days, whether on foot or on horseback, alone. However, after one has passed one's novitiate, it is pleasant to be comfortable when the comfort does not interfere with the sport; and although a man sometimes likes to hunt alone, yet often it is well to be with some old mountain hunter, a master of woodcraft, who is a first-rate hand at finding game, creeping upon it, and tracking it when wounded. With such a companion one gets much more game, and learns many things by observation instead of by painful experience.

On this trip we had with us two hunters, Tazewell Woody and Elwood Hofer, a packer who acted as cook, and a boy to herd the horses. Of the latter, there were twenty; six saddle-animals and fourteen for the packs—two or three being spare horses, to be used later in carrying the elk-antlers, sheep-horns, and other trophies. Like most hunters' pack-animals, they were either half broken, or else broken down; tough, unkempt; jaded-looking beasts of every color—sorrel, buckskin, pinto, white, bay, roan. After the day's work was over, they were turned loose to shift for themselves; and about once a week they strayed, and all hands had to spend the better part of the day hunting for them. The worst ones for straying, curiously enough, were three broken-down old "bear-baits," which went by themselves, as is generally the case with the cast-off horses of a herd. There were two sleeping-tents, another for the provisions,—in which we ate during bad weather,—and a canvas tepee, which was put up with lodge-poles, Indian fashion, like a wigwam. A tepee is more difficult to put up than an ordinary tent; but it is very convenient when there is rain or snow. A small fire kindled in the middle keeps it warm, the smoke escaping through the open top—that is, when it escapes at all; strings are passed from one pole to another, on which to hang wet clothes and shoes, and the beds are made around the edges. As an offset to the warmth and shelter, the smoke often renders it impossible even to sit upright. We had a very good camp-kit, including plenty of cooking- and eating-utensils; and among our provisions were some canned goods and sweetmeats, to give a relish to our meals of meat and bread. We had fur coats and warm clothes,—

which are chiefly needed at night,—and plenty of bedding, including water-proof canvas sheeting and a couple
of caribou-hide sleeping-bags, procured from the survivors of a party of arctic explorers. Except on rainy days I
used my buckskin hunting-shirt or tunic; in dry weather I
deem it, because of its color, texture, and durability, the
best possible garb for the still-hunter, especially in the
woods.

Starting a day's journey south of Heart Lake, we travelled and hunted on the eastern edge of the great basin,
wooded and mountainous, wherein rise the head-waters
of the mighty Snake River. There was not so much as a
spotted line—that series of blazes made with the axe,
man's first highway through the hoary forest,—but this we
did not mind, as for most of the distance we followed
well-worn elk-trails. The train travelled in Indian file. At
the head, to pick the path, rode tall, silent old Woody, a
true type of the fast-vanishing race of game hunters and
Indian fighters, a man who had been one of the California
forty-niners, and who ever since had lived the restless,
reckless life of the wilderness. Then came Ferguson and
myself; then the pack-animals, strung out in line; while
from the rear rose the varied oaths of our three companions, whose miserable duty it was to urge forward the
beasts of burden.

It is heart-breaking work to drive a pack-train
through thick timber and over mountains, where there is
either a dim trail or none. The animals have a perverse faculty for choosing the wrong turn at critical moments; and
they are continually scraping under branches and squeez-
ing between tree-trunks, to the jeopardy or destruction of

their burdens. After having been laboriously driven up a very steep incline, at the cost of severe exertion both to them and to the men, the foolish creatures turn and run down to the bottom, so that all the work has to be done over again. Some travel too slow; others travel too fast. Yet one cannot but admire the toughness of the animals, and the surefootedness with which they pick their way along the sheer mountain sides, or among boulders and over fallen logs.

As our way was so rough, we found that we had to halt at least once every hour to fix the packs. Moreover, we at the head of the column were continually being appealed to for help by the unfortunates in the rear. First it would be "that white-eyed cayuse; one side of its pack's down!" then we would be notified that the saddle-blanket of the "lop-eared Indian buckskin" had slipped back; then a shout "Look out for the pinto!" would be followed by that pleasing beast's appearance, bucking and squealing, smashing dead timber, and scattering its load to the four winds. It was no easy task to get the horses across some of the boggy places without miring; or to force them through the denser portions of the forest, where there was much down timber. Riding with a pack-train, day in and day out, becomes both monotonous and irritating, unless one is upheld by the hope of a game-country ahead, or by the delight of exploration of the unknown. Yet when buoyed by such a hope, there is pleasure in taking a train across so beautiful and wild a country as that which lay on the threshold of our hunting grounds in the Shoshones. We went over mountain passes, with ranges of scalped peaks on either hand; we skirted the edges of lovely lakes, and of streams with boulder-strewn beds; we plunged into depths of sombre woodland, broken by wet prairies. It was a picturesque sight to see the loaded pack-train stringing across one of these high mountain meadows, the motley colored line of ponies winding round the marshy spots through the bright green grass, while beyond rose the dark line of frowning forest, with lofty peaks towering in the background. Some of the meadows were beautiful with many flowers—goldenrod, purple aster, bluebells, white immortelles, and here and there masses of blood-red Indian pinks. In the park-country, on the edges of the evergreen forest, were groves of delicate quaking-aspen, the trees often growing to quite a height; their tremulous leaves were already changing to bright green and yellow, occasionally with a reddish blush. In the Rocky Mountains the aspens are almost the only deciduous trees, their foliage offering a pleasant relief to the eye after the monotony of the unending pine and spruce woods, which afford so striking a contrast to the hardwood forest east of the Mississippi.

For two days our journey was uneventful, save that we came on the camp of a squawman—one Beaver Dick, an old mountain hunter, living in a skin tepee, where dwelt his comely Indian wife and half-breed children. He had quite a herd of horses, many of them mares and colts; they had evidently been well treated, and came up to us fearlessly.

The morning of the third day of our journey was gray and lowering. Gusts of rain blew in my face as I rode at the head of the train. It still lacked an hour of noon, as we were plodding up a valley beside a rapid brook running through narrow willow-flats, the dark forest crowding down on either hand from the low foot-hills of the mountains. Suddenly the call of a bull elk came echoing down through the wet woodland on our right, beyond the brook, seemingly less than half a mile off; and was answered by a faint, far-off call from a rival on the mountain beyond. Instantly halting the train, Woody and I slipped off our horses, crossed the brook, and started to still-hunt the first bull.

In this place the forest was composed of the western tamarack; the large, tall trees stood well apart, and there was much down timber, but the ground was covered with deep wet moss, over which we trod silently. The elk was travelling up-wind, but slowly, stopping continually to paw the ground and thresh the bushes with his antlers. He was very noisy, challenging every minute or two, being doubtless much excited by the neighborhood of his rival on the mountain. We followed, Woody leading, guided by the incessant calling.

It was very exciting as we crept toward the great bull, and the challenge sounded nearer and nearer. While we were still at some distance the pealing notes were like those of a bugle, delivered in two bars, first rising, then abruptly falling; as we drew nearer they took on a harsh squealing sound. Each call made our veins thrill; it sounded like the cry of some huge beast of prey. At last we heard the roar of the challenge not eighty yards off. Stealing forward three or four yards, I saw the tips of the horns through a mass of dead timber and young growth, and I slipped to one side to get a clean shot. Seeing us, but not making out what we were, and full of fierce and insolent excitement, the wapiti bull stepped boldly toward us with a stately swinging gait. Then he stood motionless, facing us, barely fifty yards away, his handsome twelve-tined antlers tossed aloft, as he held his head with the lordly grace of his kind. I fired into his chest, and as he turned I raced forward and shot him in the flank; but the second bullet was not needed, for the first wound was mortal, and he fell before going fifty yards.

The dead elk lay among the young evergreens. The huge, shapely body was set on legs that were as strong as steel rods, and yet slender, clean, and smooth; they were in color a beautiful dark brown, contrasting well with the yellowish of the body. The neck and throat were garnished with a mane of long hair; the symmetry of the great horns set off the fine, delicate lines of the noble head. He had been wallowing, as elk are fond of doing, and the dried mud clung in patches to his flank; a stab in the haunch showed that he had been overcome in battle by some master bull who had turned him out of the herd.

We cut off the head, and bore it down to the train. The horses crowded together, snorting, with their ears pricked forward, as they smelt the blood. We also took the loins with us, as we were out of meat, though bull elk in the rutting season is not very good. The rain had changed to a steady downpour when we again got under way. Two or three miles farther we pitched camp, in a clump of pines on a hillock in the bottom of the valley, starting hot fires of pitchy stumps before the tents, to dry our wet things.

Next day opened with fog and cold rain. The drenched pack-animals, when driven into camp, stood mopingly, with drooping heads and arched backs; they groaned and grunted as the loads were placed on their backs and the cinches tightened, the packers bracing one foot against the pack to get a purchase as they hauled in on the lash-rope. A stormy morning is a trial to temper; the packs are wet and heavy, and the cold makes the work even more than usually hard on the hands. By ten we broke camp. It needs between two and three hours to break camp and get such a train properly packed; once started, our day's journey was six to eight hours, making no halt. We started up a steep, pine-clad mountain side, broken by cliffs. My hunting-shoes, though comfortable, were old and thin, and let the water through like a sieve. On the top of the first plateau, where black spruce groves were strewn across the grassy surface, we saw a band of elk, cows and calves, trotting off through the rain. Then we plunged down into a deep valley, and, crossing it, a hard climb took us to the top of a great bare table-land, bleak and wind-swept. We passed little alpine lakes, fringed with scattering dwarf evergreens. Snow lay in drifts on the north sides of the gullies; a cutting wind blew the icy rain in our faces. For two or three hours we travelled toward the farther edge of the table-land. In one place a spike bull elk stood half a mile off, in the open; he travelled to and fro, watching us.

As we neared the edge the storm lulled, and pale, watery sunshine gleamed through the rifts in the low-scudding clouds. At last our horses stood on the brink of a bold cliff. Deep down beneath our feet lay the wild and lonely valley of Two-Ocean Pass, walled in on either hand by rugged mountain chains, their flanks scarred and gashed by precipice and chasm. Beyond, in a wilderness of jagged and barren peaks, stretched the Shoshones. At the middle point of the pass, two streams welled down from either side. At first each flowed in but one bed, but soon divided into two; each of the twin branches then joined the like branch of the brook opposite, and swept one to the east and one to the west, on their long journey to the two great oceans. They ran as rapid brooks, through wet meadows and willow-flats, the eastern to the Yellowstone, the western to the Snake. The dark pine forests swept down from the flanks and lower ridges of the mountains to the edges of the marshy valley. Above them jutted gray rock peaks, snow-drifts lying in the rents that seamed their northern faces. Far below us, from a great basin at the foot of the cliff, filled with the pine forest, rose the musical challenge of a bull elk; and we saw a band of cows and calves looking like mice as they ran among the trees.

It was getting late, and after some search we failed to find any trail leading down; so at last we plunged over the brink at a venture. It was very rough scrambling, dropping from bench to bench, and in places it was not only difficult but dangerous for the loaded pack-animals. Here and there we were helped by well-beaten elk-trails, which we could follow for several hundred yards at a time. On one narrow pine-clad ledge, we met a spike bull face to face; and in scrambling down a very steep, bare, rock-strewn shoulder the loose stones started by the horses' hoofs, bounding in great leaps to the forest below, dislodged two cows.

As evening fell, we reached the bottom, and pitched camp in a beautiful point of open pine forest, thrust out into the meadow. There was good shelter, and plenty of wood, water, and grass; we built a huge fire and put up our tents, scattering them in likely places among the pines, which grew far apart and without undergrowth. We dried our steaming clothes, and ate a hearty supper of elk-meat; then we turned into our beds, warm and dry, and slept soundly under the canvas, while all night long the storm roared without. Next morning it still stormed fitfully; the high peaks and ridges round about were all capped with snow. Woody and I started on foot for an all-day tramp; the amount of game seen the day before showed that we were in a good elk-country, where the elk had been so little disturbed that they were travelling, feeding, and whistling in daylight. For three hours we walked across the forest-clad spurs of the foot-hills. We roused a small band of elk in thick timber; but they rushed off before we saw them, with much smashing of dead branches. Then we climbed to the summit of the range. The wind was light and baffling; it blew from all points, veering every few minutes. There were occasional rain-squalls; our feet and legs were well soaked; and we became chilled through whenever we sat down to listen. We caught a glimpse of a big bull feeding up-hill, and followed him; it needed smart running to overtake him, for an elk, even while feeding, has a ground-covering gait. Finally we got within a hundred and twenty-five yards, but in very thick timber, and all I could see plainly was the hip and the after-part of the flank. I waited for a chance at the shoulder, but the bull got my wind and was off before I could pull trigger. It was just one of those occasions when there are two courses to pursue, neither very good, and when one is apt to regret whichever decision is made.

At noon we came to the edge of a deep and wide gorge, and sat down shivering to await what might turn up, our fingers numb, and our wet feet icy. Suddenly the love-challenge of an elk came pealing across the gorge, through the fine, cold rain, from the heart of the forest opposite. An hour's stiff climb, down and up, brought us nearly to him; but the wind forced us to advance from below through a series of open glades. He was lying on a point of the cliff-shoulder, surrounded by his cows; and he saw us and made off. An hour afterward, as we were trudging up a steep hill-side dotted with groves of fir and spruce, a young bull of ten points, roused from his day-bed by our approach, galloped across us some sixty yards off. We were in need of better venison than can be furnished by an old rutting bull; so I instantly took a shot at the fat and tender young ten-pointer. I aimed well ahead and pulled trigger just as he came to a small gully; and he fell into it in a heap with a resounding crash. This was on the birthday of my eldest small son; so I took him home the horns, "for his very own." On the way back that afternoon I shot off the heads of two blue grouse, as they perched in the pines.

That evening the storm broke, and the weather became clear and very cold, so that the snow made the frosty mountains gleam like silver. The moon was full, and in the flood of light the wild scenery round our camp was very beautiful. As always where we camped for several days, we had fixed long tables and settles, and were most comfortable; and when we came in at nightfall, or sometimes long afterward, cold, tired, and hungry, it was sheer physical delight to get warm before the roaring fire of pitchy stumps, and then to feast ravenously on bread and beans, on stewed or roasted elk venison, on grouse and sometimes trout, and flapjacks with maple syrup.

Next morning dawned clear and cold, the sky a glorious blue. Woody and I started to hunt over the great tableland, and led our stout horses up the mountain-side, by elk-trails so bad that they had to climb like goats. All these elk-trails have one striking peculiarity. They lead through thick timber, but every now and then send off short, well-worn branches to some cliff-edge or jutting crag, commanding a view far and wide over the country beneath. Elk love to stand on these lookout points, and scan the valleys and mountains round about.

Blue grouse rose from beside our path; Clarke's crows flew past us, with a hollow, flapping sound, or lit in the pine-tops, calling and flirting their tails; the gray-clad whisky-jacks, with multitudinous cries, hopped and fluttered near us. Snow-shoe rabbits scuttled away, the big furry feet which give them their name already turning white. At last we came out on the great plateau, seamed with deep, narrow ravines. Reaches of pasture alternated with groves and open forests of varying size. Almost immediately we heard the bugle of a bull elk, and saw a big band of cows and calves on the other side of a valley. There were three bulls with them, one very large, and we tried to creep up on them; but the wind was baffling and spoiled our stalk. So we returned to our horses, mounted them, and rode a mile farther, toward a large open wood on a hill-side. When within two hundred yards we heard directly ahead the bugle of a bull, and pulled up short. In a moment I saw him walking through an open glade; he had not seen us. The slight breeze brought us down his scent. Elk have a strong characteristic smell; it is usually sweet, like that of a herd of Alderney cows; but in old bulls, while rutting, it is rank, pungent, and lasting. We stood motionless till the bull was out of sight, then stole to the wood, tied our horses, and trotted after him. He was travelling fast, occasionally calling; whereupon others in the neighborhood would answer. Evidently he had been driven out of some herd by the master bull.

He went faster than we did, and while we were vainly trying to overtake him we heard another very loud and sonorous challenge to our left. It came from a ridge-crest at the edge of the woods, among some scattered clumps of the northern nut-pine or pinyon—a queer conifer, growing very high on the mountains, its multiforked trunk and wide-spreading branches giving it the rounded top, and, at a distance, the general look of an oak rather than a pine. We at once walked toward the ridge, up-wind. In a minute or two, to our chagrin, we stumbled on an outlying spike bull, evidently kept on the outskirts of the herd by the master bull. I thought he would alarm all the rest; but, as we stood motionless, he could not see clearly what we were. He stood, ran, stood again, gazed at us, and trotted slowly off. We hurried forward as fast as we dared, and with too little care; for we suddenly came in view of two cows. As they raised their heads to look, Woody squatted down where he was, to keep their attention fixed, while I cautiously tried to slip off to one side unobserved. Favored by the neutral tint of my buckskin hunting-shirt, with which my shoes, leggings, and soft hat matched, I succeeded. As soon as I was out of sight I ran hard and came up to a hillock crested with pinyons, behind which I judged I should find the herd. As I approached the crest, their strong, sweet smell smote my nostrils. In another moment I saw the tips of a pair of mighty antlers, and I peered over the crest with my rifle at the ready. Thirty yards off, behind a clump of pinyons, stood a huge bull, his head thrown back as he rubbed his shoulders with his horns. There were several cows around him, and one saw me immediately, and took alarm. I fired into the bull's shoulder, inflicting a mortal wound; but he went off, and I raced after him at top speed, firing twice into his flank; then he stopped, very sick, and I broke his neck with a fourth bullet. An elk often hesitates in the first moments of surprise and fright, and does not get really under way for two or three hundred yards; but, when once fairly started, he may go several miles, even though mortally wounded; therefore, the hunter, after his first shot, should run forward as fast as he can, and shoot again and again until the quarry drops. In this way many animals that would otherwise be lost are obtained, especially by the man who has a repeating-rifle. Nevertheless the hunter should beware of being led astray by the ease with which he can fire half a dozen shots from his repeater; and he should aim as carefully with each shot as if it were his last. No possible rapidity of fire can atone for habitual carelessness of aim with the first shot.

The elk I thus slew was a giant. His body was the size of a steer's, and his antlers, though not unusually long, were very massive and heavy. He lay in a glade, on the edge of a great cliff. Standing on its brink we overlooked a most beautiful country, the home of all homes for the elk: a wilderness of mountains, the immense evergreen forest broken by park and glade, by meadow and pasture, by bare hill-side and barren table-land. Some five miles off lay the sheet of water known to the old hunters as Spotted Lake; two or three shallow, sedgy places, and spots of geyser formation, made pale green blotches on its wind-rippled surface. Far to the southwest, in daring beauty and majesty, the grand domes and lofty spires of the Tetons shot into the blue sky. Too sheer for the snow to rest on their sides, it yet filled the rents in their rough flanks, and lay deep between the towering pinnacles of dark rock.

That night, as on more than one night afterward, a bull elk came down whistling to within two or three hundred yards of the tents, and tried to join the horse herd. The moon had set, so I could not go after it. Elk are very restless and active throughout the night in the rutting season; but where undisturbed they feed freely in the daytime, resting for two or three hours about noon.

Next day, which was rainy, we spent in getting in the antlers and meat of the two dead elk; and I shot off the heads of two or three blue grouse on the way home. The following day I killed another bull elk, following him by the strong, not unpleasing, smell, and hitting him twice as he ran, at about eighty yards. So far I had had good luck, killing everything I had shot at; but now the luck changed, through no fault of mine, as far as I could see, and Ferguson had his innings. The day after I killed this bull he shot two fine mountain rams; and during the remainder of our hunt he killed five elk,—one cow, for meat, and four good bulls. The two rams were with three others, all old and with fine horns; Ferguson peeped over a lofty precipice and saw them coming up it only fifty yards below him. His two first and finest bulls were obtained by hard running and good shooting; the herds were on the move at the time, and only his speed of foot and soundness of wind enabled him to get near enough for a shot. One herd started before he got close, and he killed the master bull by a shot right through the heart, as it trotted past, a hundred and fifty yards distant.

As for me, during the next ten days I killed nothing save one cow for meat; and this though I hunted hard every day from morning till night, no matter what the weather. It was stormy, with hail and snow almost every day; and after working hard from dawn until nightfall, laboriously climbing the slippery mountain-sides, walking through the wet woods, and struggling across the bare plateaus and cliff-shoulders, while the violent blasts of wind drove the frozen rain in our faces, we would come in after dusk wet through and chilled to the marrow. Even when it rained in the valleys it snowed on the mountain-tops, and there was no use trying to keep our feet dry. I got three shots at bull elk, two being very hurried snap-shots at animals running in thick timber, the other a running-shot in the open, at over two hundred yards; and I missed all three. On most days I saw no bull worth shooting; the two or three I did see or hear we failed to stalk, the light, shifty wind baffling us, or else an outlying cow which we had not seen giving the alarm. There were many blue and a few ruffed grouse in the woods, and I occasionally shot off the heads of a couple on my way homeward in the evening. In racing after one elk, I leaped across a gully and so bruised and twisted my heel on a rock that, for the remainder of my stay in the mountains, I had to walk on the fore part of that foot. This did not interfere much with my walking, however, except in going down-hill.

Our ill success was in part due to sheer bad luck; but the chief element therein was the presence of a great hunting-party of Shoshone Indians. Split into bands of eight or ten each, they scoured the whole country on their tough, sure-footed ponies. They always hunted on horseback, and followed the elk at full speed wherever they went. Their method of hunting was to organize great drives, the riders strung in lines far apart; they signalled to one another by means of willow whistles, with which they also imitated the calling of the bull elk, thus tolling the animals to them, or making them betray their whereabouts. As they slew whatever they could, but by preference cows and calves, and as they were very persevering, but also very excitable and generally poor shots, so that they wasted much powder, they not only wrought havoc among the elk, but also scared the survivors out of all the country over which they hunted.

Day in and day out we plodded on. In a hunting-trip the days of long monotony in getting to the ground, and the days of unrequited toil after it has been reached, always far outnumber the red-letter days of success. But it is just these times of failure that really test the hunter. In the long run, common-sense and dogged perseverance avail him more than any other qualities. The man who does not give up, but hunts steadily and resolutely through the spells of bad luck until the luck turns, is the man who wins success in the end.

After a week at Two-Ocean Pass, we gathered our

pack-animals one frosty morning, and again set off across the mountains. A two-days' jaunt took us to the summit of Wolverine Pass, near Pinyon Peak, beside a little mountain tarn; each morning we found its surface skimmed with black ice, for the nights were cold. After three or four days, we shifted camp to the mouth of Wolverine Creek, to get off the hunting grounds of the Indians. We had used up our last elk-meat that morning, and when we were within a couple of hours' journey of our intended halting-place, Woody and I struck off on foot for a hunt. Just before sunset we came on three or four elk; a spike bull stood for a moment behind some thick evergreens a hundred yards off. Guessing at his shoulder, I fired, and he fell dead after running a few rods. I had broken the luck, after ten days of ill success.

Next morning Woody and I, with the packer, rode to where this elk lay. We loaded the meat on a pack-horse, and let the packer take both the loaded animal and our own saddle-horses back to camp, while we made a hunt on foot. We went up the steep, forest-clad mountain-side, and before we had walked an hour heard two elk whistling ahead of us. The woods were open, and quite free from undergrowth, and we were able to advance noiselessly; there was no wind, for the weather was still, clear, and cold. Both of the elk were evidently very much excited, answering each other continually; they had probably been master bulls, but had become so exhausted that their rivals had driven them from the herds, forcing them to remain in seclusion until they regained their lost strength. As we crept stealthily forward, the calling grew louder and louder, until we could hear the grunting sounds with which the challenge of the nearest ended. He was in a large wallow, which was also a lick. When we were still sixty yards off, he heard us, and rushed out, but wheeled and stood a moment to gaze, puzzled by my buckskin suit. I fired into his throat, breaking his neck, and down he went in a heap. Rushing in and turning, I called to Woody, "He's a twelve-pointer, but the horns are small!" As I spoke I heard the roar of the challenge of the other bull not two hundred yards ahead, as if in defiant answer to my shot.

Running quietly forward, I speedily caught a glimpse of his body. He was behind some fir-trees about seventy yards off, and I could not see which way he was standing, and so fired into the patch of flank which was visible, aiming high, to break the back. My aim was true, and the huge beast crashed down-hill through the evergreens, pulling himself on his fore legs for fifteen or twenty rods, his hind quarters trailing. Racing forward, I broke his neck. His antlers were the finest I ever got. A couple of whisky-jacks appeared at the first crack of the rifle with their customary astonishing familiarity and heedlessness of the hunter; they followed the wounded bull as he dragged his great carcass down the hill, and pounced with ghoulish blood-thirstiness on the gouts of blood that were sprinkled over the green herbage.

These two bulls lay only a couple of hundred yards apart, on a broad game-trail, which was as well beaten as a good bridle-path. We began to skin out the heads; and as we were finishing we heard another bull challenging far up the mountain. He came nearer and nearer, and as soon as we had ended our work we grasped our rifles and trotted toward him along the game-trail. He was very noisy, uttering his loud, singing challenge every minute or two. The trail was so broad and firm that we walked in perfect silence. After going only five or six hundred yards, we got very close indeed, and stole forward on tiptoe, listening to the roaring music. The sound came from a steep, narrow ravine, to one side of the trail, and I walked toward it with my rifle at the ready. A slight puff gave the elk my wind, and he dashed out of the ravine like a deer; but he was only thirty yards off, and my bullet went into his shoulder as he passed behind a clump of young spruce. I plunged into the ravine, scrambled out of it, and raced after him. In a minute I saw him standing with drooping head, and two more shots finished him. He also bore fine antlers. It was a great piece of luck to get three such fine bulls at the cost of half a day's light work; but we had fairly earned them, having worked hard for ten days, through rain, cold, hunger, and fatigue, to no purpose. That evening my home-coming to camp, with three elk-tongues and a brace of ruffed grouse hung at my belt, was most happy.

Next day it snowed, but we brought a pack-pony to where the three great bulls lay, and took their heads to camp; the flesh was far too strong to be worth taking, for it was just the height of the rut.

This was the end of my hunt; and a day later Hofer and I, with two pack-ponies, made a rapid push for the Upper Geyser Basin. We travelled fast. The first day was gray and overcast, a cold wind blowing strong in our faces. Toward evening we came on a bull elk in a willow thicket; he was on his knees in a hollow, thrashing and beating the willows with his antlers. At dusk we halted and went into

camp, by some small pools on the summit of the pass
north of Red Mountain. The elk were calling all around
us. We pitched our cozy tent, dragged great stumps for the
fire, cut evergreen boughs for our beds, watered the horses,
tethered them to improvised picket-pins in a grassy glade,
and then set about getting supper ready. The wind had
gone down, and snow was falling thick in large, soft flakes;
we were evidently at the beginning of a heavy snowstorm.
All night we slept soundly in our snug tent. When we
arose at dawn there was a foot and a half of snow on the
ground, and the flakes were falling as fast as ever. There is
no more tedious work than striking camp in bad weather;
and it was over two hours from the time we rose to the
time we started. It is sheer misery to untangle picket-lines
and to pack animals when the ropes are frozen; and by the
time we had loaded the two shivering, wincing pack-
ponies, and had bridled and saddled our own riding-
animals, our hands and feet were numb and stiff with cold,
though we were really hampered by our warm clothing.
My horse was a wild, nervous roan, and as I swung care-
lessly into the saddle, he suddenly began to buck before I
got my right leg over, and threw me off. My thumb was
put out of joint. I pulled it in again, and speedily caught
my horse in the dead timber. Then I treated him as what
the cowboys call a "mean horse," and mounted him carefully, so as not to let him either buck or go over backward.
However, his preliminary success had inspirited him, and
a dozen times that day he began to buck, usually choosing
a down grade, where the snow was deep, and there was
much fallen timber.

All day long we pushed steadily through the cold,

blinding snowstorm. Neither squirrels nor rabbits were abroad; and a few Clarke's crows, whisky-jacks, and chickadees were the only living things we saw. At nightfall, chilled through, we reached the Upper Geyser Basin. Here I met a party of railroad surveyors and engineers, coming in from their summer's field-work. One of them lent me a saddle-horse and a pack-pony, and we went on together, breaking our way through the snow-choked roads to the Mammoth Hot Springs, while Hofer took my own horses back to Ferguson.

I have described this hunt at length because, though I enjoyed it particularly on account of the comfort in which we travelled and the beauty of the land, yet, in point of success in finding and killing game, in value of trophies procured, and in its alternations of good and bad luck, it may fairly stand as the type of a dozen such hunts I have made. Twice I have been much more successful; the difference being due to sheer luck, as I hunted equally hard in all three instances. Thus on this trip I killed and saw nothing but elk; yet the other members of the party either saw, or saw fresh signs of, not only blacktail deer, but sheep, bear, bison, moose, cougar, and wolf. Now in 1889 I hunted over almost precisely similar country, only farther to the northwest, on the boundary between Idaho and Montana, and, with the exception of sheep, I stumbled on all the animals mentioned, and white goat in addition, so that my bag of twelve head actually included eight species—much the best bag I ever made, and the only one that could really be called out of the common. In 1884, on a trip to the Bighorn Mountains, I killed three bear, six elk and six deer. In laying in the winter stock of meat for my

ranch I often far excelled these figures as far as mere numbers went; but on no other regular hunting trip, where the
quality and not the quantity of the game was the prime
consideration, have I ever equalled them; and on several
where I worked hardest I hardly averaged a head a week.
The occasional days or weeks of phenomenal luck, are
more than earned by the many others where no luck whatever follows the very hardest work. Yet, if a man hunts
with steady resolution he is apt to strike enough lucky days
amply to repay him.

On this Shoshone trip I fired fifty-eight shots. In
preference to using the knife I generally break the neck of
an elk which is still struggling; and I fire at one as long as
it can stand, preferring to waste a few extra bullets, rather
than see an occasional head of game escape. In consequence of these two traits the nine elk I got (two running
at sixty and eighty yards, the others standing, at from
thirty to a hundred) cost me twenty-three bullets; and I
missed three shots—all three, it is but fair to say, difficult
ones. I also cut off the heads of seventeen grouse, with
twenty-two shots; and killed two ducks with ten shots—
fifty-eight in all. On the Bighorn trip I used a hundred
and two cartridges. On no other trip did I use fifty.

To me still-hunting elk in the mountains, when they
are calling, is one of the most attractive of sports, not only
because of the size and stately beauty of the quarry and the
grand nature of the trophy, but because of the magnifi-
cence of the scenery, and the stirring, manly, exciting nature of the chase itself. It yields more vigorous enjoyment
than does lurking stealthily through the grand but gloomy
monotony of the marshy woodland where dwells the

moose. The climbing among the steep forest-clad and glade-strewn mountains is just difficult enough thoroughly to test soundness in wind and limb, while without the heart-breaking fatigue of white goat hunting. The actual grapple with an angry grisly is of course far more full of strong, eager pleasure; but bear hunting is the most uncertain, and usually the least productive, of sports.

As regards strenuous, vigorous work, and pleasurable excitement the chase of the bighorn alone stands higher. But the bighorn, grand beast of the chase though he be, is surpassed in size, both of body and of horns, by certain of the giant sheep of Central Asia; whereas the wapiti is not only the most stately and beautiful of American game— far more so than the bison and moose, his only rivals in size—but is also the noblest of the stag kind throughout the world. Whoever kills him has killed the chief of his race; for he stands far above his brethren of Asia and Europe.

CHAPTER XI

The Moose; The Beast
of the Woodland

The moose is the giant of all deer; and many hunters esteem it the noblest of American game. Beyond question there are few trophies more prized than the huge shovel horns of this strange dweller in the cold northland forests.

I shot my first moose after making several fruitless hunting trips with this special game in view. The season I finally succeeded it was only after having hunted two or three weeks in vain, among the Bitter Root Mountains, and the ranges lying southeast of them.

I began about the first of September by making a trial with my old hunting friend Willis. We speedily found a country where there were moose, but of the animals themselves we never caught a glimpse. We tried to kill them by hunting in the same manner that we hunted elk; that is, by choosing a place where there was sign, and going carefully through it against or across the wind. However, this plan failed; though at that very time we succeeded in killing elk in this way, devoting one or two days to their pursuit. There were both elk and moose in the country, but they were usually found in different kinds of ground, though often close alongside one another. The former went in herds, the cows, calves, and yearlings by themselves, and they roamed through the higher and more open forests, well up towards timber line. The moose, on the contrary, were found singly or in small parties composed at the outside of a bull, a cow, and her young of two years; for the moose is practically monogamous, in strong contrast to the highly polygamous wapiti and caribou.

The moose did not seem to care much whether they lived among the summits of the mountains or not, so long as they got the right kind of country; for they were much more local in their distribution, and at this season less given to wandering than their kin with round horns. What they wished was a cool, swampy region of very dense growth; in the main chains of the northern Rockies even the valleys are high enough to be cold. Of course many of the moose lived on the wooded summits of the lower ranges; and most of them came down lower in winter than in summer, following about a fortnight after the elk; but if in a large tract of woods the cover was dense and the ground marshy, though it was in a valley no higher than the herds of the ranchmen grazed, or perchance even in the immediate neighborhood of a small frontier hamlet, then it might be chosen by some old bull who wished to lie in seclusion till his horns were grown, or by some cow with a calf to raise. Before settlers came to this high mountain region of Western Montana, a moose would often thus live in an isolated marshy tract surrounded by open country. They grazed throughout the summer on marsh plants, notably lily stems, and nibbled at the tops of the very tall natural hay of the meadows. The legs of the beast are too long and the neck too short to allow it to graze habitually on short grass; yet in the early spring when greedy for the tender blades of young, green marsh grass, the moose will often shuffle down on its knees to get at them, and it will occasionally perform the same feat to get a mouthful or two of snow in winter.

The moose which lived in isolated, exposed localities were speedily killed or driven away after the incoming of settlers; and at the time that we hunted we found no sign of them until we reached the region of continuous forest. Here, in a fortnight's hunting, we found as much sign as we wished, and plenty of it fresh; but the animals themselves we not only never saw but we never so much as heard. Often after hours of careful still-hunting or cautious tracking, we found the footprints deep in the soft earth, showing where our quarry had winded or heard us, and had noiselessly slipped away from the danger. It is astonishing how quietly a moose can steal through the woods if it wishes: and it has what is to the hunter a very provoking habit of making a half or three quarters circle before lying down, and then crouching with its head so turned that it can surely perceive any pursuer who may follow its trail. We tried every method to outwit the beasts. We attempted to track them; we beat through likely spots; sometimes we merely "sat on a log" and awaited events, by a drinking hole, meadow, mud wallow or other such place (a course of procedure which often works well in still-hunting); but all in vain.

Our main difficulty lay in the character of the woods which the moose haunted. They were choked and tangled to the last degree, consisting of a mass of thick-growing conifers, with dead timber strewn in every direction, and young growth filling the spaces between the trunks. We could not see twenty yards ahead of us, and it was almost impossible to walk without making a noise. Elk were occasionally found in these same places; but usually they frequented more open timber, where the hunting was beyond comparison easier. Perhaps more experienced hunters would have killed their game; though in such cover the best tracker and still-hunter alive cannot always reckon on success with really wary animals. But, be this as it may, we, at any rate, were completely baffled, and I began to think that this moose-hunt, like all my former ones, was doomed to end in failure.

However, a few days later I met a crabbed old trapper named Hank Griffin, who was going after beaver in the mountains, and who told me that if I would come with him he would show me moose. I jumped at the chance, and he proved as good as his word; though for the first two trials my ill luck did not change.

At the time that it finally did change we had at last reached a place where the moose were on favorable ground. A high, marshy valley stretched for several miles between two rows of stony mountains, clad with a forest of rather small fir-trees. This valley was covered with reeds, alders, and rank grass, and studded with little willow-bordered ponds and island-like clumps of spruce and graceful tamaracks.

Having surveyed the ground and found moose sign the preceding afternoon, we were up betimes in the cool morning to begin our hunt. Before sunrise we were posted on a rocky spur of the foot-hills, behind a mask of evergreens; ourselves unseen we overlooked all the valley, and we knew we could see any animal which might be either feeding away from cover or on its journey homeward from its feeding ground to its day-bed.

As it grew lighter we scanned the valley with increasing care and eagerness. The sun rose behind us; and almost as soon as it was up we made out some large beast moving among the dwarf willows beside a little lake half a mile in our front. In a few minutes the thing walked out where the bushes were thinner, and we saw that it was a young bull moose browsing on the willow tops. He had evidently nearly finished his breakfast, and he stood idly for some moments, now and then lazily cropping a mouthful of twig tips. Then he walked off with great strides in a straight line across the marsh, splashing among the wet water-plants, and ploughing through boggy spaces with the indifference begotten of vast strength and legs longer than those of any other animal on this continent. At times he entered beds of reeds which hid him from view, though their surging and bending showed the wake of his passage; at other times he walked through meadows of tall grass, the withered yellow stalks rising to his flanks, while his body loomed above them, glistening black and wet in the level sunbeams. Once he stopped for a few moments on a rise of dry ground, seemingly to enjoy the heat of the young sun; he stood motionless, save that his ears were continually pricked, and his head sometimes slightly turned, showing that even in this remote land he was on the alert. Once, with a somewhat awkward motion, he reached his hind leg forward to scratch his neck. Then he walked forward again into the marsh; where the water was quite deep he broke into the long, stretching, springy trot, which forms the characteristic gait of his kind, churning the marsh water into foam. He held his head straight forwards, the antlers resting on his shoulders.

After awhile he reached a spruce island, through which he walked to and fro; but evidently could find therein no resting-place quite to his mind, for he soon left and went on to another. Here after a little wandering he chose a point where there was some thick young growth, which hid him from view when he lay down, though not when he stood. After some turning he settled himself in his bed just as a steer would.

He could not have chosen a spot better suited for us. He was nearly at the edge of the morass, the open space between the spruce clump where he was lying and the rocky foot-hills being comparatively dry and not much over a couple of hundred yards broad; while some sixty yards from it, and between it and the hills, was a little hummock, tufted with firs, so as to afford us just the cover we needed. Keeping back from the edge of the morass we were able to walk upright through the forest, until we got to the point where he was lying in a line with this little hummock. We then dropped on our hands and knees, and crept over the soft, wet sward, where there was nothing to make a noise. Wherever the ground rose at all we crawled flat on our bellies. The air was still, for it was a very calm morning.

At last we reached the hummock, and I got into position for a shot, taking a final look at my faithful 45–90 Winchester to see that all was in order. Peering cautiously through the shielding evergreens, I at first could not make out where the moose was lying, until my eye was caught by the motion of his big ears, as he occasionally flapped them lazily forward. Even then I could not see his outline; but I knew where he was, and having pushed my rifle forward on the moss, I snapped a dry twig to make him rise. My veins were thrilling and my heart beating with that eager, fierce excitement, known only to the hunter of big game, and forming one of the keenest and strongest of the many pleasures which with him go to make up "the wild joy of living."

As the sound of the snapping twig smote his ears the moose rose nimbly to his feet, with a lightness on which one would not have reckoned in a beast so heavy of body. He stood broadside to me for a moment, his ungainly head slightly turned, while his ears twitched and his nostrils snuffed the air. Drawing a fine bead against his black hide, behind his shoulder and two thirds of his body's depth below his shaggy withers, I pressed the trigger. He neither flinched nor reeled, but started with his regular ground-covering trot through the spruces; yet I knew he was mine, for the light blood sprang from both of his nostrils, and he fell dying on his side before he had gone thirty rods.

Later in the fall I was again hunting among the lofty ranges which continue towards the southeast the chain of the Bitter Root, between Idaho and Montana. There were but two of us, and we were travelling very light, each having but one pack-pony and the saddle animal he bestrode. We were high among the mountains, and followed no regular trail. Hence our course was often one of extreme difficulty. Occasionally, we took our animals through the forest near timber line, where the slopes were not too steep; again we threaded our way through a line of glades, or skirted the foot-hills, in an open, park country; and now and then we had to cross stretches of tangled mountain forest, making but a few miles a day, at the cost of incredible toil, and accomplishing even this solely by virtue of the wonderful docility and sure-footedness of the ponies, and of my companion's skill with the axe and thorough knowledge of woodcraft.

Late one cold afternoon we came out in a high alpine valley in which there was no sign of any man's having ever been before us. Down its middle ran a clear brook. On each side was a belt of thick spruce forest, covering the lower flanks of the mountains. The trees came down in points and isolated clumps to the brook, the banks of which were thus bordered with open glades, rendering the travelling easy and rapid.

Soon after starting up this valley we entered a beaver meadow of considerable size. It was covered with lush, rank grass, and the stream wound through it rather sluggishly in long curves, which were fringed by a thick growth of dwarfed willows. In one or two places it broadened into small ponds, bearing a few lily-pads. This meadow had been all tramped up by moose. Trails led hither and thither through the grass, the willow twigs were cropped off, and the muddy banks of the little black ponds were indented by hoof-marks. Evidently most of the lilies had been plucked. The footprints were unmistakable; a moose's foot is longer and slimmer than a caribou's, while on the other hand it is much larger than an elk's, and a longer oval in shape.

Most of the sign was old, this high alpine meadow,

surrounded by snow mountains, having clearly been a favorite resort for moose in the summer; but some enormous, fresh tracks told that one or more old bulls were still
frequenting the place.

The light was already fading, and, of course, we did
not wish to camp where we were, because we would then
certainly scare the moose. Accordingly we pushed up the
valley for another mile, through an open forest, the ground
being quite free from underbrush and dead timber, and
covered with a carpet of thick moss, in which the feet sank
noiselessly. Then we came to another beaver-meadow,
which offered fine feed for the ponies. On its edge we
hastily pitched camp, just at dusk. We tossed down the
packs in a dry grove, close to the brook, and turned the
tired ponies loose in the meadow, hobbling the little mare
that carried the bell. The ground was smooth. We threw a
cross-pole from one to the other of two young spruces,
which happened to stand handily, and from it stretched
and pegged out a piece of canvas, which we were using as
a shelter tent. Beneath this we spread our bedding, laying
under it the canvas sheets in which it had been wrapped.
There was still bread left over from yesterday's baking, and
in a few moments the kettle was boiling and the frying-
pan sizzling, while one of us skinned and cut into suitable
pieces two grouse we had knocked over on our march. For
fear of frightening the moose we built but a small fire, and
went to bed soon after supper, being both tired and cold.
Fortunately, what little breeze there was blew up the valley.

At dawn I was awake, and crawled out of my buffalo
bag, shivering and yawning. My companion still slum-

bered heavily. White frost covered whatever had been left outside. The cold was sharp, and I hurriedly slipped a pair of stout moccasins on my feet, drew on my gloves and cap, and started through the ghostly woods for the meadow where we had seen the moose sign. The tufts of grass were stiff with frost; black ice skimmed the edges and quiet places of the little brook.

I walked slowly, it being difficult not to make a noise by cracking sticks or brushing against trees, in the gloom; but the forest was so open that it favored me. When I reached the edge of the beaver-meadow it was light enough to shoot, though the front sight still glimmered indistinctly. Streaks of cold red showed that the sun would soon rise.

Before leaving the shelter of the last spruces I halted to listen; and almost immediately heard a curious splashing sound from the middle of the meadow, where the brook broadened into small willow-bordered pools. I knew at once that a moose was in one of these pools, wading about and pulling up the water-lilies by seizing their slippery stems in his lips, plunging his head deep under water to do so. The moose love to feed in this way in the hot months, when they spend all the time they can in the water, feeding or lying down; nor do they altogether abandon the habit even when the weather is so cold that icicles form in their shaggy coats.

Crouching, I stole noiselessly along the edge of the willow thicket. The stream twisted through it from side to side in zigzags, so that every few rods I got a glimpse down a lane of black water. In a minute I heard a slight splashing near me; and on passing the next point of bushes, I saw the shadowy outline of the moose's hindquarters, standing in a bend of the water. In a moment he walked onwards, disappearing. I ran forward a couple of rods, and then turned in among the willows, to reach the brook where it again bent back towards me. The splashing in the water, and the rustling of the moose's body against the frozen twigs, drowned the little noise made by my moccasined feet.

I strode out on the bank at the lower end of a long narrow pool of water, dark and half frozen. In this pool, half way down and facing me, but a score of yards off, stood the mighty marsh beast, strange and uncouth in look as some monster surviving over from the Pliocene. His vast bulk loomed black and vague in the dim gray dawn; his huge antlers stood out sharply; columns of steam rose from his nostrils. For several seconds he fronted me motionless; then he began to turn, slowly, and as if he had a stiff neck. When quarter way round I fired into his shoulder; whereat he reared and bounded on the bank with a great leap, vanishing in the willows. Through these I heard him crash like a whirlwind for a dozen rods; then down he fell, and when I reached the spot he had ceased to struggle. The ball had gone through his heart.

When a moose is thus surprised at close quarters, it will often stand at gaze for a moment or two, and then turn stiffly around until headed in the right direction; once thus headed aright it starts off with extraordinary speed.

The flesh of the moose is very good; though some deem it coarse. Old hunters, who always like rich, greasy food, rank a moose's nose with a beaver's tail, as the chief of backwood delicacies; personally I never liked either. The hide of the moose, like the hide of the elk, is of very poor quality, much inferior to ordinary buckskin; caribou hide is the best of all, especially when used as webbing for snow-shoes.

The moose is very fond of frequenting swampy woods throughout the summer, and indeed late into the fall. These swampy woods are not necessarily in the lower valleys, some being found very high among the mountains. By preference it haunts those containing lakes, where it can find the long lily-roots of which it is so fond, and where it can escape the torment of the mosquitoes and deer-flies by lying completely submerged save for its nostrils. It is a bold and good swimmer, readily crossing lakes of large size; but it is of course easily slain if discovered by canoe-men while in the water. It travels well through bogs, but not as well as the caribou; and it will not venture on ice at all if it can possibly avoid it.

After the rut begins the animals roam everywhere through the woods; and where there are hardwood forests the winter-yard is usually made among them, on high ground, away from the swamps. In the mountains the deep snows drive the moose, like all other game, down to the lower valleys, in hard winters. In the summer it occasionally climbs to the very summits of the wooded ranges, to escape the flies; and it is said that in certain places where wolves are plenty the cows retire to the tops of the mountains to calve. More often, however, they select some patch of very dense cover, in a swamp or by a lake, for this purpose. Their ways of life of course vary with the nature of the country they frequent. In the towering

chains of the Rockies, clad in sombre and unbroken evergreen forests, their habits, in regard to winter- and
summer-homes, and choice of places of seclusion for cows
with young calves and bulls growing their antlers, differ
from those of their kind which haunt the comparatively
low, hilly, lake-studded country of Maine and Nova Sco-
tia, where the forests are of birch, beech, and maple,
mixed with the pine, spruce, and hemlock.

The moose being usually monogamous is never found
in great herds like the wapiti and caribou. Occasionally a
troop of fifteen or twenty individuals may be seen, but this
is rare; more often it is found singly, in pairs, or in family
parties, composed of a bull, a cow, and two or more calves
and yearlings. In yarding, two or more such families may
unite to spend the winter together in an unusually attractive locality; and during the rut many bulls are sometimes
found together, perhaps following the trail of a cow in single file.

In the fall, winter, and early spring, and in certain
places during summer, the moose feeds principally by
browsing, though always willing to vary its diet by mosses,
lichens, fungi, and ferns. In the eastern forests, with their
abundance of hardwood, the birch, maple, and moose-
wood form its favorite food. In the Rocky Mountains,
where the forests are almost purely evergreen, it feeds on
such willows, alders, and aspens as it can find, and also,
when pressed by necessity, on balsam, fir, spruce, and very
young pine. It peels the bark between its hard palate and
sharp lower teeth, to a height of seven or eight feet; these
"peelings" form conspicuous moose signs. It crops the
juicy, budding twigs and stem tops to the same height; and

if the tree is too tall it "rides" it, that is, straddles the slender trunk with its fore legs, pushing it over and walking up it until the desired branches are within reach. No beast is more destructive to the young growth of a forest than the moose. Where much persecuted it feeds in the late evening, early morning, and by moonlight. Where rarely disturbed it passes the day much as cattle do, alternately resting and feeding for two or three hours at a time.

Young moose, when caught, are easily tamed, and are very playful, delighting to gallop to and fro, kicking, striking, butting, and occasionally making grotesque faces. As they grow old they are apt to become dangerous, and even their play takes the form of a mock fight. Some lumbermen I knew on the Aroostook, in Maine, once captured a young moose, and put it in a pen of logs. A few days later they captured another, somewhat smaller, and put it in the same pen, thinking the first would be grateful at having a companion. But if it was it dissembled its feelings, for it promptly fell on the unfortunate new-comer and killed it before it could be rescued.

During the rut the bulls seek the cows far and wide, uttering continually throughout the night a short, loud roar, which can be heard at a distance of four or five miles; the cows now and then respond with low, plaintive bellows. The bulls also thrash the tree trunks with their horns, and paw big holes in soft ground; and when two rivals come together at this season they fight with the most desperate fury. It is chiefly in these battles with one another that the huge antlers are used; in contending with other foes they strike terrible blows with their fore hoofs and also sometimes lash out behind like a horse. The bear occasionally makes a prey of the moose; the cougar is a more dangerous enemy in the few districts where both animals are found at all plentifully; but next to man its most dreaded foe is the big timber wolf, that veritable scourge of all animals of the deer kind. Against all of these the moose defends itself valiantly; a cow with a calf and a rutting bull being especially dangerous opponents. In deep snows through which the great deer flounders while its adversary runs lightly on the crust, a single wolf may overcome and slaughter a big bull moose; but with a fair chance no one or two wolves would be a match for it. Desperate combats take place before a small pack of wolves can master the shovel-horned quarry, unless it is taken at a hopeless disadvantage; and in these battles the prowess of the moose is shown by the fact that it is no unusual thing for it to kill one or more of the ravenous throng; generally by a terrific blow of the foreleg, smashing a wolf's skull or breaking its back. I have known of several instances of wolves being found dead, having perished in this manner. Still the battle usually ends the other way, the wolves being careful to make the attack with the odds in their favor; and even a small pack of the ferocious brutes will in a single winter often drive the moose completely out of a given district. Both cougar and bear generally reckon on taking the moose unawares, when they jump on it. In one case that came to my knowledge a black bear was killed by a cow moose whose calf he had attacked.

In the northeast a favorite method of hunting the moose is by "calling" the bulls in the rutting season, at dawn or nightfall; the caller imitating their cries through a birch-bark trumpet. If the animals are at all wary, this kind of sport can only be carried on in still weather, as the approaching bull always tries to get the wind of the caller. It is also sometimes slain by fire-hunting, from a canoe, as the deer are killed in the Adirondacks. This, however, is but an ignoble sport; and to kill the animal while it is swimming in a lake is worse. However, there is sometimes a spice of excitement even in these unworthy methods of the chase; for a truculent moose will do its best, with hoofs and horns, to upset the boat.

The true way to kill the noble beast, however, is by fair still-hunting. There is no grander sport than still-hunting the moose, whether in the vast pine and birch forests of the northeast, or among the stupendous mountain masses of the Rockies. The moose has wonderfully keen nose and ears, though its eyesight is not remarkable. Most hunters assert that he is the wariest of all game, and the most difficult to kill. I have never been quite satisfied that this was so; it seems to me that the nature of the ground wherein it dwells helps it even more than do its own sharp senses. It is true that I made many trips in vain before killing my first moose; but then I had to hunt through tangled timber, where I could hardly move a step without noise, and could never see thirty yards ahead. If moose were found in open park-like forests like those where I first killed elk, on the Bighorn Mountains, or among brushy coulies and bare hills, like the Little Missouri Bad Lands, where I first killed blacktail deer, I doubt whether they would prove especially difficult animals to bag. My own experience is much too limited to allow me to speak with any certainty on the point; but it is borne out by what more skilled hunters have told me. In the Big Hole Basin, in southwest

Montana, moose were quite plentiful in the late 'seventies. Two or three of the old settlers, whom I know as veteran hunters and trustworthy men, have told me that in those times the moose were often found in very accessible localities; and that when such was the case they were quite as easily killed as elk. In fact, when run across by accident they frequently showed a certain clumsy slowness of apprehension which amounted to downright stupidity. One of the most successful moose-hunters I know is Col. Cecil Clay, of the Department of Law, in Washington; he it was who killed the moose composing the fine group mounted by Mr. Hornaday, in the National Museum. Col. Clay lost his right arm in the Civil War; but is an expert rifleshot nevertheless, using a short, light forty-four calibre old style Winchester carbine. With this weapon he has killed over a score of moose, by fair still-hunting; and he tells me that on similar ground he considers it if anything rather less easy to still-hunt and kill a whitetail deer than it is to kill a moose.

My friend Col. James Jones killed two moose in a day in northwestern Wyoming, not far from the Tetons; he was alone when he shot them and did not find them especially wary. Ordinarily, moose are shot at fairly close range; but another friend of mine, Mr. E. P. Rogers, once dropped one with a single bullet, at a distance of nearly three hundred yards. This happened by Bridger's Lake, near Two-Ocean Pass.

The moose has a fast walk, and its ordinary gait when going at any speed is a slashing trot. Its long legs give it a wonderful stride, enabling it to clear down-timber and high obstacles of all sorts without altering its pace. It also leaps well. If much pressed or startled it breaks into an awkward gallop, which is quite fast for a few hundred yards, but which speedily tires it out. After being disturbed by the hunter a moose usually trots a long distance before halting.

One thing which renders the chase of the moose particularly interesting is the fact that there is in it on rare occasions a spice of peril. Under certain circumstances it may be called dangerous quarry, being, properly speaking, the only animal of the deer kind which ever fairly deserves the title. In a hand to hand grapple an elk or caribou, or even under exceptional circumstances a blacktail or a whitetail, may show itself an ugly antagonist; and indeed a maddened elk may for a moment take the offensive; but the moose is the only one of the tribe with which this attitude is at all common. In bodily strength and capacity to do harm it surpasses the elk; and in temper it is far more savage and more apt to show fight when assailed by man; exactly as the elk in these respects surpasses the common deer. Two hunters with whom I was well acquainted once wintered between the Wind River Mountains and the Three Tetons, many years ago, in the days of the buffalo. They lived on game, killing it on snowshoes; for the most part wapiti and deer, but also bison, and one moose, though they saw others. The wapiti bulls kept their antlers two months longer than the moose; nevertheless, when chased they rarely made an effort to use them, while the hornless moose displayed far more pugnacity, and also ran better through the deep snow. The winter was very severe, the snows were heavy and the crusts hard; so that the hunters had little trouble in overtaking their game, although—being old mountain-men, and not hide-hunters—they killed only what was needed. Of course in such hunting they came very close to the harried game, usually after a chase of from twenty minutes to three hours. They found that the ordinary deer would scarcely charge under any circumstances; that among the wapiti it was only now and then that individuals would turn upon their pursuers—though they sometimes charged boldly; but that both the bison and especially the moose when worried and approached too near, would often turn to bay and make charge after charge in the most resolute manner, so that they had to be approached with some caution.

Under ordinary conditions, however, there is very little danger, indeed, of a moose charging. A charge does not take place once in a hundred times when the moose is killed by fair still-hunting; and it is altogether exceptional for those who assail them from boats or canoes to be put in jeopardy. Even a cow moose, with her calf, will run if she has the chance; and a rutting bull will do the same. Such a bull when wounded may walk slowly forward, grunting savagely, stamping with his forefeet, and slashing the bushes with his antlers; but, if his antagonist is any distance off, he rarely actually runs at him. Yet there are now and then found moose prone to attack on slight provocation; for these great deer differ as widely as men in courage and ferocity. Occasionally a hunter is charged in the fall when he has lured the game to him by calling, or when he has wounded it after a stalk. In one well-authenticated instance which was brought to my attention, a settler on the left bank of the St. Johns, in New Brunswick, was tramped to death by a bull moose which he had called to him and wounded. A New Yorker of my acquaintance, Dr. Merrill, was charged under rather peculiar circumstances. He stalked and mortally wounded a bull which promptly ran towards him. Between them was a gully in which it disappeared. Immediately afterwards, as he thought, it reappeared on his side of the gully, and with a second shot he dropped it. Walking forward he found to his astonishment that with his second bullet he had killed a cow moose; the bull lay dying in the gully, out of which he had scared the cow by his last rush.

However, speaking broadly, the danger to the still-hunter engaged in one of the legitimate methods of the chase is so small that it may be disregarded; for he usually kills his game at some little distance, while the moose, as a rule, only attacks if it has been greatly worried and angered, and if its pursuer is close at hand. When a moose is surprised and shot at by a hunter some way off, its one thought is of flight. Hence, the hunters who are charged by moose are generally those who follow them during the late winter and early spring, when the animals have yarded and can be killed on snow-shoes—by "crusting," as it is termed, a very destructive, and often a very unsportsman-like species of chase.

If the snow-fall is very light, moose do not yard at all; but in a hard winter they begin to make their yards in December. A "yard" is not, as some people seem to suppose, a trampled-down space, with definite boundaries; the term merely denotes the spot which a moose has chosen for its winter home, choosing it because it contains plenty of browse in the shape of young trees and saplings, and perhaps also because it is sheltered to some extent from the fiercest winds and heaviest snowdrifts. The animal travels to and fro across this space in straight lines and irregular circles after food, treading in its own footsteps, where practicable. As the snow steadily deepens, these lines of travel become beaten paths. There results finally a space half a mile square—sometimes more, sometimes very much less, according to the lay of the land, and the number of moose yarding together—where the deep snow is seamed in every direction by a network of narrow paths along which a moose can travel at speed, its back level with the snow round about. Sometimes, when moose are very plenty, many of these yards lie so close together that the beasts can readily make their way from one to another. When such is the case, the most expert snow-shoer, under the most favorable conditions, cannot overtake them, for they can then travel very fast through the paths, keeping their gait all day. In the early decades of the present century, the first settlers in Aroostook County, Maine, while moose-hunting in winter, were frequently baffled in this manner.

When hunters approach an isolated yard the moose immediately leave it and run off through the snow. If there is no crust, and if their long legs can reach the ground, the snow itself impedes them but little, because of their vast strength and endurance. Snowdrifts which render an ordinary deer absolutely helpless, and bring even an elk to a standstill, offer no impediment whatever to a moose. If, as happens very rarely, the loose snow is of such depth that even the stilt-like legs of the moose cannot touch solid earth, it flounders and struggles forward for a little time, and then sinks exhausted; for a caribou is the only large animal which can travel under such conditions. If there be a crust, even though the snow is not remarkably deep, the labor of the moose is vastly increased, as it breaks through at every step, cutting its legs and exhausting itself. A caribou, on the other hand, will go across a crust as well as a man on snow-shoes, and can never be caught by the latter, save under altogether exceptional conditions of snowfall and thaw.

"Crusting," or following game on snow-shoes, is, as the name implies, almost always practised after the middle of February, when thaws begin, and the snow crusts on top. The conditions for success in crusting moose and deer are very different. A crust through which a moose would break at every stride may carry a running deer without mishap; while the former animal would trot at ease through drifts in which the latter would be caught as if in a quicksand.

Hunting moose on snow, therefore, may be, and very often is, mere butchery; and because of this possibility or probability, and also because of the fact that it is by far the most destructive kind of hunting, and is carried on at a season when the bulls are hornless and the cows heavy with calf, it is rigidly and properly forbidden wherever there are good game-laws. Yet this kind of hunting may also be carried on under circumstances which render it if not a legitimate, yet a most exciting and manly sport, only to be followed by men of tried courage, hardihood, and skill. This is not because it ever necessitates any skill whatever in the use of the rifle, or any particular knowledge of hunting-craft; but because under the conditions spoken of the hunter must show great endurance and resolution, and must be an adept in the use of snow-shoes.

It all depends upon the depth of the snow and the state of the crust. If when the snow is very deep there comes a thaw, and if it then freezes hard, the moose are overtaken and killed with ease; for the crust cuts their legs, they sink to their bellies at every plunge, and speedily become so worn out that they can no longer keep ahead of any man who is even moderately skilful in the use of snow-shoes; though they do not, as deer so often do, sink exhausted after going a few rods from their yard. Under such circumstances a few hardy hunters or settlers, who are perfectly reckless in slaughtering game, may readily kill all the moose in a district. It is a kind of hunting which just suits the ordinary settler, who is hardy and enduring, but knows little of hunting-craft proper.

If the snow is less deep, or the crust not so heavy, the moose may travel for scores of miles before it is overtaken; and this even though the crust be strong enough to bear a man wearing snow-shoes without breaking. The chase then involves the most exhausting fatigue. Moreover, it can be carried on only by those who are very skilful in the use of snow-shoes. These snow-shoes are of two kinds. In the northeast, and in the most tangled forests of the northwest, the webbed snow-shoes are used; on the bare mountain-sides, and in the open forests of the Rockies, the long narrow wooden skees, or Norwegian snow-skates are preferred, as upon then men can travel much faster, though they are less handy in thick timber. Having donned his snow-shoes and struck the trail of a moose, the hunter may have to follow it three days if the snow is of only ordinary depth, with a moderate crust. He shuffles across the snow without halt while daylight lasts, and lies down wherever he happens to be when night strikes him, probably with a little frozen bread as his only food. The hunter thus goes through inordinate labor, and suffers from exposure; not infrequently his feet are terribly cut by the thongs of the snow-shoes, and become sore and swollen, causing great pain. When overtaken after such a severe chase, the moose is usually so exhausted as to be unable to make any resistance; in all likelihood it has run itself to a standstill. Accordingly, the quality of the fire-arms makes but little difference in this kind of hunting. Many of the most famous old moose-hunters of Maine, in the long past days, before the Civil War, when moose were plenty there, used what were known as "three dollar" guns; light, single-barrelled smooth-bores. One whom I knew used a flint-lock musket, a relic of the War of 1812. Another in the course of an exhausting three days' chase lost the lock off his cheap, percussion-cap gun; and when he overtook the moose he had to explode the cap by hammering it with a stone.

It is in "crusting," when the chase has lasted but a comparatively short time, that moose most frequently show fight; for they are not cast into a state of wild panic by a sudden and unlooked-for attack by a man who is a long distance from them, but on the contrary, after being worried and irritated, are approached very near by foes from whom they have been fleeing for hours. Nevertheless, in the majority of cases even crusted moose make not the slightest attempt at retaliation. If the chase has been very long, or if the depth of the snow and character of the crust are exceptionally disadvantageous to them, they are so utterly done out, when overtaken, that they cannot make a struggle, and may even be killed with an axe. I know of at least five men who have thus killed crusted moose with an axe; one in the Rocky Mountains, one in Minnesota, three in Maine.

But in ordinary snow a man who should thus attempt to kill a moose would merely jeopardize his own life; and it is not an uncommon thing for chased moose, when closely approached by their pursuers, even when the latter carry guns and are expert snow-shoers, to charge them with such ferocity as to put them in much peril. A brother of one of my cow-hands, a man from Maine, was once nearly killed by a cow moose. She had been in a yard with her last year's calf when started. After two or three hours' chase he overtook them. They were travelling in single file, the cow breaking her path through the snow, while the calf followed close behind, and in his nervousness sometimes literally ran up on her. The man trotted close alongside; but, before he could fire, the old cow spun round and charged him, her mane bristling and her green eyes snapping with rage. It happened that just there the snow became shallow, and the moose gained so rapidly that the man, to save his life, sprang up a tree. As he did so the cow reared and struck at him, one forefoot catching in his snow-shoe and tearing it clear off, giving his ankle a bad wrench. After watching him a minute or two she turned and continued her flight; whereupon he climbed down the tree, patched up his torn snow-shoe and limped after the moose, which he finally killed.

An old hunter named Purvis told me of an adventure

of the kind, which terminated fatally. He was hunting near the Cœur d'Alene Mountains with a mining prospector named Pingree; both were originally from New Hampshire. Late in November there came a heavy fall of snow, deep enough to soon bring a deer to a standstill, although not so deep as to hamper a moose's movement. The men bound on their skees and started to the borders of a lake, to kill some blacktail. In a thicket close to the lake's brink they suddenly came across a bull moose; a lean old fellow, still savage from the rut. Pingree, who was nearest, fired at and wounded him; whereupon he rushed straight at the man, knocked him down before he could turn round on his skees, and began to pound him with his terrible forefeet. Summoned by his comrade's despairing cries, Purvis rushed round the thickets, and shot the squealing, trampling monster through the body, and immediately after had to swing himself up a small tree to avoid its furious rush. The moose did not turn after this charge, but kept straight on, and was not seen again. The wounded man was past all help, for his chest was beaten in, and he died in a couple of hours.

CHAPTER XII

The Bison or American Buffalo

When we became a nation, in 1776, the buffaloes, the first animals to vanish when the wilderness is settled, roved to the crests of the mountains which mark the western boundaries of Pennsylvania, Virginia, and the Carolinas. They were plentiful in what are now the States of Ohio, Kentucky, and Tennessee. But by the beginning of the present century they had been driven beyond the Mississippi; and for the next eighty years they formed one of the most distinctive and characteristic features of existence on the great plains. Their numbers were countless—incredible. In vast herds of hundreds of thousands of individuals, they roamed from the Saskatchewan to the Rio Grande and westward to the Rocky Mountains. They furnished all the means of livelihood to the tribes of Horse Indians, and to the curious population of French Metis, or Half-breeds, on the Red River, as well as to those dauntless and archtypical wanderers, the white hunters and trappers. Their numbers slowly diminished, but the decrease was very gradual until after the Civil War. They were not destroyed by the settlers, but by the railways and the skin hunters.

After the ending of the Civil War, the work of constructing trans-continental railway lines was pushed forward with the utmost vigor. These supplied cheap and indispensable, but hitherto wholly lacking, means of transportation to the hunters; and at the same time the demand for buffalo robes and hides became very great, while the enormous numbers of the beasts, and the comparative ease with which they were slaughtered, attracted throngs of adventurers. The result was such a slaughter of big game as the world had never before seen; never before were so many large animals of one species destroyed in so short a time. Several million buffaloes were slain. In fifteen years from the time the destruction fairly began the great herds were exterminated. In all probability there are not now, all told, five hundred head of wild buffaloes on the American continent; and no herd of a hundred individuals has been in existence since 1884.

The first great break followed the building of the Union Pacific Railway. All the buffaloes of the middle region were then destroyed, and the others were split into two vast sets of herds, the northern and the southern. The latter were destroyed first, about 1878; the former not until 1883. My own chief experience with buffaloes was obtained in the latter year, among small bands and scattered individuals, near my ranch on the Little Missouri; I have related it elsewhere. But two of my kinsmen were more fortunate, and took part in the chase of these lordly beasts when the herds still darkened the prairie as far as the eye could see.

During the first two months of 1877, my brother Elliott, then a lad not seventeen years old, made a buffalo-hunt toward the edge of the Staked Plains in northern Texas. He was thus in at the death of the southern herds;

for all, save a few scattering bands, were destroyed within two years of this time. He was with my cousin, John Roosevelt, and they went out on the range with six other adventurers. It was a party of just such young men as frequently drift to the frontier. All were short of cash, and all were hardy, vigorous fellows, eager for excitement and adventure. My brother was much the youngest of the party, and the least experienced; but he was well-grown, strong and healthy, and very fond of boxing, wrestling, running, riding, and shooting; moreover, he had served an apprenticeship in hunting deer and turkeys. Their mess-kit, ammunition, bedding, and provisions were carried in two prairie-wagons, each drawn by four horses. In addition to the teams they had six saddle-animals—all of them shaggy, unkempt mustangs. Three or four dogs, setters and half-bred greyhounds, trotted along behind the wagons. Each man took his turn for two days as teamster and cook; and there were always two with the wagons, or camp, as the case might be, while the other six were off hunting, usually in couples. The expedition was undertaken partly for sport and partly with the hope of profit; for, after purchasing the horses and wagons, none of the party had any money left, and they were forced to rely upon selling skins and hides, and, when near the forts, meat.

They started on January 2d, and shaped their course for the head-waters of the Salt Fork of the Brazos, the centre of abundance for the great buffalo herds. During the first few days they were in the outskirts of the settled country, and shot only small game—quail and prairie fowl; then they began to kill turkey, deer, and antelope. These they swapped for flour and feed at the ranches or squalid, straggling frontier towns. On several occasions the hunters were lost, spending the night out in the open, or sleeping at a ranch, if one was found. Both towns and ranches were filled with rough customers; all of my brother's companions were muscular, hot-headed fellows; and as a consequence they were involved in several savage free fights, in which, fortunately, nobody was seriously hurt. My brother kept a very brief diary, the entries being fairly startling from their conciseness. A number of times, the mention of their arrival, either at a halting-place, a little village, or a rival buffalo-camp is followed by the laconic remark, "big fight," or "big row"; but once they evidently concluded discretion to be the better part of valor, the entry for January 20th being, "On the road—passed through Belknap—too lively, so kept on to the Brazos—very late." The buffalo-camps in particular were very jealous of one another, each party regarding itself as having exclusive right to the range it was the first to find; and on several occasions this feeling came near involving my brother and his companions in serious trouble.

While slowly driving the heavy wagons to the hunting grounds they suffered the usual hardships of plains travel. The weather, as in most Texas winters, alternated between the extremes of heat and cold. There had been little rain; in consequence water was scarce. Twice they were forced to cross wild, barren wastes, where the pools had dried up, and they suffered terribly from thirst. On the first occasion the horses were in good condition, and they travelled steadily, with only occasional short halts, for over thirty-six hours, by which time they were across the waterless country. The journal reads: "January 27th.—Big hunt—no water, and we left Quinn's block-house this morning 3 A.M.—on the go all night—hot. January 28th.—No water—hot—at seven we struck water, and by eight Stinking Creek—grand 'hurrah.' " On the second occasion, the horses were weak and travelled slowly, so the party went forty-eight hours without drinking. "February 19th.—Pulled on twenty-one miles—trail bad—freezing night, no water, and wolves after our fresh meat. 20th.— Made nineteen miles over prairie; again only mud, no water, freezing hard—frightful thirst. 21st.—Thirty miles to Clear Fork, fresh water." These entries were hurriedly jotted down at the time, by a boy who deemed it unmanly to make any especial note of hardship or suffering; but every plainsman will understand the real agony implied in working hard for two nights, one day, and portions of two others, without water, even in cool weather. During the last few miles the staggering horses were only just able to drag the lightly loaded wagon,—for they had but one with them at the time,—while the men plodded along in sullen silence, their mouths so parched that they could hardly utter a word. My own hunting and ranching were done in the north where there is more water; so I have never had a similar experience. Once I took a team in thirty-six hours across a country where there was no water; but by good luck it rained heavily in the night, so that the horses had plenty of wet grass, and I caught the rain in my slicker, and so had enough water for myself. Personally, I have but once been as long as twenty-six hours without water.

The party pitched their permanent camp in a canyon

of the Brazos known as Canyon Blanco. The last few days of their journey they travelled beside the river through a veritable hunter's paradise. The drought had forced all the animals to come to the larger watercourses, and the country was literally swarming with game. Every day, and all day long, the wagons travelled through the herds of antelopes that grazed on every side, while, whenever they approached the canyon brink, bands of deer started from the timber that fringed the river's course; often, even the deer wandered out on the prairie with the antelope. Nor was the game shy; for the hunters, both red and white, followed only the buffaloes, until the huge, shaggy herds were destroyed, and the smaller beasts were in consequence but little molested.

Once my brother shot five antelopes from a single stand, when the party were short of fresh venison; he was out of sight and to leeward, and the antelopes seemed confused rather than alarmed at the rifle-reports and the fall of their companions. As was to be expected where game was so plenty, wolves and coyotes also abounded. At night they surrounded the camp, wailing and howling in a kind of shrieking chorus throughout the hours of darkness; one night they came up so close that the frightened horses had to be hobbled and guarded. On another occasion a large wolf actually crept into camp, where he was seized by the dogs, and the yelling, writhing knot of combatants rolled over one of the sleepers; finally, the long-toothed prowler managed to shake himself loose, and vanished in the gloom. One evening they were almost as much startled by a visit of a different kind. They were just finishing supper when an Indian stalked suddenly and silently out of the surrounding darkness, squatted down in the circle of firelight, remarked gravely, "Me Tonk," and began helping himself from the stew. He belonged to the friendly tribe of Tonkaways, so his hosts speedily recovered their equanimity; as for him, he had never lost his, and he sat eating by the fire until there was literally nothing left to eat. The panic caused by his appearance was natural; for at that time the Comanches were a scourge to the buffalo-hunters, ambushing them and raiding their camps; and several bloody fights had taken place.

Their camp had been pitched near a deep pool or water-hole. On both sides the bluffs rose like walls, and where they had crumbled and lost their sheerness, the vast buffalo herds, passing and repassing for countless generations, had worn furrowed trails so deep that the backs of the beasts were but little above the surrounding soil. In the bottom, and in places along the crests of the cliffs that hemmed in the canyon-like valley, there were groves of tangled trees, tenanted by great flocks of wild turkeys. Once my brother made two really remarkable shots at a pair of these great birds. It was at dusk, and they were flying directly overhead from one cliff to the other. He had in his hand a thirty-eight calibre Ballard rifle, and, as the gobblers winged their way heavily by, he brought both down with two successive bullets. This was of course mainly a piece of mere luck; but it meant good shooting, too. The Ballard was a very accurate, handy little weapon; it belonged to me, and was the first rifle I ever owned or used. With it I had once killed a deer, the only specimen of large game I had then shot; and I presented the rifle to my brother when he went to Texas. In our happy igno-

rance we deemed it quite good enough for buffalo or anything else; but out on the plains my brother soon found
himself forced to procure a heavier and more deadly
weapon.

When camp was pitched the horses were turned loose
to graze and refresh themselves after their trying journey,
during which they had lost flesh wofully. They were
watched and tended by the two men who were always left
in camp, and, save on rare occasions, were only used to
haul in the buffalo hides. The camp-guards for the time
being acted as cooks; and, though coffee and flour both
ran short and finally gave out, fresh meat of every kind was
abundant. The camp was never without buffalo-beef, deer
and antelope venison, wild turkeys, prairie-chickens,
quails, ducks, and rabbits. The birds were simply "potted,"
as occasion required; when the quarry was deer or antelope, the hunters took the dogs with them to run down the
wounded animals. But almost the entire attention of the
hunters was given to the buffalo. After an evening spent in
lounging round the camp-fire and a sound night's sleep,
wrapped in robes and blankets, they would get up before
daybreak, snatch a hurried breakfast, and start off in couples through the chilly dawn. The great beasts were very
plentiful; in the first day's hunt twenty were slain; but the
herds were restless and ever on the move. Sometimes they
would be seen right by the camp, and again it would need
an all-day's tramp to find them. There was no difficulty in
spying them—the chief trouble with forest game; for on
the prairie a buffalo makes no effort to hide and its black,
shaggy bulk looms up as far as the eye can see. Sometimes
they were found in small parties of three or four individu-

als, sometimes in bands of about two hundred, and again in great herds of many thousands; and solitary old bulls, expelled from the herds, were common. If on broken land, among hills and ravines, there was not much difficulty in approaching from the leeward; for, though the sense of smell in the buffalo is very acute, they do not see well at a distance through their overhanging frontlets of coarse and matted hair. If, as was generally the case, they were out on the open, rolling prairie, the stalking was far more difficult. Every hollow, every earth hummock and sage-brush had to be used as cover. The hunter wriggled through the grass flat on his face, pushing himself along for perhaps a quarter of a mile by his toes and fingers, heedless of the spiny cactus. When near enough to the huge, unconscious quarry the hunter began firing, still keeping himself carefully concealed. If the smoke was blown away by the wind, and if the buffaloes caught no glimpse of the assailant, they would often stand motionless and stupid until many of their number had been slain, the hunter being careful not to fire too high, aiming just behind the shoulder, about a third of the way up the body, that his bullet might go through the lungs. Sometimes, even after they saw the man, they would act as if confused and panic-struck, huddling together and staring at the smoke puffs; but generally they were off at a lumbering gallop as soon as they had an idea of the point of danger. When once started, they ran for many miles before halting, and their pursuit on foot was extremely laborious.

One morning my cousin and brother had been left in camp as guards. They were sitting idly warming themselves in the first sunbeams, when their attention was sharply drawn to four buffaloes that were coming to the pool to drink. The beasts came down a game trail, a deep rut in the bluff, fronting where they were sitting, and they did not dare to stir for fear of being discovered. The buffaloes walked into the pool, and, after drinking their fill, stood for some time with the water running out of their mouths, idly lashing their sides with their short tails, enjoying the bright warmth of the early sunshine; then, with much splashing and the gurgling of soft mud, they left the pool and clambered up the bluff with unwieldy agility. As soon as they turned, my brother and cousin ran for their rifles, but before they got back the buffaloes had crossed the bluff crest. Climbing after them, the two hunters found, when they reached the summit, that their game, instead of halting, had struck straight off across the prairie at a slow lope, doubtless intending to rejoin the herd they had left. After a moment's consultation the men went in pursuit, excitement overcoming their knowledge that they ought not, by rights, to leave camp. They struck a steady trot, following the animals by sight until they passed over a knoll, and then trailing them. Where the grass was long, as it was for the first four or five miles, this was a work of no difficulty, and they did not break their gait, only glancing now and then at the trail. As the sun rose and the day became warm, their breathing grew quicker; and the sweat rolled off their faces as they ran across the rough prairie sward, up and down the long inclines, now and then shifting their heavy rifles from one shoulder to the other. But they were in good training, and they did not have to halt. At last they reached stretches of bare ground, sun-baked and grassless, where the trail grew dim; and here they had to go very slowly, carefully examining the faint dents and marks made in the soil by the heavy hoofs, and unravelling the trail from the mass of old footmarks. It was tedious work, but it enabled them to completely recover their breath by the time that they again struck the grassland; and but a few hundred yards from its edge, in a slight hollow, they saw the four buffaloes just entering a herd of fifty or sixty that were scattered out grazing. The herd paid no attention to the new-comers, and these immediately began to feed greedily. After a whispered consultation, the two hunters crept back, and made a long circle that brought them well to leeward of the herd, in line with a slight rise in the ground. They then crawled up to this rise and, peering through the tufts of tall, rank grass, saw the unconscious beasts a hundred and twenty-five or fifty yards away. They fired together, each mortally wounding his animal, and then, rushing in as the herd halted in confusion, and following them as they ran, impeded by numbers, hurry, and panic, they eventually got three more.

On another occasion the same two hunters nearly met with a frightful death, being overtaken by a vast herd of stampeded buffaloes. All animals that go in herds are subject to these instantaneous attacks of uncontrollable terror, under the influence of which they become perfectly mad, and rush headlong in dense masses on any form of death. Horses, and more especially cattle, often suffer from stampedes; it is a danger against which the cowboys are compelled to be perpetually on guard. A band of stampeded horses, sweeping in mad terror up a valley, will dash against a rock or tree with such violence as to leave several dead animals at its base, while the survivors race on without halting; they will overturn and destroy tents and wagons, and a man on foot caught in the rush has but a small chance for his life. A buffalo stampede is much worse—or rather was much worse, in the old days—because of the great weight and immense numbers of the beasts, which, in a fury of heedless terror, plunged over cliffs and into rivers, and bore down whatever was in their path. On the occasion in question, my brother and cousin were on their way homeward. They were just mounting one of the long, low swells, into which the prairie was broken, when they heard a low, muttering, rumbling noise, like far-off thunder. It grew steadily louder, and, not knowing what it meant, they hurried forward to the top of the rise. As they reached it, they stopped short in terror and amazement, for before them the whole prairie was black with madly rushing buffaloes.

Afterward they learned that another couple of hunters, four or five miles off, had fired into and stampeded a large herd. This herd, in its rush, gathered others, all thundering along together in uncontrollable and increasing panic.

The surprised hunters were far away from any broken ground or other place of refuge, while the vast herd of huge, plunging, maddened beasts was charging straight down on them not a quarter of a mile distant. Down they came!—thousands upon thousands, their front extending a mile in breadth, while the earth shook beneath their thunderous gallop, and, as they came closer, their shaggy frontlets loomed dimly through the columns of dust thrown up from the dry soil. The two hunters knew that their only hope for life was to split the herd, which, though it had so broad a front, was not very deep. If they failed they would inevitably be trampled to death.

Waiting until the beasts were in close range, they opened a rapid fire from their heavy breech-loading rifles, yelling at the top of their voices. For a moment the result seemed doubtful. The line thundered steadily down on them; then it swayed violently, as two or three of the brutes immediately in their front fell beneath the bullets, while their neighbors made violent efforts to press off sideways. Then a narrow wedge-shaped rift appeared in the line, and widened as it came closer, and the buffaloes, shrinking from their foes in front, strove desperately to edge away from the dangerous neighborhood; the shouts and shots were redoubled; the hunters were almost choked by the cloud of dust, through which they could see the stream of dark huge bodies passing within rifle-length on either side; and in a moment the peril was over, and the two men were left alone on the plain, unharmed, though with their nerves terribly shaken. The herd careered on toward the horizon, save five individuals which had been killed or disabled by the shots.

On another occasion, when my brother was out with one of his friends, they fired at a small herd containing an old bull; the bull charged the smoke, and the whole herd followed him. Probably they were simply stampeded, and had no hostile intention; at any rate, after the death of their leader, they rushed by without doing any damage.

But buffaloes sometimes charged with the utmost determination, and were then dangerous antagonists. My cousin, a very hardy and resolute hunter, had a narrow escape from a wounded cow which he followed up a steep bluff or sand cliff. Just as he reached the summit, he was charged, and was only saved by the sudden appearance of his dog, which distracted the cow's attention. He thus escaped with only a tumble and a few bruises.

My brother also came in for a charge, while killing the biggest bull that was slain by any of the party. He was out alone, and saw a small herd of cows and calves at some distance, with a huge bull among them, towering above them like a giant. There was no break in the ground, nor any tree nor bush near them, but, by making a half-circle, my brother managed to creep up against the wind behind a slight roll in the prairie surface, until he was within seventy-five yards of the grazing and unconscious beasts. There were some cows and calves between him and the bull, and he had to wait some moments before they shifted position, as the herd grazed onward and gave him a fair shot; in the interval they had moved so far forward that he was in plain view. His first bullet struck just behind the shoulder; the herd started and looked around, but the bull merely lifted his head and took a step forward, his tail curled up over his back. The next bullet likewise struck fair, nearly in the same place, telling with a loud "pack!" against the thick hide, and making the dust fly up from the matted hair. Instantly the great bull wheeled and charged in headlong anger, while the herd fled in the opposite direction. On the bare prairie, with no spot of refuge, it was useless to try to escape, and the hunter, with reloaded rifle, waited until the bull was not far off, then drew up his weapon and fired. Either he was nervous, or the bull at the moment bounded over some obstacle, for the ball went a little wild; nevertheless, by good luck, it broke a fore-leg, and the great beast came crashing to the earth, and was slain before it could struggle to its feet.

Two days after this event, a war party of Comanches swept down along the river. They "jumped" a neighboring camp, killing one man and wounding two more, and at the same time ran off all but three of the horses belonging to our eight adventurers. With the remaining three horses and one wagon they set out homeward. The march was hard and tedious; they lost their way and were in jeopardy from quicksands and cloudbursts; they suffered from thirst and cold, their shoes gave out, and their feet were lamed by cactus spines. At last they reached Fort Griffen in safety, and great was their ravenous rejoicing when they procured some bread—for during the final fortnight of the hunt they had been without flour or vegetables of any kind, or even coffee, and had subsisted on fresh meat "straight." Nevertheless, it was a very healthy, as well as a very pleasant and exciting experience; and I doubt if any of those who took part in it will ever forget their great buffalo-hunt on the Brazos.

My friend, Gen. W. H. Walker, of Virginia, had an experience in the early '50's with buffaloes on the upper Arkansas River, which gives some idea of their enormous numbers at that time. He was camped with a scouting party on the banks of the river, and had gone out to try to shoot some meat. There were many buffaloes in sight, scattered, according to their custom, in large bands. When he was a mile or two away from the river a dull roaring sound in the distance attracted his attention, and he saw that a herd of buffalo far to the south, away from the river, had been stampeded and was running his way. He knew that if he was caught in the open by the stampeded herd his chance for life would be small, and at once ran for the river. By desperate efforts he reached the breaks in the sheer banks just as the buffaloes reached them, and got into a position of safety on the pinnacle of a little bluff. From this point of vantage he could see the entire plain. To the very verge of the horizon the brown masses of the buffalo bands showed through the dust clouds, coming on with a thunderous roar like that of surf. Camp was a mile away, and the stampede luckily passed to one side of it. Watching his chance he finally dodged back to the tent, and all that afternoon watched the immense masses of buffalo, as band after band tore to the brink of the bluffs on one side, raced down them, rushed through the water, up the bluffs on the other side, and again off over the plain, churning the sandy, shallow stream into a ceaseless tumult. When darkness fell there was no apparent decrease in the numbers that were passing, and all through that night the continuous roar showed that the herds were still threshing across the river. Towards dawn the sound at last ceased, and General Walker arose somewhat irritated, as he had reckoned on killing an ample supply of meat, and he supposed that there would be now no bison left south of the river. To his astonishment, when he strolled up on the bluffs and looked over the plain, it was still covered far and wide with groups of buffalo, grazing quietly. Apparently there were as many on that side as ever, in spite of the many scores of thousands that must have crossed over the river during the stampede of the afternoon and night. The barren-ground caribou is the only

American animal which is now ever seen in such enormous herds.

In 1862 Mr. Clarence King, while riding along the overland trail through western Kansas, passed through a great buffalo herd, and was himself injured in an encounter with a bull. The great herd was then passing north, and Mr. King reckoned that it must have covered an area nearly seventy miles by thirty in extent; the figures representing his rough guess, made after travelling through the herd crosswise, and upon knowing how long it took to pass a given point going northward. This great herd of course was not a solid mass of buffaloes; it consisted of innumerable bands of every size, dotting the prairie within the limits given. Mr. King was mounted on a somewhat unmanageable horse. On one occasion in following a band he wounded a large bull, and became so wedged in by the maddened animals that he was unable to avoid the charge of the bull, which was at its last gasp. Coming straight toward him it leaped into the air and struck the afterpart of the saddle full with its massive forehead. The horse was hurled to the ground with a broken back, and King's leg was likewise broken, while the bull turned a complete somerset over them and never rose again.

In the recesses of the Rocky Mountains, from Colorado northward through Alberta, and in the depths of the sub-arctic forest beyond the Saskatchewan, there have always been found small numbers of the bison, locally called the mountain buffalo and wood buffalo; often indeed the old hunters term these animals "bison," although they never speak of the plains animals save as buffalo.

They form a slight variety of what was formerly the ordinary plains bison, intergrading with it; on the whole they are darker in color, with longer, thicker hair, and in consequence with the appearance of being heavier-bodied and shorter-legged. They have been sometimes spoken of as forming a separate species; but, judging from my own limited experience, and from a comparison of the many hides I have seen, I think they are really the same animal, many individuals of the two so-called varieties being quite indistinguishable. In fact the only moderate-sized herd of wild bison in existence to-day, the protected herd in the Yellowstone Park, is composed of animals intermediate in habits and coat between the mountain and plains varieties—as were all the herds of the Bighorn, Big Hole, Upper Madison, and Upper Yellowstone valleys.

However, the habitat of these wood and mountain bison yielded them shelter from hunters in a way that the plains never could, and hence they have always been harder to kill in the one place than in the other; for precisely the same reasons that have held good with the elk, which have been completely exterminated from the plains, while still abundant in many of the forest fastnesses of the Rockies. Moreover, the bison's dull eyesight is no especial harm in the woods, while it is peculiarly hurtful to the safety of any beast on the plains, where eyesight avails more than any other sense, the true game of the plains being the prong-buck, the most keen-sighted of American animals. On the other hand the bison's hearing, of little avail on the plains, is of much assistance in the woods; and its excellent nose helps equally in both places.

Though it was always more difficult to kill the bison

of the forests and mountains than the bison of the prairie, yet now that the species is, in its wild state, hovering on the brink of extinction, the difficulty is immeasurably increased. A merciless and terrible process of natural selection, in which the agents were rifle-bearing hunters, has left as the last survivors in a hopeless struggle for existence only the wariest of the bison and those gifted with the sharpest senses. That this was true of the last lingering individuals that survived the great slaughter on the plains is well shown by Mr. Hornaday in his graphic account of his campaign against the few scattered buffalo which still lived in 1886 between the Missouri and the Yellowstone, along the Big Dry. The bison of the plains and the prairies have now vanished; and so few of their brethren of the mountains and the northern forests are left, that they can just barely be reckoned among American game; but whoever is so fortunate as to find any of these animals must work his hardest, and show all his skill as a hunter if he wishes to get one.

In the fall of 1889 I heard that a very few bison were still left around the head of Wisdom River. Thither I went and hunted faithfully; there was plenty of game of other kind, but of bison not a trace did we see. Nevertheless a few days later that same year I came across these great wild cattle at a time when I had no idea of seeing them.

It was, as nearly as we could tell, in Idaho, just south of the Montana boundary line, and some twenty-five miles west of the line of Wyoming. We were camped high among the mountains, with a small pack-train. On the day in question we had gone out to find moose, but had seen no sign of them, and had then begun to climb over the higher peaks with an idea of getting sheep. The old hunter who was with me was, very fortunately, suffering from rheumatism, and he therefore carried a long staff instead of his rifle; I say fortunately, for if he had carried his rifle it would have been impossible to stop his firing at such game as bison, nor would he have spared the cows and calves.

About the middle of the afternoon we crossed a low, rocky ridge, above timber line, and saw at our feet a basin or round valley of singular beauty. Its walls were formed by steep mountains. At its upper end lay a small lake, bordered on one side by a meadow of emerald green. The lake's other side marked the edge of the frowning pine forest which filled the rest of the valley, and hung high on the sides of the gorge which formed its outlet. Beyond the lake the ground rose in a pass evidently much frequented by game in bygone days, their trails lying along it in thick zigzags, each gradually fading out after a few hundred yards, and then starting again in a little different place, as game trails so often seem to do.

We bent our steps towards these trails, and no sooner had we reached the first than the old hunter bent over it with a sharp exclamation of wonder. There in the dust were the unmistakable hoof-marks of a small band of bison, apparently but a few hours old. They were headed towards the lake. There had been a half a dozen animals in the party; one a big bull, and two calves.

We immediately turned and followed the trail. It led down to the little lake, where the beasts had spread and grazed on the tender, green blades, and had drunk their fill. The footprints then came together again, showing where the animals had gathered and walked off in single file to the forest. Evidently they had come to the pool in the early morning, walking over the game pass from some neighboring valley, and after drinking and feeding had moved into the pine forest to find some spot for their noontide rest.

It was a very still day, and there were nearly three hours of daylight left. Without a word my silent companion, who had been scanning the whole country with hawk-eyed eagerness, besides scrutinizing the sign on his hands and knees, took the trail, motioning me to follow. In a moment we entered the woods, breathing a sigh of relief as we did so; for while in the meadow we could never tell that the buffalo might not see us, if they happened to be lying in some place with a commanding lookout.

The old hunter was thoroughly roused, and he showed himself a very skilful tracker. We were much favored by the character of the forest, which was rather open, and in most places free from undergrowth and down timber. As in most Rocky Mountain forests the timber was small, not only as compared to the giant trees of the groves of the Pacific coast, but as compared to the forests of the northeast. The ground was covered with pine needles and soft moss, so that it was not difficult to walk noiselessly. Once or twice when I trod on a small dry twig, or let the nails in my shoes clink slightly against a stone, the hunter turned to me with a frown of angry impatience; but as he walked slowly, continually halting to look ahead, as well as stooping over to examine the trail, I did not find it very difficult to move silently. I kept a little behind him, and to one side, save when he crouched to take advantage of some piece of cover, and I crept in his footsteps. I did not look at the trail at all, but kept watching ahead, hoping at any moment to see the game.

It was not very long before we struck their day beds, which were made on a knoll, where the forest was open and where there was much down timber. After leaving the day beds the animals had at first fed separately around the grassy base and sides of the knoll, and had then made off in their usual single file, going straight to a small pool in the forest. After drinking they had left this pool, and travelled down towards the gorge at the mouth of the basin, the trail leading along the sides of the steep hill, which were dotted by open glades; while the roar of the cataracts by which the stream was broken ascended from below. Here we moved with redoubled caution, for the sign had grown very fresh and the animals had once more scattered and begun feeding. When the trail led across the glades we usually skirted them so as to keep in the timber.

At last, on nearing the edge of one of these glades we saw a movement among the young trees on the other side, not fifty yards away. Peering through the safe shelter yielded by some thick evergreen bushes, we speedily made out three bison, a cow, a calf, and a yearling, grazing greedily on the other side of the glade, under the fringing timber; all with their heads up-hill. Soon another cow and calf stepped out after them. I did not wish to shoot, waiting for the appearance of the big bull which I knew was accompanying them.

So for several minutes I watched the great, clumsy, shaggy beasts, as all unconscious they grazed in the open glade. Behind them rose the dark pines. At the left of the glade the ground fell away to form the side of a chasm; down in its depths the cataracts foamed and thundered; beyond, the huge mountains towered, their crests crimsoned by the sinking sun. Mixed with the eager excitement of the hunter was a certain half melancholy feeling as I gazed on these bison, themselves part of the last remnant of a doomed and nearly vanished race. Few, indeed, are the men who now have, or evermore shall have, the chance of seeing the mightiest of American beasts, in all his wild vigor, surrounded by the tremendous desolation of his far-off mountain home.

At last, when I had begun to grow very anxious lest the others should take alarm, the bull likewise appeared on the edge of the glade, and stood with outstretched head, scratching his throat against a young tree, which shook violently. I aimed low, behind his shoulder, and pulled trigger. At the crack of the rifle all the bison, without the momentary halt of terror-struck surprise so common among game, turned and raced off at headlong speed. The fringe of young pines beyond and below the glade cracked and swayed as if a whirlwind were passing, and in another moment they reached the top of a very steep incline, thickly strewn with boulders and dead timber. Down this they plunged with reckless speed; their surefootedness was a marvel in such seemingly unwieldy beasts. A column of dust obscured their passage, and under its cover they disappeared in the forest; but the trail of the bull was marked by splashes of frothy blood, and we followed it at a trot. Fifty yards beyond the border of the forest we found the stark black body stretched motionless. He was a splendid old bull, still in his full vigor, with large, sharp horns, and heavy mane and glossy coat; and I felt the most exulting pride as I handled and examined him; for I had procured a trophy such as can fall henceforth to few hunters indeed.

It was too late to dress the beast that evening; so, after taking out the tongue and cutting off enough meat for supper and breakfast, we scrambled down to near the torrent, and after some search found a good spot for camping. Hot and dusty from the day's hard tramp, I undressed and took a plunge in the stream, the icy water making me gasp. Then, having built a slight lean-to of brush, and dragged together enough dead timber to burn all night, we cut long alder twigs, sat down before some embers raked apart, and grilled and ate our buffalo meat with the utmost relish. Night had fallen; a cold wind blew up the valley; the torrent roared as it leaped past us, and drowned our words as we strove to talk over our adventures and success; while the flame of the fire flickered and danced, lighting up with continual vivid flashes the gloom of the forest round about.

CHAPTER XIII

The Black Bear

Next to the whitetail deer the black bear is the commonest and most widely distributed of American big game. It is still found quite plentifully in northern New England, in the Adirondacks, Catskills, and along the entire length of the Alleghanies, as well as in the swamps and canebrakes of the southern States. It is also common in the great forests of northern Michigan, Wisconsin, and Minnesota, and throughout the Rocky Mountains and the timbered ranges of the Pacific coast. In the East it has always ranked second only to the deer among the beasts of chase. The bear and the buck were the staple objects of pursuit of all the old hunters. They were more plentiful than the bison and elk even in the long vanished days when these two great monarchs of the forest still ranged eastward to Virginia and Pennsylvania. The wolf and the cougar were always too scarce and too shy to yield much profit to the hunter. The black bear is a timid, cowardly animal, and usually a vegetarian, though it sometimes preys on the sheep, hogs, and even cattle of the settler, and is very fond of raiding his corn and melons. Its meat is good and its fur often valuable; and in its chase there is much excitement, and occasionally a slight spice of danger, just enough to render it attractive; so it has always been eagerly followed. Yet it still holds its own, though in greatly diminished numbers, in the more thinly settled portions of the country. One of the standing riddles of American zoölogy is the fact that the black bear, which is easier killed and less prolific than the wolf, should hold its own in the land better than the latter, this being directly the reverse of what occurs in Europe, where the brown bear is generally exterminated before the wolf.

In a few wild spots in the East, in northern Maine for instance, here and there in the neighborhood of the upper Great Lakes, in the east Tennessee and Kentucky mountains and the swamps of Florida and Mississippi, there still lingers an occasional representative of the old wilderness hunters. These men live in log-cabins in the wilderness. They do their hunting on foot, occasionally with the help of a single trailing dog. In Maine they are as apt to kill moose and caribou as bear and deer; but elsewhere the two last, with an occasional cougar or wolf, are the beasts of chase which they follow. Nowadays as these old hunters die there is no one to take their places, though there are still plenty of backwoods settlers in all of the regions named who do a great deal of hunting and trapping. Such an old hunter rarely makes his appearance at the settlements except to dispose of his peltry and hides in exchange for cartridges and provisions, and he leads a life of such lonely isolation as to insure his individual characteristics developing into peculiarities. Most of the wilder districts in the eastern States still preserve memories of some such old hunter who lived his long life alone, waging ceaseless warfare on the vanishing game, whose oddities, as well as his courage, hardihood, and woodcraft, are laughingly remembered by the older settlers, and who is usually best known as having killed the last wolf or bear or cougar ever seen in the locality.

Generally the weapon mainly relied on by these old hunters is the rifle; and occasionally some old hunter will be found even to this day who uses a muzzle loader, such as Kit Carson carried in the middle of the century. There are exceptions to this rule of the rifle however. In the years after the Civil War one of the many noted hunters of southwest Virginia and east Tennessee was Wilbur Waters, sometimes called The Hunter of White Top. He often killed black bear with a knife and dogs. He spent all his life in hunting and was very successful, killing the last gang of wolves to be found in his neighborhood; and he slew innumerable bears, with no worse results to himself than an occasional bite or scratch.

In the southern States the planters living in the wilder regions have always been in the habit of following the black bear with horse and hound, many of them keeping regular packs of bear hounds. Such a pack includes not only pure-bred hounds, but also cross-bred animals, and some sharp, agile, hard-biting fierce dogs and terriers. They follow the bear and bring him to bay but do not try to kill him, although there are dogs of the big fighting breeds which can readily master a black bear if loosed at him three or four at a time; but the dogs of these southern bear-hound packs are not fitted for such work, and if they try to close with the bear he is certain to play havoc with them, disembowelling them with blows of his paws or seizing them in his arms and biting through their spines or legs. The riders follow the hounds through the canebrakes, and also try to make cutoffs and station themselves at open points where they think the bear will pass, so that they may get a shot at him. The weapons used are rifles, shotguns, and occasionally revolvers.

Sometimes, however, the hunter uses the knife. General Wade Hampton, who has probably killed more black bears than any other man living in the United States, frequently used the knife, slaying thirty or forty with his weapon. His plan was, when he found that the dogs had the bear at bay, to walk up close and cheer them on. They would instantly seize the bear in a body, and he would then rush in and stab it behind the shoulder, reaching over so as to inflict the wound on the opposite side from that where he stood. He escaped scathless from all these encounters save one, in which he was rather severely torn in the forearm. Many other hunters have used the knife, but perhaps none so frequently as he; for he was always fond of steel, as witness his feats with the "white arm" during the Civil War.

General Hampton always hunted with large packs of hounds, managed sometimes by himself and sometimes by his negro hunters. He occasionally took out forty dogs at a time. He found that all his dogs together could not kill a big fat bear, but they occasionally killed three-year-olds, or lean and poor bears. During the course of his life he has himself killed, or been in at the death of, five hundred bears, at least two thirds of them falling by his own hand. In the years just before the war he had on one occasion, in Mississippi, killed sixty-eight bears in five months. Once he killed four bears in a day; at another time three, and frequently two. The two largest bears he himself killed weighed, respectively, 408 and 410 pounds. They were both shot in Mississippi. But he saw at least one bear killed which was much larger than either of these. These figures were taken down at the time, when the animals were actually weighed on the scales. Most of his hunting for bear was done in northern Mississippi, where one of his plantations was situated, near Greenville. During the half century that he hunted, on and off, in this neighborhood, he knew of two instances where hunters were fatally wounded in the chase of the black bear. Both of the men were inexperienced, one being a raftsman who came down the river, and the other a man from Vicksburg. He was not able to learn the particulars in the last case, but the raftsman came too close to a bear that was at bay, and it broke through the dogs, rushed at and overthrew him, then lying on him, it bit him deeply in the thigh, through the femoral artery, so that he speedily bled to death.

But a black bear is not usually a formidable opponent, and though he will sometimes charge home he is much more apt to bluster and bully than actually to come to close quarters. I myself have but once seen a man who had been hurt by one of these bears. This was an Indian. He had come on the beast close up in a thick wood, and had mortally wounded it with his gun; it had then closed with him, knocking the gun out of his hand, so that he was forced to use his knife. It charged him on all fours, but in the grapple, when it had failed to throw him down, it raised itself on its hind legs, clasping him across the shoulders with its fore-paws. Apparently it had no intention of hugging, but merely sought to draw him within reach of his jaws. He fought desperately against this, using the knife freely, and striving to keep its head back; and the flow of blood weakened the animal, so that it finally fell exhausted, before being able dangerously to injure him. But it had bitten his left arm very severely, and its claws had made long gashes on his shoulders.

Black bears, like grislies, vary greatly in their modes of attack. Sometimes they rush in and bite; and again they strike with their fore-paws. Two of my cowboys were originally from Maine, where I knew them well. There they were fond of trapping bears, and caught a good many. The huge steel gins, attached by chains to heavy clogs, prevented the trapped beasts from going far; and when found they were always tied tight round some tree or bush, and usually nearly exhausted. The men killed them either with a little 32-calibre pistol or a hatchet. But once did they meet with any difficulty. On this occasion one of them incautiously approached a captured bear to knock it on the head with his hatchet, but the animal managed to partially untwist itself, and with its free fore-arm made a rapid sweep at him; he jumped back just in time, the bear's claws tearing his clothes—after which he shot it. Bears are shy and have very keen noses; they are therefore hard to kill by fair hunting, living, as they generally do, in dense forests or thick brush. They are easy enough to trap, however. Thus, these two men, though they trapped so many, never but once killed them in any other way. On this occasion one of them, in the winter, found in a great hollow log a den where a she and two well-grown cubs had taken up their abode, and shot all three with his rifle as they burst out.

Where they are much hunted, bear become purely nocturnal; but in the wilder forests I have seen them abroad at all hours, though they do not much relish the intense heat of noon. They are rather comical animals to watch feeding and going about the ordinary business of their lives. Once I spent half an hour lying at the edge of a wood and looking at a black bear some three hundred yards off across an open glade. It was in good stalking country, but the wind was unfavorable and I waited for it to shift—waited too long as it proved, for something frightened the beast and he made off before I could get a shot at him. When I first saw him he was shuffling along and rooting in the ground, so that he looked like a great pig. Then he began to turn over the stones and logs to hunt for insects, small reptiles, and the like. A moderate-sized stone he would turn over with a single clap of his paw, and then plunge his nose down into the hollow to gobble up the small creatures beneath while still dazed by the light. The big logs and rocks he would tug and worry at with both paws; once, over-exerting his clumsy strength, he lost his grip and rolled clean on his back. Under some of the logs he evidently found mice and chipmunks; then, as soon as the log was overturned, he would be seen jumping about with grotesque agility, and making quick dabs here and there, as the little, scurrying rodent turned and twisted, until at last he put his paw on it and scooped it up into his mouth. Sometimes, probably when he smelt the mice underneath, he would cautiously turn the log over with one paw, holding the other lifted and ready to strike. Now and then he would halt and sniff the air in every direction, and it was after one of these halts that he suddenly shuffled off into the woods.

Black bear generally feed on berries, nuts, insects, carrion, and the like; but at times they take to killing very large animals. In fact, they are curiously irregular in their food. They will kill deer if they can get at them; but generally the deer are too quick. Sheep and hogs are their favorite prey, especially the latter, for bears seem to have a special relish for pork. Twice I have known a black bear kill cattle. Once the victim was a bull which had got mired, and which the bear deliberately proceeded to eat alive, heedless of the bellows of the unfortunate beast. On the other occasion, a cow was surprised and slain among some bushes at the edge of a remote pasture. In the spring, soon after the long winter sleep, they are very hungry, and are especially apt to attack large beasts at this time; although during the very first days of their appearance, when they are just breaking their fast, they eat rather sparingly, and by preference the tender shoots of green grass and other herbs, or frogs and crayfish; it is not for a week or two that they seem to be overcome by lean, ravenous hunger. They will even attack and master that formidable fighter the moose, springing at it from an ambush as it passes—for a bull moose would surely be an overmatch for one of them if fronted fairly in the open. An old hunter, whom I could trust, told me that he had seen in the snow in early spring the place where a bear had sprung at two moose, which were trotting together; he missed his spring, and the moose got off, their strides after they settled down into their pace being tremendous, and showing how thoroughly they were frightened. Another time he saw a bear chase a moose into a lake, where it waded out a little distance, and then turned to bay, bidding defiance to his pursuer, the latter not daring to approach in the water. I have been told—but cannot vouch for it—that instances have been known where the bear, maddened by hunger, has gone in on a moose thus standing at bay, only to be beaten down under the water by the terrible fore-hoofs of the quarry, and to yield its life in the contest. A lumberman told me that he once saw a moose, evidently much startled, trot through a swamp, and immediately afterwards a bear came up following the tracks. He almost ran into the man, and was evidently not in a good temper, for he growled and blustered, and two or three times made feints of charging, before he finally concluded to go off.

Bears will occasionally visit hunters' or lumbermen's camps, in the absence of the owners, and play sad havoc with all that therein is, devouring everything eatable, especially if sweet, and trampling into a dirty mess whatever they do not eat. The black bear does not average more than a third the size of the grisly; but, like all its kind, it varies greatly in weight. The largest I myself ever saw weighed was in Maine, and tipped the scale at 346 pounds; but I have a perfectly authentic record of one in Maine that weighed 397, and my friend, Dr. Hart Merriam, tells me that he has seen several in the Adirondacks that when killed weighed about 350.

I have myself shot but one or two black bears, and these were obtained under circumstances of no special interest, as I merely stumbled on them while after other game, and killed them before they had a chance either to run or show fight.

CHAPTER XIV

Old Ephraim, the Grisly Bear

The king of the game beasts of temperate North America, because the most dangerous to the hunter, is the grisly bear; known to the few remaining old-time trappers of the Rockies and the Great Plains, sometimes as "Old Ephraim" and sometimes as "Moccasin Joe"—the last in allusion to his queer, half-human footprints, which look as if made by some misshapen giant, walking in moccasins.

Bear vary greatly in size and color, no less than in temper and habits. Old hunters speak much of them in their endless talks over the camp fires and in the snow-bound winter huts. They insist on many species; not merely the black and the grisly, but the brown, the cinnamon, the gray, the silver-tip, and others with names known only in certain localities, such as the range bear, the roach-back, and the smut-face. But, in spite of popular opinion to the contrary, most old hunters are very untrustworthy in dealing with points of natural history. They usually know only so much about any given game animal as will enable them to kill it. They study its habits solely with this end in view; and once slain they only examine it to see about its condition and fur. With rare exceptions they are quite incapable of passing judgment upon questions of specific identity or difference. When questioned, they not only advance perfectly impossible theories and facts in support of their views, but they rarely even agree as to the views themselves. One hunter will assert that the true grisly is only found in California, heedless of the fact that the name was first used by Lewis and Clarke as one of the titles they applied to the large bears of the plains country round the Upper Missouri, a quarter of a century before the California grisly was known to fame. Another hunter will call any big brindled bear a grisly no matter where it is found; and he and his companions will dispute by the hour as to whether a bear of large, but not extreme, size is a grisly or a silver-tip. In Oregon the cinnamon bear is a phase of the small black bear; in Montana it is the plains variety of the large mountain silver-tip. I have myself seen the skins of two bears killed on the upper waters of Tongue River; one was that of a male, one of a female, and they had evidently just mated; yet one was distinctly a "silver-tip" and the other a "cinnamon." The skin of one very big bear which I killed in the Bighorn has proved a standing puzzle to almost all the old hunters to whom I have showed it; rarely do any two of them agree as to whether it is a grisly, a silver-tip, a cinnamon, or a "smut-face." Any bear with unusually long hair on the spine and shoulders, especially if killed in the spring, when the fur is shaggy, is forthwith dubbed a "roach-back." The average sporting writer moreover joins with the more imaginative members of the "old hunter" variety in ascribing wildly various traits to these different bears. One comments on the superior prowess of the roach-back; the explanation being that a bear in early spring is apt to be ravenous from hunger. The next insists that the California grisly is the only really dangerous bear;

while another stoutly maintains that it does not compare in ferocity with what he calls the "smaller" silver-tip or cinnamon. And so on, and so on, without end. All of which is mere nonsense.

Nevertheless, it is no easy task to determine how many species or varieties of bear actually do exist in the United States, and I cannot even say without doubt that a very large set of skins and skulls would not show a nearly complete intergradation between the most widely separated individuals. However, there are certainly two very distinct types, which differ almost as widely from each other as a wapiti does from a mule deer, and which exist in the same localities in most heavily timbered portions of the Rockies. One is the small black bear, a bear which will average about two hundred pounds weight, with fine, glossy, black fur, and the fore-claws but little longer than the hinder ones; in fact the hairs of the fore-paw often reach to their tips. This bear is a tree climber. It is the only kind found east of the great plains, and it is also plentiful in the forest-clad portions of the Rockies, being common in most heavily timbered tracts throughout the United States. The other is the grisly, which weighs three or four times as much as the black, and has a pelt of coarse hair, which is in color gray, grissled, or brown of various shades. It is not a tree climber, and the fore-claws are very long, much longer than the hinder ones. It is found from the great plains west of the Mississippi to the Pacific coast. This bear inhabits indifferently lowland and mountain; the deep woods, and the barren plains where the only cover is the stunted growth fringing the streams. These two types are very distinct in every way, and their differences are not at all dependent upon mere geographical considerations; for they are often found in the same district. Thus I found them both in the Bighorn Mountains, each type being in extreme form, while the specimens I shot showed no trace of intergradation. The huge grissled, long-clawed beast, and its little glossy-coated, short-clawed, tree-climbing brother roamed over exactly the same country in those mountains; but they were as distinct in habits, and mixed as little together as moose and caribou.

On the other hand, when a sufficient number of bears, from widely separated regions are examined, the various distinguishing marks are found to be inconstant and to show a tendency—exactly how strong I cannot say—to fade into one another. The differentiation of the two species seems to be as yet scarcely completed; there are more or less imperfect connecting links, and as regards the grisly it almost seems as if the specific characters were still unstable. In the far northwest, in the basin of the Columbia, the "black" bear is as often brown as any other color; and I have seen the skins of two cubs, one black and one brown, which were shot when following the same dam. When these brown bears have coarser hair than usual their skins are with difficulty to be distinguished from those of certain varieties of the grisly. Moreover, all bears vary greatly in size; and I have seen the bodies of very large black or brown bears with short fore-claws which were fully as heavy as, or perhaps heavier than, some small but full-grown grislies with long fore-claws. These very large bears with short claws are very reluctant to climb a tree; and are almost as clumsy about it as is a young grisly.

Among the grislies the fur varies much in color and texture even among bears of the same locality; it is of course richest in the deep forest, while the bears of the dry plains and mountains are of a lighter, more washed-out hue.

A full grown grisly will usually weigh from five to seven hundred pounds; but exceptional individuals undoubtedly reach more than twelve hundredweight. The California bears are said to be much the largest. This I think is so, but I cannot say it with certainty—at any rate I have examined several skins of full-grown Californian bears which were no larger than those of many I have seen from the northern Rockies. The Alaskan bears, particularly those of the peninsula, are even bigger beasts; the skin of one which I saw in the possession of Mr. Webster, the taxidermist, was a good deal larger than the average polar bear skin; and the animal when alive, if in good condition, could hardly have weighed less than 1,400 pounds.* Bears vary wonderfully in weight, even to the extent of becoming half as heavy again, according as they are fat or lean; in this respect they are more like hogs than like any other animals.

The grisly is now chiefly a beast of the high hills and heavy timber; but this is merely because he has learned that he must rely on cover to guard him from man, and has forsaken the open ground accordingly. In old days, and in one or two very out-of-the-way places almost to the present time, he wandered at will over the plains. It is only the

---

*Both this huge Alaskan bear and the entirely distinct bear of the barren grounds differ widely from the true grisly, at least in their extreme forms.

wariness born of fear which nowadays causes him to cling
to the thick brush of the large river-bottoms throughout
the plains country. When there were no rifle-bearing
hunters in the land, to harass him and make him afraid, he
roved hither and thither at will, in burly self-confidence.
Then he cared little for cover, unless as a weather-break,
or because it happened to contain food he liked. If the
humor seized him he would roam for days over the rolling
or broken prairie, searching for roots, digging up gophers,
or perhaps following the great buffalo herds either to prey
on some unwary straggler which he was able to catch at a
disadvantage in a washout, or else to feast on the carcasses
of those which died by accident. Old hunters, survivors of
the long-vanished ages when the vast herds thronged the
high plains and were followed by the wild red tribes, and
by bands of whites who were scarcely less savage, have told
me that they often met bears under such circumstances;
and these bears were accustomed to sleep in a patch of
rank sage-brush, in the niche of a washout, or under the
lea of a boulder, seeking their food abroad even in full daylight. The bears of the Upper Missouri basin—which were
so light in color that the early explorers often alluded to
them as gray or even as "white"—were particularly given
to this life in the open. To this day that close kinsman of
the grisly known as the bear of the barren grounds con-
tinues to lead this same kind of life, in the far north. My
friend Mr. Rockhill, of Maryland, who was the first white
man to explore eastern Tibet, describes the large, grisly-
like bear of those desolate uplands as having similar
habits.

However, the grisly is a shrewd beast and shows the

usual bear-like capacity for adapting himself to changed conditions. He has in most places become a cover-haunting animal, sly in his ways, wary to a degree, and clinging to the shelter of the deepest forests in the mountains and of the most tangled thickets in the plains. Hence he has held his own far better than such game as the bison and elk. He is much less common than formerly, but he is still to be found throughout most of his former range; save of course in the immediate neighborhood of the large towns.

In most places the grisly hibernates, or as old hunters say "holes up," during the cold season, precisely as does the black bear; but as with the latter species, those animals which live farthest south spend the whole year abroad in mild seasons. The grisly rarely chooses that favorite den of his little black brother, a hollow tree or log, for his winter sleep, seeking or making some cavernous hole in the ground instead. The hole is sometimes in a slight hillock in a river bottom, but more often on a hill-side, and may be either shallow or deep. In the mountains it is generally a natural cave in the rock, but among the foot-hills and on the plains the bear usually has to take some hollow or opening, and then fashion it into a burrow to his liking with his big digging claws.

Before the cold weather sets in the bear begins to grow restless, and to roam about seeking for a good place in which to hole up. One will often try and abandon several caves or partially dug-out burrows in succession before finding a place to its taste. It always endeavors to choose a spot where there is little chance of discovery or molestation, taking great care to avoid leaving too evident trace of its work. Hence it is not often that the dens are found.

Once in its den the bear passes the cold months in lethargic sleep; yet, in all but the coldest weather, and sometimes even then, its slumber is but light, and if disturbed it will promptly leave its den, prepared for fight or flight as the occasion may require. Many times when a hunter has stumbled on the winter resting-place of a bear and has left it, as he thought, without his presence being discovered, he has returned only to find that the crafty old fellow was aware of the danger all the time, and sneaked off as soon as the coast was clear. But in very cold weather hibernating bears can hardly be wakened from their torpid lethargy.

The length of time a bear stays in its den depends of course upon the severity of the season and the latitude and altitude of the country. In the northernmost and coldest regions all the bears hole up, and spend half the year in a state of lethargy; whereas in the south only the she's with young and the fat he-bears retire for the sleep, and these but for a few weeks, and only if the season is severe.

When the bear first leaves its den the fur is in very fine order, but it speedily becomes thin and poor, and does not recover its condition until the fall. Sometimes the bear does not betray any great hunger for a few days after its appearance; but in a short while it becomes ravenous. During the early spring, when the woods are still entirely barren and lifeless, while the snow yet lies in deep drifts, the lean, hungry brute, both maddened and weakened by long fasting, is more of a flesh eater than at any other time. It is at this period that it is most apt to turn true beast of prey, and show its prowess either at the expense of the wild game, or of the flocks of the settler and the herds of the ranchman. Bears are very capricious in this respect, however. Some are confirmed game and cattle killers; others are not; while yet others either are or are not accordingly as the freak seizes them, and their ravages vary almost unaccountably, both with the season and the locality.

Throughout 1889, for instance, no cattle, so far as I heard, were killed by bears anywhere near my range on the Little Missouri in western Dakota; yet I happened to know that during that same season the ravages of the bears among the herds of the cowmen in the Big Hole Basin, in western Montana, were very destructive.

In the spring and early summer of 1888, the bears killed no cattle near my ranch; but in the late summer and early fall of that year a big bear, which we well knew by its tracks, suddenly took to cattle-killing. This was a brute which had its headquarters on some very large brush bottoms a dozen miles below my ranch house, and which ranged to and fro across the broken country flanking the river on each side. It began just before berry time, but continued its career of destruction long after the wild plums and even buffalo berries had ripened. I think that what started it was a feast on a cow which had mired and died in the bed of the creek; at least it was not until after we found that it had been feeding at the carcass and had eaten every scrap, that we discovered traces of its ravages among the livestock. It seemed to attack the animals wholly regardless of their size and strength; its victims including a large bull and a beef steer, as well as cows, yearlings, and gaunt, weak trail "doughgies," which had been brought in very late by a Texas cow-outfit—for that year several herds were driven up from the overstocked, eaten-out, and drought-stricken ranges of the far south. Judging from the signs, the crafty old grisly, as cunning as he was ferocious, usually lay in wait for the cattle when they came down to water, choosing some thicket of dense underbrush and twisted cottonwoods through which they had to pass before reaching the sand banks on the river's brink. Sometimes he pounced on them as they fed through the thick, low cover of the bottoms, where an assailant could either lie in ambush by one of the numerous cattle trails, or else creep unobserved towards some browsing beast. When within a few feet a quick rush carried him fairly on the terrified quarry; and though but a clumsy animal compared to the great cats, the grisly is far quicker than one would imagine from viewing his ordinary lumbering gait. In one or two instances the bear had apparently grappled with his victim by seizing it near the loins and striking a disabling blow over the small of the back; in at least one instance he had jumped on the animal's head, grasping it with his fore-paws, while with his fangs he tore open the throat or craunched the neck bone. Some of his victims were slain far from the river, in winding, brushy coulies of the Bad Lands, where the broken nature of the ground rendered stalking easy. Several of the ranchmen, angered at their losses, hunted their foe eagerly, but always with ill success; until one of them put poison in a carcass, and thus at last, in ignoble fashion, slew the cattle-killer.

Mr. Clarence King informs me that he was once eye-witness to a bear's killing a steer, in California. The steer was in a small pasture, and the bear climbed over, partly breaking down, the rails which barred the gateway. The steer started to run, but the grisly overtook it in four or five bounds, and struck it a tremendous blow on the flank with one paw, knocking several ribs clear away from the spine, and killing the animal outright by the shock.

Horses no less than horned cattle at times fall victims to this great bear, which usually spring on them from the edge of a clearing as they graze in some mountain pasture, or among the foot-hills; and there is no other animal of which horses seem so much afraid. Generally the bear, whether successful or unsuccessful in its raids on cattle and horses, comes off unscathed from the struggle; but this is not always the case, and it has much respect for the hoofs or horns of its should-be prey. Some horses do not seem to know how to fight at all; but others are both quick and vicious, and prove themselves very formidable foes, lashing out behind, and striking with their fore-hoofs. I have elsewhere given an instance of a stallion which beat off a bear, breaking its jaw.

Quite near my ranch, once, a cowboy in my employ found unmistakable evidence of the discomfiture of a bear by a long-horned range cow. It was in the early spring, and the cow with her new-born calf was in a brush-bordered valley. The footprints in the damp soil were very plain, and showed all that had happened. The bear had evidently come out of the bushes with a rush, probably bent merely on seizing the calf; and had slowed up when the cow instead of flying faced him. He had then begun to walk round his expected dinner in a circle, the cow fronting him and moving nervously back and forth, so that her sharp hoofs cut and trampled the ground. Finally she had charged savagely; whereupon the bear had bolted; and, whether frightened at the charge, or at the approach of some one, he had not returned.

The grisly is even fonder of sheep and pigs than is its smaller black brother. Lurking round the settler's house until after nightfall, it will vault into the fold or sty, grasp a helpless, bleating fleece-bearer, or a shrieking, struggling member of the bristly brotherhood, and bundle it out over the fence to its death. In carrying its prey a bear sometimes holds the body in its teeth, walking along on all-fours and dragging it as a wolf does. Sometimes, however, it seizes an animal in its forearms or in one of them, and walks awkwardly on three legs or two, adopting this method in lifting and pushing the body over rocks and down timber.

When a grisly can get at domestic animals it rarely seeks to molest game, the former being far less wary and more helpless. Its heaviness and clumsiness do not fit it well for a life of rapine against shy woodland creatures. Its vast strength and determined temper, however, more than make amends for lack of agility in the actual struggle with the stricken prey; its difficulty lies in seizing, not in killing, the game. Hence, when a grisly does take to game-killing, it is likely to attack bison, moose, and elk; it is rarely able to catch deer, still less sheep or antelope. In fact these smaller game animals often show but little dread of its neighborhood, and, though careful not to let it come too near, go on grazing when a bear is in full sight. Whitetail deer are frequently found at home in the same thicket in which a bear has its den, while they immediately desert the temporary abiding place of a wolf or cougar. Nevertheless, they sometimes presume too much on this confidence. A couple of years before the occurrence of the feats of cattle-killing mentioned above as happening near my ranch, either the same bear that figured in them, or another of similar tastes, took to game-hunting. The beast lived in the same succession of huge thickets which cover for two or three miles the river bottoms and the mouths of the inflowing creeks; and he suddenly made a raid on the whitetail deer which were plentiful in the dense cover. The shaggy, clumsy monster was cunning enough to kill several of these knowing creatures. The exact course of procedure I never could find out; but apparently the bear laid in wait beside the game trails, along which the deer wandered.

In the old days when the innumerable bison grazed free on the prairie, the grisly sometimes harassed their bands as it now does the herds of the ranchman. The bison was the most easily approached of all game, and the great bear could often get near some outlying straggler, in its quest after stray cows, yearlings, or calves. In default of a favorable chance to make a prey of one of these weaker members of the herds, it did not hesitate to attack the mighty bulls themselves; and perhaps the grandest sight which it was ever the good fortune of the early hunters to witness, was one of these rare battles between a hungry grisly and a powerful buffalo bull. Nowadays, however, the few last survivors of the bison are vanishing even from the inaccessible mountain fastnesses in which they sought a final refuge from their destroyers.

At present the wapiti is of all wild game that which is most likely to fall a victim to the grisly, when the big bear is in the mood to turn hunter. Wapiti are found in the same places as the grisly, and in some spots they are yet very plentiful; they are less shy and active than deer, while not powerful enough to beat off so ponderous a foe; and they live in cover where there is always a good chance either to stalk or to stumble on them. At almost any season bear will come and feast on an elk carcass; and if the food supply runs short, in early spring, or in a fall when the berry crop fails, they sometimes have to do their own killing. Twice I have come across the remains of elk, which had seemingly been slain and devoured by bears. I have never heard of elk making a fight against a bear; yet, at close quarters and at bay, a bull elk in the rutting season is an ugly foe.

A bull moose is even more formidable, being able to strike the most lightning-like blows with his terrible forefeet, his true weapons of defence. I doubt if any beast of prey would rush in on one of these woodland giants, when his horns were grown, and if he was on his guard and bent on fight. Nevertheless, the moose sometimes fall victims to the uncouth prowess of the grisly, in the thick wet forests of the high northern Rockies, where both beasts dwell. An old hunter who a dozen years ago wintered at Jackson Lake, in northwestern Wyoming, told me that when the snows got deep on the mountains the moose came down and took up their abode near the lake, on its western side. Nothing molested them during the winter. Early in the spring a grisly came out of its den, and he found its tracks in many places, as it roamed restlessly about, evidently very hungry. Finding little to eat in the bleak, snow-drifted woods, it soon began to deprecate on the moose, and killed two or three, generally by lying in wait and dashing out on them as they passed near its lurking-place. Even the bulls were at that season weak, and of course hornless, with small desire to fight; and in each case the rush of the great bear—doubtless made with the ferocity and speed which so often belie the seeming awkwardness of the animal—bore down the startled victim, taken utterly unawares before it had a chance to defend itself. In one case the bear had missed its spring; the moose going off, for a few rods, with huge jumps, and then settling down into its characteristic trot. The old hunter who followed the tracks said he would never have deemed it possible for any animal to make such strides while in a trot.

Nevertheless, the grisly is only occasionally, not normally, a formidable predatory beast, a killer of cattle and of large game. Although capable of far swifter movement than is promised by his frame of seemingly clumsy strength, and in spite of his power of charging with astonishing suddenness and speed, he yet lacks altogether the supple agility of such finished destroyers as the cougar and the wolf; and for the absence of this agility no amount of mere huge muscle can atone. He is more apt to feast on animals which have met their death by accident, or which have been killed by other beasts or by man, than to do his own killing. He is a very foul feeder, with a strong relish for carrion, and possesses a grewsome and cannibal fondness for the flesh of his own kind; a bear carcass will toll a brother bear to the ambushed hunter better than almost any other bait, unless it is the carcass of a horse.

Nor do these big bears always content themselves

merely with the carcasses of their brethren. A black bear would have a poor chance if in the clutches of a large, hungry grisly; and an old male will kill and eat a cub, especially if he finds it at a disadvantage. A rather remarkable instance of this occurred in the Yellowstone National Park, in the spring of 1891. The incident is related in the following letter written to Mr. William Hallett Phillips, of Washington, by another friend, Mr. Elwood Hofer. Hofer is an old mountain-man; I have hunted with him myself, and know his statements to be trustworthy. He was, at the time, at work in the Park getting animals for the National Museum at Washington, and was staying at Yancey's "hotel" near Tower Falls. His letter which was dated June 21st, 1891, runs in part as follows:

"I had a splendid Grizzly or Roachback cub and was going to send him into the Springs next morning the team was here, I heard a racket out side went out and found him dead an old bear that made an 9 1–2 inch track had killed and partly eaten him. Last night another one came, one that made an 8 1–2 inch track, and broke Yancy up in the milk business. You know how the cabins stand here. There is a hitching post between the saloon and old house, the little bear was killed there. In a creek close by was a milk house, last night another bear came there and smashed the whole thing up, leaving nothing but a few flattened buckets and pans and boards. I was sleeping in the old cabin, I heard the tin ware rattle but thought it was all right supposed it was cows or horses about. I don't care about the milk but the damn cuss dug up the remains of the cub I had buried in the old ditch, he visited the old meat house but found nothing. Bear are very thick in this part of the

Park, and are getting very fresh. I sent in the game to Capt. Anderson, hear its doing well."

Grislies are fond of fish; and on the Pacific slope, where the salmon run, they, like so many other beasts, travel many scores of miles and crowd down to the rivers to gorge themselves upon the fish which are thrown up on the banks. Wading into the water a bear will knock out the salmon right and left when they are running thick.

Flesh and fish do not constitute the grisly's ordinary diet. At most times the big bear is a grubber in the ground, an eater of insects, roots, nuts, and berries. Its dangerous fore-claws are normally used to overturn stones and knock rotten logs to pieces, that it may lap up the small tribes of darkness which swarm under the one and in the other. It digs up the camas roots, wild onions, and an occasional luckless woodchuck or gopher. If food is very plenty bears are lazy, but commonly they are obliged to be very industrious, it being no light task to gather enough ants, beetles, crickets, tumble-bugs, roots, and nuts to satisfy the cravings of so huge a bulk. The sign of a bear's work is, of course, evident to the most unpractised eye; and in no way can one get a better idea of the brute's power than by watching it busily working for its breakfast, shattering big logs and upsetting boulders by sheer strength. There is always a touch of the comic, as well as a touch of the strong and terrible, in a bear's look and actions. It will tug and pull, now with one paw, now with two, now on all fours, now on its hind legs, in the effort to turn over a large log or stone; and when it succeeds it jumps round to thrust its muzzle into the damp hollow and lap up the affrighted mice or beetles while they are still paralyzed by the sudden exposure.

The true time of plenty for bears is the berry season. Then they feast ravenously on huckleberries, blueberries, kinnikinic berries, buffalo berries, wild plums, elderberries, and scores of other fruits. They often smash all the bushes in a berry patch, gathering the fruit with half-luxurious, half-laborious greed, sitting on their haunches, and sweeping the berries into their mouths with dexterous paws. So absorbed do they become in their feasts on the luscious fruit that they grow reckless of their safety, and feed in broad daylight, almost at midday; while in some of the thickets, especially those of the mountain haws, they make so much noise in smashing the branches that it is a comparatively easy matter to approach them unheard. That still-hunter is in luck who in the fall finds an accessible berry-covered hill-side which is haunted by bears; but, as a rule, the berry bushes do not grow close enough together to give the hunter much chance.

Like most other wild animals, bears which have known the neighborhood of man are beasts of the darkness, or at least of the dusk and the gloaming. But they are by no means such true night-lovers as the big cats and the wolves. In regions where they know little of hunters they roam about freely in the daylight, and in cool weather are even apt to take their noontide slumbers basking in the sun. Where they are much hunted they finally almost reverse their natural habits and sleep throughout the hours of light, only venturing abroad after nightfall and before sunrise; but even yet this is not the habit of those bears which exist in the wilder localities where they are still plentiful. In these places they sleep, or at least rest, during the hours of greatest heat, and again in the middle part of the night, unless there is a full moon. They start on their rambles for food about midafternoon, and end their morning roaming soon after the sun is above the horizon. If the moon is full, however, they may feed all night long, and then wander but little in the daytime.

Aside from man, the full-grown grisly has hardly any foe to fear. Nevertheless, in the early spring, when weakened by the hunger that succeeds the winter sleep, it behooves even the grisly, if he dwells in the mountain fastnesses of the far northwest, to beware of a famished troop of great timber wolves. These northern Rocky Mountain wolves are most formidable beasts, and when many of them band together in time of famine they do not hesitate to pounce on the black bear and cougar; and even a full-grown grisly is not safe from their attacks, unless he can back up against some rock which will prevent them from assailing him from behind. A small ranchman whom I knew well, who lived near Flathead Lake, once in April found where a troop of these wolves had killed a good-sized yearling grisly. Either cougar or wolf will make a prey of a grisly which is but a few months old; while any fox, lynx, wolverine, or fisher will seize the very young cubs. The old story about wolves fearing to feast on game killed by a grisly is all nonsense. Wolves are canny beasts, and they will not approach a carcass if they think a bear is hidden nearby and likely to rush out at them; but under ordinary circumstances they will feast not only on the carcasses of the grisly's victims, but on the carcass of the grisly himself after he has been slain and left by the hunter. Of course wolves would only attack a grisly if in the most desperate straits for food, as even a victory over such an antagonist must be purchased with heavy loss of life; and a hungry grisly would devour either a wolf or a cougar, or any one of the smaller carnivora off-hand if it happened to corner it where it could not get away.

The grisly occasionally makes its den in a cave and spends therein the midday hours. But this is rare. Usually it lies in the dense shelter of the most tangled piece of woods in the neighborhood, choosing by preference some bit where the young growth is thick and the ground strewn with boulders and fallen logs. Often, especially if in a restless mood and roaming much over the country, it merely makes a temporary bed, in which it lies but once or twice; and again it may make a more permanent lair or series of lairs, spending many consecutive nights in each. Usually the lair or bed is made some distance from the feeding ground; but bold bears, in very wild localities, may lie close by a carcass, or in the middle of a berry ground. The deer-killing bear above mentioned had evidently dragged two or three of his victims to his den, which was under an impenetrable mat of bullberries and dwarf box-alders, hemmed in by a cut bank on one side and a wall of gnarled cottonwoods on the other. Round this den, and rendering it noisome, were scattered the bones of several deer and a young steer or heifer. When we found it we thought we could easily kill the bear, but the fierce, cunning beast must have seen or smelt us, for though we laid in wait for it long and patiently, it did not come back to its place; nor, on our subsequent visits, did we ever find traces of its having done so.

Bear are fond of wallowing in the water, whether in the sand, on the edge of a rapid plains river, on the muddy margin of a pond, or in the oozy moss of a clear, cold mountain spring. One hot August afternoon, as I was clambering down a steep mountain-side near Pend'Oreille lake, I heard a crash some distance below, which showed that a large beast was afoot. On making my way towards the spot, I found I had disturbed a big bear as it was lolling at ease in its bath; the discolored water showed where it had scrambled hastily out and galloped off as I approached. The spring welled out at the base of a high granite rock, forming a small pool of shimmering broken crystal. The soaked moss lay in a deep wet cushion round about, and jutted over the edges of the pool like a floating shelf. Graceful, water-loving ferns swayed to and fro. Above, the great conifers spread their murmuring branches, dimming the light, and keeping out the heat; their brown boles sprang from the ground like buttressed columns. On the barren mountain-side beyond the heat was oppressive. It was small wonder that Bruin should have sought the spot to cool his gross carcass in the fresh spring water.

The bear is a solitary beast, and although many may assemble together, in what looks like a drove, on some favorite feeding-ground—usually where the berries are thick, or by the banks of a salmon-thronged river—the association is never more than momentary, each going its own way as soon as its hunger is satisfied. The males always live alone by choice, save in the rutting season, when they seek the females. Then two or three may come together in the course of their pursuit and rough courtship of the female; and if the rivals are well matched, savage battles follow, so that many of the old males have their heads seamed with scars made by their fellows' teeth. At such times they are evil tempered and prone to attack man or beast on slight provocation.

The she brings forth her cubs, one, two, or three in number, in her winter den. They are very small and helpless things, and it is some time after she leaves her winter home before they can follow her for any distance. They stay with her throughout the summer and the fall, leaving her when the cold weather sets in. By this time they are well grown; and hence, especially if an old male has joined the she, the family may number three or four individuals, so as to make what seems like quite a little troop of bears. A small ranchman who lived a dozen miles from me on the Little Missouri once found a she-bear and three half-grown cubs feeding at a berry-patch in a ravine. He shot the old she in the small of the back, whereat she made a loud roaring and squealing. One of the cubs rushed towards her; but its sympathy proved misplaced, for she knocked it over with a hearty cuff, either out of mere temper, or because she thought her pain must be due to an unprovoked assault from one of her offspring. The hunter then killed one of the cubs, and the other two escaped. When bears are together and one is wounded by a bullet, but does not see the real assailant, it often falls tooth and nail upon its comrade, apparently attributing its injury to the latter.

Bears are hunted in many ways. Some are killed by poison; but this plan is only practised by the owners of cattle or sheep who have suffered from their ravages. Moreover, they are harder to poison than wolves. Most often they are killed in traps, which are sometimes dead-falls, on the principle of the little figure-4 trap familiar to every American country boy, sometimes log-pens in which the animal is taken alive, but generally huge steel gins. In some states there is a bounty for the destruction of grislies; and in many places their skins have a market price, although much less valuable than those of the black bear. The men who pursue them for the bounty, or for their fur, as well as the ranchmen who regard them as foes to stock, ordinarily use steel traps. The trap is very massive, needing no small strength to set, and it is usually chained to a bar or log of wood, which does not stop the bear's progress outright, but hampers and interferes with it, continually catching in tree stumps and the like. The animal when trapped makes off at once, biting at the trap and the bar; but it leaves a broad wake and sooner or later is found tangled up by the chain and bar. A bear is by no means so difficult to trap as a wolf or fox although more so than a cougar or a lynx. In wild regions a skilful trapper can often catch a great many with comparative ease. A cunning old grisly however, soon learns the danger, and is then almost impossible to trap, as it either avoids the neighborhood altogether or finds out some way by which to get at the bait without springing the trap, or else deliberately springs it first. I have been told of bears which spring traps by rolling across them, the iron jaws slipping harmlessly off the big round body. An old horse is the most common bait.

It is, of course, all right to trap bears when they are followed merely as vermin or for the sake of the fur. Occasionally, however, hunters who are out merely for sport adopt this method; but this should never be done. To shoot a trapped bear for sport is a thoroughly unsportsmanlike proceeding. A funny plea sometimes advanced in its favor is that it is "dangerous." No doubt in exceptional instances this is true; exactly as it is true that in exceptional instances it is "dangerous" for a butcher to knock over a steer in the slaughterhouse. A bear caught only by the toes may wrench itself free as the hunter comes near, and attack him with pain-maddened fury; or if followed at once, and if the trap and bar are light, it may be found in some thicket, still free, and in a frenzy of rage. But even in such cases the beast has been crippled, and though crazy with pain and anger is easily dealt with by a good shot; while ordinarily the poor brute is found in the last stages of exhaustion, tied tight to a tree where the log or bar has caught, its teeth broken to splintered stumps by rabid snaps at the cruel trap and chain. Some trappers kill the trapped grislies with a revolver; so that it may easily be seen that the sport is not normally dangerous. Two of my own cowboys, Seawell and Dow, were originally from Maine, where they had trapped a number of black bears; and they always killed them either with a hatchet or a small 32-calibre revolver. One of them, Seawell, once came near being mauled by a trapped bear, seemingly at the last gasp, which he approached incautiously with his hatchet.

There is, however, one very real danger to which the solitary bear-trapper is exposed, the danger of being caught in his own trap. The huge jaws of the gin are easy to spring and most hard to open. If an unwary passer-by should tread between them and be caught by the leg, his fate would be doubtful, though he would probable die under the steadily growing torment of the merciless iron jaws, as they pressed ever deeper into the sore flesh and broken bones. But if caught by the arms, while setting or fixing the trap, his fate would be in no doubt at all, for it would be impossible for the stoutest man to free himself by any means. Terrible stories are told of solitary mountain hunters who disappeared, and were found years later in the lonely wilderness, as mouldering skeletons, the shattered bones of the forearms still held in the rusty jaws of the gin.

Doubtless the grisly could be successfully hunted with dogs, if the latter were carefully bred and trained to the purpose, but as yet this has not been done, and though dogs are sometimes used as adjuncts in grisly hunting they are rarely of much service. It is sometimes said that very small dogs are the best for this end. But this is only so with grislies that have never been hunted. In such a case the big bear sometimes becomes so irritated with the bouncing, yapping little terriers or fice-dogs that he may try to catch them and thus permit the hunter to creep upon him. But the minute he realizes, as he speedily does, that the man is his real foe, he pays no further heed whatever to the little dogs, who can then neither bring him to bay nor hinder his flight. Ordinary hounds, of the kinds used in the South for fox, deer, wildcat, and black bear, are but little better. I have known one or two men who at different times tried to hunt the grisly with a pack of hounds and fice-dogs wonted to the chase of the black bear, but they never met with success, This was probably largely owing to the nature of the country in which they hunted, a vast tangled mass of forest and craggy mountain; but it was also due to the utter inability of the dogs to stop the quarry from breaking bay when it wished. Several times a grisly was bayed, but always in some inaccessible spot which it took hard climbing to reach, and the dogs were never able to hold the beast until the hunters came up.

Still a well-trained pack of large hounds which were both bold and cunning could doubtless bay even a grisly. Such dogs are the big half-breed hounds sometimes used in the Alleghanies of West Virginia, which are trained not merely to nip a bear, but to grip him by the hock as he runs and either throw him or twirl him round. A grisly could not disregard a wary and powerful hound capable of performing this trick, even though he paid small heed to mere barking and occasional nipping. Nor do I doubt that it would be possible to get together a pack of many large, fierce dogs, trained to dash straight at the head and hold on like a vice, which could fairly master a grisly and, though unable, of course, to kill him, would worry him breathless and hold him down so that he could be slain with ease. There have been instances in which five or six of the big so-called blood-hounds of the southern States—not pure blood-hounds at all, but huge, fierce, ban-dogs, with a cross of the ferocious Cuban blood-hound, to give them good scenting powers—have by themselves mastered the cougar and the black bear. Such instances occurred in the hunting history of my own forefathers on my mother's side, who during the last half of the eighteenth, and the first half of the present, century lived in Georgia and over the border in what are now Alabama and Florida. These big dogs can only overcome such foes by rushing in in a body and grappling all together; if they hang back, lunging and snapping, a cougar or bear will destroy them one by one. With a quarry so huge and redoubtable as the grisly, no number of dogs, however large and fierce, could overcome him unless they all rushed on him in a mass, the first in the charge seizing by the head or throat. If the dogs hung back, or if there were only a few of them, or if they did not seize around the head, they would be destroyed without an effort. It is murder to slip merely one or two close-quarter dogs at a grisly. Twice I have known a man take a large bulldog with his pack when after one of these big bears, and in each case the result was the same. In one instance the bear was trotting when the bulldog seized it by the cheek, and without so much as altering its gait, it brushed off the hanging dog with a blow from the forepaw that broke the latter's back. In the other instance the bear had come to bay, and when seized by the ear it got the dog's body up to its jaws, and tore out the life with one crunch.

A small number of dogs must rely on their activity, and must hamper the bear's escape by inflicting a severe bite and avoiding the counter-stroke. The only dog I ever heard of which, single-handed, was really of service in stopping a grisly, was a big Mexican sheep-dog, once owned by the hunter Tazewell Woody. It was an agile beast with powerful jaws, and possessed both intelligence and a fierce, resolute temper. Woody killed three grislies with its aid. It attacked with equal caution and ferocity, rushing at the bear as the latter ran, and seizing the outstretched hock with a grip of iron, stopping the bear short, but letting go before the angry beast could whirl round and seize it. It was so active and wary that it always escaped damage; and it was so strong and bit so severely that the bear could not possibly run from it at any speed. In consequence, if it once came to close quarters with its quarry, Woody could always get near enough for a shot.

Hitherto, however, the mountain hunters—as distinguished from the trappers—who have followed the grisly have relied almost solely on their rifles. In my own case about half the bears I have killed I stumbled across almost by accident; and probably this proportion holds good generally. The hunter may be after bear at the time, or he may be after blacktail deer or elk, the common game in most of the haunts of the grisly; or he may merely be travelling through the country or prospecting for gold. Suddenly he comes over the edge of a cut bank, or round the sharp spur of a mountain or the shoulder of a cliff which walls in a ravine, or else the indistinct game trail he has been following through the great trees twists sharply to one side to avoid a rock or a mass of down timber, and behold he surprises old Ephraim digging for roots, or munching berries, or slouching along the path, or perhaps rising suddenly from the lush, rank plants amid which he has been lying. Or it may be that the bear will be spied afar rooting in an open glade or on a bare hill-side.

In the still-hunt proper it is necessary to find some favorite feeding-ground, where there are many roots or berry-bearing bushes, or else to lure the grisly to a carcass. This last method of "baiting" for bear is under ordinary circumstances the only way which affords even a moderately fair chance of killing them. They are very cunning, with the sharpest of noses, and where they have had experience of hunters they dwell only in cover where it is almost impossible for the best of still-hunters to approach them.

Nevertheless, in favorable ground a man can often find and kill them by fair stalking, in berry time, or more especially in the early spring, before the snow has gone from the mountains, and while the bears are driven by hunger to roam much abroad and sometimes to seek their food in the open. In such cases the still-hunter is stirring by the earliest dawn, and walks with stealthy speed to some high point of observation from which he can overlook the feeding-grounds where he has previously discovered sign. From the coign of vantage he scans the country far and near, either with his own keen eyes or with powerful glasses; and he must combine patience and good sight with the ability to traverse long distances noiselessly and yet at speed. He may spend two or three hours sitting still and looking over a vast tract of country before he will suddenly spy a bear; or he may see nothing after the most careful search in a given place, and must then go on half a dozen miles to another, watching warily as he walks, and continuing this possibly for several days before getting a glimpse of his game. If the bear are digging roots, or otherwise procuring their food on the bare hillsides and table-lands, it is of course comparatively easy to see them; and it is under such circumstances that this kind of hunting is most successful. Once seen, the actual stalk may take two or three hours, the nature of the ground and the direction of the wind often necessitating a long circuit; perhaps a gully, a rock, or a fallen log offers a chance for an approach to within two hundred yards, and although the hunter will, if possible, get much closer than this, yet even at such a distance a bear is a large enough mark to warrant risking a shot.

Usually the berry grounds do not offer such favorable opportunities, as they often lie in thick timber, or are covered so densely with bushes as to obstruct the view; and they are rarely commanded by a favorable spot from which to spy. On the other hand, as already said, bears occasionally forget all their watchfulness while devouring fruit, and make such a noise rending and tearing the bushes that, if once found, a man can creep upon them unobserved.

CHAPTER XV

Hunting the Grisly

If out in the late fall or early spring, it is often possible to follow a bear's trail in the snow; having come upon it either by chance or hard hunting, or else having found where it leads from some carcass on which the beast has been feeding. In the pursuit one must exercise great caution, as at such times the hunter is easily seen a long way off, and game is always especially watchful for any foe that may follow its trail.

Once I killed a grisly in this manner. It was early in the fall, but snow lay on the ground, while the gray weather boded a storm. My camp was in a bleak, wind-swept valley, high among the mountains which form the divide between the head-waters of the Salmon and Clarke's Fork of the Columbia. All night I had lain in my buffalo-bag, under the lea of a windbreak of branches, in the clump of fir-trees, where I had halted the preceding evening. At my feet ran a rapid mountain torrent, its bed choked with ice-covered rocks; I had been lulled to sleep by the stream's splashing murmur, and the loud moaning of the wind along the naked cliffs. At dawn I rose and shook myself free of the buffalo robe, coated with hoar-frost. The ashes of the fire were lifeless; in the dim morning the air was bitter cold. I did not linger a moment, but snatched up my rifle, pulled on my fur cap and gloves, and strode off up a side ravine; as I walked I ate some mouthfuls of venison, left over from supper.

Two hours of toil up the steep mountain brought me to the top of a spur. The sun had risen, but was hidden behind a bank of sullen clouds. On the divide I halted, and gazed out over a vast landscape, inconceivably wild and dismal. Around me towered the stupendous mountain masses which make up the backbone of the Rockies. From my feet, as far as I could see, stretched a rugged and barren chaos of ridges and detached rock masses. Behind me, far below, the stream wound like a silver ribbon, fringed with dark conifers and the changing, dying foliage of poplar and quaking aspen. In front the bottoms of the valley were filled with the sombre evergreen forest, dotted here and there with black, ice-skimmed tarns; and the dark spruces clustered also in the higher gorges, and were scattered thinly along the mountain sides. The snow which had fallen lay in drifts and streaks, while, where the wind had scope it was blown off, and the ground left bare.

For two hours I walked onwards across the ridges and valleys. Then among some scattered spruces, where the snow lay to the depth of half a foot, I suddenly came on the fresh, broad trail of a grisly. The brute was evidently roaming restlessly about in search of a winter den, but willing, in passing, to pick up any food that lay handy. At once I took the trail, travelling above and to one side, and keeping a sharp look-out ahead. The bear was going across wind, and this made my task easy. I walked rapidly, though cautiously; and it was only in crossing the large patches of bare ground that I had to fear making a noise.

Elsewhere the snow muffled my footsteps, and made the trail so plain that I scarcely had to waste a glance upon it, bending my eyes always to the front.

At last, peering cautiously over a ridge crowned with broken rocks, I saw my quarry, a big, burly bear, with silvered fur. He had halted on an open hill-side, and was busily digging up the caches of some rock gophers or squirrels. He seemed absorbed in his work, and the stalk was easy. Slipping quietly back, I ran towards the end of the spur, and in ten minutes struck a ravine, of which one branch ran past within seventy yards of where the bear was working. In this ravine was a rather close growth of stunted evergreens, affording good cover, although in one or two places I had to lie down and crawl through the snow. When I reached the point for which I was aiming, the bear had just finished rooting, and was starting off. A slight whistle brought him to a standstill, and I drew a bead behind his shoulder, and low down, resting the rifle across the crooked branch of a dwarf spruce. At the crack he ran off at speed, making no sound, but the thick spatter of blood splashes, showing clear on the white snow, betrayed the mortal nature of the wound. For some minutes I followed the trail; and then, topping a ridge, I saw the dark bulk lying motionless in a snow drift at the foot of a low rock-wall, down which he had tumbled.

The usual practice of the still-hunter who is after grisly is to toll it to baits. The hunter either lies in ambush near the carcass, or approaches it stealthily when he thinks the bear is at its meal.

One day while camped near the Bitter Root Mountains in Montana I found that a bear had been feeding on the carcass of a moose which lay some five miles from the little open glade in which my tent was pitched, and I made up my mind to try to get a shot at it that afternoon. I stayed in camp till about three o'clock, lying lazily back on the bed of sweet-smelling evergreen boughs, watching the pack ponies as they stood under the pines on the edge of the open, stamping now and then, and switching their tails. The air was still, the sky a glorious blue; at that hour in the afternoon even the September sun was hot. The smoke from the smouldering logs of the camp fire curled thinly upwards. Little chipmunks scuttled out from their holes to the packs, which lay in a heap on the ground, and then scuttled madly back again. A couple of drab-colored whisky-jacks, with bold mien and fearless bright eyes, hopped and fluttered round, picking up the scraps, and uttering an extraordinary variety of notes, mostly discordant; so tame were they that one of them lit on my outstretched arm as I half dozed, basking in the sunshine.

When the shadows began to lengthen, I shouldered my rifle and plunged into the woods. At first my route lay along a mountain side; then for half a mile over a windfall, the dead timber piled about in crazy confusion. After that I went up the bottom of a valley by a little brook, the ground being carpeted with a sponge of soaked moss. At the head of this brook was a pond covered with water-lilies; and a scramble through a rocky pass took me into a high, wet valley, where the thick growth of spruce was broken by occasional strips of meadow. In this valley the moose carcass lay, well at the upper end.

In moccasined feet I trod softly through the soundless woods. Under the dark branches it was already dusk, and the air had the cool chill of evening. As I neared the clump where the body lay, I walked with redoubled caution, watching and listening with strained alertness. Then I heard a twig snap; and my blood leaped, for I knew the bear was at his supper. In another moment I saw his shaggy, brown form. He was working with all his awkward giant strength, trying to bury the carcass, twisting it to one side and the other with wonderful ease. Once he got angry and suddenly gave it a tremendous cuff with his paw; in his bearing he had something half humorous, half devilish. I crept up within forty yards; but for several minutes he would not keep his head still. Then something attracted his attention in the forest, and he stood motionless looking towards it, broadside to me, with his fore-paws planted on the carcass. This gave me my chance. I drew a very fine bead between his eye and ear, and pulled trigger. He dropped like a steer when struck with a pole-axe.

If there is a good hiding-place handy it is better to lie in wait at the carcass. One day on the head-waters of the Madison, I found that a bear was coming to an elk I had shot some days before; and I at once determined to ambush the beast when he came back that evening. The carcass lay in the middle of a valley a quarter of a mile broad. The bottom of this valley was covered by an open forest of tall pines; a thick jungle of smaller evergreens marked where the mountains rose on either hand. There were a number of large rocks scattered here and there, one, of very convenient shape, being only some seventy or eighty yards from the carcass. Up this I clambered. It hid me perfectly, and on its top was a carpet of soft pine needles, on which I could lie at my ease.

Hour after hour passed by. A little black woodpecker with a yellow crest ran nimbly up and down the tree trunks for some time and then flitted away with a party of chickadees and nut-hatches. Occasionally a Clarke's crow soared about overhead or clung in any position to the swaying end of a pine branch, chattering and screaming. Flocks of cross-bills, with wavy flight and plaintive calls, flew to a small mineral lick near by, where they scraped the clay with their queer little beaks.

As the westering sun sank out of sight beyond the mountains these sounds of bird-life gradually died away. Under the great pines the evening was still with the silence of primeval desolation. The sense of sadness and loneliness, the melancholy of the wilderness, came over me like a spell. Every slight noise made my pulses throb as I lay motionless on the rock gazing intently into the gathering gloom. I began to fear that it would grow too dark to shoot before the grisly came.

Suddenly and without warning, the great bear stepped out of the bushes and trod across the pine needles with such swift and silent footsteps that its bulk seemed unreal. It was very cautious, continually halting to peer around; and once it stood up on its hind legs and looked long down the valley towards the red west. As it reached the carcass I put a bullet between its shoulders. It rolled over, while the woods resounded with its savage roaring. Immediately it struggled to its feet and staggered off; and fell again to the next shot, squalling and yelling. Twice this was repeated; the brute being one of those bears which greet every wound with a great outcry, and sometimes seem to lose their feet when hit—although they will occasionally fight as savagely as their more silent brethren. In this case the wounds were mortal, and the bear died before reaching the edge of the thicket.

I spent much of the fall of 1889 hunting on the headwaters of the Salmon and Snake in Idaho, and along the Montana boundary line from the Big Hole Basin and the head of the Wisdom River to the neighborhood of Red Rock Pass and to the north and west of Henry's Lake. During the last fortnight my companion was the old mountain man, already mentioned, named Griffeth or Griffin—I cannot tell which, as he was always called either "Hank" or "Griff." He was a crabbedly honest old fellow, and a very skilful hunter; but he was worn out with age and rheumatism, and his temper had failed even faster than his bodily strength. He showed me a greater variety of game than I had ever seen before in so short a time; nor did I ever before or after make so successful a hunt. But he was an exceedingly disagreeable companion on account of his surly, moody ways. I generally had to get up first, to kindle the fire and make ready breakfast, and he was very quarrelsome. Finally, during my absence from camp one day, while not very far from Red Rock pass, he found my whiskey flask, which I kept purely for emergencies, and drank all the contents. When I came back he was quite drunk. This was unbearable, and after some high words I left him, and struck off homeward through the woods on my own account. We had with us four pack and saddle horses; and of these I took a very intelligent and gentle little bronco mare, which possessed the invaluable trait of always staying near camp, even when not hobbled. I was not hampered with much of an outfit, having only my buffalo sleeping-bag, a fur coat, and my washing kit, with a couple of spare pairs of socks and some handkerchiefs. A frying-pan, some salt, flour, baking-powder, a small chunk of salt pork, and a hatchet, made up a light pack, which, with the bedding, I fastened across the stock saddle by means of a rope and a spare packing cinch. My cartridges and knife were in my belt; my compass and matches, as always, in my pocket. I walked, while the little mare followed almost like a dog, often without my having to hold the lariat which served as halter.

The country was for the most part fairly open, as I kept near the foot-hills where glades and little prairies broke the pine forest. The trees were of small size. There was no regular trail, but the course was easy to keep, and I had no trouble of any kind save on the second day. That afternoon I was following a stream which at last "canyoned up," that is, sank to the bottom of a canyon-like ravine impassable for a horse. I started up a side valley, intending to cross from its head coulies to those of another valley which would lead in below the canyon.

However, I got enmeshed in the tangle of winding valleys at the foot of the steep mountains, and as dusk was coming on I halted and camped in a little open spot by the side of a small, noisy brook, with crystal water. The place was carpeted with soft, wet, green moss, dotted red with the kinnikinnic berries, and at its edge, under the trees where the ground was dry, I threw down the buffalo bed on the mat of sweet-smelling pine needles. Making camp took but a moment. I opened the pack, tossed the bedding on a smooth spot, knee-haltered the little mare, dragged up a few dry logs, and then strolled off, rifle on shoulder, through the frosty gloaming, to see if I could pick up a grouse for supper.

For half a mile I walked quickly and silently over the pine needles, across a succession of slight ridges separated by narrow, shallow valleys. The forest here was composed of lodge-pole pines, which on the ridges grew close together, with tall slender trunks, while in the valleys the growth was more open. Though the sun was behind the mountains there was yet plenty of light by which to shoot, but it was fading rapidly.

At last, as I was thinking of turning towards camp, I stole up to the crest of one of the ridges, and looked over into the valley some sixty yards off. Immediately I caught the loom of some large, dark object; and another glance showed me a big grisly walking slowly off with his head down. He was quartering to me, and I fired into his flank, the bullet, as I afterwards found, ranging forward and piercing one lung. At the shot he uttered a loud, moaning grunt and plunged forward at a heavy gallop, while I raced obliquely down the hill to cut him off. After going a few hundred feet he reached a laurel thicket, some thirty yards broad, and two or three times as long which he did not leave. I ran up to the edge and there halted, not liking to venture into the mass of twisted, close-growing stems and glossy foliage. Moreover, as I halted, I heard him utter a peculiar, savage kind of whine from the heart of the brush. Accordingly, I began to skirt the edge, standing on tiptoe and gazing earnestly to see if I could not catch a glimpse of his hide. When I was at the narrowest part of the thicket, he suddenly left it directly opposite, and then wheeled and stood broadside to me on the hill-side, a little above. He turned his head stiffly towards me; scarlet strings of froth hung from his lips; his eyes burned like embers in the gloom.

I held true, aiming behind the shoulder, and my bullet shattered the point or lower end of his heart, taking out a big nick. Instantly the great bear turned with a harsh roar of fury and challenge, blowing the bloody foam from his mouth, so that I saw the gleam of his white fangs; and then he charged straight at me, crashing and bounding through the laurel bushes, so that it was hard to aim. I waited until he came to a fallen tree, raking him as he topped it with a ball, which entered his chest and went through the cavity of his body, but he neither swerved nor flinched, and at the moment I did not know that I had struck him. He came steadily on, and in another second was almost upon me. I fired for his forehead, but my bullet went low, entering his open mouth, smashing his lower jaw and going into the neck. I leaped to one side almost as I pulled trigger; and through the hanging smoke the first thing I saw was his paw as he made a vicious side blow at me. The rush of his charge carried him past. As he struck he lurched forward, leaving a pool of bright blood where his muzzle hit the ground; but he recovered himself and made two or three jumps onwards, while I hurriedly jammed a couple of cartridges into the magazine, my rifle holding only four, all of which I had fired. Then he tried to pull up, but as he did so his muscles seemed suddenly to give way, his head drooped, and he rolled over and over like a shot rabbit. Each of my first three bullets had inflicted a mortal wound.

It was already twilight, and I merely opened the carcass, and then trotted back to camp. Next morning I returned and with much labor took off the skin. The fur was very fine, the animal being in excellent trim, and unusually bright-colored. Unfortunately, in packing it out I lost the skull, and had to supply its place with one of plaster. The beauty of the trophy, and the memory of the circumstances under which I procured it, make me value it perhaps more highly than any other in my house.

This is the only instance in which I have been regularly charged by a grisly. On the whole, the danger of hunting these great bears has been much exaggerated. At the beginning of the present century, when white hunters first encountered the grisly, he was doubtless an exceedingly savage beast, prone to attack without provocation, and a redoubtable foe to persons armed with the clumsy, small-bore, muzzle-loading rifles of the day. But at present bitter experience has taught him caution. He has been hunted for sport, and hunted for his pelt, and hunted for the bounty, and hunted as a dangerous enemy to stock, until, save in the very wildest districts, he has learned to be more wary than a deer, and to avoid man's presence almost as carefully as the most timid kind of game. Except in rare cases he will not attack of his own accord, and, as a rule, even when wounded his object is escape rather than battle.

Still, when fairly brought to bay, or when moved by a sudden fit of ungovernable anger, the grisly is beyond peradventure a very dangerous antagonist. The first shot, if taken at a bear a good distance off and previously unwounded and unharried, is not usually fraught with much danger, the startled animal being at the outset bent merely on flight. It is always hazardous, however, to track a wounded and worried grisly into thick cover, and the man who habitually follows and kills this chief of American game in dense timber, never abandoning the bloody trail whithersoever it leads, must show no small degree of skill and hardihood, and must not too closely count the risk to life or limb. Bears differ widely in temper, and occasionally one may be found who will not show fight, no matter how much he is bullied; but, as a rule, a hunter must be cautious in meddling with a wounded animal which has retreated into a dense thicket, and has been once or twice roused; and such a beast, when it does turn, will usually charge again and again, and fight to the last with unconquerable ferocity. The short distance at which the bear can be seen through the underbrush, the fury of his charge, and his tenacity of life make it necessary for the hunter on such occasions to have steady nerves and a fairly quick and accurate aim. It is always well to have two men in following a wounded bear under such conditions. This is not necessary, however, and a good hunter, rather than lose his quarry, will, under ordinary circumstances, follow and attack it no matter how tangled the fastness in which it has sought refuge; but he must act warily and with the utmost caution and resolution, if he wishes to escape a terrible and probably fatal mauling. An experienced hunter is rarely rash, and never heedless; he will not, when alone, follow a wounded bear into a thicket, if by the exercise of patience, skill, and knowledge of the game's habits he can avoid the necessity; but it is idle to talk of the feat as something which ought in no case to be attempted. While danger ought never to be needlessly incurred, it is yet true that the keenest zest in sport comes from its presence, and from the consequent exercise of the qualities necessary to overcome it. The most thrilling moments of an American hunter's life are those in which, with every sense on the alert, and with nerves strung to the highest point, he is following alone into the heart of its forest fastness the fresh and bloody footprints of an angered grisly; and no other triumph of American hunting can compare with the victory to be thus gained.

These big bears will not ordinarily charge from a distance of over a hundred yards; but there are exceptions to this rule. In the fall of 1890 my friend Archibald Rogers was hunting in Wyoming, south of the Yellowstone Park, and killed seven bears. One, an old he, was out on a bare table-land, grubbing for roots, when he was spied. It was early in the afternoon, and the hunters, who were on a high mountain slope, examined him for some time through their powerful glasses before making him out to be a bear. They then stalked up to the edge of the wood which fringed the table-land on one side, but could get no nearer than about three hundred yards, the plains being barren of all cover. After waiting for a couple of hours Rogers risked the shot, in despair of getting nearer, and wounded the bear, though not very seriously. The animal made off, almost broadside to, and Rogers ran forward to intercept it. As soon as it saw him it turned and rushed straight for him, not heeding his second shot, and evidently bent on charging home. Rogers then waited until it was within twenty yards, and brained it with his third bullet.

In fact bears differ individually in courage and ferocity precisely as men do, or as the Spanish bulls, of which it is said that not more than one in twenty is fit to stand the combat of the arena. One grisly can scarcely be bullied into resistance; the next may fight to the end, against any odds, without flinching, or even attack unprovoked. Hence men of limited experience in this sport, generalizing from the actions of the two or three bears each has happened to see or kill, often reach diametrically opposite conclusions as to the fighting temper and capacity of the quarry. Even old hunters—who indeed, as a class, are very narrow-minded and opinionated—often generalize just as rashly as beginners. One will portray all bears as very dangerous; another will speak and act as if he deemed them of no more consequence than so many rabbits. I knew one old hunter who had killed a score without ever seeing one show fight. On the other hand, Dr. James C. Merrill, U. S. A., who has had about as much experience with bears as I have had, informs me that he has been charged with the utmost determination three times. In each case the attack was delivered before the bear was wounded or even shot at, the animal being roused by the approach of the hunters from his day bed, and charging headlong at them from a distance of twenty or thirty paces. All three bears were killed before they could do any damage. There was a very remarkable incident connected with the killing of one of them. It occurred in the northern spurs of the Bighorn range. Dr. Merrill, in company with an old hunter, had climbed down into a deep, narrow canyon. The bottom was threaded with well-beaten elk trails. While following one of these the two men turned a corner of the canyon and were instantly charged by an old she-grisly, so close that it was only by good luck that one of the hurried shots disabled her and caused her to tumble over a cut bank where she was easily finished. They found that she had been lying directly across the game trail, on a smooth well beaten patch of bare earth, which looked as if it had been dug up, refilled, and trampled down. Looking curiously at this patch they saw a bit of hide only partially covered at one end; digging down they found the body of a well grown grisly cub. Its skull had been crushed, and the brains licked out, and there were signs of other injuries. The hunters pondered long over this strange discovery, and hazarded many guesses as to its meaning. At last they decided that probably the cub had been killed, and its brains eaten out, either by some old male-grisly or by a cougar, that the mother had returned and driven away the murderer, and that she had then buried the body and lain above it, waiting to wreak her vengeance on the first passer-by.

Old Tazewell Woody, during his thirty years' life as a hunter in the Rockies and on the great plains, killed very many grislies. He always exercised much caution in dealing with them; and, as it happened, he was by some suitable tree in almost every case when he was charged. He would accordingly climb the tree (a practice of which I do not approve however); and the bear would look up at him and pass on without stopping. Once, when he was hunting in the mountains with a companion, the latter, who was down in a valley, while Woody was on the hill-side, shot at a bear. The first thing Woody knew the wounded grisly, running up-hill, was almost on him from behind. As he turned it seized his rifle in its jaws. He wrenched the rifle round, while the bear still gripped it, and pulled trigger, sending a bullet into its shoulder; whereupon it struck him with its paw, and knocked him over the rocks. By good luck he fell in a snow bank and was not hurt in the least. Meanwhile the bear went on and they never got it.

Once he had an experience with a bear which showed a very curious mixture of rashness and cowardice. He and a companion were camped in a little tepee or wigwam, with a bright fire in front of it, lighting up the night. There was an inch of snow on the ground. Just after they went to bed a grisly came close to camp. Their dog rushed out and they could hear it bark round in the darkness for nearly an hour; then the bear drove it off and came right into camp. It went close to the fire, picking up the scraps of meat and bread, pulled a haunch of venison down from a tree, and passed and repassed in front of the tepee, paying no heed whatever to the two men, who crouched in the doorway talking to one another. Once it passed so close that Woody could almost have touched it. Finally his companion fired into it, and off it ran, badly wounded, without an attempt at retaliation. Next morning they followed its tracks in the snow, and found it a quarter of a mile away. It was near a pine and had buried itself under the loose earth, pine needles, and snow; Woody's companion almost walked over it, and putting his rifle to its ear blew out its brains.

In all his experience Woody had personally seen but four men who were badly mauled by bears. Three of these were merely wounded. One was bitten terribly in the back. Another had an arm partially chewed off. The third was a man named George Dow, and the accident happened to him on the Yellowstone, about the year 1878. He was with a pack animal at the time, leading it on a trail through a wood. Seeing a big she-bear with cubs he yelled at her; whereat she ran away, but only to çache her cubs, and in a minute, having hidden them, came racing back at him. His pack animal being slow he started to climb a tree; but before he could get far enough up she caught him, almost biting a piece out of the calf of his leg, pulled him down, bit and cuffed him two or three times, and then went on her way.

The only time Woody ever saw a man killed by a bear was once when he had given a touch of variety to his life by shipping on a New Bedford whaler which had touched at one of the Puget Sound ports. The whaler went up to a part of Alaska where bears were very plentiful and bold. One day a couple of boats' crews landed; and the men, who were armed only with an occasional harpoon or lance, scattered over the beach, one of them, a Frenchman, wading into the water after shell-fish. Suddenly a bear emerged from some bushes and charged among the astonished sailors, who scattered in every direction; but the bear, said Woody, "just had it in for that Frenchman," and went straight at him. Shrieking with terror he retreated up to his neck in the water; but the bear plunged in after him, caught him, and disembowelled him. One of the Yankee mates then fired a bomb lance into the bear's hips, and the savage beast hobbled off into the dense cover of the low scrub, where the enraged sailor folk were unable to get at it.

The truth is that while the grisly generally avoids a battle if possible, and often acts with great cowardice, it is never safe to take liberties with him; he usually fights desperately and dies hard when wounded and cornered, and exceptional individuals take the aggressive on small provocation.

During the years I lived on the frontier I came in contact with many persons who had been severely mauled or even crippled for life by grislies; and a number of cases where they killed men outright were also brought under my ken. Generally these accidents, as was natural, occurred to hunters who had roused or wounded the game.

A fighting bear sometimes uses his claws and sometimes his teeth. I have never known one to attempt to kill an antagonist by hugging, in spite of the popular belief to this effect; though he will sometimes draw an enemy towards him with his paws the better to reach him with his teeth, and to hold him so that he cannot escape from the biting. Nor does the bear often advance on his hind legs to the attack; though, if the man has come close to him in thick underbrush, or has stumbled on him in his lair unawares, he will often rise up in this fashion and strike a single blow. He will also rise in clinching with a man on horseback. In 1882 a mounted Indian was killed in this manner on one of the river bottoms some miles below where my ranch house now stands, not far from the junction of the Beaver and Little Missouri. The bear had been hunted into a thicket by a band of Indians, in whose company my informant, a white squaw-man, with whom I afterward did some trading, was travelling. One of them in the excitement of the pursuit rode across the end of the thicket; as he did so the great beast sprang at him with wonderful quickness, rising on its hind legs, and knocking over the horse and rider with a single sweep of his terrible fore-paws. It then turned on the fallen man and tore him open, and though the other Indians came promptly to his rescue and slew his assailant, they were not in time to save their comrade's life.

A bear is apt to rely mainly on his teeth or claws according to whether his efforts are directed primarily to killing his foe or to making good his own escape. In the latter event he trusts chiefly to his claws. If cornered, he of course makes a rush for freedom, and in that case he downs any man who is in his way with a sweep of his great paw, but passes on without stopping to bite him. If while sleeping or resting in thick brush some one suddenly stumbles on him close up he pursues the same course, less from anger than from fear, being surprised and startled. Moreover, if attacked at close quarters by men and dogs he strikes right and left in defence.

Sometimes what is called a charge is rather an effort to get away. In localities where he has been hunted, a bear, like every other kind of game, is always on the look-out for an attack, and is prepared at any moment for immediate flight. He seems ever to have in his mind, whether feeding, sunning himself, or merely roaming around, the direction—usually towards the thickest cover or most broken ground—in which he intends to run if molested. When shot at he instantly starts towards this place; or he may be so confused that he simply runs he knows not whither; and in either event he may take a line that leads almost directly to or by the hunter, although he had at first no thought of charging. In such a case he usually strikes a single knock-down blow and gallops on without halting, though that one blow may have taken life. If the claws are long and fairly sharp (as in early spring, or even in the fall, if the animal has been working over soft ground) they add immensely to the effect of the blow, for they cut like blunt axes. Often, however, late in the season, and if the ground has been dry and hard, or rocky, the claws are worn down nearly to the quick, and the blow is then given mainly with the under side of the paw; although even under this disadvantage a thump from a big bear will down a horse or smash in a man's breast. The hunter Hofer once lost a horse in this manner. He shot at and wounded a bear which rushed off, as ill luck would have it, past the place where his horse was picketed; probably more in fright than in anger it struck the poor beast a blow which, in the end, proved mortal.

If a bear means mischief and charges not to escape but to do damage, its aim is to grapple with or throw down its foe and bite him to death. The charge is made at a gallop, the animal sometimes coming on silently, with the mouth shut, and sometimes with the jaws open, the lips drawn back and teeth showing, uttering at the same time a succession of roars or of savage rasping snarls. Certain bears charge without any bluster and perfectly straight; while others first threaten and bully, and even when charging stop to growl, shake the head, and bite at a bush or knock holes in the ground with their fore-paws. Again, some of them charge home with a ferocious resolution which their extreme tenacity of life renders especially dangerous; while others can be turned or driven back even by a shot which is not mortal. They show the same variability in their behavior when wounded. Often a big bear, especially if charging, will receive a bullet in perfect silence, without flinching or seeming to pay any heed to it; while another will cry out and tumble about, and if charging, even though it may not abandon the attack, will pause for a moment to whine or bite at the wound.

Sometimes a single bite causes death. One of the most successful bear hunters I ever knew, an old fellow whose real name I never heard as he was always called Old Ike, was killed in this way in the spring or early summer of 1886 on one of the head-waters of the Salmon. He was a very good shot, had killed nearly a hundred bears with the rifle, and, although often charged, had never met with any accident, so that he had grown somewhat careless. On the day in question he had met a couple of mining prospectors and was travelling with them, when a grisly crossed his path. The old hunter immediately ran after it, rapidly gaining, as the bear did not hurry when it saw itself pursued, but slouched slowly forwards, occasionally turning its head to grin and growl. It soon went into a dense grove of young spruce, and as the hunter reached the edge it charged fiercely out. He fired one hasty shot, evidently wounding the animal, but not seriously enough to stop or cripple it; and as his two companions ran forward they saw the bear seize him with its wide-spread jaws, forcing him to the ground. They shouted and fired, and the beast abandoned the fallen man on the instant and sullenly retreated into the spruce thicket, whither they dared not follow it. Their friend was at his last gasp; for the whole side of the chest had been crushed in by the one bite, the lungs showing between the rent ribs.

Very often, however, a bear does not kill a man by one bite, but after throwing him lies on him, biting him to death. Usually, if no assistance is at hand, such a man is doomed; although if he pretends to be dead, and has the nerve to lie quiet under very rough treatment, it is just possible that the bear may leave him alive, perhaps after half burying what it believes to be the body. In a very few exceptional instances men of extraordinary prowess with the knife have succeeded in beating off a bear, and even in mortally wounding it, but in most cases a single-handed struggle, at close quarters, with a grisly bent on mischief, means death.

Occasionally the bear, although vicious, is also frightened, and passes on after giving one or two bites; and frequently a man who is knocked down is rescued by his friends before he is killed, the big beast mayhap using his weapons with clumsiness. So a bear may kill a foe with a single blow of its mighty fore-arm, either crushing in the head or chest by sheer force of sinew, or else tearing open the body with its formidable claws; and so on the other hand he may, and often does, merely disfigure or maim the foe by a hurried stroke. Hence it is common to see men who have escaped the clutches of a grisly, but only at the cost of features marred beyond recognition, or a body rendered almost helpless for life. Almost every old resident of western Montana or northern Idaho has known two or three unfortunates who have suffered in this manner. I have myself met one such man in Helena, and another in Missoula; both were living at least as late as 1889, the date at which I last saw them. One had been partially scalped by a bear's teeth; the animal was very old and so the fangs did not enter the skull. The other had been bitten across the face, and the wounds never entirely healed, so that his disfigured visage was hideous to behold.

Most of these accidents occur in following a wounded or worried bear into thick cover; and under such circumstances an animal apparently hopelessly disabled, or in the death throes, may with a last effort kill one or more of its assailants. In 1874 my wife's uncle, Captain Alexander Moore, U. S. A., and my friend Captain Bates, with some men of the 2d and 3d Cavalry, were scouting in Wyoming, near the Freezeout Mountains. One morning they roused a bear in the open prairie and followed it at full speed as it ran towards a small creek. At one spot in the creek beavers had built a dam, and as usual in such places there was a thick growth of bushes and willow saplings. Just as the bear reached the edge of this little jungle it was struck by several balls, both of its fore-legs being broken. Nevertheless, it managed to shove itself forward on its hind-legs, and partly rolled, partly pushed itself into the thicket, the bushes though low being so dense that its body was at once completely hidden. The thicket was a mere patch of brush, not twenty yards across in any direction. The leading troopers reached the edge almost as the bear tumbled in. One of them, a tall and powerful man named Miller, instantly dismounted and prepared to force his way in among the dwarfed willows, which were but breast-high. Among the men who had ridden up were Moore and Bates, and also the two famous scouts, Buffalo Bill—long a companion of Captain Moore,—and California Joe, Custer's faithful follower. California Joe had spent almost all his life on the plains and in the mountains, as a hunter and Indian fighter; and when he saw the trooper about to rush into the thicket he called out to him not to do so, warning him of the danger. But the man was a very reckless fellow and he answered by jeering at the old hunter for his over-caution in being afraid of a crippled bear. California Joe made no further effort to dissuade him, remarking quietly: "Very well, sonny, go in; it's your own affair." Miller then leaped off the bank on which they stood and strode into the thicket, holding his rifle at the port. Hardly had he taken three steps when the bear rose in front of him, roaring with rage and pain. It was so close that the man had no chance to fire. Its fore-arms hung useless and as it reared unsteadily on its hind-legs, lunging forward at him, he seized it by the ears and strove to hold it back. His strength was very great, and he actually kept the huge head from his face and braced himself so that he was not overthrown; but the bear twisted its muzzle from side to side, biting and tearing the man's arms and shoulders. Another soldier jumping down slew the beast with a single bullet, and rescued his comrade; but though alive he was too badly hurt to recover and died after reaching the hospital. Buffalo Bill was given the bear-skin, and I believe has it now.

The instances in which hunters who have rashly followed grislies into thick cover have been killed or severely mauled might be multiplied indefinitely. I have myself known of eight cases in which men have met their deaths in this manner.

It occasionally happens that a cunning old grisly will lie so close that the hunter almost steps on him; and he then rises suddenly with a loud, coughing growl and strikes down or seizes the man before the latter can fire off his rifle. More rarely a bear which is both vicious and crafty deliberately permits the hunter to approach fairly near to, or perhaps pass by, its hiding-place, and then suddenly charges him with such rapidity that he has barely time for the most hurried shot. The danger in such a case is of course great.

Ordinarily, however, even in the brush, the bear's object is to slink away, not to fight, and very many are killed even under the most unfavorable circumstances without accident. If an unwounded bear thinks itself unobserved it is not apt to attack; and in thick cover it is really astonishing to see how one of these large animals can hide, and how closely it will lie when there is danger. About twelve miles below my ranch there are some large river bottoms and creek bottoms covered with a matted mass of cottonwood, box-alders, bullberry bushes, rose-bushes, ash, wild plums, and other bushes. These bottoms have harbored bears ever since I first saw them; but though, often in company with a large party, I have repeatedly beaten through them, and though we must at times have been very near indeed to the game, we never so much as heard it run.

When bears are shot, as they usually must be, in open timber or on the bare mountain, the risk is very much less. Hundreds may thus be killed with comparatively little danger; yet even under these circumstances they will often charge, and sometimes make their charge good. The spice of danger, especially to a man armed with a good repeating rifle, is only enough to add zest to the chase, and the chief triumph is in outwitting the wary quarry and getting within range. Ordinarily the only excitement is in the stalk, the bear doing nothing more than keep a keen look-out and manifest the utmost anxiety to get away. As is but natural, accidents occasionally occur; yet they are usually due more to some failure in man or weapon than to the prowess of the bear. A good hunter whom I once knew, at a time when he was living in Butte, received fatal injuries from a bear he attacked in open woodland. The beast charged after the first shot, but slackened its pace on coming almost up to the man. The latter's gun jammed, and as he was endeavoring to work it he kept stepping slowly back, facing the bear which followed a few yards distant, snarling and threatening. Unfortunately while thus walking backwards the man struck a dead log and fell over it, whereupon the beast instantly sprang on him and mortally wounded him before help arrived.

On rare occasions men who are not at the time hunting it fall victims to the grisly. This is usually because they stumble on it unawares and the animal attacks them more in fear than in anger. One such case, resulting fatally, occurred near my own ranch. The man walked almost over a bear while crossing a little point of brush, in a bend of the river, and was brained with a single blow of the paw. In another instance which came to my knowledge the man escaped with a shaking up, and without even a fright. His name was Perkins, and he was out gathering huckleberries in the woods on a mountain side near Pend'Oreille Lake. Suddenly he was sent flying head over heels, by a blow which completely knocked the breath out of his body; and so instantaneous was the whole affair that all he could ever recollect about it was getting a vague glimpse of the bear just as he was bowled over. When he came to he found himself lying some distance down the hill-side, much shaken, and without his berry pail, which had rolled a hundred yards below him, but not otherwise the worse for his misadventure; while the footprints showed that the bear, after delivering the single hurried stroke at the unwitting disturber of its day-dreams, had run off up-hill as fast as it was able.

A she-bear with cubs is a proverbially dangerous beast; yet even under such conditions different grislies act in directly opposite ways. Some she-grislies, when their cubs are young, but are able to follow them about, seem always worked up to the highest pitch of anxious and jealous rage, so that they are likely to attack unprovoked any intruder or even passer-by. Others when threatened by the hunter leave their cubs to their fate without a visible qualm of any kind, and seem to think only of their own safety.

In 1882 Mr. Caspar W. Whitney, now of New York, met with a very singular adventure with a she-bear and cub. He was in Harvard when I was, but left it and, like a good many other Harvard men of that time, took to cow-punching in the West. He went on a ranch in Rio Arriba County, New Mexico, and was a keen hunter, especially fond of the chase of cougar, bear, and elk. One day while riding a stony mountain trail he saw a little grisly cub watching him from the chaparral above, and he dismounted to try to capture it; his rifle was a 40-90 Sharp's. Just as he neared the cub, he heard a growl and caught a glimpse of the old she, and he at once turned up-hill, and stood under some tall, quaking aspens. From this spot he fired at and wounded the she, then seventy yards off; and she charged furiously. He hit her again, but as she kept coming like a thunderbolt he climbed hastily up the aspen, dragging his gun with him, as it had a strap. When the bear reached the foot of the aspen she reared, and bit and clawed the slender trunk, shaking it for a moment, and he shot her through the eye. Off she sprang for a few yards, and then spun round a dozen times, as if dazed or partially stunned; for the bullet had not touched the brain. Then the vindictive and resolute beast came back to the tree and again reared up against it; this time to receive a bullet that dropped her lifeless. Mr. Whitney then climbed down and walked to where the cub had been sitting as a looker-on. The little animal did not move until he reached out his hand; when it suddenly struck at him like an angry cat, dove into the bushes, and was seen no more.

In the summer of 1888 an old-time trapper, named Charley Norton, while on Loon Creek, of the middle fork of the Salmon, meddled with a she and her cubs. She ran at him and with one blow of her paw almost knocked off his lower jaw; yet he recovered, and was alive when I last heard of him.

Yet the very next spring the cowboys with my own wagon on the Little Missouri round-up killed a mother bear which made but little more fight than a coyote. She had two cubs, and was surprised in the early morning on the prairie far from cover. There were eight or ten cowboys together at the time, just starting off on a long circle, and of course they all got down their ropes in a second, and putting spurs to their fiery little horses started toward the bears at a run, shouting and swinging their loops round their heads. For a moment the old she tried to bluster and made a half-hearted threat of charging; but her courage failed before the rapid onslaught of her yelling, rope-swinging assailants; and she took to her heels and galloped off, leaving the cubs to shift for themselves. The cowboys were close behind, however, and after half a mile's run she bolted into a shallow cave or hole in the side of a butte, where she stayed cowering and growling, until one of the men leaped off his horse, ran up to the edge of the hole, and killed her with a single bullet from his revolver, fired so close that the powder burned her hair. The unfortunate cubs were roped, and then so dragged about that they were speedily killed instead of being brought alive to camp, as ought to have been done.

In the cases mentioned above the grisly attacked only after having been itself assailed, or because it feared an assault, for itself or for its young. In the old days, however, it may almost be said that a grisly was more apt to attack than to flee. Lewis and Clarke and the early explorers who immediately succeeded them, as well as the first hunters and trappers, the "Rocky Mountain men" of the early decades of the present century, were repeatedly assailed in this manner; and not a few of the bear hunters of that period found that it was unnecessary to take much trouble about approaching their quarry, as the grisly was usually prompt to accept the challenge and to advance of its own accord, as soon as it discovered the foe. All this is changed now. Yet even at the present day an occasional vicious old bear may be found, in some far off and little trod fastness, which still keeps up the former habit of its kind. All old hunters have tales of this sort to relate, the prowess, cunning, strength, and ferocity of the grisly being favorite topics for camp-fire talk throughout the Rockies; but in most cases it is not safe to accept these stories without careful sifting.

Still, it is just as unsafe to reject them all. One of my own cowboys was once attacked by a grisly, seemingly in pure wantonness. He was riding up a creek bottom, and had just passed a clump of rose and bullberry bushes when his horse gave such a leap as almost to unseat him, and then darted madly forward. Turning round in the saddle to his utter astonishment he saw a large bear galloping after him, at the horse's heels. For a few jumps the race was close, then the horse drew away and the bear wheeled and went into a thicket of wild plums. The amazed and indignant cowboy, as soon as he could rein in his steed, drew his revolver and rode back to and around the thicket, endeavoring to provoke his late pursuer to come out and try conclusions on more equal terms; but prudent Ephraim had apparently repented of his freak of ferocious bravado, and declined to leave the secure shelter of the jungle.

Other attacks are of a much more explicable nature. Mr. Huffman, the photographer, of Miles City, informed me that once when butchering some slaughtered elk he was charged twice by a she-bear and two well-grown cubs. This was a piece of sheer bullying, undertaken solely with the purpose of driving away the man and feasting on the carcasses; for in each charge the three bears, after advancing with much blustering, roaring, and growling, halted just before coming to close quarters. In another instance a gentleman I once knew, a Mr. S. Carr, was charged by a grisly from mere ill temper at being disturbed at mealtime. The man was riding up a valley; and the bear was at an elk carcass, near a clump of firs. As soon as it became aware of the approach of the horseman, while he was yet over a hundred yards distant, it jumped on the carcass, looked at him a moment, and then ran straight for him. There was no particular reason why it should have charged, for it was fat and in good trim, though when killed its head showed scars made by the teeth of rival grislies. Apparently it had been living so well, principally on flesh, that it had become quarrelsome; and perhaps its not over sweet disposition had been soured by combats with others of its own kind. In yet another case, a grisly charged with even less excuse. An old trapper, from whom I occasionally bought fur, was toiling up a mountain pass when he spied a big bear sitting on his haunches on the hill-side above. The trapper shouted and waved his cap; whereupon, to his amazement, the bear uttered a loud "wough" and charged straight down on him—only to fall a victim to misplaced boldness.

I am even inclined to think that there have been wholly exceptional occasions when a grisly has attacked a man with the deliberate purpose of making a meal of him; when, in other words, it has started on the career of a man-eater. At least, on any other theory I find it difficult to account for an attack which once came to my knowledge. I was at Sand Point, on Pend'Oreille Lake, and met some French and Méti trappers, then in town with their bales of beaver, otter, and sable. One of them, who gave his name as Baptiste Lamoche, had his head twisted over to one side, the result of the bite of a bear. When the accident occurred he was out on a trapping trip with two companions. They had pitched camp right on the shore of a cove in a little lake, and his comrades were off fishing in a dugout or pirogue. He himself was sitting near the shore, by a little lean-to, watching some beaver meat which was sizzling over the dying embers. Suddenly, and without warning, a great bear, which had crept silently up beneath the shadows of the tall evergreens, rushed at him, with a guttural roar, and seized him before he could rise to his feet. It grasped him with its jaws at the junction of the neck and shoulder, making the teeth meet through bone, sinew, and muscle; and turning, racked off towards the forest, dragging with it the helpless and paralyzed victim. Luckily the two men in the canoe had just paddled round the point, in sight of, and close to, camp. The man in the bow, seeing the plight of their comrade, seized his rifle and fired at the bear. The bullet went through the beast's lungs, and it forthwith dropped its prey, and running off some two hundred yards, lay down on its side and died. The rescued man recovered full health and strength, but never again carried his head straight.

Old hunters and mountain-men tell many stories, not only of malicious grislies thus attacking men in camp, but also of their even dogging the footsteps of some solitary hunter and killing him when the favorable opportunity occurs. Most of these tales are mere fables; but it is possible that in altogether exceptional instances they rest on a foundation of fact. One old hunter whom I knew told me such a story. He was a truthful old fellow, and there was no doubt that he believed what he said, and that his companion was actually killed by a bear; but it is probable that he was mistaken in reading the signs of his comrade's fate, and that the latter was not dogged by the bear at all, but stumbled on him and was slain in the surprise of the moment.

At any rate, cases of wanton assaults by grislies are altogether out of the common. The ordinary hunter may live out his whole life in the wilderness and never know aught of a bear attacking a man unprovoked; and the great majority of bears are shot under circumstances of no special excitement, as they either make no fight at all, or, if they do fight, are killed before there is any risk of their doing damage. If surprised on the plains, at some distance from timber or from badly broken ground, it is no uncommon feat for a single horseman to kill them with a revolver. Twice of late years it has been performed in the neighborhood of my ranch. In both instances the men were not hunters out after game, but simply cowboys, riding over the range in early morning in pursuance of their ordinary duties among the cattle. I knew both men and have worked with them on the round-up. Like most cowboys they carried 44-calibre Colt revolvers, and were accustomed to and fairly expert in their use, and they were mounted on ordinary cow-ponies—quick, wiry, plucky little beasts. In one case the bear was seen from quite a distance, lounging across a broad table-land. The cowboy, by taking advantage of a winding and rather shallow coulie, got quite close to him. He then scrambled out of the coulie, put spurs to his pony, and raced up to within fifty yards of the astonished bear ere the latter quite understood what it was that was running at him through the gray dawn. He made no attempt at fight, but ran at top speed towards a clump of brush not far off at the head of a creek.

Before he could reach it, however, the galloping horseman was alongside, and fired three shots into his broad back. He did not turn, but ran on into the bushes and then fell over and died.

In the other case the cowboy, a Texan, was mounted on a good cutting pony, a spirited, handy, agile little animal, but excitable, and with a habit of dancing, which rendered it difficult to shoot from its back. The man was with the round-up wagon, and had been sent off by himself to make a circle through some low, barren buttes, where it was not thought more than a few head of stock would be found. On rounding the corner of a small washout he almost ran over a bear which was feeding on the carcass of a steer that had died in an alkali hole. After a moment of stunned surprise the bear hurled himself at the intruder with furious impetuosity; while the cowboy, wheeling his horse on its haunches and dashing in the spurs, carried it just clear of his assailant's headlong rush. After a few springs he reined in and once more wheeled half round, having drawn his revolver, only to find the bear again charging and almost on him. This time he fired into it, near the joining of the neck and shoulder, the bullet going downwards into the chest hollow; and again by a quick dash to one side he just avoided the rush of the beast and the sweep of its mighty fore-paw. The bear then halted for a minute, and he rode close by it at a run, firing a couple of shots, which brought on another resolute charge. The ground was somewhat rugged and broken, but his pony was as quick on its feet as a cat, and never stumbled, even when going at full speed to avoid the bear's first mad rushes. It speedily became so excited, however, as to render it almost impossible for the rider to take aim. Sometimes he would come up close to the bear and wait for it to charge, which it would do, first at a trot, or rather rack, and then at a lumbering but swift gallop; and he would fire one or two shots before being forced to run. At other times, if the bear stood still in a good place, he would run by it, firing as he rode. He spent many cartridges, and though most of them were wasted, occasionally a bullet went home. The bear fought with the most savage courage, champing its bloody jaws, roaring with rage, and looking the very incarnation of evil fury. For some minutes it made no effort to flee, either charging or standing at bay. Then it began to move slowly towards a patch of ash and wild plums in the head of a coulie, some distance off. Its pursuer rode after it, and when close enough would push by it and fire, while the bear would spin quickly round and charge as fiercely as ever, though evidently beginning to grow weak. At last, when still a couple of hundred yards from cover the man found he had used up all his cartridges, and then merely followed at a safe distance. The bear no longer paid heed to him, but walked slowly forwards, swaying its great head from side to side, while the blood streamed from between its half-opened jaws. On reaching the cover he could tell by the waving of the bushes that it walked to the middle and then halted. A few minutes afterwards some of the other cowboys rode up, having been attracted by the incessant firing. They surrounded the thicket, firing and throwing stones into the bushes. Finally, as nothing moved, they ventured in and found the indomitable grisly warrior lying dead.

Cowboys delight in nothing so much as the chance to show their skill as riders and ropers; and they always try to ride down and rope any wild animal they come across in favorable ground and close enough up. If a party of them meets a bear in the open they have great fun; and the struggle between the shouting, galloping rough-riders and their shaggy quarry is full of wild excitement and not unaccompanied by danger. The bear often throws the noose from his head so rapidly that it is a difficult matter to catch him; and his frequent charges scatter his tormentors in every direction while the horses become wild with fright over the roaring, bristling beast—for horses seem to dread a bear more than any other animal. If the bear cannot reach cover, however, his fate is sealed. Sooner or later, the noose tightens over one leg, or perchance over the neck and fore-paw, and as the rope straightens with a "pluck," the horse braces itself desperately and the bear tumbles over. Whether he regains his feet or not the cowboy keeps the rope taut; soon another noose tightens over a leg, and the bear is speedily rendered helpless.

I have known of these feats being performed several times in northern Wyoming, although never in the immediate neighborhood of my ranch. Mr. Archibald Rogers' cowhands have in this manner caught several bears, on or near his ranch on the Gray Bull, which flows into the Bighorn; and those of Mr. G. B. Grinnell have also occasionally done so. Any set of moderately good ropers and riders, who are accustomed to back one another up and act together, can accomplish the feat if they have smooth ground and plenty of room. It is, however, indeed a feat of skill and daring for a single man; and yet I have known of more than one instance in which it has been accomplished by some reckless knight of the rope and the saddle. One such occurred in 1887 on the Flathead Reservation, the hero being a half-breed; and another in 1890 at the mouth of the Bighorn, where a cowboy roped, bound, and killed a large bear single-handed.

My friend General "Red" Jackson, of Bellemeade, in the pleasant mid-county of Tennessee, once did a feat which casts into the shade even the feats of the men of the lariat. General Jackson, who afterwards became one of the ablest and most renowned of the Confederate cavalry leaders, was at the time a young officer in the Mounted Rifle Regiment, now known as the 3d United States Cavalry. It was some years before the Civil War, and the regiment was on duty in the Southwest, then the debatable land of Comanche and Apache. While on a scout after hostile Indians, the troops in their march roused a large grisly which sped off across the plain in front of them. Strict orders had been issued against firing at game, because of the nearness of the Indians. Young Jackson was a man of great strength, a keen swordsman, who always kept the finest edge on his blade, and he was on a swift and mettled Kentucky horse, which luckily had but one eye. Riding at full speed he soon overtook the quarry. As the horse hoofs sounded nearer, the grim bear ceased its flight, and whirling round stood at bay, raising itself on its hind-legs and threatening its pursuer with bared fangs and spread claws. Carefully riding his horse so that its blind side should be towards the monster, the cavalryman swept by at a run, handling his steed with such daring skill that he just cleared the blow of the dreaded fore-paw, while with one mighty sabre stroke he cleft the bear's skull, slaying the grinning beast as it stood upright.

CHAPTER XVI

The Cougar

No animal of the chase is so difficult to kill by fair still-hunting as the cougar—that beast of many names, known in the East as panther and painter, in the West as mountain lion, in the Southwest as Mexican lion, and in the southern continent as lion and puma.

Without hounds its pursuit is so uncertain that from the still-hunter's standpoint it hardly deserves to rank as game at all—though, by the way, it is itself a more skilful still-hunter than any human rival. It prefers to move abroad by night or at dusk; and in the daytime usually lies hid in some cave or tangled thicket where it is absolutely impossible even to stumble on it by chance. It is a beast of stealth and rapine; its great, velvet paws, never make a sound, and it is always on the watch whether for prey or for enemies, while it rarely leaves shelter even when it thinks itself safe. Its soft, leisurely movements and uniformity of color make it difficult to discover at best, and its extreme watchfulness helps it; but it is the cougar's reluctance to leave cover at any time, its habit of slinking off through the brush, instead of running in the open, when startled, and the way in which it lies motionless in its lair even when a man is within twenty yards, that render it so difficult to still-hunt.

In fact it is next to impossible with any hope of success regularly to hunt the cougar without dogs or bait.
Most cougars that are killed by still-hunters are shot by
accident while the man is after other game. This has been
my own experience. Although not common, cougars are
found near my ranch, where the ground is peculiarly favorable for the solitary rifleman; and for ten years I have,
off and on, devoted a day or two to their pursuit; but never
successfully. One December a large cougar took up his
abode on a densely wooded bottom two miles above the
ranch house. I did not discover his existence until I went
there one evening to kill a deer, and found that he had driven all the deer off the bottom, having killed several, as
well as a young heifer. Snow was falling at the time, but
the storm was evidently almost over; the leaves were all off
the trees and bushes; and I felt that next day there would
be such a chance to follow the cougar as fate rarely offered.
In the morning by dawn I was at the bottom, and speedily found his trail. Following it I came across his bed,
among some cedars in a dark, steep gorge, where the
buttes bordered the bottom. He had evidently just left it,
and I followed his tracks all day. But I never caught a
glimpse of him, and late in the afternoon I trudged wearily
homewards. When I went out next morning I found that
as soon as I abandoned the chase, my quarry, according to
the uncanny habit sometimes displayed by his kind, coolly
turned likewise, and deliberately dogged my footsteps to
within a mile of the ranch house; his round footprints
being as clear as writing in the snow.

This was the best chance of the kind that I ever had;
but again and again I have found fresh signs of cougar,

such as a lair which they had just left, game they had killed, or one of our venison caches which they had robbed, and have hunted for them all day without success. My failures were doubtless due in part to various shortcomings in hunter's-craft on my own part; but equally without doubt they were mainly due to the quarry's wariness and its sneaking ways.

I have seen a wild cougar alive but twice, and both times by chance. On one occasion one of my men, Merrifield, and I surprised one eating a skunk in a bullberry patch; and by our own bungling frightened it away from its unsavory repast without getting a shot.

On the other occasion luck befriended me. I was with a pack train in the Rockies, and one day, feeling lazy, and as we had no meat in camp, I determined to try for deer by lying in wait beside a recently travelled game trail. The spot I chose was a steep, pine-clad slope leading down to a little mountain lake. I hid behind a breastwork of rotten logs, with a few young evergreens in front—an excellent ambush. A broad game trail slanted down the hill directly past me. I lay perfectly quiet for about an hour, listening to the murmur of the pine forests, and the occasional call of a jay or woodpecker, and gazing eagerly along the trail in the waning light of the late afternoon. Suddenly, without noise or warning of any kind, a cougar stood in the trail before me. The unlooked for and unheralded approach of the beast was fairly ghost-like. With its head lower than its shoulders, and its long tail twitching, it slouched down the path, treading as softly as a kitten. I waited until it had passed and then fired into the short ribs, the bullet ranging forward. Throwing its tail up in the air, and giving a bound, the cougar galloped off over a slight ridge. But it did not go far; within a hundred yards I found it stretched on its side, its jaws still working convulsively.

The true way to hunt the cougar is to follow it with dogs. If the chase is conducted in this fashion, it is very exciting, and resembles on a larger scale the ordinary method of hunting the wildcat or small lynx, as practised by the sport-loving planters of the southern States. With a very little training, hounds readily and eagerly pursue the cougar, showing in this kind of chase none of the fear and disgust they are so prone to exhibit when put on the trail of the certainly no more dangerous wolf. The cougar, when the hounds are on its track, at first runs, but when hard-pressed takes to a tree, or possibly comes to bay in thick cover. Its attention is then so taken up with the hounds that it can usually be approached and shot without much difficulty; though some cougars break bay when the hunters come near, and again make off, when they can only be stopped by many large and fierce hounds. Hounds are often killed in these fights; and if hungry a cougar will pounce on any dog for food; yet, as I have elsewhere related, I know of one instance in which a small pack of big, savage hounds killed a cougar unassisted. General Wade Hampton, who with horse and hound has been the mightiest hunter America has ever seen, informs me that he has killed with his pack some sixteen cougars, during the fifty years he has hunted in South Carolina and Mississippi. I believe they were all killed in the latter State. General Hampton's hunting has been chiefly for bear and deer, though his pack also follows the lynx and the gray fox; and, of course, if good fortune throws either a wolf or a cougar in his way it is followed as the game of all others. All the cougars he killed were either treed or brought to bay in a canebrake by the hounds; and they often handled the pack very roughly in the death struggle. He found them much more dangerous antagonists than the black bear when assailed with the hunting knife, a weapon of which he was very fond. However, if his pack had held a few very large, savage dogs, put in purely for fighting when the quarry was at bay, I think the danger would have been minimized.

General Hampton followed his game on horseback; but in following the cougar with dogs this is by no means always necessary. Thus Col. Cecil Clay, of Washington, killed a cougar in West Virginia, on foot with only three or four hounds. The dogs took the cold trail, and he had to run many miles over the rough, forest-clad mountains after them. Finally they drove the cougar up a tree; where he found it, standing among the branches, in a half-erect position, its hind-feet on one limb and its fore-feet on another, while it glared down at the dogs, and switched its tail from side to side. He shot it through both shoulders, and down it came in a heap, whereupon the dogs jumped in and worried it, for its fore-legs were useless, though it managed to catch one dog in its jaws and bite him severely.

A wholly exceptional instance of the kind was related to me by my old hunting friend Willis. In his youth, in southwest Missouri, he knew a half-witted "poor white" who was very fond of hunting coons. He hunted at night, armed with an axe, and accompanied by his dog Penny, a large, savage, half-starved cur. One dark night the dog treed an animal which he could not see; so he cut down the tree, and immediately Penny jumped in and grabbed the beast. The man sung out "Hold on, Penny," seeing that the dog had seized some large, wild animal; the next moment the brute knocked the dog endways, and at the same instant the man split open its head with the axe. Great was his astonishment, and greater still the astonishment of the neighbors next day when it was found that he had actually killed a cougar. These great cats often take to trees in a perfectly foolish manner. My friend, the hunter Woody, in all his thirty years' experience in the wilds never killed but one cougar. He was lying out in camp with two dogs at the time; it was about midnight, the fire was out, and the night was pitch-black. He was roused by the furious barking of his two dogs, who had charged into the gloom, and were apparently baying at something in a tree close by. He kindled the fire, and to his astonishment found the thing in the tree to be a cougar. Coming close underneath he shot it with his revolver; thereupon it leaped down, ran some forty yards, and climbed up another tree, where it died among the branches.

If cowboys come across a cougar in open ground they invariably chase and try to rope it—as indeed they do with any wild animal. I have known several instances of cougars being roped in this way; in one the animal was brought into camp alive by two strapping cowpunchers.

The cougar sometimes stalks its prey, and sometimes lies in wait for it beside a game-trail or drinking pool— very rarely indeed does it crouch on the limb of a tree. When excited by the presence of game it is sometimes very bold. Willis once fired at some bighorn sheep, on a steep mountain-side; he missed, and immediately after his shot, a cougar made a dash into the midst of the flying band, in hopes to secure a victim. The cougar roams over long distances, and often changes its hunting ground, perhaps remaining in one place two or three months, until the game is exhausted, and then shifting to another. When it does not lie in wait it usually spends most of the night, winter and summer, in prowling restlessly around the places where it thinks it may come across prey, and it will patiently follow an animal's trail. There is no kind of game, save the full-grown grisly and buffalo, which it does not at times assail and master. It readily snaps up grisly cubs or buffalo calves; and in at least one instance, I have known of it springing on, slaying, and eating a full-grown wolf. I presume the latter was taken by surprise. On the other hand, the cougar itself has to fear the big timber wolves when maddened by the winter hunger and gathered in small parties; while a large grisly would of course be an overmatch for it twice over, though its superior agility puts it beyond the grisly's power to harm it, unless by some unlucky chance taken in a cave. Nor could a cougar overcome a bull moose, or a bull elk either, if the latter's horns were grown, save by taking it unawares. By choice, with such big game, its victims are the cows and young. The prong-horn rarely comes within reach of its spring; but it is the dreaded enemy of big-horn, white goat, and every kind of deer, while it also preys on all the smaller beasts, such as foxes, coons, rabbits, beavers, and even gophers, rats, and mice. It sometimes makes a thorny meal of the porcupine, and if sufficiently hungry attacks and eats its smaller cousin the lynx. It is not a brave animal; nor does it run its prey down in open chase. It always makes its attacks by stealth, and if possible from behind, and relies on two or three tremendous springs to bring it on the doomed creature's back. It uses its claws as well as its teeth in holding and killing the prey. If possible it always seizes a large animal by the throat, whereas the wolf's point of attack is more often the haunch or flank. Small deer or sheep it will often knock over and kill, merely using its big paws; sometimes it breaks their necks. It has a small head compared to the jaguar, and its bite is much less dangerous. Hence, as compared to its larger and bolder relative, it places more trust in its claws and less its teeth.

Though the cougar prefers woodland, it is not necessarily a beast of the dense forests only; for it is found in all the plains country, living in the scanty timber belts which fringe the streams, or among the patches of brush in the Bad Lands. The persecution of hunters however always tends to drive it into the most thickly wooded and broken fastnesses of the mountains. The she has from one to three kittens, brought forth in a cave or a secluded lair, under a dead log or in very thick brush. It is said that the old he's kill the small male kittens when they get a chance. They certainly at times during the breeding season fight desperately among themselves. Cougars are very solitary beasts; it is rare to see more than one at a time, and then only a mother and young, or a mated male and female. While she has kittens, the mother is doubly destructive to game. The young begin to kill for themselves very early. The first fall, after they are born, they attack large game, and from ignorance are bolder in making their attacks than their parents; but they are clumsy and often let the prey escape. Like all cats, cougars are comparatively easy to trap, much more so than beasts of the dog kind, such as the fox and wolf.

They are silent animals; but old hunters say that at mating time the males call loudly, while the females have a very distinct answer. They are also sometimes noisy at other seasons. I am not sure that I ever heard one; but one night, while camped in a heavily timbered coulie near Kildeer Mountains, where, as their footprints showed, the beasts were plentiful, I twice heard a loud, wailing scream ringing through the impenetrable gloom which shrouded the hills around us. My companion, an old plainsman, said that this was the cry of the cougar prowling for its prey. Certainly no man could well listen to a stranger and wilder sound.

Ordinarily the rifleman is in no danger from a hunted cougar; the beast's one idea seems to be flight, and even if its assailant is very close, it rarely charges if there is any chance for escape. Yet there are occasions when it will show fight. In the spring of 1890, a man with whom I had more than once worked on the round-up—though I never knew his name—was badly mauled by a cougar near my ranch. He was hunting with a companion and they unexpectedly came on the cougar on a shelf of sandstone above their heads, only some ten feet off. It sprang down on the man, mangled him with teeth and claws for a moment, and then ran away. Another man I knew, a hunter named Ed. Smith, who had a small ranch near Helena, was once charged by a wounded cougar; he received a couple of deep scratches, but was not seriously hurt.

Many old frontiersmen tell tales of the cougar's occasionally itself making the attack, and dogging to his death some unfortunate wayfarer. Many others laugh such tales to scorn. It is certain that if such attacks occur they are altogether exceptional, being indeed of such extreme rarity that they may be entirely disregarded in practice. I should have no more hesitation in sleeping out in a wood where there were cougars, or walking through it after nightfall, than I should have if the cougars were tomcats.

Yet it is foolish to deny that in exceptional instances attacks may occur. Cougars vary wonderfully in size, and no less in temper. Indeed I think that by nature they are as ferocious and bloodthirsty as they are cowardly; and that their habit of sometimes dogging wayfarers for miles is due to a desire for bloodshed which they lack the courage to realize. In the old days, when all wild beasts were less shy than at present, there was more danger from the cougar; and this was especially true in the dark canebrakes of some of the southern States, where the man a cougar was most likely to encounter was a nearly naked and unarmed negro. General Hampton tells me that near his Mississippi plantation, many years ago, a negro who was one of a gang engaged in building a railroad through low and wet ground was waylaid and killed by a cougar late one night as he was walking alone through the swamp.

I knew two men in Missoula who were once attacked by cougars in a very curious manner. It was in January, and they were walking home through the snow after a hunt, each carrying on his back the saddle, haunches, and hide of a deer he had slain. Just at dusk, as they were passing through a narrow ravine, the man in front heard his partner utter a sudden loud call for help. Turning, he was dumbfounded to see the man lying on his face in the snow, with a cougar which had evidently just knocked him down standing over him, grasping the deer meat; while another cougar was galloping up to assist. Swinging his rifle round he shot the first one in the brain, and it dropped motionless, whereat the second halted, wheeled, and bounded into the woods. His companion was not in the least hurt or even frightened, though greatly amazed. The cougars were not full grown, but young of the year.

Now in this case I do not believe the beasts had any real intention of attacking the men. They were young animals, bold, stupid, and very hungry. The smell of the raw meat excited them beyond control, and they probably could not make out clearly what the men were, as they walked bent under their burdens, with the deer skins on their backs. Evidently the cougars were only trying to get at the venison.

In 1886 a cougar killed an Indian near Flathead Lake. Two Indians were hunting together on horseback when they came on the cougar. It fell at once to their shots, and they dismounted and ran towards it. Just as they reached it it came to, and seized one, killing him instantly with a couple of savage bites in the throat and chest; it then raced after the other, and, as he sprung on his horse, struck him across the buttocks, inflicting a deep but not dangerous scratch. I saw this survivor a year later. He evinced great reluctance to talk of the event, and insisted that the thing which had slain his companion was not really a cougar at all, but a devil.

A she-cougar does not often attempt to avenge the loss of her young, but sometimes she does. A remarkable instance of the kind happened to my friend, Professor John Bache McMaster, in 1875. He was camped near the head of Green River, Wyoming. One afternoon he found a couple of cougar kittens, and took them into camp; they were clumsy, playful, friendly little creatures. The next afternoon he remained in camp with the cook. Happening to look up he suddenly spied the mother cougar running noiselessly down on them, her eyes glaring and tail twitching. Snatching up his rifle, he killed her when she was barely twenty yards distant.

A ranchman, named Trescott, who was at one time my neighbor, told me that while he was living on a sheep-farm in the Argentine, he found pumas very common, and killed many. They were very destructive to sheep and colts, but were singularly cowardly when dealing with men. Not only did they never attack human beings, under any stress of hunger, but they made no effective resistance when brought to bay, merely scratching and cuffing like a big cat; so that if found in a cave, it was safe to creep in and shoot them with a revolver. Jaguars, on the contrary, were very dangerous antagonists.

CHAPTER XVII

A Peccary Hunt on the Nueces

I n the United States the peccary is only found in the southernmost corner of Texas. In April, 1892, I made a flying visit to the ranch country of this region, starting from the town of Uvalde with a Texan friend, Mr. John Moore. My trip being very hurried, I had but a couple of days to devote to hunting.

Our first halting-place was at a ranch on the Frio; a low, wooden building, of many rooms, with open galleries between them, and verandas round about. The country was in some respects like, in others strangely unlike, the northern plains with which I was so well acquainted. It was for the most part covered with a scattered growth of tough, stunted mesquite trees, not dense enough to be called a forest, and yet sufficiently close to cut off the view. It was very dry, even as compared with the northern plains. The bed of the Frio was filled with coarse gravel, and for the most part dry as a bone on the surface, the water seeping through underneath, and only appearing in occasional deep holes. These deep holes or ponds never fail, even after a year's drouth; they were filled with fish. One lay quite near the ranch house, under a bold rocky bluff; at its edge grew giant cypress trees. In the hollows and by the watercourses were occasional groves of pecans, live-oaks, and elms. Strange birds hopped among the bushes; the chaparral cock—a big, handsome ground-cuckoo of remarkable habits, much given to preying on small snakes and lizards—ran over the ground with extraordinary rapidity. Beautiful swallow-tailed kingbirds with rosy plumage perched on the tops of the small trees, and soared and flitted in graceful curves above them. Blackbirds of many kinds scuttled in flocks about the corrals and outbuildings around the ranches. Mocking-birds abounded, and were very noisy, singing almost all the daytime, but with their usual irritating inequality of performance, wonderfully musical and powerful snatches of song being interspersed with imitations of other bird notes and disagreeable squalling. Throughout the trip I did not hear one of them utter the beautiful love song in which they sometimes indulge at night.

The country was all under wire fence, unlike the northern regions, the pastures however being sometimes many miles across. When we reached the Frio ranch a herd of a thousand cattle had just been gathered, and two or three hundred beeves and young stock were being cut out to be driven northward over the trail. The cattle were worked in pens much more than in the North, and on all the ranches there were chutes with steering gates, by means of which the individuals of a herd could be dexterously shifted into various corrals. The branding of the calves was done ordinarily in one of these corrals and on foot, the calf being always roped by both forelegs; otherwise the work of the cowpunchers was much like that of their brothers in the North. As a whole, however, they were distinctly more proficient with the rope, and at least half of them were Mexicans.

There were some bands of wild cattle living only in the densest timber of the river bottoms which were literally as wild as deer, and moreover very fierce and dangerous. The pursuit of these was exciting and hazardous in the extreme. The men who took part in it showed not only the utmost daring but the most consummate horsemanship and wonderful skill in the use of the rope, the coil being hurled with the force and precision of an iron quoit; a single man speedily overtaking, roping, throwing, and binding down the fiercest steer or bull.

There had been many peccaries, or, as the Mexicans and cowpunchers of the border usually call them, javalinas, round this ranch a few years before the date of my visit. Until 1886, or thereabouts, these little wild hogs were not much molested, and abounded in the dense chaparral around the lower Rio Grande. In that year, however, it was suddenly discovered that their hides had a market value, being worth four bits—that is, half a dollar—apiece; and many Mexicans and not a few shiftless Texans went into the business of hunting them as a means of livelihood. They were more easily killed than deer, and, as a result, they were speedily exterminated in many localities where they had formerly been numerous, and even where they were left were to be found only in greatly diminished numbers. On this particular Frio ranch the last little band had been killed nearly a year before. There were three of them, a boar and two sows, and a couple of the cowboys stumbled on them early one morning while out with a dog. After half a mile's chase the three peccaries ran into a hollow pecan tree, and one of the cowboys, dismounting, improvised a lance by tying his knife to the end of a pole, and killed them all.

Many anecdotes were related to me of what they had done in the old days when they were plentiful on the ranch. They were then usually found in parties of from twenty to thirty, feeding in the dense chaparral, the sows rejoining the herd with the young very soon after the birth of the latter, each sow usually having but one or two at a litter. At night they sometimes lay in the thickest cover, but always, where possible, preferred to house in a cave or big hollow log, one invariably remaining as a sentinel close to the mouth, looking out. If this sentinel were shot, another would almost certainly take his place. They were subject to freaks of stupidity, and were pugnacious to a degree. Not only would they fight if molested, but they would often attack entirely without provocation.

Once my friend Moore himself, while out with another cowboy on horseback, was attacked in sheer wantonness by a drove of these little wild hogs. The two men were riding by a grove of live-oaks along a wood-cutter's cart track, and were assailed without a moment's warning. The little creatures completely surrounded them, cutting fiercely at the horses' legs and jumping up at the riders' feet. The men, drawing their revolvers, dashed through and were closely followed by their pursuers for three or four hundred yards, although they fired right and left with good effect. Both of the horses were badly cut. On another occasion the bookkeeper of the ranch walked off to a water hole but a quarter of a mile distant, and came face to face with a peccary on a cattle trail, where the brush was thick. Instead of getting out of his way the creature charged him instantly, drove him up a small mesquite tree, and kept him there for nearly two hours, looking up at him and champing its tusks.

I spent two days hunting round this ranch but saw no peccary sign whatever, although deer were quite plentiful. Parties of wild geese and sandhill cranes occasionally flew overhead. At nightfall the poor-wills wailed everywhere through the woods, and coyotes yelped and yelled, while in the early morning the wild turkeys gobbled loudly from their roosts in the tops of the pecan trees.

Having satisfied myself that there were no javalinas left on the Frio ranch, and being nearly at the end of my holiday, I was about to abandon the effort to get any, when a passing cowman happened to mention the fact that some were still to be found on the Nueces River thirty miles or thereabouts to the southward. Thither I determined to go, and next morning Moore and I started in a buggy drawn by a redoubtable horse, named Jim Swinger, which we were allowed to use because he bucked so under the saddle that nobody on the ranch could ride him. We drove six or seven hours across the dry, waterless plains. There had been a heavy frost a few days before, which had blackened the budding mesquite trees, and their twigs still showed no signs of sprouting. Occasionally we came across open spaces where there was nothing but short brown grass. In most places, however, the leafless, sprawling mesquites were scattered rather thinly over the ground, cutting off an extensive view and merely adding to the melancholy barrenness of the landscape. The road was nothing but a couple of dusty wheel-tracks; the ground was parched, and the grass cropped close by the gaunt, starved cattle. As we drove along buzzards and great hawks occasionally soared overhead. Now and then we passed lines of wild-looking, long-horned steers, and once we came on the grazing horses of a cow-outfit, just preparing to start northward over the trail to the fattening pastures. Occasionally we encountered one or two cowpunchers: either Texans, habited exactly like their brethren in the North, with broad-brimmed gray hats, blue shirts, silk neckerchiefs, and leather leggings; or else Mexicans, more gaudily dressed, and wearing peculiarly stiff, very broad-brimmed hats, with conical tops.

Toward the end of our ride we got where the ground was more fertile, and there had recently been a sprinkling of rain. Here we came across wonderful flower prairies. In one spot I kept catching glimpses through the mesquite trees of lilac stretches which I had first thought must be ponds of water. On coming nearer they proved to be acres on acres thickly covered with beautiful lilac-colored flowers. Farther on we came to where broad bands of red flowers covered the ground for many furlongs; then their places were taken by yellow blossoms, elsewhere by white. Generally each band or patch of ground was covered densely by flowers of the same color, making a great vivid streak across the landscape; but in places they were mixed together, red, yellow, and purple, interspersed in patches and curving bands, carpeting the prairie in a strange, bright pattern.

Finally, toward evening we reached the Nueces. Where we struck it first the bed was dry, except in occasional deep, malarial-looking pools, but a short distance below there began to be a running current. Great blue herons were stalking beside these pools, and from one we flushed a white ibis. In the woods were reddish cardinal birds, much less brilliant in plumage than the true cardinals and the scarlet tanagers; and yellow-headed titmice which had already built large domed nests.

In the valley of the Nueces itself, the brush grew thick. There were great groves of pecan trees, and evergreen live-oaks stood in many places, long, wind-shaken tufts of gray moss hanging from their limbs. Many of the trees in the wet spots were of giant size, and the whole landscape was semi-tropical in character. High on a bluff shoulder overlooking the course of the river was perched the ranch house, toward which we were bending our steps; and here we were received with the hearty hospitality characteristic of the ranch country everywhere.

The son of the ranchman, a tall, well-built young fellow, told me at once that there were peccaries in the neighborhood, and that he had himself shot one but two or three days before, and volunteered to lend us horses and pilot us to the game on the morrow, with the help of his two dogs. The last were big black curs with, as we were assured, "considerable hound" in them. One was at the time staying at the ranch house, the other was four or five miles off with a Mexican goat-herder, and it was arranged that early in the morning we should ride down to the latter place, taking the first dog with us and procuring his companion when we reached the goat-herder's house.

We started after breakfast, riding powerful cowponies, well trained to gallop at full speed through the dense chaparral. The big black hound slouched at our heels. We rode down the banks of the Nueces, crossing and recrossing the stream. Here and there were long, deep pools in the bed of the river, where rushes and lilies grew and huge mailed garfish swam slowly just beneath the surface of the water. Once my two companions stopped to pull a mired cow out of a slough, hauling with ropes from their saddle horns. In places there were half-dry pools, out of the regular current of the river, the water green and fetid. The trees were very tall and large. The streamers of pale gray moss hung thickly from the branches of the live-oaks, and when many trees thus draped stood close together they bore a strangely mournful and desolate look.

We finally found the queer little hut of the Mexican goat-herder in the midst of a grove of giant pecans. On the walls were nailed the skins of different beasts, raccoons, wild-cats, and the tree-civet, with its ringed tail. The Mexican's brown wife and children were in the hut, but the man himself and the goats were off in the forest, and it took us three or four hours' search before we found him. Then it was nearly noon, and we lunched in his hut, a square building of split logs, with bare earth floor, and roof of clap-boards and bark. Our lunch consisted of goat's meat and *pan de mais*. The Mexican, a broad-chested man with a stolid Indian face, was evidently quite a sportsman, and had two or three half-starved hounds, besides the funny, hairless little house dogs, of which Mexicans seem so fond.

Having borrowed the javalina hound of which we were in search, we rode off in quest of our game, the two dogs trotting gayly ahead. The one which had been living at the ranch had evidently fared well, and was very fat; the other was little else but skin and bone, but as alert and knowing as any New York street-boy, with the same air of disreputable capacity. It was this hound which always did most in finding the javalinas and bringing them to bay, his companion's chief use being to make a noise and lend the moral support of his presence.

We rode away from the river on the dry uplands, where the timber, though thick, was small, consisting almost exclusively of the thorny mesquites. Mixed among them were prickly pears, standing as high as our heads on horseback, and Spanish bayonets, looking in the distance like small palms; and there were many other kinds of cactus, all with poisonous thorns. Two or three times the dogs got on an old trail and rushed off giving tongue, whereat we galloped madly after them, ducking and dodging through and among the clusters of spine-bearing trees and cactus, not without getting a considerable number of thorns in our hands and legs. It was very dry and hot. Where the javalinas live in droves in the river bottoms they often drink at the pools; but when some distance from water they seem to live quite comfortably on the prickly pear, slaking their thirst by eating its hard, juicy fibre.

At last, after several false alarms, and gallops which led to nothing, when it lacked but an hour of sundown we struck a band of five of the little wild hogs. They were running off through the mesquites with a peculiar hopping or bounding motion, and we all, dogs and men, tore after them instantly.

Peccaries are very fast for a few hundred yards, but speedily tire, lose their wind, and come to bay. Almost immediately one of these, a sow, as it turned out, wheeled and charged at Moore as he passed, Moore never seeing her but keeping on after another. The sow then stopped and stood still, chattering her teeth savagely, and I jumped off my horse and dropped her dead with a shot in the spine, over the shoulders. Moore meanwhile had dashed off after his pig in one direction, and killed the little beast with a shot from the saddle when it had come to bay, turning and going straight at him. Two of the peccaries got off; the remaining one, a rather large boar, was followed by the two dogs, and as soon as I had killed the sow I leaped again on my horse and made after them, guided by the yelping and baying. In less than a quarter of a mile they were on his haunches, and he wheeled and stood under a bush, charging at them when they came near him, and once catching one, inflicting an ugly cut. All the while his teeth kept going like castanets, with a rapid champing sound. I ran up close and killed him by a shot through the backbone where it joined the neck. His tusks were fine.

The few minutes' chase on horseback was great fun, and there was a certain excitement in seeing the fierce little creatures come to bay; but the true way to kill these peccaries would be with the spear. They could often be speared on horseback, and where this was impossible, by using dogs to bring them to bay they could readily be killed on foot; though, as they are very active and absolutely fearless, and inflict a most formidable bite, it would usually be safest to have two men go at one together. Peccaries are not difficult beasts to kill, because their short wind and their pugnacity make them come to bay before hounds so quickly. Two or three good dogs can bring to a halt a herd of considerable size. They then all stand in a bunch, or else with their sterns against a bank, chattering their teeth at their antagonists. When angry and at bay, they get their legs close together, their shoulders high, and their bristles all ruffled, and look the very incarnation of anger, and they fight with reckless indifference to the very last. Hunters usually treat them with a certain amount of caution; but, as a matter of fact, I know of but one case where a man was hurt by them. He had shot at and wounded one, was charged both by it and by its two companions, and started to climb a tree; but as he drew himself from the ground, one sprang at him and bit him through the calf, inflicting a very severe wound. I have known of several cases of horses being cut, however, and dogs are very commonly killed. Indeed, a dog new to the business is almost certain to get very badly scarred, and no dog that hunts steadily can escape without some injury. If it runs in right at the heads of the animals, the probabilities are that it will get killed; and, as a rule, even two good-sized hounds cannot kill a peccary, though it is no larger than either of them. However, a wary, resolute, hard-biting dog of good size speedily gets accustomed to the chase, and can kill a peccary single-handed, seizing it from behind and worrying it to death, or watching its chance and grabbing it by the back of the neck where it joins the head.

Peccaries have delicately moulded short legs, and their feet are small, the tracks looking peculiarly dainty in consequence. Hence, they do not swim well, though they take to the water if necessary. They feed on roots, prickly pears, nuts, insects, lizards, etc. They usually keep entirely separate from the droves of half-wild swine that are so often found in the same neighborhoods; but in one case, on this very ranch where I was staying, a peccary deliberately joined a party of nine pigs and associated with them. When the owner of the pigs came up to them one day the peccary manifested great suspicion at his presence, and finally sidled close up and threatened to attack him, so that he had to shoot it. The ranchman's son told me that he had never but once had a peccary assail him unprovoked, and even in this case it was his dog that was the object of attack, the peccary rushing out at it as it followed him home one evening through the chaparral. Even around this ranch the peccaries had very greatly decreased in numbers, and the survivors were learning some caution. In the old days it had been no uncommon thing for a big band to attack entirely of their own accord, and keep a hunter up a tree for hours at a time.

CHAPTER XVIII

Hunting with Hounds

In hunting American big game with hounds, several entirely distinct methods are pursued. The true wilderness hunters, the men who in the early days lived alone in, or moved in parties through, the Indian-haunted solitudes, like their successors of to-day, rarely made use of a pack of hounds, and, as a rule, did not use dogs at all. In the eastern forests occasionally an old-time hunter would own one or two track-hounds, slow, with a good nose, intelligent and obedient, of use mainly in following wounded game. Some Rocky Mountain hunters nowadays employ the same kind of dog, but the old-time trappers of the great plains and the Rockies led such wandering lives of peril and hardship that they could not readily take dogs with them. The hunters of the Alleghanies and the Adirondacks have, however, always used hounds to drive deer, killing the animal in the water or at a runway.

As soon, however, as the old wilderness hunter type passes away, hounds come into use among his successors, the rough border settlers of the backwoods and the plains. Every such settler is apt to have four or five large mongrel dogs with hound blood in them, which serve to drive off beasts of prey from the sheepfold and cattle-shed, and are also used, when the occasion suits, in regular hunting, whether after bear or deer.

Many of the southern planters have always kept packs of fox-hounds, which are used in the chase, not only of the gray and the red fox, but also of the deer, the black bear, and the wildcat. The fox the dogs themselves run down and kill, but as a rule in this kind of hunting, when after deer, bear, or even wildcat, the hunters carry guns with them on their horses, and endeavor either to get a shot at the fleeing animal by hard and dexterous riding, or else to kill the cat when treed, or the bear when it comes to bay. Such hunting is great sport.

Killing driven game by lying in wait for it to pass is the very poorest kind of sport that can be called legitimate. This is the way the deer is usually killed with hounds in the East. In the North the red fox is often killed in somewhat the same manner, being followed by a slow hound and shot at as he circles before the dog. Although this kind of fox-hunting is inferior to hunting on horseback, it nevertheless has its merits, as the man must walk and run well, shoot with some accuracy, and show considerable knowledge both of the country and of the habits of the game.

During the last score of years an entirely different type of dog from the fox-hound has firmly established itself in the field of American sport. This is the greyhound, whether the smooth-haired, or the rough-coated Scotch deer-hound. For half a century the army officers posted in the far West have occasionally had greyhounds with them, using the dogs to course jack-rabbit, coyote, and sometimes deer, antelope, and gray wolf. Many of them were devoted to this sport,—General Custer, for instance. I have myself hunted with many of the descendants of Custer's hounds. In the early '70's the ranchmen of the great plains themselves began to keep greyhounds for coursing (as indeed they had already been used for a considerable time in California, after the Pacific coast jack-rabbit), and the sport speedily assumed large proportions and a permanent form. Nowadays the ranchmen of the cattle country not only use their greyhounds after the jack-rabbit, but also after every other kind of game animal to be found there, the antelope and coyote being especial favorites. Many ranchmen soon grew to own fine packs, coursing being the sport of all sports for the plains. In Texas the wild turkey was frequently an object of the chase, and wherever the locality enabled deer to be followed in the open, as for instance in the Indian territory, and in many places in the neighborhood of the large plains rivers, the whitetail was a favorite quarry, the hunters striving to surprise it in the early morning when feeding on the prairie.

I have myself generally coursed with scratch packs, including perhaps a couple of greyhounds, a wire-haired deer-hound, and two or three long-legged mongrels. However, we generally had at least one very fast and savage dog—a strike dog—in each pack, and the others were of assistance in turning the game, sometimes in tiring it, and usually in helping to finish it at the worry. With such packs I have had many a wildly exciting ride over the great grassy plains lying near the Little Missouri and the Knife and Heart rivers. Usually our proceedings on such a hunt were perfectly simple. We started on horseback and when reaching favorable ground beat across it in a long scattered line of men and dogs. Anything that we put up, from a fox to a coyote or a prong-buck, was fair game, and was instantly followed at full speed. The animals we most frequently killed were jack-rabbits. They always gave good runs, though like other game they differed much individually in speed. The foxes did not run so well, and whether they were the little swift, or the big red prairie fox, they were speedily snapped up if the dogs had a fair showing. Once our dogs roused a blacktail buck close up out of a brush coulie where the ground was moderately smooth, and after a headlong chase of a mile they ran into him, threw him, and killed him before he could rise. (His stiff-legged bounds sent him along at a tremendous pace at first, but he seemed to tire rather easily.) On two or three occasions we killed whitetail deer, and several times antelope. Usually, however, the antelopes escaped. The bucks sometimes made a good fight, but generally they were seized while running, some dogs catching by the throat, others by the shoulders, and others again by the flank just in front of the hind-leg. Wherever the hold was obtained, if the dog made his spring cleverly, the buck was sure to come down with a crash, and if the other dogs were anywhere near he was probably killed before he could rise, although not infrequently the dogs themselves were more or less scratched in the contests. Some greyhounds, even of high breeding, proved absolutely useless from timidity, being afraid to take hold; but if they got accustomed to the chase, being worked with old dogs, and had any pluck at all, they proved singularly fearless. A big ninety-pound greyhound or Scotch deer-hound is a very formidable fighting dog; I saw one whip a big mastiff in short order, his wonderful agility being of more account than his adversary's superior weight.

The proper way to course, however, is to take the dogs out in a wagon and drive them thus until the game is seen. This prevents their being tired out. In my own hunting, most of the antelope aroused got away, the dogs being jaded when the chase began. But really fine greyhounds, accustomed to work together and to hunt this species of game, will usually render a good account of a prong-buck if two or three are slipped at once, fresh, and within a moderate distance.

Although most Westerners take more kindly to the rifle, now and then one is found who is a devotee of the hound. Such a one was an old Missourian, who may be called Mr. Cowley, whom I knew when he was living on a ranch in North Dakota, west of the Missouri. Mr. Cowley was a primitive person, of much nerve, which he showed not only in the hunting field but in the startling political conventions of the place and period. He was quite well off, but he was above the niceties of personal vanity. His hunting garb was that in which he also paid his rare formal calls—calls throughout which he always preserved the gravity of an Indian, though having a disconcerting way of suddenly tip-toeing across the room to some unfamiliar object, such as a peacock screen or a vase, feeling it gently with one forefinger, and returning with noiseless gait to his chair, unmoved, and making no comment. On the morning of a hunt he would always appear on a stout horse, clad in a long linen duster, a huge club in his hand, and his trousers working half-way up his legs. He hunted everything on all possible occasions; and he never under any circumstances shot an animal that the dogs could kill. Once when a skunk got into his house, with the direful stupidity of its perverse kind, he turned the hounds on it; a manifestation of sporting spirit which aroused the ire of even his long-suffering wife. As for his dogs, provided they could run and fight, he cared no more for their looks than for his own; he preferred the animal to be half greyhound, but the other half could be fox-hound, colley, or setter, it mattered nothing to him. They were a wicked, hard-biting crew for all that, and Mr. Cowley, in his flapping linen duster, was a first-class hunter and a good rider. He went almost mad with excitement in every chase. His pack usually hunted coyote, fox, jack-rabbit, and deer; and I have had more than one good run with it.

My own experience is too limited to allow me to pass judgment with certainty as to the relative speed of the different beasts of the chase, especially as there is so much individual variation. I consider the antelope the fleetest of all however; and in this opinion I am sustained by Col. Roger D. Williams, of Lexington, Kentucky, who, more than any other American, is entitled to speak upon coursing, and especially upon coursing large game. Col. Williams, like a true son of Kentucky, has bred his own thoroughbred horses and thoroughbred hounds for many years; and during a series of long hunting trips extending over nearly a quarter of a century he has tried his pack on almost every game animal to be found among the foot-hills of the Rockies and on the great plains. His dogs, both smooth-haired greyhounds and rough-coated deer-hounds, have been bred by him for generations with a special view to the chase of big game—not merely of hares; they are large animals, excelling not only in speed but in strength, endurance, and ferocious courage. The survivors of his old pack are literally seamed all over with the scars of innumerable battles. When several dogs were together they would stop a bull-elk, and fearlessly assail a bear or cougar. This pack scored many a triumph over blacktail, whitetail, and prong-buck. For a few hundred yards the deer were very fast; but in a run of any duration the antelope showed much greater speed, and gave the dogs far more trouble, although always overtaken in the end, if a good start had been obtained. Col. Williams is a firm believer in the power of the thoroughbred horse to outrun any animal that breathes, in a long chase; he has not infrequently run down deer, when they were jumped some miles from cover; and on two or three occasions he ran down uninjured antelope, but in each case only after a desperate ride of miles, which in one instance resulted in the death of his gallant horse.

This coursing on the prairie, especially after big game, is an exceedingly manly and attractive sport; the furious galloping, often over rough ground with an occasional deep washout or gully, the sight of the gallant hounds running and tackling, and the exhilaration of the pure air and wild surroundings, all combine to give it a peculiar zest. But there is really less need of bold and skilful horsemanship than in the otherwise less attractive and more artificial sport of fox-hunting, or riding to hounds, in a closed and long-settled country.

Those of us who are in part of southern blood have a hereditary right to be fond of cross-country riding; for our forefathers in Virginia, Georgia, or the Carolinas, have for six generations followed the fox with horse, horn, and hound. In the long-settled Northern States the sport has been less popular, though much more so now than formerly; yet it has always existed, here and there, and in certain places has been followed quite steadily.

In no place in the Northeast is hunting the wild red fox put on a more genuine and healthy basis than in the Genesee Valley, in central New York. There has always been fox-hunting in this valley, the farmers having good horses and being fond of sport; but it was conducted in a very irregular, primitive manner, until some twenty years ago Mr. Austin Wadsworth turned his attention to it. He has been master of fox-hounds ever since, and no pack in the country has yielded better sport than his, or has brought out harder riders among the men and stronger jumpers among the horses. Mr. Wadsworth began his hunting by picking up some of the various trencher-fed hounds of the neighborhood, the hunting of that period being managed on the principle of each farmer bringing to the meet the hound or hounds he happened to possess, and appearing on foot or horseback as his fancy dictated. Having gotten together some of these native hounds and started fox-hunting in localities where the ground was so open as to necessitate following the chase on horseback, Mr. Wadsworth imported a number of dogs from the best English kennels. He found these to be much faster than the American dogs and more accustomed to work together, but less enduring, and without such good noses. The American hounds were very obstinate and self-willed. Each wished to work out the trail for himself. But once found, they would puzzle it out, no matter how cold, and would follow it if necessary for a day and night. By a judicious crossing of the two Mr. Wadsworth finally got his present fine pack, which for its own particular work on its own ground would be hard to beat. The country ridden over is well wooded, and there are many foxes. The abundance of cover, however, naturally decreases the number of kills. It is a very fertile land, and there are few farming regions more beautiful, for it is prevented from being too tame in aspect by the number of bold hills and deep ravines. Most of the fences are high post-and-rails or "snake" fences, although there is an occasional stone wall, haha, or water-jump. The steepness of the ravines and the density of the timber make it necessary for a horse to be sure-footed and able to scramble anywhere, and the fences are so high that none but very good jumpers can possibly follow the pack. Most of the horses used are bred by the farmers in the neighborhood, or are from Canada, and they usually have thoroughbred or trotting-stock blood in them.

One of the pleasantest days I ever passed in the saddle was after Mr. Wadsworth's hounds. I was staying with him at the time, in company with my friend Senator Cabot Lodge, of Boston. The meet was about twelve miles distant from the house. It was only a small field of some twenty-five riders, but there was not one who did not mean going. I was mounted on a young horse, a powerful, big-boned black, a great jumper, though perhaps a trifle hot-headed. Lodge was on a fine bay, which could both run and jump. There were two or three other New Yorkers and Bostonians present, several men who had come up from Buffalo for the run, a couple of retired army officers, a number of farmers from the neighborhood; and finally several members of a noted local family of hard riders, who formed a class by themselves, all having taken naturally to every variety of horsemanship from earliest infancy.

It was a thoroughly democratic assemblage; every one was there for sport, and nobody cared an ounce how he or anybody else was dressed. Slouch hats, brown coats, corduroy breeches, and leggings, or boots, were the order of the day. We cast off in a thick wood. The dogs struck a trail almost immediately and were off with clamorous yelping, while the hunt thundered after them like a herd of buffaloes. We went headlong down the hill-side into and across a brook. Here the trail led straight up a sheer bank. Most of the riders struck off to the left for an easier place, which was unfortunate for them, for the eight of us who went straight up the side (one man's horse falling back with him) were the only ones who kept on terms with the hounds. Almost as soon as we got to the top of the bank we came out of the woods over a low but awkward rail fence, where one of our number, who was riding a very excitable sorrel colt, got a fall. This left but six, including the whip. There were two or three large fields with low fences; then we came to two high, stiff doubles, the first real jumping of the day, the fences being over four feet six, and so close together that the horses barely had a chance to gather themselves. We got over, however, crossed two or three stump-strewn fields, galloped through an open wood, picked our way across a marshy spot, jumped a small brook and two or three stiff fences, and then came a check. Soon the hounds recovered the line and swung off to the right, back across four or five fields, so as to enable the rest of the hunt, by making an angle, to come up. Then we jumped over a very high board fence into the main road, out of it again, and on over ploughed fields and grass land, separated by stiff snake fences. The run had been fast and the horses were beginning to tail. By the time we suddenly rattled down into a deep ravine and scrambled up the other side through thick timber there were but four of us left, Lodge and myself being two of the lucky ones. Beyond this ravine we came to one of the worst jumps of the day, a fence out of the wood, which was practicable only at one spot, where a kind of cattle trail led up to a panel. It was within an inch or two of five feet high. However, the horses, thoroughly trained to timber jumping and to rough and hard scrambling in awkward places, and by this time well quieted, took the bars without mistake, each one in turn trotting or cantering up to within a few yards, then making a couple of springs and bucking over with a great twist of the powerful haunches. I may explain that there was not a horse of the four that had not a record of five feet six inches in the ring. We now got into a perfect tangle of ravines, and the fox went to earth; and though we started one or two more in the course of the afternoon, we did not get another really first-class run.

At Geneseo the conditions for the enjoyment of this sport are exceptionally favorable. In the Northeast generally, although there are now a number of well-established hunts, at least nine out of ten runs are after a drag. Most of the hunts are in the neighborhood of great cities, and are mainly kept up by young men who come from them. A few of these are men of leisure, who can afford to devote their whole time to pleasure; but much the larger number are men in business, who work hard and are obliged to make their sports accommodate themselves to their more serious occupations. Once or twice a week they can get off for an afternoon's ride across country, and they then wish to be absolutely certain of having their run, and of having it at the appointed time; and the only way to insure this is to have a drag-hunt. It is not the lack of foxes that has made the sport so commonly take the form of riding to drag-hounds, but rather the fact that the majority of those who keep it up are hard-working business men who wish to make the most out of every moment of the little time they can spare from their regular occupations. A single ride across country, or an afternoon at polo, will yield more exercise, fun, and excitement than can be got out of a week's decorous and dull riding in the park, and many young fellows have waked up to this fact.

At one time I did a good deal of hunting with the Meadowbrook hounds, in the northern part of Long Island. There were plenty of foxes around us, both red and gray, but partly for the reasons given above, and partly because the covers were so large and so nearly continuous, they were not often hunted, although an effort was always made to have one run every week or so after a wild fox, in order to give a chance for the hounds to be properly worked and to prevent the runs from becoming a mere succession of steeple-chases. The sport was mainly drag-hunting, and was most exciting, as the fences were high and the pace fast. The Long Island country needs a pecu-

liar style of horse, the first requisite being that he shall be
a very good and high timber jumper. Quite a number of
crack English and Irish hunters have at different times
been imported, and some of them have turned out pretty
well; but when they first come over they are utterly unable
to cross our country, blundering badly at the high timber.
Few of them have done as well as the American horses. I
have hunted half a dozen times in England, with the
Pytchely, Essex, and North Warwickshire, and it seems to
me probable that English thoroughbreds, in a grass country, and over the peculiar kinds of obstacles they have on
the other side of the water, would gallop away from a field
of our Long Island horses; for they have speed and bottom, and are great weight carriers. But on our own
ground, where the cross-country riding is more like leaping a succession of five- and six-bar gates than anything
else, they do not as a rule, in spite of the enormous prices
paid for them, show themselves equal to the native stock.
The highest recorded jump, seven feet two inches, was
made by the American horse Filemaker, which I saw ridden in the very front by Mr. H. L. Herbert, in the hunt at
Sagamore Hill, about to be described.

When I was a member of the Meadowbrook hunt,
most of the meets were held within a dozen miles or so of
the kennels: at Farmingdale, Woodbury, Wheatly, Locust
Valley, Syosset, or near any one of twenty other queer,
quaint old Long Island hamlets. They were almost always
held in the afternoon, the business men who had come
down from the city jogging over behind the hounds to the
appointed place, where they were met by the men who had
ridden over direct from their country-houses. If the meet

was an important one, there might be a crowd of onlookers in every kind of trap, from a four-in-hand drag to a spider-wheeled buggy drawn by a pair of long-tailed trotters, the money value of which many times surpassed that of the two best hunters in the whole field. Now and then a breakfast would be given the hunt at some country-house, when the whole day was devoted to the sport; perhaps after wild foxes in the morning, with a drag in the afternoon.

After one meet, at Sagamore Hill, I had the curiosity to go on foot over the course we had taken, measuring the jumps; for it is very difficult to form a good estimate of a fence's height when in the field, and five feet of timber seems a much easier thing to take when sitting around the fire after dinner than it does when actually faced while the hounds are running. On the particular hunt in question we ran about ten miles, at a rattling pace, with only two checks, crossing somewhat more than sixty fences, most of them post-and-rails, stiff as steel, the others being of the kind called "Virginia" or snake, and not more than ten or a dozen in the whole lot under four feet in height. The highest measured five feet and half an inch, two others were four feet eleven, and nearly a third of the number averaged about four and a half. There were also several rather awkward doubles. When the hounds were cast off some forty riders were present, but the first fence was a savage one, and stopped all who did not mean genuine hard going. Twenty-six horses crossed it, one of them ridden by a lady. A mile or so farther on, before there had been a chance for much tailing, we came to a five-bar gate, out of a road—a jump of just four feet five inches from the take-off. Up to this, of course, we went one at a time, at a trot or hand-gallop, and twenty-five horses cleared it in succession without a single refusal and with but one mistake. Owing to the severity of the pace, combined with the average height of the timber (although no one fence was of phenomenally noteworthy proportions), a good many falls took place, resulting in an unusually large percentage of accidents. The master partly dislocated one knee, another man broke two ribs, and another—the present writer—broke his arm. However, almost all of us managed to struggle through to the end in time to see the death.

On this occasion I owed my broken arm to the fact that my horse, a solemn animal originally taken out of a buggy, though a very clever fencer, was too coarse to gallop alongside the blooded beasts against which he was pitted. But he was so easy in his gaits, and so quiet, being ridden with only a snaffle, that there was no difficulty in following to the end of the run. I had divers adventures on this horse. Once I tried a pair of so-called "safety" stirrups, which speedily fell out, and I had to ride through the run without any, at the cost of several tumbles. Much the best hunter I ever owned was a sorrel horse named Sagamore. He was from Geneseo, was fast, a remarkably good jumper, of great endurance, as quick on his feet as a cat, and with a dauntless heart. He never gave me a fall, and generally enabled me to see all the run.

It would be very unfair to think the sport especially dangerous on account of the occasional accidents that happen. A man who is fond of riding, but who sets a good deal of value, either for the sake of himself, his family, or his business, upon his neck and limbs, can hunt with much safety if he gets a quiet horse, a safe fencer, and does not try to stay in the front rank. Most accidents occur to men on green or wild horses, or else to those who keep in front only at the expense of pumping their mounts; and a fall with a done-out beast is always peculiarly disagreeable. Most falls, however, do no harm whatever to either horse or rider, and after they have picked themselves up and shaken themselves, the couple ought to be able to go on just as well as ever. Of course a man who wishes to keep in the first flight must expect to face a certain number of tumbles; but even he will probably not be hurt at all, and he can avoid many a mishap by easing up his horse whenever he can—that is, by always taking a gap when possible, going at the lowest panel of every fence, and not calling on his animal for all there is in him unless it cannot possibly be avoided. It must be remembered that hard riding is a very different thing from good riding; though a good rider to hounds must also at times ride hard.

Cross-country riding in the rough is not a difficult thing to learn; always provided the would-be learner is gifted with or has acquired a fairly stout heart, for a constitutionally timid person is out of place in the hunting field. A really finished cross-country rider, a man who combines hand and seat, heart and head, is of course rare; the standard is too high for most of us to hope to reach. But it is comparatively easy to acquire a light hand and a capacity to sit fairly well down in the saddle; and when a man has once got these, he will find no especial difficulty in following the hounds on a trained hunter.

Fox-hunting is a great sport, but it is as foolish to make a fetish of it as it is to decry it. The fox is hunted merely because there is no larger game to follow. As long as wolves, deer, or antelope remain in the land, and in a country where hounds and horsemen can work, no one would think of following the fox. It is pursued because the bigger beasts of the chase have been killed out. In England it has reached its present prominence only within two centuries; nobody followed the fox while the stag and boar were common. At the present day, on Exmoor, where the wild stag is still found, its chase ranks ahead of that of the fox. It is not really the hunting proper which is the point in fox-hunting. It is the horsemanship, the galloping and jumping, and the being out in the open air. Very naturally, however, men who have passed their lives as fox-hunters grow to regard the chase and the object of it alike with superstitious veneration. They attribute almost mythical characters to the animal. I know some of my good Virginian friends, for instance, who seriously believe that the Virginia red fox is a beast quite unparalleled for speed and endurance no less than for cunning. This is of course a mistake. Compared with a wolf, an antelope, or even a deer, the fox's speed and endurance do not stand very high. A good pack of hounds starting him close would speedily run into him in the open. The reason that the hunts last so long in some cases is because of the nature of the ground which favors the fox at the expense of the dogs, because of his having the advantage in the start, and because of his cunning in turning to account everything which will tell in his favor and against his pursuers. In the same way I know plenty of English friends who speak with bated breath of fox-hunting but look down upon riding to drag-hounds. Of course there is a difference in the two sports, and the fun of actually hunting the wild beast in the one case more than compensates for the fact that in the other the riding is apt to be harder and the jumping higher; but both sports are really artificial, and in their essentials alike. To any man who has hunted big game in a wild country the stress laid on the differences between them seems a little absurd, in fact cockney. It is of course nothing against either that it is artificial; so are all sports in long-civilized countries, from lacrosse to ice yachting.

It is amusing to see how natural it is for each man to glorify the sport to which he has been accustomed at the expense of any other. The old-school French sportsman, for instance, who followed the boar, stag, and hare with his hounds, always looked down upon the chase of the fox; whereas the average Englishman not only asserts but seriously believes that no other kind of chase can compare with it, although in actual fact the very points in which the Englishman is superior to the continental sportsman— that is, in hard and straight riding and jumping—are those which drag-hunting tends to develop rather more than fox-hunting proper. In the mere hunting itself the continental sportsman is often unsurpassed.

Once, beyond the Missouri, I met an expatriated German baron, an unfortunate who had failed utterly in the rough life of the frontier. He was living in a squalid little hut, almost unfurnished, but studded around with the diminutive horns of the European roebuck. These were the only treasures he had taken with him to remind him of his former life, and he was never tired of describing what fun it was to shoot roebucks when driven by the little crooked-legged *dachshunds*. There were plenty of deer

and antelope roundabout, yielding good sport to any rifleman, but this exile cared nothing for them; they were not
roebucks, and they could not be chased with his beloved
dachshunds. So, among my neighbors in the cattle country,
is a gentleman from France, a very successful ranchman,
and a thoroughly good fellow; he cares nothing for hunting big game, and will not go after it, but is devoted to
shooting cotton-tails in the snow, this being a pastime
having much resemblance to one of the recognized sports
of his own land.

However, our own people afford precisely similar instances. I have met plenty of men accustomed to killing
wild turkeys and deer with small-bore rifles in the southern forests who, when they got on the plains and in the
Rockies, were absolutely helpless. They not only failed to
become proficient in the art of killing big game at long
ranges with the large-bore rifle, at the cost of fatiguing
tramps, but they had a positive distaste for the sport and
would never allow that it equalled their own stealthy hunts
in eastern forests. So I know plenty of men, experts with
the shotgun, who honestly prefer shooting quail in the
East over well-trained setters or pointers, to the hardier,
manlier sports of the wilderness.

As it is with hunting, so it is with riding. The cowboy's
scorn of every method of riding save his own is as profound and as ignorant as is that of the school rider, jockey,
or fox-hunter. The truth is that each of these is best in his
own sphere and is at a disadvantage when made to do the
work of any of the others. For all-around riding and
horsemanship, I think the West Point graduate is somewhat ahead of any of them. Taken as a class, however, and

compared with other classes as numerous, and not with a few exceptional individuals, the cowboy, like the Rocky Mountain stage-driver, has no superiors anywhere for his own work; and they are fine fellows, these iron-nerved reinsmen and rough-riders.

When Buffalo Bill took his cowboys to Europe they made a practise in England, France, Germany, and Italy of offering to break and ride, in their own fashion, any horse given them. They were frequently given spoiled animals from the cavalry services in the different countries through which they passed, animals with which the trained horse-breakers of the European armies could do nothing; and yet in almost all cases the cowpunchers and bronco-busters with Buffalo Bill mastered these beasts as readily as they did their own western horses. At their own work of mastering and riding rough horses they could not be matched by their more civilized rivals; but I have great doubts whether they in turn would not have been beaten if they had essayed kinds of horsemanship utterly alien to their past experience, such as riding mettled thorough-breds in a steeple-chase, or the like. Other things being equal (which, however, they generally are not), a bad, big horse fed on oats offers a rather more difficult problem than a bad little horse fed on grass. After Buffalo Bill's men had returned, I occasionally heard it said that they had tried cross-country riding in England, and had shown themselves pre-eminently skilful thereat, doing better than the English fox-hunters, but this I take the liberty to disbelieve. I was in England at the time, hunted occasion-ally myself, and was with many of the men who were all the time riding in the most famous hunts; men, too, who were greatly impressed with the exhibitions of rough riding then being given by Buffalo Bill and his men, and who talked of them much; and yet I never, at the time, heard of an instance in which one of the cowboys rode to hounds with any marked success.* In the same way I have sometimes in New York or London heard of men who, it was alleged, had been out West and proved better riders than the bronco-busters themselves, just as I have heard of similar men who were able to go out hunting in the Rockies or on the plains and get more game than the western hunters; but in the course of a long experience in the West I have yet to see any of these men, whether from the eastern States or from Europe, actually show such superiority or perform such feats.

It would be interesting to compare the performances of the Australian stock-riders with those of our own cowpunchers, both in cow-work and in riding. The Australians have an entirely different kind of saddle, and the use of the rope is unknown among them. A couple of years ago the famous western rifle-shot, Carver, took some cowboys out to Australia, and I am informed that many of the Australians began themselves to practise with the rope after seeing the way it was used by the Americans. An Australian gentleman, Mr. A. J. Sage, of Melbourne, to whom I had written asking how the saddles and styles of riding compared, answered me as follows:

---

*It is, however, quite possible, now that Buffalo Bill's company has crossed the water several times, that a number of the cowboys have by practice become proficient in riding to hounds, and in steeple-chasing.

"With regard to saddles, here it is a moot question which is the better, yours or ours, for buck-jumpers. Carver's boys rode in their own saddles against our Victorians in theirs, all on Australian buckers, and honors seemed easy. Each was good in his own style, but the horses were not what I should call really good buckers, such as you might get on a back station, and so there was nothing in the show that could unseat the cowboys. It is only back in the bush that you can get a really good bucker. I have often seen one of them put both man and saddle off."

This last is a feat I have myself seen performed in the West. I suppose the amount of it is that both the American and the Australian rough riders are, for their own work, just as good as men possibly can be.

One spring I had to leave the East in the midst of the hunting season, to join a round-up in the cattle country of western Dakota, and it was curious to compare the totally different styles of riding of the cowboys and the cross-country men. A stock-saddle weighs thirty or forty pounds instead of ten or fifteen, and needs an utterly different seat from that adopted in the East. A cowboy rides with very long stirrups, sitting forked well down between his high pommel and cantle, and depends upon balance as well as on the grip of his thighs. In cutting out a steer from a herd, in breaking a vicious wild horse, in sitting a bucking bronco, in stopping a night stampede of many hundred maddened animals, or in the performance of a hundred other feats of reckless and daring horsemanship, the cowboy is absolutely unequalled; and when he has his own horse gear he sits his animal with the ease of a centaur. Yet he is quite helpless the first time he gets astride one of the small eastern saddles. One summer, while purchasing cattle in Iowa, one of my ranch foremen had to get on an ordinary saddle to ride out of town and see a bunch of steers. He is perhaps the best rider on the ranch, and will without hesitation mount and master beasts that I doubt if the boldest rider in one of our eastern hunts would care to tackle; yet his uneasiness on the new saddle was fairly comical. At first he did not dare to trot, and the least plunge of the horse bid fair to unseat him, nor did he begin to get accustomed to the situation until the very end of the journey. In fact, the two kinds of riding are so very different that a man only accustomed to one, feels almost as ill at ease when he first tries the other as if he had never sat on a horse's back before. It is rather funny to see a man who only knows one kind, and is conceited enough to think that that is really the only kind worth knowing, when first he is brought into contact with the other. Two or three times I have known men try to follow hounds on stock-saddles, which are about as ill-suited for the purpose as they well can be; while it is even more laughable to see some young fellow from the East or from England who thinks he knows entirely too much about horses to be taught by barbarians, attempt in his turn to do cow-work with his ordinary riding or hunting rig. It must be said, however, that in all probability cowboys would learn to ride well across country much sooner than the average cross-country rider would master the dashing and peculiar style of horsemanship shown by those whose life business is to guard the wandering herds of the great western plains.

Of course, riding to hounds, like all sports in long settled, thickly peopled countries, fails to develop in its followers some of the hardy qualities necessarily incident to the wilder pursuits of the mountain and the forest. While I was on the frontier I was struck by the fact that of the men from the eastern States or from England who had shown themselves at home to be good riders to hounds or had made their records as college athletes, a larger proportion failed in the life of the wilderness than was the case among those who had gained their experience in such rough pastimes as mountaineering in the high Alps, winter caribou-hunting in Canada, or deer-stalking—not deer-driving—in Scotland.

Nevertheless, of all sports possible in civilized countries, riding to hounds is perhaps the best if followed as it should be, for the sake of the strong excitement, with as much simplicity as possible, and not merely as a fashionable amusement. It tends to develop moral no less than physical qualities; the rider needs nerve and head; he must possess daring and resolution, as well as a good deal of bodily skill and a certain amount of wiry toughness and endurance.

CHAPTER XIX

Wolves and Wolf-Hounds

T he wolf is the archtype of ravin, the beast of waste and desolation. It is still found scattered thinly throughout all the wilder portions of the United States, but has everywhere retreated from the advance of civilization.

Wolves show an infinite variety in color, size, physical formation, and temper. Almost all the varieties intergrade with one another, however, so that it is very difficult to draw a hard and fast line between any two of them. Nevertheless, west of the Mississippi there are found two distinct types. One is the wolf proper, or big wolf, specifically akin to the wolves of the eastern States. The other is the little coyote, or prairie wolf. The coyote and the big wolf are found together in almost all the wilder districts from the Rio Grande to the valleys of the upper Missouri and the upper Columbia. Throughout this region there is always a sharp line of demarkation, especially in size, between the coyotes and the big wolves of any given district; but in certain districts the big wolves are very much larger than their brethren in other districts. In the upper Columbia country, for instance, they are very large; along the Rio Grande they are small. Dr. Hart Merriam informs me that, according to his experience, the coyote is largest in southern California. In many respects the coyote differs altogether in habits from its big relative. For one thing it is far more tolerant of man. In some localities coyotes are more numerous around settlements, and even in the close vicinity of large towns, than they are in the frowning and desolate fastnesses haunted by their grim elder brother.

Big wolves vary far more in color than the coyotes do. I have seen white, black, red, yellow, brown, gray, and grisled skins, and others representing every shade between, although usually each locality has its prevailing tint. The grisled, gray, and brown often have precisely the coat of the coyote. The difference in size among wolves of different localities, and even of the same locality, is quite remarkable, and so, curiously enough, is the difference in the size of the teeth, in some cases even when the body of one wolf is as big as that of another. I have seen wolves from Texas and New Mexico which were under-sized, slim animals with rather small tusks, in no way to be compared to the long-toothed giants of their race that dwell in the heavily timbered mountains of the Northwest and in the far North. As a rule, the teeth of the coyote are relatively smaller than those of the gray wolf.

Formerly wolves were incredibly abundant in certain parts of the country, notably on the great plains, where they were known as buffalo wolves, and were regular attendants on the great herds of the bison. Every traveller and hunter of the old days knew them as among the most common sights of the plains, and they followed the hunting parties and emigrant trains for the sake of the scraps left in camp. Now, however, there is no district in which they are really abundant. The wolfers, or professional wolf-hunters, who killed them by poisoning for the sake of their fur, and the cattle-men, who likewise killed them by poisoning because of their raids on the herds, have doubtless been the chief instruments in working their decimation on the plains. In the '70's, and even in the early '80's, many tens of thousands of wolves were killed by the wolfers in Montana and northern Wyoming and western Dakota. Nowadays the surviving wolves of the plains have learned caution; they no longer move abroad at midday, and still less do they dream of hanging on the footsteps of hunter and traveller. Instead of being one of the most common they have become one of the rarest sights of the plains. A hunter may wander far and wide through the plains for months nowadays and never see a wolf, though he will probably see many coyotes. However, the diminution goes on, not steadily but by fits and starts, and, moreover, the beasts now and then change their abodes, and appear in numbers in places where they have been scarce for a long period. In the present winter of 1892–'93 big wolves are more plentiful in the neighborhood of my ranch than they have been for ten years, and have worked some havoc among the cattle and young horses. The cowboys have been carrying on the usual vindictive campaign against them; a number have been poisoned, and a number of others have fallen victims to their greediness, the cowboys surprising them when gorged to repletion on the carcass of a colt or calf, and, in consequence, unable to run, so that they are easily ridden down, roped, and then dragged to death.

Yet even the slaughter wrought by man in certain localities does not seem adequate to explain the scarcity or extinction of wolves, throughout the country at large. In most places they are not followed any more eagerly than are the other large beasts of prey, and they are usually followed with less success. Of all animals the wolf is the shyest and hardest to slay. It is almost or quite as difficult to still-hunt as the cougar, and is far more difficult to kill with hounds, traps, or poison; yet it scarcely holds its own as well as the great cat, and it does not begin to hold its own as well as the bear, a beast certainly more readily killed, and one which produces fewer young at birth. Throughout the East the black bear is common in many localities from which the wolf has vanished completely. It at present exists in very scanty numbers in northern Maine and the Adirondacks; is almost or quite extinct in Pennsylvania; lingers here and there in the mountains from West Virginia to east Tennessee, and is found in Florida; but is everywhere less abundant than the bear. It is possible that this destruction of the wolves is due to some disease among them, perhaps to hydrophobia, a terrible malady from which it is known that they suffer greatly at times. Perhaps the bear is helped by its habit of hibernating, which frees it from most dangers during winter; but this cannot be the complete explanation, for in the South it does not hibernate, and yet holds its own as well as in the North. What makes it all the more curious that the American wolf should disappear sooner than the bear is that the reverse is the case with the allied species of Europe, where the bear is much sooner killed out of the land.

Indeed the differences of this sort between nearly related animals are literally inexplicable. Much of the difference in temperament between such closely allied species as the American and European bears and wolves is doubtless due to their surroundings and to the instincts they have inherited through many generations; but for much of the variation it is not possible to offer any explanation. In the same way there are certain physical differences for which it is very hard to account, as the same conditions seem to operate in directly reverse ways with different animals. No one can explain the process of natural selection which has resulted in the otter of America being larger than the otter of Europe, while the badger is smaller; in the mink being with us a much stouter animal than its Scandinavian and Russian kinsman, while the reverse is true of our sable or pine marten. No one can say why the European red deer should be a pigmy compared to its giant brother, the American wapiti; why the Old World elk should average smaller in size than the almost indistinguishable New World moose; and yet the bison of Lithuania and the Caucasus be on the whole larger and more formidable than its American cousin. In the same way no one can tell why under like conditions some game, such as the white goat and the spruce grouse, should be tamer than other closely allied species, like the mountain sheep and ruffed grouse. No one can say why on the whole the wolf of Scandinavia and northern Russia should be larger and more dangerous than the average wolf of the Rocky Mountains, while between the bears of the same regions the comparison must be exactly reversed.

The difference even among the wolves of different sections of our own country is very notable. It may be true that the species as a whole is rather weaker and less ferocious than the European wolf; but it is certainly not true of the wolves of certain localities. The great timber wolf of the central and northern chains of the Rockies and coast ranges is in every way a more formidable creature than the buffalo wolf of the plains, although they intergrade. The skins and skulls of the wolves of northwestern Montana and Washington which I have seen were quite as large and showed quite as stout claws and teeth as the skins and skulls of Russian and Scandinavian wolves, and I believe that these great timber wolves are in every way as formidable as their Old World kinsfolk. However, they live where they come in contact with a population of rifle-bearing frontier hunters, who are very different from European peasants or Asiatic tribesmen; and they have, even when most hungry, a wholesome dread of human beings. Yet I doubt if an unarmed man would be entirely safe should he, while alone in the forest in midwinter, encounter a fair-sized pack of ravenously hungry timber wolves.

A full-grown dog-wolf of the northern Rockies, in exceptional instances, reaches a height of thirty-two inches and a weight of 130 pounds; a big buffalo-wolf of the upper Missouri stands thirty or thirty-one inches at the shoulder and weighs about 110 pounds; a Texan wolf may not reach over eighty pounds. The bitch-wolves are smaller; and moreover there is often great variation even in the wolves of closely neighboring localities.

The wolves of the southern plains were not often formidable to large animals, even in the days when they most abounded. They rarely attacked the horses of the hunter, and indeed were but little regarded by these experienced animals. They were much more likely to gnaw off the lariat with which the horse was tied, than to try to molest the steed himself. They preferred to prey on young animals, or on the weak and disabled. They rarely molested a full-grown cow or steer, still less a full-grown buffalo, and, if they did attack such an animal, it was only when emboldened by numbers. In the plains of the upper Missouri and Saskatchewan the wolf was, and is, more dangerous, while in the northern Rockies his courage and ferocity attain their highest pitch. Near my own ranch the wolves have sometimes committed great depredations on cattle, but they seem to have queer freaks of slaughter. Usually they prey only upon calves and sickly animals; but in midwinter I have known one single-handed to attack and kill a well-grown steer or cow, disabling its quarry by rapid snaps at the hams or flanks. Only rarely have I known it to seize by the throat. Colts are likewise a favorite prey, but with us wolves rarely attack full-grown horses. They are sometimes very bold in their assaults, falling on the stock while immediately around the ranch houses. They even venture into the hamlet of Medora itself at night—as the coyotes sometimes do by day. In the spring of '92 we put on some eastern two-year-old steers; they arrived, and were turned loose from the stockyards, in a snowstorm, though it was in early May. Next morning we found that one had been seized, slain, and partially devoured by a big wolf at the very gate of the stockyard; probably the beast had seen it standing near the yard after nightfall, feeling miserable after its journey, in the storm and its unaccustomed surroundings, and had been emboldened to make the assault so near town by the evident helplessness of the prey.

The big timber wolves of the northern Rocky Mountains attack every four-footed beast to be found where they live. They are far from contenting themselves with hunting deer and snapping up the pigs and sheep of the farm. When the weather gets cold and food scarce they band together in small parties, perhaps of four or five individuals, and then assail anything, even a bear or a panther. A bull elk or bull moose, when on its guard, makes a most dangerous fight; but a single wolf will frequently master the cow of either animal, as well as domestic cattle and horses. In attacking such large game, however, the wolves like to act in concert, one springing at the animal's head, and attracting its attention, while the other hamstrings it. Nevertheless, one such big wolf will kill an ordinary horse. A man I knew, who was engaged in packing into the Cœur d'Alênes, once witnessed such a feat on the part of a wolf. He was taking his pack train down into a valley when he saw a horse grazing therein; it had been turned loose by another packing outfit, because it became exhausted. He lost sight of it as the trail went down a zigzag, and while it was thus out of sight he suddenly heard it utter the appalling scream, unlike and more dreadful than any other sound, which a horse only utters in extreme fright or agony. The scream was repeated, and as he came in sight again he saw that a great wolf had attacked the horse. The poor animal had been bitten terribly in its haunches and was cowering upon them, while the wolf stood and looked at it a few paces off. In a moment or two the horse partially recovered and made a desperate bound forward, starting at full gallop. Immediately the wolf was after it, overhauled it in three or four jumps, and then seized it by the hock, while its legs were extended, with such violence as to bring it completely back on its haunches. It again screamed piteously; and this time with a few savage snaps the wolf hamstrung and partially disembowelled it, and it fell over, having made no attempt to defend itself. I have heard of more than one incident of this kind. If a horse is a good fighter, however, as occasionally, though not often, happens, it is a most difficult prey for any wild beast, and some veteran horses have no fear of wolves whatsoever, well knowing that they can either strike them down with their fore-feet or repulse them by lashing out behind.

Wolves are cunning beasts and will often try to lull their prey into unsuspicion by playing round and cutting capers. I once saw a young deer and a wolf-cub together near the hut of the settler who had captured both. The wolf was just old enough to begin to feel vicious and blood-thirsty, and to show symptoms of attacking the deer. On the occasion in question he got loose and ran towards it, but it turned, and began to hit him with its fore-feet, seemingly in sport; whereat he rolled over on his back before it, and acted like a puppy at play. Soon it turned and walked off; immediately the wolf, with bristling hair, crawled after, and with a pounce seized it by the haunch, and would doubtless have murdered the bleating, struggling creature, had not the bystanders interfered.

Where there are no domestic animals, wolves feed on almost anything from a mouse to an elk. They are redoubted enemies of foxes. They are easily able to overtake them in fair chase, and kill numbers. If the fox can get into the underbrush, however, he can dodge around much faster than the wolf, and so escape pursuit. Sometimes one wolf will try to put a fox out of a cover while another waits outside to snap him up. Moreover, the wolf kills even closer kinsfolk than the fox. When pressed by hunger it will undoubtedly sometimes seize a coyote, tear it in pieces and devour it, although during most of the year the two animals live in perfect harmony. I once myself, while out in the deep snow, came across the remains of a coyote that had been killed in this manner. Wolves are also very fond of the flesh of dogs, and if they get a chance promptly kill and eat any dog they can master—and there are but few that they cannot. Nevertheless, I have been told of one instance in which a wolf struck up an extraordinary friendship with a strayed dog, and the two lived and hunted together for many months, being frequently seen by the settlers of the locality. This occurred near Thompson's Falls, Montana.

Usually wolves are found singly, in pairs, or in family parties, each having a large beat over which it regularly hunts, and also at times shifting its grounds and travelling immense distances in order to take up a temporary abode in some new locality—for they are great wanderers. It is only under stress of severe weather that they band together in packs. They prefer to creep on their prey and seize it by a sudden pounce, but, unlike the cougar, they also run it down in fair chase. Their slouching, tireless gallop enables them often to overtake deer, antelope, or other quarry; though under favorable circumstances, especially if near a lake, the latter frequently escape. Whether wolves run cunning I do not know; but I think they must, for coyotes certainly do. A coyote cannot run down a jack-rabbit; but two or three working together will often catch one.

Once I saw three start a jack, which ran right away from them; but they spread out, and followed. Pretty soon the jack turned slightly, and ran near one of the outside ones, saw it, became much frightened, and turned at right angles, so as soon to nearly run into the other outside one, which had kept straight on. This happened several times, and then the confused jack lay down under a sage-brush and was seized. So I have seen two coyotes attempting to get a newly dropped antelope kid. One would make a feint of attack, and lure the dam into a rush at him, while the other stole round to get at the kid. The dam, as always with these spirited little prong-bucks, made a good fight, and kept the assailants at bay; yet I think they would have succeeded in the end, had I not interfered. Coyotes are bold and cunning in raiding the settlers' barn-yards for lambs and hens; and they have an especial liking for tame cats. If there are coyotes in the neighborhood a cat which gets into the habit of wandering from home is surely lost.

Though, I have never known wolves to attack a man, yet in the wilder portion of the far Northwest I have heard them come around camp very close, growling so savagely as to make one almost reluctant to leave the camp fire and go out into the darkness unarmed. Once I was camped in the fall near a lonely little lake in the mountains, by the edge of quite a broad stream. Soon after nightfall three or four wolves came around camp and kept me awake by their sinister and dismal howling. Two or three times they came so close to the fire that I could hear them snap their jaws and growl, and at one time I positively thought that they intended to try to get into camp, so excited were they by the smell of the fresh meat. After a while they stopped howling; and then all was silent for an hour or so. I let the fire go out and was turning into bed when I suddenly heard some animal of considerable size come down to the stream nearly opposite me and begin to splash across, first wading, then swimming. It was pitch dark and I could not possibly see, but I felt sure it was a wolf. However after coming half-way over it changed its mind and swam back to the opposite bank; nor did I see or hear anything more of the night marauders.

Five or six times on the plains or on my ranch I have had shots at wolves, always obtained by accident and always, I regret to say, missed. Often the wolf when seen was running at full speed for cover, or else was so far off that though motionless my shots went wide of it. But once have I with my own rifle killed a wolf, and this was while travelling with a pack train in the mountains. We had been making considerable noise, and I never understood how an animal so wary permitted our near approach. He did, nevertheless, and just as we came to a little stream which we were to ford I saw him get on a dead log some thirty yards distant and walk slowly off with his eyes turned toward us. The first shot smashed his shoulders and brought him down.

The wolf is one of the animals which can only be hunted successfully with dogs. Most dogs however do not take at all kindly to the pursuit. A wolf is a terrible fighter. He will decimate a pack of hounds by rabid snaps with his giant jaws while suffering little damage himself; nor are the ordinary big dogs, supposed to be fighting dogs, able to tackle him without special training. I have known one wolf to kill a bulldog which had rushed at it with a single snap, while another which had entered the yard of a Montana ranch house slew in quick succession both of the large mastiffs by which it was assailed. The immense agility and ferocity of the wild beast, the terrible snap of his long-toothed jaws, and the admirable training in which he always is, give him a great advantage over fat, small-toothed, smooth-skinned dogs, even though they are nominally supposed to belong to the fighting classes. In the way that bench competitions are arranged nowadays this is but natural, as there is no temptation to produce a worthy class of fighting dog when the rewards are given upon technical points wholly unconnected with the dog's usefulness. A prize-winning mastiff or bulldog may be almost useless for the only purposes for which his kind is ever useful at all. A mastiff, if properly trained and of sufficient size, might possibly be able to meet a young or undersized Texan wolf; but I have never seen a dog of this variety which I would esteem a match single-handed for one of the huge timber wolves of western Montana. Even if the dog was the heavier of the two, his teeth and claws would be very much smaller and weaker and his hide less tough. Indeed I have known of but one dog which single-handed encountered and slew a wolf; this was the large vicious mongrel whose feats are recorded in my *Hunting Trips of a Ranchman.*

General Marcy of the United States Army informed me that he once chased a huge wolf which had gotten away with a small trap on its foot. It was, I believe, in Wisconsin, and he had twenty or thirty hounds with him, but they were entirely untrained to wolf-hunting, and proved unable to stop the crippled beast. Few of them would at-

tack it at all, and those that did went at it singly and with
a certain hesitation, and so each in turn was disabled by a
single terrible snap, and left bleeding on the snow. General Wade Hampton tells me that in the course of his fifty
years' hunting with horse and hound in Mississippi, he has
on several occasions tried his pack of fox-hounds (southern deer-hounds) after a wolf. He found that it was with
the greatest difficulty, however, that he could persuade
them to so much as follow the trail. Usually, as soon they
came across it, they would growl, bristle up, and then retreat with their tails between their legs. But one of his
dogs ever really tried to master a wolf by itself, and this
one paid for its temerity with its life; for while running a
wolf in a canebrake the beast turned and tore it to pieces.
Finally General Hampton succeeded in getting a number
of his hounds so they would at any rate follow the trail in
full cry, and thus drive the wolf out of the thicket, and give
a chance to the hunter to get a shot. In this way he killed
two or three.

The true way to kill wolves, however, is to hunt them
with greyhounds on the great plains. Nothing more exciting than this sport can possibly be imagined. It is not always necessary that the greyhounds should be of
absolutely pure blood. Prize-winning dogs of high pedi-
gree often prove useless for the purposes. If by careful
choice, however, a ranchman can get together a pack composed both of the smooth-haired greyhound and the
rough-haired Scotch deer-hound, he can have excellent
sport. The greyhounds sometimes do best if they have a
slight cross of bulldog in their veins; but this is not necessary. If once a greyhound can be fairly entered to the sport

and acquires confidence, then its wonderful agility, its sinewy strength and speed, and the terrible snap with which its jaws come together, render it a most formidable assailant. Nothing can possibly exceed the gallantry with which good greyhounds, when their blood is up, fling themselves on a wolf or any other foe. There does not exist, and there never has existed on the wide earth, a more perfect type of dauntless courage than such a hound. Not Cushing when he steered his little launch through the black night against the great ram Albemarle, not Custer dashing into the valley of the Rosebud to die with all his men, not Farragut himself lashed in the rigging of the Hartford as she forged past the forts to encounter her iron-clad foe, can stand as a more perfect type of dauntless valor.

Once I had the good fortune to witness a very exciting hunt of this character among the foot-hills of the northern Rockies. I was staying at the house of a friendly cow-man, whom I will call Judge Yancy Stump. Judge Yancy Stump was a Democrat who, as he phrased it, had fought for his Democracy; that is, he had been in the Confederate Army. He was at daggers drawn with his nearest neighbor, a cross-grained mountain farmer, who may be known as old man Prindle. Old man Prindle had been in the Union Army, and his Republicanism was of the blackest and most uncompromising type. There was one point, however, on which the two came together. They were exceedingly fond of hunting with hounds. The Judge had three or four track-hounds, and four of what he called swift-hounds, the latter including one pure-bred greyhound bitch of wonderful speed and temper, a dun-colored yelping animal which was a cross between a grey-hound and a fox-hound, and two others that were crosses between a greyhound and a wire-haired Scotch deer-hound. Old man Prindle's contribution to the pack consisted of two immense brindled mongrels of great strength and ferocious temper. They were unlike any dogs I have ever seen in this country. Their mother herself was a cross between a bull mastiff and a Newfoundland, while the father was described as being a big dog that belonged to a "Dutch Count." The "Dutch Count" was an outcast German noble, who had drifted to the West, and, after failing in the mines and failing in the cattle country, had died in a squalid log shanty while striving to eke out an existence as a hunter among the foot-hills. His dog, I presume, from the description given me, must have been a boar-hound or Ulm dog.

As I was very anxious to see a wolf-hunt the Judge volunteered to get one up, and asked old man Prindle to assist, for the sake of his two big fighting dogs; though the very names of the latter, General Grant and Old Abe, were gall and wormwood to the unreconstructed soul of the Judge. Still they were the only dogs anywhere around capable of tackling a savage timber wolf, and without their aid the Judge's own high-spirited animals ran a serious risk of injury, for they were altogether too game to let any beast escape without a struggle.

Luck favored us. Two wolves had killed a calf and dragged it into a long patch of dense brush where there was a little spring, the whole furnishing admirable cover for any wild beast. Early in the morning we started on horseback for this bit of cover, which was some three miles off. The party consisted of the Judge, old man Prindle, a cowboy, myself, and the dogs. The Judge and I carried our rifles and the cowboy his revolver, but old man Prindle had nothing but a heavy whip, for he swore, with many oaths, that no one should interfere with his big dogs, for by themselves they would surely "make the wolf feel sicker than a stuck hog." Our shaggy ponies racked along at a five-mile gait over the dewy prairie grass. The two big dogs trotted behind their master, grim and ferocious. The track-hounds were tied in couples, and the beautiful greyhounds loped lightly and gracefully alongside the horses. The country was fine. A mile to our right a small plains river wound in long curves between banks fringed with cottonwoods. Two or three miles to our left the foot-hills rose sheer and bare, with clumps of black pine and cedar in their gorges. We rode over gently rolling prairie, with here and there patches of brush at the bottoms of the slopes around the dry watercourses.

At last we reached a somewhat deeper valley, in which the wolves were harbored. Wolves lie close in the daytime and will not leave cover if they can help it; and as they had both food and water within we knew it was most unlikely that this couple would be gone. The valley was a couple of hundred yards broad and three or four times as long, filled with a growth of ash and dwarf elm and cedar, thorny underbrush choking the spaces between. Posting the cowboy, to whom he gave his rifle, with two greyhounds on one side of the upper end, and old man Prindle with two others on the opposite side, while I was left at the lower end to guard against the possibility of the wolves breaking back, the Judge himself rode into the thicket near me and loosened the track-hounds to let them find the wolves' trail. The big dogs also were uncoupled and allowed to go in with the hounds. Their power of scent was very poor, but they were sure to be guided aright by the baying of the hounds, and their presence would give confidence to the latter and make them ready to rout the wolves out of the thicket, which they would probably have shrunk from doing alone. There was a moment's pause of expectation after the Judge entered the thicket with his hounds. We sat motionless on our horses, eagerly looking through the keen fresh morning air. Then a clamorous baying from the thicket in which both the horseman and dogs had disappeared showed that the hounds had struck the trail of their quarry and were running on a hot scent. For a couple of minutes we could not be quite certain which way the game was going to break. The hounds ran zigzag through the brush, as we could tell by their baying, and once some yelping and a great row showed that they had come rather closer than they had expected upon at least one of the wolves.

In another minute, however, the latter found it too hot for them and bolted from the thicket. My first notice of this was seeing the cowboy, who was standing by the side of his horse, suddenly throw up his rifle and fire, while the greyhounds who had been springing high in the air, half maddened by the clamor in the thicket below, for a moment dashed off the wrong way, confused by the report of the gun. I rode for all I was worth to where the cowboy stood, and instantly caught a glimpse of two wolves, grisly-gray and brown, which having been turned by his shot had started straight over the hill across the plain toward the mountains three miles away. As soon as I saw them I saw also that the rearmost of the couple had been hit somewhere in the body and was lagging behind, the blood running from its flanks, while the two greyhounds were racing after it; and at the same moment the track-hounds and the big dogs burst out of the thicket, yelling savagely as they struck the bloody trail. The wolf was hard hit, and staggered as he ran. He did not have a hundred yards' start of the dogs, and in less than a minute one of the greyhounds ranged up and passed him with a savage snap that brought him to; and before he could recover the whole pack rushed at him. Weakened as he was he could make no effective fight against so many foes, and indeed had a chance for but one or two rapid snaps before he was thrown down and completely covered by the bodies of his enemies. Yet with one of these snaps he did damage, as a shrill yell told, and in a second an over-rash track-hound came out of the struggle with a deep gash across his shoulders. The worrying, growling, and snarling were terrific, but in a minute the heaving mass grew motionless and the dogs drew off, save one or two that still continued to worry the dead wolf as it lay stark and stiff with glazed eyes and rumpled fur.

No sooner were we satisfied that it was dead than the Judge, with cheers and oaths and crackings of his whip, urged the dogs after the other wolf. The two greyhounds that had been with old man Prindle had fortunately not been able to see the wolves when they first broke from the cover, and never saw the wounded wolf at all, starting off at full speed after the unwounded one the instant he topped the crest of the hill. He had taken advantage of a slight hollow and turned, and now the chase was crossing us half a mile away. With whip and spur we flew towards them, our two greyhounds stretching out in front and leaving us as if we were standing still, the track-hounds and big dogs running after them just ahead of the horses. Fortunately the wolf plunged for a moment into a little brushy hollow and again doubled back, and this gave us a chance to see the end of the chase from nearby. The two greyhounds which had first taken up the pursuit were then but a short distance behind. Nearer they crept until they were within ten yards, and then with a tremendous race the little bitch ran past him and inflicted a vicious bite in the big beast's ham. He whirled around like a top and his jaws clashed like those of a sprung bear-trap, but quick though he was she was quicker and just cleared his savage rush. In another moment he resumed his flight at full speed, a speed which only that of the greyhounds exceeded; but almost immediately the second greyhound ranged alongside, and though he was not able to bite, because the wolf kept running with its head turned around threatening him, yet by his feints he delayed the beast's flight so that in a moment or two the remaining couple of swift hounds arrived on the scene. For a moment the wolf and all four dogs galloped along in a bunch; then one of the greyhounds, watching his chance, pinned the beast cleverly by the hock and threw him completely over. The others jumped on it in an instant; but rising by main strength the wolf shook himself free, catching one dog by the ear and tearing it half off. Then he sat down on his haunches and the greyhounds ranged themselves around him some twenty yards off, forming a ring which forbade his retreat, though they themselves did not dare touch him. However the end was at hand. In another moment Old Abe and General Grant came running up at headlong speed and smashed into the wolf like a couple of battering-rams. He rose on his hind-legs like a wrestler as they came at him, the greyhounds also rising and bouncing up and down like rubber balls. I could just see the wolf and the first big dog locked together, as the second one made good his throat-hold. In another moment over all three tumbled, while the greyhounds and one or two of the track-hounds jumped in to take part in the killing. The big dogs more than occupied the wolf's attention and took all the punishing, while in a trice one of the greyhounds, having seized him by the hind-leg, stretched him out, and the others were biting his undefended belly. The snarling and yelling of the worry made a noise so fiendish that it was fairly bloodcurdling; then it gradually died down, and the second wolf lay limp on the plain, killed by the dogs unassisted. This wolf was rather heavier and decidedly taller than either of the big dogs, with more sinewy feet and longer fangs.

I have several times seen wolves run down and stopped by greyhounds after a break-neck gallop and a wildly exciting finish, but this was the only occasion on which I ever saw the dogs kill a big, full-grown he-wolf unaided. Nevertheless various friends of mine own packs that have performed the feat again and again. One pack, formerly kept at Fort Benton, until wolves in that neighborhood became scarce, had nearly seventy-five to its credit, most of them killed without any assistance from the hunter; killed moreover by the greyhounds alone,

there being no other dogs with the pack. These greyhounds were trained to the throat-hold, and did their own
killing in fine style; usually six or eight were slipped together. General Miles informs me that he once had great
fun in the Indian Territory hunting wolves with a pack of
greyhounds. They had with the pack a large stub-tailed
mongrel, of doubtful ancestry but most undoubted fighting capacity. When the wolf was started the greyhounds
were sure to overtake it in a mile or two; they would then
bring it to a halt and stand around it in a ring until the
fighting dog came up. The latter promptly tumbled on the
wolf, grabbing him anywhere, and often getting a terrific
wound himself at the same time. As soon as he had seized
the wolf and was rolling over with him in the grapple the
other dogs joined in the fray and dispatched the quarry
without much danger to themselves.

During the last decade many ranchmen in Colorado,
Wyoming, and Montana, have developed packs of greyhounds able to kill a wolf unassisted. Greyhounds trained
for this purpose always seize by the throat; and the light
dogs used for coursing jack-rabbits are not of much service, smooth or rough-haired greyhounds and deer-
hounds standing over thirty inches at the shoulder and
weighing over ninety pounds being the only ones that, together with speed, courage, and endurance, possess the
requisite power.

One of the most famous packs in the West was that of
the Sun River Hound Club, in Montana, started by the
stockmen of Sun River to get rid of the curse of wolves
which infested the neighborhood and worked very serious
damage to the herds and flocks. The pack was composed

of both greyhounds and deer-hounds, the best being from the kennels of Colonel Williams and of Mr. Van Hummel, of Denver; they were handled by an old plainsman and veteran wolf-hunter named Porter. In the season of '86 the astonishing number of 146 wolves were killed with these dogs. Ordinarily, as soon as the dogs seized a wolf, and threw or held it, Porter rushed in and stabbed it with his hunting-knife; one day, when out with six hounds, he thus killed no less than twelve out of the fifteen wolves started, though one of the greyhounds was killed, and all the others were cut and exhausted. But often the wolves were killed without his aid. The first time the two biggest hounds—deer-hounds or wire-haired greyhounds—were tried, when they had been at the ranch only three days, they performed such a feat. A large wolf had killed and partially eaten a sheep in a corral close to the ranch house, and Porter started on the trail, and followed him at a jog-trot nearly ten miles before the hounds sighted him. Running but a few rods, he turned viciously to bay, and the two great greyhounds struck him like stones hurled from a catapult, throwing him as they fastened on his throat; they held him down and strangled him before he could rise, two other hounds getting up just in time to help at the end of the worry.

Ordinarily, however, no two greyhounds or deer-hounds are a match for a gray wolf, but I have known of several instances in Colorado, Wyoming, and Montana, in which three strong veterans have killed one. The feat can only be performed by big dogs of the highest courage, who all act together, rush in at top speed, and seize by the throat; for the strength of the quarry is such that otherwise he will shake off the dogs, and then speedily kill them by rabid snaps with his terribly armed jaws. Where possible, half a dozen dogs should be slipped at once, to minimize the risk of injury to the pack; unless this is done, and unless the hunter helps the dogs in the worry, accidents will be frequent, and an occasional wolf will be found able to beat off, maiming or killing, a lesser number of assailants. Some hunters prefer the smooth greyhound, because of its great speed, and others the wire-coated animal, the rough deer-hound, because of its superior strength; both, if of the right kind, are dauntless fighters.

Colonel Williams' greyhounds have performed many notable feats in wolf-hunting. He spent the winter of 1875 in the Black Hills, which at that time did not contain a single settler, and fairly swarmed with game. Wolves were especially numerous and very bold and fierce, so that the dogs of the party were continually in jeopardy of their lives. On the other hand they took an ample vengeance, for many wolves were caught by the pack. Whenever possible, the horsemen kept close enough to take an immediate hand in the fight, if the quarry was a full-grown wolf, and thus save the dogs from the terrible punishment they were otherwise certain to receive. The dogs invariably throttled, rushing straight at the throat, but the wounds they themselves received were generally in the flank or belly; in several instances these wounds resulted fatally. Once or twice a wolf was caught, and held by two greyhounds until the horsemen came up; but it took at least five dogs to overcome and slay unaided a big timber wolf. Several times the feat was performed by a party of five, consisting of two greyhounds, one rough-coated deer-hound, and two cross-bloods; and once by a litter of seven young greyhounds, not yet come to their full strength.

Once or twice the so-called Russian wolf-hounds or silky coated greyhounds, the "borzois," have been imported and tried in wolf-hunting on the western plains; but hitherto they have not shown themselves equal, at either running or fighting, to the big American-bred greyhounds of the type produced by Colonel Williams and certain others of our best western breeders. Indeed I have never known any foreign greyhounds, whether Scotch, English, or from continental Europe, to perform such feats of courage, endurance, and strength, in chasing and killing dangerous game, as the homebred greyhounds of Colonel Williams.

CHAPTER XX

In Cowboy Land

O ut on the frontier, and generally among those who
spend their lives in, or on the borders of, the wilderness, life is reduced to its elemental conditions. The passions and emotions of these grim hunters of the
mountains, and wild rough-riders of the plains, are sim-
pler and stronger than those of people dwelling in more
complicated states of society. As soon as the communities
become settled and begin to grow with any rapidity, the
American instinct for law asserts itself; but in the earlier
stages each individual is obliged to be a law to himself and
to guard his rights with a strong hand. Of course the transition periods are full of incongruities. Men have not yet
adjusted their relations to morality and law with any nice-
ness. They hold strongly by certain rude virtues, and on
the other hand they quite fail to recognize even as shortcomings not a few traits that obtain scant mercy in older
communities. Many of the desperadoes, the man-killers,
and road-agents have good sides to their characters. Often
they are people who, in certain stages of civilization, do, or
have done, good work, but who, when these stages have
passed, find themselves surrounded by conditions which
accentuate their worst qualities, and make their best qualities useless. The average desperado, for instance, has, after

all, much the same standard of morals that the Norman nobles had in the days of the battle of Hastings, and, ethically and morally, he is decidedly in advance of the vikings, who were the ancestors of these same nobles— and to whom, by the way, he himself could doubtless trace a portion of his blood. If the transition from the wild lawlessness of life in the wilderness or on the border to a higher civilization were stretched out over a term of centuries, he and his descendants would doubtless accommodate themselves by degrees to the changing circumstances. But unfortunately in the far West the transition takes place with marvellous abruptness, and at an altogether unheard-of speed, and many a man's nature is unable to change with sufficient rapidity to allow him to harmonize with his environment. In consequence, unless he leaves for still wilder lands, he ends by getting hung instead of founding a family which would revere his name as that of a very capable, although not in all respects a conventionally moral, ancestor.

Most of the men with whom I was intimately thrown during my life on the frontier and in the wilderness were good fellows, hard-working, brave, resolute, and truthful. At times, of course, they were forced of necessity to do deeds which would seem startling to dwellers in cities and in old settled places; and though they waged a very stern and relentless warfare upon evil-doers whose misdeeds had immediate and tangible bad results, they showed a wide toleration of all save the most extreme classes of wrong, and were not given to inquiring too curiously into a strong man's past, or to criticising him over-harshly for a failure to discriminate in finer ethical questions. More-over, not a few of the men with whom I came in contact—with some of whom my relations were very close and friendly—had at different times led rather tough careers. This fact was accepted by them and by their companions as a fact, and nothing more. There were certain offences, such as rape, the robbery of a friend, or murder under cir-cumstances of cowardice and treachery, which were never forgiven; but the fact that when the country was wild a young fellow had gone on the road—that is, become a highwayman, or had been chief of a gang of desperadoes, horse-thieves, and cattle-killers, was scarcely held to weigh against him, being treated as a regrettable, but cer-tainly not shameful, trait of youth. He was regarded by his neighbors with the same kindly tolerance which re-spectable mediæval Scotch borderers doubtless extended to their wilder young men who would persist in raiding English cattle even in time of peace.

Of course if these men were asked outright as to their stories they would have refused to tell them or else would have lied about them; but when they had grown to regard a man as a friend and companion they would often re-count various incidents of their past lives with perfect frankness, and as they combined in a very curious degree both a decided sense of humor, and a failure to appreciate that there was anything especially remarkable in what they related, their tales were always entertaining.

Early one spring, now nearly ten years ago, I was out hunting some lost horses. They had strayed from the range three months before, and we had in a roundabout way heard that they were ranging near some broken country, where a man named Brophy had a ranch, nearly fifty miles from my own. When I started thither the weather was warm, but the second day out it grew colder and a heavy snowstorm came on. Fortunately I was able to reach the ranch all right, finding there one of the sons of a Little Beaver ranchman, and a young cowpuncher belonging to a Texas outfit, whom I knew very well. After putting my horse into the corral and throwing him down some hay I strode into the low hut, made partly of turf and partly of cottonwood logs, and speedily warmed myself before the fire. We had a good warm supper, of bread, potatoes, fried venison, and tea. My two companions grew very sociable and began to talk freely over their pipes. There were two bunks one above the other. I climbed into the upper, leaving my friends, who occupied the lower, sitting together on a bench recounting different incidents in the careers of themselves and their cronies during the winter that had just passed. Soon one of them asked the other what had become of a certain horse, a noted cutting pony, which I had myself noticed the preceding fall. The question aroused the other to the memory of a wrong which still rankled, and he began (I alter one or two of the proper names):

"Why, that was the pony that got stole. I had been workin' him on rough ground when I was out with the Three Bar outfit and he went tender forward, so I turned him loose by the Lazy B ranch, and when I come back to git him there was n't anybody at the ranch and I could n't find him. The sheep-man who lives about two miles west, under Red Clay butte, told me he seen a fellow in a wolf-skin coat, ridin' a pinto bronco, with white eyes, leadin' that pony of mine just two days before; and I hunted round till I hit his trail and then I followed to where I'd reckoned he was headin' for—the Short Pine Hills. When I got there a rancher told me he had seen the man pass on towards Cedartown, and sure enough when I struck Cedartown I found he lived there in a 'dobe house, just outside the town. There was a boom on the town and it looked pretty slick. There was two hotels and I went into the first, and I says, 'Where's the justice of the peace?' says I to the bartender.

" 'There ain't no justice of the peace,' says he, 'the justice of the peace got shot.'

" 'Well, where's the constable?' says I.

" 'Why, it was him that shot the justice of the peace!' says he; 'he's skipped the country with a bunch of horses.'

" 'Well, ain't there no officer of the law left in this town?' says I.

" 'Why, of course,' says he, 'there's a probate judge; he is over tendin' bar at the Last Chance Hotel.'

"So I went over to the Last Chance Hotel and I walked in there. 'Mornin',' says I.

" 'Mornin',' says he.

" 'You're the probate judge?' says I.

" 'That's what I am,' says he. 'What do you want?' says he.

" 'I want justice,' says I.

" 'What kind of justice do you want?' says he. 'What's it for?'

" 'It's for stealin' a horse,' says I.

" 'Then by God you'll git it,' says he. 'Who stole the horse?' says he.

" 'It is a man that lives in a 'dobe house, just outside the town there,' says I.

" 'Well, where do you come from yourself?' said he.

" 'From Medory,' said I.

"With that he lost interest and settled kind o' back, and says he, 'There wont no Cedartown jury hang a Cedartown man for stealin' a Medory man's horse,' said he.

" 'Well, what am I to do about my horse?' says I.

" 'Do?' says he; 'well, you know where the man lives, don't you?' says he; 'then sit up outside his house tonight and shoot him when he comes in,' says he, 'and skip out with the horse.'

" 'All right,' says I, 'that is what I'll do,' and I walked off.

"So I went off to his house and I laid down behind some sage-brushes to wait for him. He was not at home, but I could see his wife movin' about inside now and then, and I waited and waited, and it growed darker, and I begun to say to myself, 'Now here you are lyin' out to shoot this man when he comes home; and it's gettin' dark, and you don't know him, and if you do shoot the next man that comes into that house, like as not it won't be the fellow you 're after at all, but some perfectly innocent man a-comin' there after the other man's wife!'

"So I up and saddled the bronc' and lit out for home," concluded the narrator with the air of one justly proud of his own self-abnegating virtue.

The "town" where the judge above-mentioned dwelt

was one of those squalid, pretentiously named little clusters of makeshift dwellings which on the edge of the wild
country spring up with the rapid growth of mushrooms,
and are often no longer lived. In their earlier stages these
towns are frequently built entirely of canvas, and are subject to grotesque calamities. When the territory purchased
from the Sioux, in the Dakotas, a couple of years ago, was
thrown open to settlement, there was a furious inrush of
men on horseback and in wagons, and various ambitious
cities sprang up overnight. The new settlers were all under
the influence of that curious craze which causes every true
westerner to put unlimited faith in the unknown and un-
tried; many had left all they had in a far better farming
country, because they were true to their immemorial belief
that, wherever they were, their luck would be better if they
went somewhere else. They were always on the move, and
headed for the vague beyond. As miners see visions of all
the famous mines of history in each new camp, so these
would-be city founders saw future St. Pauls and Omahas
in every forlorn group of tents pitched by some muddy
stream in a desert of gumbo and sage-brush; and they
named both the towns and the canvas buildings in accor-
dance with their bright hopes for the morrow, rather than
with reference to the mean facts of the day. One of these
towns, which when twenty-four hours old boasted of six
saloons, a "court-house," and an "opera house," was overwhelmed by early disaster. The third day of its life a whirlwind came along and took off the opera house and half the
saloons; and the following evening lawless men nearly finished the work of the elements. The riders of a huge trail-
outfit from Texas, to their glad surprise discovered the

town and abandoned themselves to a night of roaring and lethal carousal. Next morning the city authorities were lamenting, with oaths of bitter rage, that "them hell-and-twenty Flying A cowpunchers had cut the court-house up into pants." It was true. The cowboys were in need of shaps, and with an admirable mixture of adventurousness, frugality, and ready adaptability to circumstances, had made substitutes therefor in the shape of canvas overalls, cut from the roof and walls of the shaky temple of justice.

One of my valued friends in the mountains, and one of the best hunters with whom I ever travelled, was a man who had a peculiarly light-hearted way of looking at conventional social obligations. Though in some ways a true backwoods Donatello, he was a man of much shrewdness and of great courage and resolution. Moreover, he possessed what only a few men do possess, the capacity to tell the truth. He saw facts as they were, and could tell them as they were, and he never told an untruth unless for very weighty reasons. He was pre-eminently a philosopher, of a happy, sceptical turn of mind. He had no prejudices. He never looked down, as so many hard characters do, upon a person possessing a different code of ethics. His attitude was one of broad, genial tolerance. He saw nothing out of the way in the fact that he had himself been a road-agent, a professional gambler, and a desperado at different stages of his career. On the other hand, he did not in the least hold it against any one that he had always acted within the law. At the time that I knew him he had become a man of some substance, and naturally a staunch upholder of the existing order of things. But while he never boasted of his past deeds, he never apologized for them, and evidently would have been quite as incapable of understanding that they needed an apology as he would have been incapable of being guilty of mere vulgar boastfulness. He did not often allude to his past career at all. When he did, he recited its incidents perfectly naturally and simply, as events, without any reference to or regard for their ethical significance. It was this quality which made him at times a specially pleasant companion, and always an agreeable narrator. The point of his story, or what seemed to him the point, was rarely that which struck me. It was the incidental sidelights the story threw upon his own nature and the somewhat lurid surroundings amid which he had moved.

On one occasion when we were out together we killed a bear, and after skinning it, took a bath in a lake. I noticed he had a scar on the side of his foot and asked him how he got it, to which he responded, with indifference:

"Oh, that? Why, a man shootin' at me to make me dance, that was all."

I expressed some curiosity in the matter, and he went on:

"Well, the way of it was this: It was when I was keeping a saloon in New Mexico, and there was a man there by the name of Fowler, and there was a reward on him of three thousand dollars——"

"Put on him by the State?"

"No, put on by his wife," said my friend; "and there was this——"

"Hold on," I interrupted; "put on by his wife did you say?"

"Yes, by his wife. Him and her had been keepin' a faro

bank, you see, and they quarrelled about it, so she just put a reward on him, and so——"

"Excuse me," I said "but do you mean to say that this reward was put on publicly?" to which my friend answered, with an air of gentlemanly boredom at being interrupted to gratify my thirst for irrelevant detail:

"Oh, no, not publicly. She just mentioned it to six or eight intimate personal friends."

"Go on," I responded, somewhat overcome by this instance of the primitive simplicity with which New Mexican matrimonial disputes were managed, and he continued:

"Well, two men come ridin' in to see me to borrow my guns. My guns was Colt's self-cockers. It was a new thing then, and they was the only ones in town. These come to me, and 'Simpson,' says they, 'we want to borrow your guns; we are goin' to kill Fowler.'

" 'Hold on for a moment,' said I, 'I am willin' to lend you them guns, but I ain't goin' to know what you 're goin' to do with them, no sir; but of course you can have the guns.' " Here my friend's face lightened pleasantly, and he continued:

"Well, you may easily believe I felt surprised next day when Fowler come ridin' in, and, says he, 'Simpson, here's your guns!' He had shot them two men! 'Well, Fowler,' says I, 'if I had known them men was after you, I'd never have let them have them guns nohow,' says I. That was n't true, for I did know it, but there was no cause to tell him that." I murmured my approval of such prudence, and Simpson continued, his eyes gradually brightening with the light of agreeable reminiscence:

"Well, they up and they took Fowler before the justice of the peace. The justice of the peace was a Turk."

"Now, Simpson, what do you mean by that?" I interrupted:

"Well, he come from Turkey," said Simpson, and I again sank back, wondering briefly what particular variety of Mediterranean outcast had drifted down to New Mexico to be made a justice of the peace. Simpson laughed and continued.

"That Fowler was a funny fellow. The Turk, he committed Fowler, and Fowler, he riz up and knocked him down and tromped all over him and made him let him go!"

"That was an appeal to a higher law," I observed. Simpson assented cheerily, and continued:

"Well, that Turk, he got nervous for fear Fowler he was goin' to kill him, and so he comes to me and offers me twenty-five dollars a day to protect him from Fowler; and I went to Fowler, and 'Fowler,' says I, 'that Turk 's offered me twenty-five dollars a day to protect him from you. Now, I ain't goin' to get shot for no twenty-five dollars a day, and if you are goin' to kill the Turk, just say so and go and do it; but if you ain't goin' to kill the Turk, there's no reason why I should n't earn that twenty-five dollars a day!' and Fowler, says he, 'I ain't goin' to touch the Turk; you just go right ahead and protect him.' "

So Simpson "protected" the Turk from the imaginary danger of Fowler, for about a week, at twenty-five dollars a day. Then one evening he happened to go out and met Fowler, "and," said he, "the moment I saw him I knowed he felt mean, for he begun to shoot at my feet," which cer-

tainly did seem to offer presumptive evidence of mean-
ness. Simpson continued:

"I did n't have no gun, so I just had to stand there and
take it until something distracted his attention, and I went
off home to get my gun and kill him, but I wanted to do
it perfectly lawful; so I went up to the mayor (he was
playin' poker with one of the judges), and says I to him,
'Mr. Mayor,' says I, 'I am goin' to shoot Fowler. And the
mayor he riz out of his chair and he took me by the hand,
and says he, 'Mr. Simpson, if you do I will stand by you';
and the judge, he says, 'I 'll go on your bond.' "

Fortified by this cordial approval of the executive and
judicial branches of the government, Mr. Simpson started
on his quest. Meanwhile, however, Fowler had cut up another prominent citizen, and they already had him in jail.
The friends of law and order feeling some little distrust as
to the permanency of their own zeal for righteousness,
thought it best to settle the matter before there was time
for cooling, and accordingly, headed by Simpson, the
mayor, the judge, the Turk, and other prominent citizens
of the town, they broke into the jail and hanged Fowler.
The point in the hanging which especially tickled my
friend's fancy, as he lingered over the reminiscence, was
one that was rather too ghastly to appeal to our own sense
of humor. In the Turk's mind there still rankled the memory of Fowler's very unprofessional conduct while figuring
before him as a criminal. Said Simpson, with a merry
twinkle of the eye: "Do you know that Turk, he was a right
funny fellow too after all. Just as the boys were going to
string up Fowler, says he, 'Boys, stop; one moment, gen-

tlemen,—Mr. Fowler, good-by,' and he blew a kiss to him!"

In the cow-country, and elsewhere on the wild borderland between savagery and civilization, men go quite as often by nicknames as by those to which they are lawfully entitled. Half the cowboys and hunters of my acquaintance are known by names entirely unconnected with those they inherited or received when they were christened. Occasionally some would-be desperado or make-believe mighty hunter tries to adopt what he deems a title suitable to his prowess; but such an effort is never attempted in really wild places, where it would be greeted with huge derision; for all of these names that are genuine are bestowed by outsiders, with small regard to the wishes of the person named. Ordinarily the name refers to some easily recognizable accident of origin, occupation, or aspect; as witness the innumerable Dutcheys, Frencheys, Kentucks, Texas Jacks, Bronco Bills, Bear Jones, Buckskins, Red Jims, and the like. Sometimes it is apparently meaningless; one of my cowpuncher friends is always called "Sliver" or "Splinter"—why, I have no idea. At other times some particular incident may give rise to the title: a clean-looking cowboy formerly in my employ was always known as "Muddy Bill," because he had once been bucked off his horse into a mud hole.

The grewsome genesis of one such name is given in the following letter which I have just received from an old hunting-friend in the Rockies, who took a kindly interest in a frontier cabin which the Boone and Crockett Club was putting up at the Chicago World's Fair.

"Feb 16th 1893; Der Sir: I see in the newspapers that your club the Daniel Boon and Davey Crockit you Intend to erect a fruntier Cabin at the world's Far at Chicago to represent the erley Pianears of our country I would like to see you maik a success I have all my life been a fruntiersman and feel interested in your undertaking and I hoap you wile get a good assortment of relicks I want to maik one suggestion to you that is in regard to geting a good man and a genuine Mauntanner to take charg of your haus at Chicago I want to recommend a man for you to get it is Liver-eating Johnson that is the naim he is generally called he is an olde mauntneer and large and fine looking and one of the Best Story Tellers in the country and Very Polight genteel to every one he meets I wil tel you how he got that naim Livereating in a hard Fight with the Black Feet Indians thay Faught all day Johnson and a few Whites Faught a large Body of Indians all day after the fight Johnson cam in contact with a wounded Indian and Johnson was aut of ammunition and thay faught it out with thar Knives and Johnson got away with the Indian and in the fight cut the livver out of the Indian and said to the Boys did thay want any Liver to eat that is the way he got the naim of Liver-eating Johnson

"Yours truly" etc., etc.

Frontiersmen are often as original in their theories of life as in their names; and the originality may take the form of wild savagery, of mere uncouthness, or of an odd combination of genuine humor with simple acceptance of facts as they are. On one occasion I expressed some surprise at learning that a certain Mrs. P. had suddenly married, though her husband was alive and in jail in a neighboring town; and received for answer: "Well, you see, old man Pete he skipped the country, and left his widow behind him, and so Bob Evans he up and married her!"—which was evidently felt to be a proceeding requiring no explanation whatever.

In the cow-country there is nothing more refreshing than the light-hearted belief entertained by the average man to the effect that any animal which by main force has been saddled and ridden, or harnessed and driven a couple of times, is a "broke horse." My present foreman is firmly wedded to this idea, as well as to its complement, the belief that any animals with hoofs, before any vehicle with wheels, can be driven across any country. One summer on reaching the ranch I was entertained with the usual accounts of the adventures and misadventures which had befallen my own men and my neighbors since I had been out last. In the course of the conversation my foreman remarked: "We had a great time out here about six weeks ago. There was a professor from Ann Arbor came out with his wife to see the Bad Lands, and they asked if we could rig them up a team, and we said we guessed we could, and Foley's boy and I did; but it ran away with him and broke his leg! He was here for a month. I guess he did n't mind it though." Of this I was less certain, forlorn little Medora being a "busted" cow-town, concerning which I once heard another of my men remark, in reply to an inquisitive commercial traveller: "How many people lives here? Eleven—counting the chickens—when they're all in town!"

My foreman continued: "By George, there was something that professor said afterwards that made me feel hot. I sent word up to him by Foley's boy that seein' as how it had come out we would n't charge him nothin' for the rig; and that professor he answered that he was glad we were showing him some sign of consideration, for he'd begun to believe he'd fallen into a den of sharks, and that we gave him a runaway team a purpose. That made me hot, calling that a runaway team. Why, there was one of them horses never *could* have run away before; it had n't never been druv but twice! and the other horse maybe had run away a few times, but there was lots of times he *had n't* run away. I esteemed that team full as liable not to run away as it was to run away," concluded my foreman, evidently deeming this as good a warranty of gentleness as the most exacting could require.

The definition of good behavior on the frontier is even more elastic for a saddle-horse than for a team. Last spring one of the Three-Seven riders, a magnificent horseman, was killed on the round-up near Belfield, his horse bucking and falling on him. "It was accounted a plumb gentle horse too," said my informant, "only it sometimes sulked and acted a little mean when it was cinched up behind." The unfortunate rider did not know of this failing of the "plumb gentle horse," and as soon as he was in the saddle it threw itself over sideways with a great bound, and he fell on his head, and never spoke again.

Such accidents are too common in the wild country to attract very much attention; the men accept them with grim quiet, as inevitable in such lives as theirs—lives that are harsh and narrow in their toil and their pleasure alike, and that are ever-bounded by an iron horizon of hazard and hardship. During the last year and a half three other men from the ranches in my immediate neighborhood have met their deaths in the course of their work. One, a trail boss of the OX, was drowned while swimming his herd across a swollen river. Another, one of the fancy ropers of the W Bar, was killed while roping cattle in a corral; his saddle turned, the rope twisted round him, he was pulled off, and was trampled to death by his own horse.

The fourth man, a cowpuncher named Hamilton, lost his life during the last week of October, 1891, in the first heavy snowstorm of the season. Yet he was a skilled plainsman, on ground he knew well, and just before straying himself, he successfully instructed two men who did not know the country how to get to camp. They were all three with the round-up, and were making a circle through the Bad Lands; the wagons had camped on the eastern edge of these Bad Lands, where they merge into the prairie, at the head of an old disused road, which led about due east from the Little Missouri. It was a gray, lowering day, and as darkness came on Hamilton's horse played out, and he told his two companions not to wait, as it had begun to snow, but to keep on towards the north, skirting some particularly rough buttes, and as soon as they struck the road to turn to the right and follow it out to the prairie, where they would find camp; he particularly warned them to keep a sharp look-out, so as not to pass over the dim trail unawares in the dusk and the storm. They followed his advice, and reached camp safely; and after they had left him nobody ever again saw him alive.

Evidently he himself, plodding northwards, passed over the road without seeing it in the gathering gloom; probably he struck it at some point where the ground was bad, and the dim trail in consequence disappeared entirely, as is the way with these prairie roads—making them landmarks to be used with caution. He must then have walked on and on, over rugged hills and across deep ravines, until his horse came to a standstill; he took off its saddle and picketed it to a dwarfed ash. Its frozen carcass was found, with the saddle near by, two months later. He now evidently recognized some landmark, and realized that he had passed the road, and was far to the north of the round-up wagons; but he was a resolute, self-confident man, and he determined to strike out for a line camp, which he knew lay about due east of him, two or three miles out on the prairie, on one of the head branches of Knife River. Night must have fallen by this time, and he missed the camp, probably passing it within less than a mile; but he did pass it, and with it all hopes of life, and walked wearily on to his doom, through the thick darkness and the driving snow. At last his strength failed, and he lay down in the tall grass of a little hollow. Five months later, in the early spring, the riders from the line camp found his body, resting face downwards, with the forehead on the folded arms.

Accidents of less degree are common. Men break their collar-bones, arms, or legs by falling when riding at speed over dangerous ground, when cutting cattle or trying to control a stampeded herd, or by being thrown or rolled on by bucking or rearing horses; or their horses, and on rare occasions even they themselves, are gored by fighting steers. Death by storm or in flood, death in striving to master a wild and vicious horse, or in handling maddened cattle, and too often death in brutal conflict with one of his own fellows—any one of these is the not unnatural end of the life of the dweller on the plains or in the mountains.

But a few years ago other risks had to be run from savage beasts, and from the Indians. Since I have been ranching on the Little Missouri, two men have been killed by bears in the neighborhood of my range; and in the early years of my residence there, several men living or travelling in the country were slain by small war-parties of young braves. All the old-time trappers and hunters could tell stirring tales of their encounters with Indians.

My friend, Tazewell Woody, was among the chief actors in one of the most noteworthy adventures of this kind. He was a very quiet man, and it was exceedingly difficult to get him to talk over any of his past experiences; but one day, when he was in high good-humor with me for having made three consecutive straight shots at elk, he became quite communicative, and I was able to get him to tell me one story which I had long wished to hear from his lips, having already heard of it through one of the other survivors of the incident. When he found that I already knew a good deal old Woody told me the rest.

It was in the spring of 1875, and Woody and two friends were trapping on the Yellowstone. The Sioux were very bad at the time and had killed many prospectors, hunters, cowboys, and settlers; the whites retaliated whenever they got a chance, but, as always in Indian warfare, the sly, lurking, bloodthirsty savages inflicted much more loss than they suffered.

The three men, having a dozen horses with them, were camped by the river-side in a triangular patch of brush, shaped a good deal like a common flat-iron. On reaching camp they started to put out their traps; and when he came back in the evening Woody informed his companions that he had seen a great deal of Indian sign, and that he believed there were Sioux in the neighborhood. His companions both laughed at him, assuring him that they were not Sioux at all but friendly Crows, and that they would be in camp next morning; "and sure enough," said Woody, meditatively, "they *were* in camp next morning." By dawn one of the men went down the river to look at some of the traps, while Woody started out to where the horses were, the third man remaining in camp to get breakfast. Suddenly two shots were heard down the river, and in another moment a mounted Indian swept towards the horses. Woody fired, but missed him, and he drove off five while Woody, running forward, succeeded in herding the other seven into camp. Hardly had this been accomplished before the man who had gone down the river appeared, out of breath with his desperate run, having been surprised by several Indians, and just succeeding in making his escape by dodging from bush to bush, threatening his pursuers with his rifle.

These proved to be but the forerunners of a great war party, for when the sun rose the hills around seemed black with Sioux. Had they chosen to dash right in on the camp, running the risk of losing several of their men in the charge, they could of course have eaten up the three hunters in a minute; but such a charge is rarely practised by Indians, who, although they are admirable in defensive

warfare, and even in certain kinds of offensive movements, and although from their skill in hiding they usually
inflict much more loss than they suffer when matched
against white troops, are yet very reluctant to make any
movement where the advantage gained must be offset by
considerable loss of life. The three men thought they were
surely doomed, but being veteran frontiersmen and long
inured to every kind of hardship and danger, they set to
work with cool resolution to make as effective a defence as
possible, to beat off their antagonists if they might, and if
this proved impracticable, to sell their lives as dearly as
they could. Having tethered the horses in a slight hollow,
the only one which offered any protection, each man crept
out to a point of the triangular brush patch and lay down
to await events.

In a very short while the Indians began closing in on
them, taking every advantage of cover, and then, both
from their side of the river and from the opposite bank,
opened a perfect fusillade, wasting their cartridges with a
recklessness which Indians are apt to show when excited.
The hunters could hear the hoarse commands of the
chiefs, the war-whoops, and the taunts in broken English
which some of the warriors hurled at them. Very soon all
of their horses were killed, and the brush was fairly riddled
by the incessant volleys; but the three men themselves,
lying flat on the ground and well concealed, were not
harmed. The more daring young warriors then began to
creep toward the hunters, going stealthily from one piece
of cover to the next; and now the whites in turn opened
fire. They did not shoot recklessly, as did their foes, but
coolly and quietly, endeavoring to make each shot tell.

Said Woody: "I only fired seven times all day; I reckoned on getting meat every time I pulled trigger." They had an immense advantage over their enemies, in that whereas they lay still and entirely concealed, the Indians of course had to move from cover to cover in order to approach, and so had at times to expose themselves. When the whites fired at all they fired at a man, whether moving or motionless, whom they could clearly see, while the Indians could only shoot at the smoke, which imperfectly marked the position of their unseen foes. In consequence the assailants speedily found that it was a task of hopeless danger to try in such a manner to close in on three plains veterans, men of iron nerve and skilled in the use of the rifle. Yet some of the more daring crept up very close to the patch of brush, and one actually got inside it, and was killed among the bedding that lay by the smouldering camp-fire. The wounded and such of the dead as did not lie in too exposed positions were promptly taken away by their comrades; but seven bodies fell into the hands of the three hunters. I asked Woody how many he himself had killed. He said he could only be sure of two that he got; one he shot in the head as he peeped over a bush, and the other he shot through the smoke as he attempted to rush in. "My, how that Indian did yell," said Woody, retrospectively; "*he* was no great of a Stoic." After two or three hours of this deadly skirmishing, which resulted in nothing more serious to the whites than in two of them being slightly wounded, the Sioux became disheartened by the loss they were suffering and withdrew, confining themselves thereafter to a long range and harmless fusillade. When it was dark the three men crept out to the river bed, and taking advantage of the pitchy night broke through the circle of their foes; they managed to reach the settlements without further molestation, having lost everything except their rifles.

For many years one of the most important of the wilderness dwellers was the West Point officer, and no man has played a greater part than he in the wild warfare which opened the regions beyond the Mississippi to white settlement. Since 1879, there has been but little regular Indian fighting in the North, though there have been one or two very tedious and wearisome campaigns waged against the Apaches in the South. Even in the North, however, there have been occasional uprisings which had to be quelled by the regular troops.

After my elk hunt in September, 1891, I came out through the Yellowstone Park, as I have elsewhere related, riding in company with a surveyor of the Burlington and Quincy railroad, who was just coming in from his summer's work. It was the first of October. There had been a heavy snow-storm and the snow was still falling. Riding a stout pony each, and leading another packed with our bedding, etc., we broke our way from the upper to the middle geyser basin. Here we found a troop of the 1st Cavalry camped, under the command of old friends of mine, Captain Frank Edwards and Lieutenant (now Captain) John Pitcher. They gave us hay for our horses and insisted upon our stopping to lunch, with the ready hospitality always shown by army officers. After lunch we began exchanging stories. My travelling companion, the surveyor, had that spring performed a feat of note, going through one of the canyons of the Big Horn for the first time. He went with an old mining inspector, the two of them dragging a cottonwood sledge over the ice. The walls of the canyon are so sheer and the water so rough that it can be descended only when the stream is frozen. However, after six days' labor and hardship the descent was accomplished; and the surveyor, in concluding, described his experience in going through the Crow Reservation.

This turned the conversation upon Indians, and it appeared that both of our hosts had been actors in Indian scrapes which had attracted my attention at the time they occurred, as they took place among tribes that I knew and in a country which I had sometime visited, either when hunting or when purchasing horses for the ranch. The first, which occurred to Captain Edwards, happened late in 1886, at the time when the Crow Medicine Chief, Sword-Bearer, announced himself as the Messiah of the Indian race, during one of the usual epidemics of ghost dancing. Sword-Bearer derived his name from always wearing a medicine sword—that is, a sabre painted red. He claimed to possess magic power, and, thanks to the performance of many dextrous feats of juggling, and the lucky outcome of certain prophecies, he deeply stirred the Indians, arousing the young warriors in particular to the highest pitch of excitement. They became sullen, began to paint, and armed themselves; and the agent and the settlers near by grew so apprehensive that the troops were ordered to go to the reservation. A body of cavalry, including Captain Edwards' troop, was accordingly marched thither, and found the Crow warriors, mounted on their war ponies and dressed in their striking battle-garb, waiting on a hill.

The position of troops at the beginning of such an affair is always peculiarly difficult. The settlers round-about are sure to clamor bitterly against them, no matter what they do, on the ground that they are not thorough enough and are showing favor to the savages, while on the other hand, even if they fight purely in self-defence, a large number of worthy but weak-minded sentimentalists in the East are sure to shriek about their having brutally attacked the Indians. The war authorities always insist that they must not fire the first shot under any circumstances, and such were the orders at this time. The Crows on the hill-top showed a sullen and threatening front, and the troops advanced slowly towards them and then halted for a parley. Meanwhile a mass of black thunder-clouds gathering on the horizon threatened one of those cloudbursts of extreme severity and suddenness so characteristic of the plains country. While still trying to make arrangements for a parley, a horseman started out of the Crow ranks and galloped headlong down towards the troops. It was the medicine chief, Sword-Bearer. He was painted and in his battle-dress, wearing his war-bonnet of floating, trailing eagle feathers, while the plumes of the same bird were braided in the mane and tail of his fiery little horse. On he came at a gallop almost up to the troops and then began to circle around them, calling and singing and throwing his crimson sword into the air, catching it by the hilt as it fell. Twice he rode completely around the soldiers, who stood in uncertainty, not knowing what to make of his performance, and expressly forbidden to shoot at him.

Then paying no further heed to them he rode back towards the Crows. It appears that he had told them that he would ride twice around the hostile force, and by his incantations would call down rain from heaven, which would make the hearts of the white men like water, so that they should go back to their homes. Sure enough, while the arrangements for the parley were still going forward, down came the cloudburst, drenching the command and making the ground on the hills in front nearly impassable; and before it dried a courier arrived with orders to the troops to go back to camp.

This fulfilment of Sword-Bearer's prophecy of course raised his reputation to the zenith and the young men of the tribe prepared for war, while the older chiefs, who more fully realized the power of the whites, still hung back. When the troops next appeared they came upon the entire Crow force, the women and children with their tepees being off to one side beyond a little stream while almost all the warriors of the tribe were gathered in front. Sword-Bearer started to repeat his former ride, to the intense irritation of the soldiers. Luckily, however, this time some of his young men could not be restrained. They too began to ride near the troops, and one of them was unable to refrain from firing on Captain Edwards' troop, which was in the van. This gave the soldiers their chance. They instantly responded with a volley, and Captain Edwards' troop charged. The fight lasted but a minute or two, for Sword-Bearer was struck by a bullet and fell, and as he had boasted himself invulnerable, and promised that his warriors should be invulnerable also if they would follow him, the hearts of the latter became as water and they

broke in every direction. One of the amusing, though irritating, incidents of the affair was to see the plumed and
painted warriors race headlong for the camp, plunge into
the stream, wash off their war paint, and remove their
feathers; in another moment they would be stolidly sitting
on the ground, with their blankets over their shoulders,
rising to greet the pursuing cavalry with unmoved composure and calm assurances that they had always been
friendly and had much disapproved the conduct of the
young bucks who had just been scattered on the field outside. It was much to the credit of the discipline of the army
that no bloodshed followed the fight proper. The loss to
the whites was small.

The other incident, related by Lieutenant Pitcher,
took place in 1890, near Tongue River, in northern
Wyoming. The command with which he was serving was
camped near the Cheyenne Reservation. One day two
young Cheyenne bucks, met one of the government
herders, and promptly killed him—in a sudden fit, half of
ungovernable blood lust, half of mere ferocious light-
heartedness. They then dragged his body into the brush
and left it. The disappearance of the herder of course attracted attention, and a search was organized by the cavalry. At first the Indians stoutly denied all knowledge of
the missing man; but when it became evident that the
search party would shortly find him, two or three of the
chiefs joined them, and piloted them to where the body
lay; and acknowledged that he had been murdered by two
of their band, though at first they refused to give their
names. The commander of the post demanded that the
murderers be given up. The chiefs said that they were very

sorry, that this could not be done, but that they were willing to pay over any reasonable number of ponies to make
amends for the death. This offer was of course promptly
refused, and the commander notified them that if they did
not surrender the murderers by a certain time he would
hold the whole tribe responsible and would promptly
move out and attack them. Upon this the chiefs, after
holding full counsel with the tribe, told the commander
that they had no power to surrender the murderers, but
that the latter had said that sooner than see their tribe involved in a hopeless struggle they would of their own accord come in and meet the troops anywhere the latter
chose to appoint, and die fighting. To this the commander
responded: "All right; let them come into the agency in
half an hour." The chiefs acquiesced, and withdrew.

Immediately the Indians sent mounted messengers at
speed from camp to camp, summoning all their people to
witness the act of fierce self-doom; and soon the entire
tribe of Cheyennes, many of them having their faces
blackened in token of mourning, moved down and took
up a position on the hill-side close to the agency. At the
appointed hour both young men appeared in their handsome war dress, galloped to the top of the hill near the encampment, and deliberately opened fire on the troops.
The latter merely fired a few shots to keep the young desperadoes off, while Lieutenant Pitcher and a score of cavalrymen left camp to make a circle and drive them in; they
did not wish to hurt them, but to capture and give them
over to the Indians, so that the latter might be forced
themselves to inflict the punishment. However, they were
unable to accomplish their purpose; one of the young

braves went straight at them, firing his rifle and wounding the horse of one of the cavalrymen, so that, simply in self-defence, the latter had to fire a volley, which laid low the assailant; the other, his horse having been shot, was killed in the brush, fighting to the last. All the while, from the moment the two doomed braves appeared until they fell, the Cheyennes on the hill-side had been steadily singing the death chant. When the young men had both died, and had thus averted the fate which their misdeeds would else have brought upon the tribe, the warriors took their bodies and bore them away for burial honors, the soldiers looking on in silence. Where the slain men were buried the whites never knew; but all that night they listened to the dismal wailing of the dirges with which the tribesmen celebrated their gloomy funeral rites.

Frontiersmen are not, as a rule, apt to be very superstitious. They lead lives too hard and practical, and have too little imagination in things spiritual and supernatural. I have heard but few ghost stories while living on the frontier, and these few were of a perfectly commonplace and conventional type.

But I once listened to a goblin story which rather impressed me. It was told by a grisled, weather-beaten old mountain hunter, named Bauman, who was born and had passed all his life on the frontier. He must have believed what he said, for he could hardly repress a shudder at certain points of the tale; but he was of German ancestry, and in childhood had doubtless been saturated with all kinds of ghost and goblin lore, so that many fearsome superstitions were latent in his mind; besides, he knew well the stories told by the Indian medicine men in their winter camps, of the snow-walkers, and the spectres, and the formless evil beings that haunt the forest depths, and dog and waylay the lonely wanderer who after nightfall passes through the regions where they lurk; and it may be that when overcome by the horror of the fate that befell his friend, and when oppressed by the awful dread of the un-known, he grew to attribute, both at the time and still more in remembrance, weird and elfin traits to what was merely some abnormally wicked and cunning wild beast; but whether this was so or not, no man can say.

When the event occurred Bauman was still a young man, and was trapping with a partner among the moun-tains dividing the forks of the Salmon from the head of Wisdom River. Not having had much luck, he and his partner determined to go up into a particularly wild and lonely pass through which ran a small stream said to con-tain many beaver. The pass had an evil reputation because the year before a solitary hunter who had wandered into it was there slain, seemingly by a wild beast, the half-eaten remains being afterwards found by some mining prospec-tors who had passed his camp only the night before.

The memory of this event, however, weighed very lightly with the two trappers, who were as adventurous and hardy as others of their kind. They took their two lean mountain ponies to the foot of the pass, where they left them in an open beaver meadow, the rocky timber-clad ground being from thence onwards impracticable for horses. They then struck out on foot through the vast, gloomy forest, and in about four hours reached a little open glade where they concluded to camp, as signs of game were plenty.

There was still an hour or two of daylight left, and after building a brush lean-to and throwing down and opening their packs, they started up stream. The country was very dense and hard to travel through, as there was much down timber, although here and there the sombre woodland was broken by small glades of mountain grass.

At dusk they again reached camp. The glade in which it was pitched was not many yards wide, the tall, close-set pines and firs rising round it like a wall. On one side was a little stream, beyond which rose the steep mountain-slopes, covered with the unbroken growth of the evergreen forest.

They were surprised to find that during their short absence something, apparently a bear, had visited camp, and had rummaged about among their things, scattering the contents of their packs, and in sheer wantonness destroying their lean-to. The footprints of the beast were quite plain, but at first they paid no particular heed to them, busying themselves with rebuilding the lean-to, laying out their beds and stores, and lighting the fire.

While Bauman was making ready supper, it being already dark, his companion began to examine the tracks more closely, and soon took a brand from the fire to follow them up, where the intruder had walked along a game trail after leaving the camp. When the brand flickered out, he returned and took another, repeating his inspection of the footprints very closely. Coming back to the fire, he stood by it a minute or two, peering out into the darkness, and suddenly remarked: "Bauman, that bear has been walking on two legs." Bauman laughed at this, but his partner insisted that he was right, and upon again examining the tracks with a torch, they certainly did seem to be made by but two paws, or feet. However, it was too dark to make sure. After discussing whether the footprints could possibly be those of a human being, and coming to the conclusion that they could not be, the two men rolled up in their blankets, and went to sleep under the lean-to.

At midnight Bauman was awakened by some noise, and sat up in his blankets. As he did so his nostrils were struck by a strong, wild-beast odor, and he caught the loom of a great body in the darkness at the mouth of the lean-to. Grasping his rifle, he fired at the vague, threatening shadow, but must have missed, for immediately afterwards he heard the smashing of the underwood as the thing, whatever it was, rushed off into the impenetrable blackness of the forest and the night.

After this the two men slept but little, sitting up by the rekindled fire, but they heard nothing more. In the morning they started out to look at the few traps they had set the previous evening and to put out new ones. By an unspoken agreement they kept together all day, and returned to camp towards evening.

On nearing it they saw, hardly to their astonishment, that the lean-to had been again torn down. The visitor of the preceding day had returned, and in wanton malice had tossed about their camp kit and bedding, and destroyed the shanty. The ground was marked up by its tracks, and on leaving the camp it had gone along the soft earth by the brook, where the footprints were as plain as if on snow, and, after a careful scrutiny of the trail, it certainly did seem as if, whatever the thing was, it had walked off on but two legs.

The men, thoroughly uneasy, gathered a great heap of dead logs, and kept up a roaring fire throughout the night, one or the other sitting on guard most of the time. About midnight the thing came down through the forest opposite, across the brook, and stayed there on the hill-side for nearly an hour. They could hear the branches crackle as it moved about, and several times it uttered a harsh, grating, long-drawn moan, a peculiarly sinister sound. Yet it did not venture near the fire.

In the morning the two trappers, after discussing the strange events of the last thirty-six hours, decided that they would shoulder their packs and leave the valley that afternoon. They were the more ready to do this because in spite of seeing a good deal of game sign they had caught very little fur. However, it was necessary first to go along the line of their traps and gather them, and this they started out to do.

All the morning they kept together, picking up trap after trap, each one empty. On first leaving camp they had the disagreeable sensation of being followed. In the dense spruce thickets they occasionally heard a branch snap after they had passed; and now and then there were slight rustling noises among the small pines to one side of them.

At noon they were back within a couple of miles of camp. In the high, bright sunlight their fears seemed absurd to the two armed men, accustomed as they were, through long years of lonely wandering in the wilderness to face every kind of danger from man, brute, or element. There were still three beaver traps to collect from a little pond in a wide ravine near by. Bauman volunteered to gather these and bring them in, while his companion went ahead to camp and made ready the packs.

On reaching the pond Bauman found three beaver in the traps, one of which had been pulled loose and carried into a beaver house. He took several hours in securing and preparing the beaver, and when he started homewards he marked with some uneasiness how low the sun was getting. As he hurried towards camp, under the tall trees, the silence and desolation of the forest weighed on him. His feet made no sound on the pine needles, and the slanting sun rays, striking through among the straight trunks, made a gray twilight in which objects at a distance glimmered indistinctly. There was nothing to break the ghostly stillness which, when there is no breeze, always broods over these sombre primeval forests.

At last he came to the edge of the little glade where the camp lay, and shouted as he approached it, but got no answer. The camp fire had gone out, though the thin blue smoke was still curling upwards. Near it lay the packs, wrapped and arranged. At first Bauman could see nobody; nor did he receive an answer to his call. Stepping forward he again shouted, and as he did so his eye fell on the body of his friend, stretched beside the trunk of a great fallen spruce. Rushing towards it the horrified trapper found that the body was still warm, but that the neck was broken, while there were four great fang marks in the throat.

The footprints of the unknown beast-creature, printed deep in the soft soil, told the whole story.

The unfortunate man, having finished his packing, had sat down on the spruce log with his face to the fire, and his back to the dense woods, to wait for his companion. While thus waiting, his monstrous assailant, which must have been lurking nearby in the woods, waiting for a chance to catch one of the adventurers unprepared, came silently up from behind, walking with long, noiseless steps, and seemingly still on two legs. Evidently unheard, it reached the man, and broke his neck by wrenching his head back with its forepaws, while it buried its teeth in his throat. It had not eaten the body, but apparently had romped and gambolled round it in uncouth, ferocious glee, occasionally rolling over and over it; and had then fled back into the soundless depths of the woods.

Bauman, utterly unnerved, and believing that the creature with which he had to deal was something either half human or half devil, some great goblin-beast, abandoned everything but his rifle and struck off at speed down the pass, not halting until he reached the beaver meadows where the hobbled ponies were still grazing. Mounting, he rode onwards through the night, until far beyond the reach of pursuit.

Hunting Lore

I t has been my good-luck to kill every kind of game properly belonging to the United States: though one beast which I never had a chance to slay, the jaguar, from the torrid South, sometimes comes just across the Rio Grande; nor have I ever hunted the musk-ox and polar bear in the boreal wastes where they dwell, surrounded by the frozen desolation of the uttermost North.

I have never sought to make large bags, for a hunter should not be a game butcher. It is always lawful to kill dangerous or noxious animals, like the bear, cougar, and wolf; but other game should only be shot when there is need of the meat, or for the sake of an unusually fine trophy. Killing a reasonable number of bulls, bucks, or rams does no harm whatever to the species; to slay half the males of any kind of game would not stop the natural increase, and they yield the best sport, and are the legitimate objects of the chase. Cows, does, and ewes, on the contrary, should only be killed (unless barren) in case of necessity; during my last five years' hunting I have killed but five—one by a mischance, and the other four for the table.

From its very nature, the life of the hunter is in most places evanescent; and when it has vanished there can be no real substitute in old settled countries. Shooting in a private game preserve is but a dismal parody; the manliest and healthiest features of the sport are lost with the change of conditions. We need, in the interest of the community at large, a rigid system of game laws rigidly enforced, and it is not only admissible, but one may almost say necessary, to establish, under the control of the State, great national forest reserves, which shall also be breeding grounds and nurseries for wild game; but I should much regret to see grow up in this country a system of large private game preserves, kept for the enjoyment of the very rich. One of the chief attractions of the life of the wilderness is its rugged and stalwart democracy; there every man stands for what he actually is, and can show himself to be.

There are, in different parts of our country, chances to try so many various kinds of hunting, with rifle or with horse and hound, that it is nearly impossible for one man to have experience of them all. There are many hunts I long hoped to take, but never did and never shall; they must be left for men with more time, or for those whose homes are nearer to the hunting grounds. I have never seen a grisly roped by the riders of the plains, nor a black bear killed with the knife and hounds in the southern canebrakes; though at one time I had for many years a standing invitation to witness this last feat on a plantation in Arkansas. The friend who gave it, an old backwoods planter, at one time lost almost all his hogs by the numerous bears who infested his neighborhood. He took a grimly humorous revenge each fall by doing his winter killing among the bears instead of among the hogs they had slain; for as the cold weather approached he regularly proceeded to lay in a stock of bear-bacon, scouring the canebrakes in a series of systematic hunts, bringing the quarry to bay with the help of a big pack of hard-fighting mongrels, and then killing it with his long, broad-bladed bowie.

Again, I should like to make a trial at killing peccaries with the spear, whether on foot or on horseback, and with or without dogs. I should like much to repeat the experience of a friend who cruised northward through Bering Sea, shooting walrus and polar bear; and that of two other friends who travelled with dog-sleds to the Barren Grounds, in chase of the caribou, and of that last survivor of the Ice Age, the strange musk-ox. Once in a while it must be good sport to shoot alligators by torchlight in the everglades of Florida or the bayous of Louisiana.

If the big-game hunter, the lover of the rifle, has a taste for kindred field sports with rod and shotgun, many are his chances for pleasure, though perhaps of a less intense kind. The wild turkey really deserves a place beside the deer; to kill a wary old gobbler with the small-bore rifle, by fair still-hunting, is a triumph for the best sportsman. Swans, geese, and sandhill cranes likewise may sometimes be killed with the rifle; but more often all three, save perhaps the swan, must be shot over decoys. Then there is prairie-chicken shooting on the fertile grain prairies of the middle West, from Minnesota to Texas; and killing canvas-backs from behind blinds, with the help of that fearless swimmer, the Chesapeake Bay dog. In Californian mountains and valleys live the beautiful plumed quails, and who does not know their cousin bob-white, the bird of the farm, with his cheery voice and friendly ways?

For pure fun, nothing can surpass a night scramble through the woods after coon and possum.

The salmon, whether near Puget Sound or the St. Lawrence, is the royal fish; his only rival is the giant of the warm Gulf waters, the silver-mailed tarpon; while along the Atlantic coast the great striped bass likewise yields fine sport to the men of rod and reel. Every hunter of the mountains and the northern woods knows the many kinds of spotted trout; for the black bass he cares less; and least of all for the sluggish pickerel, and his big brother of the Great Lakes, the muscallonge.

Yet the sport yielded by rod and smooth-bore is really less closely kin to the strong pleasures so beloved by the hunter who trusts in horse and rifle than are certain other outdoor pastimes, of the rougher and hardier kind. Such a pastime is snow-shoeing, whether with webbed rackets, in the vast northern forests, or with skees, on the bare slopes of the Rockies. Such is mountaineering, especially when joined with bold exploration of the unknown. Most of our mountains are of rounded shape, and though climbing them is often hard work, it is rarely difficult or dangerous, save in bad weather, or after a snowfall. But there are many of which this is not true; the Tetons, for instance, and various glacier-bearing peaks in the Northwest; while the lofty, snow-clad ranges of British Columbia and Alaska offer one of the finest fields in the world for the daring cragsman. Mountaineering is among the manliest of sports; and it is to be hoped that some of our young men with a taste for hard work and adventure among the high hills will attempt the conquest of these great untrodden mountains of their own continent. As with all pioneer work, there would be far more discomfort and danger, far more need to display resolution, hardihood, and wisdom in such an attempt than in any expedition on well known and historic ground like the Swiss Alps; but the victory would be a hundred-fold better worth winning.

The dweller or sojourner in the wilderness who most keenly loves and appreciates his wild surroundings, and all their sights and sounds, is the man who also loves and appreciates the books which tell of them.

Foremost of all American writers on outdoor life is John Burroughs; and I can scarcely suppose that any man who cares for existence outside the cities would willingly be without anything that he has ever written. To the naturalist, to the observer and lover of nature, he is of course worth many times more than any closet systematist; and though he has not been very much in really wild regions, his pages so thrill with the sights and sounds of outdoor life that nothing by any writer who is a mere professional scientist or a mere professional hunter can take their place, or do more than supplement them—for scientist and hunter alike would do well to remember that before a book can take the highest rank in any particular line it must also rank high in literature proper. Of course, for us Americans, Burroughs has a peculiar charm that he cannot have for others, no matter how much they, too, may like him; for what he writes of is our own, and he calls to our minds memories and associations that are very dear. His books make us homesick when we read them in foreign lands; for they spring from our soil as truly as *Snow-bound* or *The Biglow Papers*.*

As a woodland writer, Thoreau comes second only to Burroughs.

For natural history in the narrower sense there are still no better books than Audubon and Bachman's Mammals and Audubon's Birds. There are also good works by men like Coues and Bendire; and if Hart Merriam, of the Smithsonian, will only do for the mammals of the United States what he has already done for those of the Adirondacks, we shall have the best book of its kind in existence. Nor, among less technical writings, should one overlook such essays as those of Maurice Thompson and Olive Thorne Miller.

There have been many American hunting-books; but too often they have been very worthless, even when the writers possessed the necessary first-hand knowledge, and the rare capacity of seeing the truth. Few of the old-time hunters ever tried to write of what they had seen and

---

*I am under many obligations to the writings of Mr. Burroughs (though there are one or two of his theories from which I should dissent); and there is a piece of indebtedness in this very volume of which I have only just become aware. In my chapter on the prong-buck there is a paragraph which will at once suggest to any lover of Burroughs some sentences in his essay on "Birds and Poets." I did not notice the resemblance until happening to reread the essay after my own chapter was written, and at the time I had no idea that I was borrowing from anybody, the more so as I was thinking purely of western wilderness life and western wilderness game, with which I knew Mr. Burroughs had never been familiar. I have concluded to leave the paragraph in with this acknowledgment.

done; and of those who made the effort fewer still succeeded. Innate refinement and the literary faculty—that
is, the faculty of writing a thoroughly interesting and
readable book, full of valuable information—may exist in
uneducated people; but if they do not, no amount of experience in the field can supply their lack. However, we
have had some good works on the chase and habits of big
game, such as Caton's *Deer and Antelope of America,* Van
Dyke's *Still-Hunter,* Elliott's *Carolina Sports,* and Dodge's
Hunting Grounds of the Great West, besides the Century
Company's *Sport with Rod and Gun.* Then there is Catlin's
book, and the journals of the explorers from Lewis and
Clarke down; and occasional volumes on outdoor life,
such as Theodore Winthrop's *Canoe and Saddle,* and
Clarence King's *Mountaineering in the Sierra Nevada.*

Two or three of the great writers of American literature, notably Parkman in his *Oregon Trail* and, with less
interest, Irving in his *Trip on the Prairies* have written with
power and charm of life in the American wilderness; but
no one has arisen to do for the far western plainsmen and
Rocky Mountain trappers quite what Hermann Melville
did for the South Sea whaling folk in *Omoo* and *Moby
Dick.* The best description of these old-time dwellers
among the mountains and on the plains is to be found in
a couple of good volumes by the Englishman Ruxton.
However, the backwoodsmen proper, both in their forest
homes and when they first began to venture out on the
prairie, have been portrayed by a master hand. In a succession of wonderfully drawn characters, ranging from
"Aaron Thousandacres" to "Ishmael Bush," Fenimore
Cooper has preserved for always the likenesses of these

stark pioneer settlers and backwoods hunters; uncouth, narrow, hard, suspicious, but with all the virile virtues of a young and masterful race, a race of mighty breeders, mighty fighters, mighty commonwealth builders. As for Leatherstocking, he is one of the undying men of story; grand, simple, kindly, pure-minded, staunchly loyal, the type of the steel-thewed and iron-willed hunter-warrior.

Turning from the men of fiction to the men of real life, it is worth noting how many of the leaders among our statesmen and soldiers have sought strength and pleasure in the chase, or in kindred vigorous pastimes. Of course field sports, or at least the wilder kinds, which entail the exercise of daring, and the endurance of toil and hardship, and which lead men afar into the forests and mountains, stand above athletic exercises; exactly as among the latter, rugged outdoor games, like football and lacrosse, are much superior to mere gymnastics and calisthenics.

With a few exceptions the men among us who have stood foremost in political leadership, like their fellows who have led our armies, have been of stalwart frame and sound bodily health. When they sprang from the frontier folk, as did Lincoln and Andrew Jackson, they usually hunted much in their youth, if only as an incident in the prolonged warfare waged by themselves and their kinsmen against the wild forces of nature. Old Israel Putnam's famous wolf-killing feat comes strictly under this head. Doubtless he greatly enjoyed the excitement of the adventure; but he went into it as a matter of business, not of sport. The wolf, the last of its kind in his neighborhood, had taken heavy toll of the flocks of himself and his friends; when they found the deep cave in which it had made its den it readily beat off the dogs sent in to assail it; and so Putnam crept in himself, with his torch and his flint-lock musket, and shot the beast where it lay.

When such men lived in long settled and thickly peopled regions, they needs had to accommodate themselves to the conditions and put up with humbler forms of sport. Webster, like his great rival for Whig leadership, Henry Clay, cared much for horses, dogs, and guns; but though an outdoor man he had no chance to develop a love for big-game hunting. He was, however, very fond of the rod and shotgun. Mr. Cabot Lodge recently handed me a letter written to his grandfather by Webster, and describing a day's trout fishing. It may be worth giving for the sake of the writer, and because of the fine heartiness and zest in enjoyment which it shows:

> Sandwich, June 4,
> Saturday mor'g
> 6 o'clock

Dear Sir:

I send you eight or nine trout, which I took yesterday, in that chief of all brooks, Mashpee. I made a long day of it, and with good success, for me. John was with me, full of good advice, but did not fish—nor carry a rod.

I took 26 trouts, all weighing	17 lb.	12 oz.
The largest (you have him) weighed		
at Crokers	2 "	4 "
The 5 largest	3 "	5 "
The eight largest	11 "	8 "

I got these by following your advice; that is, *by careful & thorough* fishing of the difficult places, which others do not fish. The brook is fished, nearly every day. I entered it, not so high up as we sometimes do, between 7 & 8 o'clock, & at 12 was hardly more than half way down to the meeting house path. You see I did not hurry. The day did not hold out to fish the whole brook properly. The largest trout I took at 3 P.M. (you see I am precise) below the meeting house, under a bush on the right bank, two or three rods below the large *beeches*. It is singular, that in the whole day, I did not take two trouts out of the same hole. I found both ends, or parts of the Brook about equally productive. Small fish not plenty, in either. So many hooks get everything which is not hid away in the manner large trouts take care of themselves. I hooked one, which I suppose to be larger than any which I took, as he broke my line, by fair pulling, after I had pulled him out of his den, & was playing him in fair open water.

Of what I send you, I pray you keep what you wish yourself, send three to Mr. Ticknor, & three to Dr. Warren; or two of the larger ones, to each will perhaps be enough—& if there be any left, there is Mr. Callender & Mr. Blake, & Mr. Davis, either of them not "averse to fish." Pray let Mr. Davis *see* them—especially the large one.—As he promised to come, & fell back, I desire to excite his regrets. I hope you will have the large one on your own table.

The day was fine—not another hook in the Brook. John steady as a judge—and every thing else exactly right. I never, on the whole, had so agreeable a day's fishing tho the result, in pounds or numbers, is not great;—nor ever expect such another.

Please preserve this letter; but rehearse not these particulars to the uninitiated.

I think the Limerick *not* the best hook. Whether it pricks too soon, or for what other reason, I found, or thought I found, the fish more likely to let go his hold, from this, than from the old fashioned hook.

Yrs.

H. Cabot, Esq.   D. Webster.

The greatest of Americans, Washington, was very fond of hunting, both with rifle or fowling-piece, and especially with horse, horn, and hound. Essentially the representative of all that is best in our national life, standing high as a general, high as a statesman, and highest of all as a man, he could never have been what he was had he not taken delight in feats of hardihood, of daring, and of bodily prowess. He was strongly drawn to those field sports which demand in their follower the exercise of the manly virtues—courage, endurance, physical address. As a young man, clad in the distinctive garb of the backwoodsman, the fringed and tasselled hunting-shirt, he led the life of a frontier surveyor; and like his fellow adventurers in wilderness exploration and Indian campaigning, he was often forced to trust to the long rifle for keeping his party in food. When at his home, at Mount Vernon, he hunted from simple delight in the sport.

His manuscript diaries, preserved in the State Department at Washington, are full of entries concerning his feats in the chase; almost all of them naturally falling in the years between the ending of the French war and the opening of the Revolutionary struggle against the British, or else in the period separating his service as Commander-in-chief of the Continental armies from his term of office as President of the Republic. These entries are scattered through others dealing with his daily duties in overseeing his farm and mill, his attendance at the Virginia House of Burgesses, his journeys, the drill of the local militia, and all the various interests of his many-sided life. Fond though he was of hunting, he was wholly incapable of the career of inanity led by those who make sport, not a manly pastime, but the one serious business of their lives.

The entries in the diaries are short, and are couched in the homely vigorous English, so familiar to the readers of Washington's journals and private letters. Sometimes they are brief jottings in reference to shooting trips; such as: "Rid out with my gun"; "went pheasant hunting"; "went ducking," and "went a gunning up the Creek." But far more often they are: "Rid out with my hounds," "went a fox hunting," or "went a hunting." In their perfect simplicity and good faith they are strongly characteristic of the man. He enters his blank days and failures as conscientiously as his red-letter days of success; recording with equal care on one day, "Fox hunting with Captain Posey—catch a Fox," and another, "Went a hunting with Lord Fairfax . . . catched nothing."

Occasionally he began as early as August and continued until April; and while he sometimes made but eight or ten hunts in a season, at others he made as many in a month. Often he hunted from Mt. Vernon, going out once or twice a week, either alone or with a party of his friends and neighbors; and again he would meet with these same neighbors at one of their houses, and devote several days solely to the chase. The country was still very wild, and now and then game was encountered with which the foxhounds proved unable to cope; as witness entries like: "found both a Bear and a Fox, but got neither"; "went a hunting . . . started a Deer & then a Fox but got neither"; and "Went a hunting and after trailing a fox a good while the Dogs Raized a Deer & ran out of the Neck with it & did not some of them at least come home till the next day." If it was a small animal, however, it was soon accounted for. "Went a Hunting . . . catched a Rakoon but never found a Fox."

The woods were so dense and continuous that it was often impossible for the riders to keep close to the hounds throughout the run; though in one or two of the best covers, as the journal records, Washington "directed paths to be cut for Fox Hunting." This thickness of the timber made it difficult to keep the hounds always under control; and there are frequent allusions to their going off on their own account, as "Joined some dogs that were self hunting." Sometimes the hounds got so far away that it was impossible to tell whether they had killed or not, the journal remarking "catched nothing that we know of," or "found a fox at the head of the blind Pocoson which we suppose was killed in an hour but could not find it."

Another result of this density and continuity of cover was the frequent recurrence of days of ill success. There are many such entries as: "Went Fox hunting, but started nothing"; "Went a hunting, but catched nothing"; "found nothing"; "found a Fox and lost it." Often failure followed long and hard runs: "Started a Fox, run him four hours, took the Hounds off at night"; "found a Fox and run it 6 hours and then lost"; "Went a hunting above Darrells . . . found a fox by two Dogs but lost it upon joining the Pack." In the season of 1772–73 Washington hunted eighteen days and killed nine foxes; and though there were seasons when he was out much more often, this proportion of kills to runs was if anything above the average. At the beginning of 1768 he met with a series of blank days which might well have daunted a less patient and persevering hunter. In January and the early part of February he was out nine times without getting a thing; but his diary does not contain a word of disappointment or surprise, each successive piece of ill-luck being entered without comment, even when one day he met some more fortunate friends "who had just catched 2 foxes." At last, on February 12th, he himself "catched two foxes"; the six or eight gentlemen of the neighborhood who made up the field all went home with him to Mt. Vernon, to dine and pass the night, and in the hunt of the following day they repeated the feat of a double score. In the next seven days' hunting he killed four times.

The runs of course varied greatly in length; on one day he "found a bitch fox at Piney Branch and killed it in an hour"; on another he "killed a Dog fox after having him on foot three hours & hard running an hour and a qr."; and on yet another he "catched a fox with a bobd Tail & cut ears after 7 hours chase in which most of the Dogs were worsted." Sometimes he caught his fox in thirty-five minutes, and again he might run it nearly the whole day in vain; the average run seems to have been from an hour and a half to three hours. Sometimes the entry records merely the barren fact of the run; at others a few particulars are given, with homespun, telling directness, as: "Went a hunting with Jacky Custis and catched a Bitch Fox after three hours chace—founded it on ye. ck. by I. Soals"; or "went a Fox hunting with Lund Washington—took the drag of a fox by Isaac Gates & carrd. it tolerably well to the old Glebe then touched now and then upon a cold scent till we came into Col. Fairfaxes Neck where we found about half after three upon the Hills just above Accotinck Creek—after running till quite Dark took off the Dogs and came home."

The foxes were doubtless mostly of the gray kind, and besides going to holes they treed readily. In January, 1770, he was out seven days, killing four foxes; and two of the entries in the journal relate to foxes which treed; one, on the 10th, being, "I went a hunting in the Neck and visited the plantn. there found and killed a bitch fox after treeing it 3 t. chasg. it abt. 3 hrs.," and the other, on the 23d: "Went a hunting after breakfast & found a Fox at muddy hole & killed her (it being a bitch) after a chase of better than two hours and after treeing her twice the last of which times she fell dead out of the Tree after being therein sevl. minutes apparently." In April, 1769, he hunted four days, and on every occasion the fox treed. April 7th, "Dog fox killed, ran an hour & treed twice." April 11th, "Went a fox hunting and took a fox alive after running him to a Tree—brot him home." April 12th, "Chased the above fox an hour & 45 minutes when he treed again after which we lost him." April 13th, "Killed a dog fox after treeing him in 35 minutes."

Washington continued his fox-hunting until, in the spring of 1775, the guns of the minute-men in Massachusetts called him to the command of the Revolutionary soldiery. When the eight weary years of campaigning were over, he said good-by to the war-worn veterans whom he had led through defeat and disaster to ultimate triumph, and became once more a Virginia country gentleman. Then he took up his fox-hunting with as much zest as ever. The entries in his journal are now rather longer, and go more into detail than formerly. Thus, on December 12th, 1785, he writes that after an early breakfast he went on a hunt and found a fox at half after ten, "being first plagued with the dogs running hogs," followed on his drag for some time, then ran him hard for an hour, when there came a fault; but when four dogs which had been thrown out rejoined the pack they put the fox up afresh, and after fifty minutes' run killed him in an open field, "every Rider & every Dog being present at the Death." With his usual alternations between days like this, and days of ill-luck, he hunted steadily every season until his term of private life again drew to a close and he was called to the headship of the nation he had so largely helped to found.

In a certain kind of fox-hunting lore there is much reference to a Warwickshire squire who, when the Parliamentary and Royalist armies were forming for the battle at Edgehill, was discovered between the hostile lines, unmovedly drawing the covers for a fox. Now, this placid sportsman should by rights have been slain offhand by the first trooper who reached him, whether Cavalier or Roundhead. He had mistaken means for ends, he had confounded the healthful play which should fit a man for needful work with the work itself; and mistakes of this kind are sometimes criminal. Hardy sports of the field offer the best possible training for war; but they become contemptible when indulged in while the nation is at death-grips with her enemies.

It was not in Washington's strong nature to make such an error. Nor yet, on the other hand, was he likely to undervalue either the pleasure, or the real worth of outdoor sports. The qualities of heart, mind, and body, which made him delight in the hunting-field, and which he there exercised and developed, stood him in good stead in many a long campaign and on many a stricken field; they helped to build that stern capacity for leadership in war which he showed alike through the bitter woe of the winter at Valley Forge, on the night when he ferried his men across the half-frozen Delaware to the overthrow of the German mercenaries at Trenton, and in the brilliant feat of arms whereof the outcome was the decisive victory of Yorktown.

APPENDIX

In this volume I have avoided repeating what was contained in either of my former books, the *Hunting Trips of a Ranchman* and *Ranch Life and the Hunting Trail*. For many details of life and work in the cattle country I must refer the reader to these two volumes; and also for more full accounts of the habits and methods of hunting such game as deer and antelope. As far as I know, the description in my *Ranch Life* of the habits and the chase of the mountain sheep is the only moderately complete account thereof that has ever been published. The five game-heads figured in this volume are copied exactly from the originals, now in my home; the animals were, of course, shot by myself.

There have been many changes, both in my old hunting-grounds and my old hunting-friends, since I first followed the chase in the far western country. Where the buffalo and the Indian ranged, along the Little Missouri, the branded herds of the ranchmen now graze; the scene of my elk-hunt at Two Ocean Pass is now part of the National Forest Reserve; settlers and miners have invaded the ground where I killed bear and moose; and steamers ply on the lonely waters of Kootenai Lake. Of my hunting companions some are alive; others—among them my staunch and valued friend, Will Dow, and crabbed, surly old Hank Griffen—are dead; while yet others have drifted away, and I know not what has become of them.

I have made no effort to indicate the best kind of camp kit for hunting, for the excellent reason that it depends so much upon the kind of trip taken, and upon the circumstances of the person taking it. The hunting trip may be made with a pack-train, or with a wagon, or with a canoe, or on foot; and the hunter may have half a dozen attendants, or he may go absolutely alone. I have myself made trips under all of these circumstances. At times I have gone with two or three men, several tents, and an elaborate apparatus for cooking, cases of canned goods, and the like. On the other hand, I have made trips on horseback, with nothing whatsoever beyond what I had on, save my oil-skin slicker, a metal cup, and some hard-tack, tea, and salt in the saddle pockets; and I have gone for a week or two's journey on foot, carrying on my shoulders my blanket, a frying-pan, some salt, a little flour, a small chunk of bacon, and a hatchet. So it is with dress. The clothes should be stout, of a neutral tint; the hat should be soft, without too large a brim; the shoes heavy, and the soles studded with small nails, save when moccasins or rubber-soled shoes are worn; but within these limits there is room for plenty of variation. Avoid, however, the so-called deer-stalker's cap, which is an abomination; its peaked brim giving no protection whatsoever to the eyes when facing the sun quartering, a position in which many shots must be taken. In very cold regions, fur coats, caps, and mittens, and all-wool underclothing are necessary. I dislike rubber boots when they can possibly be avoided. In hunting in snow in the winter I use the so-called German socks and felt overshoes where possible. One winter I had an ermine cap made. It was very good for peeping over the snowy ridge crests when game was on the other side; but, except when the entire landscape was snow-covered, it was an unmitigated nuisance. In winter, webbed snow-shoes are used in the thick woods, and skees in the open country.

There is an endless variety of opinion about rifles, and all that can be said with certainty is that any good modern rifle will do. It is the man behind the rifle that counts, after the weapon has reached a certain stage of perfection. One of my friends invariably uses an old Government Springfield, a 45-calibre, with an ounce bullet. Another cares for nothing but the 40–90 Sharps', a weapon for which I myself have much partiality. Another uses always the old 45-calibre Sharps', and yet another the 45-calibre Remington. Two of the best bear and elk hunters I know prefer the 32- and 38-calibre Marlin's, with long cartridges, weapons with which I myself would not undertake to produce any good results. Yet others prefer pieces of very large calibre. The amount of it is that each one of these guns possesses some excellence which the others lack, but which is in most cases atoned for by some corresponding defect. Simplicity of mechanism is very important, but so is rapidity of fire; and it is hard to get both of them developed to the highest degree in the same piece. In the same way, flatness of trajectory, penetration, range, shock, and accuracy are all qualities which must be attained; but to get one in perfection usually means the sacrifice of some of the rest. For instance, other things being equal, the smallest calibre has the greatest penetration, but gives the least shock; while a very flat trajectory, if acquired by heavy charges of powder, means the sacrifice of accuracy. Similarly, solid and hollow pointed bullets have, respectively, their merits and demerits. There is no use of dogmatizing about weapons. Some which prove excellent for particular countries and kinds of hunting are useless in others.

There seems to be no doubt, judging from the testimony of sportsmen in South Africa and in India, that very heavy calibre double-barrelled rifles are best for use in the dense jungles and against the thick-hided game of those regions; but they are of very little value with us. In 1882 one of the buffalo hunters on the Little Missouri obtained from some Englishman a double-barrelled ten-bore rifle of the kind used against rhinoceros, buffalo, and elephant in the Old World; but it proved very inferior to the 40- and 45-calibre Sharps' buffalo guns when used under the conditions of American buffalo hunting, the tremendous shock given by the bullet not compensating for the gun's great relative deficiency in range and accuracy, while even the penetration was inferior at ordinary distances. It is largely also a matter of individual taste. At one time I possessed a very expensive double-barrelled 500 Express, by one of the crack English makers; but I never liked the gun, and could not do as well with it as with my repeater, which cost barely a sixth as much. So one day I handed it to a Scotch friend, who was manifestly ill at ease with a Winchester exactly like my own. He took to the double-barrel as naturally as I did to the repeater, and did excellent work with it. Personally, I have always preferred the Winchester. I now use a 45–90, with my old buffalo gun, a 40–90 Sharps', as spare rifle. Both, of course, have specially tested barrels, and are stocked and sighted to suit myself.

INDEX TO

HUNTING TRIPS OF A RANCHMAN

INDEX TO
THE WILDERNESS HUNTER

A Note on the Type

The principal text of this Modern Library edition was set in a digitized version of Caslon, a typeface first designed in 1722 by William Caslon. Its widespread use by most English printers in the early eighteenth century soon supplanted the Dutch typefaces that had formerly prevailed. The roman is considered a "workhorse" typeface due to its pleasant, open appearance, while the italic is exceedingly decorative.

MODERN LIBRARY IS ONLINE AT
WWW.MODERNLIBRARY.COM

MODERN LIBRARY ONLINE IS YOUR GUIDE TO CLASSIC LITERATURE ON THE WEB

THE MODERN LIBRARY E-NEWSLETTER

Our free e-mail newsletter is sent to subscribers, and features sample chapters, interviews with and essays by our authors, upcoming books, special promotions, announcements, and news.

To subscribe to the Modern Library e-newsletter, send a blank e-mail to: sub_modernlibrary@info.randomhouse.com or visit www.modernlibrary.com

THE MODERN LIBRARY WEBSITE

Check out the Modern Library website at
www.modernlibrary.com for:

- The Modern Library e-newsletter
- A list of our current and upcoming titles and series
- Reading Group Guides and exclusive author spotlights
- Special features with information on the classics and other paperback series
- Excerpts from new releases and other titles
- A list of our e-books and information on where to buy them
- The Modern Library Editorial Board's 100 Best Novels and 100 Best Nonfiction Books of the Twentieth Century written in the English language
- News and announcements

Questions? E-mail us at **modernlibrary@randomhouse.com**
For questions about examination or desk copies, please visit
the Random House Academic Resources site at
www.randomhouse.com/academic